Presidential Leadership
Politics and Policy Making

Presidential Leadership

Politics and Policy Making

George C. Edwards III
Texas A & M University

Stephen J. Wayne
The George Washington University

St. Martin's Press   New York

To Carmella and Cheryl

ISBN 0-312-64037-4
ISBN 0-312-64038-2 (paper)

Cover design: Jerry Lighter

Library of Congress Cataloging in Publication Data

Edwards, George C.
  Presidential leadership.

  Includes index.
    1. Presidents—United States.   I. Wayne, Stephen J.
II. Title.
JK516.E32   1985   353.03'1   84-18387
ISBN 0-312-64037-4
ISBN 0-312-64038-2 (paper)

Acknowledgments

Material from "Quantitative Analysis" reprinted by permission of the University of Tennessee Press. From Edwards, George C., III and Wayne, Stephen J.: STUDYING THE PRESIDENCY. Copyright © 1983 by the University of Tennessee Press.

Table 2-6 from Presidential Power in the United States by R. Tatlovich and B. W. Daynes. Copyright © 1984 by Wadsworth, Inc. Reprinted by permission of Brooks/Cole Publishing Company, Monterey, Calif. 93940.

Preface

The presidency is a much praised, much damned institution. During the early 1960s it was seen as the major innovative force within the government. People looked to the president to satisfy an increasing number of their demands. Presidential power was thought to be the key to political change.

By the late 1960s and early 1970s, this power was seen as a serious problem. Scholars blamed presidents and their excesses for involvement in the war in Southeast Asia and for the Watergate and other scandals. Restrain the "imperial" presidency became the cry.

Presidents Ford and Carter responded to this plea by attempting to deimperialize the office. Ford opened the White House to opposing views; Carter reduced the size, status, and perquisites of presidential aides. Both were careful not to exceed their constitutional and statutory powers.

Growing institutional conflict between Congress and the presidency and within the executive branch raised questions about the possibility of effective governance. Worsening economic conditions, increasing scarcity of resources, and a series of foreign policy crises produced a desire for more assertive, more directive leadership. The presidency was seen as imperiled; weakness, not strength, its problem. Disappointment in presidential performance replaced fear of presidential abuses.

The Reagan presidency has led scholars once again to reevaluate the workings of the system and the role of the president within it. Reagan's ability to achieve some of his major policy goals indicates that stalemate need not paralyze the government. But it has also given rise to fears, particularly among his critics, of the dangers that the exercise of power can produce.

Obviously, presidential leadership cuts two ways. It is desirable yet potentially harmful. It is necessary but difficult, perhaps more difficult today than in the past. Expectations of the president remain as great as ever, yet the costs of achieving those expectations have increased. This has complicated the president's leadership task and, at the same time, made that leadership more critical.

This book is about the president's leadership problems, about the obstacles to that leadership and the skills necessary to overcome them. Although it offers no simple formula for success, it does assess the costs and consequences for exercising and not exercising that leadership today. In a pluralistic system where separate institutions are forced to share powers, we believe that only effective, responsible presidential leadership can provide the coherence, direction, and support necessary to articulate and achieve national political and policy goals.

One of the difficulties we faced in writing this book was the use of singular pronouns to represent the president. Traditionally the male pronoun has been used and justified because only men have held this office. Although we have adopted this convention, we believe and hope that women (as well as members of minority groups) will have the opportunity to be elected to the presidential and vice presidential offices.

In any project of this size, the authors are indebted to many people. G. Calvin Mackenzie, Colby College; Eric Davis, Middlebury College; Richard Scher, University of Florida; Anita Pritchard, Florida Atlantic University; and Paul Light, National Academy of Public Administration, read portions of the manuscript and provided insightful criticism. Their comments greatly improved the quality of the manuscript. Terry Schiefen and Judith Schneider typed the many drafts of our chapters, often under tight deadlines. We thank them for their excellent, dependable work. Stephen Williams provided invaluable assistance with the index. Our wives have been patient and encouraging throughout. Their willingness to help in a multitude of ways has enabled us to spurn other responsibilities and concentrate on our writing. We cannot thank Carmella and Cheryl enough. It is to them that we dedicate this book.

George C. Edwards
Stephen J. Wayne

Contents

Presidential Leadership
Politics and Policy Making

1

Presidential Leadership: An Introduction

No office within American government, or for that matter most other systems, has commanded the attention, stirred the imagination, and generated the emotions that the presidency has. Considered the first among equals, it has become the dominant institution in a system designed for balanced government, the prime initiator and coordinator among separate and independent institutions, the foremost mobilizer among disparate and, often, competing interests, and the principal communications link from and to a multitude of groups and individuals. It is a many-faceted, dynamic office—charged with a plethora of responsibilities, a variety of roles, and a large range of powers.

Within it, the president is clearly the chief. Executive officials look to him for direction, coordination, and general guidance in the implementation of policy; members of Congress look to him for establishing priorities, exerting influence, and providing services; the heads of foreign governments look to him for articulating positions, conducting diplomacy, and flexing muscle; the general public looks to him for enhancing security, solving problems, and exercising symbolic and moral leadership—a big order to be sure.

Unfortunately for the president, these expectations often exceed his abilities to meet them. It is not simply a question of his skill or his personality, although both contribute to his capacity to do his job and to do it well. The problem is the system, particularly its constitutional, institutional, and political structures. The Constitution divides authority; institutions share power; and parties lack cohesion and often a sustained issue-ideological thrust.

Despite the president's position and status, he has difficulty overcoming these constraints. Nor can he easily ignore or reduce what is expected of him. As a consequence, disappointment is frequent regardless of who occupies the Oval Office.

To some extent, this has always been the case. But in recent times, the gap between expectations and performance seems to have widened. Disenchantment has increased; confidence has declined; the popularity of many presidents has plummeted during the course of their administrations. Presidential leadership has thus become more difficult and more vital if the American system is to work.

This book addresses these problems and the ability of presidents to surmount them. First and foremost, this is a book about presidential leadership, about the capacity of chief executives to fulfill their tasks, to exercise their powers, and to utilize their organizational structures. It is a book about political leadership, about public opinion, group pressures, media coverage, and presidential salesmanship before, during, and after elections. It is also a book about policy leadership, about institutions and processes, about priority setting, coalition building, and governmental implementation. Finally, it is a book about personal leadership, about incumbents in office, about their goals, national needs, and the formal and informal ways of accomplishing their objectives.

In order to understand the problems of contemporary presidential leadership, it is necessary to gain a perspective on the institution and its development. The first two parts of this chapter provide that perspective. In them we present an overview of the creation of the office and its evolution. We place particular emphasis on the growth of its policy-making roles, its advisory and administrative structures, and its political and public dimensions. In the third part of the chapter we examine recent changes in the political and policy environment and the impact of those changes on the president's job performance. We assess the sources of the institution's problems and present the dilemmas for contemporary leadership. In the final section we discuss how we will go about exploring these dilemmas.

THE ORIGINAL PRESIDENCY

The Creation of the Institution

The contemporary presidency bears little resemblance to the one the framers of the Constitution artfully designed in 1787 in Philadelphia. Their executive had more limited authority, less functional responsibility, and no explicit institutional structure or operating procedures. The times, of course, were different.

While the Constitution's framers saw the need for an independent executive empowered with its own authority, they did not begin with a consensus on the form this executive should take nor the powers it should possess. At the outset of their deliberations, two basic questions had to be answered: Should the office be entrusted to one person or to several individuals? and What combination of functions, responsibilities, and powers would yield an energetic yet safe executive?

The first of these questions was resolved early in the convention after a short but pointed discussion. James Wilson, delegate from Pennsylvania, had proposed that only a single individual could combine the characteristics of "energy, dispatch, and responsibility." Critics immediately responded that such an executive would be dangerous, "the foetus of monarchy" in the words of Edmond Randolph.

In denying the allegation that what they really wanted was a king, Wilson and James Madison sought to contrast their more limited executive with the powers of the king. As the debate intensified, Madison proposed that the institution's authority be established before the number of executives was decided. This constituted one of the most astute parliamentary moves of the Constitutional Convention. Wilson had previously declared that the prerogatives of the British monarch were not a proper guide for determining the executive's domain. They were too extensive. The American executive, he argued, should possess only executive authority, the power to execute laws and make those appointments that had not otherwise been provided for. The Convention accepted Wilson's delineation, a delineation that made it safe to entrust the office to a single individual. This was promptly done. Only later were those powers expanded through enumeration.

Wilson was primarily responsible for this enumeration as well. As a member of the committee charged with taking propositions approved by the Convention and shaping them into a constitution, he detailed the executive's powers with phraseology taken from the New York and Massachusetts constitutions. Surprisingly, his enumeration engendered little debate. The powers were not particularly controversial. Couching them in the language of two state constitutions made them more palatable. Most were quickly and quietly adopted.

Agreement on the checks to secure and restrain the executive was a little more difficult. Abuses of past executives combined with excesses of contemporary legislatures made the maintenance of an institutional balance essential. The problem was how to preserve the balance without jeopardizing the independence of the separate branches or impeding the lawful exercise of their authority. In the end the framers resolved this problem by checking those powers that they believed to be most dangerous, the ones which had been subject to greatest abuse in the previous period (appointments, treaty making, and declarations of war), while protecting the general spheres of authority from encroachment (in the executive's case by a qualified veto).

Presidential responsibility was also encouraged by the provisions for reeligibility and a short term of office. Reappointment was the great motive to good behavior. For those executives who flagrantly abused their authority, impeachment was the ultimate recourse.

The traditional weapon to defend executive authority was the veto. Theoretically, it could function to protect those executive prerogatives that were threatened by the legislature. In practice, it had frequently been employed to preclude the enactment of laws that the executive opposed. Herein lay its danger. The compromise was to give the president the veto but allow two-thirds of both houses to override it.

In summary, the relative ease with which the presidency was empowered indicates that a consensus developed on the bounds and substance of executive authority. Not only had certain traditional prerogatives been rejected but others had been readily accepted. In deciding which of these powers should be given to the new institution, the framers turned to the tenets of balanced government as articulated by the French theorist Charles de Montesquieu in his well-quoted treatise, *The Spirit of the Laws,* and practiced to some extent in the states of Massachusetts and New York.[1] Those powers which conformed to the basic division of authority were accepted; those which actually or potentially threatened the institutional balance were rejected.

Fears of potential abuse led to differing opinions on how best to constrain the branches without violating the principle of separate spheres of authority. The majority of the delegates opted for sharing powers, particularly in foreign affairs, and principally with the Senate. Their decision, reached toward the end of the convention when the pressures to compromise were greatest, exacerbated the fears of those who believed that the Senate would come to dominate the president and control the government.

Many of the opponents of the Constitution saw the sharing of powers as far more dangerous than the general grant of executive authority that was specified in Article 2. While each of the president's powers engendered some objection during the ratification debate, the most sustained criticism was directed at the relationship with the upper chamber. In the end, the proponents of the Constitution prevailed, but the debate over the efficacy of shared powers between executive and legislative branches has continued through the years.

The Scope of Article 2

In one sense what the framers did is obvious. It is written in Article 2. In another sense, however, their deliberations and decisions have been subject to constant interpretation. Unlike Article 1, where the Constitution detailed the legislative powers that were given to Congress, executive authority was stated in a more general way in Article 2: "The executive power shall be vested in a President of the United States of America." For years scholars have debated whether this designation provides the president with an undefined grant of authority or simply confers on him the title of the office.

Although the answer to this question remains in doubt, the executive portion of the president's responsibilities is relatively clear. The framers charged the president with the administration of government. He was given the task of faithfully executing the law and the capacity to do so by overseeing the executive departments. The departments were not designated by the Constitution. They were established by legislation during the first Congress. The president, however, was to have a hand in choosing the people who ran them.

The need to provide the executive with some discretion to respond to emergency or extraordinary situations was also considered essential. Heading the only institution with continuous tenure and the only one with a national perspective, the president was thought to be able to respond to events more quickly and decisively than the Congress. Traditionally this type of emergency power resided in the executive.

In his *Second Treatise of Civil Government,* the British philosopher John Locke had written of the need for such a power, which he termed a prerogative.[2] The framers agreed. Having themselves experienced a legislature unable to respond to emergencies, they desired to provide such a capacity in their constitutional arrangement and give it to the president.

The debate over the war powers illustrates their dilemma as well as their solution. Initially, the Congress was given the authority to make war. Fearing that the word "make" might preclude the executive from responding to an attack if Congress were not in session, the framers agreed to substitute the word "declare." This provided the president with flexibility but did not alter the basic intent—to have Congress decide whether or not to go to war. Even after making that decision, Congress retained powers that affected the conduct of hostilities. These powers serve to limit the president's discretion as commander-in-chief.

Similarly in foreign affairs, the president was limited in what he could do alone without the approval of the Senate or both houses. He did, however, share the treaty-making role with the upper chamber. The president exercised the initiative. But even here, the wording of the Constitution suggested that the Senate was to have a role in the negotiation of treaties as well as in their ratification.

Although executive powers were expected to expand during emergencies, they were never without limits. The exercise of discretionary powers by the executive was always tied to legislation. The president could summon Congress into special session; he was obligated to report to it on the state of the union; he could recommend necessary and expedient legislation; but it was the Congress that in the end had to decide what laws, if any, to enact. Even in the case of the veto, two-thirds of both houses would have the last word.

In short, the relatively general grant of executive authority gave the president broad discretion in the exercise of his principal responsibility—the execution of the law. Some of his powers were exclusive but others were shared. Some of them were enumerated but that enumeration was not exhaustive. The president had considerable freedom to oversee subordinates of his own choosing in his administration of government. On the other hand, his discretion in formulating policy was extremely limited. Congress, not the executive, was expected to assume that role in the normal course of events.

THE EVOLUTION OF THE PRESIDENCY

Policy-Making Roles

Although the president's constitutionally designated authority has not been formally amended, the scope of that authority has been expanded by law and precedent. Over the years, the president's policy-making powers have grown dramatically. Chief executives beginning with Washington set the contours of foreign policy. Beginning with Jefferson, they shaped it to the point of actually defining what the war policy would be. There were other early examples of presidential initiatives in foreign affairs, notably Monroe's famous doctrine that pledged United States protection of the independent states on this side of the Atlantic.

Crisis situations expanded the president's powers still further as Lincoln's actions during the Civil War demonstrated. Lincoln justified his exercise of power by the gravity of the situation. "Was it possible to lose the nation and yet preserve the Constitution?" he asked. To his own question, he replied, "I felt that measures otherwise unconstitutional might become lawful by becoming indispensable to the preservation of the Constitution through the preservation of the nation."[3]

Lincoln was not challenged by Congress during the war, but after it Congress reasserted its authority. Throughout the remainder of the century, Congress, not the president, dominated the relationship between the branches. In fact, when, as a professor of politics, Woodrow Wilson wrote his perceptive study on the American political system in the mid-1880s, he titled it *Congressional Government*.

Wilson wrote at the end of an era. By the time he became chief executive, the president's roles in both foreign and domestic affairs had expanded, and Wilson revised his book. Demands for a more activist government had encouraged Presidents McKinley and Theodore Roosevelt to work more closely and harmoniously with Congress to fashion major policy initiatives. Roosevelt was responsible for much of this activity.

Assuming an assertive posture in both foreign and domestic affairs, Roosevelt expanded the president's policy-making roles. He sent the navy halfway around the world (and then requested appropriations from Congress to return it home); he announced a corollary to the Monroe Doctrine, further involving the United States in hemispheric activities; he helped instigate a revolution in Colombia, quickly recognized the independence of insurgents on the Isthmus of Panama, and promptly entered into an agreement with them to build a canal. He was the first president to travel outside of the United States (to Mexico) and the first to help settle a war for which he won the Nobel Peace Prize. Within the domestic sphere, Roosevelt busted trusts, crusaded for conservation, and mediated a major coal strike. He was also instrumental in getting Congress to enact important legislation, including the Pure Food and Drug Act, the Meat Inspection Act, and the Hepburn (railroad) Act.

Roosevelt's theory of the presidency justified and accommodated his activism. Writing in his autobiography after his political career had ended, Roosevelt stated:

> My view was that every executive officer, and above all every executive officer in high position, was a steward of the people bound actively and affirmatively to do all he could for the people, and not to content himself with the negative merit of keeping his talents undamaged in a napkin.[4]

In contrast, William Howard Taft, Roosevelt's successor, expressed a much more restrained conception:

> The true view of the executive function is, as I conceive it, that the president can exercise no power which cannot be fairly and reasonably traced to some specific grant of power or justly implied and included within such express grant as proper and necessary to its exercise. Such specific grant must be either in the federal Constitution or in an act of Congress passed in pursuance thereof. There is no undefined residuum of power which he can exercise because it seems to him to be in the public interest.[5]

Roosevelt's *stewardship* theory has prevailed. With the exception of the three Republican presidents of the 1920s, occupants of the Oval Office in the twentieth century have assumed active political and policy-making roles. Woodrow Wilson and Franklin Roosevelt, in particular, expanded Theodore Roosevelt's initiatives in international and domestic matters.

Wilson was the first president to propose a comprehensive legislative program and the first to be involved in summitry. He was the architect of the proposal to establish a League of Nations, although he was unable to persuade the Senate to accept the treaty ending the war.

Franklin Roosevelt enlarged the president's role in economic affairs. Coming into office in the midst of the Great Depression, he initiated a series of measures to deal with the crisis and succeeded in getting Congress to enact them. He maintained the posture of an international leader, maneuvering the country's entrance into World War II and participating in the initial conferences to end the war. He also made the critical decision to develop the atomic bomb.

The modern presidency is said to have begun in the Franklin Roosevelt era. It is characterized by presidential activism in a variety of policy-making roles. Many of the practices which Roosevelt initiated or continued have been institutionalized by his successors and/or required by Congress.

Organizational Structure

The structure of the modern presidency also developed during the Roosevelt period. In 1939 the Executive Office of the President was created. Prior to that time presidents had depended largely on their department heads for administration and advice.

The Constitution did not explicitly provide for an administrative structure. It did, however, contain oblique reference to one. There was a provision in Article 2 that the president could demand in writing the opinions of subordinate officials. It was up to the first Congress to establish the executive departments as the principal administrative units of government. It created three departments (Foreign Affairs, Treasury, and War) and appointed an attorney general and a postmaster general. Since then, nine more departments and more than one hundred agencies have been established.

Throughout most of the nineteenth century it was Congress, not the president, who dominated the administration of government. Statutes specified many organizational details of the departments including their jurisdiction, staffing levels, and even operating procedures. For the most part, there was little oversight from the president.

The autonomy of the departments contributed to the influence of their secretaries, who headed them. Since the department heads were the president's principal advisers, they exercised considerable leverage in helping to design administration goals and in mobilizing congressional support. With the exception of the Jefferson, Jackson, and Lincoln administrations, strong department secretaries and weak presidents characterized executive advisory relationships.

This began to change at the outset of the twentieth century as a consequence of the president's growing influence in Congress. As that increased, the potency of the department secretaries, individually and collectively, began to decline. They lost their privileged position between president and Congress. Their support of administration proposals became less critical than it had been to the president's legislative success.

The concern that Theodore Roosevelt and particularly, William

Howard Taft evidenced toward the organization of government also contributed eventually to the president's enhanced status and power within the executive branch. Taft appointed a Committee on Economy and Efficiency to recommend improvements. Reporting in 1913, the committee urged the creation of a more hierarchial structure with the president assuming a larger administrative role.

Initially, Congress was reluctant to comply. However, sizable budget deficits, inflated by United States involvement in World War I, provided the legislature with a financial (and political) incentive to do so. Unable to control the deficits, Congress turned to the president for help. It enacted the Budget and Accounting Act of 1921, which made it a presidential responsibility to estimate the financial needs of the individual departments and agencies on a yearly basis and provided the president with an institutional mechanism to do so, the Bureau of the Budget.

When Franklin Roosevelt took office and expanded the president's domestic policy role, he needed more information, more expertise, and more staff. At first he depended on personnel provided by the executive departments. When that did not prove satisfactory, he turned to a small group of experts to advise him on how to make the organizational structure of the executive more responsive to his needs. The group, headed by Louis Brownlow, issued a report that said:

> The President needs help. His immediate staff assistance is entirely inadequate. He should be given a small number of executive assistants who would be his direct aides in dealing with the managerial agencies and administrative departments of government.[6]

The Brownlow committee urged the creation of a separate presidential office. In 1939 Congress approved the act that established the Executive Office of the President. Initially the office consisted of five units: the White House, Bureau of the Budget, and three World War II agencies (the National Resources Planning Board, the Liaison Office for Personnel Management, and the Office of Government Reports). Eventually over forty different councils, boards, and offices have been housed at one time or another in this office.

The creation of the Executive Office provided the president with a structure directly responsive to his interests. The White House became his personal office. Presidential aides performed political tasks that were dictated by the president's immediate needs, actions, and goals. Having no constitutional and statutory authority of their own and no political base other than the president's, their influence was dependent on their access to him. They did his calling.

Whereas the White House functioned as a personal extension of the president, the Budget Bureau became an institutional extension of the presidency. It coordinated the policy-making functions of the department and agencies, imposing a presidential perspective on the executive branch in the process.

During subsequent administrations, the duties of the Executive Office have been expanded and its organizational structure redesigned. Staffed by civil servants and run by political appointees, it continues to perform a variety of critical tasks. It is considered essential for an activist presidency, but its large size, its many roles, and its organizational autonomy make it difficult for the president to oversee, much less to control.

Public Dimensions

In addition to the development of the presidency as an institution and the growth of its policy-making roles, the public dimension of the office has expanded as well. This too has been a relatively recent phenomenon. Franklin Roosevelt was the first to use the mass media (radio) to communicate directly with the American people on a regular basis. His successors have used television to the same end.

For most of the nineteenth century the presidency was not a particularly visible office, although the president received his share of critical commentary. Jefferson was the first to claim a partisan mandate and Jackson the first to claim a public one.[7]

A variety of factors contributed to a more active public posture by presidents toward the beginning of the twentieth century. The growth of newsgathering organizations and the newspaper chains made it possible to communicate with more people more quickly. The advent of yellow journalism combined with the increased activism of government generated more interest in the opinions and behavior of public officials, particularly the president.

Theodore Roosevelt, more than any of his predecessors, took advantage of these developments to focus attention on himself, his policies, and his activities. He was the first president to give reporters a room in the White House and the first to hold regular meetings with the press. Using his position as "a bully pulpit," Roosevelt rallied public support for his positions and proposals.

Roosevelt's presidency prompted Professor Woodrow Wilson to revise his view that the governmental system was dominated by Congress. The president could be as big a man as he wanted, Wilson asserted in 1908. He could use his position as party and national leader to enhance his political power and thereby exert influence on Congress:

> His capacity will set the limit; and if Congress be overborne by him, it will be no fault of the makers of the Constitution—it will be from no lack of constitutional powers on its part, but only because the President has the nation behind him, and Congress has not. He has no means of compelling Congress except through public opinion.[8]

Wilson attempted to heed his own words. The enactment of his legislative program can be attributed in large part to his political leadership and public oratory. His greatest disappointment, however, his inability to persuade the Senate to ratify the treaty ending World War I, stemmed from his failure to exercise these skills successfully. Wilson, who went on a public speaking tour to build support for his position, overestimated his ability to lead public opinion and underestimated his opponents' capacity to do so.

While Theodore Roosevelt and Woodrow Wilson used the presidency as a podium, neither of them was as skillful at manipulating the press as was Franklin Roosevelt. In his first term, Franklin Roosevelt held more press conferences than any of his predecessors. Meeting frequently with small groups of reporters in the Oval Office, he used these sessions to articulate his views and float trial balloons. He also made extensive and productive use of radio in his fireside chats.

By the end of the Roosevelt era, the presidency had been permanently altered by the media. It had become the most visible national office. Coverage of the White House was constant. The president was always in the news.

The intensive and extensive media focus on the president has had three principal effects. First, it has permanently added a new role to the president's job, that of communicator-in-chief, and has required that skills commensurate with this role be exercised. Second, it has heightened public expectations of presidential performance. Advances in communications have enabled organized groups to promote the desires of their membership more effectively. The president has become the focal point for many of these increased demands on government. Third, media coverage has linked public approval more closely to the exercise of presidential power. Now more than ever, presidents need to build support outside of government to gain support within it. Taken together, these factors indicate why increased public exposure for the president has, at best, been a mixed blessing.

PROBLEMS OF CONTEMPORARY LEADERSHIP

These changes, singularly and together, have created new demands on the president which, in turn, have generated new roles and obligations for him and new criteria by which he is to be judged. These new roles and criteria, in turn, have affected perceptions of leadership. In the past, the people did not look to the president to solve most national economic, social, and political problems. Today they do. The president is expected to be a chief policymaker. He is expected to exercise a wide range of powers. Ancillary coordination, communication, and co-optation functions have followed from these expanded roles and powers.

Institutional growth has been another consequence of a more activist presidency. The size of the office has increased enormously. Prior to 1939 the president was assisted by a few aides, most of whom were detailed from executive departments and agencies. The total budget for the salaries and expenses of those working for the president was $125,804.98 in 1925. In 1939 when the Executive Office was created, it was about $250,000. Today it is about $25 million for the White House alone, and that does not include the one hundred or so detailees paid from other executive budgets. The first Executive Office of the President consisted of five agencies including the White House; forty-five years later it has ten agencies and a combined staff of approximately 1,400.

The larger staff has increased the president's capacity to perform added responsibilities and to do so with less dependence on executive departments and agencies. But the enlargement of that staff has also worked to extend the very functions and responsibilities that the staff was designed to serve. This expansion has limited the president's personal influence over what functions his presidency performs and to a lesser extent how his administration is organized to perform them.

Not only has the presidential office grown in size and solidified in organization but its policy processes have become institutionalized. Mechanisms for preparing the budget, formulating a program, building support in Congress, and advising the president whether to sign or veto legislation have developed and continued from administration to administration. These routines have also worked to shape the functions and processes they serve.

There have been significant changes in the public dimensions of the office as well. The selection process has become more individualized. Parties do not organize and mediate between candidates and the voters as they did in the past. Public expectations have increased as a consequence of longer campaigns, more personalized appeals, and many specific promises made to organized groups. Yet, the electoral coalition needed to win no longer provides the basis for governing. New coalitions have to be formed on an issue-by-issue basis.

The national media seemingly are more critical of the president than in the past. Communications from and to the public are more direct and immediate. Such communication enables the White House to measure the pulse of public opinion more accurately, but it also conditions responses, shortens the time frame, and ultimately, constrains the president's options.

Interest groups have proliferated and professionalized. Moreover, they have become more sophisticated at influencing their members and mobilizing them behind specific policy positions. No institution or individual, not the Executive Office of the President, the White House, or even the president is immune from these pressures.

Lobbying increases the political impact of many presidential decisions. It can force the president's hand, making him compromise for political reasons when he would rather not do so for policy reasons. The proliferation of professionalized interest groups makes the redistribution of resources more difficult. Over time, it increases levels of dissatisfaction among different sectors of the public. It adversely affects the president's relations with Congress.

Changes within the legislature have reinforced this organized pluralism. Congress has decentralized lawmaking, shifting power to a large number of subcommittee chairmen. Ironically, more members of Congress must now be consulted, coordinated, and cajoled at the very time when Congress has involved itself in more issues of executive policy-making and policy implementation. The president must work harder than in the past to achieve his administration's legislative goals.

He is similarly constrained within the executive branch. The continuing orientation of the bureaucracy to outside groups plus its ongoing relationships with Congress work to limit presidential influence. Most presidential appointees in the departments and agencies soon find themselves with divided loyalties.

And that is not all. External factors within the environment have enlarged policy expectations of the president but at the same time made those expectations less subject to presidential control than they were in the past. The president is expected to manage the economy, but the increasing interdependence of nations limits his ability to do so; the scarcity of some natural resources no longer permits unlimited development and forces decisions that have important political consequences; the vulnerability of the United States to nuclear attack shortens the president's reaction time and broadens the effect of national security decisions. It also contributes to the public's psychological dependence on the president and the security needs that the office serves.

Finally, events of the late 1960s and mid-1970s, United States involvement in Vietnam, the Watergate cover-up, and various congressional scandals have impugned the motives and integrity of high officials, including the president's. He no longer enjoys the benefit of doubt many of his predecessors had. This makes it more difficult for him to rally and maintain public support despite the expectation that he do so.

ORIENTATION AND ORGANIZATION OF THIS STUDY

Conceptual Focus

This book will explore the leadership problems just mentioned and the attempts by recent presidents to overcome them. It will do so by examining multiple facets of the presidency within the context of its political and policy-making roles. Our orientation will be eclectic. Instead of adopting a particular perspective, the book will present several. Instead of imposing a single thesis, it will discuss many of the hypotheses, generalizations, and conclusions which have been advanced.

The reason for utilizing a variety of approaches and presenting a body of research findings is that there is no one generally accepted theory of the presidency, no one conceptual framework with which to study the office, no one thesis, other than perhaps Richard Neustadt's on presidential power,[9] that has commanded the attention and acceptance of most presidency scholars.

Despite an abundant literature on the presidency, our understanding of how that institution works is not nearly as sophisticated as our understanding of Congress or even the Supreme Court. Much of the presidency still operates behind closed doors.

What factors have conditioned the methodology, shaped the content, and limited the findings of so much of the presidency literature? Three stand out: (1) the view that each president and administration is relatively unique; (2) the difficulty of obtaining first-hand information on the operation of the institution; (3) the absence of a comprehensive theory. Together these factors have impeded the ability to do rigorous, analytic, empirical research on the presidency.

The personalities of individual presidents and their staffs, the particular events and circumstances of their time in office, and the specific problems and actions of their administrations have led scholars to treat each presidency as if it were unique. Emphasizing the differences between presidencies rather than the similarities between them makes the identification of patterns and relations more difficult and in turn, makes it harder to generalize. Description rather than analysis and speculation rather than generalization have become the standard fare.

The relatively closed character of the institution has contributed to the problem. The presidency is not easy to observe from a distance. Public pronouncements and actions tell only part of what happens and why it happens—usually the part that the people in power wish to convey. Inside information is difficult to obtain. Decision makers, particularly those at the top of the executive bureaucracy, are not readily accessible. Their busy schedules combined with their natural reluctance to reveal information that may be embarrassing, sensitive, or in other ways controversial often make them unwilling and unresponsive sources.

Nor is dependence on journalistic accounts usually satisfactory. Journalists tend to be event oriented. They do not usually employ a time frame or perspective that is sufficiently comprehensive to permit generalizations, particularly on the institutional and behavioral aspects of the office.

The third factor that contributes to the problem is the absence of an overall theory that explains presidential behavior. Unlike other areas in political science, such as individual voting behavior in which there is a body of theory that explains and predicts who votes and why, the presidency literature has not produced an explanation of why presidents do what they do or what consequences their actions have. Nor has it been able to predict what they will do or what consequences their actions will have in the future. There are, however, many prescriptions of what presidents should do.

The nature of these problems suggests that we should cast our net as broadly as possible when examining the institution and exploring the president's leadership opportunities and problems. This is why we have decided not to focus on a single theme (which might exclude important information) but to examine a set of critical relationships. These relationships are between the president and those whose support he needs to do his job.

To function effectively an occupant of the Oval Office must be elected, build and maintain popular support, make decisions, and present, promote, and implement policies. Each of these requirements involves reciprocal relationships in which presidents influence and are influenced by others. That is why we must examine both sides of these relationships rather than focus exclusively on the president.

Relationships provide a conceptual framework for studying presidential leadership. They enable us to explain the behavioral causes and consequences of presidential activities. By stressing relationships, however, we do not suggest that legal powers, informal roles, institutional structures, and psychological factors are unimportant. Indeed, we firmly believe one cannot understand the presidency without an extensive knowledge of these matters, and we provide such a background. Our point of departure is that we discuss these matters within the context of presidential relationships rather than vice versa. Powers, roles, structures, and personality should not be viewed as ends in themselves. They are important to us for what they contribute to the president's ability to formulate, establish, and implement policies.

Outline

This book is organized into four broad sections. They deal with politics and public relations, with the person in the institution, with the policy-making process, and with the presidency's interaction with the rest of the government.

The next four chapters concern the relationship between the president and the public. In Chapters 2 and 3 we discuss nomination politics and the general election. Here we focus on the interaction between presidential candidates and the electorate. In Chapter 4 we turn to the president in office and his relations with the general public, and in Chapter 5 we examine the communications link between the incumbent and the media. In each of these chapters we explore leadership problems. Obviously, winning electoral support, gaining public approval, and obtaining favorable media coverage are critical to a president's success.

In Chapters 6 and 7 we analyze the relationship between the institution and the people in it. Specifically, we examine the interaction among the president, his White House advisers, and others who wish to affect his decisions. Here attention is directed toward presidential decision making. The institutional environment combined with the president's personal style conditions his discretion and ultimately affects his choices.

After scrutinizing the president in his office, we then discuss the formulation of public policy in and by that office. Individual chapters concern domestic, budgetary and economic, and foreign and defense policy making. In each chapter we identify and assess expectations of presidential leadership and the resources that are available for meeting these expectations.

In the fourth part of the book we turn from the presidency to the interaction that the president must have with Congress, the executive branch, and the judiciary to achieve his policy objectives. Promoting programs in Congress, implementing them in the bureaucracy, and adjudicating them in the courts are necessary if presidential leadership is to be effective.

Having explored the critical relationships between the president and the public, the president and the presidency, the president and the policy-making process, and the president and the other branches, we end with a discussion of another important but different kind of relationship, that of the president and political science. Our object in this final chapter is to demonstrate how various perspectives on the office and methods of studying it can affect what we know about the president. And we conclude where we began. If the presidency is a multifaceted institution (as we claim it is), then it can best be understood only by adopting a variety of approaches and techniques. That is why our orientation is eclectic, why we have introduced a number of themes, and why we have chosen critical presidential relationships as the conceptual framework for this study.

NOTES

1. Charles de Montesquieu, *The Spirit of the Laws*, vol. 1 (New York: Hafner, 1949).
2. Locke wrote: "Where the legislative and executive power are in distinct hands, as they are in all moderated monarchies and well-framed governments, there the good of the society requires that several things should be left to the discretion of him that has the ex-

ecutive power. For the legislators not being able to foresee and provide by laws for all that may be useful to the community, the executor of the laws, having the power in his hands, has by the common law of Nature a right to make use of it for the good of the society, in many cases where the municipal law has given no direction, till the legislative can conveniently be assembled to provide for it" (John Locke, "Second Treatise of Civil Government," in Thomas I. Cook, ed., *Two Treatises of Government* [New York: Hafner, 1956], p. 203).

3. Abraham Lincoln, "Letter dated April 8, 1964," reprinted in Harry A. Bailey, Jr., ed., *Classics of the American Presidency* (Oak Park, Ill.: 1980), p. 34.

4. Theodore Roosevelt, *The Autobiography of Theodore Roosevelt* (New York: Scribner's, 1913), p. 197.

5. William Howard Taft, *Our Chief Magistrate and His Powers* (New York: Columbia University Press, 1916), p. 138.

6. President's Committee on Administrative Management, *Report with Special Studies* (Washington, D.C.: U.S. Government Printing Office, 1937), p. 5.

7. It was during the 1820s that the electorate began to choose presidential electors directly rather than have them selected by state legislatures. This increased the value of obtaining and maintaining public support for the president. Tradition, however, required that this be done in a manner that befitted the dignity of the office. Public addresses were permitted; personal campaigning was discouraged. The party was expected to shoulder the electoral burden for its candidates. Not until William Jennings Bryan's quest for the nation's highest office in 1896 did candidates take to the stump themselves.

8. Woodrow Wilson, *Constitutional Government* (New York: Columbia University Press, 1908), pp. 70–71.

9. Richard E. Neustadt, *Presidential Power: The Politics of Leadership from FDR to Carter* (New York: Wiley, 1980), p. 26.

2

The Nomination
Process

Every four years there are two presidential selection processes: the first to nominate candidates, the second to choose between them. Both require considerable time, money, and effort.

The nominating system has evolved significantly in recent years. Rules governing delegate selection, laws regulating contributions and spending, communications controlled and uncontrolled by the candidates have all changed dramatically within the last twenty-five years. These changes have literally revolutionized the nomination process. In this chapter we will discuss that revolution and its impact on those seeking the presidency.

The chapter is organized into four parts. First we present a historical overview of the nomination process, describing its evolution from congressional caucus to brokered national conventions to popular selection of the delegates through primaries and caucuses. In the second part we examine the factors that condition that selection: party rules, finance laws, and media coverage. Emphasizing the changes that have occurred within each of these areas, we describe their impact on parties and their standard-bearers. Next, we turn to the strategy and tactics of seeking the nomination. We discuss the principal components of the campaign: building a sound organization, mounting an effective appeal, and targeting it to sufficient numbers of receptive voters. In the last part of the chapter we take this quest to the national convention and describe the unofficial and official business of these large, semipublic extravaganzas: drama and staging; rules, credentials, and platforms; and the nominations themselves. We also present a brief characterization of the successful candidates. In conclusion, we summarize changes in this process and their implications for presidential politics and government.

THE EVOLUTION OF THE SYSTEM

The nominating system began to evolve after the Constitution was written and the first two presidential elections were conducted. The framers had not concerned themselves with nominations, because there were no parties to nominate candidates. Assuming that well-qualified individuals would comprise the pool from which the president and vice president would be selected, the convention delegates directed their efforts toward encouraging an independent judgment by the electors. They considered such a judgment essential if the two *most* qualified persons were to be chosen.

Once political parties emerged, however, the notion of making an independent decision was constrained by the party's desire to choose an individual whose views were consistent with its own. This required a mechanism by which the parties could designate their nominees.

In 1796, party leaders met informally to agree on their tickets. Four years later partisan congressional caucuses met for the purposes of recommending candidates. "King Caucus," as it came to be known, constituted the principal mode of nomination until the 1820s, when factions developed within Jefferson's Republican party, the only viable party at the time. These factions eventually led to the demise of the caucus and the development of a more decentralized mode of nomination that was consistent with the increasingly sectional composition of the parties. By the 1830s national nominating conventions became the principal means for brokering those interests and uniting the party for a national campaign.

The first convention was held in 1831 by the Anti-Masons, a small but relatively active third party. Having virtually no congressional representation of its own, this party could not use a caucus of legislators to decide on its candidates. Instead, it organized a general meeting in which delegates from the state parties would choose its nominees as well as determine the party's positions on the important issues of the day. The two major parties followed suit in 1832. Thereafter conventions became the standard method for selecting nominees and for articulating policy positions.

These early conventions were informal and rowdy by contemporary standards. The delegates themselves decided on the procedures for conducting the meetings. Choosing the delegates was left to the state party and more specifically to its leadership. In most cases, public participation was minimal.

Nineteenth-century conventions served a number of purposes.

They provided a forum for party bosses. They constituted a mechanism by which agreements could be negotiated and support mobilized. By brokering interests, they helped unite disparate elements of the party, converting a conglomeration of state organizations into a national coalition for the purpose of electing a president and vice president.

The nominating system buttressed the position of party officials, but it did so at the expense of the rank and file. The influence of the leadership depended in large part on its ability to deliver the votes. To ensure loyalty, the bosses handpicked their delegations.

Demands for reform began to be heard at the beginning of the twentieth century. A number of states changed their mode of selection to primary elections to permit greater public participation. This movement, however, was short-lived. Low voter turnout in primary states, the costs of holding such an election, and the opposition of party leaders to rank-and-file involvement persuaded several state legislatures to make their primaries advisory or discontinue them entirely. As a consequence, the number of primaries declined after World War I as did the percentage of delegates selected in them (see Table 2-1).

Strong candidates avoided primaries. Running in too many of them was interpreted as a sign of weakness, not strength. It indicated the lack of national recognition and/or a failure to obtain the support of party leaders.

Those who did enter these public contests did so mainly to test their popularity rather than to win convention votes. Dwight D. Eisenhower in 1952, John F. Kennedy in 1960, and Richard M. Nixon in 1968 had to demonstrate that being a general, a Catholic, or a once-defeated presidential candidate would not be fatal to their chances. In other words, they needed to prove they could win the general election by doing well in some primaries.

With the possible exception of John Kennedy's victories in West Virginia and Wisconsin in 1960 and Barry Goldwater's in California in 1964, primaries were neither crucial nor decisive for winning the nomination until the 1970s.[1] When there was a consensus within the party on a single candidate, primaries helped confirm it; when there was not, primaries were not able to produce it. They had little to do with whether the party was united or divided at the time of the convention.

CHANGES IN THE POLITICAL ARENA

Party Reforms

Within eight years the situation was to alter dramatically. Largely as a result of the tumultuous Democratic convention of 1968 whose nominee, Hubert Humphrey, had not competed in the primaries, demands for a larger voice for the party's rank and file increased. In response to these demands, the party appointed a series of commissions to examine its rules for delegate selection and propose changes. The commissions had two basic goals: to encourage greater participation in party activities and to make the convention more representative of typical Democratic voters.

To achieve these objectives the party in the 1970s attempted to tune delegate selection more closely to popular sentiment. Delegates had to be chosen in the calendar year of the convention. In the past they had been selected up to two years prior to the convention. Fees for entering primaries were lowered or abolished. In the past, the high costs of registration had discouraged some candidates from running. Three-fourths of the delegates had to be chosen at levels no larger than congressional districts. In the past some states had elected all of their delegates at the state level, underrepresenting minorities in the process. The allocation of the delegates to candidates had to reflect fairly the popular vote which the candidates received within the state. Previously, the party had permitted winner-take-all voting by which all the delegates could be awarded to the candidate with the most votes.[2]

In nonprimary states the meetings for choosing the delegates had to be publicly announced with adequate time given for campaigning. The old system of proxy voting, whereby a state party leader would cast a large number of votes for the delegates of his choice, was abolished. State central committees were no longer permitted to appoint more than 10 percent of the delegates.

The other major objective of the reforms was to promote more equal representation of the rank and file on the delegations themselves. To achieve this aim the party required states to implement affirmative action plans for specific groups which had been subject to discrimination in the past. Native Americans, blacks, and youth were singled out, and states were required to set goals for representation on their delegations based on the proportion of the group's population within the state. With respect to women, the Democrats went one step further. Beginning in 1980 each state delegation was required to be equally divided between men and women.

One consequence of these reforms was to make primaries the preferred method of delegate selection. To avoid having their delegations challenged, many state legislatures simply had the voters choose them (see Table 2-1). A second was to tie the popular vote more closely to the allocation of convention delegates. This made the process more open and more participatory. In 1984 almost 19 million people participated in the Democratic primary campaign. This was 3.8 percent greater than in 1980.

Almost 6.5 million votes were cast in uncontested Republican primaries with 98.6 percent going to Reagan.[3] In 1968 only 12 million people participated in the preconvention nomination process. Demographic representation at the national convention has also improved (see Table 2-2).[4]

The rules changes had some negative consequences. They lengthened the process and inflated its costs. Candidate fatigue and public boredom increased. The influence of the media also grew, particularly in the early critical stages. The party became more factionalized with its

Table 2-1. Number of Presidential Primaries and Percentage of Convention Delegates from Primary States, by Party, Since 1912

	Democratic		Republican	
Year	Number of Primaries	Percentage of Delegates	Number of Primaries	Percentage of Delegates
1912	12	32.9	13	41.7
1916	20	53.5	20	58.9
1920	16	44.6	20	57.8
1924	14	35.5	17	45.3
1928	17	42.2	16	44.9
1932	16	40.0	14	37.7
1936	14	36.5	12	37.5
1940	13	35.8	13	38.8
1944	14	36.7	13	38.7
1948	14	36.3	12	36.0
1952	15	38.7	13	39.0
1956	19	42.7	19	44.8
1960	16	38.3	15	38.6
1964	17	45.7	17	45.6
1968	17	37.5	16	34.3
1972	23	60.5	22	52.7
1976	29*	72.6	28*	67.9
1980	31*	74.7	35*	74.3
1984	26	62.9	30	68.2

*Does not include Vermont, which held nonbinding presidential preference votes but chooses delegates in state caucuses and conventions.

Sources: 1912–1964, F. Christopher Arterton, "Campaign Organizations Face the Mass Media in the 1976 Presidential Nomination Process" (paper delivered at the Annual Meeting of the American Political Science Association, Washington, D.C., September 1–4, 1977); 1968–1976, Austin Ranney, *Participation in American Presidential Nominations, 1976* (Washington, D.C.: American Enterprise Institute, 1977), table 1, p. 6. Reprinted with permission of the author. The figures for 1980 were compiled by Austin Ranney from materials distributed by the Democratic National Committee; and the Republican National Committee; 1984 figures were supplied by the Democratic and Republican National Committees.

Table 2-2. The Demography of the Delegates, 1968–1984

	National Convention Delegates									
	1968		1972		1976		1980		1984	
	Dem.	*Rep.*	*Dem.*	*Rep.*	*Dem.*	*Rep.*	*Dem.*	*Rep.*	*Dem.*	*Rep.*
Women	13%	16%	40%	29%	33%	31%	49%	29%	50%	44%
Blacks	5	2	15	4	11	7	15	3	18	4
Under thirty	3	4	22	8	15		11	5	8	4
Median age (years)	(49)	(49)	(42)		(43)	(48)	(44)	(49)	(43)	(51)
Lawyers	28	22	12		16	15	13	15	17	14
Teachers	8	2	11			4	15	4	16	6
Union members			16		21	3	27	4	25	4
Attended first convention	67	66	83	78	80	78	87	84	74	61
College graduate	19		21		21	f27	20	26	20	28
Postgraduate	44	34	36		43	38	45	39	51	35
Protestant			42		47	73	47	72	49	71
Catholic			26		34	18	37	22	29	22
Jewish			9		9	3	8	3	8	2
Liberal					40	3	46	2	48	1
Moderate					47	45	42	36	42	35
Conservative					8	48	6	58	4	60

Source: CBS News Delegate Surveys, 1968 through 1980. Characteristics of the public are average values from seven CBS News/*New York Times* polls, 1980. Reprinted from Warren J. Mitofsky and Martin Plissner, "The Making of the Delegates, 1968–1980," *Public Opinion* (1980): 43. © 1980, American Enterprise Institute for Public Policy Research, Washington, D.C. 20036. 1984 data supplied by CBS News from its delegate surveys and reprinted with permission of CBS News.

state and local leadership less able to affect presidential nominations within their own areas. Party leaders were not even guaranteed a place on their own delegations. The number of party officials attending the national meetings declined (see Table 2-3).

To offset these unintended results, the Democrats reformed their reforms after their unsuccessful 1980 general election campaign. They tried to shorten the process by tightening the time-frame in which it could occur. Only two states, Iowa and New Hampshire, were given permission to hold their contests prior to the second Tuesday in March. They tried to increase the influence of elected and appointed party officials. Each state was allocated additional delegates to be selected from its members of Congress, elected officials, and party officials. All were to be unpledged, or at least not formally committed to a particular candidate. Finally, they gave states greater flexibility in determining the formula by which delegates would be allocated. States could modify but not ignore the rule that delegates be chosen in a manner that fairly reflects popular preferences. The party also raised the minimum percentage of the vote needed by candidates to obtain delegates. These changes benefited the better-known, better-organized aspirants for the nomination.

The allocation of delegates caused particular controversy during the 1984 preconvention process. Jesse Jackson alleged that the rules were biased against lesser-known, minority candidates such as himself. Jackson's delegate support fell considerably below the popular support he received in several states.

Table 2-3. Representation of Major Elected Officials at National Conventions, 1968–1984* (in percentages)

	1968	1972	1976	1980	1984
Democrats					
Governors	96	57	44	74	91
U.S. senators	61	28	18	14	56
U.S. representatives	32	12	14	14	62
Republicans					
Governors	92	80	69	68	93
U.S. senators	58	50	59	63	56
U.S. representatives	31	19	36	40	53

*Figures represent the percentages of Democratic or Republican officeholders from each group who served as delegates.

Source: Hugh L. LeBlanc, *American Political Parties* (New York: St. Martin's, 1982), p. 220. LeBlanc derived the data in this table from Warren J. Mitofsky and Martin Plissner, "The Making of the Delegates, 1968–1980," *Public Opinion* (1980), p. 43. Reprinted with permission. 1984 figures provided to author by the Republican and Democratic National Committees.

Although the Republican party (GOP) has not mandated national guidelines for the states as the Democrats have, it too has been affected by many of the changes as well. The impact on the GOP has been felt in two ways: through public pressure to broaden participation and improve the representation of minorities and through new state laws, designed to conform to Democratic rules, laws which affect the scheduling and structure of caucuses and primaries.

States are free to determine how and when nominating elections are to be conducted. However, two recent Supreme Court decisions, *Cousins v. Wigoda* (419 U.S. 477, 1975) and *Democratic Party of the U.S. v. LaFollette* (449 U.S. 897, 1981), give the party the right to reject delegates to its national convention that are not selected in conformity with its rules. These decisions have put pressure on states, particularly those whose legislature is controlled by the Democrats, to abide by its mandatory rules in order to prevent challenges to the state delegation at the national convention.

Finance Laws

While the reforms in party rules have had a profound effect, they are not the only major changes to affect the nomination process. New finance laws have had a major impact as well. They have altered the way in which money is raised and spent and the amount that is available.

Throughout most of American history candidates of both parties depended almost exclusively on large contributions to finance their campaigns. This dependence, combined with spiraling costs, secret and sometimes illegal contributions, and little public information about giving and spending, raised serious questions about the conduct of elections in a democratic society. Could officials be responsive to national needs as well as to those of their individual benefactors? Had the presidency become an office that only the wealthy could afford—or, worse yet, that only those with wealthy support could seek?

In the 1970s Congress began to address some of these issues. It enacted legislation to limit skyrocketing expenses, especially in the media, to control the influence of large contributors, and to bring them out in the open. Limits were placed on the amount of money presidential and vice presidential candidates and their families could contribute to their own campaigns and the amount that could be spent. Other legislation established a fund to subsidize the presidential nomination process and support the general election.

Faced with a threatened veto of this legislation by the Republican president Richard Nixon, the Democrats in Congress agreed to a compromise whereby the law would not take effect until after the 1972 election, in which Nixon planned to run for re-election. In that election a number of large corporations were pressured into making contributions to the Nixon reelection committee in violation of the law. The spending of campaign funds on dirty tricks and other unethical and illegal activities, including the break-in of the Democratic National Committee's headquarters at the Watergate, further aroused public ire and resulted in new and more stringent legislation.

Passed in 1974, the new law provided for public disclosure, contribution ceilings, campaign spending limits, and federal subsidies for the nomination process. Some of its provisions were highly controversial. Critics immediately charged a federal giveaway, a robbery of the Treasury. Opponents of the legislation also argued that the limits on contributions and spending violated the constitutionally guaranteed right to freedom of speech. In the landmark case of *Buckley* v. *Valeo* (424 U.S. 1, 1976), the Supreme Court agreed in part. It upheld the right of Congress to regulate the contributions and expenditures of campaign organizations but not the independent spending of individuals and groups during the campaign. The Court's decision forced Congress to enact new legislation in 1976, which it subsequently amended in 1979. The major provisions of this legislation are as follows:

- *Public Disclosure.* All contributions of $200 or more must be identified. All expenditures of $200 or more must be reported. Campaign committees are also required to file periodic reports before the election and a final report after it.

- *Contribution Limits.* In any election, contributions from individuals cannot exceed $1,000 to a single candidate, $20,000 to a national political party committee, and $5,000 to other political committees, with the total not to exceed $25,000 in any one year. Personal contributions from a candidate or that candidate's immediate family are limited to $50,000 if the candidate accepts federal funds. Candidates who do not accept federal funds are not limited in what they can contribute to their own campaign. Table 2-4 summarizes the contribution limits. Individuals and political action committees (PACs) can spend an unlimited amount on their own for candidates of their choice provided they do not consult or communicate in any way with the candidate's campaign organization.

- *Campaign Expenses.* Candidates who accept public funding are limited in the amount they can spend. During the preconvention period there is an overall ceiling as well as individual state limits. In 1984 the ceiling was $20.2 million. The state limits, based on the size of the voting-age population and a cost-of-living adjustment, ranged from approximately $440,000 in the smaller states to over

$7.5 million in the largest. Fund-raising expenses up to 20 percent of expenditures and accounting and legal fees are exempt from these spending limits.

During the general election, the federal grant cannot be exceeded. In 1984 it was $40.4 million. Candidates who do not accept federal funds have no limit on their expenditures.

- *Matching Funds.* Major party contenders who raise $5,000 in each of twenty states in contributions of $250 or less, a total of $100,000, are eligible to receive matching grants during the prenomination period, which begins January 1 of the year in which the election occurs. Only the first $250 of each contribution will be matched.

- *Communication Notices.* All authorized advertisements by candidates' organizations must state the name of the candidate or agent who authorized them. All nonauthorized advertisements must identify the person who made or financed the ad and his or her organizational affiliation, if any.

- *Compliance Procedures.* The Federal Election Commission has authority to investigate possible violations, hold hearings, and assess certain civil penalties. Its decision may be appealed to U.S district courts. The Justice Department retains the authority for criminal investigation and prosecution.

Table 2-4. Contribution Limits

	To Each Candidate or Candate Committee per Election	To National Party Committee per Calender Year	To Any Other Political Committee per Calender year	Total per Calendar Year
Individual may give	$1,000	$20,000	$5,000	$25,000
Multicandidate committee* may give	5,000	15,000	5,000	No limit
Party committees may give	1,000 or 5,000†	No limit	5,000	No limit
Other political committees may give†	1,000	20,000	5,000	No limit

*A multicandidate committee is a political action committee with more than fifty contributors which has been registered for at least six months, and, with the exception of state party committees, has made contributions to five or more federal candidates.

†Limit depends on whether or not the party committee is a multicandidate committee.

Source: Federal Election Commission, "The FEC and the Federal Campaign Finance Law" (Washington, D.C.: Government Printing Office, 1978), p. 4.

Congress had a number of objectives in enacting campaign finance legislation. It had hoped to reduce the dependence on large donors, discourage illicit contributions, broaden the base of public support, and curtail spiraling costs at the presidential level.

While all these objectives have not been achieved, the 1976 law has already had a significant impact on nomination politics. It has substantially reduced secret contributors and unexplained expenses, although it has not eliminated violations, overpayments, and improper reporting procedures. The most serious violation occurred in 1976 when Democratic candidate Governor Milton Shapp of Pennsylvania had to refund all the $300,000 he received in matching funds when it was discovered that his workers had inflated the number of contributors in several states to meet the eligibility requirements.

Dependence on large contributors has also been reduced. However, the $1,000 limit on individual donations, the $250 ceiling on matching grants, and the eligibility requirements to get federal funds have all made the solicitation of a large number of small contributions essential during the preconvention phase.

Although the law has decreased the importance that a handful of large donors had in previous campaigns, it has increased the impact of organized nonparty groups. By forming political action committees, these groups can contribute up to $5,000 to individual candidates in their primary campaign. Moreover, they can spend an unlimited amount *independently* on the candidates in educating, mobilizing, and turning out the vote. Direct contributions by PACs to aspirants for their party's nomination have not been that significant. They constitute only a small percentage of the funds candidates receive (1 percent in 1980). Independent expenditures are another matter. Having increased enormously in recent years, these expenditures can affect delegate selection on a state-by-state basis.

In his 1984 quest for the Democratic nomination, Walter Mondale was helped enormously by the activity of PACs, particularly those of organized labor. American Federation of Labor and Congress of Industrial Organizations (AFL-CIO) groups ran telephone banks, targeted union households, and mobilized large get-out-the-vote drives in districts where labor was concentrated. Not only did such efforts relieve the Mondale organization of some of this campaign activity but it reduced its financial burdens as well. In New Hampshire, for example, where Mondale's expenditures approached the legal limit, labor rented storefront offices, telephones, and other needed equipment which they allowed Mondale staffers to use at a fraction of their cost. Naturally such actions precipitated criticism by Mondale's opponents.

A major controversy developed during the 1984 preconvention contest over delegate PACs, groups organized for the purpose of electing specific individuals as delegates to the national nominating convention.

Since the Mondale committee had spent a substantial portion of its allow-able expenses early in the campaign, $13.3 million during the first three months of 1984, it encouraged the formation of these PACs to reduce its own financial outlays. A letter from a Mondale official indicated how such PACs could be established and suggested that any legal question concerning them should be referred to the campaign's legal counsel. As a consequence of these efforts, delegate PACs were organized and raised money in nineteen states. In several of them funds were used to pay the salaries of individuals who had been previously paid by the national cam-paign organization. There were even transfers of money between PACs of different states. Gary Hart, Mondale's principal opponent, charged that this activity violated the letter and spirit of the law, which prohibited collusion between the campaign organization and the PACs. After trying to sidestep the issue, Mondale was finally pressured to repay the sums his delegate PACs spent.

Despite the provisions of the law that permit PACs to organize and spend independently, the campaign finance legislation has produced greater equity. The matching-fund provision has given lesser-known candidates of the major parties a better opportunity to gain public sup-port. Previously, candidates without national visibility found it harder to raise the money necessary to run an effective campaign. For some, matching funds have increased their staying power, enabling them to continue to seek the nomination even after disappointing showings in the early primaries.[5]

By encouraging self-selection and increasing the number of candi-dates and their ability to run in more primaries, the Federal Election Cam-paign Act also enhances the prospect of a challenge to the incumbent. This has had the effect of factionalizing the national parties and ulti-mately weakening their structure. The organization of the successful can-didate is not dismantled after the nomination; it is expanded, often competing with the regular party organization.

Finally, the number of candidates vying for each party's nomination has significantly increased the amount of money spent in preconvention politics. In 1976 the expenditures of both parties totaled almost $67 mil-lion. In 1980 that figure was almost double, $128 million. Even without competition the Reagan-Bush campaign in 1984 raised and spent close to the legal limit. They received over $10 million in matching funds before the Republican convention. During the same period the Democratic con-tenders received a combined total of almost $22 million from the federal government.

Public Relations

The third major change in the nomination process has been the en-largement of its public dimension. In the past, the quest for the nomination was a relatively private affair. Candidates made their case primarily to state party leaders. There was little need to discern public attitudes, project public appeals, or build public support. Now there is.

The cast of characters is also different. In the past, preconvention campaign organizations consisted of a relatively small group of party regulars. Today that organization numbers in the hundreds at its headquarters and in the thousands in the field. Moreover, most of the principals do not hold important party positions but are professional campaigners with a partisan tinge: pollsters, media consultants, grass-roots organizers, direct-mailers, accountants and attorneys specializing in electoral politics. No candidate can be without these wizards of modern campaign technology.

Even the traits the candidates must demonstrate are different. They need less political experience but more public exposure. They need to be good actors and good orators. They should be reasonably photogenic. They must be willing to campaign continuously in the public eye through the mass media and primarily on radio and television. Nominations are no longer obtained behind closed doors. Support is acquired by personal appeals to the party's electorate.

To be credible, these appeals must be in tune with public opinion. The pulse of the voters conditions the message that is presented and the image that is created. Thus, a critical early step for any serious candidate is to have that pulse taken. A pollster must be hired and a private poll commissioned.

Polls

John F. Kennedy was the first candidate to engage a pollster in his quest for the nomination. Preconvention surveys conducted by Louis Harris in 1960 indicated that Hubert Humphrey, Kennedy's principal rival, was vulnerable in West Virginia and Wisconsin. On the basis of this information, the Kennedy campaign wisely decided to concentrate time, effort, and money in these states. Victories in both helped demonstrate Kennedy's popularity, thereby improving his chances for the nomination enormously.

Private polls are important for several reasons. They provide information about the opinions, beliefs, and attitudes of voters; they identify perceptions people have of the candidates and their positions; they suggest the kinds of appeals that are apt to be most persuasive and the groups to whom these appeals should be made. Armed with this information, media campaigns can be designed and targeted. Periodic polling allows them to be monitored over the course of the nomination process. Pollster Pat Caddell's reading of public moods in 1983 had a major impact on Gary Hart's redesigning his appeal in 1984. Discerning the desire of a sizable portion of the electorate for a new face and new ideas, Caddell urged Hart to emphasize these characteristics in Iowa and New Hampshire, which he did.

Poll results are also used to build momentum, increase morale, raise money, and affect media coverage. By indicating who can win and who should be taken seriously, polls affect the amount of attention candidates receive. In general, the more coverage they have, particularly during the early months, the more volunteers they can attract, and the more money they can raise.

There is some evidence of a relationship between standing in the polls, success in the primaries, and winning the nomination. Table 2-5 in-

Table 2-5. Public Opinion and the Nomination

Year and Party	Gallup Poll after First Primary	Final Gallup Poll before Convention	Party Nominee
1940 D	Roosevelt	Roosevelt	Roosevelt*
R	Dewey	Willkie	Willkie
1944 D	Roosevelt	Roosevelt	Roosevelt*
R	Dewey	Dewey	Dewey
1948 D	Truman	Truman	Truman
R	Stassen	Dewey	Dewey
1952 D	Kefauver	Kefauver	Stevenson
R	Eisenhower	Eisenhower	Eisenhower*
1956 D	Stevenson	Stevenson	Stevenson
R	Eisenhower	Eisenhower	Eisenhower*
1960 D	J. Kennedy	Kennedy	Kennedy*
R	Nixon	Nixon	Nixon
1964 D	—	Johnson	Johnson*
R	Lodge	Goldwater & Nixon (tie)	Goldwater
1968 D	R. Kennedy	Humphrey	Humphrey
R	Nixon	Nixon	Nixon*
1972 D	Humphrey	McGovern	McGovern
R	—	Nixon	Nixon*
1976 D	Humphrey	Carter	Carter*
R	Ford	Ford	Ford
1980 D	Carter	Carter	Carter
R	Reagan	Reagan	Reagan*
1984 D	Mondale+	Mondale+	Mondale
R	Reagan	Reagan	Reagan*

D = Democrat
R = Republican

Source: *The Gallup Poll, Public Opinion 1933–1971*, vols. 1–3 (New Yorks Random House, 1972; *Gallup Opinion Index* (Princeton, N.J.: Gallup International 1971–1980). Reprinted with permission. *Indicates general election winner. +Mondale was the choice of Democrats; he trailed Hart among self-identified Independents.

dicates how the poll leaders have done. What it does not indicate, however, is whether the public opinion leaders won because they were more popular or whether they were more popular initially because they were better known and ultimately because they looked like winners.

The benefits of appearing to be popular and electable suggest why candidates have also used their private polls for promotional purposes. Releasing favorable surveys is a standard stratagem. Nelson Rockefeller, in fact, tied his quest for the Republican nomination in 1968 to poll data. Since he did not enter the primaries, Rockefeller's aim was to convince Republican delegates that he, not Richard Nixon, would be the strongest candidate. Private surveys conducted for Rockefeller in nine large states, five important congressional districts, and in the nation as a whole one month before the Republican convention indicated that he would do better against potential Democratic candidates than Nixon. Unfortunately for Rockefeller, the final Gallup preconvention poll, fielded two days after President Eisenhower endorsed Nixon, did not support these findings. The Gallup results undercut the credibility of Rockefeller's polls as well as another national survey that had Rockefeller in the lead and effectively ended his chances for the nomination.

Media

After polls have been taken, appeals can be made. The mass media have become the principal vehicles for accomplishing this objective. This was not always the case.

When party leaders exercised the most influence, personal contact was most effective. When a relatively small number of primaries were held, personal appearances at rallies, speeches before clubs, and press conferences for local media energized rank-and-file supporters. When people received most of their information from print media, newspaper coverage, supplemented by campaign literature, educated and influenced those who were interested in politics and who would take part in the nomination process.

All this has changed. The electorate has grown in size and diversity. Primaries and multistaged caucuses have proliferated. It is now necessary to conduct simultaneous campaigns in several states. More people can be reached through the mass media, particularly radio and television.

The use of the visual and audio media has revolutionized campaigning. It has made image creation more important, brought public relations specialists into candidate organizations, and siphoned off relatively large proportions of the campaign budget for television and radio. It has also made the candidates less spontaneous. Fearful that their words and actions might be misinterpreted or misconstrued, they now tend to play it

safe. They ad lib less and follow a script more. In debates, press conferences, and interviews, candidates tend to repeat their "stump" speeches.
They sound more and more like their commercials. Even events are
staged for home video consumption.

The media, particularly television, have influenced the nomination
process in several other respects. The early contests have become more
important because of the attention they are given. New Hampshire, traditionally the first state to hold a presidential primary, produces a lot of
media coverage. For the last thirty years, it has ranked first in the amount
of attention it has received.[6] Naturally, the candidate who does surprisingly well in this primary will benefit enormously. Eugene McCarthy in
1968, George McGovern in 1972, Jimmy Carter in 1976, and Gary Hart in
1984 all gained visibility and credibility from their New Hampshire performances, even though none had a majority of the vote. Carter and Hart
had pluralities. The initial round of the Iowa caucuses, held before the
New Hampshire primary, has also received extensive attention in recent
years.

Early victories help establish front-runner status. They can provide
an important psychological boost. Being declared a winner improves
one's standing in the polls, makes fund raising easier, and aids in attracting backers who contribute to later primary success.

But media publicity can have a negative consequence as well—even
for the winner. When George Bush defeated Ronald Reagan in the 1980
Iowa caucus, he moved from having less than 10 percent support among
the Republican rank and file to 28 percent—almost as much as Reagan
had at the time.[7] He subsequently won in Puerto Rico. Much was expected of him in New Hampshire. When he lost that state to Reagan, his
defeat was magnified by his two earlier wins. Had he not been declared
winner of these first two contests, his New Hampshire performance
would not have been nearly as newsworthy.

Moreover, the media treat front-runners more harshly than challengers. There is more investigative reporting and more implicit criticism
of their candidacies. Being a front-runner guarantees not only greater
coverage but also greater scrutiny.[8]

Another way in which the media affect delegate selection is in their
interpretation of the results of primaries and caucuses. The winners are
not necessarily those who do best but those who do better than expected.
When performance exceeds expectations or does not meet them, that is
news. When performance meets expectations, it is less newsworthy.
Candidates therefore tend to underestimate their vote in public in order
to be able to indicate how satisfied they are with the results when the results are announced. Eugene McCarthy's ability to do this was a key factor in his primary challenge first of Lyndon Johnson and then of Robert
Kennedy in 1968. McCarthy contested nine primaries and won two but

minimized the impact of his seven losses using this low prediction posture. Similarly, Jimmy Carter in 1976 purposely kept his predictions low. In the words of his campaign manager Hamilton Jordan:

> It has already been established in the minds of the national press that Mo Udall is going to do well in New Hampshire. He has established that expectation. If he does not win in New Hampshire, I think now by the measuring criteria that the press is going to apply, he will have underperformed. Well, we'd never talk about winning in New Hampshire. We never talk about winning anywhere. We talk about doing well.[9]

Not only is the outcome of the primaries subject to interpretation, but so is the importance attached to particular contests. Generally speaking, the media give primaries more attention than caucuses, close elections more emphasis than one-sided ones, and statewide contests better coverage than district elections.

Candidates can affect the coverage they receive. The importance they place on individual primaries, for example, especially when a number of them occur on the same day, can affect the impact that those primaries have in the public's eye. Other tactics used to influence the media include the timing and staging of events, the release of information, and even access to the candidate and his senior aides. Major announcements are made in sufficient time to get on the evening news. Speeches are scheduled to maximize the viewing audience. Quiet periods, such as Saturday, are considered a good time to hold a press conference or schedule interviews. In addition to receiving same-day coverage by television, a Saturday event usually gets prominent treatment in the Sunday papers.

Access is another valuable commodity. At the beginning of the nomination process, access is cheap, especially for lesser-known candidates who need media attention. As the campaign progresses, access becomes more important and, at the same time, more difficult to obtain. There is more competition among journalists, the candidates have a more demanding schedule, and a larger public relations staff stands between the correspondents and the nominees. Granting interviews under these circumstances can do much to affect the quantity and quality of coverage received.

To a large extent those who report the news are dependent on this material. Many news stories come directly from the candidates themselves.[10] A study of the 1980 election by Michael Robinson and Margaret Sheehan reported:

> On UPI, just over 40 percent of the Carter news came directly from Carter, his press office, his staff, or his administration. Fewer than 10 percent came via the investigative route. On CBS, it was the same story, so to speak, only more so. A full two-thirds of the "official" news about Carter came via a Carter-controlled news source.[11]

Advertising is another way to shape and, if need be, change public perceptions. Its principal advantage is the amount of control that can be exercised over it by the candidate and his advisers. The message can be designed to create a certain effect. It also can be aired as often as money permits. Not only can advertising reach a potentially large population, but it also can be targeted to specific groups within it. Take Democratic candidate Alan Cranston's pitch to proponents for a freeze on nuclear weapons at the beginning of the 1984 presidential campaign:

> There will be no question about the purpose of the Cranston presidency. I will be the first president totally committed to stopping the arms race. I will be the only president since Franklin Roosevelt to put the full weight of his office behind getting people back to work. Full employment and ending the arms race.[12]

Political ads are not without their limitations, however. Like all commercials, they are blatantly partial, usually expensive, and require the services of skilled personnel to buy time, produce the spot, and act in it. To overcome the problem of partiality, political advertisers have gone to great lengths to project an image of authenticity and spontaneity in their commercials. To minimize costs, they have concentrated on local, less expensive media during the preconvention period. In 1980 only Republican John Connolly purchased time on the major networks. To reach a smaller but specific audience, they have used radio. To appeal to a large, more general population, they have employed television. The need for experts is reflected in the hiring of media consultants early in the campaign, often many months before the first contest. Candidates are now regularly coached, made up, and scripted before appearing on camera.

The increasing importance of the media had a major effect on the conduct of campaigns. It has made radio and television the critical communication links between candidates and the voters. Advertising in these media has become a major component of campaign strategy, although its utility varies with several factors. It is generally considered more significant in states with more voters than in those with fewer, in those that hold primaries rather than caucuses, and at the beginning of the nomination process when less is known about the candidates than at the end.

Another medium that is becoming increasingly popular in campaigns is direct mail. Computer technology has now made it possible to send letters and literature to lists of individuals organized on the basis of area, ideology, interests, partisanship, or other affiliation. The letters are tailored to the recipient and are often personalized. A return envelope for donations is usually included. In this sense direct mail can reap a dual benefit: it can inform and educate voters and it can raise money, often large amounts.

Advertising in whatever form is used to generate interest, to increase recognition, and to improve images. It can also help to mobilize and turn out voters, although it is not considered sufficient, in and of itself, to accomplish these objectives. It must be supplemented by other campaign activities.

Field Work

Candidates still need to organize at the grass roots. They need advance people to arrange for their appearances and to assemble their crowds, other politicians, and the media. They need schedulers to plan their days and decide which invitations to accept. They need local organizers to run phone banks to identify voters, and they need volunteers to ring door bells, circulate literature, and get would-be supporters to the polls. Eugene McCarthy and George McGovern recruited thousands of college students to help them in their primary efforts. In 1976 Carter's "peanut brigade," a group of Georgians who followed their candidate from state to state, was particularly effective in canvassing and organizing; the support the Reverend Jesse Jackson received from black clergy had a similar effect in 1984.

THE QUEST FOR THE NOMINATION

Greater public involvement in the nomination process has changed the strategy and tactics of those seeking the nomination. Campaigns begin much earlier than in the past. They are more broad-based. They require more money up front, an organization in place, and a game plan that targets an appeal and constructs a winning coalition.

In recent years two basic strategies have emerged. Which strategy candidates adopt depends in large part on their status at the beginning of the nomination quest. Both are predicated on certain fundamental assumptions:

1. that sufficient time and energy be devoted to personal campaigning in the pre- and early preconvention period. Only an incumbent can remain in the White House and even he can remain there too long.
2. that a strong, in-depth organization for the initial caucuses and primaries be built. Television advertising is important, but it is not possible to win by it alone.
3. that a firm financial base be established early and a spending strategy devised. All caucuses and primaries are not equal; the first ones are more important and, hence, require the allocation of greater resources.

4. that the order of events and the rules of the game be understood and, if possible, manipulated. Magnifying victories and minimizing defeats usually require that strong states be isolated and weak ones paired with strong ones.
5. that groups within the party be targeted and appeals to them be made. Over the course of the campaign, however, these appeals must be moderated and broadened. If the overall constituency is too narrow, it would be difficult to win the nomination and even more difficult to win the general election.

Non–Front-Runner Strategy

The initial goal of the non–front-runners is to establish their credibility as viable candidates. Publicly announcing one's intentions, establishing a campaign headquarters, qualifying for matching funds, and obtaining political endorsements are necessary but not sufficient conditions to do so. At the outset, the key is recognition. Over the long haul, it is momentum.

Recognition is bestowed by the media on those who do better than expected in the early primaries and caucuses; momentum is achieved by a series of prenomination victories. Together, recognition and momentum compensate for what the non–front-runners lack in reputation and appeal. That is why non–front-runners concentrate their time, efforts, and resources in the first few contests. They have no choice. Winning will provide them with opportunities later on; losing will confirm their secondary status.

Jimmy Carter's 1976 quest for the Democratic nomination is a good example of a successful non–front-runner approach. Carter began as a relatively unknown southern governor with limited financial resources and organizational support. He concentrated his efforts in Iowa and New Hampshire with the aim of doing well in these early contests. By attracting media attention, he hoped to establish his credibility as a viable candidate. Early success, he anticipated, would facilitate fund raising, organization building, and continued media coverage. Here's how Hamilton Jordan, Carter's principal strategist, described the game plan in a 1974 memo to the candidate:

> The prospect of a crowded field coupled with the new proportional representation rule does not permit much flexibility in the early primaries. No serious candidate will have the luxury of picking or choosing among the early primaries. To pursue such a strategy would cost that candidate delegate votes and increase the possibility of being lost in the crowd. I think that we have to assume that everybody will be running in the first five or six primaries.
>
> A crowded field enhances the possibility of several inconclusive primaries with four or five candidates separated by only a few percentage

points. Such a muddled picture will not continue for long as the press will begin to make "winners" of some and "losers" of others. The intense press coverage which naturally focuses on the early primaries plus the decent time intervals which separate the March and mid-April primaries dictate a serious effort in all of the first five primaries. Our "public" strategy would probably be that Florida was the first and real test of the Carter campaign and that New Hampshire would be just a warm-up. In fact, a strong, surprise showing in New Hampshire should be our goal, which would have a tremendous impact on successive primaries.[13]

The goal was achieved. Dubbed the person to beat after his victories in the Iowa caucus and New Hampshire primary, Carter's defeat of George Wallace in Florida enabled him to overcome a disappointing fourth place in Massachusetts a week earlier and become the acknowledged front-runner.

Democratic aspirants Reuben Askew, Alan Cranston, Gary Hart, Ernest Hollings, and George McGovern adopted similar strategies in 1984. Concentrating their efforts in Iowa and New Hampshire, they devoted a substantial portion of their time and budgets to both states. For Hart the effort paid off; for the others it effectively ended their candidacies. Finishing a surprising second to Walter Mondale in Iowa and ahead of John Glenn, Hart rode his unexpectedly good showing to victory the following week in New Hampshire. Contributions, volunteers, and media attention followed his success. He had become a viable candidate.

Front-Runner Strategy

For the front-runners the task is different. They have to maintain credibility, not establish it. This provides them with a little more flexibility at the outset. Their candidacy may be announced later, although their organization should still be in place early. Particular primaries and caucuses may be targeted, some can be avoided, but the first ones have to be contested. A broad-based campaign can be planned, but resources still have to be front-loaded.

The principal advantages that front-runners have are greater name recognition and a larger resource base. Status and position make it easier to raise money, establish an organization, and obtain endorsements. This enhances the front-runner's potential but it also creates expectations which may be difficult to meet. A front-runner can overcome a single defeat, but will find it more difficult to survive a string of setbacks.

Ronald Reagan's preconvention campaign in 1980 is a good example of the front-runner approach. He raised and spent a lot of his money in the early primaries and caucuses. He built in-depth organizations in many states, obtained political endorsements, and benefited from a large staff of professionals and volunteers. Concentrating his efforts in the

Northeast, where he had been weakest in 1976, Reagan amassed an early lead. Support in the South and West swelled his delegate totals. By the end of March, he had succeeded in becoming the odds-on favorite. His large lead discouraged former president Ford, who toyed with the idea of entering the contest in April, from doing so.

Reagan had an initial setback that he was able to surmount. So confident was he of winning the nomination, he ran as if he were the incumbent. He ignored other candidates, refused to debate, made few campaign appearances in Iowa, the first caucus state, and had little television advertising in that state. His loss to George Bush in Iowa caused him to adjust his strategy and his organization. He began to campaign more actively, debated other Republicans, and created strong field organizations. He won the New Hampshire primary handily.

In 1984 Democratic contenders Walter Mondale and John Glenn also used front-runner strategies. Both conducted broad-based campaigns to take advantage of their name recognition. Both concentrated their resources in areas of strength. Their strategies differed in the design and direction of their basic appeal. Glenn looked toward mainstream Democrats and took moderate to conservative positions on key policy issues. Mondale assumed a more traditional Democratic posture, supporting the party's previous positions on "bread and butter" and civil rights issues. He directed his appeal to specific groups within the electoral coalition, notably labor, educators, and minorities such as Hispanics and Jews.

Mondale's appeal turned out to be a mixed blessing. It increased the support he received from these groups, but it also made it more difficult for him to appeal to independents and Democrats who were not associated with these coalitional interests. Nonetheless, his strategy proved successful. Mondale's strong campaign organization, combined with the backing of key labor and ethnic groups, enabled him to withstand Gary Hart's initial surge and build an increasing delegate lead over his principal challenger.

NATIONAL CONVENTIONS

Theoretically, the party chooses its standard-bearers at its national convention in the summer preceding the presidential election. In practice the nominees have usually been decided upon well before the convention meets. Since most of the delegates are publicly committed, their decisions are readily predictable. Television networks and wire services provide a running total of delegate preferences throughout the nomination period.

Theoretically, the delegates make policy decisions when formulating their party's platform. In practice, platform decisions have been hammered out by representatives of the principal candidates prior to the convention.

Theoretically, conventions unify the delegates for the forthcoming election. In practice, candidate and policy disagreements are highlighted by the media, making unity more difficult to achieve.

What purpose then do conventions serve? They are part of American folklore. They ratify decisions of the voters during the primaries and the caucuses. In the event that no candidate emerges with a clear majority, they select the nominee. In the event different groups are unhappy with provisions of the platform, they serve as a court of last resort, as a final arbiter and judge. Finally, they draw attention to the parties and their nominees. They excite the faithful and implore the public to support their candidates in the general election.[14]

It is this public dimension that has gained importance in recent years. From the perspective of the party, the real function of the conventions is to show off its nominees and its policy positions; from the perspective of the candidates, it is to start building a broad-based electoral coalition; from the perspective of organized groups, it is to gain visibility and support for their positions and causes; from the perspective of the media, it is to capture the excitement and ritual of an extravaganza and to spotlight whatever drama and suspense it produces.

Public Dimensions

Television broadcasting of national conventions began in 1952. Almost immediately, a sizable audience was attracted. According to the Nielsen ratings, 20 to 30 percent of the potential audience watched the conventions between 1952 and 1968, with the number swelling during the most significant events.[15] In 1980 and again in 1984 over 150 million people saw some part of the conventions.

The large number of viewers is significant because of the potential effect conventions have on those who watch them. The conventions heighten interest, thereby increasing turnout; they arouse latent feelings, thereby raising partisan awareness; and they color perceptions, thereby affecting the public's evaluation of the candidates and their stands.[16]

Party leaders assume that the more unified the convention, the more favorable its impact on the electorate. That is why they take the media, particularly television into account when planning, staging, and scheduling their national meetings. The choice of a site, the decorations of the hall, and the selection of speakers are all made with television coverage in mind. More often than not, this attempt to create the proper visual effect has resulted in pure theater. Movie stars regularly make appearances. Color guards, marching bands, and an orchestra amuse the delegates and viewing audiences alike. Films about the party and its recent presidents are shown.

Television has changed conventions in other ways. They have become faster paced than in the past. Tedious reports and roll calls have been reduced. There are fewer candidates placed in nomination, and the speeches themselves are shorter. The length of the sessions has also been reduced.

Not only do convention planners wish to capture an audience by providing entertainment and a fast-paced meeting, they also desire to put their candidates and party in the most favorable light. To do this they have scripted the meetings, placing the major unifying events such as the keynote address and acceptance speeches during prime viewing hours and potentially discordant situations such as debate on gay rights, abortion, and busing late in the evening or in the afternoon. In the 1964 Republican convention, for example, when Goldwater partisans got wind of a series of minority platform amendments favored by Nelson Rockefeller and George Romney, they arranged to have the majority report released in its entirety in order to postpone the amendments until the early morning hours, when most potential supporters of the minority position would not be watching. In the 1964 Democratic convention, President Johnson rescheduled a movie paying tribute to President John Kennedy until after the vice presidential nomination to preclude any bandwagon for Robert Kennedy, who was to introduce the film.

Although party officials try to present a united front favoring their nominee and platform, the television networks do not. They try to generate interest by emphasizing variety, maximizing suspense, and exaggerating conflict. This attempt often requires them to focus less on the official proceedings and more on other activities, including those outside the convention hall.

Presidential nominees and their organizations try to moderate the negative effect of this coverage in a variety of ways. They make top campaign officials and members of the candidate's family available for interviews. They create photo opportunities for the press. They release personal information about the candidate and private polls to present his chances in the most favorable light.

When there is little discord, party leaders and prospective nominees may even try to create tension—albeit with a favorable outcome. The most frequent unresolved question is, who will be the vice presidential nominee? Unless an incumbent president and vice president are seeking renomination, the vice presidential recommendation of the presidential nominee is often not revealed until the morning of the nomination itself.

In 1980, the vice presidential charade reached new heights. Throughout the first three days of the Republican convention, network correspondents speculated on who would be Reagan's running mate. On the second day of the convention, unbeknown to the public, officials of the Reagan organization approached former president Ford. He expressed interest in the position. As private talks between advisers of the two men were being conducted, Ford publicly indicated his willingness to consider the vice presidency during a television interview. This immediately fueled speculation and turned the media focus from the convention proceedings to the Reagan-Ford negotiations. The negotiations did not succeed. Fearing the disappointment over the failed negotiations might divide the delegates and weaken his ability to choose his running mate, Reagan came to the convention himself late in the evening to indicate his support for George Bush.

In 1984 Mondale chose the week before the convention to announce his selection. He hoped his choice of the first woman vice presidential candidate, Geraldine A. Ferraro, would excite the delegates, mute opposition, and unite the convention behind his candidacy.

The media tend to play up various other contests, such as credentials and platform disputes. Although some of these have had a major impact on convention decisions, many have not. They simply serve to arouse the discontent of a particular minority.

Candidates understand the increasing importance of the convention's public role. They almost always adopt a healing strategy once they are certain of the nomination. At the 1980 Republican convention, for example, Reagan met with women unhappy with his stance on the Equal Rights Amendment, appeased moderates by his choice of George Bush, and appealed to Democrats and Independents with the words of Franklin Roosevelt. Similarly, in 1980 Carter gave in on a number of platform disputes to gain the support of those who opposed his nomination. Four years later Mondale agreed to support party rules changes urged by his principal opponents, Jackson and Hart. Each of them were also permitted to address the convention during prime time. In each case the object of the winning candidates was to placate those who were unhappy with the outcome of the meetings.

Official Business

Conventions still make or at least ratify major decisions. They adopt rules, accept credentials, determine platforms, and choose the standard-bearers.

Rules govern the manner in which the meetings are conducted. They can spark heated controversy, particularly if they affect the outcome of the nomination. In 1952, Eisenhower supporters at the Republican convention challenged the credentials of a sizable number of Taft delegates from southern states. Before deciding on the challenges, however, the convention adopted a "fair play" rule that prohibited these contested delegates from voting on any question, including their own credentials. This effectively prevented many Taft delegates from voting and enabled Eisenhower to win the challenges and eventually the nomination. In the 1976 Republican convention, the Reagan organization proposed a rules change that would have required Ford to indicate his choice for vice president as Reagan had done before the vote for the presidential nominee. Ford's supporters strongly opposed and subsequently defeated this rule. As a consequence, there was no way for Reagan to shake the remaining delegates loose from Ford's winning coalition.

An even more acrimonious division over party rules occurred in 1980 at the Democratic convention. At issue was a proposed requirement that delegates vote for the candidate to whom they were publicly pledged at the time they were chosen to attend the convention. Trailing Carter by about six-hundred delegates, Edward Kennedy, who had previously supported the requirement, urged an open convention in which delegates could vote their consciences rather than merely exercise their commitments. This would have required rejection of the pledged delegate rule. Naturally, the Carter organization favored the rule and strenuously lobbied for it. Carter was successful. The vote in support of the rule effectively clinched his nomination.

Disputes over the credentials of delegates have also divided conventions and influenced their outcomes. In 1912 and again in 1952, grassroots challenges to old-line party leaders generated competing delegate claims at Republican conventions. In each case the result of the challenge affected the outcome of the nomination: William Howard Taft won in the first instance and Dwight Eisenhower in the second. Approximately 7 percent of all Republican delegates were challenged between 1872 and 1956.[17]

The Democrats have also had their share of delegate disputes. Reforms following their 1968 convention have produced allegations that certain delegations have not possessed sufficient minority representation or were not chosen in a manner that conformed to party rules. The California challenge at the 1972 Democratic convention illustrates the second of these complaints.

George McGovern won the California primary. According to state law at the time, he was entitled to *all* the delegates. However, a commission, which McGovern had initially chaired, recommended that Democratic delegates be awarded in *proportion* to the popular vote a candidate received. Opponents of McGovern challenged the winner-take-all result of the California primary on the basis of the proportional rule. The party's credentials committee upheld this challenge. McGovern, now arguing in favor of a state law against proportional voting, took his case to the convention floor and won. His victory assured him of sufficient delegates to win the nomination. Winner-take-all primaries were subsequently banned by the Democrats.

A third function of conventions is to draft a platform. In recent years it too has been the subject of considerable controversy. Why? Changes in the selection process seem to have produced more issue-oriented delegates who tend to gravitate to the platform committee, and specifically, to the subcommittee considering "their" issues. This has tended to exaggerate rather than minimize the policy differences among the delegates. Television has also magnified the problem by providing publicity for platform challenges. As a consequence of these factors, the platform-drafting process has become more open and more divisive. The Republicans have suffered less than the Democrats. Being the more homogeneous and smaller of the two parties, they have been subjected to fewer and less intense pressures from organized interest groups.

Two often conflicting aims lie at the heart of the platform-drafting process. One has to do with winning the election and the other with pleasing the party's coalition. In order to maximize the vote, platforms cannot alienate. They must permit people to see what they want to see. This is accomplished by increasing the level of vagueness and ambiguity on the most controversial and emotionally charged issues. When appealing to the party's coalition, on the other hand, traditional images must be evoked and "bread and butter" positions stressed. A laundry list of promises is usually presented with something for everyone.

The tension resulting from "the electoral incentives to fudge and the coalition incentives to deliver"[18] has caused real problems for platform drafters and has resulted in documents that contain rhetoric, self-praise, and unrealistic goals. This, in turn, has led to the criticism that platforms are substantially meaningless and politically unimportant, that they bind and guide no one. There may be some truth to this criticism, but it also overstates the case.

While platforms contain rhetoric and self-praise, they also consist of goals and proposals that differentiate them from one another. In an examination of the Democratic and Republican platforms between 1944 and 1976, Gerald Pomper found that most of the differences were explained by planks made by one party but omitted by the other.[19] Over the years the Republicans have emphasized defense and general governmental matters, while the Democrats have stressed economic issues, particularly those of labor and social welfare. Significant differences have emerged in recent years over the role of government. The Democrats have been more supportive of the federal government's involvement in domestic matters, while the Republicans have placed more emphasis on the private sector to solve the nation's economic woes.

Finally, the convention must select the nominees. The decision is usually predictable and generally occurs on the first ballot. Since 1924, when the Democrats took 103 votes before they agreed on John W. Davis, there have been only four conventions (two in each party) in which more than one ballot was needed. For the Republicans this last occurred in 1948, for the Democrats in 1952.

Despite the tendency to develop a consensus well before the convention meets, there have still been attempts to defeat the front-runner at the convention itself. Two strategies for doing this have been employed. One is to release polls showing the strength of the non–front-runner and the weakness of the convention leader in the general election. The objective here is to play on the delegates' desire to nominate a winner. Rockefeller tried this in 1968 but to no avail.

A second tactic, one that has been used in more recent conventions, is to create an issue prior to the presidential balloting and win on it, thereby showing the vulnerability of the leader and raising doubts about whether he can be nominated. If the issue affects rules which affect the vote, so much the better. Reagan in 1976 and Kennedy in 1980 tried this ploy but also without success. Their defeats on key votes confirmed their status as also-rans but did not end their campaigns. With the nomination out of reach, both concentrated on the platform. For the most part, the front-runners did not accept these platform challenges, choosing instead to concede policy positions in order to obtain their opponents' backing in the forthcoming campaign. Having effectively wrapped up the nomination, they could afford to be magnanimous and were.

Characteristics of the Nominees

The nomination of a one-term southern governor by the Democrats in 1976 and a former movie actor and ex-California governor by the Republicans in 1980 indicate that changes in the preconvention process may have affected the kind of people chosen by their parties. In theory, many are qualified. The Constitution prescribes only three formal criteria for the presidency: a minimum age of thirty-five, a fourteen-year residence in the United States, and native-born status. Naturalized citizens are not eligible for the office.

In practice, a number of informal qualifications limit the pool of potential nominees. Successful candidates have usually been well known prior to the delegate selection process. Most have had promising political careers and have held high government positions.

Of all the positions from which to seek the presidential nomination, the presidency is clearly the best. Only five incumbent presidents (three of whom were vice presidents who succeeded to the office) failed in their quest for the nomination. It should be noted, however, that several others, including Truman and Johnson, were persuaded to retire rather than face tough challenges.

Over the years, there have been a variety of other paths to the White House. When the caucus system was in operation, the position of secretary of state within the administraton was regarded as a stepping stone to the nomination if the incumbent chose not to seek nother term. When

Table 2-6. Characteristics of Presidents, 1789–1984

	n		n
Sex		**Party Affiliation**	
		Republican	16
Male	39	Democrat	13
		Democratic-Republican	4
Race		Whig	3
Caucasian	39	Federalist	2
		Union Republican	1
Religion			
Catholic	1		
Jewish	0	**Ethnic Origins**	
Protestant	38	English	17
Episcopalian	10	Other Anglo-Saxon	16
Presbyterian	6	Dutch	3
Unitarian	4	Swiss-German	2
Methodist	4	Irish	1
Disc. of Christ	3		
Baptist	3	**Size of Birthplace**	
Dutch Reformed	2	Under 5,000	16
Quaker	2	5,000–19,000	15
Congregationalist	1	20,000–99,000	5
Not specified	1	100,000–515,547	3
Education Level			
College degree	26	**Office Held before Presidency**	
Some college	5		
No college	8	State legislature	1
		Governor	8
Age (when inaugurated)		Federal administration	8
35–45	2	House of Representatives	1
46–55	20	Senate	4
56–65	15	Vice-president	13
66+	2	No political experience	4

national conventions replaced the congressional caucus, the Senate became the incubator for most successful presidential candidates. After the Civil War, governors emerged as the most likely contenders, particularly for the party that did not control the White House.

In the 1960s Washington-based officials, particularly the vice president and members of the Senate, reemerged as the most viable candidates. They enjoyed the advantage of national media coverage in an age of television and national political experience at a time when the role of the government was greatly expanding. The nominations of Jimmy Carter in 1976 and Ronald Reagan in 1980 are exceptions to this recent

Table 2-6. Characteristics of Presidents, 1789–1984 (continued)

	n		n
Father's Occupation		**Mobility**	
Statesman	4	Resided in state of birth	21
Businessman	16	Resided in state not of birth	18
Skilled tradesman	6		
Military	3	**Occupation**	
Learned profession	7	Law	19
Farmer/planter	3	Military	7
		Tailor	1
State of Residence		Educator/teacher	1
South (Confederacy)	11	Engineer	1
Virginia	5	Farmer/planter	3
Tennessee	3	Actor	1
Louisiana	1	Haberdasher	1
Texas	1	Newspaper editor	1
Georgia	1	Writer	1
Non-South	28	Public service	2
Massachusetts	4		
New York	8		
Indiana	1		
New Hampshire	1		
Illinois	2		
Pennsylvania	1		
Ohio	6		
New Jersey	1		
California	2		
Missouri	1		
Michigan	1		

$N = 39$.

Grover Cleveland is counted once in these distributions.

Source: Raymond Tatalovich and Byron W. Daynes, *Presidential Power in the United States* (Monterey, Calif.: Brooks/Cole, 1984), p. 34.

trend. Both benefited from the antigovernment, anti-Washington mood of the electorate following Watergate.

There are other informal criteria, although they have less to do with qualifications for office than with public prejudices. Only white males have ever been nominated by the two major parties for president. Until 1960, no Catholic had been elected, although Governor Al Smith of New York was nominated by the Democrats in 1928. Nor has there been a candidate without a northern European heritage, a surprising commentary on a country that has regarded itself as a melting pot (see Table 2-6).

Personal matters, such as health, finance, and family life, can also be factors. After George Wallace was crippled by a would-be assassin's bullet, even his own supporters began to question his ability to withstand the rigors of the office. Today, presidential candidates are expected to release medical reports and financial statements.

Family ties have also affected nominations and elections. There have been only two bachelors elected president, James Buchanan and Grover Cleveland. During the 1884 campaign, Cleveland was accused of fathering an illegitimate child. Taunted by his opponents: "Ma, Ma, Where's my Pa? / Gone to the White House / Ha! Ha! Ha!" Cleveland admitted responsibility for the child, even though he was not certain he was the father.

In more recent times, candidates have been hurt by marital problems and allegations of sexual misconduct. The dissolution of Nelson Rockefeller's marriage and his subsequent remarriage seriously damaged his presidential aspirations in 1964, and Senator Edward Kennedy's marital problems and the Chappaquiddick incident were serious detriments to his presidential candidacy in 1980 and contributed to his decision not to seek his party's nomination in 1984. Reagan's election in 1980, however, suggests that having been divorced is no longer a relevant factor, at least for those who have been happily remarried for some time.

Finally, most recent presidential nominees have tended to be wealthy. Dwight Eisenhower, Gerald Ford, and, to a lesser extent, Richard Nixon, and Walter Mondale were exceptions. Although government subsidies have somewhat lessened the impact of personal wealth, they have not eliminated it entirely. Having a secure financial base contributes to one's ability to seek and win the nomination.

Most of the characteristics of the presidential nominee apply to the vice presidential candidate as well. However, that choice has also been affected by the perceived need for geographic, ideological, and most recently, sexual balance. Presidential aspirants have tended to select vice presidential candidates primarily as running mates and only secondarily as governing mates. Despite statements to the contrary, most attention is given to how the prospective nominee would help the ticket. Like the presidential nominee, parties have also insisted that the vice presidential aspirant possess all-American traits, including being of sound mind and body. In 1972 Senator Thomas Eagleton was forced to withdraw as the Democratic vice presidential nominee when his past psychological illness became public.

CONCLUSION

The nominating process has evolved significantly over the years. Developed initially to enable the parties to influence electoral selection, it now permits the public to affect that selection as well. With broader rank-

and-file participation has come expanded activities by candidates, expanded coverage by the mass media, and expanded public appeals by the parties.

When the presidency was created, the nomination of candidates for the office was not distinguished from the election of the president himself. The development of political parties at the turn of the century led to an informal modification of the electoral plan. At first, congressional caucuses performed the nominating function. As the parties acquired a broader, more decentralized base, the caucus system broke down and was replaced by national nominating conventions. These conventions have continued to operate, although power within them has shifted from political leaders within the states to a broader segment of the political party. The growth of primaries, the increasing impact of the mass media, and eventually the changes in party rules, finance laws, and campaign technology accelerated the movement toward more participatory nominating politics in which public support became the critical element.

On balance, these changes in the public dimension of contemporary politics have made the nomination process more democratic. They have encouraged greater rank-and-file participation in the selection of the party's nominees. They have also generated greater sensitivity by the candidates to the desires of groups within the party and to the opinions and attitudes of the general electorate.

But the costs of democracy have been high. Parties are now more factionalized; their leadership is weaker; they exercise less control over their own nominees. Unity in the general election is more difficult to achieve.

Campaigns are more onerous and more expensive. Candidates have to spend years seeking the nomination. The public is subjected to a barrage of appeals, images, promises, and positions. It is numbed by the campaign.

Not only is it more difficult to win the nomination, but it is also more difficult to govern. Contemporary campaigns hype expectations; they make alliances more fragmentary and more personal; they decrease the president's political power while they increase demands on his job. All of this has produced greater disappointment in the president's performance. It would be nice to find a way out of this dilemma but presidents have had difficulty doing so.

NOTES

1. In 1968 dissent within the Democratic party as evidenced by Senator Eugene McCarthy's surprising showing in the New Hampshire primary indicated that the incumbent, President Lyndon Johnson, would have difficulty securing renomination, much less reelection.

2. Since an object of these changes was to make delegate selection more indicative of the preferences of the voters, the party tried to prohibit those who did not consider them-

selves Democrats from participating in the Democratic primaries. It was only partially successful. Because many states did not require or even permit voters to register by party, the Democrats were forced to accept an oral affirmation of party preference, one that permitted independents and even Republicans to cross over and vote in Democratic primaries in certain states.

3. "Democratic Primaries Shaped by Small Share of Electorate," *Congressional Quarterly*, 42 (1984), 1619–1620. Although turnout in presidential primaries has increased since 1968, it is still below what it was between 1948 and 1968. In a study of eleven states holding competitive presidential primaries during this earlier period, Austin Ranney found an average of 39 percent voting in the primaries and 69 percent voting in the general election (Austin Ranney, *Participation in American Presidential Nominations, 1976* [Washington, D.C.: American Enterprise Institute, 1977], p. 24).

4. Whether the delegates of either party are more ideologically representative of its rank and file is more difficult to ascertain. The new selection process seems to encourage the election of more delegates who might be described as issue purists and fewer who might be termed partisan pragmatists. Studies have shown that convention delegates in general tend to display a greater degree of ideological consciousness and consistency in their attitudes than does the average party identifier. In general, Republican delegates tend to be more conservative than Republicans as a whole and Democratic delegates more liberal than Democrats as a whole. Sometimes, the differences between delegates and their own rank and file can be considerable. Studies of Republican delegates in 1952 and Democratic delegates in 1972 found rank and file of each party were actually closer to the positions of delegates of the *other* party than to the delegates of their own (Herbert McCloskey et al., "Issue Conflict and Consensus Among Party Leaders and Followers," *American Political Science Review* 54 [1960]:406–27; Jeane Kirkpatrick, "Representation in the American National Convention: The Case of 1972," *British Journal of Political Science* 5 [1975]:313–22).

5. Still, candidates need to obtain a minimum percentage of the vote in the primaries to remain eligible to receive federal funds. Failure to receive at least 10 percent in two consecutive primaries stops the flow of matching funds thirty days after the second primary. In order to start the flow again, a candidate must subsequently receive 20 percent of the vote. In 1984, Jesse Jackson momentarily lost his eligibility after the New Hampshire and Vermont primaries but regained it one week later by winning over 20 percent of the vote in Georgia.

6. Michael J. Robinson and Margaret A. Sheehan, *Over the Wire and on TV: CBS and UPI in Campaign '80* (New York: Russell Sage Foundation, 1983), p. 174.

7. Thomas E. Patterson, "Television and Election Strategy," in Gerald Benjamin, ed., *The Communications Revolution in Politics* (New York: Academy of Political Science, 1982), p. 26.

8. Robinson and Sheehan, *Over the Wire and on TV*, p. 243.

9. Hamilton Jordan, quoted in F. Christopher Arterton, "Campaign Organizations Face the Mass Media in the 1976 Presidential Nomination Process" (paper delivered at the Annual Meeting of the American Political Science Association, Washington, D.C., September 1–4, 1977), p. 23.

10. An analysis of news stories in 1968 in twenty papers found that candidates were the principal source of more than half of them. (Doris A. Graber, "Presidential Images in the 1968 Campaign," [paper delivered at the Annual Meeting of the Midwest Political Science Association, Chicago, April 30–May 2, 1970], p. 3).

11. Robinson and Sheehan, *Over the Wire and on TV*, p. 184.

12. Alan Cranston, quoted in Martin Schram, "4 Democrats Launch Media Blitz in New Hampshire and Iowa," *Washington Post*, January 13, 1984, p. 173.

13. Hamilton Jordan, "Memorandum to Jimmy Carter, August 4, 1974," in Martin Schram, *Running for President, 1976* (New York: Stein and Day, 1977), pp. 379–80.

14. They have also become opportunities for the national party to raise money on behalf of its candidates. In 1984 the city committees which hosted the Democratic and Republican conventions each raised $2.5 million from major corporations and individual donors. In addition, clubs were established whereby contributors received benefits in proportion to the size of their gift: convention tickets, hotel accommodations, dinners and receptions with the candidates, even photographs with the nominees if the gift was large enough.

15. Judith H. Parris, *The Convention Problem* (Washington, D.C.: Brookings Institution, 1972), p. 143.

16. Thomas E. Patterson, *The Mass Media Election* (New York: Praeger, 1980), pp. 72–74.

17. Paul T. David, Ralph M. Goldman, and Richard C. Bain, *The Politics of National Party Conventions* (Washington, D.C.: Brookings Institution, 1960), p. 263.

18. Jeff Fishel, "Agenda-Building in Presidential Campaigns: The Case of Jimmy Carter" (paper presented at the Annual Meeting of the American Political Science Association, Washington, D.C., September 1–4, 1977), p. 20.

19. Gerald M. Pomper, "Control and Influence in American Politics," *American Behavioral Scientist* 13 (1969): 223–28; Gerald M. Pomper with Susan S. Lederman, *Elections in America* (New York: Longman, 1980), p. 161.

SELECTED READINGS

Alexander, Herbert E. *Financing Politics*. Washington, D.C.: Congressional Quarterly, 1980.

Davis, James W. *National Conventions in an Age of Party Reform*. Westport, Conn.: Greenwood Press, 1983.

Goldstein, Joel. "The Influence of Money on the Prenomination Stage of the Presidential Selection Process: The Case of the 1976 Election," *Presidential Studies Quarterly* 8 (1978): 164–79.

Keech, William R., and Donald R. Matthews. *The Party's Choice*. Washington, D.C.: Brookings Institution, 1976.

Malbin, Michael J. "The Conventions, Platforms, and Issue Activists." In Austin Ranney, ed., *The American Elections of 1980*. Washington, D.C.: American Enterprise Institute, 1981.

———, ed. *Parties, Interest Groups, and Campaign Finance Laws*. Washington, D.C.: American Enterprise Institute, 1980.

Marshall, Thomas R. *Presidential Nominations in a Reform Age*. New York: Praeger, 1981.

Mitofsky, Warren J., and Martin Plissner. "The Making of the Delegates, 1968–1980," *Public Opinion* 3 (1980): 37–43.

Paletz, David L., and Martha Elson. "Television Coverage of Presidential Conventions," *Political Science Quarterly* 91 (1976):109–31.

Ranney, Austin. *Participation in American Presidential Nominations, 1976*. Washington, D.C.: American Enterprise Institute, 1977.

———. "Turnout and Representation in Presidential Primary Elections," *American Political Science Review* 66 (1972):21–37.

3

The Presidential
Election

Winning the nomination is only half the battle. The real prize comes from being elected. For the candidate the general election campaign is equally arduous. Shorter in length but with a larger and more heterogenous electorate, it requires the demonstration of similar organizational skills but different strategic plans and public appeals to build a majority coalition. For the party, the quest for the presidency is only one election among many in which it has an interest and an involvement. Like the other elections, however, the campaign is subject to its influence but not its control. For the voter the effective choice is narrower but the criteria for judgment more extensive. Personal evaluation alone is not the only factor that affects the decision whether to vote and, if so, for whom.

In this chapter we will explore these similarities and differences between the nomination process and the general election. We will do so by examining the strategic environment in which presidential elections occur, the critical factors that must be considered when planning and conducting the campaign, and the meaning of the election for the voters and new administration.

The chapter is organized into four parts. In the first we focus on the principal elements that condition the election: the Electoral College, voter attitudes, public financing, and media coverage. We assess the impact of each of these factors on the election. We then turn to the strategy and tactics of the campaign itself. We discuss how public appeals are designed and projected, how these appeals are targeted and coalitions built, and how the campaign is organized and managed. The Reagan game plan of 1980 is used as an illustration. In the third part we evaluate the election results from two perspectives: what they suggest about the moods, opinions, and attitudes of the electorate and what they portend for the president and his governing responsibilities. Part four assesses the impact of the election on governance. Does it guide the president, give him a mandate, or both?

THE STRATEGIC ENVIRONMENT

Every election occurs within an environment that shapes its activity and affects its outcome. For the presidency the Electoral College provides the legal framework for this environment, while public attitudes and group loyalties condition the political climate. Money and media constitute the principal resources and instruments by which and through which campaign objectives may be achieved. Each of these factors must be considered in the design and conduct of a presidential campaign.

The Electoral College

Of these critical elements only the Electoral College is unique. It was designed by the framers of the Constitution to solve one of their most difficult problems—how to protect the president's independence and, at the same time, have a technically sound, politically efficacious system that would be consistent with a republican form of government. Most of the delegates at the Philadelphia convention were sympathetic with a government based on consent but not with one based on direct democracy. They wanted a mechanism that would choose the most qualified person but not necessarily the most popular. And they had no precise model to follow.

Two methods had been originally proposed: selection by the legislature and election by the voters. Each, however, had its drawbacks. Legislative selection posed a potential threat to the institution of the presidency. How could the executive's independence be preserved if his election and reelection hinged on his popularity with Congress?[1] Popular election was seen as undesirable and impractical. Not only did most of the delegates lack faith in the public's ability to choose the best-qualified candidate, but they also feared that the size of the country and the poor state of its communication and transportation would preclude a national campaign. Sectional distrust and rivalry aggravated this problem, since the states were obligated to oversee the conduct of such an election. A third alternative, some type of indirect election, was proposed a number of times during the convention but it was not until near the end that election by electors was seriously considered as a possible compromise solution.

According to the terms of the Electoral College compromise, presidential electors were to be chosen by the states in a manner designated by their legislatures. In order to ensure their independence, the electors could not simultaneously hold a federal government position. The number of electors was to equal the number of senators and representatives from each state (see Appendix B). Each elector had two votes but could not cast both of them for inhabitants of his own state.[2] At a designated time the electors would vote and send the results to Congress, where they were to be announced in a joint session by the president of the Senate, the vice president. The person who received a majority of votes cast by the Electoral College would be elected president, and the one with the second highest total would be vice president. In the event that no one received a majority, the House of Representatives would choose from among the five candidates with the most electoral votes, with each state delegation casting one vote. The Senate was to determine the vice president in the event that there was a tie for second place.

The new mode of selection was defended on two grounds: it allowed state legislatures to establish the procedures for choosing electors but permitted the House of Representatives to decide if there was no Electoral College majority; it gave the larger states an advantage in the initial voting for president in accordance with the principle of majority rule but provided the smaller states with an equal voice in violation of that principle if the electoral vote was not decisive. These compromises placated sufficient interests to get the proposal adopted and subsequently ratified as part of the Constitution.

Only in the first two elections, when Washington was the unanimous choice, did the electors exercise a nonpartisan and presumably independent judgment. Within ten years from the time the federal government began to operate, the party system developed, and electors quickly became its political captives. Nominated by their party, they were expected to vote for the party's candidates, and they did. In 1800 all of the Republican electors voted for Thomas Jefferson and Aaron Burr. Since the procedure for casting ballots did not permit electors to distinguish between their presidential and vice presidential choices, the result was a tie which the House of Representatives, controlled by the Federalist party, had to break. To avoid other such situations in the future, the Constitution was amended in 1804 to provide for separate balloting for president and vice president.

The next nondecisive presidential election occurred in 1824 when four candidates received votes for president: Andrew Jackson (99 votes), John Q. Adams (84), William Crawford (41), and Henry Clay (37). The new amendment required the House of Representatives to choose from among the top three, not the top five as the Constitution had originally prescribed. Eliminated from the competition was Henry Clay, the

Speaker of the House. Clay threw his support to Adams, who won. It was alleged that Clay did so in exchange for appointment as secretary of state, a charge that he vigorously denied. After Adams became president, however, he did appoint Clay secretary of state.

Jackson, the winner of the popular vote, was outraged at the turn of events and urged the abolition of the Electoral College. Although his claim of a popular mandate in 1824 is open to question,[3] opposition to the system mounted, and a gradual democratization of the election process occurred. More and more states began to elect their electors directly on the basis of their partisan leanings. By 1832, only South Carolina retained the old practice of having its legislature do the selecting.

There was also a trend toward statewide election of the entire slate of electors. In the past some states had chosen their electors within legislative districts. Choosing the entire slate of electors on the basis of the popular vote produced a bloc electoral vote. Whichever candidate received the most popular votes in a state got all the electoral votes of that state. This had two principal effects. It maximized the state's voting power, but it also created the possibility of a disparity between the popular and electoral vote in the nation as a whole. It became possible for the candidate with the most popular votes to lose in the Electoral College if that candidate lost in the big states by small margins and won the smaller states by large margins.

This occurred in 1876, the next disputed election, when Democrat Samuel J. Tilden received 250,000 more popular votes and 19 more electoral votes than his Republican rival, Rutherford B. Hayes. However, Tilden was one short of a majority in the Electoral College. Twenty electoral votes were in dispute. Dual returns had been received from three southern states. Charges of fraud and voting irregularities were made by both parties.

Three days before the Electoral College vote was to be officially counted, Congress established a commission to resolve the dilemma. Consisting of eight Republicans and seven Democrats, the commission validated all of the Republican claims by a strictly partisan division, thereby giving Hayes a one vote victory. Tilden could have challenged the results in court but chose not to do so.

The only other election in which the popular vote winner was beaten in the Electoral College occurred in 1888. Democrat Grover Cleveland had a plurality of 95,096 popular votes but only 168 electoral votes compared with 233 for the Republican, Benjamin Harrison. Cleveland's loss of Indiana by about 3,000 votes and New York by about 15,000 led to his defeat.

Although all other popular vote leaders have won a majority of electoral votes, shifts of just a few thousand popular votes in a few states could have altered the results. Thomas E. Dewey could have denied Harry S Truman a majority in the Electoral College in 1948 with 12,487 more California votes. In 1960, a change of less than 9,000 in Illinois and Missouri would have meant that John F. Kennedy lacked an Electoral College majority. In 1968, a shift of only 55,000 votes from Richard M. Nixon to Hubert H. Humphrey in three states (New Jersey, Missouri, and New Hampshire) would have thrown the election into a Democratic House of Representatives. In 1976, a shift of only 3,687 in Hawaii and 5,559 in Ohio would have cost Jimmy Carter the election. The potential for the popular will to be thwarted remains.

POLITICS.   The Electoral College is not neutral. No system of election can be. In general, it works to the benefit of the very largest states (those with more than fourteen electoral votes) and the very smallest (those with less than four). It helps the largest states not only because of the number of electoral votes they cast but because the votes are normally cast in a bloc. The smallest states are also aided because they are over-represented in the Electoral College. By having three electoral votes, re-gardless of size, a small population state such as Alaska will have more of an advantage than it would have in a direct popular vote.

The winner-take-all system also gives an edge to pivotal groups within the larger and more competitive states. Those groups that are geo-graphically concentrated and have cohesive voting patterns derive the most benefit. Part of the opposition to changing the system has been the reluctance of these groups to give up what they perceive as their com-petitive advantage.

The Electoral College also works to the disadvantage of third and in-dependent parties. The winner-take-all system within states, when com-bined with the need for a majority within the college, makes it difficult for third parties to accumulate enough votes to win an election. To have any effect, third-party support must be geographically concentrated, as George Wallace's was in 1968 and Strom Thurmond's was in 1948, rather than evenly distributed across the country, as Henry Wallace's was in 1948 and John Anderson's was in 1980.

Periodically, proposals to alter or abolish the Electoral College have been advanced. Most of these plans would eliminate the office of elector but retain the college. One would allocate a state's electoral vote in pro-portion to its popular vote; another would determine the state's electoral vote on the basis of separate district and statewide elections; a third would use the winner-take-all system within the states but add a bonus to the popular vote winner in the nation as a whole. Only one plan, direct election, would abolish the Electoral College entirely. The popular vote winner would be elected provided that person received at least 40 percent of the popular vote. Thus far, Congress has been reluctant to approve any of these changes and seems unlikely to do so until some electoral crisis or unpopular result occurs.

Political Attitudes and Groupings

As the constitutional framework structures presidential elections, so political attitudes and group loyalties affect the conduct of campaigns. Voters do not come to the election with completely open minds. They come with preexisting views. They do not see and hear the campaign in isolation. They observe it and absorb it as part of their daily lives. In other words, their attitudes and associations affect their perceptions and influence their behavior. This is why it is important for students of presidential elections to examine public attitudes and patterns of social interaction.

Considerable research has been conducted on these subjects.[4] It suggests that people develop political attitudes early in life. Over time these attitudes become more intense and more resistant to change and therefore more important influences on voting behavior. Attitudes affect perceptions of the campaign and evaluations of the parties, the candidates, and the issues.

Of all the factors that contribute to the development of a political attitude, how an individual identifies with a political party is the most important. Party identification operates as a conceptual filter, providing clues for interpreting the issues, for judging the candidates, and for deciding if and how to vote. The stronger this identification, the more compelling the cues. Conversely, the weaker the identification, the less likely it will affect perceptions during the campaign and influence voting.

The amount of information that is known about the candidates also affects the influence of partisanship. In general, the less that is known, the more likely the people will follow their partisan inclinations when voting. Since presidential campaigns normally convey more information than do other elections, the influence of party is apt to be weaker in these higher-visibility contests.

When identification with party is weak or nonexistent, other factors, such as the personalities of the candidates and their issue positions, will be correspondingly more important. In contrast to party identification, which is a long-term stabilizing factor, candidate and issue orientations are short-term, more variable influences that change from election to election. Of the two, the image of the candidate has been more significant.

Candidate images turn on personality and policy dimensions. People tend to form general impressions about candidates on the basis of what is known about their leadership potential, decision-making capabilities, and personal traits. For an incumbent president seeking reelection, accomplishments in office provide much of the criteria for evaluation. For the challenger, experience, knowledge, confidence, and assertiveness substitute for performance. Other characteristics, such as trustworthiness, integrity, and candor, may also be important, depending on the times.

The candidates' positions on the issues, however, seem less important than their partisanship and performance/experience. Candidates themselves contribute to this effect by fudging their issue positions during the general election campaign so as to broaden their appeal and not alienate potential supporters. Staying in the mainstream tends to place the major party candidates close to one another on a variety of issues.

The low level of information and awareness that much of the electorate possesses also tends to downgrade the impact of issues on voting behavior. To be important, issues must stand out from campaign rhetoric. They must attract attention; they must hit home. Without personal impact, they are unlikely to be primary motivating factors in voting. To the extent that issue positions are not discernible, personality considerations become the critical short-term variable.

Ironically, that portion of the electorate that can be more easily persuaded—weak partisans and independents—tends to have the least information. Conversely, the most committed tend to be the most informed. They use their information to support their partisanship.

In recent years the percentage of the population identifying with a party has declined, as has the intensity of that identification. This has resulted in a more volatile electorate that decides later in the campaign whether and how to vote. In 1980, approximately half the electorate decided on their choice during the campaign with 9 percent making their judgment on election day itself.[5] The weakening of party identification has also contributed to the decline in turnout in recent years by decreasing the partisan motivation for voting (see Table 3-1).

Party identification is not the only factor that affects whether people vote. Interest in the election, concern over the outcome, feelings of civic responsibility, and a sense of political efficacy also contribute. Naturally, the person who feels more strongly about the election and its consequences is more likely to vote.

Other characteristics related to turnout include education, income, and occupational status. As people become more educated, as they move up the socioeconomic ladder, as their jobs gain in status, they are more likely to vote. Education is the most important of these variables. It has the greatest bearing on whether people vote.[6]

Candidates and their advisers must take these factors into account

Table 3-1. Participation in Presidential Elections

Year	Total Adult Popula-tion*	Total Presidential Vote	Percentage of Adult Population Voting
1824	3,964,000	363,017	9
1840	7,381,000	2,412,698	33
1860	14,676,000	4,692,710	32
1880	25,012,000	9,219,467	37
1900	40,753,000	13,974,188	35
1920	60,581,000	26,768,613	44
1932	75,768,000	39,732,000	52.4
1940	84,728,000	49,900,000	58.9
1952	99,929,000	61,551,000	61.6
1960	109,674,000	68,838,000	62.8
1964	114,085,000	70,645,000	61.9
1968	120,285,000	73,212,000	60.9
1972	140,068,000	77,719,000	55.5
1976	150,127,000	81,556,000	54.3
1980	162,761,000	86,515,000	53.2

*Restrictions based on sex, age, race, religion, and property ownership prevented a significant portion of the adult population from voting in the nineteenth and early twentieth centuries. Of those who were eligible, however, the percentage casting ballots was often quite high, particularly during the last half of the nineteenth century.

Source: Population figures for 1824 to 1920 are based on estimates and early census figures that appear in Neal R. Pierce, *The People's President* (New York: Simon and Schuster, 1968), p. 206. Population figures from 1932 to 1980 are from the U.S. Department of Commerce, Bureau of the Census, *Statistical Abstract of the United States* (Washington, D.C., 1981), p. 496.

when planning their campaign. They must also be conscious of the social basis of contemporary American politics—the racial, ethnic, religious, and even sexual groupings that comprise each party's electoral coalition.

It was during the depression that the Democrats became the majority party. They built their coalition primarily along economic lines with the bulk of it coming from those in the lower socioeconomic strata. In addition, the party maintained the support of white southerners who had voted Democratic since the Civil War.

Today, the Democrats still form the majority party, but their coalition is much more fragile than in the 1930s. White southern support has eroded within the last two decades and white labor support has also declined. The party has maintained the backing of minority religious groups (Catholics and Jews), increased its support from racial minorities (blacks and Hispanics), and cut into the traditional Republican vote in the Northeast. In recent years the Democrats have also been the beneficiaries

Table 3-2. Party Identification of Selected Groups
(in percentages)

Group	Republican	Democrat	Independent
National			
Sex	27	43	30
Male	28	40	32
Female	27	46	27
Race			
White	30	39	31
Non-white	8	73	19
Education			
College	31	35	34
High school	26	44	30
Grade school	22	58	20
Region			
East	26	45	29
Midwest	30	36	34
South	24	49	27
West	29	43	28
Age			
Total under 30	24	39	37
18–24 years	25	39	36
25–29 years	24	39	37
30–49 years	24	42	34
50 & older	32	48	20
Income			
$25,000 & over	33	35	32
$20,000–$24,999	29	41	30
$15,000–$19,999	27	42	31
$10,000–$14,999	25	44	31
$ 5,000–$ 9,999	22	52	26
Under $5,000	19	59	22

of a female vote, particularly from younger, working women (see Table 3-2).

The Republicans were the majority party before the 1930s. During the depression the GOP lost the support of much of the working class and was unable to attract new groups to its coalition. Business and professional people, however, maintained their Republican affiliation, as did nonsouthern, white Protestants.

The Republican party, composed of the population's principal majority group—white, Anglo-Saxon Protestants—has become the minority party. Today it receives much of its support from those in the upper-mid-

Table 3-2. Party Identification of Selected Groups
(in percentages)

Group	Republican	Democrat	Independent
Religion			
Protestant	31	42	27
Catholic	23	49	28
Jewish	7	58	35
Other	20	38	42
Occupation			
Professional & business	32	34	34
Clerical & sales	25	43	32
Manual workers	22	47	31
Farmers	43	31	26
Non-labor Force	29	49	22
City Size			
1,000,000 & over	25	50	25
500,000–999,999	23	43	34
50,000–499,999	26	42	32
2,500–49,999	31	39	30
Under 2,500, rural	29	42	29
Type of City			
Central city	21	50	29
Suburb	29	39	32
Non-metro area	30	41	29
Labor Union			
Labor union families	21	50	29
Non-labor union families	29	41	30

Source: *Gallup Opinion Index*, December 1981, p. 34.

dle class. The party has increased its popularity in the Sunbelt, Rocky Mountain areas, and Far West but has lost popularity in the Northeast. In recent years men have given GOP candidates at the national level more support than they have given their Democratic challengers.

The Republican coalition has not grown significantly in recent years, but the party's potential for winning presidential elections has. One of the reasons for this seeming contradiction is that the socioeconomic bases of the parties are eroding. The coalitions have become frayed. Although class, religion, and geography are still related to party identification and voting behavior, they are not as strongly related as they were in the past. Voters are less influenced by the groups with which they associate. They exercise a more independent judgment on election day, and one that is less predictable. That is why the Republicans' chances have improved even though their party has not significantly expanded.

Financial Considerations

A third factor that affects the strategic environment of presidential campaigns is the funding provided by the federal government. In the past, candidates were dependent on the generosity of their backers and the support of their party. And considerable generosity was needed to finance these national efforts.

In 1860, Lincoln spent an estimated $100,000 on his presidential campaign. One hundred years later, Kennedy and Nixon were each spending one hundred times that amount. In the twelve years following the 1960 election, expenditures quadrupled. Inflation, air travel, and television advertising contributed to the sharp rises. Table 3-3 lists the costs of the major party candidates in presidential elections from 1860 to 1972.

The spiraling costs of campaigning in the 1960s and early 1970s made candidates increasingly dependent on large donors. The number of individuals who contributed $10,000 or more grew dramatically during this period.

In addition to growing more numerous, the big contributors, often referred to as "fat cats," gave even greater amounts. In 1972, a Chicago insurance executive, W. Clement Stone, and his wife donated over $2 million to the Republicans, most of it going to Richard Nixon. Richard Mellon Scaife, heir to the Mellon fortune, gave the Nixon campaign and several other Republican candidates $1 million. The most sizable Democratic gift that year came from Stewart R. Mott, a General Motors heir, who contributed $800,000.

The rapidly rising donations and expenditures created even greater inequalities than had existed in the past. In 1964, 1968, and 1972 the Republican nominees were able to spend more than twice as much as their Democratic counterparts. This became a bone of contention, since it was assumed that money contributed to electoral success.

A cursory look at total expenditures in presidential elections lends support to this thesis. In general elections between 1860 and 1972, the winner outspent the loser twenty-one out of twenty-nine times (see Table 3-3). Republican candidates have spent more than their Democratic opponents in twenty-five out of the twenty-nine elections during this period. The four times they did not, the Democrats won. These figures would suggest that the potential for winning is affected by and affects the capacity to raise money.

The high costs of campaigning, the dependence on large donors, and the inequities in the amounts candidates received and could spend prompted a Democratically controlled Congress in the 1970s to provide for public funding of presidential elections.

The funding provision went into effect in 1976. At that time the fed-

Table 3-3. Costs of Presidential General Elections, 1860–1972 Major Party Candidates

Year	Republican		Democratic	
1860	$100,000	Lincoln*	$50,000	Douglas
1864	125,000	Lincoln*	50,000	McClellan
1868	150,000	Grant*	75,000	Seymour
1872	250,000	Grant*	50,000	Greeley
1876	950,000	Hayes*	900,000	Tilden
1880	1,100,000	Garfield*	335,000	Hancock
1884	1,300,000	Blaine	1,400,000	Cleveland*
1888	1,350,000	Harrison*	855,000	Cleveland
1892	1,700,000	Harrison	2,350,000	Cleveland*
1896	3,350,000	McKinley*	675,000	Bryan
1900	3,000,000	McKinley*	425,000	Bryan
1904	2,096,000	T. Roosevelt*	700,000	Parker
1908	1,655,518	Taft*	629,341	Bryan
1912	1,071,549	Taft	1,134,848	Wilson*
1916	2,441,565	Hughes	2,284,590	Wilson*
1920	5,417,501	Harding*	1,470,371	Cox
1924	4,020,478	Coolidge*	1,108,836	Davis
1928	6,256,111	Hoover*	5,342,350	Smith
1932	2,900,052	Hoover	2,245,975	F. Roosevelt*
1936	8,892,972	Landon	5,194,741	F. Roosevelt*
1940	3,451,310	Willkie	2,783,654	F. Roosevelt*
1944	2,828,652	Dewey	2,169,077	F. Roosevelt*
1948	2,127,296	Dewey	2,736,334	Truman*
1952	6,608,623	Eisenhower*	5,032,926	Stevenson
1956	7,778,702	Eisenhower*	5,106,651	Stevenson
1960	10,128,000	Nixon	9,797,000	Kennedy*
1964	16,026,000	Goldwater	8,757,000	Johnson*
1968†	25,402,000	Nixon*	11,594,000	Humphrey
1972	61,400,000	Nixon*	30,000,000	McGovern

*Indicates winner.
†George Wallace spent an estimated $7 million as the candidate of the American Independent party in 1968.
Source: Herbert E. Alexander, *Financing Politics* (Washington, D.C., Congressional Quarterly, 1980), p. 5.

eral contribution to the major party candidates was set at $20 million plus a cost-of-living adjustment. In 1984 when that adjustment was taken into account, each of the major candidates received $40.4 million.

The nominees of the major parties are automatically eligible for funds. Third-party candidates do not qualify until they receive 5 percent of the presidential vote. Thereafter, they are eligible to get funds equal to their proportion of the popular vote until that vote drops below 5 percent.

John Anderson, a third-party candidate in 1980, qualified but only after the election was over. He received $4.2 million for his 6.6 percent of the vote, enough to pay off his debts but not enough to have mounted a vigorous campaign. Having qualified in 1980, however, Anderson was probably eligible for funds in 1984 had he chosen to run.

The law also permits the national parties to spend two cents per citizen of voting age in support of their presidential nominees. In 1984 this amounted to $6.9 million.

The campaign finance legislation has had a major impact on the conduct of presidential elections. It has equalized spending between the major party candidates. Theoretically, this should work to the Democrats' and to the incumbent's benefit. Equal spending denies the Republicans their traditional financial edge. It also makes it more difficult for a challenger, who lacks the news-making capacity of an incumbent, to get equal public attention.

In 1976 these advantages seemed to offset one another. In 1980 they did not. Superior Republican resources at the national, state, and local levels enabled the party to mount a $9 million national media campaign and selective grass-roots efforts for many of its candidates for national and state office including president and vice president. This campaign and those efforts supplemented the activities of the Reagan-Bush committee. In contrast, the Democrats, who suffered from a weaker financial and organizational position, could not benefit the Carter-Mondale ticket nearly as much.

To maximize the impact of their funds and reach as many voters as possible, presidential candidates now spend the largest proportion of their budgets on the media. In 1984, of the $40.4 million available to his campaign, Reagan spent approximately $30 million on television advertising while Mondale spent $25 million, two-thirds of his entire budget. In both cases the bulk of these expenditures was for television advertising. The Reagan-Bush ticket was also helped by a $7 million media campaign conducted by the Republican National Committee.

In addition to media, public opinion polling has become another standard budget item. In 1980 each of the major candidates spent $1 million for survey research and analysis. The money that remains must be used to cover other essential expenses: staff salaries, transportation, advance work and press relations, literature, posters, and other campaign material. With relatively little budgeted for mobilizing at the local level, grass-roots organizing has largely been left to the dictates of state and local parties and political action committees.

A 1979 amendment to the Campaign Finance Act permits state and local political parties to spend an unlimited amount of funds on voluntary efforts to turn out the vote. The printing and distribution of literature, the operation of phone banks, and the coordination of registration and get-out-the-vote drives are all included. Reagan benefited most from these activities because of his party's superior organizational and financial position in many states.

Similarly, independent efforts by political action committees, protected by the First Amendment to the Constitution, have assumed increasing importance in presidential contests. In 1976, Democrat Carter was greatly aided by labor's efforts on his behalf in several key states. In 1980 and 1984 it was Republican Reagan who was the principal benefactor of independent spending by individuals and groups.

Finally, the law has affected and will continue to affect the major parties. Here, however, the law may be more destructive than supportive. It is not the major parties, however, but the major party candidates who receive the bulk of government support. Moreover, the prohibition against private contributions has enlarged the role and impact of PACs, further weakening the national parties' influence over the campaigns of their candidates. Limited funding has also prompted these candidates to utilize the mass media, not old-style party organizations, to reach the largest number of voters in the most cost-effective way. As a result, the two major parties have not been strengthened by the passage of a law that was designed to buttress them.

News Coverage

News coverage also affects the strategic environment. Today most people follow presidential campaigns on television. It is the prime source of news for approximately 60 percent of the population.[7] Newspapers are a distant second, being the major source of news for only about 20 percent. Radio and magazines trail far behind.

Being an action-oriented, visual medium, television reports the drama and excitement of the campaign. It does so by emphasizing the contest. Who is ahead? How are the candidates doing? Is the leader slipping? It is this horse-race aspect of the campaign that provides the principal focus. The need to stress the contest affects which issues are covered when issues are covered. The medium focuses on those that provide clear-cut differences between the candidates, those that provoke controversy, and those that can be presented in a simple, straightforward manner. These are not necessarily the issues that the candidates have stressed during their campaigns. In general, substantive, policy questions receive little in-depth coverage.[8]

Although candidates may influence their news coverage, they cannot control it. Try as they may to counter an uncomplementary evaluation and project a favorable image, it is very difficult to divert the media's focus or blunt its effect on the voters. Said Jody Powell of Jimmy Carter's efforts in 1976:

> There was no way on God's earth we could shake the fuzziness question in the general election, no matter what Carter did or said. He could have spent the whole campaign doing nothing but reading substantive speeches from morning to night and still have had that image in the national press.[9]

The time, money, and energy spent on image building suggests that it has a major impact on electoral behavior. Although there is little tangible evidence that the media campaign changes attitudes, it does generate interest, increase awareness, and perhaps affect perceptions of the candidates by the electorate. In this way, it can affect voting behavior.

Studies of presidential campaigning in the 1940s indicated that the principal impact of the print media was to activate predispositions and reinforce attitudes rather than to convert voters. Newspapers and magazines provided information but primarily to those who were most committed. The most committed, in turn, used the information to support their beliefs. Weeding out opposing views, they insulated themselves from unfavorable news and opinions that conflicted with their own.[10]

Television might have been expected to change this because it exposes the less committed to more information and the more committed to other points of view. Avoidance is more difficult, since viewers become more captive of the picture than of the printed page. Moreover, television news tends to be "more mediating, more political, more personal, more critical, [and] more thematic than old-style print."[11] Whereas newspapers describe events, indicating what candidates say and do, television presents the dramatic elements. It provides a visual slice of reality, not a compendium of people, places, and things.

Television compartmentalizes the news, fitting a large number of stories into a thirty-minute broadcast. Of necessity, this restricts the time that can be devoted to each item. Campaign stories average one and a half minutes on the evening news, the equivalent of only a few paragraphs of a printed account. This helps explain why viewers do not retain much information from it.

Two political scientists, Thomas E. Patterson and Robert D. McClure, studied how television reported the news during the 1972 campaign and found:

1. Most election issues are mentioned so infrequently that viewers could not possibly learn about them.
2. [M]ost issue references are so fleeting that they could not be expected to leave an impression on viewers.
3. [T]he candidates' issue positions generally were reported in ways guaranteed to make them elusive.[12]

"Television news adds little to the average voter's understanding of election issues," they wrote. "Network news may be fascinating. It may be highly entertaining. But it is simply not informative."[13]

From what sources, then, do people receive information? One of the most interesting findings of the Patterson and McClure study is that people actually get more information from the advertisements they see on television than from the networks' evening news programs. The reason seems to be that ads are more repetitive and more compact. When placed with other commercials in popular shows, they are difficult to avoid. In fact, television watchers pay about twice as much attention to political advertisements as they do to other kinds of commercials.

What effect does this have on the election? Who is influenced and how? Students of the electoral process suggest three principal effects for three different groups of voters.

1. *Strong partisans.* The media tend to reinforce their feelings and loyalties. Acting as a catalyst, television, radio, and newspapers move members of this group in the direction of their inclinations. In other words, it makes them more Democratic or more Republican and thus more likely to exercise their partisan judgment on election day.
2. *Weak partisans* (including those who claim they are independent but lean in a partisan direction). The campaign is too short to change their beliefs or attitudes, but it is long enough to affect their perceptions of the candidates. By providing them with more information about the candidates and their stands, the media raise doubts or remove them. By so doing either they produce cross-pressures that lead to uncertainty and may ultimately cause partisan defections or nonvoting, or they may actually reduce pressure, thereby generating a partisan response.
3. *Independents* (those with no partisan affiliation and usually little interest in politics). The media bring them into contact with the campaign. It may excite interest, arouse concern, improve knowledge, and in the end, affect judgment. In this way it increases the likelihood of voting and the influence of candidate evaluation on the voting decision itself.

THE PRESIDENTIAL CAMPAIGN

Campaigning by presidential candidates is a relatively recent phenomenon. For much of American history, personal solicitation by the party nominees was viewed as demeaning and unbecoming of the dignity and status of the presidency. It was not until 1860 that this tradition of nonparticipation by the candidates themselves was broken when Senator Stephen A. Douglas, Democratic nominee for president, spoke out on the slavery issue. Douglas did not set an immediate precedent. Presidential candidates remained on the sidelines for most of the nineteenth century. Party supporters made appeals on their behalf.

The second nominee who personally campaigned was William Jennings Bryan. Gaining the Democratic nomination following his famous "cross of gold" speech, Bryan pleaded his case for free silver to groups around the country. By his own account, he traveled more than eighteen thousand miles, made more than six hundred speeches, and, according to press estimates, spoke to almost five million people.[14] In contrast, Bryan's opponent of that year, William McKinley, campaigned from the front porch of his home.

Republican candidates did little more than front porch oratory until the 1930s, but Democrats Woodrow Wilson and Al Smith took their campaigns to the public in 1912 and 1928, respectively. By 1932 active campaigning by the nominees became the rule rather than the exception. Franklin Roosevelt crisscrossed the country by railroad, making it possible for thousands of people to see him.[15] He employed radio to reach millions of others. Roosevelt's skillful use of this communication medium demonstrated the potential that a personal appeal can have for winning and governing.

Television accelerated this potential, making it easier for a candidate to reach millions of voters. But television also created new obstacles for the nominees and their parties. The physical appearance of the candidates became more important. Attention focused on the images they presented. New game plans had to be designed. These plans contained broad public appeals, appeals that were candidate oriented, appeals that were projected by sophisticated marketing techniques, appeals that were carefully targeted to specific groups within the electorate. Additionally, large, multitiered, functionally differentiated campaign organizations had to be developed.

Constructing an Organization

A large, specialized political organization is essential to coordinate the myriad of activities which must be performed in any presidential campaign. These include advance work, scheduling, press arrangements, issue research, speech writing, polling, advertising, grass-roots organizing, accounting, budgeting, legal activities, and liaison with state and local party committees and other "friendly" groups.

Organizations vary in structure and style. Some have been very centralized, with a few individuals making most of the major decisions; others have been more decentralized. Some have worked through or in conjunction with national and state party organizations; others seem to have disregarded these groups entirely and created their own field organizations. Some have operated from a comprehensive game plan; others have adopted a more incremental approach. The Goldwater organization in 1964 and the Nixon operation in 1972 exemplified the tight, hierarchical structure in which a few individuals control decision making and access to the candidate.

There are tensions in every campaign, tensions between the candidate's organization and the party's, between the national headquarters and the field staff, between the research and operational units. Some of these tensions are the inevitable consequence of personnel operating under severe time constraints and pressures. Some are the result of the need to coordinate a large, decentralized party system for a national campaign. Some result from limited resources and the struggle over who gets how much. In Goldwater's case, however, the tensions were aggravated by his circumvention of party regulars, by his concentration of decision making in the hands of a few, and by his attempt to operate with two separate campaign organizations in many states.

The same desire for control and for circumventing the party was evident in Richard Nixon's reelection campaign in 1972. Nixon's organization was larger than Goldwater's. He had a staff of 337 paid workers and thousands of volunteers. Completely separated from the national party, his organization revealed no Republican connection, not even in title. It was called the Committee to Reelect the President (referred to by nonsympathizers as CREEP). The Nixon committee raised its own money, conducted its own public relations (including polling and campaign advertising), scheduled its own events, and even had its own security division, which planned and executed the dirty tricks and the Watergate burglary. The excesses of this division illustrate both the difficulty of overseeing all the aspects of a large campaign organization and the risk of placing nonprofessionals in key positions of responsibility. Had the more experienced Republican National Committee exercised more of an influence over the Nixon campaign, there might have been less deviation from the accepted standards of behavior.

Conflict can occur among individuals within a campaign organization itself. It normally results in a power struggle in which the losers are eased out of their positions and frequently are forced to leave the campaign. Such a struggle occurred within the Reagan organization during the preconvention campaign of 1980. John Sears, the campaign director, desired to reduce the influence of several key advisers who were personally close to Reagan. Although he was initially successful, Sears eventually lost his job on the eve of the New Hampshire primary.

Designing a Presidential Image

To become president it is necessary to act like one, to display the traits of an ideal president. Strength, boldness, and decisiveness are intrinsic to the public's image of the office. During times of crisis or periods of social anxiety these leadership characteristics are considered absolutely essential. The strength that Franklin Roosevelt was able to convey by virtue of his successful bout with polio and that Eisenhower imparted by his military command in World War II contrasted sharply with the perceptions of Stevenson in 1956, McGovern in 1972, and Carter in 1980 as weak, indecisive, and vacillating. Mondale in 1984 also suffered from the general perception that he lacked these leadership traits.

In addition to seeming strong enough to be president, it is also important to appear competent, to exhibit sufficient knowledge and skills for the job. In the public's mind, personal experience testifies to the ability to perform. However, all experience is not equal. Having held an executive or legislative office at the national level, or in a large state such as California or New York, is usually considered necessary, since the public does not think of the presidency as a position that any political novice could easily or adequately handle.

The advantage of incumbency is obvious when attempting to create a presidential image. Being president produces recognition, esteem, and clout. Presidents have an organization and mechanism through which they can affect events or at least influence their timing, help certain individuals, groups, and areas of the country, and promote certain policies and programs where it is to their political benefit to do so. The announcement of grants, and appointments, the support of legislation, even the use of White House and Cabinet officials as surrogates enhance the president's position at the expense of a challenger. It also helps to provide a record which in turn fosters an image of leadership.

While incumbency contributes to a perception of leadership, it does not guarantee it. In the 1970s the gap between expectations and performance widened in the public mind. Even presidents had to demonstrate that they were sufficiently presidential to justify being returned to office. Take the situation in which Carter found himself in the summer of 1980. With only 21 percent of the adult population approving his on-the-job performance, he had to overcome a long list of public criticisms. His pollster, Patrick Caddell, summarized these criticisms of Carter in a memorandum to the president at the beginning of his campaign:

1. Doesn't seem to have a clear view of where he is going and why; doesn't seem to understand our problems or have solutions to them.

2. Does not think in terms of vision or quality of life and articulate these.
3. Administration decision process is often incapable of bold, rapid action; in seeking the "safe" course, often miss opportunities when timing is critical.
4. Not really on top of job.
5. Not decisive.
6. Not in control of government. Doesn't seem to want to use his power and authority.
7. Boring, not exciting.
8. He is politically expedient; seems inconsistent, swings one way and then another.
9. Is a poor communicator—often press considers speeches too poor to report seriously.[16]

To improve these perceptions, Caddell wrote, "People must be given a positive reason to vote for Jimmy Carter."[17] He saw two options: laud the achievements of the administration or praise the personal qualities of the president. Fearful that an emphasis on policy accomplishments would convert the election into a referendum on the administration, he urged that personal themes be stressed. Carter was to be portrayed as a man of the people, compassionate and concerned; a moderate, flexible, decision maker; a hard-working and caring leader. Stressing these characteristics served another purpose: it highlighted public perceptions of the major weaknesses of his opponent, Ronald Reagan.

In contrast, the challenger must appear as presidential as possible. Reagan's first task in 1980 was to provide the electorate with more personal information about his leadership abilities, particularly as governor of California. Having established the personal dimension, the campaign then directed its attention to the Carter record.

Projecting an Appeal

Once a presidential image is established, it must be projected. This is done in a variety of ways: in speeches and news conferences, in press releases and interviews, and in print, radio, and television advertising. Of all these methods, advertising, particularly on television, reaches the largest audience, has the most sustained impact, and is least subject to interference by media representatives. That is why recent presidential campaigns have allocated more than half their budgets to this method of reaching the voters.

Political Advertising

To be effective, advertising must be presented in an interesting and believable way. It must maintain interest. For television, this frequently means action. The ad must move. The Carter campaign in 1976 was particularly skilled in creating such an effect. Carter was seen walking on his farm, talking with local citizens, speaking to business and professional groups, and addressing the Democratic convention. His movements gave the impression of agility, of a person who was capable of meeting the heavy and multiple responsibilities of the presidency. His 1980 ads pictured him as an active president—meeting with foreign leaders, working in the White House, talking with members of Congress. Reagan's 1980 advertising was more static. Fearful that a slick presentation would bring attention to his career as an actor, his commercials in that election presented Reagan as a talking head with as few gimmicks and diversions as possible.[18] In contrast, in 1984 Reagan's advertising had more action. It used the trappings of the presidency to demonstrate Reagan's leadership of the country.

Timing is critical. For the candidate who appears ahead, the advertising should be scheduled at a steady rate over the entire campaign in order to maintain the lead. Nixon in 1968 and 1972 and Carter in 1976 followed this course. When a candidate needs to catch up, however, a concentrated series of ads that builds toward the end of the campaign is more desirable.

Whether ads are spaced or consolidated, they are usually targeted to different sections of the country and to different groups within the electorate. The objective of targeting is to bring the campaign home, to influence specific groups of voters who share many of the same concerns. This requires that issues and positions be relevant to the audience. The candidate's appearance, message, and language must mesh. Media buyers will normally code stations by their viewers and their program format so that the messages fit the audience both demographically and regionally.

Frequently, a candidate works as hard to destroy his opponent's image as he does to build his own. This is known as confrontational advertising and has been used with regularity in presidential campaigns since 1964. That year perhaps the most famous (or infamous) negative ad was created by the Democrats. Called the daisy girl ad, it was designed to reinforce the impression that Republican candidate Barry Goldwater was a trigger-happy zealot who would not hesitate to use nuclear weapons against a Communist foe.

The advertisement began with a little girl in a meadow plucking petals from a daisy. She counted to herself softly. When she reached eleven, her voice faded and a stern-sounding male voice counted down from nine. When he got to zero, there was an explosion, the little girl disappeared, and a mushroom-shaped cloud covered the screen. The announcer stated soberly, "These are the stakes, to make a world in which all of God's children can live or go into the dark. . . . The stakes are too high for you to stay at home." The ad ended with a plea to vote for President Johnson.

The commercial was run only once. Goldwater supporters were outraged and protested vigorously. Their protest kept the issue alive. In fact, the ad itself became a news item, and parts of it were shown on television newscasts, thereby reinforcing the impression the Democrats wished to leave in the voters' minds.

In 1976, another very effective negative ad, referred to as the "Man in the Street" commercials, was created for the Ford campaign. It began with interviews of a number of people in different areas of the country who indicated their preference for Ford. The focus then gradually changed. Some people were uncertain; others voiced reservations about Carter. Most convincing were the Georgia critics. "He didn't do anything," stated one man from Atlanta. "I've tried, and all my friends have tried to remember exactly what Carter did as governor, and nobody really knows." The commercial concluded with an attractive woman, also from Georgia, saying in a thick southern accent, "It would be nice to have a president from Georgia—but not Carter." She smiled. The ad ended.

The "Man in the Street" commercials showed a contrast. They not only suggested that President Ford enjoyed broad support but also served to reinforce doubts about Carter, even among Georgians. Moreover, the fact that the people interviewed were not actors, gave the ads more credibility. They seemed like news stories, and that was not coincidental. They were so effective, in fact, that Carter adopted them in his 1980 primary and general election campaigns against Edward Kennedy and Ronald Reagan.

From the perspective of the candidates, political advertising provides the most control over what the voters see. The environment can be predetermined, the words and pictures can be created and coordinated, and the candidate can be rehearsed to produce the desired effect. News events are more difficult to influence. The candidate's message is mediated partially by the structure of the event and partially by how the media chooses to cover it. Remarks may be edited for the sake of the story. A candidate can be interrupted, his comments interpreted, and his policies evaluated. Major statements can even be ignored—if, for example, the candidate makes some goof or if hecklers are present. Anti-abortion protesters dogged Geraldine Ferraro in 1984, making abortion an issue wherever she spoke. Under these circumstances, aspirants for the presidency exercise much less leverage. They are not powerless, however. Debates are good examples of events which candidates go to great lengths to influence.

The Debates

More than any other single campaign event, presidential debates have gained public attention. It is estimated that more than half of the adult population in the United States watched all of the Kennedy-Nixon debates and almost 90 percent saw one of them.[19] The first Ford-Carter debate in 1976 attracted an estimated viewing audience of 90 million to 100 million and was seen in 35 million to 40 million homes. The Carter-Reagan debate had an audience of approximately 120 million viewers.

With so many people watching, meticulous planning goes into each debate. Representatives of the candidates study the locations, try to anticipate the questions, and brief and rehearse the candidates. Mock studios are built and the debate environment simulated. In 1980 this elaborate preparation took a bizarre twist. Those who readied Ronald Reagan for his debate obtained the briefing material which Carter's aides had prepared for him. Knowing the questions that Carter anticipated and the answers he was advised to give helped Reagan counter Carter's responses. The debate made him look good.

Candidates have viewed presidential debates as vehicles for improving their images and/or damaging their opponents. In 1960, Kennedy wanted to counter the image of being perceived as too young and inexperienced. Nixon, on the other hand, sought to maintain his stature as Eisenhower's knowledgeable and competent vice president and the obvious person to succeed his "boss" in office. In 1976, Ford saw the debates as an opportunity to appear presidential while Carter saw them as a means of shoring up his Democratic support. In 1980 the rationale from Reagan's perspective was to reassure voters about himself and his qualifications for office. For Carter, it was another chance to exaggerate the differences between himself and his opponent, between their parties, and between their issue and ideological positions. In 1984 Mondale sought to establish his leadership capabilities while Reagan reemphasized his. With the possible exception of Nixon, candidates have achieved their principal objective, but they have not benefited equally from the result.

The media tend to assess debates in terms of winners and losers. Their evaluation conditions how the public judges the results. Since most people do not follow the content very closely and do not put much faith in their own judgment, media commentary can have a considerable impact on public opinion. It can even modify the immediate impressions people have, moving them in the direction of the acknowledged winner. This happened in 1976 and again in 1980.

The debates tend to help challengers more than incumbents. Being less well known, challengers have more questions raised about them, their competence, and their capacity to be president. The debates provide an opportunity to satisfy some of these doubts in a believable setting and on a comparative basis. By appearing to be at least the equal of their incumbent opponents, the challenger's presidential images are enhanced. There are fewer reasons for voting against them.

Building a Winning Coalition

Once appeals are designed and projected they must be targeted to potentially receptive voters. When doing this, candidates must consider their political bases of support as well as the geographic foundations of the Electoral College. The goal is to build a coalition that results in winning a majority of the electoral votes, not necessarily a huge popular victory.

For the Democrats this translates into two strategic objectives: rekindle partisan loyalties and turn out a sizable vote. That the two are related in that partisanship is a motivation for voting. This is why Democratic candidates make the link between their party and themselves explicit: "McGovern, Democrat for the people;" "Carter, Democrat, a leader for a change." They direct their appeal toward the rank and file who comprise their electoral coalition.

The task for any Democratic standard-bearer is to maintain the loyalty of party supporters. To achieve this, appeals must be directed toward the major groups that make up the party's electoral coalitions. These special interest and demographic groups tend to be more highly organized and politically potent in the Democratic party than in the Republican party. Thus, Democratic candidates tend to be more issue-specific, particularly with respect to domestic economic concerns around which their coalition was originally built.

There is another reason for the Democrats' group focus. With a smaller financial base than the Republicans and weaker party structures in many of the states, Democratic candidates are more dependent upon the efforts of groups such as organized labor in getting out their vote.

In contrast, Republicans tend to make a more general appeal: "He's (Ford) making us proud again;" "The time is now for Reagan." As the smaller and more homogeneous of the two major parties, Republican candidates have less of a problem with partisan defections but more of a problem broadening their coalition base. They need the votes of Democrats and independents to win the election. Thus, it is the partisans of the majority party and, increasingly, the expanding group of independents to whom much of the campaign is directed. In 1980 Reagan focused his criticism of the Carter administration and directed it to those who were adversely affected by its policies: blue-collar workers, ethnic and religious minorities, and middle- to lower-income families. In 1984 his campaign again targeted blue-collar workers and ethnic groups.

In addition to its group orientation, campaigns also have a geo-

THE REAGAN GAME PLAN IN 1980

(1) Without alienating the Reagan base, we can beat Jimmy Carter twenty-five days from now if we continue to expand it to include more

*Independents
*Anderson voters
*Disaffected Democrats—union members, Catholics
*Urban ethnics and Hispanics

to offset Carter's larger Democratic base and the incumbency advantage.

We should *not* break any major new issue ground except in the foreign policy and highly targeted "social" issue areas. The thrust of our speeches to accomplish this condition must be directed toward:

*Inflation
*Jobs
*Economic growth and
*A more responsible and more efficient federal government

(2) Allocate all campaign resources carefully against the target list of battleground states.

We must remember that the successful outcome of many months of effort hinges on just the few percentage points we garner marginally in less than ten states.

Sufficient media funds should be available to purchase heavy spot market exposure in a few key states during the final two weeks.

The time commitments of Ronald Reagan and George Bush must be assessed and assigned against state target priorities.

Event schedules should be kept free of low-mileage meetings or events and provide sufficient personal time to *recharge* during the closing days of the campaign.

(3) Focus campaign resources to reinforce the Governor's image strengths that embody the presidential values a majority of Americans think are important:

*Leadership
*Competence
*Strength and
*Decisiveness

At the same time, we must minimize the perception that he is dangerous and uncaring.

Ultimately the voters will choose the man they believe best suited to *lead* this country in the decade of the 80s. In addition to the above general "leader perceptions" we need to reinforce, we must give the voter the opportunity to get a glimpse of the quality, skill, and experience of the men and women that a Reagan Administration would attract.

THE REAGAN GAME PLAN (continued)

(4) Reinforce through our media and spokespersons Carter's major weaknesses—that he is:

*An ineffective and error-prone leader
*Incapable of implementing policies
*Mean-spirited and unpresidential
*Too willing to use his presidential power politically, and
*Vacillating in foreign policy, creating a climate of crisis.

A sharp contrast must be drawn between Carter's political promises and his performance.

Given Carter's proclivity to mount personal and vindictive attacks, we have the opportunity to play it very cool and come out of those exchanges more "presidential" than "President" Carter. In sum, the voters do not want Carter, but are not yet quite sure of us. His outbursts help. They may be muted, but they will continue.

(5) Neutralize Carter's "October Surprise," and avoid fatal, self-inflicted blunders.

(6) Position the campaign to pick up as much of the Anderson vote as possible as Anderson fades in the stretch.

It appears Anderson has not achieved the national momentum necessary to sustain a viable candidacy. Anderson's national base may be no larger than 6–8 percent and significant only in New York, Massachusetts, and the Northeast generally.

Furthermore, on November 4th, many loyal Anderson voters will be confronted with the reality of "throwing away" their votes if they stay with Anderson. In all probability many of these voters will opt not to vote for Anderson, and will cast a vote for either Reagan or Carter because they are vehemently against one of the candidates.

Now, Carter carries more negative baggage than Reagan. Every effort should be made to appeal to these voters, giving them every reason to vote for Reagan. The target Anderson states—Illinois, Connecticut, Pennsylvania, Ohio, Michigan and New England generally.

(7) Maintain control of the thrust of our campaign by refusing to let it become event-driven especially in the last two weeks. Be prepared to end the campaign either on a hard note or a high note depending on the momentum and level of support we achieve next week.

Source: Richard B. Wirthlin, "Memorandum to Ronald Reagan, October 9, 1980," in Richard Wirthlin, Vincent Breglio, and Richard Beal, "Campaign Chronicle," Public Opinion 4 (1981):44. © 1981, American Enterprise Institute for Public Policy Research, Washington, D. C. 20036.

graphic thrust consistent with the Electoral College. The large states always receive attention. In the last two decades, the Democrats have focused on the northeastern and midwestern states. New York, Pennsylvania, Ohio, Michigan, Illinois, and Missouri form the core of the party's political base. Although the Republicans cannot concede these states, they have tended to concentrate increasingly on the Sunbelt, Far West, and Rocky Mountain areas. As Republican strength in these areas has grown, so have the party's opportunities for winning presidential elections.

Jimmy Carter's 1976 strategy was to retain the traditional Democratic states and regain the South. His goal was to win at least seventy one votes from the large industrial states. He achieved each of these objectives, but only in the South was his performance really impressive. Not since 1960 had a majority of states from this region gone Democratic. In contrast, 1984 Mondale strategy was to concentrate on the old industrial states in the rust belt (New York, New Jersey, Pennsylvania, Ohio, Michigan and Illinois), the Pacific Coast, and those that had a tradition of voting Democratic. Texas was also targeted because of its size and its large Hispanic population. Much of the west and south was conceded to Reagan and not seriously contested.

A successful strategy must address the critical objectives: the appeal for votes, the mobilization of a winning coalition, and the organization and planning of the campaign. The key decisions involve *what* appeals should be made, *how* they should be made, *to whom* they should be made, and *by whom* they should be made and, if need be, *how* they should be adjusted over the course of the election. Here's the advice Richard Wirthlin, Reagan's pollster and strategist, gave to his candidate midway through the 1980 presidential campaign.

THE MEANING OF THE ELECTION

Predicting the Results

From the candidate's perspective the name of the game is to win. From the voter's perspective, it is to decide who will govern for the next four years. Naturally, throughout the campaign there is considerable interest in what the probable results will be.

Prior to the election, pollsters tap the pulse of the electorate. Those who work for the candidates do so to help the campaigns adjust and target appeals. Those who work for the media do so to provide news on the horse race and to forecast the results.

Since 1916 there have been nationwide surveys of public sentiment during the campaign. However, some of the early polls did not accurately forecast the results. The most notable gaffes occurred in 1936 and

1948 when major surveys predicted that Landon and Dewey would win. The principal reason that a poll of over a million people conducted by a popular magazine, *The Literary Digest*, was wrong in 1936 was that the people surveyed were not randomly selected. Rather, they were taken from lists of automobile owners and telephone subscribers, hardly the average person at the height of the depression. The error in 1948 was caused by concluding the poll too early before the election.

These problems have subsequently been corrected with the result that the final preelection polls have closely reflected the popular vote. Between 1952 and 1972, the average error in the final Gallup poll was 1.65 percent; between 1972 and 1980, it was 1.5 percent. In 1980, however, it was 3.8 percent (see Table 3-4). The magnitude of Reagan's victory was underestimated.

Some of the problems in 1980 were reminiscent of those of former years. With partisan ties weakening, voting behavior has become more volatile and voters tend to make up their minds later in the campaign. In 1980, approximately 20 percent of the electorate made up their minds in the final week, approximately 9 percent on election day itself.[20] Most of the public polls, completed four days before the election, did not detect the late surge of support for Reagan. The private polls conducted by the candidates did.

The final preelection surveys are published before the election. They indicate the likely outcome, but they are not the final forecast. That comes on election night and is done by the major news networks. They, too, survey voters, but after they cast their ballots. The networks have two principal objectives in conducting these final exit polls: to forecast accurately the winner of the election ahead of the other networks and to explain the principal reasons for the result.

Here's how their polls work. A large number of precincts across the country are randomly selected. Representatives of the media, often college students, interview voters as they leave the polls. The interview is intended to measure the beliefs and attitudes of the electorate. In the course of the interview, each voter is asked to complete a printed ballot and deposit it into a sealed box. Throughout the day, these ballots are collected and tabulated and the results are telephoned to a central computer bank. After the election in a state has been completed, the findings of the poll are broadcast.

These early forecasts have engendered considerable controversy. Since the country is divided into separate time zones, projections of the results in the East and Midwest are known before voting is concluded in the Rocky Mountain and Pacific Coast states and in Alaska and Hawaii. At issue is whether these early projections affect that late voting. Although the evidence is not conclusive it does suggest a slight decline in turnout but little vote switching as a consequence of these forecasts.[21]

The issue was raised in 1980 but with a slightly different twist. When

Table 3-4. Final Preelection Polls and Results, 1948–1984

Year	Gallup Poll	Roper Poll	Harris Poll	Actual Results*
1948				
Truman	44.5	37.1		49.6
Dewey	49.5	52.2		45.1
Others	6.0	4.3		5.3
1952				
Eisenhower	51.0			55.1
Stevenson	49.0			44.4
1956				
Eisenhower	59.5	60.0		57.4
Stevenson	40.5	38.0		42.0
1960				
Kennedy	51.0	49.0		49.7
Nixon	49.0	51.0		49.5
1964				
Johnson	64.0		64.0	61.1
Goldwater	36.0		36.0	38.5
1968				
Nixon	43.0		41.0	43.4
Humphrey	42.0		45.0	42.7
Wallace	15.0		14.0	13.4
1972				
Nixon	62.0		61.0	60.7
McGovern	38.0		39.0	37.5
1976				
Carter	48.0	51.0	46.0	50.1
Ford	49.0	47.0	45.0	48.0
Others	3.0	2.0	3.0	1.9
Undecided			6.0	
1980				
Reagan	47.0		46.0	50.7
Carter	44.0		41.0	41.0
Anderson	8.0		10.0	6.6
Others				1.7
Undecided	1.0		3.0	
1984				
Reagan	59.0	52.5	56.0	59.0
Mondale	41.0	42.5	44.0	41.0
Others/Undecided		5.0	2.0	

*Except in 1948, 1976, and 1980 the percentage of votes for minor candidates is not noted in the table.

Source: Final Gallup poll, "Record of Gallup Poll Accuracy," *Gallup Opinion Index*, December 1980, p. 12. Reprinted with permission.

the early returns and private polls indicated a Reagan landslide, President Carter appeared before his supporters at 8:30 P.M. Eastern Standard Time, while polls were still open in most parts of the country, and acknowledged defeat. His concession speech was carried live on each of the major networks. Almost immediately, Carter's early announcement incurred extensive criticism, particularly from defeated West Coast Democrats. They alleged that the president's remarks discouraged many Democrats from voting, thereby contributing to their defeat as well. However, it is difficult to substantiate this claim. In general, turnout declined more in the East and Midwest than it did in the Far West. Even if there was a decline after Carter's concession, there is little evidence to suggest that Democrats behaved any differently from Republicans and independents. Hawaii, the last state to close its polls, voted for Carter.

Despite the uproar, television networks are likely to continue to depend on exit polling because it provides a wealth of information about the electorate's political and ideological preferences, issue positions, and evaluations of the candidate. This information may be correlated with demographic data to discern voting patterns and to infer the reasons for the vote.

The problem with this type of analysis is that it is time-bound (election day) and limited to a portion of the electorate (those who vote before a certain hour in the key states). It does not permit inferences about the effect of the campaign on the electorate nor about changing patterns of public opinion. To make such inferences it is necessary to interview and reinterview the same voters. Since 1948, researchers of the University of Michigan have been collecting and analyzing data collected in this manner. Their studies have provided us with our most sophisticated understanding of voting behavior.

Analyzing the Results

The Michigan analysis is premised on the concept of a normal vote, the vote that could be expected if partisanship were the only influence on the voting decision. Of course, it is not the only influence. Short-range factors, such as the evaluation of the candidates and their ideological and issue positions, interfere, reinforce, or supplement the electorate's partisan judgment. The object of the Michigan analysis is to identify these factors and their impact. In this way deviations from the expected or normal vote can be explained.

Beginning in the 1960s, partisan attitudes of the electorate began to weaken. Candidate and issue orientations became more important influences on the vote. According to the Michigan analysts, it was Kennedy's religion in 1960 that seemed to account for the closeness of the election. They estimate that he lost approximately 1.5 million popular votes because he was Catholic although he might actually have benefited in the Electoral College because of the concentration of Catholics in the large industrial states with the most electoral votes.[22]

In 1964, it was Goldwater's uncompromising ideological and issue positions that helped provide Johnson with an overwhelming victory in all areas but the Deep South.[23] Moderate Republicans and independents voted more Democratic than usual that year. Four years later, however, it was defections from the Democratic party that spurred the Wallace third-party candidacy and contributed to Nixon's triumph. In 1972, the Democrats were again divided. Over 40 percent of those who identified with the Democratic party voted for Nixon as did 66 percent of the independents and most of the Republicans. The perception of McGovern as incompetent as well as ideologically to the left of his party contributed to the larger than normal Republican vote.[24]

Short-range issue and candidate factors were also evident in 1976; but they were not of sufficient magnitude to offset the longer-term partisan inclinations of the electorate. Carter won in 1976 primarily because

Source: Copyright 1982 by Herblock in *The Washington Post*.

he was the majority party nominee and secondarily because he was from the South, the first Democrat to win the South since 1960.[25] He was also perceived as having greater potential for strong and effective leadership than his Republican opponent, President Gerald Ford.

In 1980, however, Carter lost despite the fact that he was a Democrat and because he was no longer seen as having that potential. His record as president doomed his candidacy. Reagan, in contrast, won in 1980 primarily because he was the option who had become acceptable. He did not win primarily because of his ideology, his policy positions, or his personal appeal.[26] In the words of two election analysts, "[Reagan] was the least positively evaluated candidate elected to the presidency in the history of the national election studies which date back to 1952."[27] Nonetheless, it was Reagan who offered the potential for change. When judged against Carter's performance, this potential seemed more appealing to the electorate.

If this analysis is correct, then Reagan did not receive an ideological or issue mandate from the voters in 1980 despite his sizable victory and his party's gains in Congress that year. The electorate desired change, agreed on many of the problems, but lacked a knowledge of and consensus on the solutions. Reagan's charge was to provide new and strong leadership and, by so doing, invigorate the country's economy, strengthen its defenses, enhance its prestige, and maintain peace. How he would do this was for him to determine.

The President's Mandate

Despite the postelection analyses conducted by political scientists, journalists, and politicians, the meaning of the election results often remains unclear. The reasons that people vote for a president vary. Some do so because of his party, some because of his issue stands, some because of their assessment of his potential or his performance. For most, a combination of factors contributes to their voting decision. This combination makes it difficult to discern exactly what the electorate means, desires, or envisions by its electoral choice. The president is rarely given a clear mandate for governing.

Assuming that party is the principal influence on voting behavior, what cues can a president cull from his political connection? Party platforms contain a laundry list of positions and proposals, but there are problems in using them as a guide for the new administration. First and foremost, the presidential candidate may not have exercised a major influence on the platform's formulation. Second, he may have had to accept certain compromises in the interests of party unity. It is not unusual for a nominee to disagree with one or several of the platform's positions or priorities. In addition to containing items the new president may oppose, the platform may omit some that he favors, particularly if they are controversial. There was no mention of amnesty in the 1976 Democratic platform, although Carter had publicly stated his intention to pardon Vietnam draft dodgers and war resisters if he were elected.

Other than the platform, are there any other partisan indicators to which a president might look for guidance? The parties' electoral images—the Democrats' in domestic affairs and the Republicans' in foreign affairs—suggest broad emphases but not precise directions. The issue positions and candidate evaluations of the voters are also important, but neither offers detailed guides to agenda building. While pollsters can discern a mood or even a range of views, they have difficulty assessing the intensity of public opinions, much less evaluating what it all means. Not only do people with similar attitudes and beliefs vote for a candidate for different reasons, but people with very different attitudes and beliefs vote for the same candidate. In short, the campaign may identify problems, but the vote rarely points to specific solutions.

Instead of looking to the electorate for direction, successful candidates tend to look to themselves. They should. Throughout the campaign they set the tone and generate the appeals they wish to present to the voters.

Unfortunately, the promises and positions of the candidates generate diverse expectations which are difficult to fulfill. Kennedy pledged to get the country moving again, Johnson to continue the momentum and create a Great Society, Nixon to bring a divided nation together, Carter to provide a more honest, open, responsive leadership, and Reagan to assume a new, steadier course in economic and foreign affairs. Moreover, by their ambiguity candidates encourage voters to see what they want to see and believe what they want to believe. This naturally results in disillusionment once a new president begins making decisions. The broader the electoral coalition, the more likely that some will be disappointed.

Finally, the campaign's emphasis on personal and institutional leadership also inflates expectations. By creating impressions of assertiveness, decisiveness, and potency, candidates help shape public expectations of their performance in office. Jimmy Carter contributed to the decline in his own popularity by promising more than he could deliver. Carter's problem was not unique to his presidency.

The Electoral Coalition and Governing

Not only does the selection process inflate performance expectations and create a set of diverse policy goals, it also lessens the president's power to achieve them. His political muscle has been weakened by the decline in the power of party leaders and the growth of autonomous state and congressional electoral systems.

In the past, the state party organizations were the principal units for conducting the general election campaign. Today, they are not. In the past, partisan ties united legislative and executive officials more than they currently do.

Today, presidential candidates are on their own. They essentially designate themselves to run. They create their own organizations and mount their own campaigns, but they pay a price for this independence. By winning their party's nomination, they gain a label but not an organization. In the general election, they have to utilize their own organization to perform essential campaign activities.

The personalization of the presidential electoral process has serious implications for governing. To put it simply, it makes it more difficult. The electoral process provides the president with fewer political allies in the states and in Congress. It makes his partisan appeal less effective. It fractionalizes the bases of his support.

The establishment of candidate campaign organizations and the use of out-of-state coordinators have weakened the parties, creating competition, not cooperation, within them. The competition cannot help but deplete the natural reservoir of partisan support a president needs to tap when governing.

Moreover, the democratization of the selection process has also resulted in the separation of state, congressional, and presidential elections. In the aftermath of Watergate, Jimmy Carter made much of the fact that he did not owe his nomination to the power brokers within his party or his election to them or to members of Congress. But the same can be said for members of Congress and, for that matter, governors and state legislators. Carter was not indebted to them nor were they indebted to him. The increasing independence of Congress from the presidency decreases legislators' political incentives to follow the president's lead.

The magnitude of the president's problem is compounded by public expectations of his legislative leadership. Yet that leadership is difficult to achieve because of the constitutional and political separation of institutions. Thus, the weakening of party ties during the electoral process carries over to the governing process, with adverse consequences for the president.

Finally, personality politics has produced factions within the parties. It has created a fertile environment for the growth of interest group pressures. Without strong party leaders to act as brokers and referees, groups vie for the candidate's attention and favor during the campaign and for the president's after the election is over. This group struggle provides a natural source of opposition and support for almost any presidential action or proposal. It enlarges the arena of policy-making and contributes to the multiplicity of forces that converge on most presidential decisions.

What is a president to do? How can he meet public expectations in light of the weakening of partisanship and the increased sharing of policy-making powers? How can a president lead, achieve, and satisfy pluralistic interests at the same time?

Obviously, there is no set formula for success. Forces beyond the president's control may affect the course of events. Nonetheless, the president must exercise strong political leadership. He must establish his own priorities. He must construct his own policy alliances. In doing so he must articulate his appeal clearly and convey it effectively to the general and specialized publics.

With fewer natural allies, declines in popularity are practically inevitable and usually more serious. They detract from the president's ability to accomplish his goals. The growing influence of personality on people and events makes the president's job much tougher.

CONCLUSION

The system of election designed by the framers of the Constitution has been substantially modified over the years. Theoretically the Electoral College continues to select the president, but in practice the popular vote, aggregated by states, decides the outcome.

During much of America's electoral history political parties were the principal link between candidates and the voters. They chose the nominees, organized their campaigns, mobilized their support, and stood to gain if they were elected. Moreover, partisan attitudes conditioned the perceptions and voting behavior of much of the electorate.

This has changed. Today there are more mediators and more mediums. Party professionals are less important but campaign professionals are more important. Pollsters, grass-roots organizers, and media experts now plan and run the campaigns. They discern attitudes, design and project appeals, target voters, and mobilize what they hope will be a winning coalition. They utilize the techniques of market research and the vehicles of the modern electronic age. Radio, television, direct mail, and phone banks have become the principal ways to reach voters. The influence of the party has suffered as a consequence.

The presidential campaign has become more candidate oriented. It is the candidates who now create an organization, receive federal funds, and mount highly personalized appeals. Moreover, the electorate's personal evaluation of the candidates plays an increasingly important role in their voting decision.

This personalization of the presidential selection process has serious implications for governing. It tends to inflate expectations yet reduce the capacity to achieve them. The president is more on his own. His electoral coalition is not easily converted into a governing coalition. As a consequence, disappointment in presidential performance has increased.

This, in turn, has forced presidents and their staffs to devote more time, energy, and resources to mobilizing and maintaining outside support and to worrying about reelection.

The relationship between president and public has more influence on the presidency and the policy-making process than it has had in the past. We will examine that influence in the next two chapters.

NOTES

1. The framers' solution to this problem was to grant the president a long term of office but make him ineligible for reelection. This, however, created an additional dilemma. It provided little incentive for the president to perform well and denied the country the possibility of reelecting a person whose experience and success in office might make him better qualified than anyone else. Reflecting on these concerns, delegate Gouverneur Morris urged the removal of the ineligibility clause on the grounds that it "intended to destroy the great motive to good behavior, the hope of being rewarded by a re-appointment" (Gouverneur Morris, *Records of the Federal Convention*, ed. Max Farrand [New Haven: Yale University Press, 1921], 2: 33).

2. So great was the sectional rivalry, so parochial the country, so limited the number of people with national reputations, that it was feared that electors would tend to vote primarily for those from their own states. To prevent the same states, particularly the largest ones, from exercising undue influence in the selection of both the president and vice president, this provision was included. It remains in effect today.

3. The most populous state at the time, New York, did not permit its electorate to participate in the selection of electors. Moreover, in three of the states in which Jackson won the electoral vote but lost in the House of Representatives, he had fewer popular votes than Adams. He captured the majority of electoral votes in two of these states because the electors were chosen on a district rather than statewide basis (William R. Keech, "Background Paper," in *Winner Take All: Report of the Twentieth Century Fund Task Force on Reform of the Presidential Election Process* [New York: Holmes and Meier, 1978], p. 50).

4. Much of this research has been under the direction of the Center for Political Studies at the University of Michigan. Beginning in 1952, it began conducting nationwide surveys during presidential elections. The object of these surveys was to identify the major influences on voting behavior. A random sample of the electorate was interviewed before and after the election. Respondents were asked a series of questions designed to reveal their attitudes toward the parties, candidates, and issues. On the basis of the answers, researchers constructed a model to explain voting behavior and presented it in a book entitled *The American Voter*. Published in 1960, this very important work contained both theoretical formulations and empirical findings. See Angus Campbell, et al., *The American Voter* (New York: Wiley, 1960).

5. Subsequent studies have updated and refined these findings. See Arthur H. Miller and Martin P. Wattenberg, "Policy and Performance Voting in the 1980 Election" (paper delivered at the Annual Meeting of the American Political Science Association, New York, September 3–6, 1981).

6. Raymond E. Wolfinger and Steven J. Rosenstone, "Who Votes?" (paper delivered at the Annual Meeting of the American Political Science Association, Washington, D.C., September 1–4, 1977), pp. 59–60.

7. Robert Agranoff, *The Management of Election Campaigns* (Boston: Holbrook Press, 1976), p. 311.

8. Thomas Patterson, "Television and Election Strategy," in Gerald Benjamin, ed., *The Communications Revolution in Politics* (New York: Academy of Political Science, 1982), pp. 27–28.

9. Jody Powell as quoted in F. Christopher Arterton, "The Media Politics of Presidential Campaigns," in James David Barber, ed., *The Race for the Presidency* (Englewood Cliffs, N.J.: Prentice-Hall, 1978), p. 36.

10. Paul Lazarsfeld, Bernard Berelson, and Hazel Goudet, *The People's Choice* (New York: Columbia University Press, 1948); Bernard Berelson, Paul Lazarsfeld, and William McPhee, *Voting: A Study of Opinion Formation in a Presidential Campaign* (Chicago: University of Chicago Press, 1954).

11. Michael J. Robinson and Margaret A. Sheehan, *Over the Wire and on TV: CBS and UPI in Campaign '80* (New York: Russell Sage Foundation, 1983).

12. Thomas E. Patterson and Robert D. McClure, *The Unseeing Eye* (New York: Putnam, 1976), p. 58.

13. Ibid., p. 54.

14. William J. Bryan, *The First Battle* (Port Washington, N.Y.: Kennikat Press, 1971), p. 618.

15. One reason that Roosevelt initiated the whistle-stop tour in 1932 was to overcome the whispering campaign about his physical condition. Roosevelt had been crippled by polio. To demonstrate that he was not confined to a wheelchair, he stood up when he addressed groups.

16. Patrick H. Caddell, "Memorandum on General Election Strategy," June 25, 1980, as reprinted in Elizabeth Drew, *Portrait of an Election* (New York: Simon and Schuster, 1981), p. 391.

17. Ibid., p. 400.

18. Reagan campaign officials were unhappy with these ads and subsequently changed media directors for the 1984 campaign.

19. Elihu Katz and Jacob J. Feldman, "The Debates in the Light of Research: A Survey of Surveys," in Sidney Kraus, ed., *The Great Debates* (Bloomington: Indiana University Press, 1962), p. 190.

20. CBS News/*New York Times* Poll, *New York Times*, November 9, 1980, p. 28.

21. In a 1964 survey of approximately 1,700 registered voters in California, Harold Mendelsohn found that few watched the early broadcasts and then voted. Most voted first. The impact of the early broadcasts on those who saw them and then cast ballots was about the same for supporters of Johnson and Goldwater (Harold Mendelsohn and Irving Crespi, *Polls, Television, and the New Politics* [Scranton, Pa.: Chandler, 1970], pp. 234–36). A similar study of the 1968 election conducted by other researchers arrived at a similar conclusion. (Sam Tuchman and Thomas E. Coffin, "The Influence of Election Night Television Broadcasts in a Close Election," *Public Opinion Quarterly* 35 [1971]: 315–26). However, in the 1972 election, political scientists Raymond Wolfinger and Peter Linquiti concluded that there was a small decline in the West Coast vote after the Nixon victory had been predicted (Raymond Wolfinger and Peter Linquiti, "Tuning In and Tuning Out," *Public Opinion* 4 [1981]: 57–59).

22. Philip E. Converse et al., "Stability and Change in 1960: A Reinstating Election," in Campbell et al., *Elections and the Political Order* (New York: Wiley, 1966), p. 92.

23. Philip E. Converse, Aage R. Clausen, and Warren E. Miller, "Electoral Myth and Reality: The 1964 Election," *American Political Science Review*, 59 (June 1965): 321–36.

24. Arthur H. Miller et al., "A Majority Party in Disarray: Policy Polarization in the 1972 Election" (paper presented at the Annual Meeting of the American Political Science Association, New Orleans, Louisiana, September 4–8, 1973).

25. Arthur H. Miller and Warren E. Miller, "Partisanship and Performance: Rational Choice in the 1976 Presidential Elections" (paper presented at the Annual Meeting of the American Political Science Association, Washington, D.C., September 1–4, 1977).

26. Arthur H. Miller and Martin P. Wattenberg, "Policy and Performance Voting in the 1980 Election."

27. Ibid., p. 6.

SELECTED READINGS

Adams, William C., ed. *Television Coverage of the 1980 Presidential Campaign.* Norwood, N.J.: Ablex, 1983.

Campbell, Angus, Philip E. Converse, Warren E. Miller, and Donald E. Stokes. *The American Voter*. New York: Wiley, 1960.

Kessel, John. *Presidential Campaign Politics*. 2nd ed. Homewood, Ill.: Dorsey Press, 1984.

Ladd, Everett Carll, Jr., with Charles D. Hadley. *Transformations of the American Party System*. New York: Norton, 1975.

Lengle, James I., and Byron E. Shafer, eds. *Presidential Politics*. 2nd ed. New York: St. Martin's, 1983.

Lipset, Seymour Martin, ed. *Party Coalitions in the 1980s*. San Francisco: Institute for Contemporary Studies, 1981.

Malbin, Michael J., ed. *Financing Politics in the 1980s*. Washington, D.C.: American Enterprise Institute, 1983.

Nie, Norman H., Sidney Verba, and John R. Petrocik. *The Changing American Voter*. Cambridge, Mass.: Harvard University Press, 1976.

Page, Benjamin I. *Choices and Echoes in Presidential Elections*. Chicago: University of Chicago Press, 1978.

Patterson, Thomas E. *The Mass Media Election: How Americans Choose Their President*. New York: Praeger, 1980.

Patterson, Thomas E., and Robert D. McClure. *The Unseeing Eye*. New York: Putnam, 1976.

Ranney, Austin, ed. *The Past and Future of Presidential Debates*. Washington, D.C.: American Enterprise Institute, 1979.

Robinson, Michael J., and Margaret A. Sheehan. *Over the Wire and on TV: CBS and UPI in Campaign '80*. New York: Russell Sage Foundation, 1983.

Wayne, Stephen J. *The Road to the White House*. 2nd ed. New York: St. Martin's, 1984.

Wolfinger, Raymond E., and Steven J. Rosenstone. *Who Votes?* New Haven: Yale University Press, 1980.

4

The President
and the Public

"Public sentiment is everything. With public sentiment nothing can fail, without it nothing can succeed." These words, spoken by Abraham Lincoln, pose what is perhaps the greatest challenge to any president: to obtain and maintain the public's support. As every student of the presidency quickly learns, the president is rarely in a position to command others to comply with his wishes. Instead, he must rely on persuasion. A great source of influence for the president is public approval.

Presidents want both to please the public and to avoid irritating it. They also want to lead public opinion. Accomplishing these goals is premised to a large degree on knowing what the public is thinking. Gauging public opinion is a difficult task, however. Citizens' opinions on policy are often uncrystallized and lacking in coherence. Moreover, the tools available to measure public opinion, such as polls, the mail, and election results, are far from perfect and make it difficult to infer opinion on specific issues.

The president is in the limelight of American politics, and citizens come quite naturally to organize their political thinking and focus their hopes for the future around the White House. Although this attention provides the potential for presidential leadership of the public, it is purchased at a high cost. The public's expectations of the chief executive's policy performance, personal characteristics, and private behavior tend to be high. They are also often contradictory with regard to both policy and leadership style. It is quite clear that no one can meet these expectations, yet they provide the context within which the president struggles to gain and maintain public support.

Probably the most visible political statistics in American life are the frequent measurements of the public's approval of the president. Political commentators duly note whether the president is doing better or worse than in the last poll (sort of a political batting average). But on what bases do people arrive at their evaluations of the president? Certain predispositions in the public, such as party affiliation and the positivity bias (a proclivity to evaluate people favorably), provide an important component of the explanation of presidential approval. Job-related personal characteristics and the president's handling of, and stands on, the issues are also important. On the other hand, the president's personality and the personal effects and short-run success of policies play a less important role.

Presidents are not passive followers of public opinion. In the words of Franklin Roosevelt, "All our great Presidents were *leaders* of thought at times when certain historic ideas in the life of the nation had to be clarified." His cousin, Theodore Roosevelt, added: "People used to say of me that I . . . divined what the people were going to think. I did not 'divine.' . . . I simply made up my mind what they ought to think, and then did my best to get them to think it."[1] In 1982, polls showed that the public wanted to lower the federal deficit and did not want to cut social programs. They were willing to defer upcoming tax cuts and decrease planned military spending to accomplish these goals.[2] President Reagan refused to go along.

Presidents offer several rationales for not following public opinion. President Nixon claimed he was not really acting contrary to public opinion at all but rather he represented the "silent majority" who did not express its opinion in activist politics. Similarly, presidents may argue that their actions are on behalf of underrepresented groups, such as the poor or an ethnic minority. The extreme case of this technique, of course, is for a president to say that he is representing a future (probably unborn) generation. This kind of rationale is used today on behalf of environmental and energy policies designed to save natural resources for the future population. Presidents have also wrapped themselves in the mantle of the courageous statesman following his principles and fighting the tides of public opinion.

Whatever the reasons given, presidents have generally not been content only to follow public opinion on issues or to let their approval ratings reach some "natural" level. Instead, they usually have engaged in substantial efforts to lead the public. Sometimes their goals have been to gain long-term support for themselves, while at other times they have been more interested in obtaining support for a specific program. Often both goals are present.

In this chapter we explore the president's attempts to understand public opinion and the public's expectations and evaluations of the chief executive. We are interested in both the nature of the public's attitudes and, even more important, *why* it holds them. Such study will deepen our understanding not only of expectations and evaluations but of the obstacles the White House faces in measuring public opinion. We also examine presidential efforts to influence public opinion, including appealing directly to the public, employing symbols, controlling information, and engaging in public relations activities. We do not assume, of course, that presidents are always successful in influencing the public. Thus, we are equally concerned with the effectiveness of the various techniques of opinion leadership presidents use.

UNDERSTANDING PUBLIC OPINION

Presidents need public support, and understanding public opinion can be a considerable advantage to them in gaining and maintaining it. At the very least, presidents want to avoid needlessly antagonizing the public. Thus, presidents need reliable estimates of public reactions to the actions they are contemplating. It is equally useful for presidents to know what actions and policies, either symbolic or substantive, the public wants. No politician wants to overlook opportunities to please constituents and, perhaps even more significant, to avoid frustrating them. By knowing what the public desires, a president may use his discretion to gain its favor when he feels the relevant actions or policies are justified.

In addition, presidents often want to lead public opinion to support them and their policies. To do this they need to know the views of various segments of the public, whom they need to influence and on what issues, and how far people can be moved. Presidents usually do not want to use their limited resources on hopeless ventures. Nor do they want to be too far ahead of the public. If they are, they risk losing their followers and alienating segments of the population.

Americans' Opinions

Before a president can understand what opinions the public holds, citizens must have opinions. Although Americans are usually willing to express opinions on a wide variety of issues, we generally cannot interpret their responses as reflecting crystallized and coherent views. Citizens' opinions are often rife with contradictions, because they fail to give their views much thought and do not consider the implications of their policy stands for other issues. A national poll in January 1981 showed that the American people placed a very high priority on balancing the budget. At the same time, majorities favored maintaining or increasing spending on defense policy, social security cost-of-living increases, highways, mass transit, pollution control, unemployment, and student aid.[3]

A poll in April of the same year found that, of those with an opinion, people overwhelmingly favored the president's budget-cutting proposals—in the abstract. When asked about specific policies, however, majorities favored maintaining or increasing expenditures for policies as diverse as aid to the arts, energy research, job programs, legal services for the poor, student loans, and defense (on which the president himself wanted to increase spending).[4]

Policy making is a very complex enterprise, and most voters do not have the time, expertise, or inclination to think extensively about most issues, especially those as distant from their everyday experiences as federal regulations, nuclear strategy, and bureaucratic reorganizations. This may come as a surprise to those who work in the White House and who deal with politics and policy twelve to eighteen hours a day, but it is something that they must accept if they are to understand public opinion. In the words of former vice president Hubert Humphrey:

> People do not pay as much attention to political commentary as the politicians themselves do. Particularly in Washington we read, analyze, and read again every story. Every nuance contains implications of cosmic importance, or so we think. Though national problems are of interest and concern, the average citizen is busy with other things. He has his mind on his job, his family, maybe his plans for a vacation, his favorite athletic teams and their success. His personal problems invariably take precedence over what seems so important to us. Mostly, he reads the headlines and possibly a few lead paragraphs.[5]

In early 1979 a poll found that only 23 percent of the public knew the two countries engaged in the SALT II negotiations,[6] although the talks between the United States and the Soviet Union had been going on for seven years and the proposed treaty that resulted was one of the major issues of the day. Certainly the most important and most visible issues before the country in 1981 were President Reagan's budget and tax proposals. Yet in a national poll taken in late June, 53 percent of the people did not have an opinion on the president's budget proposals and 47 percent had no opinion on his proposed cuts in income taxes.[7]

In sum, anyone attempting to understand American public opinion operates under the handicap that many people do not have opinions on issues of significance to the president, and many of the opinions that the public expresses are neither crystallized, coherent, nor informed. Nevertheless, sometimes opinions are widely held, such as on issues that touch the public directly like economic conditions and civil rights. Moreover, the president may desire to know the distribution of the opinions that do exist. Under these circumstances, what means can the president rely upon to measure public opinion?

Public Opinion Polls

One common tool for measuring public attitudes is public opinion polls. Whether they are commissioned especially on behalf of the White House or by various of the mass media, they allow the president to learn how a cross section of the population feels about a specific policy, conditions in their lives, or his performance in office.

In an attempt to understand public opinion on matters of special concern to them, recent presidents have commissioned their own polls. Franklin D. Roosevelt was the first president to pay much attention to polls, which were, of course, just being scientifically developed during his tenure in office. Presidents Kennedy, Johnson, Nixon, Ford, Carter, and Reagan all have retained private polling firms to provide them with soundings of American public opinion. In some cases pollsters have also played a larger role as high-level political advisers.

Despite their widespread use in the modern White House, public opinion polls are not completely dependable instruments for measuring public opinion. An important limitation of polls is that questions usually do not attempt to measure the intensity with which opinions are held. People with intense views will probably be more likely to act on those views to reward or punish politicians than people who state a preference but for whom the issue is incidental and a matter of indifference.

A related problem with polls is that the questions asked of the public seldom mesh with the decisions that a president faces. He rarely considers issues in the "yes/no" terms presented by most polls. Evidence of widespread support for a program does not indicate how the public stands on most of the specific provisions under consideration. Yet such details do not lend themselves to mass polling, because they require specialized knowledge that few Americans possess.

Another problem with polls is that responses may reflect the particular wording of the choices presented to citizens, especially for those people who lack crystallized opinions on issues. If questions are of the "agree/disagree" variety, there is a bias toward the "agree" alternative. If the "official" government position is indicated in a question, this often elicits a bias toward that position, especially on foreign policy issues. Public attitudes toward China softened considerably after the president began making overtures toward establishing relations with the People's Republic.

On policies that are very controversial, it may be impossible to ascertain public attitudes without some "contamination" by the use of "loaded" symbols in the questions. When people were asked in a 1981 poll whether federal "welfare" programs should be turned over to state and local governments, 39 percent replied in the affirmative. In a survey the following month only 15 percent favored turning over federal programs for "aid to the needy" to state and local governments.[8]

A final limitation of polls from the president's perspective is that, unless he pays for them, polls are not taken at his convenience. If opinion on an issue is measured at all, it is likely to be a one-time measurement, so the president will not be able to learn of changes in public opinion. Thus, the president cannot rely upon public polls to inform him of what the public is thinking on a given issue at a particular time.

Questions that inevitably arise when discussing presidents and polls include the following: How should presidents use public opinion data? Does use of these data constrain presidents rather than indicate where their persuasive efforts should be focused? Do presidents, in effect, substitute followship for leadership?

According to President Carter's chief media adviser, Gerald Rafshoon, "If we ever went into the president's office and said, 'We think you ought to do this or that to increase your standing in the polls,' he'd throw us out." Instead of using polls to determine his policies, Carter used them to measure how effective he was in getting his message across to the public and to determine the obstacles in his path. During the Carter administration pollster Patrick Caddell commented:

> This White House uses polls as a kind of a guidepost to determine the direction and distance the President has to go in terms of getting the public to move in favor of positions which he feels are necessary for the country. They are a sounding board for that kind of movement. And they are obviously an indicator of political successes or problems that the President has.[9]

Other presidents have not been captives of public opinion polls either, but all recent presidents have used polls in their efforts to lead. According to one close White House observer, "perhaps more than any other Administration, the Reagan White House uses polling, public opinion analyses and media and marketing research as contributory elements in the decision-making process and the selling of the presidency." Reagan's pollsters meet regularly with the president and his top aides. Their most important function is to determine when the nation's mood is amenable to the president's proposals. The White House wants the timing of the presidential agenda to be compatible with the political climate to maximize the probabilities of achieving the president's objectives.[10]

Presidential Election Results

If presidents cannot always rely on polls to inform them about public opinion, theoretically they can gain valuable insights through interpretation of their own electoral support. In other words, perhaps they can learn what voters are thinking when they cast their ballots for president.

Before such an approach can be useful for a president seeking to understand public opinion, the following conditions must be met:

1. Voters must have opinions of policies.
2. Voters must know candidates' stands on the issues.
3. The candidates that voters support must offer them the alternatives they desire.
4. There must be a large turnout.
5. Voters must vote on the basis of issues.
6. The president must be able to correlate voter support with voters' policy views.

As we saw in Chapter 3, these conditions rarely occur, making presidential election results a tenuous basis for interpreting public opinion.

Mail from the Public

The mail is another potential means for the president to learn about public opinions. Although estimates vary and record keeping is inconsistent, there can be no doubt that the White House receives a tremendous volume of communications from the public. President Reagan received 100,000 letters and telegrams in the two weeks following the unveiling of his economic program in February 1981,[11] and typically he receives between 12,000 and 20,000 pieces of mail daily.[12] Naturally, a president can read only a negligible percentage of this avalanche of messages. The White House staff screens the mail and keeps a log that summarizes opinion on critical issues. Correspondence that requires a response is forwarded to relevant agencies.

The president usually reads only a few items from a day's mail, and these are communications from personal friends, prominent and influential citizens, and interest group leaders. He may answer a few letters from ordinary citizens, primarily as a public relations gesture. President Reagan receives a weekly selection of the mail and the overall numbers, pro and con, on relevant issues. Mail from important individuals and organizations the president wants to rebuff is usually answered by his top assistants.

Even if the president could read the mail, this would not necessarily provide a useful guide to what the public is thinking about policy issues, since most of the mail does not focus on the issues with which the president must deal. In addition, those who communicate with the White House are not a cross section of the American people. They overrepresent the middle and upper classes and people who agree with the president.

Understanding Public Opinion in Perspective

Presidents find it difficult to understand public opinion. There is potential for slippage between what the public wants, what it is understood to want, and what it receives. There is also the potential for the president to exceed the boundaries of what the public will find acceptable. There is no lack of examples of the White House being surprised by public reaction to events and presidential actions. These range from President Nixon's decision to invade Cambodia in 1970 to Ronald Reagan's efforts to halt increases in social security benefits in 1981.[13]

Even if presidents feel they understand public opinion on a particular issue, they do not necessarily follow it. A typical line in a presidential address to the nation on a specific issue goes something like, "Although the action I am taking may be unpopular, I am doing what I feel is in the best interests of the country." For example, in a speech on the invasion of Cambodia in 1970 President Nixon stated:

> I would rather be a one-term president and do what I believe is right than to be a two-term president at the cost of seeing America become a second-rate power and to see this nation accept the first defeat in its proud 190-year history.[14]

Presidents often feel, with good reason, that they know more about policy than most members of the public and that they sometimes have to lead public opinion instead of merely following it. Gerald Ford expressed this view:

> I do not think a President should run the country on the basis of the polls. The public in so many cases does not have a full comprehension of a problem. A President ought to listen to the people, but he cannot make hard decisions just by reading the polls once a week. It just does not work, and what the President ought to do is make the hard decisions and then go out and educate the people on why a decision that was necessarily unpopular was made.[15]

PUBLIC EXPECTATIONS OF THE PRESIDENT

When a new president assumes his responsibilities as chief executive, he enters into a set of relationships, the contours of which are largely beyond his control. The nations with which he will negotiate, the Congress he must persuade, and the bureaucracy he is to manage, for example, have existed long before he arrives in the White House. They have well-established routines and boundaries within which they function. These set the context of the president's relationships with them.

Public evaluations of the president also occur within an established environment: public expectations. The public has demanding expectations of what the president should be, how he should act, and what his policies should accomplish. It is up to him to live up to these expectations. Although some presidents may succeed in educating the public to alter their expectations over time, the public's views change slowly and usually the changes that take place only create additional burdens for the president. In addition, the static nature of the president's personal characteristics and leadership style and the constraints on his power and capacity to choose the most effective policies that are inherent in governing in the American political system limit his ability to meet the public's expectations. Frustration on the part of both the president and the public is inevitable in such a situation.

High Expectations

The public's expectations of the president in the area of policy are substantial and include his ensuring peace, prosperity, and security. Table 4-1 shows the results of polls taken in December 1976 and 1980 following the elections of Presidents Carter and Reagan, respectively. Performance expectations of each president are quite high and cover a broad range of policy areas. As President Carter told a group of visiting journalists in 1979, "The President is naturally held to be responsible for the state of the economy . . . [and] for the inconveniences, or disappointments, or the concerns of the American people."[16] We want the good life, and we look to the president to provide it.

Later in this book we will see that the president's influence on public policy and its consequences is quite limited most of the time. Nevertheless, as Table 4-2 indicates, the public holds the president responsible for them anyway. To quote President Carter again: "When things go bad

Table 4-1. Early Expectations of Presidents Carter and Reagan

Policy	%Feel Can Expect	
	Carter	Reagan
Reduce unemployment	72	69
Reduce inflation	*	66
Reduce cost of government	59	70
Increase government efficiency	81	89
Deal effectively with foreign policy	79	77
Strengthen national defense	81	76

*Not available.

Source: "Early Expectations: Comparing Chief Executives," *Public Opinion*, February–March 1981, p. 39.

Table 4-2. Policy Expectations of the President

President Carter at Least Partly to Blame for:	% Agreeing
Continued inflation	78
High energy prices	68
Gasoline shortage	61

Source: NBC-AP Poll, Summer 1979, cited in Thomas E. Cronin, "Looking for Leadership, 1980," *Public Opinion*, February–March 1980, p. 15.

you [the president] get entirely too much blame. And I have to admit that when things go good, you get entirely too much credit."[17] Since conditions emphasized in the press seem to be bad more often than good, it is usually blame that presidents receive.

In addition to expecting successful policies from the White House, Americans expect their presidents to be extraordinary individuals. (This, of course, buttresses the public's policy expectations.) As Table 4-3 shows, the public expects the president to be intelligent, cool in a crisis, competent, and highly ethical and to possess a sense of humor. Substantial percentages also want him to have imagination and charisma. Obviously, it is not easy to meet these expectations, and, as we have seen, presidents are watched very carefully to see whether they do.

The public has not only high expectations for the president's official performance but also lofty expectations for his private behavior. Table 4-4 provides the results of asking poll respondents if they would strongly object if the president acted in certain ways. As we can see, substantial percentages of the population would not merely object but would strongly object if the president engaged in behavior that is very common in American society. For example, when the Watergate tapes revealed that President Nixon frequently used profane and obscene language in his private conversations, many Americans were outraged. Many people were probably more upset by the president's language than by the substance of his statements. We demand that the president's public and private life be exemplary.

Table 4-3. Public Expectations of the Personal Characteristics of Presidents

Characteristic	% Feel Important
Intelligence	82
Sound judgment in a crisis	81
Competence, ability to get job done	74
High ethical standards	66
Sense of humor	50
Imagination	42
Personal charm, style, charisma	33

Source: Gallup Poll, Fall 1979.

Table 4-4. Public Expectations of the Private Behavior of Presidents

Behavior	% Would Strongly Object
If he smoked marijuana occasionally	70
If he told ethnic or racial jokes in private	43
If he were not a member of a church	38
If he used tranquilizers occasionally	36
If he used profane language in private	33
If he had seen a psychiatrist	30
If he wore blue jeans occasionally in the Oval Office	21
If he were divorced	17
If he had a cocktail before dinner each night	14

Source: Gallup Poll, Fall 1979.

It is interesting that the public seems to be aware of both the increasing difficulty of being president and its own rising expectations of his performance. The public overwhelmingly believes that the president's job is more difficult than in the past and that he is likely to receive more criticism in the press (see Table 4-5). Moreover, it believes that expectations of the president are higher than in the past. Nevertheless, those who feel the president's tasks are more challenging than in the past do not take this fact into consideration when they evaluate his performance.

In addition, there is a substantial gap between the expectations the public has of what the president should accomplish (and for which it will hold him accountable) and the degree of success the public expects the president to have in meeting its expectations. For example, when Jimmy Carter took office 63 percent of the people felt he could not stop inflation and 50 percent believed he could not balance the budget.[18] The fact that the juxtaposition of these views might be unfair to the president does not

Table 4-5. Changing Perceptions of the Difficulty of Being President

Perceptions Compared to the Past	% Agreeing
The public's expectations of the president are higher.	73
Congress is more difficult to deal with.	75
The problems the president must solve are more difficult.	77
The press is more critical of the president.	76

Source: Gallup Poll, Fall 1979.

seem to disturb many of his constituents. Under such conditions we should not be surprised that recent presidents have often been unpopular.

What is perhaps more surprising is the fact that expectations of the president remain high despite the disappointment many Americans have experienced in the performance of their presidents over the past generation. The tenacity with which Americans maintain high expectations of the president may be due in large part to the encouragement they receive from presidential candidates to do so. The extremely lengthy process by which we select our presidents lends itself to political hyperbole. For one year out of every four we are enticed to expect more from our president than we are currently receiving. Evidently we take this rhetoric to heart and hold our presidents to ever higher standards, independent of the reasonableness of these expectations.

High expectations of presidents are also supported by our political socialization; we are often taught American history organized by presidential eras. Implicit in much of this teaching is the view that great presidents were largely responsible for the freedom and prosperity Americans enjoy. From such lessons it is a short step to our presuming that contemporary presidents can be wise and effective leaders and, therefore, that we should expect them to be so.

Those most attentive to the presidency and politics are as susceptible to the influence of a "remembered" past in their expectations as are other citizens. Professor Richard Neustadt's comments about reactions in Washington to Jimmy Carter are especially insightful:

> Almost from the outset of his term, and savagely at intervals since his first summer, press commentators and congressional critics have deplored Carter's deficiencies in ways suggestive of a markedly higher standard, apparently compounded out of pieces of performance by the Presidents since Truman, as Washingtonians recall them. . . .
>
> Too much is expected of a President in Carter's shoes . . . Washingtonians, like less attentive publics, tend to project on the Presidency expectations far exceeding anyone's assured capacity to carry through.[19]

Yet another factor encouraging high expectations of the White House is the prominence of the president. He is our national spokesman, the personification of our nation—the closest thing we have to a royal sovereign. Upon his election he and his family dominate the news in America. The president's great visibility naturally induces us to focus our attention and thus our demands and expectations upon him.

Related to the president's prominence is our tendency to personalize. Issues of public policy are often extremely complex. To simplify them we tend to think of issues in terms of personalities, especially the president's. It is easier to blame a specific person for our personal and societal problems than it is to analyze and comprehend the complicated mix of factors that really cause these problems. Similarly, it is easier to project our frustrations onto a single individual than it is to deal with the contradictions and selfishness in our own policy demands. At the midpoint of his term in office President Carter reflected: "I can see why it is difficult for a President to serve two terms. You are the personification of problems and when you address a problem even successfully you become identified with it."[20]

Part of the explanation for the public's high expectations of the president probably lies in its lack of understanding of the context in which the president functions. We shall see in later chapters that the president's basic power situation in our constitutional system is one of weakness rather than strength. Yet this is widely misperceived by the public. In 1979, for example, only 36 percent of the people felt the president had too little power, and 49 percent felt his power was "just right."[21]

Do high expectations of the president affect the public's evaluations of his performance? Although we lack sufficient data to reach a definitive conclusion, there is reason to believe that they do. Sometimes the negative impact of high expectations in the public's support for the president is of the chief executive's own making. Jimmy Carter provides a good example of a president who was his own worst enemy in this regard. Both before and after taking office he set very high standards for himself and his administration and assured the public that he would live up to them. Unfortunately, he was unable to keep many of his promises, such as balancing the budget and keeping his administration free from scandal. Reagan, too, set his goals high. He promised a balanced budget by 1984, only to be plagued with the largest deficits in the nation's history.

We have, of course, no way to calculate precisely the influence of such unkept promises on the president's standing with the public, and none of them alone is probably of much significance. Yet their collective impact undoubtedly depresses the president's approval ratings because they help to undermine the aura of statesmanship and competence that attracted support in his election campaign. Perhaps presidents should lower expectations, especially at the beginning of their terms, so they will not mortgage their reputation and prestige to nuances of governing they have not yet learned.

Contradictory Expectations

The contradictions in the public's expectations of the president present an additional obstacle to presidents in their efforts to gain public support. With contradictory expectations it is very difficult to escape criticism and loss of approval—no matter what they do.

Contradictory expectations of the president deal with either the content of policy or his style of performance. Our expectations of policy are

Table 4-6. Public Expectations of the President's Leadership Style

Characteristic	% Feel Important
Placing country's interest ahead of politics	83
Taking firm stand on issues	75
Compassion, concern for little man/average citizen	70
Ability to anticipate the nation's needs	68
Saying what one believes, even if unpopular	64
Ability to inspire confidence	63
Forcefulness, decisiveness	59
Having consistent positions on issues	52
Flexibility, willingness to compromise	52
Political savvy, know-how	51
Having modern, up-to-date ideas and solutions	51
Loyalty to one's party	30

Source: Gallup Poll, Fall 1979.

confused and seemingly unlimited. We want taxes and the cost of government to decrease, yet we do not want a decrease in public services. We desire plentiful gasoline, but not at a higher price. We wish inflation to be controlled, but not at the expense of higher unemployment or interest rates. We yearn for a clean environment, yet we are anxious to have industrial development.

It is true, of course, that the public is not entirely to blame for holding these contradictory expectations. Presidential candidates often enthusiastically encourage voters to believe that they will produce the proverbial situation in which the people can have their cake and eat it, too. In the 1980 presidential campaign Ronald Reagan promised, among other things, to slash government expenditures, substantially reduce taxes, increase military spending, balance the budget, and maintain government services.

Expectations of the president's leadership style are also crucial in the public's evaluation of the president. Table 4-6 lists some of these performance expectations. The table suggests that people want a president who embodies a variety of traits, some of which are contradictory.

1. We expect the president to be a *leader*, an independent figure who speaks out and takes stands on the issues even if his views are unpopular. We also expect the president to preempt problems by anticipating them before they arise. Similarly, we count on the president to provide novel solutions to the country's problems. To meet these expectations the president must be ahead of public opinion, acting on problems that may be obscure to the general populace and contributing ideas that are different from those currently in vogue in discussions of policy.

In sharp contrast to our expectations for presidential leadership are our expectations that the chief executive be *responsive* to public opinion and that he be constrained by majority rule as represented in Congress. The public overwhelmingly desires Congress to have final authority in policy disagreements with the president, and it does not want the president to be able to act against majority opinion.[22]

The contradictory expectations of leadership versus responsiveness place the president in a no-win situation. If he attempts to lead, he may be criticized for losing contact with his constituents and being unrepresentative. Conversely, if he tries to reflect the views of the populace, he may be reproached for failing to lead and for not solving the country's problems.

2. We expect our presidents to be open-minded politicians in the American tradition and thus exhibit *flexibility* and willingness to compromise on policy differences. At the same time we also expect the president to be *decisive* and to take firm and consistent stands on the issues. These expectations are also incompatible, and presidents can expect to be criticized for being rigid and inflexible when they are standing firm on an issue. Ronald Reagan suffered such a fate in 1982 when he refused to yield on defense spending in the face of massive deficits. Presidents will also be disparaged for being weak and indecisive when they do compromise.

3. A large majority of the public wants the president to be a *statesman*, to place the country's interests ahead of politics. Yet a majority of the same public also desires their president to be a skilled *politician*, and a substantial minority favors the president's exercising loyalty to his political party. If the president acts statesmanlike, he may be criticized for being too far above the political fray, for being an ineffective idealist and insufficiently solicitous of his party supporters. Jimmy Carter began his term on such a note when he attempted to cut back on "pork barrel" water projects. If he emphasizes a party program, however, the president may be criticized for being a crass politician, without concern for the broader national interest.

4. Americans like their presidents to run *open* administrations. We desire a free flow of ideas within the governing circles in Washington, and we want the workings of government to be visible to us and not sheltered behind closed doors. At the same time we want to feel that the president is *in control* of things and that the government is not sailing rudderless. If a president allows internal dissent in White House decision making and does not try to hide or succeed in hiding this dissent from the public, he will

inevitably be reproached for not being in control of his own aides. But if he should attempt either to stifle dissent or to conceal it from the public, he will be accused of being isolated, undemocratic, unable to accept criticism, and of attempting to muzzle opposition.

5. Finally, Americans want their presidents to be able to *relate* to the average person in order to inspire confidence in the White House and to have compassion and concern for the typical citizen. Yet, as we have seen throughout our discussion of expectations, the public also expects the president to possess characteristics far *different* from their own and to act in ways that are beyond the capabilities of most people. To confuse the matter further, we also expect the president to act with a special dignity befitting the leader of our country and the free world and to live and entertain in splendor. In other words, presidents are not supposed to resemble the common man at all.

If a president seems too common, he may be disparaged for being just that—"common." One only has to think of the political cartoons of Harry Truman and Gerald Ford, implying that they were really not up to the job of president. On the other hand, if a president seems too different, appears too cerebral, or engages in too much pomp, he will likely be denounced as snobbish and isolated from the people and as being too regal for Americans' tastes. Again, one has to think back only to the Nixon White House to recall such criticisms.

Public Expectations in Perspective

In his search for public support the president finds himself confronted by more than just the public's general inattentiveness to politics and policy. An additional obstacle to the chief executive's obtaining and maintaining public support is citizens' expectations. These expectations are wide-ranging and include the president's private behavior, personal characteristics, leadership style, and policy performance. What is worse, the public's expectations are high and sometimes contradictory, making them very difficult to meet. Moreover, since a president's personality, personal characteristics, and leadership style are largely set by the time he takes office, it is in the area of policy in which he has the most flexibility to act to satisfy the public. Still, limits on policy making, which we will discuss in later chapters, severely constrain the president's ability to achieve his programmatic goals.

This is the context of the public's evaluations of the president, and it is not a particularly favorable one for the White House. Tension between public expectations and presidential performance is inevitable, and it is likely to lower his support in the country. The president enters his relationship with the public fighting an uphill battle. In the next section we examine factors that may directly influence the public's evaluations of the president's performance throughout his tenure.

PUBLIC APPROVAL OF THE PRESIDENT

The most visible and significant aspect of the president's relations with the public is his level of approval. The president's efforts to understand and lead public opinion and his efforts to influence the press's portrayal of him are aimed at achieving public support. This support is related to his success in dealing with others, especially the Congress. The higher the public's level of approval of the president, the more support his programs receive.[23]

Whether they are based on perceptions encouraged by the White House, the press, or other political actors, or based on detached and careful study, Americans hold opinions about the president and his policies. People are also affected, sometimes quite directly, by the impact of foreign and domestic policies. In this section we examine the economy, war, foreign policy, issue stands, the president's personality and personal characteristics, and international events as possible explanations for presidential approval. Regarding specific policies, we are concerned with whether evaluations of the president's performance, the success of the president's policies, or people's personal experiences of those policies are most influential in determining presidential approval.

In addition, there are certain less dynamic factors in the form of predispositions that citizens hold, such as political party identification and the positivity bias, that may strongly influence their evaluations of the president. Party in particular not only directly affects opinions of the president but also mediates the impact of other variables. Thus it is important that we examine predispositions as well as more specific opinions about the president and his policies.

Party Identification

Evaluations of the president's performance reflect the underlying partisan loyalties of the public. Members of the president's party are predisposed to approve of his performance and members of the opposition party are predisposed to be less approving. Independents, those without explicit partisan attachments, fall between the Democrats and Republicans in their levels of approval of the president. Table 4-7 shows the average level of approval of the president for each of these groups in the 1953–1983 period. The average absolute difference in support between

Table 4-7. Average Yearly Presidential Approval by Partisan Groups, 1953–1983

		Partisan Group % Approval		
Year	Party of President	Democrats	Republicans	Independents
1953	R	56	87	67
1954	R	49	87	69
1955	R	56	91	74
1956	R	56	93	75
1957	R	47	86	66
1958	R	36	82	56
1959	R	48	88	66
1960	R	44	87	64
1961	D	87	58	72
1962	D	86	49	69
1963	D	79	44	62
1964	D	84	62	69
1965	D	79	49	59
1966	D	65	31	44
1967	D	59	27	38
1968	D	58	27	36
1969	R	50	83	61
1970	R	42	83	57
1971	R	36	79	49
1972	R	41	86	58
1973	R	26	71	43
1974	R	24	60	35
1975	R	33	66	45
1976	R	36	71	51
1977	D	73	46	60
1978	D	56	28	42
1979	D	47	25	35
1980	D	54	26	36
1981	R	40	85	59
1982	R	24	79	46
1983	R	24	79	47

R = Republican
D = Democrat
Source: Gallup Poll.

Democrats and Republicans is 36 percentage points, a very substantial figure. Independents fall in between, averaging a difference of 17 percentage points from Democrats and 19 percentage points from Republicans.

The impact of partisanship on evaluations of the president can also be seen by examining presidential approval at a cross section of time. In

July of 1974, shortly before he resigned, Richard Nixon's overall support stood at 25 percent. Approval among Democrats had diminished to a meager 13 percent, and among Independents he received only a 23 percent approval rating. Yet even at the height of the Watergate crisis, 52 percent of Republicans gave the president their approval. Five years later, at the end of July 1979, Jimmy Carter, a Democratic president, saw his approval fall to an overall 29 percent. Republican approval stood at only 18 percent. Democrats, on the other hand, were more than twice as likely to support Carter, giving him 37 percent approval. Independents were in the middle at 27 percent.

Party identification, then, is an important determinant of presidential approval. Since the percentage of the population affiliating with one of the two major parties has been decreasing, a somewhat smaller percentage of the population is strongly predisposed to support or withhold support from the president because of party affiliation. As a result, presidential approval should be more variable, a prediction supported by the increased volatility of the polls since the 1970s.

Positivity Bias

Another predisposing factor is the "positivity bias," which one authority defines as the tendency "to show evaluation of public figures and institutions in a generally positive direction."[24] Americans have a general disposition to prefer, to learn, and to expect positive relationships more than negative relationships and to perceive stimuli as positive rather than negative. They tend to have favorable opinions of people.

The causes of the positivity bias are not well known, but it seems to have the greatest potential for influence in ambiguous situations, such as the beginning of a president's term. New occupants of the White House are unknown to the public as chief executives and therefore may receive the benefit of the doubt in the public's evaluation of them.

Although positivity should encourage presidential approval throughout a president's tenure, it should be especially important at the beginning of a new president's term, when he lacks a track record. One way to see the impact of positivity bias is to compare the electoral percentages by which presidents first won election with their approval in the first Gallup poll taken after their election. Such a comparison is made in Table 4-8 (President Ford is excluded because he never won an election for the presidency). The figures clearly show that, with the exception of Ronald Reagan, a substantially larger percentage of the people are willing to give new presidents their approval at the beginning of their terms than were willing to vote for them two months earlier.

As presidents perform their duties, they become better known to citizens, who have more basis for judgments about them. Moreover, the

Table 4-8. Comparison of Electoral Percentages and Postinaugural Approval

President	% of Popular Vote in First Election	% Approval in First Postinaugural Poll
Eisenhower	55	69
Kennedy	50	72
Johnson	61	71
Nixon	43	60
Carter	50	66
Reagan	51	51

Source: Gallup Poll.

public may begin to perceive greater implications of presidential policies for their own lives as time passes. If these are viewed unfavorably, people may be more open to, and pay more attention to, negative information about the president.

A related factor may be at work in affecting presidents' approval by the public early in their terms. As the people have little basis on which to evaluate the president, they may turn to others for cues. A new chief executive is generally treated favorably in the press. Moreover, there is excitement and symbolism inherent in the peaceful transfer of power, inaugural festivities, and "new beginnings." All of this creates a very positive environment in which initial evaluations of elected presidents take place and buttresses any tendency toward the positivity bias.

Several studies have found evidence of what some authors term a *fait accompli*, or bandwagon effect. In other words, after an election people, especially those who voted for the loser, tend to view the winner more favorably than they did before the election. The depolarization of politics following an election and the positivity bias itself probably help to create an environment conducive to attitude change.[25]

The Persistence of Approval

We have seen that presidents typically begin their initial terms with the benefit of substantial support from the public. But how long does this honeymoon last? Conventional wisdom seems to indicate that presidents soon have to begin making hard choices that inevitably alienate segments of the population. Additional support for this view comes from a revealing response of President Carter in 1979 to a reporter's question concerning whether it was reasonable to expect the president to rate very highly with the American people. The president answered:

> In this present political environment, it is almost impossible. There are times of euphoria that sweep the Nation immediately after an election or after an inauguration day or maybe after a notable success, like the Camp David Ac-

Source: B.C. by Johnny Hart, by permission of Johnny Hart and News Group Chicago, Inc.

cords, when there is a surge of popularity for a President. But most of the decisions that have to be made by a President are inherently not popular ones. They are contentious.[26]

Despite the reasonableness of these expectations, presidential honeymoons are not always short-lived. When we examine shifts in presidents' approval ratings, we find that although declines certainly do take place, they are neither inevitable nor swift. Eisenhower maintained his standing in the public very well for two complete terms. Kennedy and Nixon held their public support for two years, as did Ford, once he suffered his sharp initial decline. Johnson's and Carter's approval losses were steeper, although Johnson's initial ratings were inflated by the unique emotional climate at the time he assumed office. The same was true, of course, for Ford.

Thus, honeymoons are not necessarily fleeting phenomena in which new occupants of the White House receive a breathing period from the public. Instead, the president's constituents seem to be willing to give a new chief executive the benefit of the doubt for some time. In January 1982 over 70 percent of the public felt it would not be fair to judge President Reagan's economic program passed in mid-1981 until at least the end of 1982.[27] It is up to each president to exploit this goodwill and build solid support for his administration in the public.

Long-Term Decline

In addition to examining approval levels within presidential terms, we also need to look for trends in public support across presidents. As we can see in Table 4-9, from 1953 through 1965, with the single exception of 1958, at least 60 percent of the public approved the president on the average. Support from two out of three Americans was not unusual. Starting in 1966, approval levels changed dramatically. Since that time, support from even half the public has been the exception rather than the rule.

Table 4-9. Average Yearly Presidential Approval, 1953–1980

Year	President	% Approval
1953	Eisenhower	68
1954	Eisenhower	66
1955	Eisenhower	71
1956	Eisenhower	73
1957	Eisenhower	64
1958	Eisenhower	54
1959	Eisenhower	64
1960	Eisenhower	61
1961	Kennedy	76
1962	Kennedy	71
1963	Kennedy	65
1964	Johnson	75
1965	Johnson	66
1966	Johnson	50
1967	Johnson	44
1968	Johnson	43
1969	Nixon	63
1970	Nixon	58
1971	Nixon	51
1972	Nixon	58
1973	Nixon	43
1974	Nixon/Ford	36
1975	Ford	44
1976	Ford	49
1977	Carter	63
1978	Carter	45
1979	Carter	38
1980	Carter	42
1981	Reagan	58
1982	Reagan	44
1983	Reagan	44

Source: Gallup Poll.

What happened? We cannot provide a definitive answer to this question, but it seems reasonable to argue that the war in Vietnam, a highly divisive policy following an era of peace, had a destructive effect on President Johnson's approval levels. Although Richard Nixon rebounded somewhat from his predecessor's low standing in the polls in 1966–1968, he did not rise back to pre-1966 levels, and Watergate sent his approval levels to new lows.

Just how much residual effect the factors of Vietnam and Watergate have had on the approval levels of the presidents that followed is impossible to determine with certainty. We do know that President Ford's pardon of Nixon tied him to Watergate and that his public support plummeted immediately following his announcement. Moreover, a 1974 survey of Wisconsin residents found that 55 percent of the respondents agreed that Watergate had reduced their confidence in the office of president.[28]

We also know that Presidents Carter and Reagan have not enjoyed high levels of approval. Ronald Reagan, as we saw in Table 4-8, began his term with less public approval than any president in our study. Like his predecessor, he was below the 50 percent level by his second year in office. Although it is possible that the generally low levels of support for recent presidents is purely a product of their individual actions and characteristics, it is difficult not to conclude that the events of the late 1960s and early 1970s have weakened the predispositions of many Americans to support the president.

Personality or Policy?

A factor that we commonly associate with someone's being approved is personality. When focusing on presidents or other public figures, there may be a tendency to evaluate them more on style than substance. The fact that Americans pay relatively little detailed attention to politics and policy adds further support to the view that the president's personality plays a large role in the public's approval of him.

Dwight Eisenhower was unique among modern presidents in that his public standing preceded and was independent of his involvement in partisan politics. He was a likeable war hero who had recently been a principal leader in the highly consensual policy of defeating Germany in World War II. His image following the war was so apolitical that both parties approached him about running for president under their labels.

Nevertheless, as Table 4-7 indicates, Eisenhower was evaluated by the public as a partisan figure. Republicans were much more likely to approve his handling of the presidency than were Democrats. Moreover, the differences between the approval levels of the two groups of party identifiers are typical of those for other presidents. Thus, the personal component of Eisenhower's public support may have kept his overall level of approval high, but it did not protect him from evaluations as a partisan figure or from fluctuations in approval related to other conditions and events in the public's environment.

Personality may buttress presidential approval, but it is not a dynamic factor. In other words, it cannot explain shifts in the president's standing with the public. Sharp changes in approval have occurred for presidents whose public manners have remained unaltered. Although impressions the public holds of the president's personality form early and change slowly, what the public feels ought to be and the way people evaluate what they see can change more rapidly. "Cleverness" can soon be viewed as "deceit," "reaching down for details" as "a penchant for the trivial," "evaluating all the alternatives" as "indecisiveness," "charm" as "commonness" or, even worse, "vulgarity," "staying above politics" as "naivete." The contradictory expectations the people hold of the president help to set the scene for these changing interpretations of presidential behavior, allowing the public to switch emphasis in what it looks for in a president and how it evaluates what it sees.

In addition, the public may "like" presidents but still disapprove of the way they are handling their jobs. A poll near the middle of President Carter's term found that almost twice as many people liked the president as approved of the manner in which he was handling the presidency.[29] In November 1981 the Gallup Poll found that 74 percent of the public approved of President Reagan as a person, but only 49 percent approved of his performance as president.[30]

Thus, although we cannot specify the contribution of personality to presidential approval, we do know that policy matters play a large role in evaluations of presidents. Some political scientists have found that presidential approval increases when the news is good and decreases when the news is bad.[31] We do not know whether it is the ratio of good news to bad news per se that explains levels and shifts of presidential approval, or whether it is the more specific events and conditions occurring in the country and the world that are reported in the news that have this influence. Nevertheless, this research shows that changes in presidential approval are in large part a response to what people see happening in the world and not merely a reaction to a particular personality. It is the president's actions and the consequences of policies that are reported in the news. And, as we should expect in light of the findings in the previous section, the president's approval is affected whether or not he is responsible for these policy outcomes.

The Economy

The state of the economy has a pervasive influence on our lives. The conventional view is that people's evaluations of the president are affected strongly by their personal economic circumstances. That is, people are more likely to approve of the president if they feel they are prospering personally than if they feel they are not. Lyndon Johnson, for example, believed that "the family pocketbook was the root-and-branch crucial connection to all his plans and hopes for the future."[32]

Yet there is plenty of reason to be skeptical of the role of short-term self-interest in evaluations of the president.[33] People differentiate their own circumstances from those of the country as a whole. In January 1981 the Gallup Poll found that although 81 percent of the public was dissatisfied with the way things were going in the country, 83 percent were satisfied with the way things were going in their personal lives.[34] People may evaluate the president in terms of the state of the economy as a whole, rather than its effect on them personally, or they may simply evaluate how well the president is handling economic policy, regardless of the short-term impact of his actions. In fact, the public may approve of a president who is struggling with a difficult situation even if he is not meeting with great tangible success. Franklin Roosevelt in 1933 and 1934 seems to be such a case.

This reasoning regarding the public's evaluation of the president applies to other factors besides the economy. The war in Vietnam may have influenced citizens' evaluations of the president because of how they viewed it as a general policy rather than how it affected them personally. Jimmy Carter's standing in the public may have benefited from favorable public perceptions of his handling of the Iranian hostage crisis, despite the fact the hostages were held for more than fourteen months.

When we examine survey data, we find results in line with this theorizing.[35] Whether people and their families feel financially better or worse off over the past year or expect to be in the coming year, whether they or their families have experienced unemployment, or whether they have been hurt by inflation has little or no bearing on their approval of the president. The same is true when we ask people their views about the state of the economy itself, including evaluations of past and future conditions, price levels, unemployment, and the economy in general. When we turn to the public's evaluation of the president's *handling* of the economy, however, we find a different picture. Citizens' evaluations of the president's handling of unemployment, inflation, and the economy in general are related strongly to overall presidential approval. In sum, the public evaluates the president's role in the economy more on the basis of his performance than on its view of the state of the economy.

War

War is frequently discussed as a factor in presidential approval. The reasons for this attention are obvious: wars disrupt and sometimes polarize society and are very costly in terms of lives and money. The president, moreover, in his role as commander-in-chief, is inevitably closely identified with war policy. Unlike the economy, war, fortunately, is not always with us. We do have some relevant data from polls taken during the war in Vietnam, however.

As in the case of the impact of the economy on presidential approval, the personal circumstances of individuals do not seem to affect their evaluations of the president. Persons who had a member of their immediate family or close friends or relatives in the armed services as a result of the war in Vietnam did not evaluate the president differently from those who were not as directly touched by the war. We find, however, that the public's evaluations of the president's handling of the war strongly influenced overall presidential approval.

Other Issues

When we examine public opinion on other issues, ranging from national health insurance to federal aid to minorities, we find that citizens' policy differences with the president are modestly related to their evaluations of his performance in office. Once again, however, people's direct evaluations of the president's actions in policy areas such as energy, the Iranian hostage crisis, and crime control exert the strongest influence on their overall evaluations of his performances.

Personal Characteristics

Much of the commentary on the president in the press and in other forums focuses on his personal characteristics, especially integrity, intelligence, and leadership abilities. When the public is asked about such job-related characteristics, its responses are clearly related to its evaluations of the president. Thus the public's evaluations of the president's personal characteristics must be included in the list of factors that influence its approval of his performance in office.

Rally Events

To this point we have examined factors that may affect presidential approval systematically over time, but sometimes public opinion takes sudden jumps. One popular explanation for these surges of support are "rally events." John Mueller, in his seminal definition of the concept, defined a rally event as one that is international, directly involves the United States and particularly the president, and is specific, dramatic, and sharply focused. Such events confront the nation as a whole, are salient to the public, and gain public attention and interest.[36]

The preponderance of evidence indicates that the rally phenomenon rarely appears and that the events that generate it are highly idiosyncratic and do not seem to differ significantly from other events that were not followed by surges in presidential approval. Moreover, the events that cause sudden increases in public support are not restricted to international affairs, and most international events that would seem to be potential rally events fail to generate much additional approval of the president.

Summary

Public approval of the president is the product of many factors. At the base of evaluations of the president is the predisposition of many people to support the president. Political party identification provides the basic underpinning of approval or disapproval and mediates the impact of other factors. The positivity bias and the bandwagon effect buttress approval levels, at least for a while.

Changes in approval levels appear to be due primarily to the public's evaluation of how the president is handling policy areas such as the economy, war, energy, and foreign affairs. Citizens seem to focus on the president's efforts and his stands on issues rather than on his personality or how his policies affect them personally or even whether his policies are successful in the short run. Job-related personal characteristics of the president also play an important role in influencing the degree of presidential approval. Conversely, rally events may provide an occasional increment of support, but in general they do not seem to be very significant.

DIRECT OPINION LEADERSHIP

The most visible and obvious technique employed by presidents to lead public opinion is to seek the public's support directly. Presidents frequently attempt to influence public opinion with speeches over television or radio or in person to large groups. Not all presidents are effective speakers, however, and not all look good under the glare of hot lights and the unflattering gaze of television cameras. Moreover, the public is not always receptive to the president's message.

All presidents since Truman have had media advice from experts on lighting, makeup, stage settings, camera angles, clothing, pacing of delivery, and other facets of making speeches. Despite this aid and despite the experience that politicians inevitably have in speaking, presidential speeches aimed at directly leading public opinion have typically not been very impressive. Only Kennedy and Reagan have mastered the art of speaking to the camera.

No matter how effective a president might be as a speaker, he still must contend with the predisposition of his audience. The president cannot depend upon an attentive audience. Most people are not very interested in politics. The relative importance the typical person attaches to a president's address is illustrated by the attention President Carter gave to setting the date for his 1978 State of the Union message. He had to be careful to avoid preempting prime time on the night that offered the current season's most popular shows—"Laverne and Shirley," "Happy Days," and "Three's Company"—and thus irritating the shows' loyal viewers.[37] Cable television, with its multitude of stations, has complicated this problem.

The public's general lack of interest in politics constrains the president's leadership of public opinion in the long run as well as on a given day. Although he has unparalleled access to the American people, the president cannot make too much use of this situation. If he does, his speeches will become commonplace and will lose their drama and interest. That is why presidents do not make appeals to the public, particularly on television, very often. Some presidents, such as Reagan and Nixon, have turned to radio and midday addresses to reserve prime-time televised addresses for their most important speeches.

Television is a medium in which visual interest, action, and conflict are most effective. Presidential speeches are unlikely to contain these characteristics. Although some addresses to the nation, such as President Johnson's televised demand for a voting rights act before a joint session of Congress in 1965, occur at moments of high drama, they do not typically do so.

Presidents not only have to contend with the medium but they also must concern themselves with their messages. The most effective speeches seem to be those whose goals are general support and image building rather than specific support. They focus on simple themes rather than complex details. Calvin Coolidge used this method successfully in his radio speeches, as did Franklin Roosevelt in his famous "fireside chats." The limitation of such an approach, of course, is that general support cannot always be translated into public backing for specific policies.

Success of Appeals

We should not be surprised, then, that direct appeals to the public often fail. Shortly after becoming president, Jimmy Carter made a televised appeal to the American people on the energy crisis, calling it the "moral equivalent of war." One year later the Gallup Poll found that exactly the same percentage of the public (41 percent) felt the energy situation was "very serious" as before Carter's speech.[38]

In perhaps that most famous presidential public appeal, Woodrow Wilson took his case on behalf of the League of Nations directly to the American people in a nationwide tour. His goal was to pressure the Senate into ratifying the Treaty of Versailles, which contained provisions for setting up the league. He failed in his goal, however, and permanently damaged his health when he suffered a severe stroke en route.

Despite the limitations of their abilities to exercise direct opinion leadership over the public, presidents are aided by the willingness of Americans to *follow* their lead, especially on foreign policy. Foreign policy is more distant from the lives of most Americans than is domestic policy and is therefore seen as more complex and based on specialized knowledge. Thus people tend to defer more to the president on foreign issues than on domestic ones that they can relate more easily and directly to their own experience. Studies have shown public opinion undergoing changes in line with presidents' policies on testing nuclear weapons, relations with the People's Republic of China, and both the escalation and de-escalation of the war in Vietnam.[39]

In a survey taken right after the United States' invasion of Cambodia in 1970, the Gallup Poll found dramatic evidence that the public sometimes takes its cues on public policy issues from the president. When asked if they "approved of President Nixon's decision," 51 percent of the respondents replied in the affirmative. However, when asked in the *same* poll if they approved of sending American troops into Cambodia, 58 percent disapproved and only 28 percent approved.[40] When the sample of the public was asked about the same specific action without mentioning the president's name, many more disapproved. Another study described the Family Assistance Plan and asked a sample of citizens whether they favored it. Forty-eight percent did favor it, 40 percent opposed it, and 12 percent were indecisive. When another sample was told that the plan was President Nixon's, support increased slightly to 50 percent and, more significantly, opposition decreased to 25 percent, while 24 percent fell into the "indecisive" category.[41]

Such studies are rare and it is difficult to be sure that the public is really not aware of the president's actions and thus already influenced by them. In an effort to overcome this problem, one scholar ascertained public opinion on six potential responses to the hostage crisis in Iran. Then he asked those who opposed each option if they would change their view

Table 4-10. Reconsidering Policy Opinions in Response to the President

Policy	% Original Approval	% Approval after Reconsideration	% Change Due to President
Wait and see	58	83	25
Return Shah to Iran	21	53	32
Send Shah elsewhere	74	87	13
Naval blockade	62	85	23
Threaten to send troops	43	73	30
Send troops	29	62	33

Source: Lee Sigeiman, "Gauging the Public Response to Presidential Leadership," *Presidential Studies Quarterly* 10 (Summer 1980): 431.

"if President Carter considered this action necessary." The policy options and the public's responses to them are shown in Table 4-10.[42] In each case a substantial percentage of the public changed its opinion in deference to the supposed opinion of the president. Similarly, a poll of Utah residents found that two-thirds of them opposed basing the deployment of MX missiles in Utah and Nevada. But an equal number said they would definitely or probably support President Reagan if he decided to go ahead and base the missiles in those states.[43]

Not all results are so positive, however. In one study different sample groups were asked whether they supported a domestic policy proposal dealing with welfare and a proposal dealing with foreign aid. One of the groups was told President Carter supported the proposals. The authors found that attaching the president's name to either proposal not only failed to increase support for them but actually had a negative effect because those who disapproved of Carter reacted very strongly against proposals they thought were his.[44] The limited evidence available indicates that presidents are much more likely to be successful in influencing public opinion when they have high approval ratings themselves.[45]

As we learned earlier, the public generally does not have crystallized opinions on issues and is therefore often easy to sway in the short run. But this volatility also means that any opinion change is subject to slippage. As issues fade into the background or as issue positions confront the realities of daily life, opinions that were altered in response to presidential leadership may quickly be forgotten. This is especially likely to occur where the president's influence on public opinion seems to be greatest: foreign policy.

A balanced view of the president's ability to lead public opinion directly must take into consideration both the potential for and the obstacles to leadership. As in so many other presidential relationships, the direct leadership of public opinion provides opportunities, especially in foreign policy, but no guarantees of success. It is for this reason that presidents often rely on more subtle methods of opinion leadership.

INFORMATION CONTROL

A technique for influencing public opinion that is much less direct than appeals to the public is information control. This comes in many forms, ranging from withholding information from the public to lying. If the public is unaware of a situation or has a distorted view of it, then the president may have more flexibility in achieving what he desires. Often the president desires public passivity as much as he wants public support.

Withholding Information

One means of influencing public opinion through information control is to withhold from the public information it needs to evaluate the president and his policies. The war in Vietnam provides many examples of the president and other high officials withholding crucial information from the American people about very important policy matters, including the nature and extent of our involvement, especially in the early years of the war, and U.S. activities in Laos and Cambodia.

In other areas of foreign policy the public has been kept equally in the dark. Americans were not informed that between 1962 and 1973 the United States engaged in covert actions to prevent Salvador Allende from coming to power in Chile and then aiding his opponents once he was elected. In 1975, the United States secretly intervened in the civil war in Angola.

Pertinent information is also withheld on domestic policies. President Nixon favored federal subsidies for the Supersonic Transport plane and therefore withheld a negative assessment of the airplane by his own advisers (done at public expense). In the Johnson administration attempts were made to keep secret the results of the Coleman report on educational opportunity as well as an evaluation of Head Start programs. The presidents perceived the information contained in these reports to be contrary to their self-interest. Each of these reports was eventually released, but not until members of Congress or the media had discovered them and applied pressure for their publication, often after the information was no longer relevant to the formulation of public policy.

The classification of information under the rubric of "national security" is a frequently used means of withholding information. Most people support secrecy in handling national security affairs, especially in such matters as defense plans and strategy, weapons technology, troop movements, the details of current diplomatic negotiations, the methods and sources of covert intelligence gathering, and similar information about the defense, negotiations, and intelligence gathering of other nations. However, there has been controversy over the amount of information classified and whether classification is used by the president and other high officials to influence public opinion. When officials withhold information that might aid the public in evaluating their performance in office and in answering general questions of public policy but that might embarrass them if made public, they may provide a distorted view of reality and increase or maintain support for themselves.

De-emphasis of Information

A president can also employ more subtle methods of manipulating information in an effort to influence public opinion. He can, for example, order that information collected by the government be de-emphasized. When the economy was not doing well in 1971, the White House ordered the Bureau of Labor Statistics to discontinue its monthly briefing of the press on prices and unemployment. Similarly, during the war in Vietnam the Defense Department gave much more attention in its public announcements to deserters from enemy forces than to deserters from the armed forces of our South Vietnamese allies. In each case the government possessed information that might negatively influence public perceptions of the president and his administration. It chose not to emphasize this "bad news."

Collection of Information

Going a step further, a president can simply not order that information on a policy be collected. This, of course, prevents the public from fully evaluating his performance. President Johnson had invested a great deal in his Great Society domestic programs and did not want to cut back on them when large amounts of funds were needed for the war in Vietnam. Although warned by the Council of Economic Advisers at the end of 1965 of the need for a tax increase to avoid the inflation that would result from having *both* guns and butter, he refused to request one. Instead Johnson kept the precise expenditures on the war from Congress and the public. No serious effort was ever made to determine the true costs of U.S. involvement in the war in Vietnam, and Americans felt the ravages of inflation for years to come.

Timing of the Release of Information

Sometimes information is provided, but the timing of its release is used to try to influence public opinion. On November 2, 1970, the White House announced the most recent casualty figures from Vietnam. They were a five-year low and their announcement was made on Monday instead of Thursday as usual, presumably because the 1970 congressional elections were being held the next day. The Carter administration revealed that the Pentagon had developed a new technology that made aircraft virtually invisible to enemy detection devices. This disclosure coincided with an administration effort during the 1980 presidential election campaign to show that it was working to strengthen national defense. Taking the opposite tack, the Ford administration announced that the country was in a recession one week after the 1974 congressional elections.

Obfuscation of Information

Presidents and their aides may also attempt to obscure or distort the truth in order to confuse or mislead the public. President Eisenhower regularly gave purposefully ambiguous answers at his press conferences.[46] A classic example of this technique is an answer Nixon's press secretary Ron Ziegler gave to a reporter's question about the Watergate tapes.

> I would feel that most of the conversations that took place in those areas of the White House that did have the recording system would, in almost their entirety, be in existence, but the special prosecutor, the court, and I think, the American people are sufficiently familiar with the recording system to know where the recording devices existed and to know the situation in terms of the recording process, but I feel, although the process has not been undertaken yet in preparation of the material to abide by the court decision, really, what the answer to that question is.[47]

Distortion comes in many forms. One of the most common is to provide impressive statistics without going into the details of how they were compiled. In 1982 President Reagan told the American people more than half the stores investigated by the government were selling items that were prohibited for purchase with food stamps. He mitted the fact that the stores that were investigated were ones already suspected of abuse.

Presidents have also used tricks to make budgets appear smaller. In his last year in office President Johnson introduced the "unified budget," which included trust funds previously *excluded* from the budget, such as those for social security, unemployment benefits, highway construction, and retirement pensions of railroad workers. The fact that the trust funds were running a surplus allowed him to cut the size of the projected federal deficit—at least on paper, because these surplus trust funds cannot be used to cover the deficit in the regular budget. President Nixon introduced the "full employment" budget in fiscal 1972. His ruse was to calculate the federal revenues not at what was expected but at what they would be if there were full employment (which there was not). This subterfuge allowed him to show a smaller overall deficit. In more recent times presidents (and Congress) have used what are termed "off-budget" expenditures to reduce the size of the budget—on paper.[48]

It is not only what goes into compiling a "fact" that is important for the public's evaluation of it, but also the context of events in which the "fact" occurs. In 1964 Lyndon Johnson went before Congress to ask for a resolution supporting U.S. retaliation against North Vietnam for two attacks on U.S. ships in the Gulf of Tonkin. The Gulf of Tonkin Resolution was subsequently passed with only two dissenting votes and marked the watershed of U.S. military actions in Vietnam. As the president desired, it was passed in the context of strong public support for retaliating against "unprovoked" attacks against Americans.

The public might have been less enthusiastic in its backing of military reprisals, however, if it had known what the president knew about the context in which the North Vietnamese actions took place. First, the United States had secretly been gathering intelligence and supporting covert South Vietnamese operations against North Vietnam for several years before the incidents in the Gulf of Tonkin. Some of these activities were going on in the vicinity at the time of the attacks on U.S. ships, and the North Vietnamese might have thought our ships were involved.

The second piece of crucial contextual information that was withheld from the American people was that there was considerable reason to doubt that the second attack ever occurred! As President Johnson later said (in private, of course), "For all I know, our Navy was shooting whales out there."[49] Although it is possible that at the time the president had honestly concluded that the attack had in fact occurred, there is little doubt that the public's approval of U.S. retaliatory actions would have been more restrained if it had had this information.

Attempts to distort information are not always successful. By 1967 two-thirds of the American people felt the Johnson administration was not telling them all it should know about the Vietnam War. In 1971 a similar percentage felt the same way about the Nixon administration.[50] Out of such attitudes emerged the credibility gap and low levels of popular standing for these presidents.

Prevarication

The most extreme form of information control is lying. Do presidents lie? The answer is yes. The range of lies is great and includes the topics of the U.S. military situation in Vietnam; the U.S. role in the 1954 coup in Guatemala; the U-2 incident; the U.S. role in the Bay of Pigs invasion; the presence of missiles in Cuba in 1962; the U.S. role in the overthrow of President Diem of South Vietnam; the attempted bribery by the United States of the prime minister of Singapore; the motivations behind the U.S. invasion of the Dominican Republic in 1965; the reasons that the USS *Liberty* was sunk by our Israeli allies in the 1967 Six-Day War; U.S. attempts to prevent the election of Marxist Salvador Allende as president of Chile; the Watergate cover-up; presidential plans for appointments, travel, and policies; and even the president's review of requests to use the White House tennis courts.[51]

In his press conference on September 28, 1982, President Reagan responded to questions on the economy with descriptions about the growth of the gross national product, the rate of increase in the unemployment rate under his predecessor, the proportion of the population in the work force, and the increase in the purchasing power of the average family. All of these were assertions about the economy's performance, and all of them were motivated by a desire to put it in the best possible light. Unfortunately, all of these statements were also untrue![52] Whether the president's responses were carefully planned or the result of his misunderstanding of the statistics is unclear.

Information Control in Perspective

What can we conclude from our discussion of information control? Perhaps the most obvious pattern that we have found is that it is most common in the national security area. The reason is simple: it is difficult for the public to challenge official statements about events in other countries, especially military activities, which often are shrouded in secrecy. It is much easier to be skeptical about domestic activities that American reporters can scrutinize and to which they can provide alternative views. In addition, the public can relate many domestic policies to their own experiences more easily than they can relate most foreign and military policies. When officials' statements do not correspond to people's experiences, they have a built-in basis for skepticism.

Information control is employed to deny information not only to a foreign adversary but also to the American public. In virtually all of the examples involving national security policy, from the U-2 flight over the Soviet Union to the secret bombing of Cambodia, the "enemy" knew the truth. Only the American public was left in the dark.

Information control is an unfortunate and, regrettably, a common technique used by presidents. Their goal is to influence public opinion by controlling the information upon which the public bases its evaluations of chief executives and their policies and upon which it determines if there is cause for concern. Although we have no way to measure the impact of these efforts, it is probably safe to say that some are successful and some lead to embarrassment and a loss of credibility for the president and his administration.

THE USE OF SYMBOLS

The language used in political discourse may have an influence on public opinion independent of the subject under discussion. One important aspect of political language is the use of symbols, things that are simple or familiar that stand for things complex or unfamiliar. Symbols are frequently used to describe politicians, events, issues, or some other aspect of the political world. Naturally, symbols are not synonyms for what they describe. The choice of symbols inevitably highlights certain aspects of an issue or event and conceals others. Thus, if presidents can get a substantial segment of the public to adopt symbols favorable to them, they will be in a position to influence public opinion.

Because of the potential power of symbols in shaping public opinion, presidents have encouraged the public to adopt certain symbols as representative of their administrations. Franklin Roosevelt dubbed his administration the "New Deal," and Harry Truman termed his the "Fair Deal." Each symbol was an oversimplification for new and extremely complex policies, but each served to reassure many Americans that these policies were for their good. Similarly, John Kennedy's "New Frontier" and Lyndon Johnson's "Great Society" served as attractive symbols of their administrations.

Symbols are also used to describe specific policies. President Johnson declared a "War on Poverty" despite the fact that many saw the "war" as more of a skirmish. President Nixon went to considerable efforts to have the public view the January 1973 peace agreement ending the involvement of American troops in Vietnam as "peace with honor," clearly a controversial conclusion. He also claimed his administration represented "law and order," a claim that is especially ironic in light of the Watergate debacle.

Perhaps the most important and effective televised address President Reagan made to the nation in 1981 was his July 27 speech seeking the public's support for his tax cut bill. In it he went to great lengths to present his plan as "bipartisan." It was crucial that he convince the public that this controversial legislation was supported by members of both parties and was therefore, by implication, fair. Despite the fact that House Democrats voted overwhelmingly against the president's proposal two days later, he described it as "bipartisan" *eleven* times in the span of a few minutes! No one was to miss the point.

As these examples indicate, symbols can be manipulated in attempts not only to lead public opinion but also deliberately to mislead it. During the Watergate controversy Richard Nixon repeatedly referred to his unwillingness to cooperate fully with Congress and the special prosecutor as necessary to protect the office of the presidency (a powerful symbol), not himself as a particular president.

The White House tries to label opponents as well as policies. President Nixon's chief of staff, H. R. Haldeman, accused critics of Nixon's Vietnam peace plan of being traitors, and the president made no disclaimer. Vice President Agnew classified administration critics as "radical-liberals" and "effete snobs."

The presidency uniquely lends itself to symbolic manipulation. In his role as chief of state the president personifies the government and our nation's heritage. Presidents use this opportunity to enhance their public standing. They are frequently seen on television welcoming heads of state or other dignitaries to the White House, dedicating federal projects, speaking before national groups, or performing ceremonial functions, such as laying a wreath at the Tomb of the Unknown Soldier in Arlington National Cemetery.

The president's foreign travels provide even greater opportunities to be viewed as the representative of America and as a statesman above partisan politics. As he deals with the leaders of other nations on matters of international importance and as he is greeted by cheering crowds of Egyptians, Poles, or Italians, Americans naturally take pride in him as the representative of our country, the embodiment of our goals, and the bearer of our goodwill. As we shall see, presidents are aware of this and may schedule activities so they will be covered on prime-time television.

The president also participates in many ceremonial roles dealing with domestic matters. These include having his picture taken with the winner of the national spelling bee, the teacher of the year, or the March of Dimes poster child; lighting the national Christmas tree; and issuing proclamations celebrating national holidays such as Thanksgiving and Veterans Day and lesser-known celebrations such as National Pickle Week.

All of this activity as chief of state, the president hopes, will help foster the view that he is a fitting head of state and competent to run the country and make important and difficult decisions. He wants to try to relieve some of the fears and anxieties of the public and provide hope for and confidence in the future. If he is successful in projecting an image of dignity and ability, which may or may not be accurate, he will make it easier for people to vest their allegiance in him as a visible, human source of authority and to accept decisions they might otherwise oppose.

While engaging in these and other functions, the president often makes appeals to patriotism, traditions, and our history (and its greatness) to move the public to support him, reminding people of their common interests. He also frequently invokes the names of great leaders of the past, such as Lincoln or Wilson, who made difficult decisions on the basis of high principles, and relates himself or his decisions to them.

Presidents also make gestures to show that they are really "one of the people." President Carter made considerable use of this technique, desiring to be seen as a people's president. He invited hundreds of thousands of people to his inauguration and walked (instead of riding) down Pennsylvania Avenue from the Capitol to the White House after taking the oath of office. Later he conducted a "fireside chat" over national television, seated before a blazing fire and dressed casually in a sweater instead of a suit. He also staged a press conference in which private individuals could call in from around the country and directly ask him questions.

Despite the considerable efforts presidents make to manipulate symbols, they are not always successful. The Nixon administration tried to find a slogan that captured its essence, including the "New Federalism," the "New American Revolution," the "Generation of Peace," and the "Open Door," but none of these metaphors caught on with the press or the public. Gerald Ford wore a WIN (for "Whip Inflation Now") button during a televised address before a joint session of Congress to represent his economic priorities, but it only became an object of derision.

Many observers feel that a president's failure to lead the public to adopt broad symbols for his administration can cause severe problems in relations with the public. Jimmy Carter faced a great deal of criticism for lacking a unifying theme and cohesion in the programs, for failing to inspire the public with a sense of purpose, an idea to follow. Instead of providing the country with a sense of his vision and priorities, he emphasized discrete problem solving. In other words, he had an analytic but not synthetic approach to government.

PUBLIC RELATIONS

In its efforts to mold public opinion, the White House and subordinate departments employ public relations techniques modeled after those of commercial advertising firms. No one really knows how many federal employees work on public relations or how much money they spend. It is illegal for the government to hire "publicity experts" unless Congress specifically authorizes such positions (which it rarely does). Therefore, the various executive departments hire "information" experts and others to engage in public relations. Many of these employees answer questions from the press and the public and prepare information about government programs. Others prepare advertisements asking citizens to join in such widely supported activities as antilittering or fire-prevention campaigns. Nevertheless, the line between *information* and *propaganda* is vague and often crossed.

The White House as an Ad Agency

One indicator of the importance of public relations to contemporary presidents is the presence of advertising specialists in the White House. President Carter put Gerald Rafshoon, the advertising director for his 1976 campaign, on the White House staff. His role was that of a general adviser with special responsibilities for developing and coordinating public relations. These responsibilities included orchestrating the president's public appearances and scheduling and coordinating public appearances by other administration officials to help ensure that they publicized the president's policies and had maximum impact and that their public postures were consistent and not distracting.

The use of public relations specialists was hardly novel. One of President Johnson's closest aides, Jack Valenti, came to the White House from the advertising business and went into the motion picture industry when he left. Richard Nixon carried the hiring of public relations experts further than any other president. His chief of staff, H. R. Haldeman, his press secretary and later close adviser, Ron Ziegler, and several other aides came to the White House from advertising firms.

Aside from serving as an indicator of the importance presidents place on public relations, the presence of these aides may influence the substance and especially the timing of policy. Since no president will admit to making policy decisions on the basis of advice from image makers, this assertion is difficult to prove. Carter aide Gerald Rafshoon told one reporter: "I try to tell the President how these things [policies] will be perceived, but I have nothing to do with making up policy."[53] He did, however, advise the president to take such actions as increasing the defense budget, firing his adviser on women's affairs, and resurrecting some of the trappings of the imperial presidency.[54]

Being human, all presidents are subject to the temptation to do the most popular thing. For example, an analysis of President Johnson's public statements on Vietnam shows that he varied their content—that is, their "hawkishness"—with the audience he was addressing.[55] The potential for subordinating substance to style is clearly present.

There is also the potential for running the White House like an advertising agency. Since an advertising specialist's orientation is to stress a uniform image, the power of such persons can be a centralizing force in an administration. Emphasis on "team play" inevitably leads to the discouragement of dissent and irregularity because it blunts the impact of the president's image. The parallels between this description and the Nixon White House are striking.

Spreading the Word

The primary goal of White House public relations efforts is to build support for the president and his policies. Part of this job is "getting the word out" about the president, his views, and his accomplishments. Lyndon Johnson constantly sought more publicity and even arranged to have favorable articles placed in the *Congressional Record* with prefatory remarks provided by the White House. Richard Nixon took a special interest in public relations. His office of communications tried to stimulate books on Nixon, suggested ideas for feature articles about the president and his family, wrote speeches for leading administration officials, attempted to exercise more control over the public relations of the executive branch, held regional press briefings to publicize younger members of the administration, stacked a televised press conference with Nixon supporters, and pressured the Bureau of Labor Statistics to issue announcements of the number of new jobs created in the economy (as the unemployment rate failed to fall). The office also placed representatives of the administration on television shows and lecture platforms and dispersed information to editors, commentators, and reporters and to ethnic, religious, geographic, professional, and other types of groups interested in particular policies.

Reaching the enormous television audience of about 50 million viewers of the evening news is especially important to the White House, and the president's staff builds his schedule around efforts to do so. As President Ford's deputy press secretary put it: "Whenever possible, everything was done to take into account the need for coverage. After all, most of the events are done for coverage. Why else are you doing them?"[56]

Public relations efforts may focus on certain presidential characteristics. Photographs portraying the president as a family man or pet owner are common. In January 1976 President Ford held a special budget briefing so he could display that he was "competent," a subject over which there had been considerable debate in the press.[57]

Many aspects of public relations were employed in the early days of the Reagan administration. The president focused on his priority item: the economy. Publicity was carefully planned at the time of his first speech urging budgetary reductions. Press briefings were held, and administration officials appeared on all three Sunday interview shows—"Issues and Answers," "Meet the Press," and "Face the Nation"—"Nightline," the "MacNeil-Lehrer Report," and one of the morning news shows. Throughout, the White House paid close attention to the image of the president as well, trying to portray him as busy and engaged in important decision making, not remote and passive.

The president and his aides tailor messages they wish to transmit to the public to the needs of the press. President Carter emphasized short two- or three-minute statements to the White House press over longer addresses, because he knew that is all that would be shown on the evening news broadcasts. Similarly, announcements are timed so that reporters can meet their papers' deadlines. Those made too late in the evening will not appear in the next morning's newspapers and those made too late in the afternoon will miss publication in the evening papers. Naturally, if the White House wants to decrease the coverage of an event, it can wait until after the evening news programs to announce it. Then it might be buried among the next day's occurrences. It can also pass the word to administration officials to avoid appearing on interview programs or holding press conferences.

Media Events

In addition to general efforts to publicize the president, the White House has often staged "media events" in hope of obtaining additional public support. President Nixon was second to none in his use of media events. He engaged in live "conversations" with the press; allowed NBC television to film his activities in a day in the White House; became the first president to veto a bill on television; twice chatted informally with Barbara Walters on the "Today" show; was interviewed as a sports fan during halftime at the Texas-Arkansas football game; delivered a halftime message during a professional football game; made a "phone call" before 125 million viewers to the astronauts on the moon and personally greeted them when they landed in the Pacific; and chose to give a televised speech to students at Kansas State University, where he knew he would be enthusiastically received. The wedding reception of his daughter Tricia on the lawn of the White House naturally received widespread coverage.

Nixon's trip to China in 1972 was probably the greatest media event of all. The White House obtained agreement from the Chinese to allow live television coverage, and the networks sent three large cargo planes of equipment and more than one hundred technicians, producers, and executives to do the job. Of course, the White House was not passive in obtaining media coverage. The president's plane arrived in Peking and returned to Washington during prime time. The latter was accomplished only by sitting on the ground in Anchorage, Alaska, for nine hours! The president was very much aware of the huge viewing audience. In his opening remarks at the first banquet in Peking, he referred to the fact that "more people are seeing and hearing what we say than on any other occasion in the whole history of the world."

Presidents Carter and Reagan engaged in most of the public relations activities of their predecessors and added a few innovations of their own. In addition to staging a call-in and several town meetings, Carter also traveled to New York City to sign the bill authorizing federal aid to the city. The White House signing of the Camp David Accords between Egypt and Israel on prime-time television was a spectacular media event. President Reagan had been in office for less than two months when NBC filmed "A Day with President Reagan" and *Time* did a similar story. Both days were atypically active for the president.

Public relations efforts sometimes go to extraordinary lengths to attempt to influence public opinion. The Nixon White House organized an extensive letter-writing program. Women in Washington wrote fifty or sixty individualized letters each week and then sent them to Republicans around the country to be signed and mailed to various publications that had criticized the president in one way or another. One presidential aide estimated that 15 to 20 percent of these letters were published. The White House also worked with state committees to set up grass-roots letter-writing operations. Following one of the president's televised speeches on Vietnam, the White House sent itself telegrams of support. The telegrams, stacked in piles on the president's desk the morning after his speech, made for impressive wire service and television pictures, indicating intense public support for his actions. Frequently, H. R. Haldeman, the White House chief of staff, ordered individually worded telegrams sent to members of Congress from around the country thanking or criticizing them, depending upon their support of the administration. Calls and letters also went on to critics. The president himself was aware of and interested in these tactics.

Interpreting Events

Presidents also use public relations to attempt to have their interpretation of events accepted by the public. President Ford once hailed as a "hundred-percent" victory a vaguely worded promise from Congress to hold down spending. As his press secretary wrote later, the congressional action "wasn't a victory at all." Similarly, the president told his staff not to be unduly optimistic about the economy so that when things were better the White House would appear in a better light and be more credible.[58]

Discrediting Opponents

Public relations can be used to discredit opponents as well as to build support for a president or his policies. In September 1977, White House press secretary Jody Powell passed along to at least two newspapers unsubstantiated allegations (which later proved to be false) that Republican Senator Charles Percy had improperly used corporate aircraft and the facilities of a Chicago bank in his 1972 reelection campaign. A high-ranking aide to Richard Nixon planted a story in *Life* magazine on Senator Joseph Tydings of Maryland in 1970 when the senator was up for reelection. The aide also organized a "paper" committee to run ads against Tydings on the eve of the election, with no time for reply. The story falsely accused him of financial misdeeds.

Access to the Public

Presidents have easy access to the public, especially through television. By simply asking for coverage of a presidential speech or allowing a speech or news conference to be televised, the White House can usually gain substantial free publicity. The president can also agree to appear on a special televised interview. Such offers will usually be readily accepted, since the president is the premier interviewee in the country.

The president may also be able to gain access to network television for others. During the 1968 Democratic National Convention, President Johnson was concerned that the delegates would pass an antiwar provision for the party platform. Therefore, he called the president of CBS and elicited a promise that Secretary of State Dean Rusk's speech defending Johnson's policies would be covered in prime time. Another time he suggested that the networks give Rusk and Secretary of Defense Robert McNamara air time to discuss the war in Vietnam. Two days later they appeared on a special one-hour edition of "Meet the Press."

Almost everyone agrees that the president should have access to free television air time for his major policy statements, news conferences, or national addresses, and the television networks are happy to carry these appearances. But there is a question about the president's possibly having too free an access to the public, access that may be exploited for partisan or public relations purposes. Should the White House be able to decide what should be covered and what should not?

The problem is really one of equal time for the opposition rather than simply of presidential access. Currently the opposition party gets free air time to present only its own State of the Union message in reply to the president's and an occasional opportunity to comment on other speeches. Moreover, the opposition party typically receives less favorable air time than the president and often does not receive a monopoly of time on all three networks as the president does. In early 1981 the networks gave the Democrats a half hour to respond to President Reagan's televised presentation of his economic program to a joint session of Congress. Two of the networks put the Democrats opposite "Dallas," one of the most popular shows on television. When these factors are combined with the differences in prestige of the speakers, it is no surprise that the ratings of the opposition are considerably lower than the president's.

CONCLUSION

The president's relations with the public are complex. He needs its support in order to play an effective leadership role, yet he has a difficult time obtaining it. Expectations are high and contradictory and the public's desires are hard to ascertain. Although the public appears to award or withhold its support of the chief executive largely on job-performance grounds, its perceptions of issues and the president's actions are hazy. Just how the public reaches its conclusions about the president's performance is not well understood. It does seem, however, that there is ample opportunity for the president, directly and through the press, to influence public perceptions.

Given this environment, presidents are not content to follow public opinion. In their search for public support they invest substantial amounts of time, energy, ingenuity, and manpower in techniques that include direct appeals to the public, use of symbols, information control, and public relations. Some of this activity is quite legitimate, and some is not. Some of it follows Richard Nixon's view that "It's not *what* Presidents do but how they do it that matters."[59]

There is no guarantee of success in these efforts, however, and they often fail to achieve their desired effects. As President Carter's press secretary, Jody Powell, put it:

> Communications and the management of them, the impact is marginal. The substance of what you do and what happens to you over the long haul is more important, particularly on the big things like the economy. . . . Poor communications comes up after a problem is already there, if an economic program doesn't work, if it is ill-conceived, or if circumstances change. . . . The ability to turn a sow's ear into silk purses is limited. You can make it into a silkier sow's ear, that's all.[60]

Nevertheless, presidents continue to employ these tactics, adding their own wrinkles to those of their predecessors as they seek public support.

NOTES

1. Quoted in Emmett John Hughes, "Presidency vs. Jimmy Carter," *Fortune*, December 4, 1978, pp. 62, 64; our italics.
2. Jon Margolis, "Polls Show Americans Have Changed Their Minds since Reagan's Election," *Bryan-College Station Eagle*, March 21, 1982, p. 11A.
3. *CBS News/The New York Times Poll*, February 2, 1981, p. 4.
4. *CBS News/The New York Times Poll*, April 29, 1981, Part I, p. 3.
5. Hubert H. Humphrey, *The Education of a Public Man: My Life and Politics* (Garden City, N.Y.: Doubleday, 1976), p. 180.
6. "Opinion Roundup," *Public Opinion*, March-May 1979, p. 27.
7. *CBS News/The New York Times Poll*, June 30, 1981, pp. 7–8.
8. Advisory Commission on Intergovernmental Relations, *Changing Public Attitudes on Governments and Taxes* (Washington, D.C.: Advisory Commission on Intergovernmental Relations, 1981), pp. 1–4.
9. See Dom Bonafede, "Carter and the Polls—If You Live by Them, You May Die by Them," *National Journal*, August 19, 1978, pp. 1312–13.
10. Dom Bonafede, "As Pollster to the President, Wirthlin Is Where the Action Is," *National Journal*, December 12, 1981, pp. 2184–88.
11. "Slow Motion," *Wall Street Journal*, March 6, 1981, p. 1.
12. "White House Pen Pal," *Newsweek*, March 22, 1981, p. 31.
13. See, for example, Saul Pett, "Interview Draws Rare Portrait of Carter," *New Orleans Times-Picayune*, October 23, 1977, sec. 1, p. 13; Richard M. Nixon, *RN: The Memoirs of Richard Nixon* (New York: Grosset and Dunlap, 1978), pp. 935, 945; Herbert G. Klein, *Making It Perfectly Clear* (Garden City, N.Y.: Doubleday, 1980), p. 341.
14. Richard M. Nixon, "Address to the Nation on the Situation in Southeast Asia,"

Public Papers of the President of the United States: Richard Nixon, 1970 (Washington, D.C.: U.S. Government Printing Office, 1971), p. 410.

15. Gerald R. Ford, "Imperiled, Not Imperial," *Time*, November 10, 1980, p. 31.

16. Office of the White House Press Secretary, "Remarks of the President at a Meeting with Non-Washington Editors and Broadcasters," September 21, 1979, p. 12.

17. President Carter, quoted in Godfrey Hodgson, *All Things to All Men: The False Promise of the Modern American Presidency* (New York: Simon and Schuster, 1980), p. 25.

18. "The Reagan Presidency—Same Old Expectations," *CBS News/The New York Times Poll*, January 1981, p. 2.

19. Richard E. Neustadt, *Presidential Power: The Politics of Leadership from FDR to Carter* (New York: Wiley, 1980), pp. 210–12.

20. "Carter Interview," *Congressional Quarterly Weekly Report*, November 25, 1978, p. 3354.

21. Gallup Poll, *Attitudes toward the Presidency*, January 1980, p. 21.

22. Jack Dennis, "Dimensions of Public Support for the Presidency" (paper presented at the Annual Meeting of the Midwest Political Science Association, Chicago, April 1975), tables 4, 8; Hazel Erskine, "The Polls: Presidential Power," *Public Opinion Quarterly* 37 (Fall 1973): 492, 495.

23. See George C. Edwards III, *Presidential Influence in Congress* (San Francisco: Freeman, 1980), chap. 4.

24. David O. Sears, "Political Socialization," in Fred I. Greenstein and Nelson Polsby, eds., *Micropolitical Theory*, vol. 2 of *Handbook of Political Science* (Reading, Mass.: Addison-Wesley, 1975), p. 177.

25. See George C. Edwards III, *The Public Presidency* (New York: St. Martin's, 1983), p. 261, n. 13.

26. "Remarks of the President at a Meeting with Non-Washington Editors and Broadcasters," pp. 11–12.

27. *CBS News/The New York Times Poll, Part I*, January 1982, table 34.

28. "Institutions: Confidence Even in Difficult Times," *Public Opinion*, June–July 1981, p. 33.

29. *Gallup Opinion Index*, November 1978, pp. 8–9.

30. "Reagan: A Likeable Guy," *Public Opinion*, December–January 1981, p. 24.

31. Richard A. Brody and Benjamin I. Page, "The Impact of Events on Presidential Popularity: The Johnson and Nixon Administrations," in Aaron Wildavsky, ed., *Perspectives on the Presidency* (Boston: Little, Brown, 1975), pp. 136–48, for example.

32. Jack Valenti, *A Very Human President* (New York: Norton, 1975), p. 151.

33. On this subject see Edwards, *The Public Presidency*, p. 227 and sources cited therein.

34. *Public Opinion*, June–July 1981, p. 36.

35. For a more in-depth analysis of presidential approval, see Edwards, *The Public Presidency*, chap. 6.

36. John E. Mueller, *War, Presidents, and Public Opinion* (New York: Wiley, 1970), pp. 208–13.

37. "Prime Concern," *Newsweek*, December 19, 1977, p. 17.

38. "Carter Fails to Educate Public on Energy Crisis," *New Orleans Times-Picayune*, April 30, 1978, sec. 1, p. 21.

39. Eugene J. Rossi, "Mass and Attentive Opinion on Nuclear Weapons Test and Fallout, 1954–1963," *Public Opinion Quarterly* 29 (Summer 1965), pp. 280–97; Robert S. Erikson, Norman R. Luttbeg, and Kent L. Tedin, *American Public Opinion: Its Origins, Content, and Impact*, 2nd ed. (New York: Wiley, 1980), p. 144; Mueller, *War, Presidents, and Public Opinion*, pp. 69–74.

40. Michael Wheeler, *Lies, Damn Lies, and Statistics: The Manipulation of Public Opinion in America* (New York: Liveright, 1976), pp. 146–47.

41. Carey Rosen, "A Test of Presidential Leadership of Public Opinion: The Split-Ballot Technique," *Polity* 6 (Winter 1973): 282–90.

42. Lee Sigelman, "Gauging the Public Response to Presidential Leadership," *Presidential Studies Quarterly* 10 (Summer 1980): 427–33. See also Pamela Johnston Conover and Lee Sigelman, "Presidential Influence and Public Opinion: The Case of the Iranian Hostage Crisis," *Social Science Quarterly* 63 (June 1982): 249–64.

43. "Most Utah Residents Say 'No' to MX Missile Deployment," *Bryan-College Station Eagle,* September 15, 1981, p. 5A.

44. Lee Sigelman and Carol K. Sigelman, "Presidential Leadership of Public Opinion: From 'Benevolent Leader' to Kiss of Death?" *Experimental Study of Politics* 7, no. 3 (1981): 1–22.

45. Benjamin I. Page and Robert Y. Shapiro, "Presidents as Opinion Leaders: Some New Evidence," *Policy Studies Journal* 12 (June 1984): 649–61.

46. Fred I. Greenstein, "Eisenhower as an Activist President: A Look at New Evidence," *Political Science Quarterly* 94 (Winter 1979–80): 588–90.

47. Israel Shenker, "Obfuscation Foes against Ziegler and an Air Attache," *New York Times,* November 28, 1974, sec. 1, p. 35.

48. These expenditures are primarily federal loans to the public for specified investment and assistance projects, federal guarantees of loans made by private issuers, and lending activities of federally sponsored enterprises, such as the Farm Credit Administration, Federal Home Loan Bank system, Student Marketing Association, and the Federal National Mortgage Association. Although they involve billions of dollars of outlays, these funds are not included in the regular budget.

49. Joseph C. Goulden, *Truth Is the First Casualty* (Chicago: Rand McNally, 1969), p. 160.

50. Mueller, *War, Presidents, and Public Opinion,* pp. 112–13.

51. For a more complete discussion see Edwards, *The Public Presidency,* pp. 60–64.

52. Dick Kirschten, "Reagan and Reality," *National Journal,* October 16, 1982, p. 1765.

53. "Rafshoon and Co.," *Newsweek,* January 29, 1979, p. 22.

54. Sidney Blumenthal, *The Permanent Campaign: Inside the World of Elite Political Operatives* (Boston: Beacon Press, 1980), pp. 50–51; David L. Paletz and Robert M. Entman, *Media—Power—Politics* (New York: Free Press, 1981), p. 74.

55. Lawrence C. Miller and Lee Sigelman, "Is the Audience the Message? A Note on LBJ's Vietnam Statements," *Public Opinion Quarterly* 42 (Spring 1978): 71–80.

56. Michael Baruch Grossman and Martha Joynt Kumar, *Portraying the President: The White House and the News Media* (Baltimore: Johns Hopkins University Press, 1981), p. 29.

57. Ibid., p. 234.

58. Ron Nessen, *It Sure Looks Different from the Inside* (Chicago: Playboy Press, 1978), pp. 88–89.

59. John Ehrlichman, *Witness to Power: The Nixon Years* (New York: Simon and Schuster, 1982), pp. 267.

60. Jody Powell, quoted in Michael Baruch Grossman and Martha Joynt Kumar, "Carter, Reagan, and the Media: Have the Rules Changed or the Poles of the Spectrum of Success?" (paper presented at the Annual Meeting of the American Political Science Association, New York, September 3–6, 1981), pp. 18, 26.

SELECTED READINGS

Brody, Richard A., and Benjamin I. Page. "The Impact of Events on Presidential Popularity: The Johnson and Nixon Administration." In Aaron Wildavsky, ed., *Perspectives on the Presidency.* Boston: Little, Brown, 1975.

Cronin, Thomas E. "The Presidency and Its Paradoxes." In Thomas E. Cronin and Rexford G. Tugwell, eds., *The Presidency Reappraised,* 2nd ed. (New York: Praeger, 1977).

———. "The Presidency Public Relations Script." In Rexford G. Tugwell and Thomas E. Cronin, eds., *The Presidency Reappraised.* New York: Praeger, 1974.

Edwards, George C., III. *The Public Presidency.* New York: St. Martin's, 1983.

Graber, Doris, ed. *The President and the Public.* Philadelphia: Institute for the Study of Human Issues, 1982.

Grossman, Michael Baruch, and Martha Joynt Kumar. *Portraying the Presi-*

dent: The White House and the News Media. Baltimore: Johns Hopkins University Press, 1981.

Gustafson, Merlin. "The President's Mail (Is It Worthwhile to Write to the President?)" *Presidential Studies Quarterly* 8 (Winter 1978): 36–44.

Kernell, Samuel. "Explaining Presidential Popularity." *American Political Science Review* 72 (June 1978): 506–22.

Kinder, Donald R. "Presidents, Prosperity, and Public Opinion," *Public Opinion Quarterly* 45 (Spring 1981): 1–21.

Klein, Herbert G. *Making It Perfectly Clear*. Garden City, N.Y.: Doubleday, 1980.

Lau, Richard, and David O. Sears. "Cognitive Links between Economic Grievances and Political Responses." *Political Behavior* 3, no. 4 (1981): 279–302.

Lee, Jong R. "Rallying around the Flag: Foreign Policy Events and Presidential Popularity." *Presidential Studies Quarterly* 7 (Fall 1977): 252–55.

Miller, Lawrence C., and Lee Sigelman. "Is the Audience the Message? A Note on LBJ's Vietnam Statements." *Public Opinion Quarterly* 42 (Spring 1978): 71–80.

Minow, Newton; John B. Martin; and Lee M. Mitchell. *Presidential Television*. New York: Basic Books, 1973.

Mueller, John E. *War, Presidents, and Public Opinion*. Chaps. 9–10. New York: Wiley, 1970.

Page, Benjamin I., and Robert Y. Shapiro. "Presidents as Opinion Leaders: Some New Evidence." *Policy Studies Journal* 12 (June 1984): 649–61.

Sigelman, Lee. "Gauging the Public Response to Presidential Leadership." *Presidential Studies Quarterly* 10 (Summer 1980): 427–33.

Sigelman, Lee, and Carol K. Sigelman. "Presidential Leadership of Public Opinion: From 'Benevolent Leader' to Kiss of Death?" *Experimental Study of Politics* 7, no. 3 (1981): 1–22.

Sniderman, Paul, and Richard A. Brody, "Coping: The Ethic of Self-Reliance," *American Journal of Political Science* 21 (August 1977): 501–22.

Wayne, Stephen J. "Great Expectations: What People Want from Presidents." In Thomas E. Cronin, ed., *Rethinking the Presidency*. Boston: Little, Brown, 1982.

Wise, David. *The Politics of Lying: Government Deception, Secrecy, and Power*. New York: Vintage, 1973.

5

The President
and the Press

Despite all their efforts to lead public opinion, presidents do not directly reach the American people on a day-to-day basis. It is the press that provides people with most of what they know about the chief executive, his policies, and the consequences of his policies. The media also interpret and analyze presidential activities, even the president's direct appeals to the public.

The press is thus the principal intermediary between the president and the public, and relations with the press are an important aspect of the president's efforts to lead public opinion. If the press portrays the president in a favorable light, he will face fewer obstacles in obtaining public support. If, on the the other hand, the press is hostile toward his administration, the president's talk will be more difficult.

Because of the importance of the press to the president, the White House goes to great lengths to encourage the media to project a positive image of the president and his policies. These efforts include coordinating the news, holding press conferences, and providing a range of services such as formal briefings, interviews, photo opportunities, background sessions, travel accommodations, and daily handouts. On occasion it also resorts to attempts to punish the press for coverage the president perceives as unfair, unfavorable, or both.

In addition to the chief executive's efforts to influence the media, there is another side of this relationship we must examine: the content of the news. Ultimately, it is the written and spoken word that concerns the president. Leaks of confidential information and what is seen in the White House as superficial and biased reporting exacerbate the tensions inherent in presidential-press relations. Presidents commonly view the press as a major obstacle to their obtaining and maintaining public support. Criticism of media coverage as being trivial and distorted and as violating confidences is a standard feature of most administrations. The White House feels that this type of reporting hinders its efforts to develop public appreciation for the president and his policies.

In this chapter we examine the nature and structure of presidential relationships with the press, emphasizing both the context of these relationships and the White House's attempts to obtain favorable coverage. We also discuss issues in presidential-press relations, especially the nature and consequences of media coverage of the presidency.

THE EVOLUTION OF MEDIA COVERAGE

Today we are accustomed to turning to our newspapers or television sets to learn conveniently about what the president has said or done. Things have not always been this way. Before the Civil War, newspapers were generally small, heavily partisan, and limited in circulation. Between 1860 and 1920 a number of changes occurred that permanently altered the relationships between the president and the press.

Several technological innovations, including the electric printing press, the telegraph, the typewriter, the telephone, linotype, and wood-pulp paper, made it both possible and economical to produce mass circulation newspapers carrying recent national news. Aside from the sales efforts of the newspapers themselves, the increasing literacy of the population helped to create a market for these papers.

The increased interest in national affairs as a result of the new importance of the national government also helped newspapers. The government began to regulate the economy with the Interstate Commerce Commission and its antitrust efforts. It expanded its role in world affairs with the Spanish-American War and World War I. Both of these events kindled support for and great interest in the activities of the government in Washington. The increased interest in national affairs was also caused by the renewed prominence of the presidency following an era of congressional ascendancy. Theodore Roosevelt took an activist view of the presidency and exploited the new opportunities to reach the public provided by the mass-circulation press. He used the White House as a "bully pulpit" to dramatize himself and the issues in which he was interested. He sought and gained extensive access to the press in order to forge a more personal relationship with the American people.

Ever since the first Roosevelt occupied the White House, news about the president has played an increasingly prominent role in the printed press, both in absolute terms and relative to coverage of Congress or the national government as a whole. Recent research has found that almost three-fourths of national government news focuses on the president.[1]

Presidents have found that they need the press because it is their primary link to the people. The press, in turn, finds coverage of the president indispensable in satisfying its audience and in reporting on the most significant political events. The advent of radio and television has only heightened these mutual needs.

AN ADVERSARIAL RELATIONSHIP

The history of presidential-press relations has not involved unlimited goodwill. President George Washington complained that the "calumnies" against his administration were "outrages of common decency" motivated by the desire to destroy confidence in the new government.[2] John Adams was so upset at criticism in the press that he supported the Sedition Act and jailed some opposition journalists under its authority.

Thomas Jefferson, certainly one of our greatest defenders of freedom, became so exasperated with the press as president that he argued that "even the least informed of the people have learned that nothing in a newspaper is to be believed." He also felt that "newspapers, for the most part, present only the caricature of disaffected minds. Indeed, the abuses of freedom of the press have been carried to a length never before known or borne by any civilized nation." These observations, it should be noted, come from the man who earlier had written that "were it left to me to decide whether we should have a government without newspapers or newspapers without a government, I should not hesitate to prefer the latter."[3]

Almost two centuries later things have not changed very much. Although all presidents have supported the abstract right of the press to criticize them freely, most have not found this criticism very comfortable while in office. They have viewed some of the press as misrepresenting (perhaps maliciously) their views and actions, failing to perceive the correctness of their policies, and dedicated to impeding their goals.

No matter who is in the White House or who reports on him, presidents and the press tend to be in conflict. Presidents are inherently policy advocates. They will naturally assess the press in terms of its aiding or hindering their goals. The press, on the other hand, has the responsibility for presenting reality. While the press may fail in its efforts, it will assess itself on that criterion. The president wants to control the amount and timing of information about his administration, while the press wants all the information that exists without delay. As long as their goals are different, presidents and the press are likely to be adversaries.

THE WHITE HOUSE PRESS

Who are the reporters that regularly cover the White House? The regulars represent diverse media constituencies. These include daily newspapers like the *Washington Post* and the *New York Times;* weekly newsmagazines like *Time* and *Newsweek;* the wire services like the Associated Press (AP) and United Press International (UPI); newspaper chains like Hearst, Scripps-Howard, Newhouse, and Knight; the television and radio networks; the foreign press; and "opinion" magazines like the *New Republic* and the *National Review.* In addition, photographers, columnists, television commentators, and magazine writers are regularly involved in White House–press interactions. In 1981 about 1,700 persons had White House press credentials. Fortunately, not everyone shows up at once. About 60 reporters and 15 photographers regularly cover the White House, and the total of both increases to more than 100 when an important announcement is expected.

The great majority of daily newspapers in America have no Washington correspondents, much less someone assigned to cover the White House. The same can be said for almost all of the country's individual television and radio stations. These papers and stations rely heavily upon the AP and UPI wire services, each of which covers the White House continously and in detail with three full-time reporters.

WHITE HOUSE PRESS OPERATION

The White House's relations with the media occupy a substantial portion of the time of a large number of aides. About one-third of the high-level White House staff are directly involved in media relations and policy of one type or another and most of the staff are involved at some time in influencing the media's portrayal of the president.

The person in the White House who most often deals directly with the press is the president's press secretary. Probably the central function of press secretaries is to serve as conduits of information from the White House to the press. They must be sure that clear statements of administration policies have been prepared on important policy matters. The press secretaries usually conduct the daily press briefings, giving prepared announcements and answering questions. In forming their answers they often do not have specific orders on what to say or not to say. They must be able to think on their feet to ensure that they accurately reflect the president's views. Sometimes these views may be unclear, however, or the president may not wish to articulate his views. Therefore, press secretaries may seem to be evasive or unimaginative in public settings. They also hold private meetings with individual reporters, where the information provided can be more candid and speculative.

To be effective in the conduit role the press secretary must maintain credibility with reporters. Credibility rests on at least two important pillars: (1) truth and (2) access to and respect of the president and senior White House officials. If a press secretary is viewed as not telling the truth or as not being close to top decision makers (and therefore not well informed), he will not be an effective presidential spokesman, because the press will give little credence to what he says. Credibility problems have arisen for several press secretaries, including Ron Ziegler (Nixon) and Ron Nessen (Ford), as a result of the first and second pillars, respectively.

Press secretaries also serve as conduits from the press to the president. They must sometimes explain the needs of the press to the president. For example, all of Johnson's press secretaries tried to persuade the president to issue advance information on his travel plans to the press. When he refused, they provided it anyway and then had it expunged from the briefing transcript so the president would not see it. Press secretaries also try to inform the White House staff of the press's needs and the rules of the game, and they help reporters gain access to staff members.

Press secretaries are typically not involved in substantive decisions, but they do give the president advice, usually on what information should be released, by whom, in what form, and to what audience. They also advise the president on rehearsals for press conferences and on how to project his image and use it to his political advantage.

Since the time of William Loeb, Theodore Roosevelt's press secretary, the White House has attempted to coordinate executive-branch news. Presidents have assigned aides to clear the appointments of departmental public affairs officials, to keep in touch with the officials to learn what news is forthcoming from the departments, and to meet with them to explain the president's policy views and try to prevent conflicting statements from emanating from the White House and other units of the executive branch. Specialists have had responsibility for coordinating national security news.

Of course, such tactics do not always work. President Ford wanted to announce the success of the *Mayaguez* operation from the White House, but he found to his disappointment that the Pentagon had already done so, making any presidential announcement anticlimactic. At the beginning of his second year in office, President Reagan issued an order that required advance White House approval of television appearances by cabinet members and other top officials, but it soon lapsed.

Coordinating the news from the White House itself has also been a presidential goal. Presidents have sometimes monitored and attempted to limit the press contacts of White House aides, who have annoyed their bosses by using the media for their own purposes. President Reagan, for example, instituted a policy midway through his administration that required his assistant for communications, David Gergen, to approve any interview requested by a member of the media for any White House official. All requests were monitored and entered on a computer so the White House could keep tabs on whom reporters wanted to see. Since even the White House press cannot wander through the East or West wings on their own, the only way to speak to aides without administration approval was to call them at home, a practice discouraged by presidential assistants and generally avoided by the media. Such efforts to limit press access are exceptional, however, and have proved to be largely fruitless.

Recent administrations have also made an effort to coordinate publicity functions within the White House, attempting to present the news in the most favorable light, such as preventing two major stories from breaking on the same day, smothering bad news with more positive news, and timing announcements for maximum effect.

All recent presidents, including Eisenhower, who had a reputation to the contrary, have read several newspapers each day, especially the *New York Times* and the *Washington Post*. Kennedy and Johnson were also very attentive to television news programs. Johnson had a television cabinet with three screens so he could watch all three networks at once. But even this was not enough to satisfy his thirst for news. He also had teletypes that carried the latest reports from the AP and UPI wire services installed in the Oval Office, and he monitored them regularly.

President Nixon rarely watched television news and did not peruse large numbers of newspapers or magazines, but he was extremely interested in press coverage of his administration. He had his staff prepare a daily news summary of newspapers, magazines, television news, and the AP and UPI news wires. Often this summary triggered ideas for the president, who gave orders to aides to follow up on something he read. The news summary also went to White House assistants. Subsequent presidents have continued the news summary, altering it to meet their individual needs, and have circulated it to top officials in their administrations. The Carter White House instituted a separate magazine survey and even a weekly summary of Jewish publications when it became concerned about a possible backlash within the American Jewish community against the administration's Middle East policy.

PRESS CONFERENCES

The best-known direct interaction between the president and the press is the presidential press conference. The frequency of press conferences has varied over time. Franklin Roosevelt held about seven a month; Truman cut this figure in half. Eisenhower further reduced their frequency, holding about two press conferences each month, a rate maintained by Kennedy, Johnson, and Carter, and somewhat bettered by Ford. The deviant case was Richard Nixon, who held only about one press conference every two months. Ronald Reagan has also averaged only about one formal press conference every two months, despite his press secretary's promise at the beginning of his term that the president would hold formal televised press conferences "no less than once a month."[4] Such figures should not be accepted at face value, however. What presidents count as press conferences varies considerably, and the figures for average frequency of press conferences may conceal wide fluctuations in the time between conferences.

Naturally, the more time that has elapsed between press conferences, the more events and governmental actions that will have transpired since the last press conference. The more that has transpired, the more wide-ranging the questions asked of the president are likely to be. And the more wide-ranging the questions, the more superficial the coverage of any one topic is likely to be.

The notice presidents provide of their upcoming press conferences is no more uniform than their frequency of holding them. The short notice for many press conferences has advantages for presidents. If press conferences are not publicly scheduled until shortly before they take place, it is easier for presidents to cancel them if they find it convenient. In addition, short notice gives reporters less time to prepare probing questions. Moreover, many specialty reporters who cover all of Washington, who can ask detailed questions, and who can be less concerned with remaining on good terms with the president will miss impromptu press conferences.

Another factor that has perhaps reduced the utility of the press conferences for eliciting useful information about government has been their increasing size. Modern presidents have generally employed a large room (such as the State Department auditorium or the East Room in the White House) for press conferences, usually relying upon public address systems. The increased number of reporters covering press conferences and the setting in which they take place has inevitably made them more formal. More reporters mean more persons with different concerns and thus less likelihood of follow-up questions to cover a subject in depth. Spontaneity in questions and answers has largely been lost.

Presidents have taken other steps that have contributed to the formalization of press conferences. Beginning with Truman, they have undergone formal briefings and "dry runs" in preparation for questions that might be asked. Presidents have asked their aides and the departments and agencies to submit to them possible questions and suggested answers, and sometimes they call for further information. In 1982 President Reagan began holding full-scale mock news conferences. Guessing at questions is not too difficult. There are obvious areas of concern, and questions raised at White House and departmental briefings and other meetings with reporters provide useful cues. The president also can anticipate the interests of individual reporters, and he has discretion over whom to recognize. In Reagan's news conferences, reporters were assigned seats, and the president, using a seating chart, called them by name. In one case Reagan called a reporter only to discover that he was not even attending the conference. The reporter, watching the news conference in his living room at home, asked a question anyway but only his family heard it. The next day the newspapers had a field day reporting the incident.

The change in the nature of the presidential press conferences from semiprivate to public events has diminished their utility in transmitting information from the president to the press. Since every word they say is transmitted verbatim to millions of people, presidents cannot speak as candidly as, say, Franklin D. Roosevelt could. Nor can they speculate freely about their potential actions or evaluations of persons, events, or circumstances. Instead, they must choose their words carefully, and their responses to questions are often not terribly enlightening.

Presidents like Truman have frequently begun their press conferences with carefully prepared opening statements. Examples include President Kennedy's 1962 blast at the steel companies for raising their prices (eventually leading to the increases being rescinded) and President Carter's five-minute monologue on his administration's accomplishments in a televised press conference during the 1980 presidential election. Lyndon Johnson was especially likely to deliver an opening statement. These statements have given presidents an opportunity to reach the public on their own terms. Opening statements have also further reduced the opportunities for questions while at the same time focusing questions on issues of the president's choosing (contained in the statement).

Because the president is in control of his press conference, he can avoid the harder questions. Sometimes presidents state that they will not entertain questions on certain topics. They may also evade questions with clever rhetoric or simply answer with a "no comment." Or they can use a question as a vehicle to say something they planned ahead of time. If necessary they can reverse the attack and focus on the questioner, or conversely, they can call on a friendly reporter for a "soft" question. Eisenhower used a skilled evasiveness and impenetrable syntax to avoid direct answers to embarrassing or politically sensitive questions, something not unusual among presidents.

Presidents and their staffs have sometimes found it convenient to plant questions with the press. In other words, they end up asking themselves questions. This practice started at least as early as Franklin Roosevelt, and Eisenhower and Johnson often made use of it.

Many of the questions asked the president involve trivial topics. One reason for this is deference to the president. Reporters meet the president in his territory, not theirs, and dutifully rise when he enters the room. An adversarial relationship may exist outside the press conference, but it is rarely reflected during the sessions themselves. The author of a study of press conferences between 1961 and 1975 found only two occasions in fifteen years when the number of hostile questions asked by reporters at any press conference exceeded three.[5]

The artificial nature of press conferences, especially on television, may lead to distortions. On the one hand, a truly spontaneous answer to a question may be candid, but it also may be foolish or expose the president's ignorance of an area. Generalizations based on such a reply may be inaccurate because the president may actually be well informed but require more than a few seconds to think about a complex problem. On the other hand, some presidents may be glib, charming, and attractive, and therefore perform well in a spontaneous press conference but really not be very competent. The advent of television has further increased the potential for distortion, since a president's physical attractiveness, delivery, and flair for the dramatic may leave more of an impression on the public's mind than the substance of his answers.

In sum, presidential press conferences are often not very informative. In the more formal and less spontaneous press conferences that characterize the more recent era, the president has a substantial opportunity to control the image he projects. He often begins with a prepared announcement, his answers to most questions are equally prepared, and he has leeway on when he will hold the conference and whom he will call upon. While the press conference does provide the president an opportunity to focus national attention upon himself, stimulate public opinion, and criticize or support various political actors, and while the preconference briefing may serve as a useful device for informing the president across a broad spectrum of issues, we cannot depend upon it for revealing the real president, and the nature of television may distort more than it reveals.

SERVICES FOR THE PRESS

In order to get their messages across to the American people and to influence the tone and content of the press's presentation of those messages, presidents have provided services for the press. One of the most important is the backgrounder. The president's comments to reporters may be "on the record" (remarks may be attributed to the speaker); "on background" (a specific source cannot be identified but the source's position and status can—such as a "White House source"); "deep background" (no attribution); or "off the record" (the information reporters receive may not be used in a story). For purposes of convenience we shall term all sessions between White House officials (including the president) and the press that are not "on the record" as "backgrounders." All recent presidents, especially Johnson and Ford, have engaged in background discussion with reporters, although President Nixon's involvement was rare. Some presidents, especially Eisenhower and Nixon, have relied heavily upon their principal foreign policy advisers to brief reporters on foreign affairs.

The most common type of presidential discussion with reporters on a background basis is a briefing. In these sessions the president typically explains a policy's development and what it is expected to accomplish. Interestingly, the president does not appear to stress the substance of policy. He seldom makes "hard" news statements in background briefings, because this would irritate absent members of the press. The reporters watch the president perform, and since the president controls the conditions of these briefings, the chances of making a favorable impression are good.

Reporters tend to view middle-level aides as the best information sources. They have in-depth knowledge about the substance of programs, and they are generally free from the constraints of high visibility, so they are in a good position to provide useful backgrounders. Backgrounders are particularly important for these officials because presidents are generally intolerant of staff members who seek publicity for themselves, and most interviews with White House staff are on this basis. Sometimes aides say more than their superiors would like in order to prod the president in a particular policy direction.

Backgrounders have a number of advantages for the White House. Avoiding direct quotation allows officials to speak on sensitive foreign policy and domestic policy matters candidly and in depth, something domestic politics and international diplomacy would not tolerate if speakers were held directly accountable for their words. The White House hopes such discussions will help it communicate its point of view more clearly and serve to educate journalists, perhaps preparing them for future policies, and make them more sympathetic to the president's position in their reporting. An impressive performance in a background session can show the White House to be competent and perhaps elicit the benefit of the doubt in future stories. Moreover, background sessions can be used to scotch rumors and limit undesirable speculation about presidential plans and internal White House affairs.

On the other hand, backgrounders may be aimed at the public (in the form of trial balloons that the White House can disclaim if they meet with disapproval) or at policymakers in Washington. They may also be directed at other countries. To discourage the Soviet Union's support of India in its war with Pakistan, Henry Kissinger told reporters in a backgrounder that the Soviet policy might lead to the cancellation of

President Nixon's trip to Moscow. Since the statement was not officially attributed to Kissinger, it constituted less of a public threat to the Soviet Union, while at the same time it communicated the president's message.[6]

Reporters have generally been happy to go along with protecting the identities of "spokesmen" and "sources" (although an experienced observer can identify most of them), because the system provides them more information than they would have without it. This increase of information available to reporters adds to the information available to the public, and it probably helps advance journalistic careers as well.

Backgrounders, of course, have also provided the White House opportunities to disseminate misleading or self-serving propaganda anonymously. Sometimes such propaganda concerns intramural warfare, an especially common theme in the Ford administration but also appearing in the Nixon and other administrations.

In addition to the more informal sessions, briefings are held each weekday for the White House press (they were held twice daily until the Nixon administration). In the daily briefings reporters are provided with information about appointments and resignations; decisions of the president to sign or not to sign routine bills and explanations for his actions; and the president's schedule (whom he will see that day, what meetings he has, what his future travel plans are, and when the press can see him). More significantly from the standpoint of the press, the briefing provides presidential reactions to events, the White House "line" on issues and whether it has changed, and a reading of the president's moods and ideas. This information is obtained through prepared statements or answers to reporters' queries. Responses to the latter are often prepared ahead of time by the White House staff. The daily briefings, of course, also provide the press with an opportunity to have the president's views placed on the public record, which eases the burdens of reporting.

Usually the president's press secretary or his deputy presides over these briefings, although sometimes the president participates. White House staff members and executive-branch officials with substantial expertise in specific policy areas such as the budget or foreign affairs sometimes brief the press and answer questions at the daily briefing or at special briefings, especially when the White House is launching a major publicity campaign.

Interviews with the president and top White House staff members are a valuable commodity to the press, and sometimes the White House uses them for its purposes. During the 1980 primaries, Jimmy Carter was angered by the *Boston Globe's* pro-Kennedy slant. Thus, his staff arranged an exclusive presidential interview with the *Globe's* rival, the *Boston Herald American.*[7]

In a less subtle move, President Nixon traded an exclusive interview to Hugh Sidney of *Time* for a cover story on him. In order to obtain an interview with President Ford, even the venerable Walter Cronkite agreed to use only questions the president could handle easily. At other times the White House may give exclusives to a paper like the *New York Times* in return for getting a story in which it is interested a prominent place in the paper.[8]

Providing the press exclusive information may be as ingratiating as an exclusive interview and may be used to distract reporters from more embarrassing stories. At other times the White House may trade advance notice of a story for information reporters possess about developments elsewhere in the government that are not clear to the president and his staff.

Recent presidents, with the exception of Richard Nixon, have regularly cultivated elite reporters and columnists, the editors and publishers of leading newspapers, and network news producers and executives with small favors, social flattery, and small background dinners at the White House. (Nixon turned these chores over to top aides). Indeed, since the 1960s the White House has had first a special person and then an office for media liaison to deal directly with the representatives of news organizations, such as editors, publishers, and producers, in addition to the press office that deals with reporters' routine needs.

There are many additional services that the White House provides for the press. It gives reporters transcripts of briefings and presidential speeches and daily handouts announcing a myriad of information about the president and his policies, including advance notice of travel plans and upcoming stories. Major announcements are timed to accommodate the deadlines of newspapers, magazines, and television networks.

Photographers covering the president are highly dependent on the White House press office, which provides facilities for photographers on presidential trips and arranges photo opportunities, making sure they will produce the most flattering shots of the president (such as Johnson's left profile). President Reagan even prohibited impromptu questions from reporters at photographing sessions. Moreover, the official White House photographers provide many of the photographs of the president that the media use. Naturally, these are screened so that the president is presented favorably.

When the president goes on trips, at home or abroad, extensive preparations are made for the press. These preparations include arranging transportation and lodging for the press, installing equipment for radio and television broadcasting, obtaining telephones for reporters, erecting platforms for photographers, preparing a detailed account of where and with whom the president will be at particular times, providing elaborate information about the countries the president is visiting, forming pools of press members to cover the president closely (as in a motorcade), and scheduling the press plane to arrive before the president's so the press can cover his arrival.

As many of these services suggest, the press is especially dependent upon the White House staff in covering presidential trips, particularly foreign trips. The number of sources of information is generally reduced, as is the access of the press to the principal figures they wish to cover. Thus the president's aides are in a good position to manipulate press coverage to their advantage. Coverage of foreign trips is generally favorable, although perhaps less so than in the past now that reporters with expertise in foreign affairs accompany the president, and the press points out the relationship of the trip and its goals and accomplishments to the president's domestic political problems.

Even in Washington, however, reporters are very much in a controlled environment. They may not freely roam the halls of the White House, interviewing whomever they please. They are highly dependent upon the press officer for access to officials, and about half their interviews are with the press secretary and his staff. Much of their time is spent waiting for something to happen or watching the president at formal or ceremonial events. Since most news stories about such occurrences show the president in a favorable light, the press office does everything possible to help reporters record these activities. Similarly, the White House is happy to provide photographs featuring the president's "warm," "human," or "family" side. These please editors and the public alike.

Briefings, press releases, and the like can be used to divert the media's attention from embarrassing matters. The Reagan White House adopted a strategy of blitzing the media with information to divert its attention after the press raised questions about the president's sleeping through Libyan attacks on U.S. forces off the coast of Africa.[9] More frequently, the White House, by adopting an active approach to the press, gains an opportunity to shape the media's agenda for the day. Through announcements and press releases it attempts to focus attention on what will reflect positively on the president. Such information frequently generates questions from reporters and subsequent news stories. Representatives of the smaller papers, who have few resources, are more heavily dependent upon White House–provided news than are the larger news bureaus, including the major networks. They are the most likely to follow the White House's agenda. Moreover, since White House reporters, especially the wire services, are under pressure to file daily "hard news" reports, the White House is in a strong position to help by providing information, much of it trivial and all of it designed to reflect positively on the president. As a Ford official put it: "You can predict what the press is going to do with a story. It is almost by formula. Because of this they are usable."[10]

Many observers, including journalists, feel that the press tends to parrot the White House line, so conveniently provided at a briefing or in a press release, especially early in a president's term. The pressure among journalists to be first with a story increases the potential for White House manipulation inherent in this deferential approach, as concerns for accuracy give way to career interests.

Presidents have undoubtedly hoped that the handouts, briefings, and other services they and their staffs provide for reporters will gain them some goodwill. They may also hope that these services will keep the White House press from digging too deeply into presidential affairs. In addition, they want to keep reporters interested in the president's agenda, because bored journalists are more negative in their reporting and may base their stories on trivial incidents like the president's stumbling on a plane.

In addition, the White House controls a commodity of considerable value to the press: information on the president's personal life. Most reporters are under pressure to provide stories on the minutiae of the president's life, no matter what he does. Some White House aides have found that the provision of such information can co-opt journalists or sidetrack them from producing critical stories. Some reporters will exploit the opportunity to please their editors instead of digging into more significant subjects; others reciprocate their favorable treatment by the White House with positive stories about the president.

Seeing yet another opportunity to influence the press, the White House has provided services for the local as well as the national and Washington-based media. Relations with the local media took a significant step forward in the Nixon administration. In an effort to bypass the more liberal national press and to develop goodwill, President Nixon held briefings for local news executives given by himself or senior administration officials. He also sent administration briefing teams around the country to discuss his legislative proposals with local media representatives. The local press, they found, was very responsive to this attention, often giving the president substantial publicity and using the White House story ideas and sometimes even the background materials it provided. Special mailings of news releases and documents to newspapers, television and radio stations, journal writers, citizens groups, and private individuals were also made.

Subsequent presidents learned that dealing directly with the nonnational press was very useful in obtaining coverage of the president's message in the local and specialty media. Once the Washington press reports an issue, it tends to drop it and move on to the next one, yet repetition is necessary to convey the president's views to the generally inattentive public. Moreover, the Washington press tends to place more emphasis on the support of or opposition to a program than on its substance, although the White House wants to communicate the latter.

The Nixon administration's efforts at dealing with the local press were continued and expanded. Gerald Ford invited local news announcers to the White House for taped personal interviews to be used exclusively in their home stations. He also held press conferences for reporters from the local press. Every other week President Carter had local newspapers and broadcast journalists come to Washington to meet him and be briefed by administration officials. The information provided in these meetings was not released to the general press for twenty four hours so that the out-of-town journalists could file their exclusive stories. At the end of 1978 the White House began to provide 30- and 40-second taped radio spots free of charge to radio stations that called a toll-free White House number.

Presidents who engage in servicing (and lobbying) the local media undoubtedly hope that they will receive a sympathetic hearing from journalists grateful to be invited to the White House and perhaps susceptible to presidential charm. They also hope that by providing information directly to the local media they can evade the closer scrutiny of the Washington- and New York–based national media, with its greater resources to challenge White House versions of events and policies and to investigate areas of government not covered by briefings or press releases. Naturally, they hope they can also create some goodwill that will be reflected in news stories on the local level.

HARASSMENT OF THE PRESS

The White House can wield the stick as well as offer the carrot. While the Nixon administration did not ignore the latter, it emphasized the former—with a vengeance. The president and his aides were obsessed with the press and spent a disproportionate amount of time dealing with it, and they allowed the personalities and views of reporters to affect their working relationship with the press as a whole. The president regularly spoke of the press (to his staff) as the "enemy," as something to be hated and beaten.[11] At the end of direct American involvement in the Vietnam War he told reporters: "We finally have achieved a peace with honor. I know it gags some of you to write that phrase, but that is true."

Open hostility, however, was not the full story of the Nixon White House's relations with the press. This attitude led to harassment of the press and attempts to pressure it into quiescence. These attempts took many forms. One was a steady stream of criticism of the printed and electronic press by administration officials and by the president himself. They criticized the reporters for being prejudiced against the president and unrepresentative of the American people and for distorting the news and emphasizing negative instead of positive events. Complaints were made directly to the news organizations and reporters as well as to the public.

It is significant that the Nixon White House was not at all bothered by press treatment that was favorable to it. When it attacked the networks, it focused more on CBS and NBC than ABC, whose coverage was more favorable. When the Nixon White House criticized newspapers, it concentrated its wrath on the "Eastern" press, especially the *Washington Post* and *New York Times*, the two most prominent newspapers in the country. The editorial pages of both these papers are oriented toward a more liberal viewpoint. Most other papers, however, are not. Nixon was quite content to receive their support and was not concerned that the liberal point of view was not better represented in their coverage of the news.

The Nixon administration did not limit its efforts at harassing the press to mere criticism. Some reporters had their phones tapped or their taxes audited. One even was the focus of a full FBI field investigation aimed at discovering something negative in his past to discredit him. Others were excluded from White House press pools, briefings, and presidential and vice presidential trips or had their access to administration officials restricted. The White House also instituted antitrust suits against the networks and threatened them with the loss of the five highly profitable local television stations they each owned, and it inspired challenges to the license renewals of television stations owned by the *Washington Post*. Efforts were also made to have affiliates pressure their networks to provide more positive coverage of the administration and to force the Public Broadcasting Service to devote fewer resources to coverage and analysis of national news.

Despite the substantial time and energy the Nixon administration devoted to intimidating the press, the results were meager. Moreover, attempts to punish reporters and their organizations by cutting off their access to administration sources, for example, were undermined by White House aides who ignored orders to do so.

Other presidents have been angered by press coverage and have occasionally criticized and harassed reporters, of course. Nevertheless, such episodes have not been characteristic of past administrations. Nixon added an extra dimension to the adversarial relations between the president and the press. He preferred to bludgeon the press into submission. Failing that, he tried to discredit the press by creating doubt in the public's mind that the press was treating his administration fairly. He hoped that the public would pay less attention to the press criticism of him and his policies and also that he would have an acceptable excuse to avoid meeting the press directly.

INFORMATION LEAKS

In early 1982 President Reagan read the riot act to his cabinet, denouncing the release of confidential information to the press by anonymous sources as one of the major problems facing his administration. He was particularly concerned about leaks regarding his upcoming budget proposals for defense spending, a number of foreign policy matters, and the urban enterprise zones proposal that he wanted to save for his State of the Union message.[12] The president's frustration is evident in the quip with which he opened a press conference held at about the same time: "I was going to have an opening statement, but I decided that what I was going to say I wanted to get a lot of attention so I'm going to wait and leak it."

President Reagan was hardly the first president to be upset by leaks. Sometimes they can be potentially quite serious, as when the U.S. negotiating strategy in the first SALT talks was disclosed during the Nixon administration. When the *Pentagon Papers* were leaked to the public, President Nixon felt that there was a danger that other countries would lose confidence in our ability to keep secrets and that information on the delicate negotiations then in progress with China might also be leaked, endangering the possibility of rapprochement.[13] At other times they are just embarrassing, as when internal dissent in the administration is revealed to the public. President Johnson feared leaks would signal what he was thinking, and he would lose his freedom of action as a result.

Who leaks information? The best answer is "everybody." Presidents themselves do so, sometimes inadvertently. As Lyndon Johnson once put it: "I have enough trouble with myself. I ought not to have to put up with everybody else too."[14] Top presidential aides may also reveal more than they intend. When a leak regarding President Reagan's willingness to compromise on his 1981 tax bill appeared in the *New York Times*, White House aides traced down the source of the story and found it was budget director David Stockman.[15] A year earlier a leak revealing secret CIA arms shipments to Afghan rebels was attributed to the office of the president's chief national security adviser.[16]

Most leaks, however, are deliberately planted. As one close presidential aide put it, "99 percent of all significant secrets are spilled by the principals or at their direction."[17] Presidents are included in those who purposefully leak. *Newsweek* used to hold space open for the items John Kennedy would phone in to his friend Benjamin Bradlee right before the magazine's deadline.[18] There are many reasons for leaks. They may be used as trial balloons to test public or congressional reaction to ideas and proposals or to stimulate public concern about an issue. Both the Ford

and Carter White House used this technique to test reaction to a tax sur-
charge on gasoline. When the reaction turned out to be negative, they denied ever contemplating such a policy. At other times information is
leaked to reporters who will use it to write favorable articles on a policy.

Diplomacy is an area in which delicate communications play an important role. Leaks are often used to send signals to other nations of our
friendship, anger, or willingness to compromise. At the same time they
provide the president with the opportunity to disavow publicly or to
reinterpret what some might view as, for example, an overly "tough"
stance or an unexpected change in policy.

Leaks may also be used to influence personnel matters. The release
of information letting a reluctant official know his superiors wish him to
leave can force him to resign and thus save the problem of firing him. The
release of information on an appointment before it is made places the
president in an awkward position and can help ensure that he follows
through on it or prematurely denies he has such plans.

Some leaks are designed to force the president's hand on policy decisions. During the Indian-Pakistani War, President Nixon maintained a
publicly neutral stance but was really favoring Pakistan. When this was
leaked there was inevitably pressure to be neutral in action as well as in

" I HAD TO SWITCH YOUR LIE DETECTOR TEST THIS AFTERNOON FROM 3 TO 1
BECAUSE YOU'RE SCHEDULED TO LEAK SOME INFORATION AT 2 ! "

Source: Reprinted by permission: Tribune Company Syndicate, Inc.

rhetoric. Conversely, in the case of Lyndon Johnson, a leak that he was thinking about a decision could ensure that he would take no such action.

Leaks may serve a number of other functions for individuals. They may make one feel important or help one gain favor with reporters. Leaks may also be used to criticize and intimidate personal or political adversaries in the White House itself or protect and enhance reputations. In the Ford administration, White House counsel Robert Hartmann and the chief of staff Richard Cheney often attacked each other anonymously in the press. Several members of the White House staff attacked Press Secretary Ron Nessen in an effort to persuade the president to replace him. When negotiations with North Vietnam broke down in late 1972, White House aides employed leaks to dissociate the president from his national security adviser.

Presidents sometimes leak information for their own political purposes. Lyndon Johnson leaked information on nuclear weapons to answer Barry Goldwater in the 1964 presidential election. A Nixon aide leaked a false story to the *Wall Street Journal* that the president was considering seeking legislation to reduce the independence of the Federal Reserve Board and that the board's chairman, Arthur Burns, was a hypocrite because he sought a personal salary increase while he was asking the rest of the country to dampen its demands. The UPI received a somewhat similar story. These leaks were attempts to make Burns more responsive to White House demands. The Nixon White House often employed leaks as a political tactic.

In all of these cases government officials were using the press for their purposes and not vice versa. Although reporters may well be aware of being used, the competitive pressure of the news business makes it difficult for them to pass up an exclusive story. Nevertheless, most good reporting, even investigative reporting, does not rely heavily upon leaks. Instead, reporters put together stories by bits and pieces.

It is generally fruitless to try to discover the source of a leak. Nevertheless, some presidents have tried. The Reagan administration has added new sophistication to the effort to trace leakers. Reporters are required to make appointments when they visit top officials. These are logged into a computer. When the president's aides find an offending story based on an unidentified source, they can check the computer to learn which officials have been talking to the reporter. Such measures, of course, cannot stop an official who desires to leak information from doing so and hiding his identity from the White House.

SUPERFICIALITY OF PRESS COVERAGE

Early in this century Woodrow Wilson complained that most reporters were "interested in the personal and trivial rather than in principles of policies."[19] Things have not changed much in the ensuing generations. In a background briefing in 1979 President Carter complained to reporters: "I would really like for you all as people who relay Washington events to the world to take a look at the substantive questions I have to face as a president and quit dealing almost exclusively with personalities."[20] In this section we examine the questions of the superficiality of the coverage of the presidency and the reasons for it.

Today media coverage of national news is characterized by brevity and simplicity. Editors do not want to bore or confuse their viewers, listeners, or readers. They often resort to the use of themes ("another example of rivalries within the White House"), symbols (a supermarket checkout line may represent inflation), and personification (an unemployed mother of five) to simplify issues. Moreover, most reporting is about events, actions taken or words spoken by public figures, especially if the events are dramatic and colorful, such as ceremonies and parades. Conflict between clearly identifiable antagonists (the president versus the Speaker of the House) is highly prized, particularly if there is something tangible at stake, such as the passage of a bill.

The amount of information transmitted under such conditions is very limited. This type of news coverage is ill-equipped to deal with the ambiguities and uncertainties of most complex events and issues. Moreover, it provides little in the way of the background and contextual information that is essential for understanding political events. Although the electronic media, especially television, are the most typical source of news for Americans, they do the poorest job of providing information to the public. According to CBS anchorman Dan Rather, "you simply cannot be a well-informed citizen by just watching the news on television."[21]

Human interest stories, especially those about the president and his family, are novel and easier for the public to relate to than are complex matters of public policy. They are always in high demand. Nancy Reagan's new White House china received more attention in the press than most issues. Scandals involving public persons of all kinds receive high priority coverage. Disasters and incidents of violence make for excellent film presentations, are novel, contain ample action, and are portrayed in easily understood terms. The intricacies of a presidential tax proposal are not so fortunate.

Focusing more specifically on media coverage of the presidency, studies show that coverage of presidential election campaigns is basically trivial, especially on television. Issue coverage is spotty. The issue stands of candidates are usually old news to reporters who must suffer through hearing the same speech, with slight variations added for local audience appeal, again and again. The issue stands are not viewed as news. In general, substantive issues are reported in terms of their impact on the election rather than in terms of their merits.[22]

Clear-cut issue differences between candidates have the potential for confrontation, even if the drama results from skillful tape editing, and these differences are emphasized within the space allotted to issue coverage. Such issues are not typical, however. Media coverage does not reflect the blend of issues advocated by the candidates. Moreover, the press generally ignores issues that the candidates neglect, even though they may be significant to the typical citizen. What does receive extensive coverage, as we saw in Chapter 3, is the "horse race," the campaign as opposed to what the campaign is ostensibly about. Stories feature conflict, make brief points, are easily understood (often in either/or terms), and, especially on television, have film value.

In the second debate between Gerald Ford and Jimmy Carter during the 1976 presidential campaign, Ford made a slip of the tongue and said that Eastern Europe was "free from Soviet domination." Everyone, including the president, knew that he had misspoken. Unfortunately for Ford, he refused to admit his error for several days while the press had a field day speculating about his basic understanding of world politics.

Superficial news coverage is not limited to elections. Most of the White House press's activity comes under the heading of the "body watch." In other words, reporters focus on the most visible layer of the president's personal and official activities and provide the public with a step-by-step account. They are interested in what the president is going to do, how his actions will affect others, how he views policies and individuals, how he presents himself, and whose stars are rising and falling, rather than in the substance of policies or the fundamental processes operating in the executive branch.

Editors expect this type of coverage and reporters do not want to risk missing a story. As the Washington bureau chief of *Newsweek* said: "The worst thing in the world that could happen to you is for the President of the United States to choke on a piece of meat, and for you not to be there."[23] The emphasis of news coverage is on short-run, "instant history." Perspective on the events of the day is secondary. Thus, embarrassing items such as blunders and contradictions made by the president and his staff are widely reported, especially if the president is low in the polls (providing a consistent theme). Similarly, major presidential addresses are often reported in terms of how the president looked, how he spoke, and the number of times he received applause as much as in terms of what he had to say.

Presidential slips of the tongue or behavior are often blown out of all proportion. President Nixon once termed mass murderer Charles Manson as guilty before his trial had ended. Since almost everyone else in the country probably also felt Manson was guilty, the president's slip was not really extraordinary. Nevertheless, it was treated as such by the press. When he gave his press secretary, Ron Ziegler, a shove in New Orleans, speculation immediately began about the president's mental state.

At other times words are lifted out of context. When Richard Nixon described the persons "blowing up the campuses" as "bums," the press extended the adjective to all students, something the president had not meant. The uproar following this "news" can well be imagined.

In its constant search for "news," the press, especially the electronic media, is reluctant to devote repeated attention to an issue, although this might be necessary to explain it adequately to the public. As a deputy press secretary in the Carter administration said: "We have to keep sending out our message if we expect people to understand. The Washington Press corps will explain a policy once and then it will feature the politics of the issue."[24] This is one incentive for the president to meet with the non-Washington press.

One of the causes of superficial press coverage of the presidency is the demands of news organizations for information that is new and different, personal and intimate, revealing and unexpected. According to the White House correspondent for a major newspaper chain: "It's a lot easier for me to get [my stories] into several newspapers in the chain with a story about Amy [President Carter's daughter] than with a story about an important policy decision. If they use both, the Amy story is likely to get on page one, while the policy story will be buried on page 29."[25] Similarly, as ABC White House correspondent Sam Donaldson commented, "A clip of a convalescent Reagan waving from his window at some circus elephants is going to push an analytical piece about tax cuts off the air every time."[26]

Given the emphasis on the short-run and the demand for details of the president's activities, reporters typically cover several stories each day and face continual deadlines. There is little time for reflection, analysis, or comprehensive coverage.

A related factor contributing to the trivialization of the news is the great deal of money and manpower spent on covering the president, including following him around the globe and on vacations. Because of this investment and because of the public's interest in the president, reporters must come up with something every day. Newsworthy happenings do not necessarily occur every day, however, so reporters either emphasize the trivial or blow events out of proportion. Similarly, the White House press often focuses on the exact wording of an announcement in an effort to detect a change in policy. Frequently they find significance where none really exists.

There are more than organizational imperatives at work in influencing coverage of the president, however. Reporters' backgrounds and personal interests also underlie the trivialization of the news. They are often ill at ease with abstractions, and when they talk to each other about politics, they emphasize the superficial aspects—who will be elected, what bills will pass, personalities, who has power.

The typical White House reporter lacks special background on the presidency and sees no need to have such background. Moreover, the White House press frequently lacks policy expertise relevant to understanding the issues with which the president deals. Thus, its focus on politics and personalities rather than on issues is not surprising.

To delve more deeply into the presidency and policy requires not only substantial expertise but also certain technical skills. Washington reporters in general and White House reporters in particular do little documentary research. They are trained to do interviews and transmit handouts from press secretaries and public information officials rather than to conduct research. Moreover, in-depth research requires a slower pace and advance planning, and journalists tend to be comfortable with neither.

Sometimes several factors influence coverage of the presidency at the same time. Despite the glamour attached to investigate reporting following the Watergate scandal, not much of it takes place. Most reporters are unwilling or unable to take the time necessary for investigative work and the coordination required with other reporters and news bureau staff to cover all leads successfully. The ethic of journalism is to go it alone, and the incentives are generally to get news out fast. Similarly, the slowness of the process of using the Freedom of Information Act to force the release of documents inhibits its use. A final hindrance to investigative reporting is the reluctance of many editors to publish analyses sharply divergent from the president's position without some confirmation from what they consider to be an authoritative source who would be willing to go on the record in opposition to the president.

Not only does the press provide superficial coverage of the stories it reports, but many important stories about the presidency are missed altogether because of the emphasis of the media. Implementation of policy, the predominant activity of the executive branch, is very poorly covered because it is not fast-breaking news, it takes place mostly in the field, away from the reporters' natural territory, and it requires documentary analysis and interaction with civil servants who are neither famous nor experts at public relations. Similarly, the White House press misses most of the flow of information and options to the president from the rest of the executive branch.

BIAS IN PRESS COVERAGE

Bias is the most politically charged issue in presidential-press relations. Bias is also an elusive concept with many dimensions. Although we typically envision bias as news coverage favoring identifiable persons, parties, or points of view, there are more subtle and more pervasive forms of bias that are not motivated by the goal of furthering careers or policies.

A large number of studies covering topics such as presidential election campaigns, the war in Vietnam, and local news conclude that the news media are not biased *systematically* toward a particular person, party, or ideology, as measured in the amount or favorability of coverage. The bias found in such studies is inconsistent; the news is typically characterized by neutrality.[27]

Some people may equate objectivity with passivity and feel that the press should do no more than report what others present to it. This simple passing on of news is what occurs much of the time, and it is a fundamental reason for the superficiality of news coverage. Sometimes, however, reporters may feel the necessity of setting the story in a meaningful context. The construction of such a context may entail reporting what was *not* said as well as what was said, what had occurred before, and what political implications may be involved in a statement, policy, or event. If the press is passive, it can be more easily manipulated, even representing fiction as fact.

This discussion of the general neutrality of news coverage in the mass media pertains most directly to television, newspaper, and radio reporting. Columnists, commentators, and editorial writers usually cannot even pretend to be neutral. Newspaper endorsements for presidential candidates overwhelmingly favor Republicans. In 1972, 93 percent of the newspapers making endorsements supported Richard Nixon over George McGovern.[28] Newsmagazines are sometimes less neutral than newspapers or television. In the 1940s, 1950s, and 1960s Henry Luce used *Time* to criticize Harry Truman, to campaign for his view of a China policy, to help elect Dwight Eisenhower as president, and to support the war in Vietnam, and the magazine has continued to favor Republican presidents. Unfair but picturesque adjectives are often used in newsmagazines to liven up stories. So are cartoons and drawings, which are generally unflattering to the president.

A number of factors help to explain why most mass media news coverage is not biased systematically toward a particular person, party, or ideology. Reporters generally are not personally partisan or ideological; nor are they politically aligned or holders of strong political beliefs. Journalists are typically not intellectuals or deeply concerned with public policy. Moreover, they share journalism's professional norm of objectivity.

The organizational processes of story selection and editing provide opportunities for softening judgments of reporters. The rotation of assignments and rewards for objective newsgathering are further protections against bias. Local television station owners and newspaper publishers are in a position to apply pressure regarding the presentation of the news, and, although they rarely do so, their potential to act may restrain reporters.

Self-interest also plays a role in constraining bias. Individual reporters may earn a poor reputation if others view them as biased. The television networks, newspapers, newsmagazines, and the wire services, which provide most of the Washington news for newspapers, have a direct financial stake in attracting viewers and subscribers and do not want to lose their audience by appearing biased, especially when there are multiple versions of the same story available to major news outlets. Slander and libel laws; the Federal Communications Commission's "fairness doctrine," requiring electronic media news coverage of diverse points of view; and the "political attack" rule, providing those personally criticized on the electronic media with an opportunity to respond, are all formal limitations on bias.

To conclude that the news contains little explicit partisan or ideological bias is not to argue that the news does not distort reality in its coverage. It does. Even under the best of conditions, some distortion is inevitable due to simple error or such factors as lack of careful checking of facts, the efforts of the news source to deceive, and short deadlines.

In a very important sense, values are pervasive in the news, and it is difficult to imagine how it could be otherwise. As members of our society, journalists are imbued with such values as democracy, capitalism, and individualism, and these unconsciously receive positive treatment in the media. Similarly, journalists have concepts of what is "new," "abnormal," and "wrong" and notions of how the world works (e.g., how power is distributed) and how to draw inferences that guide them in their efforts to gather and present the news.

Journalism also contains a structural bias. Selecting, presenting, editing, and interpreting the news inevitably require judgments about what stories to cover and what to report about them, because there is simply not enough space for everything. Thus the news can never mirror reality. In addition, the particular ways in which the news is gathered and presented have consequences for distortion in news coverage.

We have already seen that the news is fundamentally superficial and oversimplified and is often overblown, all of which provides the public a distorted view of, among other things, presidential activities, statements, policies, and options. The emphasis on action and the deviant (and therefore "newsworthy" items) rather than on patterns of behavior and the implication that most stories represent more general themes of national significance contribute further to this distortion. Personalizing the news downplays structural and other impersonal factors that may be far more important in understanding the economy, for example, than individual political actors.

We have also seen that the press prefers to frame the news in themes, which both simplify complex issues and events and provide continuity of persons, institutions, and issues. Once these themes are established, the press tends to maintain them in subsequent stories. Of necessity, themes emphasize some information at the expense of other data, often determining what information is most relevant to news coverage and the context in which it is presented.

Once a stereotype of President Ford as a "bumbler" was established, every stumble was magnified in coverage of him. He was repeatedly forced to defend his intelligence, and many of his acts and statements were reported as efforts to "act" presidential. Once Ford was typecast, his image was repeatedly reinforced and was very difficult to overcome.

Sometimes themes are established by the press to attract an audience for coverage of an event. A study of television coverage of the 1972 Democratic National Convention found that, although they were neutral as to partisanship, the networks portrayed the convention as more disorderly and conflictual than it actually was. Television's requirements for themes and conflict encouraged reporters to focus on differences between delegates, and the technique of switching from camera to camera gave the impression of rapidly shifting action.[29]

Reporters often fail to alert readers and viewers about the tentativeness of much of what the press reports. Although sources may be unreliable, motives obscure, facts disputed or confused, and meanings unclear, the news is presented in a straightforward manner that communicates little notion of uncertainty. Similarly, reporters often do not make it clear that they have made inferences in their reporting. Such presentations enhance the credibility of journalists who deliver the news, but they provide the potential for distortion in the process.

Some observers feel that the press is biased against whomever holds office at the moment and that reporters want to expose them in the media. Reporters hold disparaging views of most politicians and public officials, finding them self-serving, lacking in integrity and competence, hypocritical, and preoccupied with reelection. Thus it is not surprising that journalists see a need to expose and debunk them through general derogation. This orientation may be characterized as neither liberal nor conservative, but reformist.

White House reporters are always looking to expose conflicts of interest and other shady behavior of public officials. Moreover, many of their inquiries revolve around the question, "Is he up to the job?" Reporters who are confined in the White House all day may attempt to make up for their lack of investigative reporting with sarcastic and accusatory questioning. Moreover, the desire to keep the public interested and the need for continuous coverage may create a subconscious bias in the press against the presidency that leads to critical stories.

News coverage of the presidency often tends to emphasize the negative (although the negative stories are typically presented in a neutral manner). In the 1980 election campaign the press portrayed President Carter as mean and Ronald Reagan as imprecise rather than Carter as precise and Reagan as nice. The emphasis, in other words, was on the candidates' negative qualities. As the following excerpt from Jimmy Carter's diary regarding a visit to Panama in 1978 illustrates, "objective" reporting can be misleading:

> I told the Army troops that I was in the Navy for 11 years, and they booed. I told them that we depended on the Army to keep the Canal open, and they cheered. Later, the news reports said that there were boos and cheers during my speech. I reckon that was an accurate report![30]

On the other hand, one could argue that the press is biased *toward* the White House. Their general respect for the presidency is often transferred to individual presidents. Framed at a respectful distance by the television camera, the president is typically portrayed with an aura of dignity working in a context of rationality and coherence on activities benefiting the public. Word selection often reflects this orientation as well. In addition, journalists follow conventions that protect politicians and public officials from revelations of private misconduct.

The White House enjoys a consistent pattern of favorable coverage in newspapers, magazines, and network news. The most favorable coverage comes in the first year of a president's term, before he has a record to criticize and critics for reporters to interview. Coverage focuses on human interest stories of the president and his appointees and their personalities, goals, and plans. The president is pictured in a positive light as a policymaker dealing with problems. Controversies over solutions arise later. Newspaper headlines also favor the president, and news of foreign affairs provides basic support for the policies and personalities of the administration.[31]

MEDIA EFFECTS

The most significant question about the substance of media coverage, of course, is about the impact it has, if any, on public opinion. Unfortunately, we know very little about this subject. Most studies on media effects have focused on attitude changes, especially in voting for presidential candidates, and have typically found little or no evidence of influence. Reinforcement of existing attitudes and opinions has been the strongest effect of the media.[32] There are other ways to look for media effects, however. The public appears to be a fairly passive audience and usually does not do a great deal of perceptual screening of the news. Repeated coverage of an issue or person by all the media, television's use of themes and simple story lines, and the vividness of live coverage of visually exciting events can buttress the media's effect on the public.

The media are more likely to influence perceptions than attitudes. The press can influence the perceptions of what public figures stand for and what their personalities are like, what issues are important, and what is at stake. By raising certain issues or personal characteristics to prominence, the salience of attitudes that people already hold may change and thus alter their evaluations of, say, presidential performance, without their attitudes themselves changing.

The public's information on and criteria for evaluating candidates parallel what is presented in the media: campaign performance, personality traits, mannerisms, and personal background rather than issue positions, ability to govern, and relevant experience. Moreover, what the press emphasizes about elections (the horse race) is what the people say is important about them, what they discuss about them in private conversations, and what they remember about them.[33]

While it cannot be conclusively proven that media coverage contributes to the public's de-emphasis of the professional capacities and policy plans of candidates, it is reasonable to speculate that the press's emphasis on the horse race and personality traits encourages the public to view campaigns in these terms. Thus, although the press may not directly influence voters to support a particular candidate, it probably amplifies the public's predispositions to view public affairs through personalities rather than more complex factors.

Earlier we saw that the press gave substantial coverage to President Ford's misstatement about Soviet domination of Eastern Europe. This coverage had an impact on the public. Polls show that most people did not realize the president made an error until they were told so by the press. After that, pro-Ford evaluations of the debate declined noticeably as voters' concerns for competence in foreign policy making became salient.[34]

The press probably has the greatest effect on public perceptions of individuals and issues between election campaigns, when people are less likely to activate their partisan defenses. The prominant coverage of Gerald Ford's alleged physical clumsiness was naturally translated into suggestions of mental ineptitude. In the president's own words:

> Every time I stumbled or bumped my head or fell in the snow, reporters zeroed in on that to the exclusion of almost everything else. The news coverage was harmful, but even more damaging was the fact that Johnny Carson and

Chevy Chase used my "missteps" for their jokes. Their antics—and I'll admit that I laughed at them myself—helped create the public perception of me as a stumbler. And that wasn't funny.[35]

Once such an image is established in the mass media, it is very difficult to change, as reporters continue to emphasize behavior that is consistent with their previously established themes.

During the Iranian hostage crisis ABC originated a nightly program entitled "America Held Hostage," Walter Cronkite provided "countdown" on the number of days of the crisis at the end of each evening's news on CBS, many feature stories on the hostages and their families were reported in all the media, and the press gave complete coverage to "demonstrations" in front of the U.S. embassy in Tehran. The latter were often artificially created for consumption by Americans. This crisis gave President Carter's approval rating a tremendous boost, at least for a while. Conversely, when the *Pueblo* was captured by North Korea, there were many more American captives, but there were also no television cameras and few reporters to cover the situation. Thus the incident played a much smaller role in American politics.

Those with only marginal concern for politics may be especially susceptible to the impact of the media because they have few alternative sources of information and less-developed political allegiances. Thus, they have fewer strongly held attitudes to overcome. Similarly, coverage of new issues that are removed from the experiences of people and their political convictions is more likely to influence public opinion than coverage of continuing issues.

Almost all citizens are basically ignorant of such areas of the world as Central America, Afghanistan, and Poland. The press plays a pivotal role in shaping perceptions of the personalities and issues involved in conflicts abroad (generally only conflicts receive coverage) and the United States' stake in the outcomes of the disputes. In such situations we have seen that there is substantial potential for distortion. The public is heavily dependent on the media for information and has little basis for challenging what it reads and sees in the news. The illustrations of the conflict—scenes of combat or demonstrations, for example—may become the essence of the issue in the public's mind. The underlying problems, which the president must confront, may be largely ignored.

The president needs an understanding by the public of the difficulty of his job and the nature of the problems he faces. The role of the press here can be critical. Watching television news seems to do little to inform viewers about public affairs; reading the printed media is more useful. This may be because reading requires more active cognitive processing of information than watching television, and there is more information presented in newspapers.

We have seen that press coverage of the president is superficial, oversimplified, and often overblown, providing the public a distorted picture of White House activities. This trivialization of the news drowns out coverage of more important matters, often leaving the public ill-informed about matters with which the president must deal, ranging from the renegotiation of the Panama Canal Treaty to funding social security benefits. The preoccupation of the press with personality and the results of policies does little to help the public appreciate the complexity of presidential decision making, the trade-offs involved in policy choices, and the broad trends outside the president's control.

In the previous chapter we saw that the president's access to the media is at least a potential advantage in influencing public opinion. The press's focus on the president has disadvantages as well. It inevitably leaves the impression that the president *is* the federal government and crucial to our prosperity and happiness. This naturally encourages the public to focus its expectations on the White House. So does the national frame of reference provided by a truly mass media and the press's penchant for linking its coverage of even small matters with responses from the president or presidential spokesmen.

Moreover, the extraordinary attention the press devotes to the president magnifies his flaws. Even completely unsubstantial charges against the president may make the news because of his prominence. Familiarity may not breed contempt, but it certainly may diminish the aura of grandeur around the chief executive.

Similarly, commentary following presidential speeches and press conferences may influence what viewers remember and may affect their opinions.[36] Although the impact of commentary on presidential addresses and press conferences is unclear, it is probably safe to argue that it is a constraint on the president's ability to lead public opinion. In the words of two observers,

> Critical instant analysis undermines presidential authority by transforming him from presentor to protagonist. . . . Credible, familiar, apparently disinterested newsmen and -women, experts too, usually agreeing with each other, comment on the self-interested performance of a politician. Usually the president's rhetoric is deflated, the mood he has striven to create dissipated.[37]

CONCLUSION

The mass media play a prominent role in the public presidency, providing the public with most of its information about the White House and mediating the president's communications with his constituents. Presidents need the press in order to reach the public, and presidential-press relations are an important complement to the chief executive's efforts at leading public opinion. Through attempting to coordinate news, holding press conferences, and providing a wide range of services for the press, the White House tries to influence its portrayal in the news. On occasion, the inevitable adversarial nature of presidential-press relations leads to open warfare and various forms of harassment of the press.

Presidential-press relations pose many obstacles to the president's efforts to obtain and maintain public support. Although it is probably not true that press coverage of the White House is biased along partisan or ideological lines or toward or against a particular president, it frequently presents a distorted picture to the public and fails to impart an appropriate perspective from which to view complex events. Moreover, presidents are continuously harassed by leaks to the press and are faced with superficial, over-simplified coverage that devotes little attention to substantive discussion of policies and often focuses on trivial matters. This type of reporting undoubtedly affects public perceptions of the president, usually in a negative way. It is no wonder that chief executives generally see the press as a hindrance to their efforts to develop appreciation for their performance and policies.

Before leaving this chapter, however, it is important to put it in perspective. Americans benefit greatly from a free press. We should not forget this as we examine the media's flaws. The same press that provides superficial coverage of the presidency also alerts us to abuses of authority and to attempts to mislead public opinion. It is also much less biased than the heavily partisan newspapers that were typical early in our nation's history. The press is an essential pillar in the structure of a free society.

Moreover, perhaps the fundamental reason that the press's coverage is much less than its critics would like it to be is that it must appeal to the general public. When the public, or a sizable segment of it, demands more of the mass media, it undoubtedly will receive it. In short, although mass media coverage of the presidency is often poor, it could be much worse and it is probably about what the public desires. The media reflect as well as influence American society.

NOTES

1. Elmer E. Cornwell, Jr.,"Presidential News: The Expanding Public Image," *Journalism Quarterly* 36 (Summer 1959): 275–83; Alan P. Balutis,"The Presidency and the Press: The Expanding Presidential Image," *Presidential Studies Quarterly* 7 (Fall 1977): 244–51.

2. Richard Harris, "The Presidency and the Press," *New Yorker*, October 1, 1973, p. 122; Dom Bonafede, "Powell and the Press—A New Mood in the White House," *National Journal*, June 25, 1977, p. 981.

3. Harris, "The Presidency and the Press," p. 122, Peter Forbath and Carey Winfrey, *The Adversaries: The President and the Press* (Cleveland: Regal Books, 1974), p. 5.

4. Dick Kirschten, "Life in the White House Fish Bowl—Brady Takes Charge as Press Chief," *National Journal*, January 31, 1981, p. 180.

5. Jarol B. Manheim, "The Honeymoon's Over: The News Conference and the Development of Presidential Style," *Journal of Politics* 41 (February 1979): 60–61.

6. Doris A. Graber, *Mass Media and American Politics* (Washington, D.C.: Congressional Quarterly Press, 1980), p. 207.

7. "Carter Gets Even with the *Boston Globe*," *Newsweek*, February 25, 1980, p. 21.

8. Michael Baruch Grossman and Martha Joynt Kumar, *Portraying the President: The White House and the Media* (Baltimore: Johns Hopkins University Press, 1981), pp. 59–60, 63–64, 280–81.

9. Dom Bonafede, "The Washington Press—It Magnifies the President's Flaws and Blemishes," *National Journal*, May 1, 1982, pp. 267–71.

10. David L. Paletz and Robert M. Entman, *Media—Power—Politics* (New York: Free Press, 1981), pp. 55–56.

11. See William Safire, *Before the Fall: An Inside View of the Pre-Watergate White House* (New York: Doubleday, 1975), especially pp. 75, 321–23, 341–65. See also John Ehrlichman, *Witness to Power: The Nixon Years* (New York: Simon and Schuster, 1982), p. 264.

12. "Reagan Outburst on Leaks," *Newsweek*, January 18, 1982, p. 23; Walter S. Mossberg, "Reagan Prepares Curbs on U.S. Officials to Restrict News Leaks on Foreign Policy," *Wall Street Journal*, January 13, 1982, p. 7.

13. Safire, *Before the Fall*, p. 373; Henry Kissinger, *Years of Upheaval* (Boston: Little, Brown, 1981), p. 116.

14. Lyndon Johnson, quoted in George Christian, *The President Steps Down: A Personal Memoir of the Transfer of Power* (New York: Macmillan, 1970), p. 203.

15. "The U.S. vs. William Colby," *Newsweek*, September 28, 1981, p. 30.

16. "The Tattletale White House," *Newsweek*, February 25, 1980, p. 21.

17. Robert T. Hartmann, *Palace Politics: An Inside Account of the Ford Years* (New York: McGraw-Hill, 1980), p. 38.

18. William J. Lanouette, "The Washington Press Corps—Is It All That Powerful?" *National Journal*, June 2, 1979, p. 898.

19. Woodrow Wilson, quoted in William Small, *To Kill a Messenger: Television News and the Real World* (New York: Hastings, 1970), p. 221.

20. President Carter, quoted in Michael Baruch Grossman and Martha Joynt Kumar, "Carter, Reagan, and the Media: Have the Rules Really Changed or the Poles of the Spectrum of Success?" (paper presented at the Annual Meeting of the American Political Science Association, New York, September 3–6, 1981), p. 8.

21. Hoyt Purvis, ed., *The Presidency and the Press* (Austin, Tex.: Lyndon B. Johnson School of Public Affairs, 1976), p. 56.

22. See George C. Edwards III, *The Public Presidency* (New York: St. Martin's, 1983), p. 149 and sources cited therein.

23. Grossman and Kumar, *Portraying the President*, p. 43.

24. Quoted in Ibid., p. 26.

25. Ibid., p. 231.

26. Quoted in "Washington Press Corps," *Newsweek*, May 25, 1981, p. 90.

27. See Edwards, *The Public Presidency*, p. 156 and sources cited therein.

28. John P. Robinson, "The Press as King-Maker: What Surveys from Last Five Campaigns Show," *Journalism Quarterly* 51 (Winter 1974): 587–94, 606.

29. David L. Paletz and Martha Elson, "Television Coverage of Presidential Conventions: Now You See It, Now You Don't," *Political Science Quarterly* 91 (Spring 1976): 109–31.

30. Jimmy Carter, *Keeping Faith: Memoirs of a President* (New York: Bantam, 1982), pp. 179–80.

31. On this topic see Edwards, *The Public Presidency*, p. 162 and sources cited therein.

32. For an overview, see Cliff Zukin, "Mass Communication and Public Opinion," in Dan D. Nimmo and Keith R. Sanders, eds., *Handbook of Political Communication* (Beverly Hills: Sage, 1981), pp. 359–90.

33. Thomas E. Patterson, *The Mass Media Election: How Americans Choose Their President* (New York: Praeger, 1980), pp. 84–86, 98–100, 105, chap. 12; Doris A. Graber, "Personal Qualities in Presidential Images: The Contribution of the Press," *Midwest Journal of Political Science* 16 (February 1972): 295; Graber, *Mass Media and American Politics*, pp. 184–85.

34. Frederick T. Steeper, "Public Response to Gerald Ford's Statements on Eastern

Europe in the Second Debate," in George F. Bishop, Robert G. Meadow, and Marilyn Jackson-Beeck, eds., *The Presidential Debates: Media, Electoral, and Public Perspectives* (New York: Praeger, 1978), pp. 81–101.

35. Gerald R. Ford, *A Time to Heal: The Autobiography of Gerald R. Ford* (New York: Harper and Row, 1979), p. 289; see also pp. 343–44.

36. Dwight F. Davis, Lynda Lee Kaid, and Donald Singleton, "Information Effects of Political Commentary," *Experimental Study of Politics* 6 (June 1977), pp. 45–68; Lynda Lee Kaid, Donald L. Singleton, and Dwight Davis, "Instant Analysis of Televised Political Addresses: The Speaker versus the Commentator," in Brent D. Ruben, *Communication Yearbook I* (New Brunswick, N.J.: Transaction Books, 1977), pp. 453–64; John Havick, "The Impact of a Televised State of the Union Message and the Instant Analysis: An Experiment," unpublished paper, Georgia Institute of Technology, 1980, typescript).

37. Paletz and Entman, *Media—Power—Politics*, p. 70.

SELECTED READINGS

Abel, Elie, ed. *What's News: The Media in American Society*. San Francisco: Institute for Contemporary Studies, 1981.

Braestrup, Peter. *Big Story*. Garden City, N.Y.: Anchor, 1978.

Christian, George. *The President Steps Down: A Personal Memoir of the Transfer of Power*. New York: Macmillan, 1970.

Edwards, George C., III. *The Public Presidency*. Chaps. 3 and 4. New York: St. Martin's, 1983.

Epstein, Edward Jay. *News from Nowhere: Television and the News*. New York: Vintage, 1973.

Gans, Herbert J. *Deciding What's News*. New York: Vintage, 1979.

Graber, Doris A. *Mass Media and American Politics*. Washington, D.C.: Congressional Quarterly Press, 1980.

Grossman, Michael Baruch, and Martha Joynt Kumar. *Portraying the President: The White House and the News Media*. Baltimore: Johns Hopkins University Press, 1981.

Hess, Stephen. *The Washington Reporters*. Washington, D.C.: Brookings Institution, 1981.

Hofstetter, Richard C. *Bias in the News: Network Television Coverage of the 1972 Election Campaign*. Columbus: Ohio State University Press, 1976.

Iyengar, Shanto; Mark D. Peters; and Donald R. Kinder. "Experimental Demonstrations of the 'Not-so-Minimal' Consequences of Television News Programs." *American Political Science Review* 76 (December 1982): 848–58.

Kaid, Lynda Lee; Donald L. Singleton; and Dwight Davis. "Instant Analysis of Televised Political Addresses: The Speaker versus the Commentator." In Brent D. Ruben, ed., *Communication Yearbook I*. New Brunswick, N.J.: Transaction Books, 1977.

Keogh, James. *President Nixon and the Press*. New York: Funk and Wagnalls, 1972.

Klein, Herbert G. *Making It Perfectly Clear*. Garden City, N.Y.: Doubleday, 1980.

Lammers, William W. "Presidential Press Conference Schedules: Who Hides and When?" *Political Science Quarterly* 96 (Summer 1981): 261–78.

Manheim, Jarol B. "The Honeymoon's Over: The News Conference and the Development of Presidential Style." *Journal of Politics* 41 (February 1979): 55–74.

Minow, Newton; John B. Martin; and Lee M. Mitchell. *Presidential Television.* New York: Basic Books, 1973.

Morgan, Edward R.; Max Ways; Clark Mollenhoff; Peter Lisagor; and Herbert G. Klein. *The Presidency and the Press Conference.* Washington, D.C.: American Enterprise Institute, 1971.

Nessen, Ron. *It Sure Looks Different from the Inside.* Chicago: Playboy Press, 1978.

Paletz, David L., and Robert M. Entman. *Media—Power—Politics.* New York: Free Press, 1981.

Patterson, Thomas E. *The Mass Media Election: How Americans Choose Their President.* New York: Praeger, 1980.

Porter, William E. *Assault on the Media: The Nixon Years.* Ann Arbor: University of Michigan Press, 1976.

Purvis, Hoyt, ed. *The Presidency and the Press.* Austin, Tex.: Lyndon B. Johnson School of Public Affairs, 1976.

Robinson, Michael Jay. "The Impact of Instant Analysis." *Journal of Communication* 27 (Spring 1977): 17–23.

Robinson, Michael Jay, and Margaret A. Sheehan. *Over the Wire and On TV: CBS and UPI in Campaign '80.* New York: Russell Sage Foundation, 1983.

Safire, William. *Before the Fall: An Inside View of the Pre-Watergate White House.* New York: Doubleday, 1975.

Steeper, Frederick T. "Public Response to Gerald Ford's Statements on Eastern Europe in the Second Debate." In George F. Bishop, Robert G. Meadow, and Marilyn Jackson-Beeck, *The Presidential Debates: Media, Electoral, and Public Perspectives.* New York: Praeger, 1978.

Wise, David. *The Politics of Lying: Government Deception, Secrecy, and Power.* New York: Vintage, 1973.

6

The Presidential Office

A president's tasks are many and varied. The job is too big for any one person to perform. Presidents need help. They need help in making, promoting, and implementing their decisions. They need help in attending to the symbolic and ceremonial functions of the office. They need help in articulating their beliefs, communicating their policy, and responding to public moods, opinions, and expectations.

The executive departments and agencies were obviously intended to provide such help, but they alone have not been sufficient. Their interests, needs, and ongoing responsibilities have not been synonymous with the president's all the time or even most of the time. Besides, they serve a number of masters. In addition to the chief executive, they must look to Congress for their programs and budgets and to their clientele for policy requests and political support. With an increasing number of issues overlapping departmental jurisdictions and an increasing number of matters requiring presidential attention, presidents have found it necessary to turn to other advisory bodies and institutional structures for assistance.

We will focus on those that have had a direct and continuing influence on major presidential actions and decisions: the cabinet, the Executive Office, senior White House aides, and more recently, the vice president. Beginning with the oldest of these advisory bodies, the cabinet, we briefly describe its creation, evolution, and its demise. We then explore the institutionalization of advisory responsibilities in the Executive Office. Here the emphasis is on the growth of this bureaucracy within a bureaucracy and its impact on the president and the performance of his presidential responsibilities. After a historical sketch of the evolution of the White House, we examine patterns of staffing and their relationship to the personal style and policy objectives of the president. In the final section we assess the increasing impact of the vice presidential office.

ORGANIZING EXECUTIVE ADVICE

The Evolution of the Cabinet

The Constitution did not create a separate advisory council for the president. The framers had discussed the idea but rejected it largely out of the fear that the president might try to sidestep responsibility for his own actions by using his council as a foil. In order to avoid the fiction, popular in England at the time, that the king could do no wrong, that any harmful action he committed was always the result of poor or even pernicious advice from his counselors, the Constitution designated that the president could demand written opinions of his subordinates. Having these in writing, it was hoped, would pinpoint responsibility.

Although presidents had been expected to use their department secretaries in both administrative and advisory capacities, there was no expectation that they would function as the principal body of advisers. However, in 1791, when George Washington prepared to leave the capital city, he authorized his vice president, secretaries of state, treasury, war, and the chief justice to consult with each other on governmental matters during his absence. The following year, the president began to meet more frequently with the four heads of the executive departments but without the vice president and the chief justice. During the undeclared naval war with France, these meetings became more frequent. It was James Madison who referred to this group as the president's cabinet. The name stuck. Jefferson's resignation as secretary of state in 1794 in protest over the administration's policies fixed the partisan nature of the group. Members were expected to provide counsel as well as support.

For the next 140 years, the cabinet functioned as the president's principal advisory body for both foreign and domestic affairs. Administrative positions on controversial proposals were often thrashed out at cabinet meetings. Presidents also turned to their cabinets for help in supporting them on Capitol Hill. The personal relationships between the individual secretaries and members of Congress often put the cabinet officials in a better position than the president to obtain this support. Strong cabinets and weak presidents characterized executive advisory relationships during most of the nineteenth century.

The president's position began to change as his capacity for exerting personal influence improved. The ability to shape public opinion and mobilize partisan support, evident during the Theodore Roosevelt and Woodrow Wilson administrations, strengthened the president's hand in dealing with Congress and with his own department heads. Beginning in 1921, the power to affect department and agency decision making through the budget process also contributed to a stronger presidency.

As a consequence of these changes, cabinet meetings became more of a forum for discussion than a mechanism for making decisions. Franklin Roosevelt even trivialized the forum. His practice was to go around the table asking each participant what was on his or her mind. Frequently after the session, several secretaries remained to discuss their important business with him.

Although Truman emphasized the importance of the cabinet upon taking office (as have all of his successors), he did not meet with it regularly. Rather than utilizing his department secretaries as an advisory body, he turned to them individually as Roosevelt had done and relied on a few senior staff aides in the White House for help in formulating policy.

The cabinet enjoyed a resurgence under Eisenhower, meeting some 230 times during his eight years in office. The president personally presided over most of these meetings and used his presence to achieve consensus on policy. The sessions themselves often featured elaborate presentations of proposals by individual department heads and their staffs. These presentations, replete with visual aides and supporting materials, were the prelude to final decisions on the administration's legislative program prior to its presentation to Congress.

Eisenhower's use of the cabinet, however, has been the exception, not the rule, for contemporary presidents. Kennedy and Johnson rarely met with their cabinets, and Nixon, despite his announced intention to revert to a cabinet system, held few meetings and relegated department heads to positions of lesser importance in his administration.

Ford and Carter paid lip service to cabinet government but neither used the cabinet as a decision-making body. They held cabinet meetings at the beginning of their administrations and then slowly discontinued them. Carter, for example, met with the cabinet every week during his first year in office, every other week during his second year, once a month during his third year, and sporadically during his final year.

Reagan, too, has met less frequently with the full cabinet as his presidency has progressed. However, within his administration, department heads and their assistants have worked closely with presidential aides to formulate and coordinate major policy initiatives. They have done this within the structure of a cabinet council system. Organized on the basis of broad policy areas, the councils, composed of various departmental secretaries, performed some of the same advisory functions that the cabinet as a group did during and before the Eisenhower administration. They deliberated policy recommendations, developed administration positions, and helped coordinate the implementation of key presidential decisions. Staff support was provided by the White House. Nominally chaired by the president, the councils were run in the president's absence by one of the department heads who had been designated as chairman pro tempore.

The Cabinet's Demise

While the cabinet council system has not been an unqualified success (see Chapter 8), it has addressed and partially overcome one of the principal weaknesses of the contemporary cabinet—its size and its diversity. Table 6-1 lists the departmental components of the contemporary cabinet. In addition to the secretaries, the vice president, senior White House aides, and other executive officials of cabinet rank may attend its sessions. The increasingly technical nature of policy making and the need for highly specialized information also made it difficult for secretaries to be sufficiently versed in the intricacies of issue areas outside of their own to carry on an intelligent discussion. At best this limited participation at cabinet meetings to the few who were informed and competent; at worst it reduced the level of the discussion and extended the time of debate.

There are other reasons for the cabinet's decline. Increasing pressure from outside groups forced secretaries to assume more of an advocacy role for their respective departments (referred to as "going native"), particularly in meetings in which they had to go on the record or even in closed sessions where minutes were kept (and could be leaked to the press). The tendency to advocate department interests increased over the course of an administration. The cabinet meetings thus became more confrontational and less useful as a device for reaching a consensus or building one after policy decisions had been made.

Moreover, the need and desire to extend personal influence discouraged department secretaries from discussing their concerns in a group setting. Cabinet members usually prefer the president's ear alone, and contemporary presidents, beginning with Franklin Roosevelt, encouraged one-on-one situations to maximize their own flexibility, increase their own bargaining power, and conserve their own time.

These factors help explain why recent presidents have met with their cabinets less as their administrations have progressed.[1] They also suggest why presidents have increasingly differentiated among their secretaries in seeking advice. The heads of certain departments have tended to exercise closer and more collaborative relationships with the president. These tend to be the most influential secretaries, those who comprise the so-called inner cabinet. According to political scientist Thomas E. Cronin, they include the heads of the first departments: State, Treasury, Justice, and Defense.[2]

Table 6-1. The Cabinet, 1985

Department	Year Created	President	Fiscal 1984 Rankings	
			Budget	Personnel Authority
State	1789	Washington	12	9
Treasury	1789	Washington	3	3
Interior	1849	Polk	10	5
Agriculture	1862	Lincoln	4	4
Justice	1870	Grant	10	7
Commerce (formerly part of Department of Commerce and labor, 1903)	1913	Wilson	13	8
Labor (formerly part of Department of Commerce and Labor, 1903)	1913	Wilson	5	10
Defense (consolidated Department of War, 1789, and Department of Navy, 1798)	1947	Truman	2	1
Housing and Urban Development	1965	Johnson	9	12
Transportation	1966	Johnson	6	6
Energy	1977	Carter	8	11
Health and Human Services (formerly part of Department of Health, Education, and Welfare, 1953)	1980	Carter	1	2
Education (formerly part of Department of Health, Education, and Welfare, 1953)	1980	Carter	7	13

In contrast, the other secretaries, who are considered members of the outer cabinet, tend to have a more distant relationship with the president because of the nature of their departments and clientele. "These departments experience heavy and often conflicting pressures from clientele groups, from congressional interests, and from state and local governments, pressures that often run counter to presidential priorities."[3] Advocating departmental interests and exercising administrative responsibilities make it more difficult for secretaries to perceive problems from the president's perspective and recommend solutions that accord with his needs rather than theirs. This has given presidents little choice but to develop their own institutional and personal staffs.

The Executive Office

The Executive Office of the President (EOP) was established by executive order in 1939. Its title, however, is a misnomer. Its functions are not primarily executive nor is it (or was it ever) a single office.

The principal objective of the EOP has always been to help the president perform central, nondelegable tasks, including those involved in his expanded policy-making roles. For the most part, administrative responsibilities have been avoided. The various offices in the EOP have not taken over the ongoing responsibilities of the departments and agencies, although they have helped coordinate some interagency projects.

Nor is the Executive Office a single monolithic agency. It has always consisted of a number of specialized staffs. The first EOP was composed of five separate units, including the Bureau of the Budget and the White House. Over the years forty-six different boards, offices, and councils have been placed within its purview. Table 6-2 lists its former components while Figure 6-1 lists its current units.

While the EOP has evolved in size and function, it has not done so in a systematic, carefully planned way. Rather, its development has been a product of historical accident, the needs of different administrations, and the goals of different presidents. Most chief executives have changed the Executive Office in some way, adding or deleting some of its units. Some have attempted to overhaul it entirely. The most extensive reorganization occurred during the first term of the Nixon presidency.

Unhappy with the piecemeal expansion of the executive that had occurred prior to 1968, President Nixon appointed a council at the beginning of his administration to review the entire executive-branch structure including the organization and operation of the EOP. Meeting over a fourteen-month period, this advisory council proposed a set of recommendations to centralize and streamline the executive branch, thereby making it more responsive to the president's political needs. Included was a recommendation to create a separate domestic policy-making staff, the Domestic Council, and another to reorganize and retitle the Bureau of the Budget.

The changes not only affected the composition of the Executive Office but decision making within it. More political positions, filled by presidential nominees, were created. This had the effect of decreasing the role and influence of civil servants. It also shifted power from the departments and agencies to the presidency. Political appointees in the upper echelon of the White House and the Office of Management and

Table 6-2. Former Units in the Executive Office of the President

	Years
National Resources Planning Board	1939–1943
Office of Government Reports	1939–1948
Liaison Office for Personnel Management	1939–1945
Office of Emergency Management	1940–1943
War Agencies	1943–1946
National Security Resources Board	1947–1953
Office of Defense Mobilization	1952–1958
Office of the Director for Mutual Security	1951–1953
Telecommunications Adviser	1951–1953
Operations Coordinating Board	1953–1961
President's Advisory Committee on Government Organization	1953–1960
President's Board of Consultants on Foreign Intelligence Activities	1956–1961
National Aeronautics and Space Council	1958–1973
Office of Civil and Defense Mobilization	1958–1961
Office of Emergency Planning (Preparedness)	1961–1973
Office of Economic Opportunity	1964–1975
President's Committee on Consumer Interests— Office of Special Assistant for Consumer Affairs	1964–1966
National Council on Marine Resources and Engineering Development	1966–1971
President's Council on Youth Opportunity— Office of Special Assistant for Youth	1967–1971
Council of Urban Affairs	1969–1970
Office of Intergovernmental Relations	1969–1972
Council for Rural Affairs	1969–1970
President's Foreign Intelligence Advisory Board	1961–1977
Office of Telecommunications Policy	1970–1978
Cost of Living Council	1971–1974
Council on International Economic Policy	1971–1978
Office of Consumer Affairs	1971–1973
Special Action Office for Drug Abuse Prevention	1971–1975
Federal Property Council/Property Review Board	1973–1978, 1981–1984
Energy Policy Office	1973–1975
Council on Wage and Price Stability	1974–1981
Presidential Clemency Board	1974–1975
Economic Policy Board	1974–1977
Energy Resources Council	1974–1978
Office of Drug Abuse Policy	1976–1978
Intelligence Oversight Board	1976–1983

Figure 6-1. Executive Office of the President

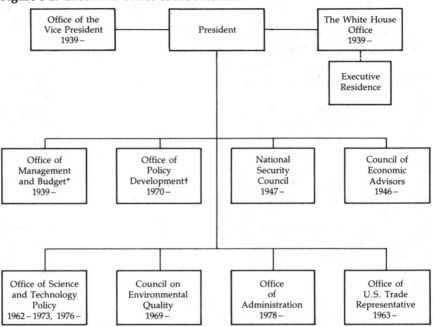

*Titled Bureau of the Budget, 1939–1970.
†Titled Domestic Council, 1970–1976; Domestic Policy Staff, 1977–1980.

Budget (OMB) dominated activities, ran the processes, advised the president, and made sure that his wishes were carried out.

Criticism of the hierarchical structure of the Nixon presidency, the heavy-handed tactics of his principal aides, and the inaccessibility of the president to others in the executive branch and Congress led to a moderating effect and less-centralized control during the Ford and Carter presidencies. Ford was more accessible to department and agency heads and more receptive to their input than was his predecessor. He did not use the EOP to impose a perspective on them as the Nixon administration attempted to do. Carter, too, gave his department secretaries considerable latitude in articulating and promoting their positions and in administering their own departments.

Carter also reorganized the EOP. As a candidate, he had promised to reduce the size of the presidency. As president, he decreased the number of EOP offices from nineteen to twelve and reduced its personnel by more than 250, saving an estimated $6 million in the process.[4] The smaller EOP did not, however, increase the president's capacity to manage the government. Unable to impose discipline on the various departments and agencies, Carter was eventually forced to fire two cabinet secretaries who consistently undercut his position on Capitol Hill and in their own departments.

President Reagan did not make major structural changes in his Executive Office although he did eliminate several units and retitled others.

Consequences of Structural Change

The transformations that have occurred in the EOP have made the structure of that office more consistent with the personal styles of individual presidents. This has resulted in short-term advantages for the president, but long-term disadvantages for the presidency. Together, they have produced instability in organization, irregularity in operations, and turnover in personnel. Relations between the president and executive-branch agencies have been subject to continuing uncertainty with each new administration. Transitions between administrations have been made more arduous. The wheel has to be reinvented constantly.

Despite the initial objective of the office to help the president oversee the operational responsibilities and policy-making efforts of the executive departments and agencies, not to substitute for them, separate policy-making units have been established. Despite the initial desire to staff the EOP with civil servants, political appointees have increased in number and influence. Despite the initial goal to keep the Executive Office small in size and general in capabilities, it has become a large, highly specialized, presidential bureaucracy.

This growth, differentiation, and politicization has worked at cross-purposes. On one hand, it has increased the political sensitivity of the president; on the other, it may have decreased his capacity to obtain neutral policy advice. Discontinuities in policy between and even within administrations have resulted.

There is another problem. Politicization has caused the presidency's institutional memory to fade. Turnover among its political appointees and career officials has increased, often placing the president's people at a competitive disadvantage when dealing substantively with officials from other departments and agencies.

Although the establishment of a presidential bureaucracy has increased the presidency's discretion and extended its influence, it has also generated internal rivalry and competition. Senior presidential aides enjoy considerable status by virtue of their access to and influence on the president. They also exercise considerable authority within their functional areas. This status and that authority have contributed to tension between department and agency heads and the White House which, in turn, has accentuated problems of maintaining loyalty and mobilizing support within an administration. Information leaks are now a perennial presidential problem.

While the establishment of an institutional mechanism within the presidency has increased the president's ability to meet the multiple demands of his office, it has also helped perpetuate those demands. Bureaucracies have a self-perpetuating character of their own. By performing functions and meeting expectations, these structures encourage those expectations to persist. Subsequent presidents who do not meet them are criticized.

Finally, the development of the presidency has enhanced the institution's power, but it has probably decreased the president's personal influence on that institution. A chief executive is either forced to immerse himself in the details of administration, consuming valuable time and energy in the process, or delegate that responsibility to others. If he chooses to delegate, as most presidents have done, then he faces the danger of having key operational and policy decisions shaped by others acting on his behalf. His presidency becomes theirs. His failure to delegate, on the other hand, can cloud his perspective. It can prevent him from seeing the big picture as he tries to set national goals and devise national policy.

PROVIDING A PRESIDENTIAL STAFFING SYSTEM

In addition to the support the institution requires, presidents need assistants to help them perform their personal duties and responsibilities. Until the creation of an official White House staff in 1939, that help was mainly clerical and frequently in short supply.

The Early Years

For the first seventy years, Congress did not even provide the president with secretarial support. Early presidents were expected to write their own speeches and answer their own correspondence. Most employed a few aides and paid them out of their own executive salary. These assistants tended to be young and undistinguished. Frequently, they were related to the president. They were paid low salaries and generally performed menial tasks.

In 1857 Congress enacted a separate appropriation for a secretary, but the position did not assume great importance or even much potential at the time. If anything, the quality of the secretaries actually employed by presidents declined. Andrew Johnson's aide, his son Robert, was an alcoholic; Grant's secretary, General Orville E. Babcock, was indicted for fraud; Hayes's assistant, William Rogers, was generally regarded as incompetent.[5]

The secretary's role and influence began to expand with the administration of Chester Arthur. Daniel G. Rollings, who had assisted Arthur as vice president, helped him draft speeches and legislative messages.[6] Grover Cleveland's chief aide performed a variety of political and personal tasks. His influence was reflected by the press corps' attribution of him: assistant president; he was the first presidential assistant to receive such an appellation.

In the twentieth century, the secretary's functions were gradually increased. Roosevelt's principal aide, William Loeb, Jr., began to deal with the press on a regular basis. Wilson's secretary, Joseph Tumulty, controlled access to the Oval Office and functioned as an appointments secretary, political adviser, administrative manager, and public relations aide.

The number of presidential assistants also began to increase during this period. Whereas Benjamin Harrison could house his entire staff on the second floor of the White House near his own living quarters, in McKinley's administration a separate group of offices had to be constructed outside the mansion for the president's staff. When the West Wing was completed in 1909, the president's aides occupied an even larger space near the president's office.

Hoover doubled the number of his administrative aides from two to four and was also helped by more than forty others: clerks, typists, messengers, and so on. Franklin Roosevelt expanded presidential support still further. In addition to a small administrative staff, he had key aides, budgeted to the executive departments but available for White House work. The creation of a separate White House unit as part of the Executive Office enabled Roosevelt to move several of these individuals to the official White House staff, but it did not end the practice of using detailees for presidential tasks.

The Personalized White House, 1939 to the Mid-1960s

In establishing the first White House office, Roosevelt designed a highly personal staff system. Six key administrative aides performed action-forcing assignments for the president, ones that were dictated by Roosevelt's immediate needs and activities. The president ran the staff operation himself, making assignments, receiving reports, and generally coordinating activities. Presidential assistants were expected to be anonymous. They were given general responsibilities. No one exercised exclusive jurisdiction over "their" function or program. On the contrary, lines of authority were purposely blurred and assignments overlapped. Roosevelt even encouraged competition among his aides to maximize his information and extend his influence. According to Richard E. Neustadt, he enjoyed "bruised egos."[7]

The organization of Roosevelt's White House was a prescription for personal control. It satisfied Roosevelt's needs. It was not, however, a model his successors could easily follow, because it conformed to Roosevelt's style, not theirs. The increasing responsibilities of the presidency dictated a larger, more specialized arrangement.

The White Houses of Truman and Eisenhower were more highly structured and more carefully differentiated than Roosevelt's, although senior aides in both administrations continued to operate with a great deal of informality with one another and enjoyed easy access to the president. Of the two staffs, Eisenhower's was the larger and the more hierarchical. Areas of responsibility were more clearly designated. Eisenhower personally had a penchant for organization and adopted a system along the lines of the one he experienced in the military. A chief of staff oversaw the operation and regulated the flow of visitors and memoranda to the Oval Office. Unlike Roosevelt and Truman, who desired to maximize their information and involvement, Eisenhower preferred a system that relieved him of numerous detailed decisions. He desired to set general policy and then work behind the scenes to build political support for it. To some extent he used his staff as a shield to enhance his own flexibility.

While the Roosevelt, Truman, and Eisenhower operations differed somewhat in size, structure, and style, they had much in common. By contemporary standards they were small and they performed a range of activities for the president. They operated more as a personal extension of the president than as an institutional extension of the presidency. With the exception of Eisenhower's chief of staff, Sherman Adams, presidential aides did not possess the status and clout of department secretaries. Their influence stemmed from their mediating role, their ability to obtain information, and their proximity to the president. When the White House called, the president's personal interests were usually the reason why.

The Institutionalized White House, 1960s–

Changes began to occur in the 1960s. They had a profound effect not only on the way the White House was structured and how it worked but on the operation of the entire executive branch itself. Presidential aides became better known, exercised more power, and tended to monopolize the president's attention and his time. The White House grew in size, specialization, and responsibilities.

The most notable change during the Kennedy-Johnson period was the institutionalization of policy-making functions by and in the White House. Senior presidential aides became the principal policy advisers. They supervised their own staffs which were based in the Executive Office. These staffs competed with the departments and agencies for influence. The institutionalization of policy making in the White House had three major effects. First, it gave the president more discretion and allowed him to take more personal credit for policy developed by his administration. Second, it gave the presidency a capacity to formulate policy distinct from and independent of the departments and agencies. Third, it accelerated the shift of power from the departments and agencies to the White House. Cabinet secretaries were no longer the president's only advisers within their respective spheres. In some cases they were not even primary advisers. Their status declined accordingly while that of the president's assistants increased.

The growth of the White House naturally affected the relationship between the president and his aides, particularly at the middle and lower levels of the White House. Informality was replaced by a more formal arrangement. Personal interaction with the president became more difficult and less frequent for most members of the staff. The president's time became an even more precious and closely guarded commodity.

How the president related to his senior aides was still a matter of personal style. Kennedy consciously attempted to emulate Franklin Roosevelt's model but without the internal competition that Roosevelt generated. Senior Kennedy staffers, many of whom had worked together on the 1960 election campaign, were a close-knit group. They operated in an ad hoc, collegial manner. Many of the recommendations for major presidential decisions and actions were the product of group decisions.

Lyndon Johnson inherited Kennedy's staff structure and did little to change it initially beyond the appointment of several additional aides. Over the course of his administration, however, the jurisdiction of those who worked in the White House became more clearly defined. Policy advisers, in particular, exercised considerable influence within their respective spheres.

Nixon gave his senior policy aides even greater power and enlarged their functions accordingly. His White House was the most hierarchically structured and centrally managed to date. Ironically, Nixon had begun his presidency by announcing a return to a cabinet form of government in which the heads of the principal executive departments would be the prime initiators and implementors of administration policy. He contemplated a small White House staff composed of a handful of senior advisers to help him meet presidential responsibilities and provide political advice.

Nixon's personal style, however, made the operation of this type of staffing system difficult. After a relatively short time, changes were made that resulted in a large, specialized White House staff that numbered 535 at its height. Sizable policy staffs in the national security and domestic areas supported presidential activities.

The Nixon White House had clear lines of authority. It also had vertical patterns of decision making. From a managerial perspective the

White House operated smoothly. From a political perspective there were problems which impeded the president's ability to make and implement policy.

The system insulated the president from the departments and agencies, members of Congress, and even from many of his own staff. Access to Nixon was limited to a few top aides. The difficulty of communicating with the president produced dissatisfaction with White House decision-making procedures, although in the short run it also enhanced the clout of the White House aides who coordinated the processes and saw the president on a regular basis.

After his reelection in 1972, Nixon sought to expand his personal and political influence by transferring trusted White House officials to important positions in the departments and agencies. The events of Watergate aborted the plan, immobilized the White House, and raised doubts about the wisdom of having a large personal staff whose blind loyalty to the president impaired their judgment and his.

Ford and Carter both reacted to the Nixon experience in slightly different ways. Ford improved access to the president; Carter cut down on the size and status of the White House and the perquisites of those working there.

At first, both presidents also tried to structure their White Houses like the spokes of a wheel with themselves at the hub. Theoretically, top aides, operating autonomously within their own offices but collegially as a staff, were to have direct and easy access to the president. There was to be no chief of staff.

In practice, the system did not work well. Turf battles quickly erupted within the White House and between it and other executive agencies. These internal disputes plagued both administrations for most of their time in office.

Presidential advising was also adversely affected. The presentation of a wide range of options to the president was not assured. Each administration had difficulty establishing and articulating priorities. Presidential interests were not always protected.

Eventually, a more efficient operating structure did emerge in each administration. Coordination between the White House and the departments improved. Better organization for dealing with outside groups was created. Lines of authority were more clearly designated. A chief of staff was appointed. Each president began to use his own time more wisely.

The lessons of the Ford and Carter experiences were not lost on Ronald Reagan and those who advised him. What were these lessons? First, the White House had grown too large and too specialized during the 1970s to operate effectively without a tight administrative structure and efficient operating procedures. Second, while considerable autonomy was necessary for those engaged in policy making and consensus building, the individual offices in the White House that dealt with these activities had to be coordinated if the administration was to speak in a single voice and act in a unified manner. Third, although White House involvement in a host of presidential activities could not be easily reduced, the activities and initiatives of the president could be more carefully marshaled.

The Reagan approach was to maintain a large, structurally differentiated White House staff, even expanding it to include more outreach efforts. However, a more centralized management orientation was imposed. Attempts to coordinate the input of departments more effectively into the policy-making process were also made. The trick was to foster department initiatives without reducing presidential influence or abdicating White House responsibilities. To do so, the Reagan administration rejected the idea of a super cabinet and instituted its own system of councils tied to the White House through a secretariat staffed by presidential assistants.

The functional differentiation of the Reagan White House resembled that of previous administrations. The traditional policy-making and constituency-building offices that had come to be regarded as necessary were established. What was different was the attempt to distinguish between operational and policy responsibilities in the White House organization. An operational division charged with mobilizing support for the president's program reported to the chief of staff. The policy division charged with developing the program was coordinated by a counsellor to the president.

Linking the policy and operational branches was a triumvirate consisting of chief of staff, James Baker, deputy chief of staff, Michael Deaver, and counsellor, Edwin Meese. Together they orchestrated the staff's activity, monitoring the operation of the different White House units, briefing the president, and acting on his behalf. A legislative strategy group, operating out of the chief of staff's office, coordinated the administration's congressional initiatives. The principal units of the Reagan White House and the lines of authority are shown in Figure 6-2.

Trends in White House Staffing

Since its creation, the White House has undergone significant growth. It has become more specialized. Greater presidential needs and responsibilities have resulted in a larger and more functionally differentiated office. Every recent president has added to the structure. Eisenhower established a congressional liaison office; Kennedy created a national security adviser and staff; Johnson instituted a domestic counterpart; Nixon expanded both policy staffs as well as the press and com-

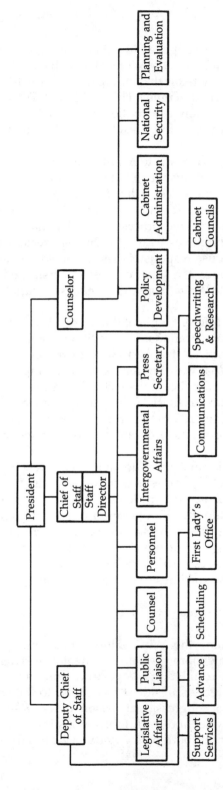

Figure 6-2. Principal Operating and Policy Offices in the Reagan White House

munications offices; Ford added an economic assistant and a modest public liaison operation; Carter vastly enlarged the public liaison function as well as created an office for intergovernmental affairs; Reagan added a new unit of planning and evaluation, a political affairs office, and a secretariat for cabinet administration. Most of these units have remained. Although the number of officials budgeted to the White House has been reduced, the functions and capabilities of the office are larger than ever.

The institutional components reflect these functions. There is little a president can do to alter them as long as the expectations and obligations he inherits remain large. He may tinker with the structure, but he cannot radically change it.

Over time, the White House becomes more important to the president. Over time, his need for a more centrally managed and efficiently run staff becomes obvious in large part because a president finds that he has to depend increasingly on his assistants and not on his department and agency heads for information, advice, and operational needs.

White House staffs tend to expand over the course of an administration, and presidents come to rely increasingly on their staffs as leaks and loyalty problems surface and as press and public criticism mounts. Ironically, the larger and more powerful the staff becomes, the more resistant it is to the president's personal control. Like any large organization, it develops a structure and a routine of its own.

Moreover, the staff operation tends to exhibit self-perpetuating tendencies. These tendencies may even be reinforced as personnel leave and subordinates are promoted to replace them. Turfs are established and protected. Standard operating procedures evolve. The White House achieves greater autonomy over priority decision making. It begins to engulf the president as he depends increasingly on it.

The president exerts the most influence on his staff at the top among his senior aides. His style affects their interaction with him, their priorities, and to a lesser extent, their operation of their offices. Whether he chooses to overlap their jurisdiction or carefully delineate their authority, to have them compete or operate in a collegial manner, to delegate decision making or get involved in the details himself is his prerogative, although there are consequences for each of these ways of doing business.

Evaluating the Staffing System

There have been three basic models which presidents have employed to organize their White Houses: the *collegial* model that Kennedy used and Carter attempted to employ; the *competitive* system which Roosevelt engineered; and the *central management* model that characterized the Nixon presidency, and to a lesser extent, the Eisenhower and Reagan White Houses. Each of these staffing arrangements has its pros and cons.

The collegial system is characterized by a relatively small group of senior aides who work informally together to advise the president and plan and coordinate administration positions and responses. The key ingredient is their working together. The system is predicated on the ability of the president's top assistants to adopt a team approach and generate loyalty and to do so without centralized direction and control.

The danger is that the team will be too cohesive, their perceptions too uniform, and their advice too complementary. The psychologist Irving Janis refers to this problem as "groupthink" and suggests that it is most apt to occur in crisis situations. What happens, according to Janis, is that the crisis generates a desire for unity among policy advisers. Critical opinions are suspended and a consensus is produced.[8]

A number of high-level administration decisions may have been influenced by this groupthink effect. The reaction to Pearl Harbor, the response to North Korean aggression, and the escalation of the war in Vietnam are three modern examples. The ill-fated decision by almost all of Kennedy's advisers to support an invasion of the Bay of Pigs in Cuba in 1961 is another. When that mission failed, President Kennedy took steps to avoid a repetition of this groupthink mentality. He would constantly question his advisers and frequently absent himself from their deliberations.

Other presidents have also tried to ensure candor and encourage dissent among their aides. Ford would request opposing points of view in meetings he attended. Carter insisted that he be presented with a wide range of options.

Occasionally a system that begins as collegial can end as competitive. Some competition is inevitable within the White House and between it and other executive agencies. It stems from the people involved, the stake they develop in their positions, the sheer size of government and the difficulty of communicating within it. A presidential candidate tends to attract highly motivated people. Frequently these people are ambitious and use their campaign positions as an entrée to the White House. Once there, they drive themselves, often becoming fatigued and lowering their tolerance in the process. Moreover, they frequently develop proprietary interests in projects with which they have been associated. These interests breed competition with those who have differing perspectives, concerns, and goals.

Presidents can moderate the effect that excessive competition produces, but they cannot eliminate it altogether. A president's style and attitudes shape those of his associates and condition the climate within the White House. This was poignantly illustrated during the Nixon years when that atmosphere could be described as brutally efficient and increasingly belligerent toward critics. Aides had to demonstrate their loyalty by proving how tough they were, how long they could work, and how many sacrifices they could make. There was little compassion from the president on down and no patience for poor quality work or missed deadlines.

Presidents Ford and Carter were more tolerant, more open, and less imposing. They permitted a looser operation. There were fewer penalties for nonperformance. Senior aides who did not produce quality staff work were circumvented rather than removed. Internal rivalries persisted, however, within the Ford White House and between the Carter White House and some department and agency heads.

Staff competition, of course, does not always adversely affect the running of the White House, although it does tend to make working conditions less pleasant. The Franklin Roosevelt experience suggests the benefits which a competitive staff structure can reap for a president interested in maximizing his information, options, and influence. A competitive system encourages diversity. It minimizes indispensibility. It keeps assistants on their toes.

On the other hand, a competitive environment also encourages self-interested behavior that can warp vision, overextend arguments, and lead to inaccurate or unbalanced presentations of issues and options. With the increasing number of participants who try to affect presidential decisions and actions, this competition naturally makes cooperation more arduous to achieve.

To coordinate advisers and relieve the president from being over-burdened with detailed decisions, a central management structure with clear lines of authority has been used. In such a system senior aides are given authority within their functional areas but report through a hierarchy that organizes and coordinates the entire operation.

The problem with such an arrangement is that it can be too efficient. Important decisions can get made before they reach the Oval Office. At the top, presidential assistants can become assistant presidents. Down the line, middle-level officials operate outside of the president's purview. If carried to an extreme, such a system can imprison the chief executive for whom it was designed.

And that is not all. A centrally managed system aggravates the proclivity toward isolation that White Houses usually evidence over time. It can work to insulate the president and those around him from public criticism. The risk, similar to the groupthink effect, is that sufficient weight will not be given to countervailing views. Bad policy decisions and poor political judgments can result.

What is a president to do? Which structural model in whole or part would best facilitate the achievement of his policy objectives and political goals and do so at the least cost? The answer depends on the president's personal style and the kinds of decisions that need to be made during his administration.

In general, those presidents who wish to maximize their involvement, their discretion, and their influence benefit more from a fluid advisory relationship. On the other hand, those who prefer to make the final decision themselves, leaving the burden of soliciting and coordinating advice to others are better served by a more formal arrangement. Kennedy, Johnson, and Carter fall into the first category; Nixon, Ford, and Reagan into the second.

Presidents who wish to depart from existing policy, particularly that which is based on strong outside interests, would tend to gain from the flexible advisory arrangement. The less formal the structure, the more quickly it can respond to changing conditions and the more easily it can produce innovative policy. Kennedy is an example of a president who had these objectives, who desired new and creative policy. Johnson is another. Nixon and Carter, in contrast, were less interested in innovation and more interested in obtaining the careful analysis that a well-staffed White House policy operation could produce.

INVOLVING THE VICE PRESIDENT

Enlargement of Responsibilities

Presidential support has been supplemented in recent years by the activities of the vice president and his staff. These activities range from providing policy advice and making political appeals, to performing a variety of ceremonial functions. It was not always this way.

For years the vice presidency was regarded as a position of little importance. It was the brunt of jokes and laments. The nation's first vice president, John Adams, complained, "My country has in its wisdom contrived for me the most insignificant office that ever the invention of man contrived or his imagination conceived."[9] Thomas Jefferson, the second person to hold the office, was not quite as critical. Describing his job as "honorable and easy," he added, "I am unable to decide whether I would rather have it or not have it."[10]

Throughout most of the nineteenth century, the vice president performed very limited functions. Other than succeeding to the presidency, the holder of this position had only one designated constitutional responsibility—presiding over the Senate and voting in case of a tie. Nor did presidents enlarge these responsibilities very much. Vice presidents played only a peripheral role within their respective administrations, so much so that when Professor Woodrow Wilson wrote his treatise on American government in the 1880s, he devoted only one paragraph to the vice president. "The chief embarrassment in . . . explaining how little there is to be said about it," Wilson concluded, is that "one has evidently said all there is to say."[11] John Nance Garner, Franklin Roosevelt's first vice president, offered perhaps the most earthy refrain in his much-quoted comment that the office was "hardly worth a pitcher of spit."

Were Adams, Jefferson, and Garner alive today, they would have to reevaluate their assessments. The position has increased enormously in importance. Roosevelt's sudden death, Eisenhower's illnesses, and Kennedy's assassination cast attention on the vice president and generated support for clarifying succession during presidential disability and for filling the vice presidency should it become vacant. These events also contributed to the enhancement of the office by encouraging presidents to do more to prepare their vice president for the number one job.

Eisenhower was the first of the modern presidents to upgrade the vice president's role. He invited Richard Nixon, his vice president, to attend cabinet, National Security Council, and legislative strategy meetings. During his illnesses, Nixon presided over these sessions. In addition, as vice president, Nixon was sent on a number of well-publicized trips for the administration.

Lyndon Johnson was also involved in a variety of activities. As John Kennedy's vice president, he helped coordinate administration efforts to eliminate racial discrimination and promote exploration of outer space. He participated in legislative lobbying efforts, joining Kennedy in the White House breakfasts for congressional leaders. He also traveled abroad on behalf of the administration. Nonetheless, Johnson was not enamored with the job. To biographer Doris Kearns, he stated:

> Everytime I came into John Kennedy's presence, I felt like a goddamn raven hovering over his shoulder. Away from the Oval Office, it was even worse. The Vice Presidency is filled with trips around the world, chauffeurs, men saluting, people clapping, chairmanships of councils, but in the end, it is nothing. I detested every minute of it."[12]

Despite their own experiences, neither Johnson nor Nixon added new responsibilities to the office, although both continued to have their vice presidents perform a variety of ceremonial, diplomatic, and political roles, such as chairing committees, making speeches, and representing the administration at international and national events. Hubert Humphrey and Spiro Agnew were not influential presidential advisers. Neither exercised major influence on the formulation of important policy initiatives within their administrations.

Nelson Rockefeller, Gerald Ford's vice president, had the opportunity to do so. He was the first to be given an important policy-making role—to oversee the development of domestic programs for the administration. Upon taking office, Rockefeller instituted a series of meetings with cabinet officials and public forums around the country to identify major issues and ways of dealing with them. Before these sessions had generated many proposals, however, Rockefeller, under criticism from conservative Republicans, announced his intention not to seek the vice presidency in 1976. He subsequently removed himself from an active policy-making and advisory role.

Whereas Rockefeller did not realize the vice president's potential as a presidential adviser, Walter Mondale did. As Jimmy Carter's vice president, he exercised considerable influence on the president and his administration. With an office in the West Wing of the White House and a staff integrated with the president's, Mondale saw Carter on a regular basis. While he had no ongoing administrative responsibilities, he was given *carte blanche* to be included in any conference, see any paper, and participate in any study that he desired. Carter's "expansive agenda" also provided opportunities for Mondale to shape policy, and he did.[13]

Mondale was instrumental in improving congressional relations. He headed a priority-setting mechanism, facilitated administration lobbying on key bills, was instrumental in the establishment of a public liaison operation in the White House, and used his own political connections to groups outside the government to improve coalition building for the president.

One reason for Mondale's success was his willingness to exercise power behind the scenes and not become the focus of public attention. He let the president take the credit. According to political scientist Paul C. Light, the Rockefeller and Mondale experiences suggest four rules that should be followed if vice presidents are to exercise influence successfully. In Light's words, these rules are:

1. Never complain to the press. One of Rockefeller's continuing problems in the Ford administration was his high profile in the press. Leaks were easily traced to the Vice President's office.
2. Never take credit from the President. The Vice President must remember who is President and who is not. According to Mondale, once Carter made a decision, "I wouldn't rag him."
3. Fall in line. No matter how much the Vice President opposes a presidential decision, he or she must support the final policy. The Vice President does not have to become a vocal supporter or lobbyist, but must fall in line like any other staffer.
4. Share the dirty work. Though the Vice President may not like endless travel (and nights in Holiday Inns, as Mondale once said), but it is all part of being a team player. Mondale, for example, was on the road 600 days during his term.[14]

George Bush, Reagan's vice president, has followed these rules. He, too, has performed a variety of symbolic and ceremonial roles. When

President Reagan wished to demonstrate his administration's concern with crisis management, drug enforcement, and government relations, he did so by appointing Bush to head committees studying these issues. Bush has also served as a personal envoy of the president's in visits to North Atlantic Treaty Organization (NATO) countries, on a fact-finding trip to Lebanon, and by attending the funeral of Soviet leader Yuri V. Andropov.

The expanded role for the vice president has resulted in an enlarged budget and supporting staff for the office. In 1961 Lyndon Johnson had only twenty professional and clerical aides. Today the vice president has approximately seventy with a budget in the neighborhood of $2 million. That staff is divided into two groups, one charged with helping the vice president perform his legislative functions and the other, his executive responsibilities. The legislative office, the smaller of the two, arranges meetings with members of Congress, and aids the vice president in his role as president of the Senate. It is located in the Senate chamber. The executive office, housed in the Executive Office Building next to the White House, handles domestic and international policy questions, administrative responsibilities, and media coverage, as well as appointments, travel, and scheduling.

Significantly, the vice president now has a West Wing office down the hall from the president's. Mondale was the first to be given such an office; the closest his predecessors had gotten was the building next door.

Having an office in the West Wing has both symbolic value and practical significance. It places the vice president at the center of power. It allows him and his staff to interact informally with others in the White House, including the president. Bush described the environment as follows:

> The atmosphere is such that I can go down there and say, "Look, after this next meeting, I'd love to stick my head in for two seconds to tell him [the president] something." I don't think I've ever done that and anyone ever said, "Don't do that," or "What do you want to talk about?" He has an openness about him in that relationship.[15]

Stepping Stone to Power

From its very modest beginnings, the vice presidency has emerged as an office of status and influence. It routinely provides its occupant with national media exposure, Washington political experience, and more recently, the opportunity to influence public policy. It has become a stepping stone to power, the most desirable position from which to seek the presidency (other than the presidency itself). Walter Mondale describes it as the best training of all for the number one job.

I don't know of any other office, outside of the presidency, that informs an officer more fully about the realities of presidential government, about the realities of federal government and the duties of the presidency that remotely compares to that of the Vice President as it is now being used.

I'm privy to all the same secret information as the President. I have unlimited access to the President. I'm usually with him when all the central decisions are being made. I've been through several of these crises now that a President inevitably confronts, and I see how they work. I've been through the budget process, I've been through diplomatic ventures, I've been through a host of congressional fights as seen from the presidential perspective.

I spent 12 years in the Senate. I learned a lot there, but I learned more here about the realities of presidential responsibilities. I learned more about our country and the world the last three years than I could any other way.[16]

The growth of the vice presidency has not only benefited the vice president, it has worked to the president's advantage as well. It has provided the president with additional institutional resources for the performance of his ceremonial and symbolic functions; it has provided him with additional personal resources for the exercise of his political and public opinion roles; and it has provided the president with additional policy advice from an official who shares his national and political perspective.

Each of these advantages, however, can become a disadvantage if the vice president rivals the president for political influence, policy direction, or personal power. Presidents want strong and loyal support, but they do not relish internal opposition, particularly from those who are a heartbeat or an election away from replacing them. That is why the vice president's influence is still dependent to a much larger extent on the president's personal needs than on the institutional responsibilities of his office.

Finally, the evolution of the vice presidency indicates why the criteria for filling the office should evolve as well. In the past, vice presidential candidates such as George Bush and Geraldine Ferraro have been selected primarily for their electibility, for their contributions to the ticket. If presidents are to obtain maximum benefit from their vice presidents today, then they must choose their running mates on the basis of their capacity to govern as well. It is as simple as that.

CONCLUSION

The founding fathers undoubtedly would have been surprised and probably dismayed by the growth and institutionalization of the presidential office. They conceived of the president as a chief executive and envisioned his need for subordinates and advisers. Still, nothing in their deliberations suggests an institution as large, complex, and influential as the presidential office has become.

Most of this growth has occurred in the twentieth century; much of it since World War II. The office has evolved considerably over the years. It has grown larger, more specialized, and increasingly politicized. It has developed an independent capacity to advise and inform the president, to formulate and prioritize policy, to orchestrate and oversee department and agency input, and to build public and congressional support.

As a result of this growth, senior presidential aides have become more important, more prestigious, and more visible. They occupy more of the president's time. In contrast, department secretaries have lost some of their status and influence, their access to the president, and their control over advice within their department's primary spheres. Instead of being the president's only or principal advisers, they became several among many.

Not only has the creation and maintenance of a presidential office occurred at the expense of the departments and agencies, but it may also have occurred at some cost to the president. While the influence of the presidency and its capacity to affect policy has undoubtedly been enhanced, the president's personal ability to oversee his staff has not. In fact, it has been made more difficult by the large size and number of functional responsibilities of the Executive Office.

One resource that presidents have utilized to lighten their institutional and personal duties has been the vice presidency. Beginning in the 1950s, vice presidents performed a variety of important diplomatic, political, and ceremonial functions for the president. Beginning in the 1960s, they assumed more active legislative and executive liaison roles. Beginning in the 1970s they exerted more influence as policy advisers, agenda setters, and coalition builders.

These activities have enhanced the status and attractiveness of the vice presidency. They have benefited the presidency as well. The fear that the vice president's influence may come at the president's expense, however, has affected the scope and conduct of the vice president's responsibilities. Ultimately, it is the president who must decide how important his vice president will be and what he will do for the administration.

In conclusion, the expansion of the presidential office has been a mixed blessing. Created to meet increased expectations, it has generated new ones. Designed to coordinate and facilitate executive-branch decision making, it has produced serious tensions between the White House and the departments. Tailored to systematize advice to the president, it has proliferated that advice and sometimes has worked to isolate the president from his advisers.

Yet, its expansion has obviously been necessary. It has been both a cause and effect of the growth of government, of the executive branch, and of the president's responsibilities. In the foreseeable future, the shape of the presidency may undergo modest adjustment, but the institution is not likely to shrink. If the past is any indication, it is likely to grow.

NOTES

1. The need to develop policy is most acute at the beginning of an administration when cabinet input is desired. Toward the end, the implementation of that policy, often the prerogative of a single department, consumes more time. The increasing constraints on a president's time resulting from periods of extended foreign travel or the quest for reelection also make it difficult for presidents to continue to meet with their cabinet on a regular basis.
2. Thomas E. Cronin, *The State of the Presidency* (Boston: Little, Brown, 1980), p. 276.
3. Ibid., p. 283.
4. Donald L. Maggin, "How Carter reorganized the EOP," *Management Review* 67 (May 1978): 16.
5. William C. Spragens, "White House Staffs (1789–1974)," in Bradley D. Nash et al. *Organizing and Staffing the Presidency* (New York: Center for the Study of the Presidency, 1980), pp. 20–21.
6. Ibid., p. 21.
7. Richard E. Neustadt, "Approaches to Staffing the Presidency," *American Political Science Review* 54 (December 1963):857.
8. Irving Janis, *Victims of Groupthink* (Boston: Houghton Mifflin, 1972).
9. John Adams, *The Works of John Adams*, ed. C. F. Adams (Boston: Little, Brown, 1850), 1:289.
10. Thomas Jefferson, *The Writings of Thomas Jefferson*, ed. P. L. Ford (New York: Putnam 1896), 1:98–99.
11. Woodrow Wilson, *Congressional Government* (1885; reprint, New York: Meridian Books, 1956), p. 162.
12. Lyndon Johnson as quoted in Doris Kearns, *Lyndon Johnson and the American Dream* (New York: Harper and Row, 1976), p. 164.
13. Paul C. Light, "Second Counts: Filling the New Vice Presidency" (paper presented at the Brookings Institution, Washington, D.C., 1984), p. 18.
14. Ibid., 20–21.
15. George Bush, quoted in Dick Kirschten "George Bush—Keeping His Profile Low So He Can Keep His Influence High," *National Journal*, June 20, 1981, p. 1097.
16. Walter Mondale as quoted in Dom Bonafede, "Mondale, the President's Preacher, Spreads the Gospel of Jimmy Carter, *National Journal*, December 1, 1979, p. 2016.

SELECTED READINGS

Cronin, Thomas E. *The State of the Presidency*. Boston: Little, Brown, 1980.

Goldstein, Joel K. *The Modern American Vice Presidency*. Princeton: Princeton University Press, 1982.

Hess, Stephen. *Organizing the Presidency*. Washington, D.C.: Brookings Institution, 1976.

Hoxie, R. Gordon. "The Cabinet in the American Presidency, 1789–1984," *Presidential Studies Quarterly* 4 (Spring 1984): 209–30.

Janis, Irving. *Victims of Groupthink*. Boston: Houghton Mifflin, 1972.

Johnson, Richard Tanner. *Managing the White House.* New York: Harper and Row, 1974.

Kessel, John H. *Presidential Parties.* Homewood, Ill.: Dorsey Press, 1984.

Light, Paul C. *Vice Presidential Power.* Baltimore: Johns Hopkins University Press, 1984.

Nash, Bradley D., with Milton S. Eisenhower, R. Gordon Hoxie, and William C. Spragens. *Organizing and Staffing the Presidency.* New York: Center for the Study of the Presidency, 1980.

Reedy, George. *The Twilight of the Presidency.* New York: World, 1970.

7

Presidential Decision Making

The essence of the president's job is making decisions—about foreign affairs, economic policy, and literally hundreds of other important matters. The task is a difficult one, and there are many obstacles to rational decision making. At the core of presidential decisions are the options and information available to him. As President Truman wrote after leaving office, "By and large a President's performance in office is as effective as the information he has and the information he gets."[1]

In his classic study of presidential power, Richard Neustadt alerted future presidents that they would need information, including tangible details, and choices—before they were preempted by the passage of events.[2] Such data would help to construct a necessary frame of reference for decision making, but no president can assume that any person or advisory system will provide him the options and information he requires. Thus, presidents must reach out widely for them.

In addition to actions the president can take in the White House, Neustadt argues, he needs to bring certain personal traits into office with him. These traits include a sense of direction for his policies and the country; a self-confident, secure personality; a sensitivity to his personal power stakes in an issue; and a sense of perspective (a sense of proportion and capacity for detachment).

It seems clear, then, that the options and information a president receives are influenced by many factors, including time constraints, the White House organization, the president's advisers and his decision-making style, the bureaucracy, and the president's personality. In this chapter we examine the ways in which these aspects of the president's environment affect his decision making. Figure 7-1 is a visual representation of the influences on presidential decision making, ranging from the broad context in which decisions take place in the outer circles to the more immediate influences on decisions in the inner circles.

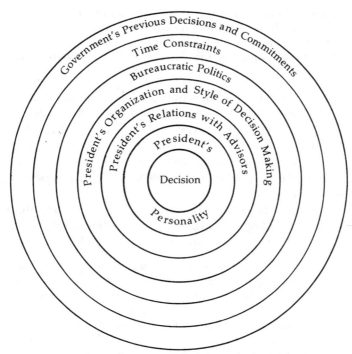

Figure 7-1. Influences on Presidential Decision Making

Before proceeding, however, it is important that we understand that the president operates under severe constraints in his decision making, no matter what his approach to making decisions. As Kennedy aide Theodore Sorensen has observed:

> We assume that the President makes decisions. . . . Presidents rarely, if ever make decisions . . . in the sense of writing their conclusions largely on a clean slate. They make choices. They select options. They exercise judgments. But the basic decisions, which confine their choices, have all too often been previously made by past events or circumstances, by other nations, by pressures or predecessors or even subordinates.[3]

Thus, the president's decisions usually fall within parameters set by prior commitments of the government that obligate it to spend money, defend allies, maintain services, or protect rights.

TIME CONSTRAINTS

The diverse obligations of the president and his top aides impose severe constraints on the amount of time they can devote to generating and evaluating options and information. According to a Carter aide:

> When the President asks to see all the potential alternatives, it is an impossible request. Not only do we have to limit the range to the few that just might work but we have to cut back to save on time. The staff already has too much to do without attempting that kind of analysis—it involves too much time.[4]

Overloaded advisers may rely on others, equally overloaded, to bring crucial information to the attention of the president. Several of President Truman's advisers believed there was a serious danger of Chinese intervention in the Korean War if the president attempted to reunite all of Korea under a non-communist government. However, no one went to him to argue that he should reverse General MacArthur's orders. Each person thought that someone else would do it.[5]

The president and his advisers rarely have the luxury of anticipating new issues. According to Zbigniew Brzezinski, President Carter's national security adviser, at the time the fateful revolution in Iran began,

> our decision making circuits were heavily overloaded. The fall of 1978 was the time of the Camp David process and its aftermath. This was also the time of the stepped-up SALT negotiations, and during the critical December days we would literally rush from one meeting, in which the most complex positions on telemetry encryption or cruise missile definition would be hammered out, to another meeting on the fate of Iran. The fall . . . was also the period of the critical phase in the secret U.S.–Chinese negotiations. . . . In addition, the crisis in Nicaragua was beginning to preoccupy and absorb us. Finally, [Secretary of State] Cy Vance was heavily involved in key negotiations abroad, notably in the Middle East, while for [Secretary of Defense] Harold Brown this was the period of most difficult battles with the President over the defense budget. . . . It was unfortunately not a time in which undivided attention could be focused easily and early on what became a fatal strategic and political turning point.[6]

Sometimes deadlines make it necessary for the president and his aides to cease the consideration of information and options and make a decision. In the words of President Reagan's budget director, David Stockman:

> I just wish that there were more hours in the day or that we didn't have to do this so fast. I have these stacks of briefing books and I've got to make decisions about specific options. . . . I don't have time, trying to put this whole package together in three weeks, so you just start making snap judgments.[7]

Because of such time limits, the less controversial parts of elaborate policies often receive too little attention and contain too much logrolling.

If a study about an issue is not available when policymakers must make a decision, the report will go unread. If the report is required by a certain date and more than one person has been engaged to produce it, there is an incentive for the participants to "soften" their views in order to reach a consensus. This in turn can mask problems inherent in the policies they recommend. Moreover, the pressure of hammering together a report under a strict deadline may make it quite incoherent.

ORGANIZATION AND STYLE OF DECISION MAKING

Each president is unique and has broad discretion in structuring his decision making in the White House. There are many ways to do this, and each has consequences for the effectiveness of the advisory system. In this section we explore the ways in which the organization and style of the presidential advisory process can affect the president's consideration of options and information.

White House Organization

Many commentators on the presidency stress the formal aspects of White House organization, but they may be overemphasized, at least as they relate to presidential decision making. As Kennedy aide Theodore Sorensen has commented,

> To be preoccupied with form and structure—to ascribe to . . . reform and structure a capacity to end bad decisions—is too often to overlook the more dynamic and fluid forces on which presidential decisions are based.[8]

There is virtual unanimity among observers of the presidency that one cannot develop an ideal organization for the White House that is appropriate for every president. The organization of the White House will inevitably reflect the personality and work habits of the incumbent. Moreover, the chief executive's personal style will dominate any organizational scheme. If a president has a penchant for acting without adequate study, he will defeat any advisory system that he has established in the White House. According to an experienced presidential aide, "The nature of the *man* is absolutely crucial and decisive, altogether overriding the issue of organization."[9]

White House structure may also reflect the goals of presidents. Those like Franklin Roosevelt, John Kennedy, and Lyndon Johnson who were concerned with producing innovative policies have displayed a tendency toward more flexible staff arrangements. They require a wide range and variety of ideas more than they need order and attention to precise details.

Organizational charts may also be misleading. When asked by a fellow White House assistant about drawing up an organization chart of the Johnson White House, Bill Moyers replied:

> Such an exercise is a gross misuse of a good man's time; nothing useful can come from it since the White House staff reflects the personal needs of the

President rather than a structural design. . . . There is no pattern to it that can be fitted to a chart.[10]

Henry Kissinger adds that the influence of a presidential assistant "derives almost exclusively from the confidence of the President, not from administrative arrangements."[11]

We should not be surprised, then, that top Carter aides sometimes "walked" their memos into the president's office when he was gone, circumventing the prescribed system for the circulation of memoranda to the president (to ensure that all relevant views were gathered), and then made sure that their memos were on top of the president's pile. President Eisenhower's decision-making process was really much more fluid than the rigid hierarchy that would appear on an organization chart. Nixon adviser John Connally regularly bypassed the White House chain of command.

Sometimes what appears to be crucial presidential consultation with his advisers is actually much less. One of the crucial moments in America's involvement in Vietnam came in July 1965 when President Johnson committed the United States to large-scale combat operations. In his memoirs Johnson goes to considerable lengths to show that he considered very carefully all the alternatives available at the time. The detailed account by one of his aides of the dialogue between Johnson and some of his advisers shows the president probing deeply for answers, challenging the premises and factual bases of options, and playing the devil's advocate. Yet a presidency scholar has argued persuasively that this "debate" was really a charade, staged by the president to lend legitimacy to the decision he already had made.[12] Richard Nixon has been accused of similar behavior.

After analyzing sources of decisional problems in foreign policy, political scientist Alexander George concluded that "there appears to be no single structural formula by which the chief executive and his staff can convert the functional expertise and diversity of viewpoints of the many offices concerned with international affairs into consistently effective policies and decisions."[13] We may confidently add that this is also true for domestic policy decisions.

On the other hand, organization does make a difference. As we saw in the previous chapter, the two most common White House organizational schemes are the hierarchical and the "spokes of the wheel." Recent presidents have found that they require a chief of staff to coordinate the flow of White House business and to give them time to focus on priorities and reflect on questions of basic strategy.

Both Gerald Ford and Jimmy Carter began their tenures trying to employ the spokes of the wheel approach, but both had to alter their organizational scheme to establish more of a hierarchical system headed by a chief of staff. The following comments by President Ford explain why this was necessary and also indicate the significance of organization:

> Initially, when I became President, I did not want to have a powerful chief of staff. . . . I was aware of the trouble . . . top assistants had caused my predecessors. I was determined to be my own chief of staff. . . . I would have five or six senior assistants with different areas of responsibility . . . and they would be able to see me at regular intervals during the day. . . . But as I was to discover soon enough, it simply didn't work. Because power in Washington is measured by how much access a person has to the President, almost everyone wanted more access than I had access to give. I wanted to have an "open" door, but it was very difficult; my working days grew longer and longer, and the demands on my time were hindering my effectiveness. Someone . . . had to be responsible for scheduling appointments, coordinating the paper flow, following up on decisions I had made and giving me status reports on projects and policy development. I didn't like the idea of calling this person chief of staff, but that in fact was the role he would fill.[14]

Hierarchical staff organizations save the president's time and promote thorough evaluation of options. Yet many observers of the presidency are concerned with such arrangements because the hierarchy that screens information may also distort it. This does not occur because presidential aides "capture" the president, however. Even in the Nixon administration, with its famed "palace guard" around the president, whatever isolation occurred in the Oval Office was with the full concurrence and encouragement of the president. The president used his staff to serve his own needs and to keep out those whom he did not want to see. Moreover, we lack systematic evidence that Nixon's chiefs of staff provided Nixon with a distorted view of the issues with which he desired to deal.

The president's staff also needs to sift issues so that only those requiring his involvement will be presented to him. If he attempts to solve all the problems that come to the White House, he will spread his and his advisers' attention too thinly, wasting time and scarce resources. In addition, the more the president does, the more problems for which others will hold him accountable. Presidents Ford and Carter had tendencies toward becoming involved in relatively minor matters and both have been criticized, even by their own aides, for lacking the appropriate breadth of vision and understanding necessary to shape and guide the government.

Presidents, such as Eisenhower, Nixon, Ford, and Reagan, often want their advisers to reach a consensus on an issue and make a recommendation to them before it receives much consideration in the Oval Office. This does not mean that they will accept the recommendation, however. Gerald Ford's description of his approach is typical:

I myself liked to have consensus developed before a problem came to my desk for decision, but then I reserved the right to go behind that consensus to find out what the differing views were in the process. In that way I got a feel as to whether it was just a weak compromise or whether it was a legitimate one that provided the best answer.[15]

The Form of Advice

Different presidents prefer to receive advice in different forms. Presidents Nixon and Carter preferred to reach their decisions on the basis of written memoranda on the pros and cons of various options. In contrast, Presidents Eisenhower, Kennedy, Johnson, Ford, and Reagan used memos to focus discussion but frequently discussed issues with advisers in relatively open settings.

There are advantages and disadvantages of both the verbal and paper approaches. The latter requires that options that go to the president be thoroughly "staffed out," that is, that relevant officials comment upon them after careful analysis. As Henry Kissinger explains, if this does not occur,

> the danger is real that plausibility is confused with truth and verbal fluency overwhelms cool analaysis. . . . in the absence of staff work, decisions may be made which the facts do not support, where individuals talk to impress and not to elucidate at a time when precision is crucial. The temptation . . . is . . . to allow a fleeting and superficial consensus to ratify unexamined assumptions. There are the simultaneous risks of paralysis and recklessness. Principals cannot really know the consequences of their recommendations unless those recommendations have been translated into specific operational terms.[16]

Reviewing advice on paper also saves the president time and protects the confidentiality of communications. It may also provide an outlet for those who find it difficult to express themselves directly to the president to articulate their views. The most vociferous critic out of the president's presence can become the meekest lamb when meeting the president personally. This inhibition in speech is not unusual. President Carter found that people's oral skills often deserted them when they were in the Oval Office. He had a somewhat similar experience of his own in his first debate with President Ford in 1976.

On the other hand, the requirement that communications to the president be written and thoroughly researched may deny the chief executive access to some useful information and ideas. Some aides simply resist writing memos, as did Jody Powell, one of President Carter's closest advisers. Face-to-face discussions with advisers may also provide the president with information that is not reflected in the written word. Direct confrontation between advocates of diverse positions allows the participants to pinpoint their critiques of each other's positions and raise relevant follow-up points. Oral discussions also provide opportunities for advisers to highlight crucial nuances in arguments and for presidents to learn the intensity of officials' views. This may alert the chief executive to the level of support he may expect from officials who oppose his ultimate decision. In addition, some ideas, especially those that are highly sensitive, can be best or perhaps only advanced personally and informally in the give-and-take of conversation, and some may not be ready for memoranda but deserve mention so the president will be aware of the fullest range of options.

In order for face-to-face discussions among advisers and the chief executive to be useful, the president must be able to accommodate the interpersonal tensions inherent in an advisory system of close give-and-take. Yet not all presidents possess this tolerance. Richard Nixon's personality was not amenable to dealing with oral confrontations. He dreaded meeting new people, especially if they were in a position to rebuff or contradict him. To avoid tension, he spoke elliptically and had a tendency to agree with whomever he was speaking (only to disavow it later). Thus, the president conducted as much business as possible by memos, in which he was more likely to express his true views and less likely to meet with opposition. To avoid confrontations he sometimes called carefully constructed meetings that included one dissenter and began by agreeing with that person and then allowed himself to be talked out of that position, leaving the holdout isolated and more likely to join in a consensus view.

Nixon's aversion to open disagreement both affected the quality of his decision-making process and led him to alter policy decisions to achieve consensus. According to national security adviser Henry Kissinger:

> So much time, effort, and ingenuity were spent in trying to organize a consensus of the senior advisers that there was too little left to consider the weaknesses in the plan or to impose discipline on the rest of the government. There was no role for a devil's advocate. At every meeting, to gain the acquiescence of the potential recalcitrant, Nixon would offer so many modifications that the complex plan he was seeking to promote was eventually consumed. . . . Each of these steps may have been minor; the cumulative impact was considerable.[17]

The oral approach also carries the danger that the president will decide on the basis of the last person he talked to instead of on the basis of careful consideration of alternatives. President Ford sometimes did this, as when he agreed to support Secretary of Labor John Dunlap on a common situs picketing bill, only to face the opposition of the rest of his cabinet and top advisers when the bill passed. The president vetoed the bill amidst embarrassing publicity on his policy reversal, angering labor interests, which felt betrayed, and undercutting his secretary of labor, who resigned over the matter.

Another requirement for the oral approach to be effective is that the president must not dominate the discussion. If he does, he may not devote sufficient attention to the advice he receives and may influence that advice by his comments. According to Hamilton Jordan, Jimmy Carter's White House chief of staff,

> I had learned when Jimmy Carter was Governor that if I wanted to change his mind or challenge him on something that was important or complicated, it was best to do it in writing. If I went into his office to argue with him, armed with five reasons to do something, I would rarely get beyond point one before he was aggressively countering it. I seldom got to the second or third point.[18]

Similarly, another Carter aide found the president formidable in face-to-face encounters and that the president often persuaded him to his view, even though upon reflection he concluded the president was actually wrong on the matter. When personally confronted, the president's ego may be on the defense; written differences of opinion may be easier to accept.

Multiple Advocacy

Closely related to the form in which the president receives advice is the range of options he receives and the effectiveness with which they are presented. The president should not be dependent upon a single channel of information. This occurred when the president and other high officials, including the Joint Chiefs of Staff, relied upon the CIA's estimates of the success of the 1961 invasion of Cuba at the Bay of Pigs. It occurred again in 1965 when the president relied upon the U.S. embassy in the Dominican Republic for the information that led to the U.S. invasion of the island. Moreover, the key assumptions of alternatives should be evaluated by officials who did not develop them and thus have no personal stake in them. Only the CIA evaluated the Bay of Pigs plan, with disastrous consequences.

Quality decision making requires more than that the president be presented with a diversity of views. It is also necessary that each point of view be represented by an effective advocate. This is not always the case, however, because there are differences among advisers in persuasive skills, intellectual ability, policy expertise, power, status, standing with the president, and analytical staff support. These disparities may distort the decision-making process by giving some viewpoints an undue advantage. As Kennedy aide Theodore Sorensen has observed, "The most formidable debater is not necessarily the most informed, and the most reticent may sometimes be the wisest."[19]

Nevertheless, presidents are susceptible to being influenced by the form as well as the substance of an argument. For example, observers found that Daniel Moynihan, a liberal Democratic adviser to Richard Nixon, was often more influential with the president than Nixon's old friend and staunch Republican Arthur Burns. According to a Nixon aide:

> He [Moynihan] was one of the very few people on the White House staff who had operated in the Washington bureaucracy and understood it. He had an extensive network of contacts throughout HEW [Department of Health, Education and Welfare] and OEO [Office of Economic Opportunity] . . . who flooded him with research data and other information. And he had great persuasive resources. In the sea of dark gray and blue that surrounded Nixon, Moynihan, in his cream-colored suit and red bow tie, gleamed like a playful porpoise. He was a charming Irish rogue, a delightful dinner companion, a fascinating teller of tales. His presence lighted the gloom of national policy deliberations, and even his opponents liked to have him around. The President liked to read his memoranda, sometimes even searching through the pile on his desk to find them.[20]

Similarly, executive-branch officials favoring escalation in the war in Vietnam had several advantages in advocating their views. They were in daily contact with each other and had access to substantial staff aid and classified information. They could therefore coordinate their activities, prepare elaborately detailed predictions of the consequences of escalation, and be sure of a serious hearing. The dissenters from this view generally worked at lower levels in the hierarchy, did not coordinate their activities with those of other dissenters, and proceeded without adequate staff assistance. They could only offer personal judgments on various aspects of the war and hope someone would listen.

Multiple advocacy forces a larger number of issues to the top, that is, to the president; debate and give-and-take on a large number of issues require a substantial commitment of time on the part of both the president and his staff, and time is a scarce commodity in the White House. According to a Ford assistant, "Multiple advocacy is very nice on paper. It just can't work in the White House. We don't have the time to make sure all the advisors have access to the President. This is not a day-care; it is survival of the fittest."[21] In addition, the president may not be interested in all his advisers have to offer on a policy about which he cares little.

Multiple advocacy also runs a considerable risk of increasing staff conflict. The president must engage in the delicate balancing act of being in firm control of the process of decision making while encouraging free and open discussion. This is difficult enough to accomplish while he is considering options. It is even more of a challenge after he decides on a course of action, because it it not uncommon for both winners and losers among presidential advisers to be less than gracious and turn to backstabbing and leaks to the press. Some political scientists have suggested that the president needs a process manager to balance the resources of his advisers and strengthen the weaker advocates, ensure that all options are articulated and have effective advocates, set up additional channels of information, arrange for independent evaluations of decisional premises and options when necessary, and generally monitor the decision-making process and identify and correct any malfunctions. This delicate role can easily be undermined if the custodian is also a policy adviser, presidential spokesman, enforcer of decisions, administrative operator, or watchdog for the president's power stakes. He must remain an "honest broker" concerned with the process of advising the president. He must also keep his own staff small so that it will not become specialized and circumvent established channels of advice.

In some decision-making stiuations an adviser may adopt the role of "devil's advocate" in order to provide a challenge to the dominant point of view. The devil's advocate may relieve some of the stress of decision making because officials feel they have considered all sides of an issue, and there may be some public relations benefits for the president when the word is spread that he considered the full range of views. Decision makers may also benefit from listening to and rebutting challenges to their course of action, and those least enthusiastic about a decision may be more willing to join in a consensus view if there has been debate before it is reached.

Nevertheless, the devil's advocate does not necessarily improve the quality of White House decision making. Since the devil's advocate is playing a role and is not a true dissenter, he is unlikely to persist in opposition or try to form coalitions or employ all his resources to persuade others. He is not really engaged in a truly competitive struggle. Moreover, officials may discount ahead of time the comments of one who persistently plays the devil's advocate role. Yet if devil's advocacy is not routinized, there is no assurance it will be operating when it is needed to provide balance to an argument.

Even if a president chooses to consider a range of viewpoints, he may not benefit fully from them. For example, Gerald Ford has been criticized for falling back on his experience as a legislator and reaching decisions by weighing the views of others and then leaning in the direction of the consensus opinion. Presidential authority is diluted when the chief executive bases decisions on the number of advisers on a side rather than on his own informed judgment.

PRESIDENTIAL RELATIONSHIPS WITH ADVISERS

The president requires the services of personal aides to carry out his duties. Since he must rely so heavily upon his aides and work so closely with them, he naturally chooses persons of similar attitudes and compatible personalities. Moreover, strong personalities, which typically characterize presidents, create environments to their liking and weed out irritations.

Many, perhaps most, people find it difficult to stand up to the president and disagree with him. There is evidence that President Reagan's aides had growing doubts about his economic policies even in 1981 but did not relay them to the president until after the program was enacted. At times advisers are strong advocates of a position before a meeting with the president and then completely switch their arguments during the meeting after they learn the president has accepted the opposite view. It was because of this phenomenon that President Kennedy often absented himself from meetings of his advisers during the Cuban missile crisis. He wanted everyone to feel free to speak his mind.

Sometimes advisers find it difficult to disagree with the president because of the latter's strong, dynamic, or magnetic personality. These traits are certainly not unusual in successful politicians, especially presidents. Former White House assistant Chester Cooper has written that President Johnson often polled his foreign policy advisers one at a time to discover their views on policies regarding the war in Vietnam. Each

"All those in favor say 'Aye.'"
"Aye."   "Aye."   "Aye."
     "Aye."   "Aye."

Source: Drawing by H. Martin; © 1979 The New Yorker Magazine, Inc.

would respond "I agree," although Cooper, and undoubtedly others, did *not* agree. Cooper even dreamed of answering no, but he never did.[22] Other Johnson administration officials report of a similar tendency of those around the president to tell him what they thought he wanted to hear about the war rather than what they really thought.

One reason for the reluctance of presidential aides to challenge the president is that they are completely dependent upon him for their jobs, their advancement, and the gratification of their egos. Cabinet members are nearly as dependent, although they may have support in Congress or from interest groups. Because aides usually desire to perpetuate their positions, they may refrain from giving the president "unpleasant" information or from fighting losing battles on behalf of their principles. Even Nixon's White House chief of staff H. R. Haldeman felt that he had to survive in his own job and therefore failed to fight sufficiently the dark side of the president's character.

Thus, the president often finds it difficult to evoke critical responses from those around him. Gerald Ford observed:

> Few people, with the possible exception of his wife, will ever tell a President that he is a fool. There's a majesty to the office that inhibits even your closest friends from saying what is really on their minds. They won't tell you that you just made a lousy speech or bungled a chance to get your point across. . . . You can tell them you want the blunt truth; you can leave instructions on every bulletin board, but the guarded response you get never varies.
>
> And yet the President—any President—needs to hear straight talk. He needs to be needled once in a while, if only to be brought down from the false pedestal that the office provides. He needs to be told that he is, after all, only another human being with the same virtues and weaknesses as anyone else. And he needs to be reminded of this constantly if he's going to keep his perspective.[23]

All of these tendencies may be reenforced by a president who "punishes" aides who present options and information he does not like. Lyndon Johnson was such a person. He forced top aides and officials to leave his administration for dissent over Vietnam, and he went so far as to reduce contact with such key people as Secretaries of Defense Robert McNamara and Clark Clifford and Vice President Hubert Humphrey.

Johnson's press secretary George Reedy observed that the White House had an inner political life of its own. Thus, the staff carefully studied the president's psyche to gain and maintain access to him. They wanted to be around when there was good news to report and discreetly absent when the news was bad, hoping someone else would receive the blame. Naturally, this gamesmanship helped to distort Johnson's view of reality.

Richard Nixon had little interest in critiques of his weak points, and those who attempted to criticize him did not maintain their influence very long. Even as secure and personable a president as Franklin Roosevelt is reported to have allowed only those who did not challenge him to remain around.

The dampening effect that behavior like Johnson's or Nixon's can have on discussions even outside the Oval Office can be substantial. Office of Congressional Relations chief Lawrence O'Brien and Vice President Hubert Humphrey were in constant contact for months before they became aware of each other's views on Vietnam. Because President Johnson equated criticism with disloyalty, even the highest officials in the White House kept their dissent to themselves.

Strong presidents may also, in effect, tell their advisers what advice to offer them. In 1965 President Johnson complained to the army chief of staff that he needed solutions other than bombing to stop the Communists from taking over South Vietnam and sent the general, who was reluctant to escalate the war, to Vietnam. When he returned, the president urged the Joint Chiefs of Staff to propose measures "to kill more VC" (Viet Cong). It is not surprising that five days later the chiefs submitted their first recommendation for direct use of American troops in combat.

Richard Nixon sometimes sought out advisers who would tell him what he wanted to hear. He turned to John Connally for "tough" advice, such as when he wanted someone to urge him to mine the harbor at Haiphong, North Vietnam. A Nixon aide once observed the president and Connally cruising down the Potomac on the presidential yacht, the *Sequoia*, as Nixon was trying to talk his adviser into recommending that he institute wage and price controls on the economy.

A president with heightened fears of security leaks may place loyalty above either competence, independence, or openness as a criterion for evaluating and relying upon advisers. He may also control the information flow tightly and keep even insiders in the dark. One of the reasons President Johnson relied so heavily on a group of five or six high officials (called the Tuesday lunch group) to advise him on the Vietnam War was that he felt the larger National Security Council leaked too much information. According to Secretary of State Dean Rusk, "The Tuesday luncheons were where the really important issues regarding Vietnam were discussed in great detail. This was where the real decisions were made. And everyone there knew how to keep his mouth shut."[24]

Ironically, one inhibition on freedom of dissension in the White House and in the upper levels of the bureaucracy is public opinion. If the president allows open discussion of policy views, then there will inevitably be disagreement. This disagreement is often then presented in the press as evidence that the president is not in control and that the White House lacks a sense of direction. Thus, by being open the president may lose some public support and by being closed to options and information he may make poor decisions.

Feuding and infighting for power and access to the president among ambitious aides is also an obstacle to rational decision making. This rivalry takes several forms. One of the most common techniques is to attack rivals through leaks to the press that they are out of favor with the president or not competent to carry out their duties. Sometimes the leaks place competitors for power in a favorable context but one that will displease the president, who may value credit and publicity for himself rather than his aides. In recent years the Nixon, Ford, and Reagan administrations stand out for the extent of their internal feuding and infighting.

All of this feuding encourages self-interested behavior by presidential advisers that may distort their vision and cause them to overextend their arguments and present unbalanced discussions of options and their consequences to the president. There is also a tendency for competing advisers to seek to aggrandize influence and monopolize the counsel on which presidential decisions are based, providing insufficient information, analysis, and deliberation for decisions. Staff rivalry also detracts from the efficiency of White House operations as it wastes time and lowers staff morale. Moreover, publicity on feuding in the White House can embarrass the president when it is covered in the press, which it inevitably is.

High officials in Washington know that their ability to function effectively with the bureaucracy depends on being known for their effectiveness with the president. Former secretary of state Dean Rusk argues that "the real organization of government at higher echelons is . . . how confidence flows down from the President."[25] To maintain their reputations for effectiveness with the president, officials may not strongly advocate positions that they consider sound if they feel the president is unlikely to adopt their proposals. An official does not usually want to be known as one whose advice the president rejected.

An additional potential hindrance to sound advice for the president is the loss of perspective by White House aides. Because working in the White House is a unique experience, a narrowing of viewpoint may easily occur. Especially for top aides, the environment is luxurious, secure, and heady, and the exercise of power is an everyday experience. The potential for isolation is real, and the chief executive must fight these insulating tendencies. President Johnson was very sensitive about his aides losing perspective, and thus he closely controlled the use of White House perks and stripped his staff of pretensions with a "merciless persistency."[26]

An adviser's conception of his job influences his delivery of information and options. President Eisenhower's secretaries of defense, Charles Wilson and Neil McElroy, considered themselves managers of the department and did not become heavily involved in disputes over foreign policy or strategic doctrine. By contrast, Secretary of Defense Robert McNamara adopted an aggressive stance as an adviser. But

McNamara's colleague, Secretary of State Dean Rusk, did not consider it his job to participate in policy disputes with his colleagues or the president. In fact, many observers thought he did not effectively present State Department views on Vietnam or other foreign policy issues.

BUREAUCRATIC POLITICS AND DECISION MAKING

A primary source of options and information for the president is the bureaucracy. Yet it is not a neutral instrument. Individuals and the agencies they represent have interests of their own to advance and protect and do not necessarily view issues from the president's perspective. Moreover, the structure of the flow of information and the development of options may also hinder decision making in the White House.

Organizational Parochialism

Government agencies have a tendency toward inbreeding. The selective recruitment of new staff helps to develop homogeneous attitudes. Those attracted to work for government agencies are likely to support the policies carried out by those agencies, whether they be in the fields of social welfare, agriculture, or national defense. Naturally, agencies prefer hiring like-minded persons. Within each agency the distribution of rewards creates further pressure to view things from the perspective of the status quo. Personnel who do not support established organizational goals and approaches to meeting them are unlikely to be promoted to important positions. Moreover, all but a few high-level policymakers spend their careers within one agency or department. Since people want to believe in what they do for a living, this long association strongly influences the attitudes of bureaucrats.

Related to longtime service in an agency is the relatively narrow range of each agency's responsibilities. Officials in the Department of Education, for example, do not deal with the budget for the entire national government but only with the part that pertains to their programs. It is up to others to recommend to the president what is best for national defense, health, or housing. With each bureaucratic unit focusing on its own programs, there are few people to view these programs from a wider, national perspective.

Influences from outside an agency also encourage parochial views among bureaucrats. When interest groups and congressional committees support an agency, they expect continued bureaucratic support in return. Since these outsiders generally favor the policies the bureaucracy has been carrying out all along (which the outsiders probably helped initiate), what they really want is "more of the same."

All of these factors result in a relatively uniform environment in which policy making takes place. Intraorganizational communications pass mainly among persons who share similar frames of reference and who reinforce bureaucratic parochialism by their continued association.

The influence of parochialism is strong enough that even some presidential appointees, who are in office for only short periods of time, adopt the narrow views of their bureaucratic units. The Nixon White House felt that even close associates of the president were "captured" by the bureaucracy. The dependence of such officials on their subordinates for information and advice, the need to maintain organizational morale by supporting established viewpoints, and pressures from their agencies' clienteles combine to discourage high-ranking officials from maintaining broad views of the public interest.

President Nixon observed that "it is inevitable when an individual has been in a Cabinet position or, for that matter, holds any position in Government, after a certain length of time he becomes an advocate of the status quo; rather than running the bureaucracy, the bureaucracy runs him."[27] Thus, parochialism can lead officials to see different faces on the same issue. In 1977 President Carter asked Congress for an authorization for a 20 percent cutback in wheat acreage and the placing of several million tons of food and feed grains in reserve. This proposal followed an intense internal debate in which the Department of Agriculture, reacting to the demands of farmers, wanted an even bigger cutback; the Treasury Department and the Council of Economic Advisers opposed any cutback out of concern for future consumer prices and the export potential of the United States should food shortages develop; and the State Department was concerned about the proposal's effect on international negotiations regarding an international grain reserve. In other words, policymakers in different bureaucratic units with different responsibilities saw the same policy in a different light and reacted differently to it.

It was to combat this parochialism that President Reagan went to considerable lengths to insulate his new cabinet appointees from the traditional agency arguments in defense of programs the White House had slated for cuts. They received their initial briefings from the president and citizens groups rather than the bureaucracy, were often assigned deputies with close personal and ideological ties to the White House, and were given little time to react to the president's proposals.

Maintaining the Organization

As a result of parochialism in the bureaucracy, career officials come to believe that the health of their organization and its programs is vital to the national interest. In their eyes, this well-being depends in turn on the organization's fulfilling its missions, securing the necessary resources (personnel, money, authority), and maintaining its influence. Organizational personnel can pursue their personal quests for power and prestige, the goals of their organization, and the national interest all at the same time without perceiving any role conflicts. Moreover, policymakers in different organizational units are prone to see different faces on the same issue because of their different organizational needs.

The single-mindedness of policymakers attached to various agencies causes them to raise options and gather information that support the interests of their organization and avoid or oppose options and information that challenge those interests. In this way, the goals of maintaining an organization may displace the goals of solving the problems for which the organization was created. As one former high White House official has written, "For many cabinet officers, the important question was whether their department would have the principal responsibility for the new program—not the hard choices that lay hidden within it."[28]

Within most organizations there is a dominant view of the *essence* of the organization's mission and the attitudes, skills, and experience employees should have to carry out that mission. Organizations usually propose options they believe will build upon and reinforce the essential aspects of their organizations. Although its bombing campaigns had not had unqualified success in previous wars, the air force lobbied for strategic bombing and deep interdiction in the war in Vietnam. One way to do this was to argue for bombing as a central feature of U.S. policy in order to show its utility. The lack of success only reinforced the air force's efforts to step up bombing even further; the air force never admitted it was not accomplishing its objectives. An organization will also vigorously resist efforts of others to take away, decrease, or share its essence and the resources deemed necessary to realize that essence.

In their struggles over roles and missions, bureaucrats may distort the information and options provided to senior officials. In Vietnam the air force and navy were each concerned that the other might encroach on its bombing missions: the navy was also concerned about justifying the high cost of its aircraft carriers. Thus, they competed in their efforts at air warfare. The aspect of this interservice competition that was most damaging to the accuracy of the perceptions high-level decision makers had of American success in the war was the battle over the relative effectiveness of each service's air warfare. Each was concerned for future budgets and missions and could not let the other get the upper hand. Thus, each exaggerated its own performance, expecting the other to do likewise.

Budgets are another vital component of strategies to maintain an organization. This is true for grant-awarding agencies, as well as for agencies with large operational capabilities like the military services and the

Department of Agriculture. Because staff within governmental organizations generally believe their work is vital to the national interest, and because conventional wisdom stipulates that a larger budget enables an organization to perform its functions more effectively, units normally request an increase in funding and fight decreases. The size of a group's budget not only determines the resources available for its services but also serves as a sign of the importance others attach to the organization's functions.

Agency personnel also examine any substantive proposal to ascertain its impact on the budget. They rarely suggest adding a new function to their responsibilities if it must be financed from monies already allocated for ongoing activities. Moreover, components of large organizations, like units in the military or the Department of Health and Human Services, are concerned about maintaining or increasing their percentage of the larger unit's budget.

An organization's staff are likely to raise and support options that give them autonomy. In their view they know best how to perform their essential mission. They resist options that would place control in the hands of higher officials or require close coordination with other organizations. This desire for autonomy helps explain why several agencies independently gather and evaluate national security intelligence from their own perspective. As Richard Nixon complained when he was disappointed in the intelligence reports he received, "Those guys spend all their time fighting each other."[29]

Because organizations seek to create and maintain autonomous jurisdictions, they rarely oppose each other's projects. This self-imposed restraint reduces the conflict between organizations and correspondingly reduces the options and information available to the president. In dealing with their superiors, the leaders of an organization often guard their autonomy by presenting only one option for a new program. The rationale is that if higher officials cannot choose among options, they cannot interfere with the organization's preference.

Once an agency of government has responsibility for a program, it has a tendency to evaluate it positively. Thus,

> After the American presence in Vietnam was increased and the programs enlarged . . . each bureaucratic organization then had its own stakes. The military had to prove that American arms and advice could succeed. The Foreign Service had to prove that it could bring about political stability in Saigon and build a nation. The CIA had to prove, especially after the Bay of Pigs fiasco, that it could handle covert action and covert paramilitary operations lest it chance having its operational missions in general questioned. The Agency for International Development (AID), like the State Department and the military, had to prove that pacification could work and that advice and millions of dollars in assistance could bring political returns. . . . by

1965 almost all career professionals became holier than the Pope on the subject of U.S. interests in Vietnam.[30]

Organizational and Personal Influence

To achieve the policies they desire, organizations and individuals seek influence. In pursuing power, officials often further distort the processes of generating options and gathering information for the president. One way for organizations to increase their influence is to defer to one another's expertise. The operations of all large-scale organizations, including governments, require a considerable degree of specialization and expertise. Those who possess this expertise, whether within executive agencies or congressional committees, naturally believe they know best about a subject in their field, and they therefore desire primary influence on the resolution of issues in their subject area. Because each set of experts has a stake in deference to expertise (they each receive benefits from it), reciprocal deference to expertise becomes an important theme in policy making. One result of this reciprocity is that fewer challenges to expert views are aired than might otherwise be the case.

For several decades there has been an implicit agreement between the Departments of State and Defense that each would stay out of the other's affairs. During the war in Vietnam the State Department often took no part in shaping war policies and refrained from airing its views on many of them. Contributing to this restraint was Secretary of Defense McNamara's adamant belief that the State Department should not challenge the military's appraisal of the actual progress of the war. Once when the director of the State Department's Bureau of Intelligence and Research attempted to do so, McNamara forcefully elicited a promise from Secretary of State Dean Rusk that such a challenge would not recur. He thus deliberately blocked the flow of information on the war. This meant that policymakers had to defer to Defense Department assessments that were often inaccurate and biased toward military rather than political solutions.

Although deference to expertise is not always a satisfactory way of resolving conflicts in policy making, it is often the only possible course of action. Governmental agencies are the sole source of data and analysis on many issues. As their work becomes more and more specialized, it becomes more and more difficult to check their information and evaluations. This problem is exacerbated by a need for secrecy on most national security policies, which makes it necessary to limit even further the number of participants in the policy-making process.

To take full advantage of deference to expertise and to increase their influence further, organizations seek to prevent their own experts from disseminating conflicting information and options. Contrary information and evaluations undercut the credibility of a unit's position. Moreover, by presenting several real options, a unit increases the range of possible policy decisions and commensurately decreases the probability that the option favored by the unit's leaders will be selected. Thus, the Joint Chiefs of Staff rarely disagree in their recommendations. The relevant departments never really presented President Carter options on welfare reform, in part because they were afraid he would select an alternative they opposed. No one would insist to the president that reform would be costly, because they feared he would then reject reform efforts.[31]

If there are disagreements among the experts of an organizational unit, efforts to produce an appearance of unanimity can reduce the experts' recommendations to broad generalizations. A record of agreement on the least disputed common denominators usually fails to mention many controversial points that may be crucial to the ultimate success of the policy at issue. When compromise positions reach the president in a form that suggests a unified consensual judgment, they can give him a false sense of security because he may lack an awareness of the potential problems buried within the recommendations. For example, in the early days of bombing North Vietnam the army wanted to show infiltration was increasing (to bolster its requests for more troops), while the air force wanted to show success in stopping it. They worked out a compromise in which the Defense Intelligence Agency (DIA) each month reported that "enemy infiltration continued at a rate higher than last month; however, the cumulative effect of United States bombing has seriously degraded his ability to mount a large-scale offensive." It should be noted that there was no evidence the enemy was considering such an offensive.[32]

For bureaucrats interested in their own careers, the prospect of a deferred promotion or even dismissal makes them reluctant to report information that undercuts the official stands of their organizations. The example of the Foreign Service officers who frankly (and accurately) reported on the strength of the Communists in China during the late 1940s is not quickly forgotten in the bureaucracy. They were driven from the Foreign Service for allegedly pro-Communist sympathies. Twenty years later, the Foreign Service's memory of these incidents may have inhibited candid reporting on the weakness of the South Vietnamese regime and the strength of the Viet Cong. In addition, senior officials at the State Department are still complaining about the Foreign Service's lack of creativity.

Some officials anticipate sanctions even in the absence of their being exercised. One of the most embarrassing incidents of Jimmy Carter's early presidency was the scandal surrounding Bert Lance, his close friend and the director of the Office of Management and Budget. Lance eventually resigned under pressure after details of his business and personal financial dealings were made public. For our purposes the question is, Why did the president not know of these problems?

At least a large part of the answer seems to be that officials responsible for reviewing Lance's background soft-pedaled the reports in an effort to cultivate the goodwill of the new administration. The deputy comptroller general (who was acting comptroller) later testified that he knew of Lance's problems but downplayed them to avoid losing his job. Indeed, he hoped to be appointed comptroller general. It also appears that the relevant U.S. attorney closed his investigation of Lance early, over the objections of several of his subordinates, hoping not to irritate the new president so that he could keep his job and qualify for a federal pension.

At times an illusion of competition conceals a basic consensus. Rivalry among the military organizations has reached legendary proportions, but much of it is superficial. Interorganizational competition among the armed services has primarily been over jurisdictional matters (which service should do what) rather than over questions of substantive policy.

Experts also create an illusion of competition when they agree to compare their preferred action to infeasible alternatives. Lyndon Johnson's advisers have been criticized for juxtapositioning in 1964 their favored option of bombing North Vietnam against two phony options (in effect, blow up the world or scuttle and run).

Bureaucratic Structure

The structure of administrative organizations is one of the factors that impedes the flow of options and information to higher-level decision makers. Most bureaucracies have a hierarchical structure, and the information on which decisions are based usually passes from bottom to top. At each step in this ladder of communication, personnel screen the information from the previous stage. Such screening is necessary because presidents cannot absorb all the detailed information that exists on an issue and must have subordinates summarize and synthesize information as it proceeds upward. The longer the communication chain, the greater the chance that judgments will replace facts; nuances or caveats will be excluded; subordinates will paint a positive face on a situation to improve their own image or that of their organization; human error will distort the overall picture; and the speculations of "experts" will be reported as fact.

Screening, summarizing, and human error are not the only pitfalls in the transmission of information. When subordinates are asked to transmit information that can be used to evaluate their performance, they have a tendency to distort information to put themselves in the most favorable light. Body counts of killed enemy soldiers in Vietnam, made by the troops who had faced them in combat, were notoriously unreliable and became even more so as they were padded at each higher level of the military hierarchy to demonstrate successful operations. Equally inaccurate were the estimates of bombing damage, made by the pilots flying the bombing missions.

Following the North Vietnamese Tet offensive in 1968, the United Nations ambassador, Arthur Goldberg, visited Vietnam for the president and was briefed on U.S. performance. According to Goldberg,

> The briefing indicated that the enemy had lost 80,000 men killed in the Tet offensive. I asked the general what the normal ratio of killed to wounded would be. He said, as I recall, ten to one. And I said that was a big figure and that . . . could we consider three to one to be a conservative figure for those rendered ineffective by wounds? And he said yes. And then I asked the question, "How many effectives do you think they have operating in the field?" And he said something like 230,000. And I said, "Well, General, I am not a great mathematician but with 80,000 killed and with a wounded ratio of three to one, or 240,000 wounded, for a total of 320,000, who the hell are we fighting?"[33]

Subordinates sometimes distort facts by not reporting those that indicate danger. President Kennedy was not apprised of the following problems with the contingency plan for the Bay of Pigs: the men participating in the invasion had not been told to go to the mountains if the invasion failed; there was a large swamp between the beach and the mountains which supposedly offered refuge; and only one-third of the men had received guerrilla training. Instead, he was simply informed that if the invasion failed, the men would go to the mountains and carry out guerrilla warfare. At other times subordinates may exaggerate the evidence in support of their favored alternative in order to increase the probability of its being chosen.

Even in the hierarchical executive branch, the president cannot depend on information being centralized. There was a great deal of information pointing to the Japanese attack on Pearl Harbor, for example, but it was never fully organized. No one brings forward all the political, economic, social, military, and diplomatic considerations of a policy in a recognizable manner for the president's deliberation because the bureaucracy relevant to any policy is too decentralized and too large and produces too much paper to coordinate information effectively.

The president may attempt to compensate for the problems of hierarchy be sending personal aides or outsiders to assess a situation directly and propose options. However, the person assigned to the task may determine the nature of the report more than the situation itself. When President Kennedy sent General Maxwell Taylor and Walt Rostow on a fact-finding mission to South Vietnam, their recommendations for military action could have been predicted on the basis of their views before they left on the trip. Moreover, the president cannot bypass senior officials very often without lowering their morale and undercutting their operational authority.

President Kennedy's chief White House national security adviser, McGeorge Bundy, ordered that cables to the State Department, the Central Intelligence Agency (CIA), and the Pentagon be sent directly to the White House and not just to the Washington headquarters of those departments where they could be summarized and analyzed for transmittal to the president. But this practice could not correct the distortion that may have gone into the cables in the first place, and someone had to summarize and synthesize the tremendous volume of information before it reached the president.

Organizations use routines or standard operating procedures (SOPs) to gather and process information in a methodical fashion. However, the character of the SOPs may delay the recognition of critical information, distort the quality of information, and limit the options presented to policymakers.

In the case of the Cuban missile crisis, several weeks before the president was aware of the missiles there was a good deal of information in the United States intelligence system pointing to their presence. But the time required by SOPs to sort out raw information and double check it delayed recognition of the new situation. Organizational routines also masked signs forecasting the 1974 leftist coup in Portugal. Officials from the intelligence services of the CIA, the Defense Department, and the State Department testified after the event that their routines did not focus much attention on Portugal, and they could not shift personnel rapidly to a new area of concern.

SOPs affect not only *if* and *when* information is collected but also the substance of the information. In Vietnam the military's concentration on the technical aspects of bombing caused it to substitute a set of short-run physical objectives for the ultimate political goals of the war. Military reports emphasized physical destruction per se rather than the political impact of such destruction. The enemy's capacity to recruit more men or rebuild a structure never seemed to enter into the calculations.

Standard operating procedures give disproportionate weight to information entering the system from regular channels. For example, in the early stages of the Vietnam War, the routines gave undue credence to the reports of South Vietnamese officials without questioning whether the information favored South Vietnamese interests more than those of the United States and without giving proper weight to the opposing views of journalists and others outside the regular flow of information.

SOPs structure the process of decision making by preselecting those who will be asked for advice and predetermining when they will be asked. There are routine ways of invading foreign countries and of determining agency budgets. Some persons will be involved at earlier stages than others, and some will be viewed as having more legitimate and expert voices in policy discussions. When Lyndon Johnson limited his circle of personnel advisers on the war in Vietnam to a half-dozen top officials, those at a lower rung in the foreign policy hierarchy found it harder to have their dissents heard. In addition, there was little opportunity for others in the cabinet to challenge the war policy because they were not in the right decision-making channels.

Purely analytic units often have problems in being heard. According to Henry Kissinger,

> I can think of no exception to the rule that advisers without a clear-cut area of responsibility eventually are pushed to the periphery by day-to-day operators. The other White House aides resent interference in their spheres. The schedulers become increasingly hesitant in finding time on the President's calendar.[34]

Thus, information is most likely to influence policy making if the position of those who have it ensures they must be consulted before a decision is made.

Standard operating procedures also affect the nature of the alternatives proposed by bureaucratic units. They typically propose their standard ways of doing things rather than innovative solutions to problems. These standard policies may not be appropriate for the problem at hand. The original mission of the Economic Development Administration was to aid economically depressed *regions* such as Appalachia, principally by developing the economic infrastructure (including roads and electric power) and attracting industry. When the agency tried to aid the *city* of Oakland, it based its proposals on what it considered standard alternatives. But Oakland was in a prosperous area with a highly developed economic infrastructure, a great deal of manufacturing, and plenty of capital. The city's problems were those of unemployed minorities, and the SOPs of the Economic Development Administration did not allow the agency to deal with those types of problems.

As a result of problems with established routines, presidents often create special task forces of "outside" experts to develop new programs. Such bodies, brought together for a new purpose, are less likely than established agencies to be blinded by SOPs.

Because only decision makers directly responsible for a policy are normally consulted on "secret" matters, fewer advisers contribute to secret deliberations than to debate on more open issues. This reduces the range of options that are considered in a secret decision and limits the analysis of the few options that are considered. The secrecy of President Johnson's Tuesday lunch group, which made the important decisions on the war in Vietnam, prevented an advance agenda. Thus, decisions were made without a full review of the options beforehand. Secrecy also makes it easier for those directly involved to dismiss (intentionally or unintentionally) the dissenting or offbeat ideas of outsiders as the products of ignorance, which is unfortunate because secret information is often inaccurate or misleading. President Kennedy wished he had not been successful in persuading the *New York Times* not to publish the plans for the Bay of Pigs invasion; he afterward felt that publicity might have elicited some useful critiques.

PERSONALITY AND DECISION MAKING

The structure of the presidential advisory system, the relationships among the president and his staff, and general patterns of bureaucratic behavior are not the only factors that affect presidential decision making. The personal needs, values, and beliefs of those involved also leave their mark. We have already seen that personality affects how presidents organize the White House and acquire information. In this section we focus on how the personal traits of presidents and their advisers affect their processing of information and consideration of options.

Managing Inconsistency

The environment in which the president operates is complex and uncertain. Yet the human mind is not comfortable with these characteristics. It has certain cognitive needs and prefers stable views, not continuous consideration of options. Lyndon Johnson became obsessed with the correctness of his views on the war in Vietnam. He simply had to feel he was right or else he would have to open himself to the pain of reliving his old decisions and options.

It does not follow that the president should not continue to consider options and information once a policy decision has been made. The decision may have been a poor one. Yet busy aides are typically reluctant to risk irritating an even busier president by attempting to reopen a question he thought was settled. In the words of two close observers of decision making:

> Once a president sets policy, it becomes a herculean task for senior officials and bureaucrats to argue against it. Presidents have to make clear up and down the line that they want to hear criticisms and alternatives from their subordinates before they read them in the press, and that dissenters will be rewarded as well as team players. They should press for agreement on coherent policies but also leave the door open to revising judgment.[35]

It is especially difficult to review decisions regarding national security while fighting is taking place. Speaking from experience, Vice President Hubert Humphrey wrote: "Once a wartime decision has been made and men's lives have been lost, once resources are committed—and most dangerously, once a nation's honor has been committed—what you are doing becomes almost Holy Writ. Any division, dissension, or diversion is suspect."[36]

It is very difficult for any president to maintain an open mind throughout his consideration of advice. Just before he ordered the attempt to rescue the American hostages in Iran, President Carter cornered his foreign policy advisers and told them, "Before I make up my mind, I want to know your reactions." But according to one of his closest advisers, "The President might say—or even believe—he hadn't made up his mind, but I know he had."[37]

Decision makers often experience stress as they try to cope with the complexity of decisions, especially in times of crisis. In a revealing incident President Warren G. Harding explained to a friend:

> John, I can't make a damn thing out of this tax problem. I listen to one side and they seem right, and then God! I talk to the other side and they seem just as right, and there I am where I started. I know somewhere there is a book that would give me the truth, but hell, I couldn't read the book. I know somewhere there is an economist who knows the truth, but I don't know where to find him and haven't the sense to know him and trust him when I did find him. God, what a job![38]

Fortunately, most of those occupying the Oval Office have had a greater intellectual capacity than Harding.

The mind simplifies in order to deal with the complexities of the world and resolves uncertainty by ignoring or de-emphasizing information that contradicts existing beliefs. These mental activities occur through unconsciously operating inference mechanisms that function to some extent in everyone's mind. Those mechanisms may have as great an influence on a person's beliefs as objective evidence. Consequently, most policymakers remain unreceptive to a major revision of their beliefs in response to new information, especially if they have had success in the past with applying their general beliefs to specific decisions or if they have held their beliefs for a long time. Moreover, they are unlikely to search for information that challenges their views or for options contrary to those they advocate.

One relatively simple technique for managing inconsistency consists in attaching very negative consequences to alternatives, as top policymakers did to the option of "scuttle and run" from Vietnam. By concluding that the role of the United States in international relations would be seriously diminished by such action, decision makers dismissed an alternative that was widely advocated outside the government.

Related to this mechanism of predicting undesirable consequences is that of making inferences based on selected indicators to show that a particular situation could not possibly occur. If policymakers accept this inference of impossibility, there is no need for them to consider information pointing to the "impossible" situation, alternatives to prevent or respond to it, or what effect it would have on the alternatives that *are* being considered. Before the massive North Vietnamese Tet offensive in early 1968, planning regarding the war was based on the assumption that no such offensive was possible; top U.S. officials paid little heed to information that contradicted this assumption. Data on the size and firepower of South Vietnamese forces, the number of hamlets pacified, and the number of Communists killed provided welcomed positive feedback on U.S. policy and were accepted as signs of progress; policymakers never realistically weighed those indicators against the size of the task at hand. Another, classic example of the inference of impossibility was the belief that the Japanese could not attack Pearl Harbor. Because they were not expecting an attack, U.S. officials did not notice the signs pointing toward it. Instead, they paid attention to signals supporting their current expectations of enemy behavior.

Another means of reducing inconsistency and thereby decreasing the pressure to consider alternatives is similar to what we commonly term "wishful thinking." Information inconsistent with ongoing policy may be de-emphasized by believing that undesirable conditions are only temporary and will ameliorate in response to current policy. Officials used this type of reasoning to garner support for the continued escalation of the war in Vietnam. All that was needed to force the enemy to succumb, they argued, was to keep up the pressure. More generally, in the face of contradictory or ambiguous indicators of the progress of the war, they listened most carefully to the optimistic rather than the pessimistic reports or the caveats to positive assessments and hoped for the best. As two authorities on decision making on the war in Vietnam have written, "the human mind's capacity to perceive and balance evidence with perfect rationality is limited, and men are peculiarly able to combine pessimism and optimism, doubt and confidence, recognition of negative evidence and persistence in positive assumptions, all at the same time."[39]

Yet another means of resolving uncertainty and simplifying decision making is reasoning by analogy. The conclusions supported by this type of reasoning seem to have strength independent of the available evidence, probably because the analogies simplify and provide a coherent framework for ambiguous and inconsistent information.

Metaphors and similes simplify a complex and ambiguous reality by relating it to a relatively simple and well-understood concept. If one is then used as the basis of an analogy, the possibilities for error are considerable. Part of the theoretical underpinning for the war in Vietnam was often characterized as the "domino theory" of international relations, which holds that the United States must prevent countries from falling to the Communists because once one country falls, the one next to it will fall, and then the next—just like falling dominoes. The simplistic nature of the metaphor indicates how much room exists for differences between it and reality.

Decision makers often employ historical analogies. One frequently used to support opposition to the imperialistic ventures of other nations is "Munich," referring to the attempts of the allies to placate Hitler by legitimizing his control over Czechoslovakia. The problem is that one can infer too much from similarities that may only be superficial. Analogies are never perfect and may not hold under all conditions. Sometimes what appears to some to be "appeasement" may be a sensible response to a complex action by another nation.

Officials also use analogies when they project their own thinking onto others, reasoning that the latter will see things as they do. Such reasoning is not always correct, however. Economic forecasts, such as those by President Reagan's advisers in 1981 that people would work harder and save and invest more in response to a large tax cut—something that did not happen, at least in the following two years—are often criticized for being based on assumptions that people will respond to economic policy in a "rational" manner. In 1950 President Truman and his advisers concluded that the Chinese would not intervene in the Korean War because it would not be in their interests (as the U.S. saw them) to do so.

Discrediting the source of information and options is another means of reducing the complexity and resolving the contradictions with which policymakers have to deal. At first, President Johnson handled the critics of his war policy quite well, inviting them to his office and talking to them for hours. But as opposition increased and polls indicated a dip in his popularity, he responded to criticism by discrediting its source. He maintained that Senator William Fulbright (the chairman of the Senate Foreign Relations Committee) was upset at not being named secretary of state; the liberals in Congress were angry at him because he hadn't gone to Harvard, because the Great Society was more successful than the New Frontier, and because he had blocked Robert Kennedy from the presidency; the columnists opposed him to make a bigger splash and to follow James Reston and Walter Lippman; and the young were hostile because they were ignorant.

At other times presidents may simply avoid information they fear will force them to face disagreeable decisions that complicate their lives and produce additional stress. Richard Nixon is a classic example. In his memoirs he writes of putting off confronting his own attorney general, John Mitchell, because of his hypersensitivity and desire not to know the truth about Mitchell's involvement in Watergate in case it was unpleasant. He just could not bring himself to talk to Mitchell personally. Similarly, the president found it too painful to discuss Watergate with experienced officials he had brought back to the White House to help restore confidence in his administration. It was easier to rely solely on those personally close to him in dealing with the scandal. Referring to Nixon's ability to engage in self-delusion and avoid unpleasant facts, White House chief of staff H.R. Haldeman argues that the "failure to face the irrefutable facts, even when it was absolutely clear that they were irrefutable, was one of our fatal flaws in handling Watergate at every step."[40]

Each of the cognitive processes that reduce uncertainty and complexity can be a reasonable response to a situation. The point is that people are likely to rely on them not by conscious choice but because of the human need for certainty and simplicity. In each of the examples cited above the president and his advisers made use of an inference mechanism that diverted their attention from vital information and led them to ignore appropriate options. Potential actions that were considered disastrous would have been far less so than those that were taken, situations thought to be impossible actually occurred, hoped-for results from policies never materialized, inferences were based upon inappropriate analogies, and worthwhile criticism was rejected. Thus, the inference mechanisms that top decision makers employ to manage inconsistency clearly may jeopardize rational decision making.

Maintaining Self-Esteem

In addition to simplicity and certainty, presidents and their aides have other psychological needs for which they must provide. One of the most important of these is the need to maintain self-esteem. We all have egos and we all have defensive mechanisms to protect them. Presidents with similar values and skills of political leadership can have very different careers and behave quite differently, depending on inner self-confidence and self-esteem. Personal needs may be displaced onto political objects and influence decision making.

A president may manifest ego defenses when he denies that his actions caused a problem or that there is a problem, assertions that make it unnecessary to reconsider policies or examine new options. Lyndon Johnson's discrediting of the sources of criticism served to protect his self-esteem. The more his popularity plunged, the more he needed evidence that *he* was not at fault. The intellectuals, the press, the liberals, and the Kennedys provided convenient scapegoats for the causes of his problem, and his feeling of martyrdom temporarily increased his self-esteem. He found protection in the world of his imagination.

When the 1965 Watts riot broke out, Johnson at first refused to look at the cables, take calls, or make decisions about how to deal with the crisis. He simply refused to acknowledge that it was happening. His first perceptions of the rioting seemed to be in terms of the harm the rioters had done to *him*, indicating a connection between the event and Johnson's ego. Although he sometimes seemed to understand the frustrations behind the rioting in Watts and other cities, he never seemed to understand that he might bear partial responsibility for the conditions causing those frustrations.

A prominent psychological analysis of the presidency is that of political scientist James David Barber.[41] He develops four "character" types based on two dimensions: (1) how much energy the president invests in the presidency and (2) the affect of the president toward this activity. These types, he argues, represent clusters of personality characteristics that produce significant behavioral tendencies.

Barber particularly focuses on those who are active and positive about themselves and those who are active but negative about themselves. "Active-positive" presidents, including Franklin D. Roosevelt, Harry Truman, John Kennedy, Gerald Ford, and Jimmy Carter, are secure, self-confident men who are open to new people and experiences and have a capacity for personal growth and a willingness to admit mistakes. They focus on achieving results they see as beneficial to the country but are flexible in pursuit of their goals and are pragmatic and willing to compromise.

"Active-negative" presidents, such as Woodrow Wilson, Lyndon Johnson, and Richard Nixon, on the other hand, are insecure personalities who pursue inner phantoms to try to compensate for their insecurity. They are driven, compulsive individuals who desire power for its own sake to compensate for their low self-esteem, but they never achieve a sense of satisfaction. Barber argues that these presidents are tragedy-prone figures who undergo a process of rigidification in their decision making when an issue poses a challenge to their self-esteem.

Although Barber's analysis is creative and provocative, it has received a substantial amount of criticism from other political scientists. They argue, for example, that he has not tied his diagnoses closely to psychological theory, that his concepts are vague, that his classifications of presidents are sometimes in error, and that all modern presidents are "active." Moreover, many analysts feel Barber has largely ignored coping strategies that presidents may use to deal with their inner needs and fails to consider alternative explanations for the behavior he discusses. Finally, an analysis that focuses on pathological behavior tells us little about presidential decision making in the absence of unspecified conditions that trigger rigidification, especially when we realize that secure presidents may have deficient values, beliefs, or political skills, and many successful people are successes because they are driven by insecurity.

The president and his advisers also reduce uncertainty (and its accompanying doubt and anxiety) and sustain self-esteem by operating as part of a group. In a cohesive group, particularly one that operates under stress, is insulated from outside experts, and has a leader who actively promotes his own alternatives, unconscious processes sometimes occur that produce what one author has termed "groupthink."[42] Under conditions of groupthink, a group's members become excessively optimistic about the effectiveness and morality of their decisions while underestimating the difficulty of their task or discounting the skill and morality of those opposing them. As a result, they disregard warnings that would force them to reconsider their assumptions and thereby take greater risks than they would agree to take individually.

To protect itself from uncertainty and anxiety the group may develop an illusion of unanimity. It may also impose direct pressure on any member who challenges the group's illusions or commitments. More subtle self-censorship of deviation from the group's apparent consensus may take place, and self-appointed "mindguards" whose task is to protect the group from adverse information may emerge.

These group dynamics bolster the personality characteristics that incline leaders to overlook the unfavorable consequences of their actions. The tendencies toward conformity are usually strongest in those who are most fearful of disapproval and rejection. And the more threats there are to the self-esteem of members of a cohesive group, the more they will tend to seek consensus at the expense of critical thinking.

Other Psychic Needs

Presidents have many other psychic needs that may affect their consideration of information and options. Much remains unclear about this subject, but the scope and significance of these needs are great. For example, the bombing of North Vietnam may have satisfied several of President Johnson's psychological needs. It provided relief from the pressures and debates of decision making; it was an action that accomplished something. The bombing also helped him ease his fear of appearing weak, and it supported his self-deceiving conjecture that the end of the war was in sight, which would enable him to free funds for his Great Society programs.

World View

Presidents and their aides bring to office sets of beliefs about politics, policy, human nature, and social causality, in other words, beliefs about how the world works and why it does so. We sometimes refer to a set of such beliefs as a "world view." These beliefs serve decision makers by providing a frame of reference for raising and evaluating policy options, filtering information and giving it meaning, establishing potential boundaries of action, and supplying an approach to decision making itself. Beliefs also help busy officials cope with complex decisions to which they can devote limited time, and they predispose them to act in certain directions.

During the Cuban missile crisis President Kennedy precluded diplomatic and nonmilitary responses to the situation at the outset and actually considered a fairly narrow range of military options (contrary to much conventional wisdom). He believed that the presence of Soviet missiles in Cuba greatly increased the threat to the national security of the United States and that the Soviet Union would remove the missiles only if forced to do so by the threat of American military sanctions.

Although sets of beliefs are inevitable and help to simplify the world, they can be dysfunctional as well. This is perhaps most dramatically illustrated in the case of surprise attacks by one country on another. In these situations beliefs often interfere with effective analysis, because "the primary problem in major strategic surprise is not intelligence but political disbelief."[43]

Let us turn to the October 1973 war in the Middle East as an illustration. Months before it occurred, American (and Israeli) foreign policy officials had plenty of information pointing to an attack on Israel by Egypt and Syria, but they dismissed this evidence and concluded that war was improbable. Even as military operations were taking place, intelligence agencies discounted them as indicators of full-scale war. The fundamental problem in analysis was the preconceptions of officials, which led them to misinterpret the available facts. Since they knew Egypt and Syria could not win such a war, their definition of rationality led them to conclude that the two countries would not initiate one. They ignored the possibility of the two countries starting an unwinnable war for psychological reasons, that is, to restore their self-respect.

Decisions about U.S. participation in the war in Vietnam were also molded by the views of top officials. The premises they shared included the contentions that a non-Communist Vietnam was important to the security and credibility of the United States; the war-torn country was a critical testing ground of U.S. ability to counter Communist support for wars of national liberation; communism was a world conspiracy; South Vietnam would fall to the North without American aid; and if South Vietnam fell to communism, other countries would shortly follow. When these views were coupled with President Johnson's more general premises that all problems were solvable and that the United States could do anything, U.S. intervention was a foregone conclusion.

The doctrinal consensus on Vietnam made it difficult to challenge U.S. policy. Defining doctrine in terms of necessity foreclosed policy options. As a result, "no comprehensive and systematic examination of

Vietnam's importance to the United States was ever undertaken within the executive branch. Debates revolved around how to do things better and whether they could be done, not whether they were worth doing."[44]

A president's view of a problem and proposed response to it is especially likely to foreclose consideration of alternatives in a crisis when there is a premium on rapid and decisive action. The North Korean invasion of South Korea in 1950 and the civil war in the Dominican Republic in 1965 were seen by Presidents Truman and Johnson, respectively, as threats to the United States, and they decided virtually immediately that American armed forces would be employed in those countries.

CONCLUSION

The president faces an enormously difficult and complex task in making decisions on a wide range of issues. He must work within the parameters of the national government's prior commitments and is further constrained by the limited time he can devote to considering options and information on any one policy. In addition, the president faces a number of other potential hazards in reaching decisions.

There are a variety of ways for him to organize the White House and acquire advice. Not all of them are equally useful in ensuring that the president is presented with a full range of options, each supported with effective advocacy. Moreover, the president may experience problems with his aides' reluctance to present candid advice, which may be aggravated by the president himself, and with their efforts to increase their influence.

Bureaucratic politics also play a role in determining the options and information the president receives and the form in which he receives it. Agencies and their personnel inevitably have narrower perspectives than the White House and desire to maintain and expand their programs, status, and influence. Those ambitions often bias the options and information they present to the White House. The ways in which bureaucratic units collect, process, and transmit options and information and the secrecy that sometimes accompanies them may add further distortion to what the president sees.

The personal traits of presidents and their advisers also leave their mark on decisions. The complexity and uncertainty surrounding most presidential decisions create a stressful situation and a need for consistency. In response, presidents and their aides often resort to unconsciously operating inference mechanisms that may be inappropriate for the situation at hand. Decisions may also threaten the president's self-esteem and activate ego defenses that may or may not aid him in maintaining his perspective on an issue. All officials bring certain world views into office with them, outlooks that make thinking about public affairs manageable but that also may screen out or distort useful options and information.

It is important that the president be sensitive to the many obstacles to effective decision making and attempt to avoid or compensate for them as best he can, realizing that perfectly rational decision making is unattainable.

NOTES

1. Harry S. Truman, "Limit CIA Role to Intelligence," *Washington Post*, December 22, 1963, p. 11.

2. Richard E. Neustadt, *Presidential Power: The Politics of Leadership from FDR to Carter* (New York: Wiley, 1980), chaps. 6 and 7.

3. Theodore Sorensen, quoted in John C. Donovan, *The Politics of Poverty*, 2nd ed. (Indianapolis: Pegasus, 1973), p. 111.

4. Quoted in Paul C. Light, *The President's Agenda: Domestic Policy Choice from Kennedy to Carter* (Baltimore: Johns Hopkins University Press, 1982), p. 179.

5. Neustadt, *Presidential Power*, pp. 106–7.

6. Zbigniew Brzezinski, *Power and Principle: Memoirs of a National Security Adviser, 1977–1981* (New York: Farrar, Straus, and Giroux, 1983), p. 358; see also p. 396.

7. David Stockman, quoted in William Greider, "The Education of David Stockman," *Atlantic*, December 1981, p. 34.

8. Theodore C. Sorensen, *Decision-Making in the White House: The Olive Branch or the Arrows* (New York: Columbia University Press, 1963), p. 3.

9. Bryce Harlow, quoted in Emmet John Hughes, *The Living Presidency: The Resources and Dilemmas of the American Presidential Office* (Baltimore: Penguin, 1973), p. 345.

10. Bill Moyers, quoted in Larry Berman, "Political Scientists in Presidential Libraries: How Not to Be a Stranger in a Strange Land" (paper presented at the Annual Meeting of the American Political Science Association, Washington, D.C., September 1979), n. 52.

11. Henry Kissinger, *White House Years* (Boston: Little, Brown, 1979), p. 47; see also p. 1455.

12. Larry Berman, *Planning a Tragedy: The Americanization of the War in Vietnam* (New York: Norton, 1982).

13. Alexander L. George, "The Case for Multiple Advocacy in Making Foreign Policy," *American Political Science Review* 66 (September 1972): 766.

14. Gerald R. Ford, *A Time to Heal: The Autobiography of Gerald R. Ford* (New York: Harper and Row, 1979), p. 147; see also p. 186.

15. Gerald R. Ford, "Imperiled, Not Imperial," *Time*, November 10, 1980, p. 31.

16. Kissinger, *White House Years*, p. 602; see also p. 40.

17. Ibid., p. 996.

18. Hamilton Jordan, *Crisis: The Last Year of the Carter Presidency* (New York: Putnam, 1982), p. 42.

19. Sorensen, *Decision-Making in the White House*, p. 62.

20. Martin Anderson, *Welfare: The Political Economy of Welfare Reform in the United States* (Stanford, Calif.: Hoover Institution Press, 1978), p. 6.

21. Quoted in Light, *The President's Agenda*, p. 200.

22. Chester L. Cooper, *The Lost Crusade: America In Vietnam* (New York: Dodd, Mead, 1970), p. 223.

23. Ford, *A Time to Heal*, pp. 187–88.

24. Dean Rusk, quoted in Leon V. Sigal, *Reporters and Officials: The Organization and Politics of Newsmaking* (Lexington, Mass.: Heath, 1973), p. 147.

25. "Mr. Secretary: On the Eve of Emeritus," *Life*, January 17, 1969, p. 62B.

26. Jack Valenti, *A Very Human President* (New York: Norton, 1975), pp. 115–16.

27. Richard M. Nixon, *Public Papers of the Presidents: Richard Nixon, 1972* (Washington, D.C.: U.S. Government Printing Office, 1974), p. 1150.

28. Harry McPherson, *A Political Education* (Boston: Little, Brown, 1972), p. 298.

29. H. R. Haldeman, *The Ends of Power* (New York: Times Books, 1978), p. 107.

30. Leslie H. Gelb with Richard K. Betts, *The Irony of Vietnam: The System Worked* (Washington, D.C.: Brookings Institution, 1979), p. 239.

31. Laurence E. Lynn, Jr., and David def. Whitman, *The President as Policymaker: Jimmy Carter and Welfare Reform* (Philadelphia: Temple University Press, 1981), pp. 116, 269.

32. Patrick J. McGarvey, *C.I.A.: The Myth and the Madness* (Baltimore: Penguin, 1973), p. 130; see also pp. 28–30, 125.

33. Arthur Goldberg, quoted in Herbert Y. Schandler, *The Unmaking of a President: Lyndon Johnson and Vietnam* (Princeton: Princeton University Press, 1977), pp. 260–61.

34. Henry Kissinger, *Years of Upheaval* (Boston: Little, Brown, 1982), p. 74.

35. Gelb with Betts, *The Irony of Vietnam*, p. 365.

36. Hubert H. Humphrey, *The Education of a Public Man: My Life and Politics* (Garden City, N.Y.: Doubleday, 1976), p. 351.

37. Jordan, *Crisis*, p. 250.

38. Warren G. Harding, quoted in William Allen White, *Masks in a Pageant* (New York: Macmillan, 1928), pp. 422–23.

39. Gelb with Betts, *The Irony of Vietnam*, p. 130.

40. Haldeman, *The Ends of Power*, p. 34.

41. James David Barber, *The Presidential Character: Predicting Performance in the White House*, 2nd ed. (Englewood Cliffs, N.J.: Prentice-Hall, 1977).

42. Irving L. Janis, *Groupthink: Psychological Studies of Policy Decisions and Fiascoes*, 2nd ed. (Boston: Houghton Mifflin, 1982).

43. Richard K. Betts, *Surprise Attack: Lessons for Defense Planning* (Washington, D.C.: Brookings Institution, 1982).

44. Gelb with Betts, *The Irony of Vietnam*, p. 190; see also pp. 353–54, 365–67.

SELECTED READINGS

Allison, Graham. *Essence of Decision: Explaining the Cuban Missile Crisis.* Boston: Little, Brown, 1971.

Anderson, Paul A. "Decision Making by Objection and the Cuban Missile Crisis," *Administrative Science Quarterly* 28 (June 1983): 201–22.

Barber, James David. *The Presidential Character: Predicting Performance in the White House.* 2nd ed. Englewood Cliffs, N.J.: Prentice-Hall, 1977.

Berman, Larry. *Planning a Tragedy: The Americanization of the War in Vietnam.* New York: Norton, 1982.

Betts, Richard K. *Surprise Attack: Lessons for Defense Planning.* Washington, D.C.: Brookings Institution, 1982.

Buchanan, Bruce. *The Presidential Experience: What the Office Means to the Man.* Englewood Cliffs, N.J.: Prentice-Hall, 1978.

Destler, I. M. *Presidents, Bureaucrats, and Foreign Policy: The Politics of Organizational Reform.* Princeton: Princeton University Press, 1972.

Downs, Anthony. *Inside Bureaucracy.* Boston: Little, Brown, 1967.

Edwards, George C., III, and Ira Sharkansky. *The Policy Predicament: Making and Implementing Public Policy.* San Francisco: Freeman, 1978.

Gelb, Leslie H., with Richard K. Betts. *The Irony of Vietnam: The System Worked.* Washington, D.C.: Brookings Institution, 1979.

George, Alexander L. *Presidential Decisionmaking in Foreign Policy: The Effective use of Information and Advice.* Boulder, Colo.: Westview Press, 1980.

George, Alexander L., and Juliette L. George. *Woodrow Wilson and Colonel House: A Personality Study.* New York: Dover, 1964.

Halperin, Morton H. *Bureaucratic Politics and Foreign Policy.* Washington, D.C.: Brookings Institution, 1974.

Janis, Irving L. *Groupthink: Psychological Studies of Policy Decisions and Fiascoes.* 2nd ed. Boston: Houghton Mifflin, 1982.

Kessel, John H. "The Structures of the Reagan White House." *American Journal of Political Science* 28 (May 1984): 231–258.

March, James G., and Herbert A. Simon. *Organizations.* New York: Wiley, 1958.

Neustadt, Richard E. *Presidential Power: The Politics of Leadership from FDR to Carter.* New York: Wiley, 1980.

Simon, Herbert A. *Administrative Behavior: A Study of Decision-Making Processes in Administration Organization.* 2nd ed. New York: Free Press, 1957.

Sorensen, Theodore C. *Decision-Making in the White House: The Olive Branch or the Arrows.* New York: Columbia University Press, 1963.

Steinbruner, John D. *The Cybernetic Theory of Decision: New Dimensions of Political Analysis.* Princeton: Princeton University Press, 1974.

8

Domestic Policy Making

The framers of the Constitution gave the president a policy role, but they did not expect him to dominate the process. Yet that is precisely what has occurred. Seizing on the initiative which the Constitution provides, and which their central perspective, institutional structure, and political support facilitate, presidents have become chief policymakers. Today, the public expects the president to establish and achieve national goals. He is expected to redeem campaign promises, to respond to policy emergencies, and to propose on a regular basis solutions to the country's social, economic, and political ills. Failure to address critical issues and rectify national problems will likely result in public criticism and even electoral defeat the next time around.

The president's domestic policy role did not evolve gradually. It developed in response to severe policy problems during the twentieth century. In the first part of the chapter we describe those responses, chronicling the growth of the president's role.

In the second part we discuss the mechanism and processes that were established to help meet these enlarged responsibilities. Initially we focus on the work of the Office of Management and Budget (known as the Bureau of the Budget prior to 1970) in the clearance and coordination of presidential policy initiatives emanating from the executive departments and agencies. We then turn to the White House and to the development of a domestic policy office. In this section we also examine the impact of differing organizational models, policy goals, and personal styles on the policy making. Finally, we look at policy-making strategies: How can external forces be accommodated? How can internal agendas be constructed and accomplished? How can an administration in office for a limited period of time devise and implement long-range policy goals? We place particular emphasis on the politics of agenda building—the content, packaging, and timing of domestic policy proposals.

THE DEVELOPMENT OF A POLICY ROLE

The framers of the Constitution did not envision the president as chief domestic policymaker. They did, however, anticipate that the institution would include a policy-making role. Within the framework of the separation of powers, the president was given the duty to recommend necessary and expedient legislation. He also had latitude in the execution of the law. Taken together, this duty and that discretion provided the constitutional basis upon which a substantial policy-making role could be built.

For the first one hundred years, presidents recommended measures, took positions, and occasionally even drafted bills, but they did not formulate domestic policy on a regular basis. Beginning with Theodore Roosevelt and continuing with Woodrow Wilson, presidential participation in the policy-making process expanded. Theodore Roosevelt developed a close relationship with the Speaker of the House, Joseph Cannon. The two consulted each other frequently on most major policy initiatives. Cannon's power as Speaker and party leader enabled him to gain support for proposals Roosevelt initiated or favored.

Woodrow Wilson expanded the president's role even further. Seeing his responsibilities as analogous to the British prime minister's— to propose an integrated set of measures which addressed social and economic problems and then to utilize his personal and political influence to get them enacted—Wilson personally supervised the development of policy in his administration. He chose priorities, helped formulate legislation, and exhorted his cabinet and members of Congress to support it. Wilson himself went to Congress on several occasions and was the first president since John Adams to use the State of the Union address to articulate his goals directly to Congress.

Wilson's program, known as New Freedoms, included labor measures, tariff reform, and consumer protection. He introduced legislation that led to the creation of the Federal Reserve system. Working primarily with the leaders of his party on Capitol Hill, he secured the passage of many of his domestic proposals, including the Adamson Act (which provided an eight-hour day for railroad workers), the Clayton Anti-Trust Act, and the act that established the Federal Trade Commission. He led the country into World War I but was unable to obtain Senate approval for the Treaty of Versailles, the agreement ending hostilities.

Wilson's Republican successors (Harding, Coolidge, and Hoover) did not expand the presidency's policy-making responsibilities. Their conservative philosophy undoubtedly influenced their conception of a limited role. This philosophy, combined with the dispersal of power in

Congress, did not encourage extensive legislative activity or an aggressive presidential posture. From the perspective of the 1920s, the Republican interlude was a return to "normalcy," as Warren Harding termed it. From today's perspective it was a brief respite in the growth of the president's domestic role.

Institutionalizing Presidential Initiatives

Franklin Roosevelt, more than any other individual, enlarged the president's domestic role and shaped the contemporary expectations of the job. Coming into office in the throes of a depression, Roosevelt believed it absolutely essential for the president to take the policy initiative. In his first inaugural address, he stated:

> I am prepared under my constitutional duty to recommend the measures that a stricken Nation in the midst of a stricken world may required. These measures or such other measures as Congress may build out of its experience and wisdom, I shall seek within my constitutional authority to bring to speedy adoption.[1]

Having a sizable Democratic majority that was inclined to support his initiatives and being the kind of person who was not averse to using his personal influence to get them adopted, Roosevelt quickly and dramatically became deeply involved in the policy process.

During the first one hundred days of the New Deal, Roosevelt and his aides formulated a series of measures to address the nation's most pressing economic problems. Designed to regulate and stimulate financial, agricultural, and business sectors, these proposals, which Congress enacted into law, also created new executive and regulatory agencies. This expanded the bureaucracy, but it did not necessarily improve the president's ability to oversee the implementation of "his" laws.

In the period from 1934 to 1936 another series of programs, fashioned by the president and his aides, was subsequently passed by Congress. Known as the second phase of the New Deal, these proposals included labor reform, social security, soil conservation, and various public works projects. New administrative structures were also established to administer these programs.

By the end of the Roosevelt era, the president's role as domestic policymaker was firmly established. In fact, when Harry S. Truman, Roosevelt's successor, asked Congress for legislation to combat inflation, he was criticized by the Republican majority for not presenting a draft bill. When Eisenhower failed to propose a legislative program during his first year as president, he was criticized from both sides of the aisle. "Don't expect us to start from scratch on what you people want," an irate member of the House Foreign Affairs Committee told an Eisenhower official.

"That's not the way we do things here. You draft the bills and we work them over."[2]

Whereas Roosevelt extended presidential initiatives primarily into the economic sphere, Presidents Kennedy and Johnson expanded them to include social welfare and civil rights measures.[3] Medical aid to the elderly, public housing, community health, minimum wages, and conservation and education programs plus a variety of civil rights policies were crafted during their administrations. By the end of the 1960s the domestic policy initiative was firmly established in the White House.

Presidents were expected to set their policy agendas and determine the contours of legislative debate; they were expected to draft legislation and to work for its enactment. As time went on, they were also expected to mobilize public coalitions in support of their legislative proposals. And where Congress was slow in acting or obstructionist in its response, presidents were expected to find other ways of fulfilling their policy promises. Executive orders and other administrative actions became vehicles by which they could accomplish some of their policy goals. Republican presidents in particular, when confronted by Democratic Congresses, resorted to their executive powers to achieve their policy goals.

Changing Policy Environment

That the 1960s were a period of unbridled prosperity, replete with low inflation and high employment, permitted the expansion of government services. Most elements of the society benefited. Even the president reaped political advantage from his policy-making role. As the chief provider, he was charged with finding solutions to the country's domestic ills. These solutions took the form of federal programs to the disadvantaged. However, the weakening of the economy in the 1970s and early 1980s cast doubt about these programmatic solutions. It also placed increasing burdens on the president in the performance of his policy-making role.

Higher inflation, greater unemployment, declining productivity, increasing foreign competition, and decreasing natural resources limited the capacity of the federal government to respond to economic and social ills. Beginning with the Nixon administration and continuing through the Reagan years, presidents attempted to slow the federal government's involvement in the domestic sector. President Nixon initiated a program of New Federalism in which the national government's revenues were to be shared with the states in exchange for a larger state and local role in providing social services. President Reagan carried this initiative one step further. In an attempt to shrink the public sector and reduce the responsibility of the federal government, he proposed a swap in which the states would take over the welfare and food stamp programs while the federal government would run the medicare program. Nixon's revenue-sharing policy was enacted; the Reagan program was not.

In addition to the devolution of federal responsibilities to the states, recent presidents have also supported a reduction or at least retrenchment of other domestic programs. Carter vetoed appropriations for nineteen water projects much to the dismay of their supporters in Congress. Reagan proposed user fees for those using federal facilities, including waterways. His budget cut spending for a variety of social services, thereby shrinking the domestic proportion of the total outlays.

Consolidating and eliminating federal programs has been one response to changing economic conditions and shifting public moods. Less regulatory activity has been another. The Carter administration successfully pushed the deregulation of the airline, railroad, and trucking industries while the Reagan administration relaxed the enforcement of those regulations which conflicted with its policy, particularly in the areas of consumer protection, worker safety, and the environment. In addition, the administration created a new division in the Office of Management and Budget to review all executive regulations to make sure that they were necessary and conformed to administration guidelines.

Reducing government programs, expenditures, and regulations has not been easy. Presidents have had to overcome countervailing pressures from various constituencies interested in protecting and promoting programs which benefited them. Moreover, presidents have found it necessary to pursue policies for which large constituencies have been lacking. Raising social security taxes or cutting benefits is a good example.

In 1983 the social security system was on the verge of bankruptcy. Revenues were insufficient to pay ongoing obligations. Something had to be done, but none of the remedies proved to be popular. Each threatened to affect adversely a segment of the population. After a couple of false starts, President Reagan appointed a commmission out of which developed an informal negotiating group. Meeting behind closed doors, this group fashioned a compromise which the leadership of both parties, including the president, accepted and supported. Without presidential backing such a solution would not have been possible.[4]

Winning in a No-Win Role

The social security problem is not unique. Contemporary presidents are in a bind. How can they meet public needs with existing economic resources? How can they build political support for constituentless, but necessary, national solutions? How can they maintain their electoral and governing coalitions without being captive of the interests of those within these coalitions? These problems have led one astute observer,

Paul C. Light, to conclude that domestic policy making places the president in a no-win situation: "The cost of presidential policy has grown, while the President's ability to influence outcomes has declined."[5]

How can presidents overcome this dilemma? How can they meet contemporary expectations of their policy-making role? In the next part of this chapter, we will explore this question by examining the mechanisms and processes which have been developed to aid the president in this increasingly difficult task.

THE OMB AND THE EXECUTIVE BRANCH

A president cannot make policy alone. He needs others to provide him with information and expertise, to coordinate and implement his decisions and actions, to articulate his positions publicly and privately, and to build coalitions in support of them on Capitol Hill and within the executive branch. Initially many of these functions were performed by the Bureau of the Budget, working in conjunction with a small White House staff.

Exercising Central Clearance

The Bureau of the Budget was originally established in 1921 to help the president prepare an annual budget and submit it to Congress. In performing this function the budget agency annually reviewed the requests for funds of the executive departments and agencies. Beginning in the 1930s, this centralized clearance process was extended to include all executive-branch requests for legislation, regardless of whether or not money would be expended. In each case, the budget officials had to decide whether the proposal was in accord with the president's program, consistent with the president's objectives, or at the very least, not opposed by the president. Any proposal which the Bureau of the Budget believed conflicted with presidential policy could not be advanced by the departments and agencies.

In making their judgments, the analysts in the Budget Bureau used presidential campaign statements, major addresses and reports, and special messages to Congress. "From there on, it was just a question of common sense," stated Roger Jones, the Budget Bureau official who supervised this process during much of the Truman and Eisenhower periods.[6]

If there was a major issue about which the Budget Bureau was uncertain how the president's program applied or what the program actually was, the White House would be consulted. This situation was rare, however. As a consequence, the Budget Bureau's decision was usually final. Although an appeal could be made to the White House by the departments and agencies, the practice was not encouraged and was rarely successful. Presidents wanted the clearance procedure to work, and it did. In fact the process was extended to include the positions that departments and agencies take on legislation, and the testimony their officials present to Congress.

The legislature also found the process useful. Beginning in 1947, standing committees of both houses requested that the Bureau of the Budget indicate the president's position on legislation that did not originate in the executive departments and agencies.[7]

From the president's perspective, central clearance provided a number of benefits: (1) it provided a mechanism for imprinting a presidential seal of approval on those proposals that the administration supported and withholding it from those it opposed; (2) it made the departments and agencies more aware of each other's views; (3) it helped resolve interagency disputes and promote interagency coordination. One of its most important functions was the resolution of conflict. Rather than kill a proposal, the Budget Bureau tried to have the objectionable parts removed and mediate the differences between the agencies.

From the department's perspective, however, the clearance requirement was seen as a constraint and the Bureau of the Budget as the policing agency. The civil servants who worked in the budget agency were regarded as the people who said no.

The central clearance process continues to operate today in much the same manner as it did in the past. However, it has become more politicized in the sense that civil servants play a less important role and political appointees a more important one. It is the political appointees in the Office of Management and Budget and in the White House who make the critical decisions on what does or does not accord with the program of the president.

Coordinating Executive Advice

In addition to applying the president's position on the policy proposals and the stands of the executive agencies, the Budget Bureau performs another coordinating function. It solicits and summarizes recommendations on enrolled bills, legislation which has passed both houses of Congress and is awaiting presidential action.

After Congress has enacted the legislation, the Office of Management and Budget circulates copies of it to all executive-branch units that have been involved in its development, would be involved in its implementation, or have a substantive interest in the program itself. The departments and agencies have forty-eight hours in which to make a recommendation to the president. Their recommendations, accompanied by supporting arguments and frequently by drafts of signing and veto statements, are then summarized by the OMB, which adds a recommendation of its own and sends the entire file to the White House within the first five days of the ten-day period the president has to approve or disapprove the legislation. A similar process designed to solicit the views of key White House aides was also begun in 1965. A diagram of the enrolled bill process is shown in Figure 8-1.

Today, when presidents are ready to make decisions on pending legislation, they have the benefit of the advice of a large number of executive officials. And because they have limited time and expertise of their own, they usually follow it.

Of all the executive participants in the process, presidents seem to be most influenced by the OMB and secondarily by the principal agency into whose jurisdiction the legislation falls. An OMB recommendation to approve the bill is almost always accepted. As the agency that says no most often, its advice to the president to sign the legislation seems to be regarded as an all-clear signal by the White House. Rarely does a president disregard this opportunity to approve legislation. On the other hand, the OMB's advice to veto might be ignored if there is significant political pressure to support legislation.

A study of executive recommendations and presidential actions on enrolled bills during the Nixon and Ford administrations revealed that the OMB's recommendation to veto was followed only about half the time.[8] If other executive agencies also urged the president to disapprove the legislation, the chances of his vetoing it increased. In general, the more unified the advice, the more likely it will be taken. See Tables 8-1 and 8-2.

It is interesting to note that as far as acts of Congress are concerned, the White House does *not* seem to play a critical role on *most* bills. Although presidential aides may take sides, they rarely stand alone and oppose the executive agencies in their recommendations to the president.

As with central clearance, the OMB has remained the principal cue-giver on enrolled bills over the years. Its position in these processes, its orientations, and its institutional resources account for its influence.

Presenting an Annual Program

Since 1948, presidents have developed an annual legislative program and presented it to Congress in the form of special and required messages and addresses. This programming process developed out of the president's need to articulate his policy goals and to generate a record on which to appeal to voters. It also satisfied the need of Congress for an agenda upon which to focus its activities.

During the Truman and Eisenhower administrations, the Bureau of

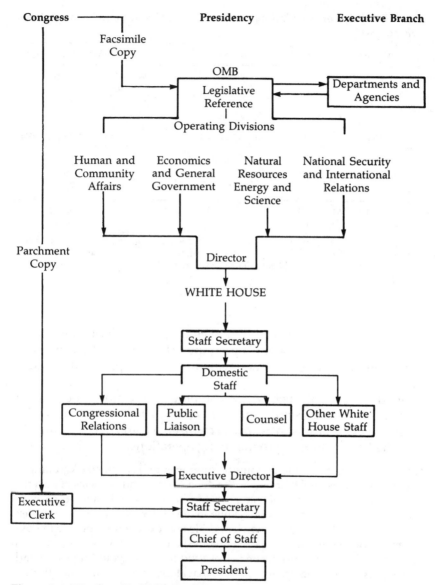

Figure 8-1 The Enrolled Bill Process

the Budget coordinated the mechanism that produced this program for the president. It did so initially as part of its annual budget review process. When departments and agencies were asked to submit their budgets for the next fiscal year, they were also asked to submit ideas for new proposals that would require funding. The Budget Bureau collected these

Table 8-1. OMB Recommendations and Presidents Nixon's and Ford's Actions (in Percentages)*

President Nixon	OMB Approval	OMB Disapproval
Approval	96.3	56.6
Disapproval	3.7	43.4
Total	41.5	58.5
President Ford	OMB Approval	OMB Disapproval
Approval	92.0	43.5
Disapproval	8.0	56.5
Total	26.6	73.4

*Percentages have been rounded.

Nixon: N = 130; Ford: N = 94.

Source: Stephen J. Wayne, Richard L. Cole, and James F. C. Hyde, Jr., "Advising the President on Legislation: Patterns of Executive Branch Influence" (paper presented at the Annual Meeting of the American Political Science Association, Washington, D.C., September 1–4, 1977) p. 29.

ideas and forwarded them to the White House, which decided which of them to include in the president's program. The State of the Union address became the vehicle for announcing these policy proposals to Congress.

From the president's perspective, tapping a wide range of executive ideas and goals proved useful. It increased administration options. In the words of Clark Clifford, who as special counsel to Harry Truman initially directed the White House's programming operations:

> The purpose of obtaining this information was to have the background of the needs and also the opinions of the departments and agencies of government so that we would be able to extract from that voluminous source of information a legislative program. While much of it was self-serving, at least we felt that we had tapped knowledgeable and experienced people in government. Sometimes in that general request a real pearl would appear. It is like a diver swimming around and all of a sudden there would appear a pearl as large as a hen's egg. In my opinion, that alone would justify the effort.[9]

During the Truman and Eisenhower period, the departments and agencies were the major source for presidential policy initiatives. They helped draft proposed legislation, executive orders, and regulations. The Budget Bureau coordinated the process and worked out disagreements.

This departmental orientation to policy making ended in the 1960s. The desire of Presidents Kennedy and Johnson to generate new initiatives, combined with their view of the bureaucracy as a pretty conservative place where innovative ideas were not likely to originate, resulted

Table 8-2. Recommendations of OMB and Lead Agency and Presidential Action (in Percentages)*

	OMB Approval		OMB Disapproval	
President Nixon	Lead Agency Approval	Lead Agency Disapproval	Lead Agency Approval	Lead Agency Disapproval
Approval	97.0	94.4	70.3	44.8
Disapproval	3.0	5.6	29.7	55.2
Total	28.2	14.4	31.6	24.8
	OMB Approval		OMB Disapproval	
President Ford	Lead Agency Approval	Lead Agency Disapproval	Lead Agency Approval	Lead Agency Disapproval
Approval	95.2	100.0	58.6	30.0
Disapproval	4.8	0.0	41.4	69.7
Total	24.4	4.0	33.7	38.4

*Percentages have been rounded.

Nixon: $N = 117$; Ford: $N = 86$.

Source: Stephen J. Wayne, Richard L. Cole, and James F. C. Hyde, Jr. "Advising the President on Legislation: Patterns of Executive Branch Influence" (paper presented at the Annual Meeting of the American Political Science Association, Washington, D.C., September 1–4, 1977), p. 30.

in a shift of focus from inside the executive branch to outside the government. In the words of President Johnson:

> I had watched this programming process for years, and I was convinced that it did not encourage enough fresh or creative ideas. The bureaucracy of the government is too preoccupied with day to day operations, and there is strong bureaucratic inertia dedicated to preserving the status quo. As a result, only the most powerful ideas can survive. Moreover, the cumbersome organization of government is simply not equipped to solve complex problems that cut across departmental jurisdictions.[10]

To generate new ideas, both Kennedy and Johnson set up task forces composed of campaign supporters, academicians, business and labor leaders, but not bureaucrats. Their job was to investigate a problem and present the president with a solution without regard to political considerations or costs. These factors were taken into account by the president and his aides when deciding which of the proposals to pursue.

Under Johnson the number of task forces increased, but their composition and their recommendations were secret. The purpose of the secrecy was to enable the president to take credit for ideas he liked but at the same time not be burdened by those he did not. The secrecy also permitted the president to ascertain the opinions of influential members of Congress without embarrassment to him or them. The Johnson aide who communicated with those in Congress would normally preface his remarks with the comment, "The president hasn't decided to do this, but if he did, how would you respond."

The high priority on new domestic policy proposals in both the Kennedy and Johnson administrations and the desire of both presidents to be personally involved in their development put an even greater burden for their initiation, coordination, and synthesis on White House aides. Moreover, the size of this effort and the number of task forces that were involved forced an expansion in the personnel who regularly dealt with domestic policy matters. By the mid-1960s, a separate White House staff was created to systematize the programming operation. This staff, although small and fairly general by contemporary standards, was the forerunner of the larger, more differentiated structure that functioned as an operating arm of the presidency thereafter.

As a consequence of the growing White House role in policy making, the status and influence of the departments and agencies and the people who ran them declined. A two-track programming system eventually emerged with the departments and agencies on the second track. While they continued to submit proposals with their annual budget estimates, these submissions had less of an impact on the president's major domestic objectives. As power shifted to the White House, the Budget Bureau's influence also declined.

THE DOMESTIC POLICY OFFICE AND
THE WHITE HOUSE

The first domestic policy office was organized by the White House in 1965 to coordinate Lyndon Johnson's Great Society program. Charged with staffing Johnson's outside task forces and then reviewing their recommendations, the office developed policy initiatives for the president and then converted them into a legislative format, an executive order, or a departmental regulation.

President Nixon enlarged and institutionalized this White House policy-making operation. In 1970 he created a Domestic Council composed of his domestic cabinet secretaries and a supporting staff. Organized as a separate unit in the EOP and directed by a senior White House aide, the staff quickly assumed dominance over the process. The council met infrequently. In fact, cabinet secretaries had difficulty even communicating with the president on an individual basis, much less as a group.

Since Nixon preferred a memorandum or option paper, the policy debate had to be in written form. Moreover, since he preferred a formal hierarchical mode of operation, proposals, memos, and option papers had to be sent through official channels. John Ehrlichman, Nixon's chief domestic adviser and executive director of the council, supervised staff operations. All domestic policy documents to and from the president passed through his office.

The council's work was done primarily by committees organized on the basis of projects or missions. Composed of subcabinet departmental officials but organized and run by Ehrlichman's staff, the committees operated as internal task forces. Their functions were similar to the Johnson external task forces—to examine issues, conduct studies, and prepare recommendations for the president. Once a course of action was chosen by the president, the committees reconvened for the purpose of implementing his decision.

The Domestic Council staff member who presided over the group had to make certain that recommendations to the president were in conformity with his basic goals and that the options he selected were properly translated into legislative proposals or executive actions. In this way a White House orientation was imposed on the policy-making process.

The Nixon council system was subsequently modified in 1972. Its staff was reduced in size. Senior personnel were reassigned to other departments and agencies. Some have contended that this was a thinly veiled attempt by the president to rein-in the executive bureaucracy.[12]

As part of the policy reorganization, three cabinet secretaries were given additional responsibilities for coordinating domestic policy within three broad areas: human resources, natural resources, and community development. The events of Watergate, culminating first in Ehrlichman's resignation and eventually in Nixon's, ended this "super cabinet" experiment but did not deter future presidents from trying to exercise as tight control as possible over the domestic policy-making activities of their departments and agencies.

The domestic policy office has been continued in each subsequent administration. Its title, however, has changed, perhaps more for symbolic reasons than anything else. New administrations, not wanting their domestic proposals emanating from an office associated in any way with their predecessor, changed its name. The Carter administration called it the Domestic Policy Staff, and the Reagan administration titled it the Office of Policy Development. Although its principal functions have remained essentially the same—the development and/or coordination of major policy initiatives for the president—the degree to which the office has controlled policy making has varied. During its heyday in the Nixon administration, the Domestic Council was the principal policy unit. It ran the process by which major administration initiatives were developed, and its executive director was the president's main domestic adviser. In contrast, during the Ford period, the council played a much less important role. Weak leadership of its policy staff, an emphasis on economic matters, and Ford's desire for broader participation in key administration decisions helped shift power away from the White House and toward the departments and agencies.

Under Carter, the office was resuscitated, although it did not become the sole advisory body for domestic policy as it had been during the Nixon years. It did, however, become the principal coordinating mechanism for presenting and evaluating a range of opinions and options to the president. Stuart Eizenstat, head of the office and Carter's chief domestic adviser, was an important and influential presidential aide.

Ronald Reagan's penchant for turning to his department secretaries for advice combined with his opposition to new and costly domestic programs once again reduced the influence and shifted the role of the White House's domestic policy staff. It performed largely administrative tasks, providing institutional support for the cabinet councils and helping the president with other policy matters that required his attention. The office's low status and limited impact generated considerable turnover in its staff. Reagan had three assistants for domestic policy in the first three years of his administration.

The size of the domestic staff has varied from a high of approximately eighty at the end of Nixon's first term to about thirty to forty in other administrations. About half of the staff have been professionals; the remainder have been supporting personnel. A senior presidential assistant has headed the office. Frequently, his deputy has coordinated the day-to-day operations.

Over the years, members of the domestic policy group have worked closely with department and agency officials in developing major administrative programs, particularly policy that cuts across department and agency lines. They have also from time to time solicited and coordinated ideas for new policy from outside sources.

In performing this role, the staff has played both broker and advocate. As broker it has mediated among the varying positions of the departments, agencies, and outside groups. As advocate it has recommended specific courses of action to the president. The recommendations that it has made have often put the domestic staff into conflict with the departments and agencies.

In the course of its operation, the policy staff has worked closely with the OMB. In general, priority policy making has been the prerogative of the president's domestic advisers while the clearance and coordination of less important policy matters remain the job of the OMB. Conflict and cooperation have alternately characterized the relationship between these two presidential staffs. From time to time turf battles have also erupted between those responsible for economic advice and those charged with domestic policy making. This was particularly evident in the Ford administration.

Structural Orientation

The relationship between the domestic policy staff and the executive departments and agencies has been critical to the success of the president's policy efforts. While most presidents-elect ritually promise to institute a cabinet government, upon taking office, they often find this undesirable.

In general, contemporary presidents have adopted one of two approaches to policy making. They have either assumed a White House orientation in which their senior aides dominate the process or they have adopted a cabinet orientation in which department secretaries exercise greater influence. The Nixon, and to a lesser extent, Carter presidencies illustrate the first approach and the Reagan presidency exemplifies the latter.

In the White House approach strong, influential domestic advisers funnel recommendations to the president. They filter and broker ideas. Their influence stems primarily from their control of the information flow to and from the president and the analytic network upon which that information rests.

The senior advisers tend to be advocates as well as mediators. Presidents rely on them for advice. This enhances their status and provides them with greater influence, not only with the president but also with others who wish to affect his policy judgments.

Finally, in a White House-oriented system the head of the domestic policy office oversees his staff's operation. In both approaches the policy office links the departments to the White House. However, when the White House exercises dominance, the domestic policy office controls that linkage and thereby exercises greater influence over how presidential goals are converted into administration policies.

In contrast, the cabinet approach is less centralized. Cabinet secretaries, individually and collectively, have a greater impact. The White House policy office functions more as a liaison and secretariat than as a process overseer. It coordinates executive-branch activity rather than dominates it. The senior adviser is more of a broker than an advocate.

President Reagan utilized this approach in his cabinet council system. The councils, consisting of six to eleven department heads, were organized on the basis of substantive issue areas. Reagan established seven of them: economic affairs, commerce and trade, human resources, natural resources and environment, food and agriculture, legal policy, and management and administration.

The function of the councils was to develop policy with the purview of the president's basic objectives. They formulated administration positions on pending legislation, reviewed and cleared policy reports, and helped coordinate and resolve management issues. Working groups of subcabinet officials performed much of the early fact-finding. During his first fifteen months in office, Reagan attended approximately 14 percent of the council's meetings.[13]

Stylistic Differences

In addition to the structural orientations presidents have adopted, their policy goals and personal styles have also affected White House policy making. The desire for innovative policy, particularly evident during the Kennedy-Johnson period, spurred the development of new sources for ideas and programs. The departments were supplemented by outside task forces. Similarly, the goals of retrenchment and consolidation, particularly evident during the Reagan administration, turned the focus back to executive officials appointed by the president who shared the president's ideological and policy perspectives.

While Kennedy and Johnson did not believe the bureaucracy could develop innovative policy, they were confident that civil servants would be able and willing to implement that policy once it had been initiated. Reagan lacked that confidence. He did not believe that career bureaucrats could be trusted to execute the demise of their own programs.

All recent presidents have tried to keep tabs on their principal policy objectives by using their staff to promote and protect their interests. How this staff worked and how much power it wielded related in part to the style of the president and his penchant for exercising central authority. Those presidents who wished to involve themselves in the details of decision making seemed to have more flexible staff structures. Johnson and Carter, in particular, had domestic policy offices that facilitated their reaching down the policy-making chain to make decisions. Both presidents had difficulty delegating authority to others. In contrast, Ford and Reagan were delegators who relied on their advisers for recommendations on what decisions to make and when to make them. Their policy operations were designed to relieve them of making the less important policy judgments. The difference was that Reagan had a more structured ideological perspective. It shaped the contours of his administration's decision making more than did Ford's pragmatic views.

Nixon, too, was a delegator. In contrast to Ford and Reagan, however, he did not enjoy or encourage debate among his subordinates.

Rather he preferred a system that produced option papers from which he could make judgments. Like Carter, he desired detailed written analyses and ranges of alternatives from which he could choose.

STRATEGIES FOR POLICY MAKING

The organizational component is only one aspect of policy making. Presidents obviously need a mechanism to help them design and coordinate their program, but that mechanism alone cannot ensure their program's success. Policy must be strategically accomplished. External interests must be accommodated; agendas must be artfully constructed and promoted; and long-term, national objectives must be maintained, despite the persistance of parochial perspectives and short-term goals.

Accommodating External Forces

Changes within the political and institutional environment, the decentralization of power in Congress, growth of single-issue groups, and weakening of partisan coalitions have increased and diversified pressures on the presidency. This has affected the policy-making process in two principal ways. It has made it more sensitive to outside interests, and it has required that the president devote more personal and institutional resources to the achievement of his domestic policy goals.

Prior to the 1970s the Bureau of the Budget and, to a lesser extent, the White House were relatively invulnerable to external groups seeking to influence their decisions. The Budget Bureau considered itself a presidential agency. It had only one principal constituent, the president. Civil servants, not political appointees, ran the process and made most of the decisions. They were expected to do so within the framework of the president's objectives but on the basis of the merits of the issue.

Taking political factors into account was the job of senior presidential aides in the White House. They worked in a relatively closed environment. While leaders of the president's party, influential supporters, and friends could gain access, the general public, including most of the organized groups, were excluded. Congress and the bureaucracy were the principal turfs on which groups fought their political battles. The Bureau of the Budget and the White House were distanced from the fray.

This began to change in the 1970s. The reorganization of the Budget Bureau into the Office of Management and Budget and the creation of a number of political positions to oversee its operation, the increase in the size of the policy staffs in the White House and their growth in power and influence, and the need to mobilize interest groups behind the president's program all contributed to this increased receptivity to outside pressures. The reaction of Presidents Ford and Carter to Watergate, particularly to Nixon's closed presidency, provided further impetus to open the White House to public view and political influence.

Lobbyists, who themselves were increasing in number, began to contact administration officials directly in the OMB and in the policy office to try to affect their judgments. The White House, in turn, began to utilize interest group and community leaders in building coalitions behind their programs. By the mid-1970s a separate unit within the White House had been established to accomplish this objective. Known as the Public Liaison Office, it became the primary link between the administration and interest group leaders.

The office functioned primarily as a conduit. It provided access for those outside the government who wished to affect administration policies. It also provided public relations opportunities for the president. Literally thousands of group representatives and community leaders have been invited to the White House to meet administration officials and hear them promote their programs. The effect of these activities has been to aid the president in getting his proposals through Congress and accepted by significant segments of the American people.

Recent administrations have worked hard to build political support on an issue-by-issue basis. They have used business, labor, and trade associations to ascertain congressional opinion and affect congressional decision making. They have encouraged letter writing and telephone campaigns; they have even gotten interest groups to contribute to the administration's electoral efforts. In doing this, they have not admitted to "lobbying" but to educating and providing channels of communication, since federal law prohibits the use of government funds to lobby for executive policies in Congress.

In addition to the work of the Public Liaison Office, other units have also been established to communicate with state and local governments and with party officials and political leaders around the country. A larger, more sophisticated White House communications operation has also been established to market the president and his policy objectives more effectively with the general population. By the 1980s more than one-third of the people who worked in the White House were involved in public relations activities of one type or another.

Building a Policy Agenda

The changing institutional and political environment for policy has also affected the content of agendas. In recent years their scope has become more modest while the policies within them have become more complex. Moreover, their promotion has become more closely tied to the cycle of decreasing presidential influence.

In the past, agendas tended to be laundry lists of proposals designed to appeal to as broad a segment of electoral supporters as possible. Franklin Roosevelt's New Deal, Truman's Fair Deal, Kennedy's New Frontier, Johnson's Great Society, even Nixon's New Federalism programs fit into this category. The depressed American economy of the 1930s, the increasing social consciousness of the 1960s, the democratizing of the nomination process in the 1970s, and the expansion of the electoral period during the past decade have all contributed to the demands for a large and diverse policy agenda.

The way in which presidents formulated their domestic programs also contributed to the same end. By soliciting proposals from a variety of sources and established interests, presidents have generated multiple pressures on their own programs. The most effective way to deal with these pressures had been to accommodate them in packages that included something for almost everyone.

While these pressures have persisted and even increased, the president's ability to achieve them has diminished. Resources have become more scarce; a huge national debt has developed. The government lacks the revenues to meet a plethora of policy demands. The system has become more pluralistic. Greater effort must be exerted to mobilize majority coalitions. This has increased the costs of domestic policy making for the president. It is required that more time, energy, and institutional resources be devoted to these activities.

One consequence of increasing costs and decreasing resources has been the need to limit items in the domestic agenda. Another has been to move them more quickly. A third imperative for the president is to avoid excessive involvement in the details of his administration's policy while maintaining a long-term, national perspective.

LIMITING THE ITEMS   The expansion of governmental activities has generated more groups with a stake in public policy. Today, there are more opinions to hear, more interests to balance, more agendas to combine. This has produced, in the words of Hugh Heclo, more "policy congestion."[14]

It has also increased the complexity of many issues with which contemporary administrations must deal. One policy decision affects another. Spheres of jurisdiction overlap. Distinctions between domestic and international concerns are no longer as clear-cut.

The task for the president and his aides is to sort out the relationships among the competing interests and complex issues and to integrate them into a single comprehensive program. One way to do this has already been discussed—create an institutional mechanism that imposes a presidential perspective as the Bureau of the Budget did prior to 1965 and the domestic policy office has done since then. Another tactic is to reduce the agenda to a few critical items and bind them together in some fashion. The Reagan administration has employed this strategy as well.

Upon taking office, President Reagan translated his campaign stands—government is too large and costly, taxes are too high, defense is too weak, and regulations are too numerous—into two basic legislative intiatives, budget and tax reform, and two basic executive ones, a hiring freeze and a reduction of regulations. These items constituted the administration's entire agenda for its first two years in office.

Limiting items helps the president set the pace and tone of public debate. It helps focus public attention on certain presidential activities. This contributes to the perception that the president is in command.

There is, of course, a negative side to limiting the agenda. Some people's expectations will not be satisfied. For the Reagan administration it was the social objectives of the conservatives that were postponed.[15]

In addition to limiting the items in the president's agenda, it is necessary to package them artfully. Presenting a few key proposals rather than a comprehensive set of policies reduces the number of instances in which supporters of the president can disagree. It encourages them to rally behind his policies, while it forces others to choose sides. Fewer positions and roll-call votes make it easier to concentrate resources and mobilize winning coalitions. Reagan followed this strategy in his 1981 and 1982 budget battles with the Democrats in Congress. By getting the House of Representatives to agree to an up or down vote on its final budget resolutions, the president improved his chances of obtaining the level of expenditures he desired.

MOVING THEM QUICKLY　　　Another strategic consequence of the increased costs of domestic policy making is that an administration's priorities must be established and moved quickly. No longer does a president and his entourage have the luxury of waiting several months before they formulate their principal policy proposals. The reason is that electoral cycles, department pressures, and public moods tend to decrease presidential influence over time. As members of Congress position themselves for the next election, as bureaucrats and their clientele begin to assert their claims on political appointees, as segments of the winning coalition become disillusioned, as the outparty begins to coalesce in opposition to the incumbent, it is more difficult for a president to achieve domestic policy goals.

Carter found this out the hard way. He used the first six months in office to develop policies to implement his election promises. By the time these proposals were readied for Congress, Carter's honeymoon had ended and his policies got stuck in a legislative labyrinth.

Eventually the Carter administration did develop a legislative priority mechanism. Vice President Mondale headed a group of senior advisers who met at the beginning of the year to establish and order goals and schedule them over the course of the legislative calendar. Carter's midterm successes in Congress suggest that this policy mechanism may have had some effect.

The Reagan administration learned from the Carter experience. With its agenda in place prior to taking office, Reagan seized on his unexpectedly large electoral victory in 1980 to claim a mandate for his economic program and then moved quickly to obtain its enactment. Proposals that were developed later in the administration such as the New Federalism and urban enterprise zone plans met with considerably more congressional resistance.

The dilemma presidents face is that their influence is greatest when their knowledge is least. This makes "a move it or lose it" strategy[16] as dangerous as it may be necessary. A good example would be the Reagan administration's initial suggestions for reducing the gap between social security revenues and expenditures. Deep cuts were proposed in the benefits of those who chose to retire early. Following a huge public outcry, the Republican controlled Senate went on record with a vote of ninety-six to zero against this proposal.

Not only do presidents not have sufficient time to educate themselves before making critical policy judgments, they may not have time to develop innovative policy at all. According to Paul C. Light, declining influence requires presidents to look for available alternatives among existing options and take the first acceptable one. This may be the policy that raises the fewest objections, the one that has resulted in the most compromise, and consequently, the one able to muster the most support within the executive branch. That support makes it most acceptable to the largest number of decision makers even though it may not be the best solution.[17]

DISCERNING THE FOREST FROM THE TREES   Constraints on time and energy suggest another lesson for contemporary presidents. They should not involve themselves too deeply in the details of decision making, although they must provide general policy guidance. Jimmy Carter is a case in point. Finding it difficult to delegate, he spent considerable time becoming an expert in the various policy issues in which he was interested or which came to his attention. At the beginning of his administration he read around 400 pages of papers and memos a day! James

Fallows, a former Carter speech writer, describes his boss as "the perfectionist accustomed to thinking that to do a job right you must do it yourself."[18] Fallows illustrated:

> He [Carter] would leave for a weekend at Camp David laden with thick briefing books, would pore over budget tables to check the arithmetic, and during his first six months in office, would personally review all requests to use the White House tennis court. . . . After six months had passed, Carter learned that this was ridiculous, as he learned about other details he would have to pass by if he was to use his time well. But his preference was still to try to do it all.[19]

Naturally, this prodigious effort took its toll and Carter was eventually forced to cut back.

In contrast, Reagan took the opposite track. While he articulated a strong ideological perspective, he left most of the details to senior White House and cabinet officials. This exposed him to the charge that he was manipulated by his staff. On the other hand, it distanced him both from the problems that resulted from these decisions and from the decision makers themselves.

SUSTAINING A NATIONAL PERSPECTIVE   Reagan's ideological perspective helped him tackle another policy-making problem that besets contemporary presidents—how to sustain a national perspective in the light of continuous parochial pressures. Ideology provides a rationale for including (and excluding) certain items in a policy agenda and linking them to one another in a way that makes sense to partisan supporters. It helps transform an electoral coalition into a policy one. It is also useful in overcoming the tendencies that frequently lead executive officials to adopt views and advocate interests that are at variance with the president's.

The Reagan administration employed ideology in converting electoral promises into tangible policy goals. It was also used as a criterion for appointment. Cabinet and subcabinet officials were nominated in part because they shared the president's views. They were expected to impose those views on their agencies rather than the other way around.

Ideology, in short, can be a unifying tool. It can build support by simplifying and focusing. It is not without its dangers, however. Rigid adherence to an ideological perspective makes compromise difficult. As it unites supporters so too can it unify opponents, thereby polarizing the policy positions. It can blind adherents to the nuances of proposals and the need for adjustment and change. Pragmatic solutions may be disregarded. Policy is apt to be more precipitous and extreme. Continuity between administrations of differing ideological perspectives is more difficult to achieve.

On the other hand, lack of an overarching ideological or conceptual framework can produce the same problem within an administration. Critics have contended that policy inconsistencies in the Carter administration were due in part to this problem. Again as James Fallows observed:

> I came to think that Carter believes fifty things, but no one thing. He holds explicit, thorough positions on every issue under the sun, but he has no large view of the relations between them, no line indicating which goals (reducing unemployment? human rights?) will take precedence over which (inflation control? a SALT treaty?) when the goals conflict.[20]

MANTAINING A LONG-RANGE VIEW   Another related problem to promoting policy consistency is maintaining a long-range perspective. In making policy, everyday emergencies tend to drive out future planning. This limits the outlook of those involved in policy making to the short term and rarely beyond the next election.

Contemporary White Houses have attempted to design a longer-range domestic planning capability but without much success. In 1975 President Ford asked Vice President Rockefeller to provide leadership and direction for the establishment of social goals. However, Rockefeller's decision not to run for office one year later abruptly ended this effort. A second attempt in the spring of 1976 to relieve some of the policy staff's operational responsibilities so they could devote more time to planning for future needs met with a similar fate.

The most ambitious effort to create a longer-range, policy-making capability has been the creation of the Office for Planning and Evaluation in the Reagan administration. Charged with developing strategic plans for the president's agenda and schedule, the office fashioned a series of six-month blueprints for the administration. As part of this effort scenarios of possible responses to international and national crises and events were designed. Within two years, however, the focus shifted from policy to politics. Data from public opinion polls were analyzed to discern shifting public moods and to anticipate the type and timing of presidential actions that would be of most benefit to the administration.

One of the lasting legacies of this office's work will probably be its use of sophisticated information and communication technology to serve the policy needs of the presidency. The Carter White House has begun to employ computers for tracking correspondence and grants, but the Reagan administration broadened their application to include the drafting, editing, and transmission of speeches and messages, the processing of presidential correspondence, and the scheduling of meetings, tracking of legislation, and monitoring of executive operations.

The White House has also expanded its access to commercial and governmental data bases. An electronic mail capability has been established within the Executive Office and between its various units and a growing number of executive departments and agencies. There is even a portable electronic mail unit that travels with the president.[21] In short, the White House is beginning to take advantage of advances in technology to make, communicate, and sell public policy.

CONCLUSION

The president has become the nation's principal domestic policy-maker. His role developed primarily in the twentieth century and largely as a consequence of social, economic, and political problems which required solutions by the federal government. With a national perspective, a large staff structure, and the ability to focus public attention and mobilize support, the president has been in a better position than Congress to propose policy and get it adopted. The electoral process has provided him with further incentives to do so.

Since Franklin Roosevelt's administration, the president's domestic policy initiative has been firmly established. Congress, the executive, and the public look to him for leadership. He is expected to present and promote a comprehensive policy program.

The mechanism necessary to accomplish this task took form and became institutionalized over the two decades beginning with Truman's presidency. The Budget Bureau provided the resources and managed the processes with its senior civil servants working closely with the White House to coordinate and clear policy proposals emanating from the departments and agencies. Initially, the preparation of an annual legislative program by the president further enlarged the Budget Bureau's responsibilities. Once the White House turned from departments and agencies to task forces for its policy ideas, however, the budget agency's influence declined and the White House's increased.

Since the mid-1960s the president's chief policy aides have dominated the policy-making process. They, in turn, have depended on their assistants to monitor and integrate the input of others. The White House has also become more involved in building support for these priorities. Separate presidential offices charged with policy development and political liaison have now become standard.

The development of these structures has enhanced the presidency's influence but not necessarily the president's. Although the incumbent's goals and style still shape domestic policy making, they cannot control it. A president is dependent on his staff for deciding when he should be involved, what options he should consider, how those options are presented to him, and how they should be articulated and promoted inside and outside the government.

Changes within the political system have made the president's tasks more burdensome. Competing demands, complex issues, and confrontational politics have made it more difficult for the chief policymaker to design programs and obtain support for them. His dilemma is that expectations of his role exceed his resources for achieving his goals. This has affected strategies for policymaking.

Today, a president must accommodate external forces and mobilize them into a policy coalition. He must establish priorities quickly, even before taking office, and then package, promote, and cycle them throughout his administration. Finally, he must work to establish and maintain a longer-term, national perspective.

These tasks are not easy. They require skillful personal and institutional leadership. A president cannot dictate policy outcomes but he can affect them. His reputation and even the fate of his presidency may hinge on how well he does so.

NOTES

1. Franklin D. Roosevelt, "First Inaugural Address," March 4, 1933, as appears in the *Congressional Record*, 73rd Cong., Special Sess., pp. 5–6.
2. As quoted in Richard E. Neustadt, "Presidency and Legislation: Planning the President's Program," *American Political Science Review* 49 (December 1955): 1015.
3. The one major exception was the social security program.
4. For an excellent discussion of the politics of the compromise see Paul C. Light, *Artful Work* (New York: Random House, 1985).
5. Paul C. Light, *The President's Agenda* (Baltimore: Johns Hopkins University Press, 1982), p. 217.
6. Roger Jones as quoted in Stephen J. Wayne, *The Legislative Presidency* (New York: Harper and Row, 1978), p. 72.
7. For its part the Bureau of the Budget, and later the Office of Management and Budget, also maintained a *watch list* of all objectionable legislation introduced or modified by the Congress which the president might consider vetoing.
8. Stephen J. Wayne, Richard L. Cole, and James F. C. Hyde, Jr., "Advising the President on Enrolled Legislation," *Political Science Quarterly* 94 (Summer 1979): 303–17.
9. Clark Clifford as quoted in Wayne, *The Legislative Presidency*, p. 104.
10. Lyndon B. Johnson, *The Vantage Point: Perspectives of the Presidency 1963–1969* (New York: Holt, Rinehart and Winston, 1971), pp. 326–27.
11. Quoted in Doris Kearns, *Lyndon Johnson and the American Dream* (New York: Harper and Row, 1976), p. 223.
12. Richard P. Nathan, *The Plot That Failed* (New York: Wiley, 1975).
13. The councils functioned unevenly: The one concerned with economic policy met most frequently (as much as the others combined) and had the most impact on policy within its sphere. Others were not nearly as active. For an excellent discussion on the councils and their operation see Chester A. Newland, "A Mid-Term Appraisal—The Reagan Presidency: Limited Government and Political Administration," *Public Administration Review*, January/February 1983, pp. 6–10.
14. Hugh Heclo, "One Executive Branch or Many?" in Anthony King, ed., *Both Ends of the Avenue* (Washington, D.C.: American Enterprise Institute, 1983), p. 32.
15. Being a Republican and having a narrower constituency contributed to Reagan's ability to focus on economic matters. In contrast, Democratic presidents find themselves under greater pressures from a more heterogeneous group of supporters to involve the federal government in a greater range of social and economic programs.

16. Light,*The President's Agenda*, p. 218.
17. Ibid., p. 219.
18. James Fallows, "The Passionless Presidency," *Atlantic*, May 1979, p. 38.
19. Ibid.
20. Ibid., p. 42.
21. Charlotte Saikowski, "Computers' Whir Replaces Typists' Tap-Tap at White House," *Christian Science Monitor*, April 26, 1984, p. 1.

SELECTED READINGS

Heclo, Hugh. "One Executive Branch or Many?" In Anthony King, ed., *Both Ends of the Avenue*. Washington, D.C.: American Enterprise Institute, 1983.

Helmer, John, and Louis Maisel. "Analytical Problems in the Study of Presidential Advice: The Domestic Council Staff in Flux." *Presidential Studies Quarterly* (Winter 1978): 45–67.

Light, Paul C. *The President's Agenda*. Baltimore: Johns Hopkins University Press, 1982.

Nathan, Richard P. "The Reagan Presidency in Domestic Affairs." In Fred I. Greenstein, ed., *The Reagan Presidency*. Baltimore: Johns Hopkins University Press, 1983.

Newland, Chester. "A Mid-Term Appraisal—The Reagan Presidency: Limited Government and Political Administration." *Public Administration Review* (January/February 1983): 1–20.

Salamon, Lester M. "Federal Regulation: A New Arena for Presidential Power?" In Hugh Heclo and Lester M. Salamon, eds., *The Illusion of Presidential Government*. Boulder, Colo.: Westview Press, 1981.

Shull, Steven A. *Domestic Policy Formation: Presidential-Congressional Partnership?* Westport, Conn.: Greenwood Press, 1983.

Wayne, Stephen J. *The Legislative Presidency*. New York: Harper and Row, 1978.

Wayne, Stephen J.; Richard L. Cole; and James F. C. Hyde, Jr. "Advising the President on Enrolled Legislation." *Political Science Quarterly* (Summer 1979): 303–16.

Wyszomirski, Margaret J. "A Domestic Policy Office: Presidential Office in Search of a Role." *Policy Studies Journal* (June 1984): 705–718.

9

Budgetary and Economic Policy Making

Presidents have always been concerned with the costs of government and the state of the economy, but that concern has never been greater than it is today. With a budget exceeding $900 billion, with a national debt exceeding $1.5 trillion, with federal revenues tied to economic conditions, with the private sector increasingly dependent on public expenditures, almost any substantive policy decision a president makes has significant budgetary and economic implications. Similarly, almost any major budget and economic decision has important political consequences.

Like it or not, presidents and their staffs must devote increasing time and resources to budgetary and economic matters. Their popularity, their reelectability, and their reputation often hinge on the performance of these policy-making responsibilities.

In this chapter we will explore those responsibilities and their evolution. Beginning with a historic overview of the executive budget, we will look at the development of a presidential budget office and the creation of a budget review process and then note the evolving role of Congress in budgetary matters.

In the second part of the chapter we will explore presidential policy making within the economic sphere, describing the development of a presidential role, the creation of an advisory mechanism, and the politics of economic decision making. A concluding section summarizes the trends in budget and economic policy making.

THE FEDERAL BUDGET

The budget is a document that forecasts revenue and estimates the expenditures of the federal government. It does so for a fiscal year, a twelve-month period beginning October 1 and continuing through the following September 30. Since the primary purpose of the budget is to allocate limited funds, that allocation is, by definition, highly political. Competition for limited resources is inevitable.

A presidential budget has been required since 1921. The Budget and Accounting Act of that year made the president responsible for presenting a budget for executive departments and agencies to the Congress. Prior to that time agencies perfunctorily submitted their estimates to the secretary of the treasury, who passed them on to the legislature. The president played a minor role in this process.

The 1921 act, a response to a series of budget deficits incurred at the beginning of the twentieth century and magnified by World War I, established a bureau within the Department of the Treasury to handle these new presidential responsibilities. Acting as a surrogate for the president, this division organized and ran a process that solicited yearly expenditure estimates from the departments and agencies, evaluated and adjusted them according to the president's goals, and finally combined them in a comprehensive executive budget. This budget review cycle has continued through the years.

The budget, however, has changed rather dramatically.[1] In its early years it was relatively small by contemporary standards, oriented toward the executive agencies, and utilized primarily as a vehicle for *controlling federal spending*. Since the primary object of the budget was to make the national government more economical, to eliminate the deficits, and to keep a lid on spending, federal outlays were substantially reduced during this initial period, 1921–1930.[2]

Total government expenditures were in the range of $2 billion to $3 billion. Most of the money went directly to the departments and agencies for the costs of running the government. There were relatively few public works projects that required direct funding.

The Great Depression of the 1930s had a major effect on the character of the budget. Increased demands for government intervention in the economy culminated in Roosevelt's New Deal programs. Followed by World War II and the cold war, this larger governmental role greatly accelerated spending in domestic and defense areas. Fortunately, the economic recovery, beginning in the late 1940s and continuing through the 1950s, provided substantially more revenues for these increasing expenditures. These developments not only expanded the size of the budget but also moved it into an *incremental* phase.

During this phase, which reached its zenith in the 1960s, the budget highlighted new programs and maintained existing ones. Agencies assumed that the costs of their ongoing programs would be met in addition to whatever priority legislation the president wished to introduce.

While the departments continued to administer their programs, more and more of the outlays went to third parties. Programs designed

to help the invalid and the poor, senior citizens, veterans, and others provided direct payments to individuals from the treasury. Particularly since
the 1970s these so-called "entitlement" programs have consumed an
ever-increasing proportion of government expenditures, expenditures
that are not easily subject to presidential control.

The reason they are not is that these programs and others like them
legally entitle individuals to benefits as long as they meet stated eligibility
requirements. These entitlements are independent of specific appropriations by Congress. (In 1974, Congress decided to peg social security
payments to the consumer price index, forsaking decision making even
on the levels of benefits. The president does not have the authority to
change these payments.) Congress has obligated itself to provide whatever funds are required to serve those who qualify.

Other major uncontrollable annual expenditures are outlays from
prior contracts and obligations (which the government is committed to
pay), interest on the national debt, general revenue sharing (a state and
community entitlement program), payments for farm price supports,
and deficits in the operation of the United States Postal Service.

Today, a smaller and smaller proportion of the budget is subject to
presidential discretion (see Figures 9-1 and 9-2). For Carter's last budget

Figure 9-1. Growth in Social Contract Spending* 1963–1981
CONSTANT (1983 $) OUTLAYS

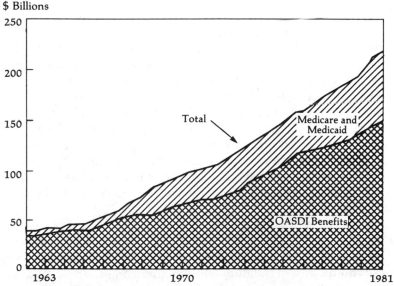

*Includes spending for basic retirement and disability income and health care services.

Source: *Budget of the United States, Fiscal 1984.* Washington, D.C.: Government Printing Office, pp. 3–6.

Figure 9-2. Growth in Other Entitlement Programs, 1970–1981*
CONSTANT (1983 $) OUTLAYS

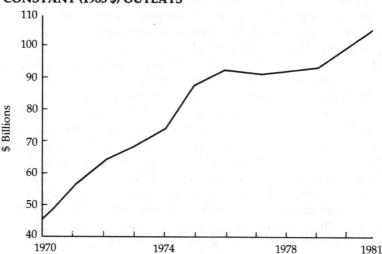

*Does not include social contract spending for retirement, disability, and health care services.

Source: *Budget of the United States, Fiscal 1984*. Washington, D.C.: Government Printing Office, pp. 3–8.

(fiscal 1982), the percentage of expenditures required by existing legislation exceeded 75 percent of the total (see Figure 9-3).

The payments to third parties have had another important effect. They have increased the political ramifications of budget decisions. Instead of primarily affecting departments and agencies, the budget now has a direct impact on those outside the government. As a consequence, outside constituencies such as veterans, senior citizens, farmers, labor, and others have organized to protect and extend their benefits. They regularly exert pressure on budget makers. This pressure makes it more difficult to use the budget as a device for controlling spending. By the late 1970s, the end of phase two, the budget demonstrated more of the president's weaknesses than his strengths; he was responsible for it yet controlled little of it.

The third phase of the budget began in the Reagan administration, although its seeds were sown in the economic problems of the previous decade: the decline in the nation's productivity and its industrial competitiveness and the rise in inflation and unemployment. These factors, along with a steadily increasing national debt and sizable deficits, led those inside and outside the government to question the wisdom of ever-

Figure 9-3. The Composition of Federal Spending

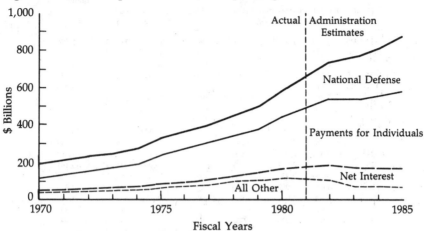

Source: U.S. Congress, Congressional Budget Office, "An Analysis of the President's Budgetary Proposal for Fiscal Year, 1983," p. xxvii.

increasing government expenditures within the domestic sphere, particularly when the economy was weak (see Table 9-1).

Upon taking office, President Reagan took the lead in reordering of national priorities and used the budget to achieve this objective. *Incremental* increases gave way to *decremental* adjustments. The proportion of the budget devoted to domestic discretionary spending was cut; entitlement programs such as social security were adjusted; money for defense was increased.

These changes affected the budget's orientation more than they affected overall outlays. Instead of distributing an expanding base of resources, the budget redistributed a declining one. This increased the competition and division among the agencies and outside groups concerned with "their" expenditures. With different interests and groups vying to protect and promote their own programs, a consensus supporting the budget was harder to achieve. Congress found it more difficult to enact budgetary policy. It spent more time on budget matters and had more votes on budget questions. Other issues were driven off the legislative calendar as a result.

The president also had to devote more time and energy to his budget activities, not merely to formulating the budget but to obtaining congressional approval for it. As the principal policymaker and coalition builder, he had little option. His policy success was dependent, in large part, on his ability to get his budget proposals enacted into law.

Table 9-1. Budget Receipts and Outlays, 1789–1989[1]
(in millions of dollars)

Fiscal Year	Budget Receipts	Budget Outlays	Budget Surplus or Deficit (−)	Fiscal Year	Budget Receipts	Budget Outlays	Budget Surplus or Deficit (−)
1789–1849	1,160	1,090	+70	1965	116,833	118,430	−1,596
1850–1900	14,462	15,453	−991	1966	130,856	134,652	−3,796
1901–1905	2,797	2,678	+119	1967	148,906	157,608	−8,702
1906–1910	3,143	3,196	−52	1968	152,973	178,134	−25,161
1911–1915	3,517	3,568	−49	1969	186,882	183,645	+3,236
1916–1920	17,286	40,195	−22,909	1970	192,807	195,652	−2,845
1921	5,571	5,062	+509	1971	187,139	210,172	−23,033
1922	4,026	3,289	+736	1972	207,309	230,681	−23,373
1923	3,853	3,140	+713	1973	230,799	245,647	−14,849
1924	3,871	2,908	+963	1974	263,224	267,912	−4,688
1925	3,641	2,924	+717	1975	279,090	324,245	−45,154
1926	3,795	2,930	+865	1976	298,060	364,473	−66,413
1927	4,013	2,857	+1,155	TQ[2]	81,232	94,188	−12,956
1928	3,900	2,961	+939	1977	355,559	400,506	−44,948
1929	3,862	3,127	+734	1978	399,561	448,368	−48,807
1930	4,058	3,320	+738	1979	463,302	490,997	−27,694
				1980	517,112	576,675	−59,563
1931	3,116	3,577	−462				
1932	1,924	4,659	−2,735	1981	599,272	657,204	−57,932
1933	1,997	4,598	−2,602	1982	617,766	728,375	−110,609
1934	3,015	6,645	−3,630	1983	600,562	795,969	−195,407
1935	3,706	6,497	−2,791	1984 est	670,071	853,760	−183,689
1936	3,997	8,422	−4,425	1985 est	745,127	925,492	−180,365
1937	4,956	7,733	−2,777	1986 est	814,940	992,072	−177,132
1938	5,588	6,765	−1,177	1987 est	887,829	1,068,293	−180,464
1939	4,979	8,841	−3,862	1988 est	978,303	1,130,335	−152,032
1940	6,361	9,456	−3,095	1989 est	1,060,304	1,183,698	−123,394

1941	8,621	13,634	−5,013
1942	14,350	35,114	−20,764
1943	23,649	78,533	−54,884
1944	44,276	91,280	−47,004
1945	45,216	92,690	−47,474
1946	39,327	55,183	−15,856
1947	38,394	34,532	+3,862
1948	41,774	29,773	+12,001
1949	39,437	38,834	+603
1950	39,485	42,597	−3,112
1951	51,646	45,546	+6,100
1952	66,204	67,721	−1,517
1953	69,574	76,107	−6,533
1954	69,719	70,890	−1,170
1955	65,469	68,509	−3,041
1956	74,547	70,460	+4,087
1957	79,990	76,741	+3,249
1958	79,636	82,575	−2,939
1959	79,249	92,104	−12,855
1960	92,492	92,223	+269
1961	94,389	97,795	−3,406
1962	99,676	106,813	−7,137
1963	106,560	111,311	−4,751
1964	112,662	118,584	−5,922

Totals, including outlays of off-budget Federal entities[3]

Fiscal Year	Outlays of Off-Budget Federal Entities	Total Outlays	Total Surplus or Deficit (−)
1973	60	245,707	−14,908
1974	1,447	269,359	−6,135
1975	8,088	332,332	−53,242
1976	7,307	371,779	−73,719
TQ	1,785	95,973	−14,741
1977	8,700	409,206	−53,647
1978	10,359	458,726	−59,166
1979	12,467	503,464	−40,162
1980	14,245	590,920	−73,808
1981	21,005	678,209	−78,936
1982	17,331	745,706	−127,940
1983	12,357	808,327	−207,764
1984 est	16,196	869,956	−199,884
1985 est	14,814	940,307	−195,179
1986 est	8,789	1,000,861	−185,922
1987 est	7,221	1,075,513	−187,685
1988 est	7,631	1,137,967	−159,664
1989 est	4,767	1,188,465	−128,161

[1]Data for 1789–1939 are for the administrative budget: data for 1940 and all following years are for the unified budget.
[2]In calendar year 1976, the Federal fiscal year was converted from a July 1–June 30 basis to an Oct. 1–Sept. 30 basis. The TQ refers to the transition quarter from July 1 to Sept. 30, 1976.
[3]Off-budget Federal entity outlays begin in 1973.

Source: *The United States Budget in Brief, Fiscal 1985*, Washington, D.C.: Government Printing Office, p. 84.

THE EXECUTIVE BUDGETARY PROCESS

There are four principal stages in the executive phase of the process. In the first, the overall guidelines of the budget are established. They are conditioned by the objectives of the president, the state of the economy, and the commitments of legislation, past and present. In the second stage, the departments and agencies prepare their estimates in accordance with these guidelines. Personnel from the Office of Management and Budget examine these estimates in a formal review process in stage 3. Stage 4 begins with the president being briefed by the budget director, hearing appeals from the department and agency heads, and making the final decisions. The budget is then printed and sent to Congress in January. These stages of the budgetary process are detailed below.

The Budgetary Process

Approximate Times	Actions
	Budget Policy Development
March, 1st year	Senior economic advisers review outlook for the current and future fiscal years; predict effects on revenues and spending programs and report to the President.
April–May	OMB conducts spring planning review sessions, exploring funding implications of major issues or programs that will be considered in the fall budget review. OMB sets overall guidelines for the agency budget submissions and sends these, along with instructions on preparing their proposed budgets, to the agencies.
	Agencies' Preparation of Proposed Budgets
July–August	Agencies develop their proposed budgets.
September	Agencies send OMB their proposed budgets for the fiscal year that begins 13 months later.
	OMB Review and President's Decision
September–October	OMB staff analyzes proposed budgets, holds hearings with agencies.
October–November	Economic advisers again review outlook for fiscal year that begins next October. Director holds agency by agency reviews at which he considers agency requests, staff recommendations and decides on recommendations to the President.

December	OMB transmits proposed budget and economic advisers' findings to the President. OMB gives agencies their recommended budget levels—also known as "the mark." President reviews OMB recommendations and decides on totals for agencies and programs. Possible appeals by agencies to the President. OMB prepares budget documents for transmittal to Congress.
January, 2nd year	President delivers his proposed budget to Congress. OMB sends "allowance letter" to each agency giving its total within the President's budget and also transmitting "planning numbers" for the next two fiscal years.

Source: The Office of Management and Budget, May 1982, pp. 13–14.

THE BUDGET MAKERS

The President

The president bears the primary responsibility for the executive phase of the budget. Increasingly, he is also expected to play a major role in the legislative phase as well. In each, he can exercise influence but cannot dictate the outcome.

There are various ways a president can affect the executive budget. His goals dictate its priorities and shape its initial guidelines; his policies determine the new big-item expenditures; his decisions resolve interagency disputes. He hears last-minute appeals and makes the final judgments on them. The budget presented to the Congress must meet with his approval. However, since his discretion extends to less than 25 percent of the total outlays, much of *his* budget has been predetermined by decisions of his predecessors and their Congresses.

In affecting a portion of the budget, presidents can get involved in detailed decision making, if they desire. Some have done so. Ford and Carter spent considerable time on budget matters. Nixon did not. He took little interest in the budget and delegated considerable authority to his budget director.

Ronald Reagan has taken a slightly different tack. Interested in setting broad budget policy, he has not been intimately involved in its implementation. Rather, he has been content to establish the priorities and make decisions on items brought to his attention. Reagan has left the detailed evaluation of agency estimates to officials in the Office of Management and Budget. By avoiding details, Reagan has distanced himself from internal and external pressures to spend. This has made it easier for him to achieve one of his primary objectives—cutting domestic spending.

The Office of Management and Budget

When the Bureau of the Budget (BOB) was first created in 1921 as a unit within the Department of the Treasury, its initial charge was to "assemble, correlate, revise, reduce, or increase the estimates of the several departments or establishments."[3] In 1939 it was moved to the newly created Executive Office of the President, where it has remained ever since. In 1970 its title was changed from the Bureau of the Budget to the Office of Management and Budget and its functions broadened to include management responsibilities.

Despite the fact that the Budget Bureau was housed in the Treasury Department for its first eighteen years, it functioned as an important, powerful, and independent presidential agency. During this early phase of its existence, the bureau exercised central oversight over the budget. It operated according to a standard rule that departmental estimates equal to or less than the previous year's were automatically approved, while estimates for more money had to receive the authorization of the budget director, and in some cases, even the president.

The objectives of promoting economical government and controlling spending contributed to the bureau's power. Since most of the outlays prior to the mid-1930s went to the executive departments and agencies, there was little interest in the budget outside the government. The lack of public visibility and external pressure worked to the bureau's advantage. Its decisions were final unless overruled by the president, an infrequent practice in those days. Executive agencies were forbidden to circumvent the process by going directly to Congress for funds.

As the budget expanded, so did the size and functions of the budget agency and the interest in its decisions. In the 1920s and the 1930s, the bureau consisted of fewer than 45 employees.[4] New responsibilities generated by World War II and the clearance of legislative policy matters enlarged the staff to more than 500 by 1949 and created an institutional memory upon which the White House grew increasingly to depend.[5]

Most of the people who worked in the bureau were civil servants. Initially, there were only two political appointees, the director and the deputy director. The latter, by tradition, was chosen from the ranks of the professionals who had worked their way up in the agency. As a consequence of its nonpartisan character, the Budget Bureau was particularly well suited to provide the president with "advice on the merits" as opposed to "advice on the politics." Moreover, its invulnerability to outside pressures, relative invisibility to the press, and accessibility to the president and his senior aides heightened its mystique and enhanced its clout.

Changes in the organization, influence, and roles of the BOB began to occur in the 1960s. These changes were a consequence of the increasing size of the White House staff, the increasing number of initiatives that emanated from it, and the increasing suspicion of the political loyalties of civil servants by new presidents and their staffs. Singularly and together, these factors decreased the agency's influence within the executive branch. While it continued to run the budget review process and decide on routine budget matters, key issues became the more or less exclusive province of senior White House aides.

Changes in the character of the budget also worked to affect the bureau's role and ultimately its power. With less emphasis placed on limiting expenditures and more on highlighting programs, political policymakers, not career budget analysts, became the key players. With more requests emanating from the departments and agencies, budget review focused on the size of their increments rather than the merits of their existing programs. With an increasing percentage of the budget consisting of uncontrollable items, the Budget Bureau was limited in what it could cut and how much it could save. As a consequence of all these factors, the BOB's influence declined while expenditures continued to expand. In the words of Allen Schick, "Agencies became more vigorous (and successful) in pressing their claims for larger budget shares. The relationship (between the Budget Bureau and the executive agencies) became more a matter of bargaining, and less one in which high authority dictated the outcome."[6]

Executive agencies acquired new allies and new bargaining chips in their efforts to maintain and increase spending. Outside groups, which benefited from the programs, supported agency requests on Capitol Hill, thereby creating an environment that made it difficult for the president to sustain cuts in these programs. Welfare organizations desire food stamps; farm organizations back price supports; veteran organizations lobby for increased benefits. All put pressure on the budget. As a result, it grew. An expanding economy funded this growth.

Prior to the 1970s these external political pressures were felt indirectly by the bureau. After 1970 the budget agency itself became more directly subjected to outside influences. Changes in the organization and orientation of the agency were primarily responsible for its increased sensitivity to political matters.

A reorganization in July 1970 gave the Budget Bureau its new name, Office of Management and Budget, a new structure, and more political appointees (see Figure 9-4). Four new positions were added. Titled program associate directors (PADs), the executive officials nominated by the president to these positions were given operational responsibility over budget, legislative, and management functions within their respective programmatic areas: national security and international affairs, economics and general government activity, natural resources, and human resources. Civil servants who had previously exercised policy judgments on budgetary and legislative matters were relegated to positions of lesser importance in the organizational hierarchy.

The politicization of the OMB has continued. Presidents Carter and Reagan added additional political positions and staffed them with people who shared their beliefs and perspectives. Today there are approximately two dozen senior political appointees in the OMB.

The functions of the office also expanded during this period. Nixon and Ford used it to improve management techniques and evaluate existing programs. Carter set up a division within the agency to oversee reorganization efforts. Reagan used the office to decrease the size of the federal workforce, increase oversight of executive regulations, and achieve sizable cuts in domestic programs.

In recent times the OMB's political sensitivities and its expanded functions have contributed to its influence. The willingness of presidents to use the agency to promote their objectives have worked to the same end. However, the OMB's ability to effect change has varied over the course of an administration. In the beginning its institutional resources are most valuable in overcoming departmental interests and congressional opposition to achieve presidential goals. In the end its nay-saying abilities are apt to be most effective in maintaining the president's course.

How the Reagan administration achieved its 1981 budget cuts illustrates the advantage the OMB can give a president in his first year in office. In January 1981, before many of the departments were fully staffed and their secretaries had been fully briefed about their budget needs, the OMB proposed major reductions in domestic programs. Almost immediately, budget working groups were established. Composed of key White House personnel, budget officials, and appropriate department secretaries and their aides, the groups reviewed the proposed cuts and made recommendations to the president. In most cases the recommendations supported the cuts. Why? The president had stated his goals, the OMB had a near monopoly over budget information, and the composition of the groups was stacked against the departments. The secretaries were not in a position to advocate their departments' interests even if they wanted to. As a result, sizable reductions were proposed in twelve

Figure 9-4. The Office of Management and Budget, 1984

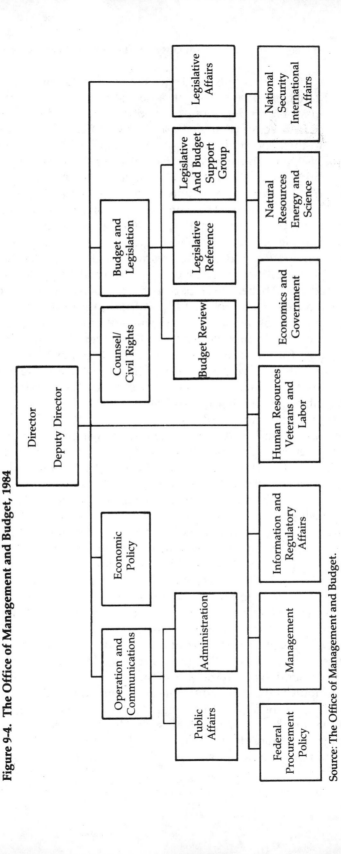

Source: The Office of Management and Budget.

major entitlement programs and in much discretionary spending in only three weeks.[7] Although the Reagan administration attempted to maintain its centralized control over the budgetary process, it was not as successful in subsequent years.

Over time, however, the advantages which the OMB can give a president decline. The inevitability of pressure to maintain existing benefits, the relatively small amount of discretionary spending, and the need to develop its own constituency-oriented programs limit the OMB's ability to effect major change over the course of an administration.

The Executive Departments and Agencies

While the OMB is the principal participant in the executive phase of the budgetary process, it is not the only one. In one way or another every single executive agency has an impact on the budget, mostly on its own.

Departments and agencies are asked to submit yearly estimates for their programs and operational costs. They are expected to defend these estimates before the OMB and the Congress. They may also have to appeal to the president if funding for a particular program is threatened.

Most agencies have a division that coordinates their budget preparation and another that facilitates their legislative activity. In deciding how much to request, agencies have limited discretion. A large percentage of their budget is required by existing legislation, either by formulas written into the law or by long-term commitments. Even within the discretionary portion there are presidential guidelines to follow, ceilings that cannot be exceeded, and administrative costs that must be met.

Nonetheless, the agencies have an advantage. In a bottom-up system they specify their needs. The OMB reacts to department and agency estimates rather than the other way around. According to Allen Schick, "this arrangement is oriented to incremental growth in expenditure, for once demands have been presented to OMB, they strongly influence the outcome."[8]

Agencies tend to request funds within an acceptable range but toward the top of that range. They anticipate that the OMB will revise these requests downward. This expectation contributes to their tendency to pad their estimates and the OMB's inclination to cut them. In general, the agencies that are most aggressive in requesting funds for their programs enjoy the greatest political support.

Budget decisions of an agency frequently have impact beyond that agency. In the 1980s the large increase in defense expenditures came at the expense of domestic programs. Even within the Department of Defense, the intense rivalry among the army, navy, and air force has a major impact on how that department allocates its requests.

The president and his advisers establish the guidelines; the departments and agencies make their estimates; the OMB evaluates those estimates; but Congress has the last word.

The Congress

The Constitution requires that the Congress appropriate all funds which the government spends and raise all revenues which it collects. Congress meets this requirement by the passage of separate appropriation bills and revenue measures. During most of the nineteenth century, policy committees of each house drafted the legislation which appropriated money for the departments and agencies within their jurisdiction. There was no comprehensive national budget.

Following the passage of the Budget and Accounting Act of 1921 in which Congress required the president to present such a budget, the legislature centralized its own spending authority in two appropriation committees. These committees, however, did not consider the budget as a whole. Rather, using the president's executive estimates as guidelines, they drafted individual bills for the separate departments. In many instances, Congress's appropriations did not match the president's budget estimates. Supplemental money bills, passed during the year, also magnified the difference between the president's requests and the appropriations made by Congress. The legislature's consideration of the budget was fragmented and highly political. Members could publicly support the president's goals yet push for exceptions for their own pet projects.

After several abortive attempts to pass a comprehensive budget rather than simply separate appropriation bills, Congress enacted legislation in 1974 that enabled it to do so. The Budget and Impoundment Control Act of that year established a congressional budget process, two congressional committees, and a Congressional Budget Office (CBO) to provide it with an alternate budget capacity. The process set up a timetable for considering the budget; the committees were charged with drafting advisory and binding budget resolutions that the Congress could not exceed; and the CBO provided staff support for revenue and expenditure estimates.

While the Budget and Impoundment Control Act improved the capacity of Congress to consider a comprehensive budget, it did not force the legislature to abide by its own budget decisions. Separate appropriation bills still determined the actual expenditures; separate tax bills still determined the actual revenues. Thus, a gap between budget goals and appropriation and revenue measures was still possible, even probable. The 1974 act, however, did provide a procedure by which Congress could direct its committees to legislate within the guidelines of its budget decisions. This is known as reconciliation and was used for the first time in 1980.

THE CONGRESSIONAL BUDGETARY PROCESS

The congressional phase of the process begins with the budget committees of each House considering the president's request. In stage two the committees report their targets for revenue and expenditures and Congress enacts an advisory budget resolution. During the third phase the authorization and appropriation committees draft their legislation within the guidelines of the budget resolution. In the final stage Congress enacts a second budget resolution and has the power, if it desires, to reconcile differences between its revenue, appropriations and budget committees.

These stages of the process are enumerated below:

February, 2nd year	Budget committees hold hearings as background for concurrent resolution.
March	By March 15, each standing committee sends its budget estimates to House and Senate budget committees.
April	By April 1, budget committees receive fiscal policy report of the Congressional Budget Office.
May	By May 15, first concurrent resolution in which House and Senate agree on budget targets for receipts, budget authorities and outlays is passed.
June 1	OMB sends Congress an update of the President's January budget.
June–September	Authorization and Appropriations bills are considered and adopted by both chambers of Congress.
September	By September 15, second concurrent resolution sets budget ceilings and a floor for expected income.
	By September 25, discrepancies must be reconciled.
	Fiscal Year Begins
October	The fiscal year begins October 1. If Congress has not enacted appropriation bills, it must enact a resolution to continue spending at the current rate or some other rate. Failure to do so will deny money to the government and eventually force its closure.

During the Fiscal Year:
Agencies carry out programs as approved by Congress in appropriations acts and other legislation. OMB oversees agencies' spending, analyzes their progress and effectiveness, and reports to the President from time to time on agencies' operations.

September, 3rd year   The fiscal year ends on September 30.

Source: The Office of Management and Budget, May 1982, pp. 13–15, as amended by the authors.

Reconciliation is a comprehensive, action-forcing process that forces Congress to consider the budget as a whole and enables it to enforce its budgetary decisions on its standing committees. Reconciliation is not a required procedure. Congress must choose to use it. Moreover, it is difficult to use successfully because it involves the participation of many individuals from many committees. Here's how it works: First, Congress adopts a resolution that instructs certain committees to effect savings of specific amounts. Second, these committees recommend changes in laws under their jurisdiction, changes which would achieve the required savings. Third, these revenue and expenditure figures are then formally incorporated into a second *binding* budget resolution by the Congress. Once this is done, the legislature cannot consider bills that would exceed spending or fall short of the revenues specified in the budget.

The value of reconciliation is that it can be used to overcome the parochial, constituency-oriented pressures that normally afflict the congressional budgetary process. Ronald Reagan took advantage of reconciliation in 1981 and 1982 by getting the Democratic House of Representatives to agree to a vote *without* amendments on a binding budget resolution that reconciled the differences between its budget estimates, authorization bills, and revenue measures. In this way he was able to achieve many of his policy objectives through the mechanism of a budget.

The Budget and Impoundment Control Act has not lessened the importance of presidential involvement in the congressional phase of the budgetary process. The president's critical assessments of the economy and his targets for funding continue to provide the basis for Congress's initial deliberations. Over the course of the legislature's budget hearings, mark-up, and floor debate, the president may adjust his projections and requests. In fact, Congress requires a mid-year update. At each stage presidential influence is important if the president's budget proposals are to prevail. With Congress having an alternate budget-making capacity, the president's budget is no longer the only one in town.

Once the budget has been enacted and appropriation bills or continuing resolutions passed, the president's influence is fairly limited. He can exercise his negative as Reagan did in 1982 by vetoing or threatening to veto appropriation bills that exceeded his budget requests. His ability to defer spending or impound funds appropriated by Congress has been constrained by the 1974 act. According to this law, any presidential proposal to rescind expenditures must be approved by both houses of Congress within forty-five days; any presidential proposal to defer spending can be reversed by the action of the House or the Senate within a year.

THE BUDGET AND PRESIDENTIAL DECISION MAKING

The impediments on presidential influence in Congress explain why presidents in recent times have been more successful in articulating their budgets than in getting them enacted into law. With over half of the Senate and a fourth of the House serving on budget, appropriations, or revenue committees, the task is difficult for the president, his aides, and party leaders on the Hill. Their political clout and legislative skills are necessary to make the effort a success, although the clout and skills, in and of themselves, may not be sufficient. It is almost always the case that compromises must be made by the president to salvage some of his priorities and claim to victory.

Ronald Reagan is a good example of a president who effectively mobilized a majority coalition for his budget in the first two years of his administration. To do so, he had to meet with many members of Congress, individually and collectively; make major public appeals to generate support; and organize interest group leaders, particularly in the financial and business communities, to back his proposals. Reagan even used the veto to deter Congress from passing bills that exceeded his budget, a practice that Nixon and Ford also followed.

Reagan's success, however, came at a high cost. Legislative lobbying consumed much of his time and budget and tax matters much of the Congress's agenda. Fewer major legislative proposals were enacted into law during this period than in previous administrations.

ECONOMIC POLICY MAKING

Presidents have been involved in the budgetary process since 1921, but not until the administration of Franklin Roosevelt in the 1930s have they been concerned on a regular basis with economic policy making.

Prior to that time presidential activities were generally limited to initiating or supporting proposals to correct specific problems that had arisen within the economy. Theodore Roosevelt's trust-busting and Woodrow Wilson's labor reforms are two examples of these early forms of presidential involvement.

The depth of the depression, the degree of public panic, and Herbert Hoover's resounding election defeat signaled the beginning of a more comprehensive presidential role in the economy. No longer could presidents enjoy the luxury of standing on the sidelines. Franklin Roosevelt's activism became the model for his Democratic successors. Even Republicans found that there was no turning back.

Congress expected and even required this involvement. The Employment Act of 1946 obligated the president to prime the economy to maximize employment and production. The Taft-Hartley Act of 1947 gave the president the power to intervene in labor-management disputes that threatened the nation's security and well-being. In each case Congress not only acknowledged an expanded presidential role but created mechanisms to help the executive fulfill it.

Every president since Roosevelt has strived to meet these expanded expectations. Their policies, however, have differed. Truman, Kennedy, and Reagan desired to lower taxes to stimulate economic growth. Eisenhower and Ford tried to achieve savings by cutting government spending. Johnson obtained a surtax to help pay for the costs of the Vietnam War and his Great Society programs, while Nixon implemented wage and price controls to reduce inflation and stabilize the economy. Carter tried a variety of revenue and budget measures to deal with the high inflation and stagnant economy which plagued his presidency.

Differing fiscal approaches lay at the core of these presidential policies. A fiscal strategy is a plan to manipulate government revenue and expenditures to influence economic conditions. In contrast, a monetary approach regulates the supply of money to affect change. Presidents cannot affect monetary policy, generally the prerogative of the Federal Reserve Board (FED), nearly as much as they can influence fiscal policy. However, even with fiscal policy, as pointed out in the previous section, it is the Congress which enacts appropriations and revenue bills. Although the president can influence the legislature's actions, he cannot control them.

Until recently, fiscal strategies were predicated on Keynesian economics. John Maynard Keynes, an eminent British economist, argued that increases in government spending and reductions in government taxes would stimulate demand and invigorate the economy during periods of sluggish activity. The only trouble with adopting such a policy is that it also results initially in budget deficits. Keynes was not worried about these deficits, however, because he believed that in the long run a vibrant economy would generate greater revenues, reducing or eliminating the difference between expenditures and income. With the exception of Eisenhower, Presidents Truman through Nixon subscribed to this belief.

An expanding economy coupled with relatively low unemployment and inflation during most of the 1950s and 1960s seemed to confirm the merits of the Keynesian approach. By the beginning of the 1970s, however, economic conditions began to change. Budget deficits increased, the rate of growth declined, and inflation rose dramatically throughout the decade. Other economic theories began to command attention.

Monetarists, led by Professor Milton Friedman of the University of Chicago, contended that the supply of money was the key to sound economic growth. Increasing interest rates would reduce the amount of money in circulation, decreasing inflationary pressure and cooling the economy. Lowering interest rates, on the other hand, would have the opposite effect, stimulating demand and output by making borrowing cheaper and more money available. In periods of high inflation and an overheated economy, a tight money policy made sense. But when inflation was high and the economy stagnant, it did not. It was precisely this condition in the late 1970s that gave credence to still another economic strategy—supply-side economics.

The supply-side philosophy combined the Keynesian approach to generating demand with the monetarist's desire to regulate currency. Tax cuts stimulate spending while money supply controls inflation. Ronald Reagan, an advocate of this approach, sought to implement the fiscal component of this strategy as president. He proposed budgets that increased defense expenditures, cut domestic programs, and substantially reduced corporate and personal federal income taxes. Congress enacted the bulk of his requests during his first two years in office although he was forced to modify his tax stand in 1982 because of the need for additional revenues and the desirability of closing tax loopholes.

While the tax cuts eventually stimulated the economy, the nation also suffered the largest budget deficit in its history (which in the short run also acted as an economic stimulus). Reagan, who had promised to achieve a balanced budget during his 1980 campaign for the presidency (as had Franklin Roosevelt in 1932), and who had supported a balanced budget amendment while president, argued that the deficit was "institutional" and would be eventually reduced by a vigorous economy. He believed that a stimulated economy would produce greatly increased revenues for the government. When that did not occur, Reagan proposed a down-payment on the deficit, a plan to reduce expenditures to cut the size of the deficit. Much debate ensued over the Reagan plan and others proposed by members of the House and Senate.

The success of Reagan's economic program, or any president's program, for that matter, is hard to measure. Mixed economic indicators, differing time frames, competing priorities, and changing world conditions make comparison and evaluation difficult. Nonetheless, the expectation that the president will propose economic policy, will mobilize support for it, and will consider its success critical to his administration is widespread. The issue is not whether the president will be a maker of economic policy but what kind of economic policies he will make. To help him with these efforts, an economic advisory mechanism within the presidency has been created.

ECONOMIC POLICYMAKERS

The Department of the Treasury

Most of the president's economic advisory structure has been established by Congress. The Treasury Department was the first executive-branch agency to play a major role in the financial affairs of government. Charged with responsibility for collecting and dispersing federal funds, its functions have gradually expanded to include debt financing, import controls, and drug enforcement. Even the Coast Guard falls under its purview.

Representing the financial community, this department has exercised a conservative influence throughout the years on matters of economic policy. Its orientation is to promote stability and long-term growth. The secretary of the treasury has become the nation's chief economic spokesman.

The Federal Reserve Board

The second oldest government agency concerned with economic policy is the Federal Reserve Board (known as the FED). However, it is not a presidential agency. Created by legislation in 1913, its principal function is to regulate monetary policy. It does so by adjusting the discount rate that commercial banks must pay when they borrow money from one of the member banks in the Federal Reserve System. The percentage of deposits that commercial banks must maintain is also regulated by the FED. A third way the Federal Reserve Board can affect the money supply is by requesting its regional banks to buy or sell government securities on the open market.

The FED operates with considerable autonomy from the president and Congress. Its members, nominated by the president and appointed with the advice and consent of the Senate, serve for fourteen years. Its chairman, designated by the president from members of the board of governors, has a four-year term that does not coincide with the president's. This increases the chairman's independence.

Over the years there has been some tension between the FED's monetary policy and the president's fiscal policy. This was evident in the Reagan years when the president desired lower interest rates to stimulate spending and the FED kept higher rates as a hedge against inflation. Although the administration publicly vented some of its displeasure, there was little it could do beyond "gentle persuasion" to change the FED's policy. In the end President Reagan muted his criticism and reappointed Paul A. Volcker as chairman of the FED.

The Council of Economic Advisers

The economic advisory units within the Executive Office of the President are the Council of Economic Advisers (CEA) and the Office of Management and Budget. Both have been established by statute. The Employment Act of 1946 created the CEA and charged it with advising the president on macroeconomic policy. This included analyzing economic conditions, forecasting trends, and preparing the president's annual economic report to the Congress. In addition to providing the president with long-term advice, the council has become increasingly involved in short-term microeconomic issues such as trade policy, deregulation, even credit and housing programs. It has avoided operational responsibilities, however.

The council is small and specialized. It is composed of three members appointed by the president with the advice and consent of the Senate. They serve at the president's discretion. The chairman is the principal link to the White House and to the president's other economic advisers.

The council is supported by a small staff, approximately twenty-five professionals, mostly economists, who come primarily from the academic community. Members of the council are also drawn from academia and frequently have worked on the council's staff prior to their appointment. All but two of the chairmen have been university professors.

The academic orientation of the council has made it less subject to outside pressures than other economic advisory units. As a consequence, when strong political pressures are exerted, the chairman of the council can take a longer-term, less partisan perspective than can some of the president's other advisers. This was particularly evident during the third and fourth years of the Reagan administration, when council chairman Martin Feldstein frequently clashed with the administration's public position on interest rates and the deficit. After two years in office, Feldstein returned to his academic position.

In general, the council has declined in influence as economic policy has become more political and as the number of economic advisers has

I THINK FELDSTEIN IS SENDING THE WRONG SIGNAL TO THE MARKETS AGAIN.

DEFICITS

Source: By Dan Wasserman, © Los Angeles Times Syndicate. Reprinted by permission.

proliferated. Nonetheless, the personal relationship of the chairman and the president remains the key to the council's impact on economic policy making. Arthur Burns (Eisenhower), Walter Heller (Kennedy), and Alan Greenspan (Ford) were three chairmen who had their president's confidence and were able to exercise considerable influence on economic decisions.

The Office of Management and Budget

The OMB also performs economic advisory functions for the president. Not only does its director participate in the initial forecasts for revenue and expenditures as budget planning gets under way, but he and his associates continually analyze and evaluate the merits of department and agency requests. Revisions of the initial budget forecasts are also the responsibility of the OMB. The director regularly meets with the president's senior economic advisers.

THE COORDINATION OF ECONOMIC ADVICE

In addition to using the Treasury Department, the Council of Economic Advisers, and the OMB in an advisory capacity, presidents have also concocted a number of other institutional arrangements for soliciting and coordinating recommendations and advice. The origins and organizations of these groups have varied.

Two political scientists, Erwin Hargrove and Michael Nelson, suggest that the pattern of economic advising since World War II can be described in stages.[9] In the first, 1946 to 1960, a broad, relatively unstructured relationship existed among the chairman of the Council of Economic Advisers, the director of the Bureau of the Budget, and the secretaries of the treasury, commerce, and agriculture. These individuals, both collectively and individually, provided the president with advice, advocacy, and administration within the economic sphere.

Beginning in 1960 and continuing through the end of the Nixon administration, relationships among the president's primary economic advisers became institutionalized. A troika, consisting of the heads of the three major advisory bodies, the Treasury Department, the OMB, and the CEA, met on a regular basis to coordinate policy. Within the group a rough division of authority emerged with the secretary of the treasury becoming the major spokesman and revenue adviser, the chairman of the council the principal forecaster and analyst, and the budget director the chief overseer of expenditures. Other cabinet secretaries, who had previously rendered economic advice, were generally excluded. This had the effect of reducing the impact of outside forces on the group and maximizing the range of presidential decisions.

The third phase of economic advising commenced in the 1970s. It is characterized by more participants and more external influences on policy judgments. With national economies more interdependent, foreign, defense, and national security affairs have greater impact on economic decisions and vice versa. As a consequence, the secretaries of state and defense, the president's national security adviser, and his special representative for trade negotiations all have legitimate concerns about the country's economic policy. Similarly, the explosion of federal programs in the 1960s, particularly entitlement programs, has created a large public constituency interested in and affected by economic decisions.

To cope with a policy-making process that has become more fragmentary, pluralistic, and political, recent administrations have had to devise mechanisms, consistent with its president's particular style of decision making, that permit a range of views to be presented and a range of interests to be accommodated, yet at the same time, that work to coordinate these concerns, to maximize the president's discretion, and to articulate his decisions in a single voice.

In the Ford administration an Economic Policy Board (EPB) performed these functions. The board, consisting of practically the entire cabinet, was run by an executive committee composed of the president's chief economic advisers and those domestic department heads who had an ongoing interest in a range of broad economic issues. Meeting three to four times a week, this executive committee functioned as a policy forum and conduit. The president attended its sessions on an average of once a week. The EPB was supported by a staff structure tied to the office of the president's assistant for economic affairs, a new position Ford had created. The head of this office presented the board's recommendations to the president and saw that the president's decisions were properly executed.

During the Carter presidency a more informal economic policy group emerged. While its composition was similar to Ford's EPB, Carter's organization lacked a staff back-up and a regular meeting schedule. Over time, key White House personnel, particularly domestic aide Stuart Eizenstat, became more involved in the details of economic policy decisions.

President Reagan reverted to the Ford model although he did not resurrect his Economic Policy Board. Rather, Reagan utilized cabinet councils, principally the one on economic affairs, for coordination and advice. Meeting several times a week, with the president occasionally in attendance, the Council on Economic Affairs discussed a range of policy issues from budgets and taxes to foreign investment, strategic reserves, and banking institutions.[10] Other cabinet councils also considered issues that had an economic content and impact.[11]

In addition to the cabinet councils, the Reagan administration also regularized less formal contacts among the president's principal economic advisers and their deputies. Two groups, one consisting of the chiefs of the treasury, the OMB, and the CEA and the other composed of their assistants, met separately on a weekly basis to prepare assumptions and forecast trends in the economy.

The advantage of the more formal arrangement for Ford and Reagan was that it relieved them of day-to-day decision making but still permitted them the opportunity to establish broad policy guidelines. In both administrations economic groups developed a range of options from which each president made his decisions. In contrast, the Carter system maximized the president's personal involvement, but it also placed greater decisional responsibilities on his shoulders. Carter liked to make decisions and calculate their costs and benefits himself, but he did not possess an overarching economic philosophy to guide his choices. As a result, his policy lacked consistency and coherence. Eventually, he lost interest in economic matters.

THE POLITICS OF ECONOMIC DECISION MAKING

Economic policy making has become more political, more pragmatic, and less stable. These changes have affected the advice the president receives as well as the accommodations he must make.

The recommendation process is more sensitive to outside pressures from Congress, the bureaucracy, and organized interest groups, each of which has its own interests to protect and its own political axes to grind. Members of Congress must consider the economic impact on their constituencies, while department and agency heads must be responsive to their clientele, and organized groups must placate their supporters. To the extent that economic decisions require coalition building to become public policy, presidents must take these varied interests into account.

The politicization of economic decision making has made long-range planning more difficult. The election cycle must be considered when calculating the effect of policy change. Policymakers key recoveries to their own benefit whenever possible.

Not only do short-run considerations such as elections tend to drive economic decisions, but they also enhance the pragmatic character of the decisions themselves. Presidents are more inclined to strive for what is politically feasible than what may be theoretically optimal or ideologically desirable. The experience of the Reagan administration is a case in point. Coming into office with clear-cut views of how it wished to stimulate the economy, the administration was forced to compromise its initial budget and tax proposals in order to get them enacted into law.[12] The compromises became more extensive as the next presidential election approached and presidential influence in Congress declined. Pragmatic considerations, in short, muted the administration's ideological perspective but at the same time enhanced the chances for the passage of its legislative proposals.

The impact of politics on economic policy decisions has had another effect. It has made those decisions less stable over time. Unanticipated events and unintended consequences have forced presidents frequently to adjust their economic programs. President Ford was forced to abandon his Whip Inflation Now (WIN) program as economic conditions deteriorated and the country fell into a recession. President Carter had to recant a promise to provide tax payers with a fifty dollar rebate as the budget deficit soared. President Reagan had to support the largest tax increase in the nation's history (referred to as a revenue enhancement plan) one year after getting his massive tax cut through Congress.

Another factor that contributes to fluctuations in economic policy is the economy itself. Although presidents are ritually blamed for unfavorable conditions and are expected to improve them, many events and situations are beyond their immediate control. Existing laws establish levels of revenue and high percentages of expenditures. Interest rates dictate the cost of government borrowing while cost-of-living adjustments (COLAs) automatically raise federal outlays. Presidents inherit these laws which they are sworn to enforce. Over time they can try to change them, but as recent presidents have discovered, change is not easy.

Similarly, international forces and events affect the American economy. The rise in the price of imported oil in the mid-1970s contributed to the inflation in the United States at the end of the decade. The reindustrialization of West Germany and Japan and the growth of new industries in Asia have adversely affected American competition in steel, shipbuilding, textile, and automobile manufacturing. The weakness and strength of the U.S. dollar affect the flow of trade and tourism, the stability of financial markets, and the ability of countries to meet their foreign debts. All of these factors have short and long-term consequences. All of them interfere with the president's ability to manipulate the economy along the lines he desires despite the fact that the president is ritually blamed for the economy's poor performance and lauded for its success.

These external factors also affect the process of making economic decisions. They have made that process more complex. They have produced more people inside and outside the government who are interested in economic decisions. More interests must be balanced, more coordination is necessary, more time must be devoted to economic affairs. The burdens on the president and his advisers are greater; economic issues have more political impact; yet presidential control is more difficult to achieve. In no other policy area (except possibly the budget) are presidential limits more discernible. The increased complexity of the economic decision-making process compounds the president's leadership problem.

CONCLUSION

Presidential responsibility has been enlarged in budgetary and economic spheres. That enlargement has been a product of need, statute, and precedent. Acknowledging its inability to fashion comprehensive budget and economic policy, Congress has required the president to do so. This requirement, coupled with the expanded role of the federal government, has forced presidents and their staffs to devote increasing resources to these activities.

It has not been easy. Expectations of presidential performance have grown, but the president's capacity to affect budgetary and economic matters has not kept pace. Much of the budget is dictated by existing law and policy commitments. Presidents can affect discretionary funding, but even here political pressures often undercut their efforts to reorder spending priorities and revenue measures. Similarly, within the economic sphere, a myriad of forces from within the country and abroad are not easily subject to the president's control. These factors mute presidential efforts to stimulate the economy, but at the same time, make those efforts more important.

To help the president fulfill expectations of leadership within these areas, advisory mechanisms have developed and decision-making processes have evolved. The OMB continues to be the principal unit to provide the president with budget advice and oversee spending requests. However, the needs of the departments and agencies, the concerns of the House and Senate, and the interests of organized groups have involved many more participants in the budgetary and economic policy-making processes. This involvement has increased the complexity of these processes and has made them more political and less easily subject to presidential control.

For the president this has meant that he must devote more attention to economic matters (including the budget), he must weigh more interests in making critical judgments, and he must use more skills in articulating an administration position. For the presidency these changes have placed greater stress on the organizational mechanism that coordinates and integrates the policy decisions and builds support for them inside and outside the government. For budgetary policy they have made it more difficult to control expenditures, although Reagan has demonstrated that priorities can be reordered. For economic policy they have produced a short-term perspective with more variation within and between administrations, a policy that tends to emphasize political feasibility.

In short, presidential roles have increased but presidential influence has declined within the budgetary and economic spheres. Presidents have less ability to control the factors that affect their judgments. Yet those judgments are increasingly expected to solve national problems and promote national prosperity. As a consequence, presidents and their aides must devote more time to budgetary and economic policy formulation, promotion, and implementation. They must coordinate support within the executive, build coalitions within Congress, balance interests, and maintain the confidence of the general public—a tall order to be sure.

NOTES

1. Our description of the evolution of the budget is based primarily on Allen Schick's discussion and analysis in his paper, "The Politics of Budgeting: Can Incrementalism Survive in a Decremental Age?" (paper presented at the Annual Meeting of the American Political Science Association, Denver, Colorado, September 2–5, 1982).

2. In 1920 federal expenditures totaled $6.357 billion. By 1930 they had been reduced to $3.32 billion.

3. Louis Fisher, *Presidential Spending Power* (Princeton: Princeton University Press, 1975), p. 35.

4. Larry Berman, *The Office of Management and Budget and the Presidency, 1921–1979* (Princeton: Princeton University Press, 1979), p. 8.

5. Ibid., p. 102.

6. Schick, "The Politics of Budgeting," p. 7.

7. For a description of this process see William Greider, "The Education of David Stockman," *Atlantic*, December 1981, pp. 33–34.

8. Allen Schick, "The Budget as an Instrument of Presidential Policy" (paper presented at the Urban Institute Conference on Governance: The Reagan Era and Beyond, Washington, D.C., December 15–16, 1983), p. 34.

9. Erwin C. Hargrove and Michael Nelson, *Presidents' Politics and Policy* (New York: Knopf, 1984), pp. 186–189.

10. Task forces operating at the subcabinet level supplemented the council's deliberations with working papers and in-depth studies. An executive secretary from the president's domestic policy office provided White House staff support and coordination [Murray L. Weidenbaum, "Economic Policymaking in the Reagan Administration," *Presidential Studies Quarterly* 12 (Winter, 1982): 95].

11. These cabinet councils included the Council on Commerce and Trade (business issues), the Council on Human Resources (health policy and social security), the Council on Food and Agriculture (agricultural land policy), and the Council on Natural Resources and Environment (energy issues).

12. Hugh Heclo and Rudolph G. Penner, "Fiscal and Political Strategy in the Reagan Administration," in Fred I. Greenstein, ed., *The Reagan Presidency* (Baltimore: Johns Hopkins University Press, 1983); Allen Schick, "How the Budget Was Won and Lost," in Norman J. Ornstein, ed., *President and Congress* (Washington, D.C.: American Enterprise Institute, 1982).

SELECTED READINGS

Berman, Larry. *The Office of Management and Budget and the Presidency, 1921–1979.* Princeton: Princeton University Press, 1979.

Fisher, Louis. *Presidential Spending Powers.* Princeton: Princeton University Press, 1975.

Greider, William. "The Education of David Stockman." *Atlantic*, December 1981:27–54.

Heclo, Hugh, and Rudolph G. Penner. "Fiscal and Political Strategy in the Reagan Administration." In Fred I. Greenstein, ed., *The Reagan Presidency.* Baltimore: Johns Hopkins University Press, 1983.

Mowery, David C.; Mark S. Kamlet; and John P. Crecine. "Presidential Management of Budgetary and Fiscal Policymaking." *Political Science Quarterly* 95 (Fall 1980):395–426.

Porter, Roger B. "Economic Advice to the President." *Political Science Quarterly* 98 (1983):403–26.

————. *Presidential Decision Making: The Economic Policy Board.* Cambridge: Cambridge University Press, 1980.

Schick, Allen. "How the Budget Was Won and Lost." In Norman J. Ornstein, ed., *President and Congress.* Washington, D.C.: American Enterprise Institute, 1982.

————. *Reconciliation and the Congressional Budget Process.* Washington, D.C.: American Enterprise Institute, 1981.

Stein, Herbert. *Presidential Economics: The Making of Economic Policy from Roosevelt to Reagan and Beyond.* New York: Simon and Schuster, 1984.

Weidenbaum, Murray L. "Economic Policy Making in the Reagan Administration." *Presidential Studies Quarterly* 12 (Winter 1982):95–99.

10

Foreign and Defense Policy Making

Few would question the president's obligation to preserve and protect the nation. Few would deny him the constitutional and statutory authority to do so. Few would dispute his need to perform a variety of roles with the help of a responsive supporting staff. Still, the extent of the president's powers, the scope of his roles, and the nature of his advisory system have all been subject to controversy.

In this chapter we will examine the president's multiple responsibilities in foreign and military affairs and the debate over how these responsibilities have been and should be met. After describing the president's formal authority first in theory and then practice, we turn to the expansion of the president's policy-making role, identifying the factors which have contributed to that expansion and the success presidents have had in achieving their policy goals. Changes in the international and domestic environment, particularly within the last decade, have presented leadership problems. We discuss those problems and their impact on presidential policy making and then go on to describe the advisory mechanism that has been created to help the president coordinate, formulate, articulate, and implement foreign and military policy. We examine this mechanism and assess its effect on policy, the presidency, and the governmental system.

CONSTITUTIONAL AND STATUTORY AUTHORITY

The Original Design

The president's powers in foreign affairs and national defense have expanded significantly beyond their original design. The framers of the Constitution anticipated a policy-making role for the president, but they did not desire the executive to dominate that role. On the contrary, their fear that a president might pursue personal interests at the expense of the nation's welfare led them to divide and share responsibilities in such a way that the executive lacked the authority to conclude policy on his own. Whether or not to go to war was to be the decision of Congress. The president had discretion to react in times of emergency but presumably not to establish permanent war policy. The expectation was that he would summon Congress to do so. The president could, however, terminate hostilities.

Short of war, the executive was given a broad prerogative in foreign affairs. He could initiate treaties in conjunction with the Senate; their approval required the concurrence of two-thirds of the upper chamber. Within foreign and military spheres the president was expected to exercise executive authority. This included nominating ambassadors and receiving them. Senate approval was required for the appointment to take effect. The performance of the ceremonial duties of a head of state was also seen as a presidential duty. Similarly, the president could nominate military officials and nominally, at least, command them. How command was to work in practice, however, was not enumerated.

In performing these executive responsibilities, the president would inevitably make decisions that had policy implications. The framers did not fear this. They anticipated that Congress by virtue of its power to appropriate money, authorize programs, and regulate commerce, would establish the contours of that policy.

The Exercise of Powers

TREATY MAKING   Treaty making was to be jointly exercised with the Senate. An incident that occurred early in the Washington administration, however, soured this arrangement and presaged the difficulties that the president would have in dealing with the upper chamber as both an advisory and consenting body. In August 1789, President Washington came to the Senate to request its advice on a treaty with the Indians of West Georgia. Armed with thirteen questions prepared by his secretary of war, General Knox, Washington desired the Senate's guidance in the negotiations. Instead, he was treated to a long, discursive discussion that reached no decision. Forced to return two days later for what turned out to be insipid advice, Washington did not personally go back to the Senate for its counsel. Instead, he and his successors turned to their principal department heads for advice and to the Senate primarily for its consent as required by the Constitution.

The experience had a profound effect on presidential-senatorial relations. It discouraged the president from involving the Senate in the negotiation phase of treaty making. While some consultation continued, presidents began to do more on their own. Woodrow Wilson's refusal to consider senatorial opinion in the negotiations on the Versailles Treaty represents one of the most flagrant examples of chief executive's going it alone.

Historically, the Senate has approved without modification about 70 percent of the approximately 1,600 treaties that have been submitted to it by the president since 1789. Only 16 of those that have come to a vote have been voted down (the most famous probably being the Treaty of Versailles ending World War I and establishing the League of Nations). However, many other proposed treaties have been withdrawn by the president because of opposition in the Senate and thus have never come up for a vote. About 150 have been withdrawn since World War II, including the SALT (strategic arms limitation talks) II treaty proposed by President Carter and withdrawn to protest the Soviet Union's armed presence in Afghanistan.

Not only can the Senate approve treaties without modification or reject them outright, but it can also approve them with reservations or with amendments, thereby requiring changes or deletions. In early 1978 the Senate consented to two treaties dealing with the Panama Canal. It added a reservation to one of them stating that the United States had a right to use military force, if necessary, to keep the canal open.

Once a change has been made to a treaty, it usually must go to the president and the other country or countries who are parties to the treaty for approval.[1] Additions and deletions are not always approved, however, and many treaties have failed for this reason.

From time to time the House of Representatives has also attempted to impose itself in the treaty-making process, but frequently without success. Arguing that the Congress as a body is empowered to deal with foreign commerce, military affairs, war, and international policy, it has proposed legislation and used its appropriations authority to this end. Both the president and the Senate have resisted the lower chamber's intrusion into their exclusive domain, however.

Whereas Senate consent is necessary for the ratification of treaties, it has not been considered essential for their termination. When President Carter ended a long-standing defense treaty with the Chinese Nationalists on Taiwan, he did not request the approval of the Senate. The legality of Carter's action, challenged by Senator Barry Goldwater, was upheld in court.

FORMULATING EXECUTIVE AGREEMENTS   The need to obtain the Senate's consent has encouraged recent presidents to enter into executive agreements in order to avoid the formal treaty-ratification process. The number of such agreements has mushroomed in recent years as indicated in Table 10-1. As of January 1, 1983, there were 966 treaties and 6,571 executive agreements in force.

An executive agreement is concluded by the president on behalf of

Table 10-1. Treaties and Executive Agreements, 1789–1982

Period	Treaties	Executive Agreements
1789–1839	60	27
1839–1889	215	238
1889–1939	524	917
1940–1970	310	5,653
1971–1982	201	3,779

Source: Figures for 1789–1970, Louis Fisher, *President and Congress* (Macmillan, 1972), p. 45. 1971–1982 provided to the author by Department of State, Washington, D.C.

the United States with the head of government of another country. Unlike a treaty, it does not require a two-thirds vote of the Senate. Thus, when President Tyler failed to get the Senate to approve a treaty annexing Texas, he entered into an executive agreement to do so. Most executive agreements do not even need formal congressional approval, although some may require legislation to implement them. Such legislation is subject to a simple majority vote of both houses.

Unlike treaties, executive agreements do not supersede statutes with which they conflict. Otherwise, they are just as binding as treaties and have been used for such famous compacts as the destroyer-bases deal with Great Britain in 1940, the Yalta and Potsdam agreements in 1945, and the Vietnam peace agreement of 1973.

Presidents have been careful in their choice of instruments for making international agreements. In recent years treaties have dealt with subjects such as shrimp, the protection of Mexican archaeological artifacts, dumping wastes at sea, and the maintenance of lights in the Red Sea; executive agreements have also been used to end wars and to establish or expand military bases in other countries. In 1972, as a result of SALT, President Nixon signed a treaty limiting the defensive weapons of the Soviet Union and the United States and an executive agreement limiting the offensive weapons of each country. Although most executive agreements are routine and deal with noncontroversial subjects such as food deliveries or customs enforcement, some implement important and controversial policies.

To influence executive agreements, Congress needs to know about them before they are finalized, while options are still open. Even more basic, it needs to know that the agreements even exist. In 1969 and 1970, the Senate Foreign Relations Committee discovered that presidents had covertly entered into a number of significant agreements with South Vietnam, South Korea, Thailand, Laos, Ethiopia, Spain, and other countries. In response to these actions Congress passed the Case Act of 1972, which requires the secretary of state to transmit to Congress within sixty days the text of any international agreement other than treaties to which the United States is a party. If the president feels publication of an agreement would jeopardize national security, he may transmit the text only to members of the Senate Foreign Relations and House Foreign Affairs committees under an injunction of secrecy that only he (or his successors) may remove.

Presidents Nixon and Ford did not fully comply with the Case Act, however. Some agreements were not submitted to Congress and others were submitted after the sixty-day period. Consequently, in 1977 Congress passed legislation requiring any department or agency of the U.S. government that enters into any international agreement on behalf of the United States to transmit the text to the State Department within twenty days of its signing. Neither of these two laws actually limits the president's power to act without Congress in defense and foreign affairs. Yet their passage indicates that Congress is increasingly unwilling to defer blindly to the president's judgment.

RECOGNIZING AND NOT RECOGNIZING COUNTRIES   In addition to negotiating treaties and formulating executive agreements, presidents can initiate or terminate relations with other countries. The right of recognition has traditionally been considered a presidential responsibility. George Washington exercised it when he received Citizen Genêt and thereby recognized the new French Republic in 1789. Presidents have even extended this to acknowledging the rights of a people who lack a state and to continuing to recognize a government that has been removed from power. The Senate has no role in this process other than to consent to the choice of the American ambassador.

Recognizing countries can be controversial. In 1933 Franklin D. Roosevelt recognized the government of the Soviet Union, fifteen years after it was constituted and functioning. In 1979 Jimmy Carter extended recognition to the government that controlled mainland China, the People's Republic, following a period of thirty years of nonrecognition. In 1984 Ronald Reagan announced the resumption of formal diplomatic relations with the Vatican. Each of these actions provoked criticism about the merits of the president's judgment, but not his right to make it.

Presidents can also end relations. Before war ensues it is customary to sever relations with adversaries. Similarly, events short of war can also result in a disruption of diplomatic activity. The revolutionary activities of Cuba and Iran led Presidents Eisenhower and Carter to cut formal ties with these countries. However, some contact was maintained by an "interests section" that operated out of the embassy of a friendly country.

There are other actions that presidents can take to register their disapproval of the policies of other countries. Recalling an ambassador, instituting a trade embargo, reducing economic or military assistance, boycotting the Olympics, are all devices which contemporary presidents have employed to sanction the actions of others.

MAKING WAR   The Constitution gives Congress the sole power to declare war, a power it has exercised only five times (in 1812, 1846, 1898, 1917, 1941). Such full-scale wars as those in Korea and Vietnam were not officially declared by Congress. In addition, presidents have employed a more limited use of force abroad without a declaration of war or statutory authority on approximately one hundred occasions, about half of which lasted more than thirty days.

The roles as commander-in-chief, head of state, and head of government have undoubtedly contributed to the capacity of presidents to commit the nation to battle. Armed with a near-monopoly of first-hand information, a potential for engaging public support, and an oath to provide for the common defense, they have used their prerogatives to broaden their constitutional powers. Jefferson ordered the navy and marines to retaliate against the Barbary pirates who threatened American shipping. Polk ordered the army into disputed territory with Mexico to protect Texas's claim to its borders. Lincoln instituted a blockade of the South and imposed other sanctions to put down the southern insurrection. Recent instances include the orders of President Eisenhower to send armed forces to Lebanon in 1958, of President Kennedy to blockade Cuba in 1962, of President Johnson to dispatch troops to the Dominican Republic in 1965, of President Nixon to bomb Cambodia in 1970, of President Ford to attack Cambodia to rescue the crew of the *Mayaquez* (a U.S. merchant ship seized by Cambodia in 1975), of President Carter to rescue the American hostages in Iran, and of President Reagan to send an armed force to the Caribbean island of Grenada in 1983 as well as marines to Lebanon that year.

Theoretically, Congress could have resisted such executive actions. In practice it has been unable and unwilling to do so. The House of Representatives condemned Polk, but after the Mexican War had been concluded. Congress forced Nixon to end bombing in Cambodia, but only after that action had been carried on for more than two years. During periods of crises, Congress finds it difficult, if not impossible, to oppose the president.

The war in Vietnam, which stirred up deep dissent at home, was the last straw. In 1973 Congress passed the War Powers Resolution over President Nixon's veto. It requires that the president consult with Congress "in every possible instance" involving the use of American troops in hostile or potentially hostile situations. The president must report to Congress in writing within forty-eight hours after ordering U.S. armed forces into hostilities. More significantly, the military action must stop sixty days after the submission of this report unless Congress declares war, authorizes the use of force, extends the sixty-day period, or is unable to meet because of an attack upon the United States. At any time Congress can end the use of American armed forces by passing a concurrent resolution (which is not subject to a presidential veto).[2] The president may extend the use of force for thirty additional days if he deems it necessary to protect departing American troops.

The law has aroused considerable debate about just what consultation means and whether the president could, in sixty days of hostilities, place the United States in a position from which Congress could not extract it. These issues were not resolved by the applications of the War Powers Resolution since its passage: the evacuations from Southeast Asia in April 1975, the rescue of the *Mayaquez* from Cambodia in May 1975, and the attempted rescue of the hostages from Iran in 1980 and the Grenada invasion of 1983. Each of these operations was brief and broadly supported by the general public.

It is unclear the extent to which the War Powers Resolution applied to the United States peacekeeping force in Lebanon in 1983. President Reagan claimed the authority to commit American troops under his powers as commander-in-chief. Members of Congress believed that the War Powers Resolution should have taken effect. The issue was not whether the president could send troops but how long they could stay without congressional authorization. A compromise was eventually reached that established an eighteen-month period in which American armed forces could remain. The troops were withdrawn before this period elapsed.

The type of presidential actions that the War Powers Resolution seems designed to prevent, the long-term conventional limited wars similar to Korea and Vietnam, seem to be those that are least likely to occur if the political climate that has existed in the United States since the mid-1970s persists. However, if that climate were to change, the propensity of Congress to support military action initiated by the president would probably increase as well. In general, the shorter the time frame and the quicker the needed response, the less likely Congress can play an important role.

Although Congress is not likely to oppose presidential involvement in emergency situations which threaten the national security or adversely affect American interests abroad, its propensity for influencing presidential policy in nonemergency situations has increased. Congress's power to authorize conscription or maintain an all-volunteer military, to appropriate money for defense, even to affect the sales of arms has been greater in peacetime. Since the war in Vietnam, presidents can no longer count on bipartisan support for military actions, alliances, and aid. In 1981 President Reagan had to use all of his persuasive powers to keep Congress from preventing a sale of special reconnaissance aircraft known as AWACS (Airborne Warning and Control System) to Saudi Arabia.

COMMANDING THE MILITARY   The president's powers as commander-in-chief have also been expanded. The initial concept of this role was unclear. Did the framers of the Constitution vest the president with a title, civilian head of the military, or empower him with operational authority? Over the years, presidents began to behave as if they had operational authority. Lincoln used the crisis of the Civil War to institute a series of military actions including a blockade of the South, the arrest of suspected traitors, activation of the state militia, establishment of military courts in areas of civil insurrection, and suspension of the writ of habeas corpus. Lincoln also got involved in the conduct of the war and the selection of field commanders.

Other presidents have also expanded the operational component of their commander-in-chief responsibilities. Franklin Roosevelt ordered the internment of persons of Japanese ancestry on the West Coast, chose the principal theaters of operations and points of invasion, and established a map room in the White House to keep abreast of developments in World War II. Harry Truman ordered the use of atomic weapons in that war, forbade American planes to cross the Chinese border during the Korean War, and dismissed his Pacific commander, Douglas MacArthur. John Kennedy personally monitored the Bay of Pigs invasion and the blockade of Cuba during the missile crisis. Lyndon Johnson approved strategic and tactical military decisions in Vietnam including the bombing of targets and mining of ports, while Richard Nixon extended the bombing to Cambodia.

Ronald Reagan has been a particularly active military commander. In addition to his commitment of American forces in Lebanon and Grenada and approving their military actions, he ordered the stationing of air and naval forces near the coast of Libya, sent U.S. warships and personnel to Central America and approved clandestine operations of the Central Intelligence Agency in that area, and took a strong interest in military strategy and tactics. He was the first president in twenty-five years to review a war game conducted by the Defense Department and national security staff.[3] Moreover, Reagan initiated and later endorsed a National Security Council directive that developed strategic plans for fighting and winning prolonged nuclear and conventional wars.[4] The destructiveness of nuclear weapons combined with this rapid deployment and delivery suggests that presidents can no longer leave war making to their military commanders. The ultimate responsibility for how war is to be conducted rests with the civilian commander, the president.

THE EXPANSION OF A POLICY-MAKING ROLE

Incentives for Presidential Leadership

The growth of the president's authority in foreign and military affairs has been the consequence of several factors: the increasing involvement of the United States within the international community; the public's desire for strong, personal leadership to direct that involvement; and the political ramifications of that leadership on the administration and its policy goals.

Since the end of World War II, the United States has been a dominant economic, military, and political power. It has tried to shape international developments, aiding its allies and resisting its adversaries, building its defenses yet promoting peaceful coexistence, fostering its interests yet supporting international cooperation. The industrial capacity, technological skills, and resource base of the United States were essential to the revitalization of the economies of countries in Western Europe and Asia following the destruction during World War II. The economic strength of the United States has also been an important source of technical, financial, and agricultural aid to the Third World which needs the products and skills of an advanced technological society. The United States, in turn, has become increasingly dependent on the natural resources of developing countries, particularly those that produce energy. Today the economies of many nations, rich and poor, are more interdependent than ever before.

Resource dependency and economic interdependency have contributed to the incentives for American involvement. No longer can the United States afford to adopt an isolationist policy nor can the president avoid international affairs, at least not for long. Held accountable for the performance of the domestic economy, a president has no choice but to tackle international problems as well.

The technological advances in armaments, particularly nuclear weapons, and the continued competition and conflict with the Soviet Union have forced presidents to be continuously concerned about military preparedness, strategic planning, alliance building, and arms control. The vulnerability of all nations, the proliferation of nuclear weapons, and the persistence of armed conflict require the president to promote the common defense and peaceful coexistence at the same time.

Not only have world events forced the president to emphasize foreign and military affairs, but domestic political forces have also done so. The public looks to the president in time of crisis for leadership. He is the person around which the country can rally, a unifying figure, the personification of the state.[5]

In the short run, crisis situations may increase the public's approval of the president. When American hostages were seized in Iran in 1979, public approval of Carter's performance rose. Over time, when he was unable to obtain their release, his approval level declined. This suggests that in the long run the persistence of the crisis works to the president's disadvantage. He is expected to resolve the problem in a manner favorable to American national interests.

In addition to the short-run support that crises can generate for a president, foreign policy leadership benefits the incumbent in other respects. It contributes to the image of nonpartisan, national leadership. This is particularly useful during reelection campaigns when strength, assertiveness, will, and direction are seen as most desirable presidential traits.

The public wants to feel secure. People look to the president to satisfy that feeling. The nation's security in modern times has been a source of continuous concern and is a recurring campaign issue. The results of recent presidential elections testify to its importance. In 1972, 1976, and 1980 those candidates perceived as less competent in foreign affairs lost. Each suffered from the view that they lacked the firmness, know-how, and decisiveness to keep the nation secure.[6]

The difficulties faced by presidents in formulating a policy agenda and in developing a consensus for it are not usually as arduous in foreign and military affairs as they are in domestic ones. The normal partisanship that characterizes domestic policy debate is less evident on foreign and defense policy, although it is usually not absent. As the president's ability to effect domestic change decreases, his incentive to get involved in foreign affairs increases.

Taken together, these factors have encouraged the president to assume a dominant role in foreign affairs. They have also contributed to his ability to achieve his political goals. This emphasis and that success led one political scientist, Aaron Wildavsky, to conclude that there are really two presidents: one domestic and one foreign.

Policy Goals and Presidential Success: The Two Presidencies Thesis

According to Wildavsky, presidents tend to get their way in the foreign policy realm far more often than in the domestic one. He added, "Although presidents have rivals for power in foreign affairs, the rivals do not usually succeed. Presidents prevail not only because they may have superior resources but because their potential opponents are weak, divided or believe that they should not control foreign policy."[7]

Wildavsky supported his argument with a study of congressional action on presidential proposals from 1948 through 1964. In this examination of congressional role calls, he found that presidents had significantly better records in foreign and defense policy. He concluded: "When refugees and immigration—which Congress considers primarily a domestic concern—are removed from the general foreign policy area, it is clear that Presidents prevail about 70 per cent of the time in defense and foreign policy, compared with 40 per cent in the domestic sphere."[8]

Wildavsky wrote in the mid-1960s after an era of bipartisanship in foreign affairs. He wrote after the emergence of the United States as a world power, after Presidents Roosevelt, Truman, Eisenhower, and Kennedy established America's position as a leader of the Western world, container of communism, and promoter of international cooperation. He wrote before the Vietnam War.

The unpopularity of that war led to recriminations against the presidents who directed that effort and against the presidency itself. In an effort to deter future presidential action that lacked popular and congressional support, Congress passed a series of statutes designed to constrain executive discretion in hostile or potentially hostile situations. As a consequence, presidents still retain the policy initiative, but Congress has improved its capacity to modify that initiative and to say no.

Political and institutional changes during the 1970s have contributed to Congress's more assertive posture in foreign affairs. The domestic impact of foreign policy has become more pronounced, blurring the old distinction between foreign and domestic affairs and creating new incentives for legislative involvement. No longer could it be said that "politics stops at the water's edge."

With more committees and subcommittees dealing with international issues; more staff and better information facilities at their disposal; more foreign travel by legislators and their aides; more groups, governments, and individuals trying to affect policy judgments, members of Congress, individually and collectively, have become less disposed to acquiesce in the president's initiatives. Some have even taken matters into their own hands. At the height of the Iranian hostage crisis, Representative George Hansen went to Tehran to try to obtain the release of the hostages. He failed, but Democratic presidential candidate Jesse Jackson did get Syria to release a captured American flier in 1984.

With presidential policy making subject to greater scrutiny, scholars have begun to reexamine Wildavsky's thesis. The results of that reexamination thus far have been mixed.[9] In general, scholars have found that presidents are still more likely to get their way in Congress on national security policy than on domestic policy but they are also more likely to lose than in the past.[10] Moreover, they must fight harder to win. President Reagan had to use all his persuasive powers to prevent Congress from halting the sale of AWACS aircraft to Saudi Arabia in 1981, and he had to agree to demonstrate increased flexibility in arms control negotiations in order to obtain congressional funding of the MX missile. In noncrisis situations it appears likely that the age of bipartisanship is over.

Although Congress has become more reluctant to ratify presidential policy quickly, preferring instead to debate and modify it, the general public, party leaders, and elected officials continue to look to the president for guidance. A 1979 Gallup poll found that almost twice as many people saw the making of foreign policy as a presidential responsibility than saw it as a congressional one.

The increasing interest and involvement of Congress in foreign policy decisions places the president in a dilemma. How can he lead without followers? How can he be expected to make policy and be held accountable for it if he cannot be assured of its enactment? This problem is why presidents need policy advisers and coalition builders to succeed. It is to that advisory mechanism that we now turn.

THE DEVELOPMENT OF AN ADVISORY SYSTEM

The Executive Departments

Throughout the nineteenth century and well into the twentieth, the secretary of state was the president's principal foreign policy adviser. He provided information and advice as well as implemented policy decisions. In performing this role, the secretary has been assisted by a staff of career officials, who were organized primarily on the basis of five regional bureaus.

Over the years the State Department has become more specialized. Functional divisions dealing with economics and business, international organization, environmental and scientific affairs, and public and congressional relations have supplemented the political bureaus. Nonetheless, the department remains relatively small. Its 1982 budget outlays of $2.2 billion pales by comparison to the Defense Department's $186.7 billion as does the size of its work force (23,545 compared to over 1 million civilians for the Defense Department). One reason that the State Department has not grown dramatically as American involvement in world affairs has increased is that a variety of old and new agencies now also participate in international activities.

There is an intelligence community. Consisting of almost forty separate agencies, it is dominated by the Central Intelligence Agency, National Security Agency, and the Defense Intelligence Agency. There is a United States Information Agency (USIA), which operates libraries; sponsors cultural, scientific, and educational programs; coordinates press relations; and runs the Voice of America, a worldwide radio network. There is a special trade representative, an Arms Control and Disarmament Agency, and a National Aeronautics and Space Administration (NASA). Many of the principal executive departments also have international divisions and ongoing interests in international affairs. The State Department no longer enjoys a monopoly.

The proliferation of agencies with international activities has presented the president with several problems: how to balance competing perspectives and interests within his administration; how to coordinate and integrate policy advice; how to articulate policy with a single voice; and how to do all of this without jeopardizing his own goals or sacrificing his own discretion in the decision-making process. The resolution of these problems has proved difficult. Solutions have varied with the style and goals of the president and the institutional needs of his office.

President Franklin Roosevelt relied primarily on his White House staff. Presidential aides provided liaison with the military and State departments, acted as personal emissaries of the president to other governments, and funneled information and advice to Roosevelt. He, in turn, directed their activities.

Partially in reaction to the ad hoc nature of Roosevelt's advisory system and his reliance on personal aides rather than department heads, Congress enacted the National Security Act of 1947. This law, which combined the separate military departments into a single defense agency and established the Central Intelligence Agency, acknowledged presidential responsibilities within the national security sphere and provided a mechanism for meeting these responsibilities, the National Security Council (NSC).

The National Security Council

The National Security Council initially consisted of four statutory members: the president, vice president, secretary of state, and secretary of defense. It also included a number of advisory members such as the director of the CIA and the chairman of the Joint Chiefs of Staff. Beginning with Truman, presidents provided it with staff support.

The council's charge was advisory but its mandate was broad: to help define goals and priorities, to coordinate and integrate domestic, foreign, and military policies, and to suggest specific courses of action—all within the national security sphere. The participation of executive heads on the council was designed to integrate political advice, minimize fragmentation and internal rivalry, and advance national rather than departmental and parochial interests.

In the Truman presidency, the council functioned as a forum for discussion. Truman used it only sporadically until the Korean War, when he began meeting with it on a regular basis. During this period the council performed an important advisory role.

President Eisenhower expanded this role, converting the NSC into a policy-making body. It operated as a planning board for developing general policy positions. A White House secretariat, headed by a special assistant to the president for national security affairs, helped provide organizational support.

As an advisory body the council reached its zenith during the 1950s.

Eisenhower's penchant for using formal organizations to establish broad objectives meshed well with the capacity of the National Security Council to provide an integrated set of policy recommendations. Beginning with Kennedy, however, the council's policy-making function was eliminated and its advisory role declined. Although it continued to meet, often for symbolic purposes, its principal responsibilities were assumed by a special assistant to the president for national security affairs and his staff.

The NSC enjoyed a mild resurgence during the Reagan administration. Functioning within a cabinet council system, it has helped coordinate policy among the various agencies involved in national security issues. A major component of that job has been to oversee the implementation of key presidential decisions.

The decline of the NSC's role as an advisory body has coincided with the development of a sizable staffing structure for the president's special assistant for national security affairs. Presidents have increasingly turned to that assistant for information, advice, and internal coordination.

The Special Assistant for National Security Affairs

Kennedy was the first president to create the position of special assistant for national security affairs. His purpose was to integrate the growing diversity of executive-branch perspectives and views and to do so without the burden of a large support system. Moreover, his preferred style of decision making was to interact with a few key aides rather than preside over a cabinetlike body.

Kennedy's involvement in the management of foreign and defense policy enhanced the role of his national security adviser at the expense of senior officials in the State and Defense departments. Power shifted from these departments to the White House. This shift continued and accelerated in subsequent administrations. Increasing reliance by presidents on their national security adviser enhanced the prestige and influence of the adviser and in the process produced tension with the secretary of state.

The national security office grew. The staff approached 150 policy experts and supporting personnel by 1972. The reach of the president's assistant expanded. Not only was he able to offer advice on a wider range of issues, but increasingly, he was able to act as the president's personal representative, negotiator, and spokesman. Dr. Henry Kissinger, who served in this position during the Nixon and Ford administrations, performed all of these roles. In addition, he presided over an elaborate system of interagency committees that fortified his position and undercut that of the department heads. In this way he controlled the flow of information and ideas to the president. Traditional departmental interests were muted.

Kissinger's personal relationships, particularly with President Nixon, prevented others from circumventing his authority. Moreover, his "closed" style of operating, combined with Nixon's penchant to consult primarily, sometimes exclusively, with his national security adviser, reduced the influence of others. Secretary of State William Rogers was not even informed of the president's China initiative until it was under way. For all intents and purposes, the traditional policy functions of the secretary of state had been eclipsed. After Rogers resigned in 1972, Nixon made it official. He appointed Kissinger to head the State Department yet allowed him to continue in his national security position.

Ford disengaged the positions in 1974, appointing Kissinger's principal assistant to replace him. With this disengagement came a reversion of the adviser's responsibilities to those which were performed during the Kennedy period: briefing the president, acting as a liaison to the departments, and coordinating presidential responses after decisions had been made. This reduced role was short-lived, however. The Kissinger model was restored during the Carter administration by one of Kissinger's former students, Dr. Zbigniew Brzezinski. Assuming functions of adviser, advocate, and sometimes spokesman, Carter's assistant for national security affairs clashed frequently with Secretary of State Cyrus Vance.

While Brzezinski did not retain the elaborate substructure of standing committees and working groups that characterized the Kissinger operation, most important studies, option papers, and memos to the

"FIRST OF ALL I WANT YOU TO ISSUE A STATEMENT DENYING IT"

Source: Pat Oliphant, © 1971 Universal Press Syndicate. Reprinted by permission.

president were still routed through his office. Of his own role, Brzezinski stated:

> I work very closely with the President. I'm his adviser in foreign policy and security matters. And I'm the coordinator for him of all the work that comes for his decision from the State Department, from Defense and from the CIA. Finally, and expressly so, the President wishes me and my staff to help him play an innovative role, that is to say, to try to look beyond the problems of the immediate and help him define a larger and more distant sense of direction.[11]

Unlike the Nixon-Kissinger arrangement, the Carter-Brzezinski one was not exclusive. The President consulted with others for policy advice. Brzezinski's voice was one among several, although probably the most influential.

Still another attempt to change the relationship between the president, his adviser, and the secretary of state occurred at the beginning of the Reagan administration. Desiring to have the department heads play a larger advisory role and avoid the tension that had been created between the White House and other executive branch units, Reagan reduced the influence and visibility of his national security adviser and had him report to Edwin Meese, counsellor to the president, who was charged with policy coordination in both domestic and national security affairs.

Tension between the State Department and White House persisted, however. Fueled by clashing personalities, policy perspectives, and institutional interests, these tensions eventually led to the resignation of the secretary of state, Alexander Haig, and the upgrading of the White House national security operation under a new director and with new personnel. As a consequence of these changes, the national security adviser again became more important to and influential with the president.

What happened to Reagan has also happened to other presidents. As administration priorities shift and national security policy becomes more important, there is a tendency for the White House adviser to become dominant. It was this recognition that prompted White House chief of staff James Baker and deputy chief Michael Deaver to try to persuade Reagan to appoint Baker to the national security position when it became vacant in 1983. They were unsuccessful but their attempt indicated the importance they attached to that position within the White House hierarchy and with the president.

ASSESSING THE ADVISORY SYSTEM

As we have seen, presidents tend to rely more on their national security adviser for policy advice over the course of their administration. Why? For one thing, presidents seem to become more interested in making foreign policy. They see their ability to do so as more critical to their administration's popularity and to their own political success.

If policy matters become more important to the president, it is natural for him to try to maximize his discretion when dealing with them, to exercise more central control, to act quickly and decisively and to do so in a manner that is consistent with his basic beliefs and his policy objectives. Naturally, presidents do not enjoy resistance to their policy from outside the administration much less within it (although the policy might benefit from such resistance). From the president's perspective reliance on *his* national security operation tends to facilitate these objectives.

There are several reasons for this. The national security adviser has one constituent, the president. The secretary of state has several: other governments, other departments, organized interest groups, and the department's own diverse bureaucracy. Second, the national security assistant is more apt to be on the president's wavelength with a staff of policy experts chosen in large part because of their acceptable political and ideological views. The secretary of state is supported by a department composed predominantly of civil servants who have survived precisely because they do not enunciate partisan views or see the world primarily in ideological terms. The national security adviser and his staff can be more ideological and partisan than the secretary of state.

Moreover, the national security staff, unburdened by administrative responsibilities, can respond more rapidly and less visibly to presidential needs and requests, particularly emergencies. In contrast, the State Department, like any large organization, tends to move more slowly. It adheres to established procedures, utilizes regular channels, and speaks in carefully measured tones. Presidents have become impatient with it and distrustful of it. Particularly fearful of leaks, some have even tried to avoid involving the department entirely on very sensitive matters.[12]

Not only does a White House office enjoy institutional advantages in responding to presidential needs, but the head of it also enjoys several personal advantages. He has better access to the president, including an office in the West Wing and a daily briefing/discussion with the president. He has fewer operational responsibilities, hence more time to focus on immediate problems that demand presidential decisions or actions. In contrast, the secretary of state must deal with a wider range of policy and administrative matters, including diplomatic and ceremonial functions.

It is easy to see why presidents have turned to their national security adviser. In addition to exercising more discretion within the most supportive environment, they can more easily engage in top-down decision making and formulate policies that are consistent with their political beliefs and ideological convictions. Moreover, the policies themselves are apt to be more innovative and consist of fewer compromises than would result if a larger number of executive and legislative officials were involved.

These advantages, however, are offset by several major disadvantages. I. M. Destler, a leading student of national security policy making, lists three:

1. Policy judgments are less predictable when those with longer-term interests and perspectives are not consulted or their opinions are not seriously considered. Continuity is harder to achieve.
2. The president may lose touch with important institutional and/or political realities. When his decisional environment is more supportive, it is also less apt to consider discordant factors which question the basic thrust of his policy initiatives.
3. Comprehensive integration of the policy is more difficult. Traditionally, the president's national security staff emphasizes political and strategic matters, not defense and international economic issues. It competes with the State Department rather than systematically coordinates policy matters.

According to Destler, "the recent evolution of White House policy staffing responds to the president's immediate needs, and caters to his personal convenience, but does not serve his broader, long-term need to lead a strong, loyal, and responsive government."[13]

Does a president have any other options? There are those like Destler who propose that the input of the department heads be strengthened and that their ties to the president be made closer. They argue for more effective coordination among these senior executive officials and a less visible, more process oriented, White House staff structure and adviser.

In contrast, Zbigniew Brzezinski, Carter's national security adviser, has urged that the White House national security operation be upgraded. He would have its head coordinate the policy recommendations of the State and Defense Departments and the CIA. According to the Brzezinski plan, the secretary of state would be the chief diplomat, charged primarily with the conduct of foreign policy, not the making of it.[14]

A third option, originally proposed by Alexander George in the early 1970s, is a multiple advocacy structure (briefly mentioned in Chapter 7) in which a range of viewpoints is presented to the president who is the final judge and jury rolled into one.[15] Key to this model is a custodian manager, based in the White House, who coordinates the divergent opinions and makes sure that the president hears a variety of well-argued positions. The custodian is both a broker and facilitator but not an advocate. His job is to ensure the competitive nature of policy making and to make certain that the president has a range of well-studied options from which to choose.

Which of these advisory structures is best? The answer depends on the president, his personality, policy goals, and institutional needs. As noted in previous chapters, style is an important influence on how a president interacts with his aides. Eisenhower thrived in group settings. Eliciting a team approach that emphasized consensus building from within, his national security mechanism provided internal coordination for a cabinet-based, advisory model. In contrast, Nixon's introverted personality, his secretive manner, and his need for power led him to adopt a hierarchical model in national security staffing. Jimmy Carter provided a third extreme. His desire to get involved in details, to evaluate a range of alternatives, but ultimately to make his own judgment caused him to utilize a variation of multiple advocacy—with the undesirable consequences. His policy seemed to lack both direction and consistency.

A second component that affects the advisory structure is the goals themselves and the extent to which the president has made up his mind. Does he desire to reach a judgment or to exercise one he has reached? Lyndon Johnson's conviction about the Vietnam War cast him in the role of advocate. As a consequence, he wanted (although perhaps did not benefit from) a mechanism that supported his views.

Having a strong ideological bent shapes decision making. Reagan desired an advisory system that would produce a policy consensus *within* his conceptual framework and a mechanism for implementing his basic goals but one which relieved him of day-to-day decisional responsibilities. In contrast, Carter opted for a structure that processed information without filtering it too much. What he wanted from his advisers were choices not consensus.

Whereas style and goals explain differences in advisory systems, the institutional needs of the presidency have fostered some of the basic trends evident since the Eisenhower administration: the growth and specialization of a White House national security staffing structure, the increasing reliance on this structure over the course of an administration, and the advisory and advocacy roles of the national security adviser often in conflict with the secretary of state.

In short, presidents have to be comfortable with the system and the system has to work. It needs to generate information and ideas, to organize and manage competing viewpoints, and to help define and achieve a president's basic goals. It should provide *continuity* in policy and promote the *integration* of policies.[16] It should enable the president to exercise strong and steady leadership.

CONCLUSION

The limited role that the framers of the Constitution envisioned for the president in foreign and military affairs has been expanded significantly. Today the president is expected to take the policy-making initiative in both spheres. He is expected to oversee the conduct of war and diplomacy. He is also expected to perform the symbolic duties of chief of state and commander-in-chief.

Although presidential expectations have increased, the ability of the president to meet these expectations has declined. That decline is a product of several factors: the increasing domestic impact of foreign policy, the proliferation of groups and governments trying to affect policy decisions, and the more assertive role Congress has assumed. No longer does the legislature more or less automatically defer to presidential initiatives. As a consequence, presidents have had to devote more time and increasing resources to the performance of their policy-making responsibilities. They have had to make greater efforts at coordination within the executive branch and at consensus building outside of it.

Despite the increasing obstacles they face, presidents continue to emphasize foreign policy matters, particularly as their administrations progress. There are psychological, political, and policy reasons for doing so. As foreign policy leaders they can act as unifying figures, overcome perceptions of partisanship, and work to achieve specific policy goals. Demonstrating leadership in this manner stands to increase their popularity, improve their reelectability, and enhance their place in history— all very desirable personal goals.

With foreign and defense policy so important, presidents have turned increasingly to their national security staff for help. Established in 1960 and expanded in size and specialization since then, this internal White House mechanism has provided a cadre of loyal policy experts to help presidents with the everyday problems with which they have to deal. The national security staff functions primarily to inform and advise the president and secondarily to handle his correspondence, speeches, and briefings. It has increased the president's information, maximized his discretion, and created the capacity for rapid and decisive responses. However, it has done all of this at a cost: an increase in tension between the White House and executive-branch agencies, a decrease in the continuity of policy within and between administrations, and a constricting of vision and limiting of perspectives.

NOTES

1. Actually, all treaties approved by two-thirds of the Senate must be signed by the president before they go into effect.

2. The Supreme Court's legislative veto decision, *Immigration and Naturalization* v. *Chadha* (103 S. Ct. 2764) (June 23, 1983), calls into question the use of concurrent resolutions as a means of restricting executive activity.

3. Richard Halloran, "Reagan as Military Commander," *New York Times Magazine*, January 15, 1984, p. 57.

4. Ibid.

5. Fred I. Greenstein, "Popular Images of the President," *American Journal of Psychiatry* 122 (1965):523–29.

6. For an excellent discussion of impact of foreign policy on electoral politics and vice versa see Valerie Bunce, "The Electoral Cycle and Presidential Foreign Policy-Making" (paper presented at the Annual Meeting of the American Political Science Association, New York, September 3–6, 1981).

7. Aaron Wildavsky, "The Two Presidencies," in Aaron Wildavsky, ed., *Perspectives on the Presidency* (Boston: Little, Brown, 1975), p. 452.

8. Ibid., p. 449.

9. One difficulty with Wildavsky's analysis was that it was based on *all* presidential initiatives on which Congress conducted roll-call votes. Many of these concerned minor, noncontroversial items. Lee Sigelman attempted to overcome this problem by examining only key votes on major issues between 1957 and 1978. His findings were quite different from Wildavsky's. According to Professor Sigelman, not only did the Congress not back the president more often in foreign and defense policy than in domestic affairs, but since 1973 its presidential support in all areas has weakened (Lee Sigelman, "A Reassessment of the Two Presidencies Thesis," *Journal of Politics* 41 (1979):1201–1205).

10. Wildavsky's study had revealed a 30 percent difference in Congress's enactment of foreign and domestic policy initiatives by the president. An examination of the ten years following the period of Wildavsky's research found only a 9 percent margin (Lance T. Leloup and Steven A. Shull, "Congress versus the Executive: The 'Two Presidencies' Reconsidered," *Social Science Quarterly* 59 [1979]:707). Still another analysis of presidential-congressional relations, this one from 1957 through 1980, revealed more presidential success on foreign policy matters but declining support for the president in general. This decline was most pronounced in the Senate and on domestic matters (Harvey G. Zeidenstein, "The Two Presidencies Thesis is Alive and Well and Has been Living in the U.S. Senate Since 1973," *Presidential Studies Quarterly* 2 (1981):511–25.

11. Zbigniew Brzezinski, quoted in Dom Bonafede, "Brzezinski—Stepping Out of His Backstage Role," *National Journal* 9 (October 15, 1977):1596.

12. The national security staff has also been a source of leaks. Kissinger had the telephones of one of his principal aides tapped. Similarly, a "mole" on the national security staff during the Carter administration allegedly provided information to the Reagan election campaign.

13. I. M. Destler, "National Security II: The Rise of the Assistant (1961–1981)," in Hugh Heclo and Lester M. Salamon, eds., *The Illusion of Presidential Government* (Boulder, Colo.: Westview Press, 1981), p. 278.

14. Zbigniew Brzezinski, "Deciding Who Makes Foreign Policy," *New York Times Magazine*, September 18, 1983.

15. Alexander George, "The Case for Multiple Advocacy in Making Foreign Policy," *American Political Science Review* 66 (1972):751–85.

16. Destler, "National Security II," p. 279.

SELECTED READINGS

Berman, Larry. *Planning a Tragedy*. New York: Norton, 1982.

Crabb, Cecil V., Jr., and Pat M. Holt. *Invitation to Struggle: Congress, the President, and Foreign Policy*. Washington, D.C.: Congressional Quarterly Press, 1980.

Destler, I. M. "National Security Management: What Presidents Have Wrought." *Political Science Quarterly* 95 (Winter 1980/1981):573–88.

———. "The Evolution of Reagan Foreign Policy." In Fred I. Greenstein, ed., *The Reagan Presidency: An Early Assessment*. Baltimore: Johns Hopkins University Press, 1983.

George, Alexander. *Presidential Decision Making in Foreign Policy: The Effective Use of Information and Advice*. Boulder, Colo.: Westview Press, 1980.

Hunter, Robert E. *Presidential Control of Foreign Policy*. New York: Praeger, 1982.

Rockman, Bert A. "America's Department of State: Irregular and Regular Syndromes of Policy Making." *American Political Science Review* 75 (1981):911–27.

Sigelman, Lee. "A Reassessment of the Two Presidencies Thesis." *Journal of Politics* 41 (1979):1195–1205.

Wildavsky, Aaron. "The Two Presidencies." In Aaron Wildavsky, ed., *Perspectives on the Presidencies*. Boston: Little, Brown, 1975.

11

Presidential Influence in Congress

If one were to write a job description of the presidency, near the top of the list of presidential responsibilities would be that for working with Congress. According to Lyndon Johnson, "There is only one way for a President to deal with Congress, and that is continuously, incessantly, and without interruption."[1] Since our system of separation of powers is really one of *shared* powers, the president can rarely operate independently of Congress. Although he requires Congress's cooperation, he cannot depend on it. Thus, one of the president's most difficult and frustrating tasks is trying to persuade Congress to support his policies.

In this chapter we examine the president's relationship with Congress. Because it is important to understand the context of presidential-congressional interaction, we begin with a discussion of the president's formal legislative powers and the inevitable sources of conflict between the two branches. We then move to an examination of the potential sources of presidential influence in Congress, including party leadership, public support, and legislative skills. In our discussion we emphasize both how presidents attempt to persuade members of Congress and the utility of each source of influence.

FORMAL LEGISLATIVE POWERS

Presidents today have a central role in the legislative process. They are expected to formulate and promote policies. They are expected to coordinate them within the executive branch, to introduce them to Congress, and to mobilize support for them on Capitol Hill and, increasingly, with the general public.

These expectations suggest a broad scope of legislative authority for the president. In actuality, his constitutional powers are quite limited. Only four duties and responsibilities were designed by Article 2: (1) to inform Congress from time to time on the state of the union; (2) to recommend necessary and expedient legislation; (3) to summon Congress into special session and adjourn it if the two houses cannot agree on adjournment; and (4) to exercise a qualified veto.

With the exception of the veto, these responsibilities stem primarily from the president's unique position within the political system: the only official other than the vice president who was to have continuous tenure, a national perspective, and the ability to respond quickly and decisively to emergencies. As the framers of the Constitution saw it, these job-related qualifications placed the president in a unique position to inform Congress, to recommend legislation, and to summon it into session if necessary.

The rationale for the veto was different. Justified within the Constitutional Convention as a defensive weapon, it was proposed as a device by which the president could prevent his powers from being usurped by the legislature. The founding fathers feared that the institutional balance would become undone and that the Congress would be the likely perpetrator. The extent to which their fears were justified and the use of the veto as a political and constitutional weapon are examined later in this chapter.

Over the years presidents have used their legislative responsibilities to enlarge their congressional influence. The State of the Union message is a good example. In the nineteenth century it was a routine message dealing primarily with the actions of the executive departments and agencies for the previous year. Beginning with Jefferson and continuing through Theodore Roosevelt, the address was sent to the Congress to be read by the clerk of the House and then distributed to the members. Woodrow Wilson revived the practice of the first two presidents and delivered the speech himself. Subsequently, presidents have timed the address to maximize its public exposure. Today it is an important vehicle by which presidents can articulate the legislative goals of their administration, recite their accomplishments, present their agenda, and try to mobilize support for their programs.

Similarly, presidents have transformed their responsibility to recommend necessary and expedient legislation into an annual agenda-setting function. While nineteenth-century presidents formulated some legislative proposals and even drafted bills in the White House, it was not until the twentieth century that the practice of presidential programming developed on a regular basis. Wilson and Franklin Roosevelt submitted comprehensive legislative proposals to Congress. Truman packaged them in the State of the Union address. With the exception of Eisenhower in his first year in office, every subsequent president has followed the Truman tradition.

To some extent the Congress has found the president's legislative initatives advantageous. In some cases it has insisted upon them. For example, the 1921 Budget and Accounting Act, the 1946 Employment Act, and the 1974 Budget Act require the president to provide Congress with annual reports and an annual executive budget.

The calling of special sessions by the president has fallen into disuse. The length of the current legislative year combined with changes in the calendar have made this function largely obsolete. The last special session occurred in 1948. In the past, however, presidents frequently would call special sessions after their inauguration to gain support for their objectives and to initiate "their" Congress. Until the passage of the Twentieth Amendment in 1933, Congress began its session on or about December 1. This made every other session of Congress "a lame duck" and forced a newly elected president to wait nine months for the newly elected Congress. Between the Lincoln and Franklin Roosevelt administrations there were nineteen special sessions.

SOURCES OF CONFLICT BETWEEN THE EXECUTIVE AND LEGISLATIVE BRANCHES

The president must influence Congress because he generally cannot act without its consent. Under our constitutional system of separation of powers, Congress must pass legislation and can override vetoes. The Senate must ratify treaties and confirm presidential appointments to the cabinet, the federal courts, regulatory commissions, and other high offices. Yet these overlapping powers do not explain the president's need to influence Congress. Theoretically, the two branches could be in agreement. Likewise, the president and some members of Congress will always disagree because of their personalities or past histories. Yet these differences are not the source of systematic conflict, which lies in the structure and processes of American politics.

Different Constituencies

In "The Federalist No. 46," James Madison focused on the greatest source of conflict between the president and Congress: their different constituencies. "The members of the federal legislature will likely attach themselves too much to local objects. . . . Measures will too often be decided according to their probable effect, not on the national prosperity and happiness, but on the prejudices, interests, and pursuits of the governments and the people of the individual states."[2]

Only the president (and his vice presidential running mate) is chosen in a national election. Each member of Congress is elected by only a fraction of the populace. Inevitably, the president must form a broader electoral coalition in order to win his office than any member of Congress. Moreover, two-thirds of the senators are not elected at the same time as the president, and the remaining senators and all the House members seem to be increasingly insulated from the causes of presidential victories. In addition, the Senate overrepresents rural states because each state has two senators regardless of its population. Thus, the whole that the president represents is different from the sum of the parts that each legislator represents. Each member of Congress will give special access to the interests that he or she represents, but Congress as a body has difficulty representing the nation as a whole.

The consequences of the two branches having different constituencies arise at many stages of policy making. The responsiveness of members of Congress to narrow constituencies hinders good policy analysis. Members tend to support broad legislative action in the short run, not cautious policy experimentation, because this produces the quickest benefits for the most people. But such an approach may waste scarce resources or spread them too thinly to accomplish the goals of policies.

In predicting the consequences of various policy alternatives, Congress is often responsive to the desires of narrow segments of public opinion. Congress has recently tried to impose its views on the president in the area of foreign policy more aggressively than it has in the past. In 1974 the Senate attempted to influence the Soviet Union to liberalize its restrictions on the emigration of Jews and other Soviet citizens by making this a condition for international trade benefits. In that same year, Congress cut off aid to Turkey in an attempt to reduce that country's aggressiveness toward Greece and the Greek population on Cyprus. Both tactics were consistent with the desires of influential groups in the United States but contrary to the wishes of the president. Also, neither attempt seemed to accomplish its purpose.

Similarly, members of Congress often show little interest in realistic evaluation of the costs and benefits of policy alternatives. They are more interested in funding pork-barrel water projects or maintaining unneeded defense plants or bases in their districts. President Carter's first real battle with Congress in 1977 was over the water projects. He wanted to end several projects for which he felt the costs exceeded the benefits. After a substantial battle, a compromise was reached in which he got about half of what he wanted. The following January, Secretary of Interior Cecil Andrus told a press conference, "If you think I'm going to walk up to the Hill with another hit list and go through the agony and heartburn I went through last year, I can only say, 'I'm not stupid.' "[3]

Internal Structure

The internal structures of the executive and legislative branches also cause differences between the president and Congress. The executive branch is hierarchically organized, facilitating the president's examining a broad range of viewpoints on an issue and then weighing and balancing various interests. This structure also helps the president to view the trade-offs among various policies. Since one person, the president, must support all the major policies emanating from the executive branch, he is virtually forced to take a comprehensive view of those policies.

Members of Congress frequently do not take such a broad view. Each house of Congress is highly decentralized, which each member jealously guarding his or her independence and power. The party structure, unlike the situation in many countries, is not a unifying force within the U.S. legislature, as we shall see later. Committee memberships are frequently unrepresentative of each chamber, and members of each committee tend to defer to members of the other committees in exchange for the same deference in return. Thus, members representing special interests have a disproportionate say over policy regarding those interests.

Indeed, one of the functions of decentralizing power and responsibility in Congress is to allow for specialization in various policy areas. However, because of specialization, legislators make decisions about many of the policies with which Congress must deal in form only. In actuality they tend to rely upon the cues of party leaders, state party delegations, relevant committee leaders of their party, and other colleagues to decide how to vote. These cue givers, however, are chosen because they represent constituencies or ideologies that are similar to those of the member who is consulting them. They also do not represent a cross section of viewpoints.

Members of Congress are not generally in a position to make trade-offs between policies. Because of its decentralization, Congress usually considers policies serially, that is, without reference to other policies. Without an integrating mechanism, members have few means by which to set and enforce priorities and to emphasize the policies with which the president is most concerned, particularly when Congress is controlled by the opposition party. In addition, Congress has little capability, except within the context of the budget, to examine two policies, like education and health care, in relation to each other. Not knowing that giving up something on one policy will result in a greater return on another policy, members have little incentive to engage in trade-offs. Congress is also poorly organized to deal comprehensively with major policy domains. It distributes its workload among committees with jurisdictions that often do not cover entire policy areas such as welfare, national security, or economic stability.

Thus, while the structure of Congress ensures that a diversity of views will be heard and that many interests will have access to the legislative process, it does not follow that *each* member will hear all the views and see the proponents of each interest. Indeed, the decentralization of Congress almost guarantees that the information available to it as a whole is not a synthesis of the information available to each legislator. The Congress as a whole does not ask questions; individual members do. Thus, not all members receive the answers.

The hierarchical structure of the executive branch, with the president at the pinnacle, forces the president to take responsibility for the entire executive branch. Moreover, when the president exercises power, it is clear who is acting and who should be held accountable. Congress, on the other hand, is not responsible for implementing policies, and each member is relatively obscure compared with the president. Since Congress is so decentralized, any member can disclaim responsibility for policies or their consequences. Members of Congress, therefore, can and do make irresponsible or self-serving decisions and then let the president take the blame. They are often more interested in the immediate distribution of the benefits of policies to their constituents than in the ultimate consequences of policies. The short-run results please the interested parties and can easily be attributed to congressional actions; long-term effects are more obscure, as are their causes. Thus, members of Congress can gain points for reelection while evading accountability for their actions.

All of this can be very frustrating to the president. As Gerald Ford, who spent most of his adult life in Congress, wrote after leaving the White House,

> When I was in the Congress myself, I thought it fulfilled its constitutional obligations in a very responsible way, but after I became President, my perspective changed. It seemed to me that Congress was beginning to disintegrate as an organized legislative body. It wasn't answering the nation's challenges domestically because it was too fragmented. It responded too often to single-issue special interest groups and it therefore wound up dealing with minutiae instead of attacking serious problems in a coherent way.[4]

Information and Expertise

A third source of conflict between the president and Congress is the difference in information and expertise available to them. Despite the substantial increase in congressional staff in recent years, including the expansion or addition of analytic units such as the General Accounting Office, the Congressional Research Service in the Library of Congress, the Office of Technology Assessment, and the Congressional Budget Office, members of Congress rarely have available to them expertise of the quantity and quality that is available to the president.

Aside from the fact that the executive branch includes nearly 5 million civilian and military employees plus hundreds of advisory committees while Congress employs only about 30,000 persons (including

"THE BUTLER DID IT"

Source: Copyright 1983 by Herblock in *Washington Post National Weekly Edition.*

supporting agencies), the expertise of the two branches differs. Members of Congress tend to hire generalists, even on committee staffs. Sometimes these individuals develop great expertise in a particular field, but more often they are only amateurs compared with their counterparts in the executive branch. Many are selected to serve legislators' needs and desires, which have little to do with policy analysis, and neither house has a merit system, a tenured career service, or a central facility for recruiting the best available talent.

Congress is especially at a disadvantage in matters concerning foreign policy and national security policy, matters in which the president relies on classified information that is generally unavailable to Congress. Furthermore, Congress is often overwhelmed by the complexity of domestic policy. When the Senate considered reform of the U.S. Criminal Code in early 1978, it had to rely almost totally upon the Judiciary Committee, and throughout the debate it accepted hundreds of committee amendments offered in single packages.

Because the president and Congress have different information and expertise available to them, they may well see issues from different perspectives. The president's views will generally be buttressed with more data and handled more expertly. This may give him different views and more confidence in his views.

Time Perspectives

The Constitution limits the president to two terms or a maximum of ten years if he completes the unfinished term of a predecessor. If presidents are activists, and virtually all modern presidents are forced to be in one way or another, they can waste no time in pushing for the adoption of their policies, be they a new economic program as President Reagan proposed or the myriad of domestic initiatives President Carter sent to Congress.[5] These proposals were in addition to routine legislation for maintaining ongoing programs that both presidents had to support.

Congress has a different timetable. Its members tend to be careerists and therefore do not have the same compulsion to enact policies rapidly. This sluggish approach is aggravated by the decentralization of Congress. Because no one has the authority to push through legislation, a great deal of negotiating and compromising must take place on all but a few noncontroversial (and usually unimportant) issues. This process can take years. President Nixon proposed revenue sharing in 1969; it passed in 1972. President Truman proposed a national health plan in 1948; a limited version (medicare) was passed in 1965. Moreover, the decentralization of Congress provides "veto points" at virtually every stage of the legislative process. At these points intense minorities can rule over weak majorities. Senate filibusters, in which a minority of senators keep the majority from voting on a bill, are also well-known forms of this veto point phenomena.

The most obvious consequences of Congress's sluggishness in handling legislation is that the president is not likely to get much of what he wants now until later, if at all. In a nationally televised interview after his first year in office, President Carter commented that it was easier for him to study and propose an energy policy to Congress than it was for Congress to pass it. Thus, he had to exert influence on Congress. A second consequence is that presidential policies may be passed too late to become fully effective. For example, when John Kennedy became president, he inherited a slumping economy. His economic advisers advised a tax cut to stimulate the economy, which Kennedy proposed to Congress in late 1962. The bill did not pass until January 1964, denying the economy a much-needed stimulus for an entire year. And this action was taken quite soon for Congress. The Senate would probably have held the bill longer if it had not been spurred by the assassination of the president.

We have seen that the structure of American government exerts strong pressure on the two branches to represent different sets of interests and to view policies differently. This in turn sets the stage for conflict and virtually compels a president to try to influence Congress.

PARTY LEADERSHIP

"What the Constitution separates our political parties do not combine."[6] Richard Neustadt wrote these words nearly a quarter of a century ago to help explain why presidents could not simply assume support from the members of their party in Congress. The challenge of presidential party leadership in Congress remains just as great and is just as important today as it was when Neustadt wrote his famous treatise on presidential power.

Party Support of the President

Representatives and senators of the president's party are almost always the nucleus of coalitions supporting the president's programs. As one Nixon aide put it: "You turn to your party members first. If we couldn't move our own people, we felt the opportunities were pretty slim."[7] No matter what other resources a president may have, without seats in Congress held by his party, he will usually find it very difficult to move his legislative program through Congress. Table 11-1 shows the annual average support given to the president by members of each party in the House and the Senate where the losing side won at least 20 percent of the vote. Table 11-2 shows summary measures of partisan presidential support for the period 1953–1983.

Two important points emerge from an examination of these tables. First, there is a great deal of slippage within the president's party in terms of party loyalty. Second, there is a substantial difference between the levels of presidential support by members of the two parties, with the gap generally exceeding 25 percent. Four Republican and three Democratic presidents are covered by the tables, and although the presidents of each party varied considerably in their policies, personalities, and political environments, their fellow partisans in Congress gave them considerably more support then they gave presidents of the opposition party.

Although the president receives more support from members of his party than from the opposition, it does not follow that this is necessarily due to their shared party affiliation. It is difficult to tell whether a member of the president's party votes for the president's policies because of shared party affiliation, basic agreement with those policies, or some other factor. Undoubtedly, members of the same party share many policy preferences and have similar electoral coalitions supporting them. In 1981 President Reagan won several crucial votes in Congress on his taxing and spending proposals. He was immediately credited with extraor-

Table 11-1. Average Presidential Support by Party, 1953–1983 (in percentages)

Year	President's Party	House Democrats	House Republicans	Senate Democrats	Senate Republicans
1953	R	45	70	42	66
1954	R	34	74	36	74
1955	R	42	52	37	70
1956	R	38	72	35	69
1957	R	48	52	44	69
1958	R	52	55	37	66
1959	R	34	72	28	73
1960	R	46	64	41	66
1961	D	73	26	68	31
1962	D	72	30	64	31
1963	D	75	21	63	37
1964	D	78	26	63	56
1965	D	75	24	64	44
1966	D	67	20	53	35
1967	D	70	28	56	42
1968	D	63	36	46	41
1969	R	48	57	42	65
1970	R	41	60	35	63
1971	R	41	71	33	65
1972	R	46	68	34	66
1973	R	31	65	24	64
1974	R	38	59	31	53
1975	R	37	68	36	67
1976	R	32	67	29	62
1977	D	61	32	62	39
1978	D	65	34	64	36
1979	D	64	26	67	39
1980	D	63	31	60	38
1981	R	39	72	33	81
1982	R	30	61	35	72
1983	R	28	71	39	73

Only nonunanimous votes are given.

R = Republican.
D = Democrat.

dinary party leadership because nearly 100 percent of the Republicans in Congress supported his programs. If we examine voting on budget resolutions under Democrat Jimmy Carter, however, we find nearly the same degree of Republican party unity in the House. Thus, we should not necessarily ascribe Reagan's success to party loyalty. Republican

Table 11-2. Average Congressional Support for Presidents by Party, 1953–1983

	% Support	
	Democratic Presidents	Republican Presidents
House Democrats	69	39
House Republicans	28	65
Senate Democrats	61	35
Senate Republicans	39	68

members of the House had been voting a conservative line well before Ronald Reagan came to Washington.

The greatest impact of party affiliation is in the foreign policy area. Republicans have a tendency to be more supportive of internationalist foreign policies when there is a Republican president. They are also more likely to accept governmental economic activity under a Republican president. Democrats, on the other hand, have a tendency to move in the opposite direction when the opposition controls the White House. The events of 1981 parallel these findings. With a conservative Republican in the White House, many Republicans in Congress shifted to supporting foreign aid and increasing the national debt ceiling. Supporting these policies was anathema to Republicans under the previous Democratic administration of Jimmy Carter.

Another way to see the influence of party affiliation in voting is to examine votes to override a presidential veto. In most cases many members of the president's party who voted for the bill when it was originally passed switch and vote against the bill after their party leader has vetoed it.

Leading the Party

That members of the president's own party are more open to his influence is clear. Members of the president's party typically have personal loyalties or emotional commitments to their party and their party leader, which the president can often translate into votes when necessary. Thus, members of the president's party vote with him when they can, giving him the benefit of the doubt, especially if their own opinion on an issue is weak. Moreover, this proclivity for supporting the president increases the effectiveness of other sources of party influence.

One of these sources is the desire of members of the presidential party not to embarrass "their" administration. This attitude stems from two motivations. The first is related to the sentiments discussed above, but the second is more utilitarian. Members of the president's party have an incentive to make him look good because his standing in the public may influence their own chances for reelection. A president may also find it easier to obtain party unity behind his program if his party regains control of one or both houses of Congress at the time of his election. Many new members may feel a sense of gratification for the president's coattails. Moreover, the prospect of exercising the power to govern may provide a catalyst for party loyalty while the loss of power may temporarily demoralize the opposition party. All of the motivations to support the president are, of course, buttressed by basic distrust of the opposition party.

Working with Congressional Leaders

Each party has a set of floor and committee leaders in the House and Senate, and in theory they should be a valuable resource for their party's leader in the White House. Because of their role perceptions and because they are susceptible to the same sentiments and pressures toward party loyalty as are other members of Congress, floor leaders of the president's party in Congress are usually very supportive of the White House. In the month before Ronald Reagan's inauguration, the new Senate majority leader, Howard Baker, declared, "I intend to try to help Ronald Reagan [carry out] the commitments he made during the campaign."[8]

Yet party floor leaders are not always dependable supporters. They certainly are not simply extensions of the White House. As one presidential aide said of Senate majority leader Robert Byrd in 1977, "God, is he independent. He ain't our man—he's the Senate's man."[9] There is little the White House can do in such a situation. Presidents do not lobby for candidates for congressional party leadership positions and virtually always remain neutral during the selection process. They have no desire to alienate important members of Congress whose support they will need.

Similarly, committee chairpersons and ranking minority members are usually determined by seniority. Furthermore, the chairpersons always come from the majority party in the chamber, which often is not the president's. For all practical purposes, the president plays no role at all in determining the holders of these important positions. Moreover, the norm of supporting a president of one's party is weaker for committee leaders than for floor leaders.

Presidents and their staff typically work closely with their party's legislative leaders, meeting regularly for breakfast when Congress is in session. Sometimes these meetings include the leaders of the opposition party as well. These gatherings provide opportunities for an exchange of views and for the president to keep communication channels open and maintain morale. The significance of these efforts has varied, however.

On one extreme, Nixon's meetings were often pro forma, serving more as a symbolic ritual than a mechanism for leadership. On the other, Johnson used them as strategy sessions, integrating congressional leaders into the White House legislative liaison operation.

Equally as important as the congressional party leaders' relations with the president are their relations with their party colleagues in Congress. Major changes have occurred in the past fifteen years that have weakened the ability of party leaders to produce votes for the president. According to former president Gerald Ford:

> Today a President really does not have the kind of clout with the Congress that he had 30 years ago, even in matters that affect national security. There is not the kind of teamwork that existed in the '50s, even if the President and a majority of the Congress belong to the same party.
>
> The main reason for this change is the erosion of the leadership in the Congress. Party leaders have lost the power to tell their troops that something is really significant and to get them to respond accordingly. The days of Sam Rayburn, Lyndon Johnson and Everett Dirksen are gone. That has adversely affected the Congress's ability to do things even in very difficult circumstances involving the national interest.[10]

One reason that party leaders have lost much of their power over their "followers" is the increased dispersion of power in Congress, especially the House. The face of Congress has changed over the past two decades. Seniority is no longer an automatic path to committee or subcommittee chairs, and chairpersons must be more responsive to the desires of committee members. There are also more subcommittees and more subcommittee chairpersons now, and these subcommittees have a more important role in handling legislation. While the power of subcommittees has increased, that of the Southern oligarchies has declined. Members of both parties have larger personal, committee, and subcommittee staffs at their disposal as well as new service adjuncts such as the Congressional Budget Office. This new freedom and these additional resources, combined with more opportunities to amend legislation, make it easier for members of Congress to challenge the White House and the congressional leadership and to provide alternatives to the president's policies.

The president's program is also now subject to more cross-cutting demands within Congress as a result of split and joint committee referrals for some legislation. This further complicates the task of influencing members of Congress, because it is difficult to lobby several committees at once with the limited resources available to the president.

Yet other reforms have increased the burden of leaders. The increased number of roll-call votes and thus the increased visibility of representatives' voting behavior have generated more pressure on House members to abandon party loyalty, making it more difficult for the president to gain passage of legislation. Reforms that have opened committee and subcommittee hearings to the public have had the same effect. There has also been a heavy turnover in the personnel of Congress in recent years, and new members have brought with them new approaches to legislating. They are less likely to adopt the norms of apprenticeship and specialization than were their predecessors in their first terms. Instead, they have eagerly taken an active role in all legislation. They place a heavy emphasis on individualism and much less on party regularity.

Thus, congressional party leaders now have more decision makers to influence. They can no longer rely on dealing with the congressional aristocracy and expect the rest of the members to follow. According to one Johnson assistant:

> In 1965, there were maybe ten or twelve people who you needed to corral in the House and Senate. Without those people, you were in for a tough time. Now, I'd put that figure upwards of one hundred. Believe it, there are so many people who have a shot at derailing a bill that the President has to double his effort for even routine decisions.[11]

Although the party leadership at least in theory possesses sanctions that it can exercise to enforce party discipline, including exercising discretion on committee assignments, patronage, campaign funds, trips abroad, and aid with members' pet bills, in reality this discretion exists primarily on paper. Most rewards are considered a matter of right, and it is the leadership's job to see that they are distributed equitably. Party leaders do not dare to withhold benefits because they fear being overturned by the rank and file. Threats of sanctions in such a situation are unconvincing and thus rarely occur.

Obstacles to Party Unity

The primary obstacle to party cohesion in support of the president is the lack of consensus among his party's members on policies, especially if the president happens to be a Democrat. This diversity of views often reflects the diversity of constituencies represented by party members. The frequent defection from support of Democratic presidents by the conservative Southern Democrats, or "boll weevils," is one of the most prominent features of American politics. Under presidents Kennedy, Johnson, and Carter there was approximately a 25 percentage point difference between Northern and Southern Democrats in support of the presidents on nonunanimous votes.

Republican presidents often lack stable coalitions as well. As we noted earlier, Ronald Reagan received nearly unanimous support from his party on his 1981 proposals to reduce taxes and expenditures. The next year, when he proposed legislation to increase taxes, to restrict abortions and forced busing for integration, and to allow school prayer, things were different. Republicans were in the forefront of the opposition to these policies.

The issues of the 1970s and 1980s, such as energy, welfare reform, social security financing, deregulation, containment of medical costs, and the social issues mentioned above lack either sizable constituencies, common underlying principles, or both. Yet these are necessary to provide the basis for consensus among party members.

A shift in the status of party members may present another obstacle to party unity. Just as regaining power may encourage party unity, having to share it may strain intraparty relations. When a party that has had a majority in Congress regains the White House, committee and floor leaders of that party will typically be less influential because they will be expected to take their lead on major issues from the president. This may cause tensions within the party, and make party discipline more difficult.

Yet other obstacles may confront a president trying to mobilize his party in Congress. If the president's party has just regained the presidency but remains a minority in Congress, its members need to adjust from their past stance as the opposition minority to one of a "governing" minority. This is not always easily done, however, as Richard Nixon found when he sought Republican votes for budget deficits.

Further difficulties may stem from the fact that the winning presidential candidate may not be the natural leader of his party. Indeed, as in the case of Jimmy Carter, he may have campaigned against the party establishment and not identified with whatever party program existed. Such a new president may arrive in Washington in an atmosphere of hostility and suspicion that is not conducive to intraparty harmony. Appeals for party loyalty under such conditions may fall on less than receptive ears.

Midterm Election Campaigning

Members of Congress who are of the president's party are more likely to support him than are members of the opposition party, and presidents do their best to exploit the potential of partisan support. Nevertheless, such actions are inevitably at the margins of coalition building, because they take place within the confines of the partisan balance of the Congress. To exploit fully the benefits of party leadership, a president needs as many of his fellow partisans in Congress as possible. Once members of Congress are elected, however, they almost never change their party affiliation, and the rare instances when they do have not resulted from presidential persuasion. Thus, if presidents are to alter the party composition of Congress, they must help to elect additional members of their party. One way to accomplish this goal is to campaign for candidates in midterm congressional elections.

Sometimes presidents are so unpopular that the candidates of their party do not want their support. President Johnson adopted a low profile during the 1966 campaign because of his lack of public support (below 50 percent in the Gallup Poll). In 1974, before he resigned, President Nixon wanted invitations to campaign for Republicans to prove that he wasn't political poison, but he had few offers as the Watergate crisis reached a head.

Nevertheless, modern presidents have often taken an active role in midterm congressional elections. In 1970, President Nixon was heavily involved in the congressional elections. He chose Vice President Agnew to carry the main burden of making speeches and offered him the services of several White House aides and speech writers. Nevertheless, behind the scenes Nixon was running the show, making strategic decisions such as selecting issues to raise and to avoid, labeling particular Democratic candidates as "radicals," encouraging people (mostly representatives) to run for the Senate, and deciding whom to support. He also made numerous campaign speeches. President Carter also was an active campaigner in 1978, speaking on behalf of Democratic candidates all across the country. Ronald Reagan did the same in 1982, although some candidates asked him to stay away because of the recession, with which many voters identified him.

Presidential efforts in midterm elections have had quite limited success. As Table 11-3 shows, a recurring feature of American politics is the decrease in representation of the president's party in Congress in midterm congressional elections. We can also see this as far back as Woodrow Wilson's efforts in 1918, which were rewarded by the loss of both houses of Congress.

Table 11-3. Changes in Congressional Representation of the President's Party in Midterm Elections

Year	House		Senate	
	Losses	Gains	Losses	Gains
1954	18	0	1	0
1958	47	0	13	0
1962	4	0	0	4
1966	47	0	3	0
1970	12	0	0	2
1974	47	0	5	0
1978	11	0	3	0
1982	26	0	0	0

Presidential Coattails

A second way in which the president may influence the partisan composition of Congress is through his coattails. Presidential coattails are part of the lore of American politics. Politicians project them in their calculations, journalists attribute them in their reporting, historians recount them, and political scientists analyze them. Yet we really know little about coattails. Most significantly, we have limited understanding of how they affect the outcomes in congressional elections. A coattail victory is a victory for a representative of the president's party in which presidential coattail votes provide the increment of the vote necessary to win the seat.

Coattail victories, whether they bring in new members or preserve the seats of incumbents, can have significant payoffs for the president in terms of support for the administration's programs. Moreover, it is possible that those members of the president's party who won close elections may provide him an extra increment of support out of a sense of gratitude for the votes they perceive they received due to presidential coattails or out of a sense of responsiveness to their constituents' support for the president.

Over the eight presidential elections from 1952 through 1980, there was a total of 76 coattail victories or an average of 9.5 per election. These results are presented in Table 11-4. The largest number of coattail victories (17) occurred in the Johnson landslide of 1964, and the fewest (4) resulted from Jimmy Carter's narrow victory in 1976. Most House seats are too safe for a party, and especially for an incumbent, to have the election outcome affected by the presidential election.

Thus, presidents cannot expect personally to carry like-minded running mates into office to provide additional support for their programs. To the contrary, rather than being amenable to voting for the president's

Table 11-4. Coattail Victories

Year	President	No. of Coattail Victories
1952	Eisenhower	13
1956	Eisenhower	8
1960	Kennedy	7
1964	Johnson	17
1968	Nixon	10
1972	Nixon	12
1976	Carter	4
1980	Reagan	5

Source: George C. Edwards III, *The Public Presidency* (New York: St. Martin's, 1983), p. 86.

policies due to shared convictions, representatives are free to focus on parochial matters and to respond to narrow constituency interests. Similarly, although we cannot know the extent to which representatives have felt gratitude to presidents for their coattails and thus have given them additional legislative support in the past, we do know that any such gratitude is rarely warranted. The more representatives are aware of the independence of their elections from the president's, the less likely they are to feel that they must "thank" the president with an additional increment of support.

Bipartisanship

On July 27, 1981, President Reagan delivered an exceptionally important and effective televised address to the nation seeking the public's support for his tax cut bill. In it he went to great lengths to present his plan as "bipartisan." It was crucial that he convince the public that this controversial legislation was supported by members of both parties and was therefore, by implication, fair. Thus, he described it as "bipartisan" *eleven* times in the span of a few minutes! No one was to miss the point. The president required the votes of Democrats in the House to pass his bill, and he wanted their constituents to apply pressure to them to support it.

Despite a president's advantage in dealing with members of his party in Congress, he is often forced to solicit bipartisan support. There are several reasons for this. First, the opposition party may control one or both houses of Congress. Even if the president received total support from all members of his party, he would still need support from some members of the opposition. For instance, since 1953 there have been fourteen years (1955 through 1960 and 1969 through 1976) when the Republicans held the White House but the Democrats had control of the legislative branch. Since 1981 Republicans have had a majority in the Senate only.

A second reason for bipartisanship is that no matter how large the representation of the president's party in Congress, he cannot always depend upon it for support. Tables 11-1 and 11-2 show clearly that members of the president's own party frequently oppose him. As Jimmy Carter wrote, "I learned the hard way that there was no party loyalty or discipline when a complicated or controversial issue was at stake—none."[12] Southern Democrats support Democratic presidents less consistently than do Northern Democrats, particularly on civil rights legislation.

Not only do partisan strategies often fail, but they also may provoke the other party into a more unified posture of opposition. "Where there is confrontation, there can be no consensus," and consensus is often required to legislate changes on important issues. The president is also inhibited in his partisanship by pressures to be "president of all the people" rather than a highly partisan figure. This role expectation of being somewhat above the political fray undoubtedly constrains presidents in their role as party leader.

Despite the frequent necessity of a bipartisan strategy, it is not without costs. Bipartisanship often creates a strain with the extremists within the president's party as a Republican president tries to appeal to the left for Democratic votes and a Democratic president to the right for Republican votes. Although it is true that the Republican right wing and Democratic left wing may find it difficult to forge a coalition in favor of alternatives to their own president's policies, it is not true that they must therefore support their president. Instead, they may complicate a president's strategy by joining those who oppose his policies.

PUBLIC SUPPORT

Although congressional seats held by members of the president's party may be a necessary condition for presidential success in Congress, they are not a sufficient one. The president needs public support as well. In the words of Eisenhower aide and presidential authority Emmet John Hughes, "Beyond all tricks of history and all quirks of Presidents, there would appear to be one unchallengeable truth: the dependence of Presidential authority on popular support."[13]

In his memoirs, President Johnson wrote, "Presidential popularity is a major source of strength in gaining cooperation from Congress."[14] Thus, following his landslide electoral victory, he assembled the congressional liaison officials from the various departments and told them that his victory at the polls "might be more of a loophole than a mandate" and that since his popularity could decrease rapidly, they would have to use it to their advantage while it lasted.[15]

President Carter's aides were quite explicit about the importance of Carter's popularity in their efforts to influence Congress. One stated that the "only way to keep those guys [Congress] honest is to keep our popularity high."[16] The president's legislative liaison officials generally agreed that their effectiveness with Congress ultimately depended upon the president's ability to influence public opinion. As one of them said, "When you go up to the Hill and the latest polls show Carter isn't doing well, there isn't much reason for a member to go along with him. There's little we can do if the member isn't persuaded on the issue."[17]

Why is presidential approval or popularity such an important source of influence in Congress? According to a senior aide to President Carter:

> When the President is low in public opinion polls, the Members of Congress see little hazard in bucking him. . . . After all, very few Congressmen examine an issue solely on its merits; they are politicians and they think politically. I'm not saying they make only politically expedient choices. But they

read the polls and from that they feel secure in turning their backs on the President with political impunity. Unquestionably, the success of the President's policies bears a tremendous relationship to his popularity in the polls.[18]

Members of Congress are concerned with public opinion, either because they feel they ought to represent the public's wishes or because they desire to increase their chances for reelection. In an environment of limited information on public preferences and the potential of serious electoral challenges, members of Congress "run scared" and anticipate public reactions to their support of or opposition to the most visible figure in American politics: the president. According to Johnson aide Harry McPherson, members of Congress "listened hard for evidence of how the President stood in their states in order that they might know how to treat him."[19] Richard Nixon tells us that presidential popularity polls affect the ability of presidents to lead because politicians pay attention to them.[20]

A president high in the polls is more likely to obtain congressional support for his policies than one who is low. To illustrate this point, let us examine congressional support for Richard Nixon in 1972 and 1973. In 1973 President Nixon won only 51 percent of the votes in Congress on issues on which he took a stand, by far the lowest percentage of any recent president. Moreover, his record for 1973 would have been even lower without the many routine votes that took place at the end of the year. His support decreased among all party groups in Congress, especially Democrats.

Why did this happen? Nixon had just won one of the greatest landslide victories in history, carrying every state except Massachusetts (and the District of Columbia). There were twelve more Republicans in the House and two more in the Senate in 1973 than in 1972, when he received considerably more support. Moreover, American military involvement in Vietnam ended at the time of his second inauguration and therefore should have been less of an irritation to Congress. Nixon had also made changes to improve his personal relations with Congress. Bob Haldeman and John Ehrlichman, who were disliked for their arrogance and formed the cornerstone of the so-called Berlin Wall around the president, were early victims of Watergate. The ineffective Vice President Spiro Agnew fell to his own tragedy, and the president brought Bryce Harlow and Melvin Laird into the White House and nominated Gerald Ford as vice president. These three men were experienced in dealing with Congress, which liked and respected them. The president held more bipartisan leadership meetings, more meetings with the Republican leadership, and more meetings with the Republican rank and file and had more social contact with members of Congress than ever before. All of these actions should have increased rather than lowered Nixon's support in Congress. What, then, explains the decline in support for the president?

One might argue that Congress was angered by Nixon's arrogant approach toward it and his unique conception of the separation of powers, which involved massive impoundments, waging an undeclared war, and an extensive claim of executive privilege. However, just because members of Congress were alienated by one or more actions by the president, they would not necessarily oppose him on pieces of legislation that were unrelated to those actions (as almost all legislation was). In addition, the three types of acts noted above were prevalent well before 1973. The most reasonable explanation for Richard Nixon's substantial decline in support among members of Congress in 1973 is his equally substantial decline in public approval, primarily because of Watergate. In December 1972 his overall approval stood at 62 percent; one year later his popularity had plummeted 33 points to 29 percent. Without public support his legislative program languished.

Public approval is a necessary but not a sufficient source of influence in Congress. It is most useful in combination with party supporters in each house of Congress. If either approval or seats are lacking, the president's legislative program will be in for rough sledding. The consequences of the absence of each source of influence are described by two presidential assistants, the first to Nixon and the second to Carter:

> Nineteen seventy-two did not help us. It was similar to Eisenhower in 1956. We had tremendous public and electoral support. But that and a dime couldn't buy a cup of coffee. It was still a question of what we didn't have: what we didn't have was enough Republican congressmen.

> The 292 Democrats in Congress were potential supporters—that was only three fewer than LBJ had. But with the close election and the drop in approval, they remained that way: potential. We couldn't force them to be active supporters.[21]

The fact that presidential approval is an important potential source of influence in Congress provides a strong incentive for the president to gain popular support. This is not solely determined by the president himself, however, as we learned earlier. Thus, although presidential approval is an effective source of presidential influence, it is not one he can manipulate easily.

PRESIDENTIAL LEGISLATIVE SKILLS

In this section of our discussion of presidential influence in Congress we examine other White House efforts to persuade members of Congress to support the president's legislative proposals. These include the president's personal appeals for support, bargaining, providing services and amenities, pressuring, consulting with Congress, and carefully timing the introduction of his proposals. Some of these activities are aimed at building goodwill in the long run and others at obtaining votes from individual members of Congress on specific issues.

Whatever the immediate goal, the nature of the legislative process in America demands that the president apply his legislative skills in a wide range of situations. In the words of one presidential aide:

> Senator A might come with us if Senator B, an admired friend, could be persuaded to talk to him. Senator C wanted a major project out of Chairman D's committee; maybe D, a supporter of our bill, would release it in exchange for C's commitment. Senator E might be reached through people in his home state. If Senator F could not vote with us on final passage, could he vote with us on key amendments? Could G take a trip? Would the President call Senator H?[22]

Congressional Liaison

Although the Constitution establishes separate institutions, the operation of the government requires those institutions to work together. The president is expected to propose legislation and to get it enacted into law. As our previous discussion suggests, he needs all the help he can get. To assist him in these efforts as well as with his other ongoing legislative responsibilities, a congressional liaison staff, based in the White House, has operated since 1953. The size of this staff and the duties it performs has expanded significantly in recent years.

The growth of the president's liaison mechanism has occurred in three stages. In its initial phase during the Eisenhower administration, the congressional relations office was small in size, adopted a low profile, and utilized a bipartisan approach in dealing with Congress. Cautious of infringing on the legislature's prerogatives or of operating on its turf, the president's agents worked the phones from the White House rather than the halls of Congress, communicated mainly with and through the legislative leadership, and used gentle persuasion rather than arm-twisting to achieve their goals. Eisenhower, himself, was not heavily involved in the details of legislation although he did have contact with members of Congress, especially with the Republican leaders.

The congressional relations office assumed a more aggressive posture in its second phase, which occurred during the Kennedy-Johnson years. With a larger and more comprehensive legislative agenda to advocate, the staff expanded its size and its functions. In addition to pushing major White House policy initiatives, the president's liaison team began funneling legislative views into the executive decision-making process. The increasing development of policy by the White House made this input desirable from a congressional perspective.

Presidential assistants involved in legislation became more numerous, more visible, and more partisan. Attempts were made to organize executive department and agency liaison staffs more effectively behind the president's major priorities. Pressures were exerted on committee chairs, informal legislative groups, and in general, on more members on more issues. Rewards were also more generously bestowed. "The White House certainly remembers who its friends are," Lawrence F. O'Brien, head of the office, both warned and promised legislators early in the Kennedy administration.[23]

In an effort to improve the atmosphere for the administration on Capitol Hill and to meet an increasing need of Congress, the White House began providing casework services for members and their staffs. This care and feeding operation soon became a congressional expectation, one that subsequent White Houses could not shirk. Social lobbying increased as well.

By the end of the 1960s certain functions had come to be regarded as traditional liaison activities. In addition to catering to the constituency needs of members of Congress, these included gathering intelligence, tracking legislation, coordinating department and agency efforts, and working with the leadership on priority programs. These functions continue to be performed today, but the level of White House involvement and the scope of its activities have expanded even further. The principal reason for that expansion is the difficulty that contemporary presidents have had in mobilizing majority coalitions in support of their policy proposals.

Phase three in the evolution of the presidency's liaison mechanism began in the Carter administration. Frustrated by its inability to get Congress to enact its policy recommendations in the first year and a half of the administration, the Carter White House began to broaden its interaction with Congress and utilize outside forces to help build legislative support. The president increased the size of his congressional relations office despite his highly publicized reduction of White House personnel. Much of that increase was in support staff to aid in executive-branch coordination and casework. Internal task forces on key initiatives were formed to coordinate the administration's congressional activities. A mechanism for setting priorities for highly visible issues was established. More sophisticated information retrieval systems and computerized mail logs were developed to process congressional mail and assess voting patterns. Even the president, a private person by nature, began to interact more regularly with members of Congress, particularly the leadership. There were more White House social events for legislators of both parties.

In conjunction with these changes, other presidential offices got more involved with Congress and the legislative process. Although it did not solicit congressional views, the domestic policy staff became more receptive to them. Members of Congress and their staffs were given opportunities to affect the development of proposed legislation *before* it was sent to Congress. A public liaison office was established to organize outside groups and community leaders into coalitions behind the administration's proposals. Once established, these coalitions, orchestrated by the White House, mounted grass-roots efforts and directed them toward Congress. They identified the positions of members on key issues, targeted those who were wavering, had them contacted by group representatives from their own constituencies, and supplemented these activities by organizing mass letter-writing and telephoning campaigns. These constituency-based pressures were designed to make it easier for members of Congress to vote with the president regardless of their party affiliation.

During the Reagan presidency a legislative strategy group, consisting of senior presidential aides, operated out of the chief of staff's office to coordinate these "outreach" efforts and tie them to administrative lobbying on Capitol Hill. Other White House offices, in addition to congressional relations and public liaison, also got involved in congressional affairs. A newly constituted political office handled patronage and other party-related matters. In addition to organizing state and local officials behind other administration initiatives, an intergovernmental affairs office promoted the president's New Federalism proposals.

In summary, congressional liaison has developed and expanded because it serves the needs of *both* executive and legislative branches. For the Congress, it helps integrate legislative views into executive policy making, it services constituency needs, it forces the president to indicate his legislative priorities, it provides channels for reaching compromises, and it helps the leadership to form majority coalitions. For the president, it enables him to gain a congressional perspective, to communicate his views to Congress, to mobilize support for his programs, and to reach accommodations with the legislature. Such efforts to bridge the constitutional separation have helped to overcome some of the obstacles to the formulation of public policy.

We now turn to the legislative skills that the president and his liaison aides must utilize in their efforts to win support for the administration's proposals on Capitol Hill.

Personal Appeals

A special aspect of presidential involvement in the legislative process is the personal appeal for votes. According to presidential scholar Richard Neustadt, "when the chips are down, there is no substitute for the President's own footwork, his personal negotiation, his direct appeal, his voice and no other's on the telephone."[24] Members of Congress are as subject to flattery as other people and are impressed when the president calls.

Calls from the president must be relatively rare to maintain their usefulness. If the president calls too often, his calls will have less impact. Moreover, members might begin to expect calls, for which the president has limited time, or they may resent too much high-level pressure being applied to them. On the other hand, they may exploit a call and say that they are uncertain about an issue in order to extract a favor from the president. In addition, the president does not want to commit his prestige to a bill by personal lobbying and then lose. Also, his staff's credibility when speaking for him will decrease the more he speaks for himself.

Presidents become intensely involved only after the long winnowing process of lining up votes is almost done and their calls are needed to win on an important issue, a situation that arises only a few times a year. When presidents do call about a vote, they focus on key members of Congress, whose votes serve as cues for other members, and members who are uncommitted or weakly committed in either direction. They identify the latter by studying the head counts prepared by the White House congressional liaison office.

Despite the prestige of their office, their invocations of national interest, and their persuasiveness, presidents often fail in their personal appeals. President Eisenhower liked to depend heavily on charm and reason, but in 1953 he tried to persuade Republican chairman Daniel Reed of the House Ways and Means Committee to support the continuance of the excess profits tax and to oppose a tax cut. "I used every possible reason, argument, and device, and every kind of personal and indirect contact," he wrote, "to bring Chairman Reed to my way of thinking." But he failed.[25] Lyndon Johnson was renowned for his persuasiveness but nevertheless failed on many issues, ranging from civil rights and education to medicare and the Panama uprising. "No matter how many times I told Congress to do something," he wrote, "I could never force it to act."[26] If Eisenhower and Johnson often failed in their efforts at persuasion, we should not be surprised that other presidents did also.

Bargaining

It is part of the conventional wisdom that the White House regularly "buys" votes through bargains struck with members of Congress, and this certainly does occur at times. Yet we obtain a more accurate perspective when we listen to Kennedy-Johnson legislative liaison chief Lawrence O'Brien, who said near the end of his government service, "This suggestion that you trade the bridge or the dam or some project for a vote . . . it's just not the case."[27] Similarly, William Timmons, O'Brien's counterpart in the Nixon administration, maintains that there were no blatant trades for votes in his experience.[28]

The president cannot bargain with Congress as a whole because it is too large and decentralized for one bargain to satisfy everyone. Also, the president's time is limited, as are his resources—only so many appointive jobs are available and the federal budget is limited. Moreover, funding for public works projects is in the hands of Congress. In addition, if many direct bargains are struck, word will rapidly spread, everyone will want to trade, and persuasive efforts will fail. Thus, most of the bargains that are reached are implicit. The lack of respectability surrounding bargaining also encourages implicitness.

Fortunately for the president, bargaining with everyone in Congress is not necessary. Except on vetoes and treaties, he needs only a simple majority of those voting. A large part of Congress can be "written off" on any given vote. Moreover, as we have seen, the president generally starts with a substantial core of party support and then adds to this number those of the other party who agree with his views on ideological or policy grounds. Others may support him on the basis of goodwill that he has generated through his services or because of public support for him or his policies. Thus, the president needs to bargain only if all these groups do not provide a majority for crucial votes, and he need bargain only with enough people to provide him with that majority.

Since resources are scarce, the president will usually try to use them for bargaining with powerful members of Congress, such as committee chairs or those whose votes are the most important. There is no guarantee that a tendered bargain will be accepted, however. The members may not desire what the president offers, or they may be able to obtain what they want on their own. This is, of course, particularly true of the most powerful members, whose support the president needs most. Sometimes members of Congress do not want to trade at all because of constituency opinion or personal views. At other times the president is unwilling to bargain.

Most of the pressure for bargaining actually comes from the Hill. When the White House calls and asks for support, representatives and senators frequently raise a question regarding some request that they have made. In the words of an Eisenhower aide, "Every time we make a special appeal to a Congressman to change his position, he eventually comes back with a request for a favor ranging in importance from one of the President's packages of matches to a judgeship or cabinet appointment for a 'worthy constituent.' "[29]

More general bargains also take place. In the words of Nixon's chief congressional aide, William Timmons: "I think they [members of Congress] knew that we would try our best to help them on all kinds of requests if they supported the President, and we did. It kind of goes without saying." His successor in the Ford administration, Max Fried-ersdorf, added his assurance that people who want things want to be in the position of supporting the president. This implicit trading on "accounts" is more common than explicit bargaining.[30]

For the White House, a member of Congress indebted to the president is easier to approach and ask for a vote. For the member, previous support increases the chances of a request being honored. Thus, office-holders at both ends of Pennsylvania Avenue want to be in the other's favor. The degree of debt determines the strategy used in presidential requests for support. While services and favors increase the president's chances of obtaining support, they are not usually exchanged for votes directly. They are strategic and not tactical weapons.

This point is illustrated in the following statement by Lawrence O'Brien, discussing various White House services for Congress:

> [There is] no single element of [them] that is overridingly important, but [in] the over-all activity . . . in putting the package together over a period of years [we] can only hope the Member up there has the view that the White House is interested in him and his problems . . . and therefore when we have our problems—we will get favorable reaction at least from the sense of giving us a hearing, seriously considering our viewpoint, if he feels that we in turn understand his problem.[31]

Services and Amenities

Since a member of Congress who is indebted to the president is easier to approach and ask for a vote, the White House provides many services and amenities for representatives and senators. Although these favors may be bestowed on any member of Congress, they actually go disproportionately to members of the president's party. Personal amenities used to create goodwill include social contact with the president, flattery, rides on Air Force One, visits to Camp David, birthday greetings, theater tickets for the presidential box, invitations to bill-signing ceremonies, pictures with the president, briefings, and a plethora of others, the number and variety of which are limited only by the imagination of the president and his staff.

Also, the White House often helps members of Congress with their constituents. A wide range of services is offered, including greetings to elderly and other "worthy" constituents, signed presidential photographs, presidential tie clasps and other White House memorabilia, reprints of speeches, information about government programs, White House pressure on agencies in favor of constituents, passing the nominations of constituents on to agencies, influence on local editorial writers, ceremonial appointments to commissions, meetings with the president, and arguments to be used to explain votes to constituents. The president may also help members of Congress please constituents through patronage, pork-barrel projects and government contracts, and aid with legislation of special interest to particular constituencies.

Campaign aid is yet another service the White House can provide party members, and the president may dangle it before them to entice support. This aid may come in various forms, including campaign speeches by the president and executive officials for congressional candidates, funds and advice from the party national committees, presidential endorsements, pictures with the president, and letters of appreciation from the president. Some aid is more ingenious, as when Lawrence O'Brien, then postmaster general, held a stamp dedication ceremony, complete with parade and associated festivities, in Representative Stan Greigg's hometown in 1966.

When it created a Political Affairs Office, the Reagan administration formalized an activity in which White House staff members have long engaged. A principal function is to secure support for the president in Congress, and it is closely tied to the Republican National Committee and the House and Senate Republican Campaign Committees. Officials from each unit meet weekly to coordinate their activities. Not only is the office a liaison between the president and the campaign arena, but it is also a place where Republicans in Congress can come for favors.

All administrations are not equally active in providing services and amenities for members of Congress. The Johnson and Reagan White House fall on the "active" end of this spectrum while the Nixon and Carter presidencies fall on the other end. Yet the important point is that any such differences are relatively small in comparison to the efforts made by every recent administration to develop goodwill among its party members in Congress.

Pressure

In 1982 one of President Reagan's aides told of how he persuaded two Republican members of the House to vote for the president's budget cuts. The representatives feared the political repercussions in their constituencies of supporting the president, so the aide promised them the maximum campaign aid the law allows a party to give a candidate and won their votes. When asked what would have happened if the congressmen had not given in, the aide replied, "I would have nailed them to the wall."[32]

Thus, just as the president can offer the carrot, he can also wield the stick. Moreover, the increased resources available to the White House in recent years provide increased opportunities to levy sanctions in the form of the withholding of favors. As the deputy chairman of the Republican National Committee said, there is more money than ever "to play hardball with. We're loaded for bear."[33] The threats of such actions are effective primarily with members of the president's party, of course, because members of the opposition party do not expect to receive many favors from the president.

Although sanctions or threats of sanctions are far from an everyday occurrence, they do occur. These may take the form of excluding a member from White House social events, denying routine requests for White House tour tickets, and shutting off access to see the president. Each of these personal slights sends a signal of presidential displeasure.

Sometimes the arm-twisting is more severe and includes cutting projects in a district or state from the budget, cutting off patronage to a member, and refusing White House help in fund-raising and campaign activities. The Reagan White House let it be known that campaign aid in the form of party funds and technical advice, appearances by top administration officials at fund-raisers and during campaigns, and the encouragement of PAC contributions was contingent upon support for the president. The White House Political Affairs Office let junior Republicans in Congress know that it was watching their votes and public statements closely and warned them not to oppose the president. In the words of the office's director, "We will help our friends first."[34]

Sheer psychological pressure also plays a role in presidential party leadership. One freshman congressman reported that when he told President Reagan he could not support his 1982 proposal to increase taxes, the president "got red-faced, pounded the table and yelled at me." Similarly, the director of the White House Political Affairs Office, Ed Rollins, described the pressures the White House put on Republican Senator Roger Jepsen on the issue of selling AWACS planes to Saudi Arabia: "We just beat his brains out. That's all. We just took Jepsen and beat his brains out."[35]

Such heavy-handed arm-twisting is unusual, however. More typical is the orchestration of pressure by others. The Reagan White House has been especially effective in this regard. Operating through party channels, its Political Affairs Office, and its Office of Public Liaison, the administration has been able to generate pressure from party members' constituents, campaign contributors, political activists, business leaders, state officials, interest groups, party officials, and, of course, cabinet members. The Office of Legislative Affairs is also in regular communication with the president's party cohorts. Such efforts are by no means restricted to party members, of course, but they are the primary focus because of their general proclivity to support the president and the reverse situation among the opposition.

Despite the resources available to the president, if members of Congress wish to oppose the White House, there is little the president can do to stop them. This is true for those in his party as well as those in the opposition. The primary reason is that the parties are highly decentralized; national party leaders do not control those aspects of politics that are of vital concern to members of Congress: nominations and elections. Members of Congress are largely self-recruited, gain their party's nominations by their own efforts and not the party's, and provide most of the money and organizational support needed for their elections. Presidents can do little to influence the results of these activities, and usually they don't even try. As President Kennedy said in 1962, "Party loyalty or responsibility means damn little. They've got to take care of themselves first. They [House members] all have to run this year—I don't and I couldn't hurt most of them if I wanted to."[36]

Process Matters

In addition to the skills we have discussed above, many of which involve matters tangential to a specific bill, there are also many things a president can do that are more directly related to the legislative process per se that may increase the probabilities of his proposals passing. Presidents can consult with members of Congress at each stage of the legislative process. Congressional input may be especially important *before* a bill is introduced, as the White House is drafting a program and estimating its prospects for passage. Involving members of Congress in this process and clearing legislation in advance with key members and interest groups can ease the path for a president's bills by preempting opposition and garnering advance commitments. So can giving members advance warning of legislation and appointments. This is an important courtesy in Washington, as politicians do not like being blindsided.

Presidents usually have many more proposals than Congress can handle at once or than they can lobby for at once. Congress can easily become bogged down with too much legislation, and it needs the president's help in establishing its agenda. Thus, it is important that the White House indicate its priority issues to Congress. Otherwise, presidential proposals back up and compete with each other for congressional attention, something for which Jimmy Carter was criticized.

Carter's troubles were aggravated by the fact that many of his major proposals had to pass through the Senate Finance and the House Ways and Means committees. He made the mistake of sending to them his economic stimulus package; hospital cost containment bill; social security, welfare, and tax reform legislation; and his urban assistance program all within his first year in office. This many issues simply clogged up the legislative process.

Timing is another important aspect of presidential-congressional relations. Presidents who are ready with legislation early in the first year of their terms stand a better chance of success than those who must wait many months to draft legislation. The glow of the president's electoral victory begins to fade before long so the honeymoon period must be exploited quickly. Similarly, when a proposal has cleared Congress, the White House should be ready to replace it with another so as not to waste opportunities.

Yet most presidents find it difficult to orchestrate legislation in this way, both because of the complexity of drafting modern legislation and the protracted nature of the legislature process. While Kennedy, Johnson, and Reagan were ready to submit proposals to Congress soon after taking office, Eisenhower, Nixon, Ford, and Carter were not. Moreover, waiting for one program to pass before submitting another may mean never submitting the latter at all.

The Context of Influence

In our discussion of the president's legislative skills, it is important that we keep in mind the general context in which he operates. Contemporary presidents serve during the post-Vietnam and post-Watergate period of congressional assertiveness. The diminished deference to the president by individual members of Congress and by the institution as a whole naturally makes presidential influence more problematical. Vietnam, Watergate, and a sagging economy have also combined to make the public more skeptical of government policies. The optimism of the race to the moon and the idealism that fueled the war on poverty in the 1960s has been replaced by anxiety over nuclear weapons, energy resources, and inflation. For a president who desires to establish new programs, the outlook is not promising.

Current presidents also have the misfortune to preside during a period of substantial economic scarcity, whereas the Kennedy-Johnson years were characterized by stable prices, sustained economic growth, and general prosperity. The prosperity of the 1960s provided the federal government with the funds for new policies, with little risk. Taxes did not have to be raised and sacrifices did not have to be made in order to help the underprivileged. In the late 1970s and 1980s resources are more limited, helping to make the passage of new welfare or health programs, for example, more problematical. When resources are scarce, presidents are faced with internal competition for them and the breakdown of supporting coalitions. They must choose between policies rather than building coalitions for several policies through logrolling.

In light of the above discussion, it is not surprising that the relations of recent presidents with Congress are often characterized by stalemate. The environment for presidential influence has been deteriorating.

THE VETO

Sometimes not only does the president fail to win passage of his proposals but Congress passes legislation to which he is strongly opposed. Since all bills and joint resolutions except those proposing constitutional amendments must be presented to the president for his approval, the president has another opportunity to influence legislation: the veto.

When Congress passes an item that must be submitted to the president, the president has several options. Within ten days (Sundays excepted) of its presentation the president may (1) sign the measure, in which case it becomes the law of the land, (2) withhold his signature and return the measure to the house in which it originated with a message stating his reasons for withholding approval, or (3) do nothing. When the president returns a bill or joint resolution to Congress, he has *vetoed* the measure. It can then become law only if each house of Congress repasses it by a two-thirds majority of those present. Congress may override the presidential veto at any time before it adjourns *sine die*.

Early presidents exercised their veto power sparingly and ostensibly for the purpose of voiding legislation they deemed to be unconstitutional in its content or sloppy and improper in design. The first six presidents vetoed a total of eight bills; the seventh president, Andrew Jackson, vetoed twelve. Jackson used his negative to prevent legislation he opposed from becoming law. His example was followed by others. Through 1982, a total of 1,395 bills and resolutions were vetoed, almost half by Franklin Roosevelt (635).

The president can veto only an entire bill. Unlike most state governors, he does not have an *item veto*, which allows just specific provisions of a bill to be vetoed. As a result of this constraint, members of Congress use a number of strategies to avoid a possible veto of a particular proposal. For example, Congress may add increased appropriations or *riders* (i.e., nongermane provisions) that the president might not want to bills that the president otherwise desires. Thus, he must accept these unattractive provisions in order to gain the legislation that he wants. In most such cases, the president does not use his veto. For example, after President Carter vetoed a bill providing for increased salaries for Public Health Service physicians, Congress added the pay raise to mental health services legislation, a pet project of First Lady Rosalyn Carter. The president signed the bill.

An unofficial item veto occurs when a president signs a bill but states that he will disregard selected provisions or provides interpretations of key clauses. Both actions may significantly modify the bill. President Eisenhower stated that the sections of the 1959 Mutual Security Act dealing with the provision of documents to Congress would not alter the constitutional right of the president to keep secrets. He made a similar statement regarding the Availability of Information Act of 1958, leaving it ineffectual. More dramatically, in 1971 President Nixon signed a bill containing a statement urging the president to set a date for U.S. withdrawal from military actions in Southeast Asia. He said that he would ignore that part of the act, regarding it "without binding force or effect." President Ford, concerned about the concept of the legislative veto, signed two bills in 1976, one dealing with defense appropriations and the other with veterans affairs, but declared that the legislative veto provision in each bill would be treated as a "nullity." The legality of such presidential statements has never been established.

If the president does nothing after he receives a measure from Congress, it becomes law after ten days (Sundays excepted) if Congress remains in session. If it has adjourned during the ten-day period, thus preventing the president from returning the bill to the house of its origination, the bill is *pocket vetoed*. A pocket veto kills a piece of legislation just as a regular veto does. Traditionally somewhat fewer than half of all vetoes have been pocket vetoes. Table 11-5 presents data on the vetoes by recent presidents.

Presidents have sometimes attempted to use the pocket veto by taking no action on measures sent to them just before Congress went into a temporary recess, claiming that the recess prevented them from returning their veto for congressional consideration. (In 1964 President Johnson pocket vetoed a bill during a congressional recess and then recalled and signed it.) However, in 1976 after the Nixon and Ford White Houses had lost litigation on the issue, the Ford administration promised that the president would not use the pocket veto during congressional recesses as long as an official of Congress was designated to be on hand to receive his vetoes. Since Congress is in session nearly all year, most people thought only an adjournment sine die would provide the opportunity for a pocket veto. Ronald Reagan used the pocket veto during a recess at the end of the 1981 session without apparent problems, but thirty-three House Democrats filed suit in federal court to challenge his pocket veto during the congressional recess at the end of 1983 of a bill making aid to El Salvador dependent on human rights progress. In 1984 a federal appeals court ruled against the president.

The last column in Table 11-5 shows that vetoes are rarely used. Not only are the absolute numbers low, but fewer than 1 percent of the bills passed by Congress (which number several hundred per session) are vetoed. The table also shows that presidents who faced Congresses controlled by the opposition party (Eisenhower, Nixon, and Ford) used more vetoes, as we would expect. They were more likely to be presented with legislation that they opposed.

Table 11-6 illustrates another important fact about vetoes. Regular

Table 11-5. Regular and Pocket Vetoes

President	No. of Regular Vetoes	No. of Pocket Vetoes	Total Vetoes
Eisenhower	73	108	181
Kennedy	12	9	21
Johnson	16	14	30
Nixon	26	17	43
Ford	48	18	66
Carter	13	18	31
Reagan*	18	21	39

*For 1981–1984.

vetoes are generally sustained, but overriding does occur, especially when the president's party is in the minority in Congress. Some very important legislation is passed over the president's veto. In the post–World War II era such legislation includes the Taft-Hartley Labor Relations Act (1947), the McCarran-Walter Immigration Act (1952), the McCarran-Wood Internal Security Act (1950), and the War Powers Resolution (1973).

Sometimes presidents choose not to veto a bill either because, as mentioned earlier, they feel the good in the legislation outweighs the bad or because they do not want their veto to be overridden. Thus, President Ford did not veto the 1975 food stamp legislation, which he opposed, because only forty-six members of the House and Senate had supported his own proposal.

When a bill is introduced in either house of Congress, the chamber's parliamentarian classifies it as public or private. Generally, public bills relate to public matters and deal with individuals by classifications or categories, such as college students or the elderly. A private bill, on the other hand, names a particular individual or entity who is to receive relief, such as payment of a pension or a claim against the government or the granting of citizenship. Up until 1969 presidents usually vetoed more private than public bills. Recent presidents have vetoed very few private bills, however.

The veto is an inherently negative element in the president's arsenal, but sometimes it may be used as a threat to shape legislation. For example, in late 1978 President Carter threatened to veto any bill that allowed tuition tax credits. As a result, Congress seems to have dropped such a provision, which had already passed the Senate. Nevertheless, once exercised, a veto can only say no. At that point, the threat has failed and the chances of the president's legislative proposals passing in the forms that he desires are diminished. Moreover, the threat must be exercised with caution lest it be used too often and be too easily overcome. Thus, while a president's vetoes are normally successful in stopping legislation,

Table 11-6. Vetoes Overridden

President	No. of Regular Vetoes	No. of Vetoes Overridden	% Vetoes Overridden
Eisenhower	73	2	3
Kennedy	12	0	0
Johnson	16	0	0
Nixon	26	7	27
Ford	48	12	25
Carter	13	2	15
Reagan*	18	4	21

*For 1981–1984.

they are less effective when used as threats to pass his own legislation, and they are utilized in this way only in exceptional cases.

CONCLUSION

The president faces an uphill battle in dealing with Congress. His formal powers of recommending legislation to Congress and vetoing bills help set the legislature's agenda and prevent some of what he opposes from passing. Yet these prerogatives are of only marginal help. Conflict between the executive and legislative branches is inherent in our system of government. The overlapping powers of the two branches, their representation of different constituencies, the contrast of the hierarchical, expert nature of the executive and the decentralized, generalist Congress and the different time frames within which they operate guarantee that, except in extraordinary circumstances, conflict between them will remain a central feature of American politics.

Despite the substantial obstacles to presidential success in Congress, the chief executive's assets are unimpressive. Party leadership is a potential source of influence in Congress, and the president receives considerably more support from members of his party than from the opposition. Much, or even most, of this support is the result of members of the same party sharing similar policy views rather than the influence of the president's party leadership. Nevertheless, the president works closely with his party and its leaders in Congress and gains some increment of support as a result of party loyalty. Party support is undependable, however, as constituency interests, a lack of policy consensus, and other factors intervene and diminish the importance of the party label. Congressional party leaders are typically in weak positions to move their troops in the president's direction. Ideally, the president could influence the election of members of his party to Congress, but presidential coattails are very short and midterm campaigning seems to have limited pay-offs. Thus, the president generally has to seek support from opposition party members, but his efforts at bipartisanship, although necessary, may strain relations with the less moderate wing of his own party.

The president is more likely to receive support in Congress when he has the public's approval than when he sits low in the polls. Unfortunately, as we have seen in Chapter 4, the president cannot depend on the public's support, nor can he be sure of being able to mobilize new support. Moreover, public approval is usually a necessary but not a sufficient source of influence. Even a president high in the polls will find it difficult to pass his program if his party lacks a substantial number of congressional seats.

The White House engages in a large-scale legislative liaison effort to create goodwill and influence votes on a more personal level. Bargains are consummated, services and amenities are provided, arms are twisted, presidential phone calls are made, and advance consultation is done. Yet there are severe limits on a president's time and resources. The president can also increase his chances of success if he moves his program early in his tenure and does not let it clog the legislative process. However, many presidents find it difficult or impossible to control Congress's agenda so neatly. Although presidential legislative skills are crucial in winning some votes, their importance is often exaggerated by those who focus more on the unique than the general. Thus, the president must constantly struggle to succeed in having his policies enacted into law.

NOTES

1. Lyndon Johnson, quoted in Doris Kearns, *Lyndon Johnson and the American Dream* (New York: Harper and Row, 1976), p. 226.

2. James Madison, "The Federalist No. 46," in *The Federalist* (New York: Modern Library, 1937), p. 307.

3. Cecil Andrus, quoted in "Water Policy: Battle over Benefits," *Congressional Quarterly Weekly Report*, March 4, 1978, p. 565.

4. Gerald R. Ford, *A Time to Heal: The Autobiography of Gerald R. Ford* (New York: Harper and Row, 1979), p. 150.

5. President Carter's first-year proposals included a new Department of Energy, reform of the welfare system, reform of the financing of the social security system, several energy policy proposals, executive-branch reorganization legislation, public jobs, ending expenditures for the B-1 bomber, several water resource projects, and the Clinch River breeder reactor project, legislation to hold down hospital costs, an air pollution bill, new housing programs, a series of election laws, food stamp reform, a strip-mining bill, a wiretap bill, two Panama Canal treaties, a tax cut, common-site picketing for labor unions, a new minimum wage bill, user fees for inland waterways, new target prices for some agricultural commodities, and the creation of the largest number of new federal judgeships in history.

6. Richard E. Neustadt, *Presidential Power: The Politics of Leadership from FDR to Carter* (New York: Wiley, 1980), p. 26.

7. Quoted in Paul C. Light, *The President's Agenda: Domestic Policy Choice from Kennedy to Carter* (Baltimore: Johns Hopkins University Press, 1982), p. 135.

8. Howard Baker, quoted in James L. Sundquist, *The Decline and Resurgence of Congress* (Washington, D.C.: Brookings Institution, 1981), p. 402.

9. "Jimmy's 'Oracle,' " *Newsweek*, October 3, 1977, p. 27.

10. Gerald R. Ford, "Imperiled, Not Imperial," *Time*, November 10, 1980, p. 30.

11. Quoted in Light, *The President's Agenda*, p. 211.

12. Jimmy Carter, *Keeping Faith: Memoirs of a President* (New York: Bantam, 1982), p. 80.

13. Emmet John Hughes, *The Living Presidency* (Baltimore: Penguin, 1974), p. 68.

14. Lyndon B. Johnson, *The Vantage Point: Perspectives of the Presidency, 1963–1969* (New York: Popular Library, 1971), p. 443.

15. Ibid., p. 323.

16. "Run, Run, Run," *Newsweek*, May 2, 1977, p. 38.

17. "Carter Seeks More Effective Use of Departmental Lobbyists' Skills," *Congressional Quarterly Weekly Report*, March 4, 1978, p. 585.

18. Dom Bonafede, "The Strained Relationship," *National Journal*, May 19, 1979, p. 830.

19. Harry McPherson, *A Political Education* (Boston: Little, Brown, 1972), pp. 246–47.

20. Richard M. Nixon, *RN: The Memoirs of Richard Nixon* (New York: Grosset and Dunlap, 1977), p. 753.

21. Quoted in Light, *The President's Agenda*, pp. 29 and 31; see more generally pp. 28–31.

22. McPherson, *A Political Education*, p. 192.

23. Lawrence F. O'Brien, quoted in Neil McNeil, *Forge of Democracy* (New York: McKay, 1963), p. 260.

24. Richard E. Neustadt, "Presidency and Legislation: Planning the President's Program," in Aaron Wildavsky, ed., *The Presidency* (Boston: Little, Brown, 1969), p. 596.

25. Dwight D. Eisenhower, *Mandate for Change, 1953–1956* (New York: Signet, 1963), pp. 254–55.

26. Johnson, *The Vantage Point*, p. 40.

27. "Larry O'Brien Discusses White House Contacts with Capitol Hill," in Aaron Wildavsky, ed., *The Presidency* (Boston: Little, Brown, 1969), p. 481.

28. William Timmons, quoted in "Turning Screws: Winning Votes in Congress," *Congressional Quarterly Weekly Report*, April 24, 1976, p. 954.

29. Gary W. Reichard, *The Reaffirmation of Republicanism: Eisenhower and the Eighty-Third Congress* (Knoxville: University of Tennessee Press, 1975), p. 173.

30. William Timmons, quoted in "Turning Screws," pp. 952–53.

31. "Larry O'Brien Discusses," p. 485.

32. Quoted in "Playing Hardball," *Wall Street Journal*, August 18, 1982, p. 1.

33. Quoted in ibid.

34. Quoted in Dick Kirschten, "Reagan's Political Chief Robbins: 'We Will Help Our Friends First,' " *National Journal*, June 12, 1982, p. 1054.

35. Ed Rollins, quoted in "Playing Hardball," p. 15.

36. President Kennedy, quoted in Theodore Sorensen, *Kennedy* (New York: Bantam, 1966), p. 387.

SELECTED READINGS

Davis, Eric. "Legislative Reform and the Decline of Presidential Influence on Capitol Hill." *British Journal of Political Science* 9 (October 1979):465–79.

Edwards, George C., III. *Presidential Influence in Congress* (San Francisco: Freeman, 1980).

———. *The Public Presidency* (New York: St. Martin's, 1983).

Fisher, Louis. *The Constitution between Friends* (New York: St. Martin's, 1978).

Harmel, Robert, ed. *Presidents and Their Parties: Leadership or Neglect?* (New York: Praeger, 1984).

Light, Paul C. *The President's Agenda: Domestic Policy Choice from Kennedy to Carter* (Baltimore: Johns Hopkins University Press, 1982).

Neustadt, Richard E. *Presidential Power: The Politics of Leadership from FDR to Carter* (New York: Wiley, 1980).

Ornstein, Norman J., ed. *President and Congress: Assessing Reagan's First Year* (Washington, D.C.: American Enterprise Institute, 1982).

Ragsdale, Lyn. "The Fiction of Congressional Elections as Presidential Events." *American Politics Quarterly* 8 (October 1980):375–98.

Wayne, Stephen J. *The Legislative Presidency* (New York: Harper and Row, 1978).

12

Presidential Policy Implementation

Public policies are rarely self-executing. Perhaps the only public policy that executes itself is the president's decision to recognize a foreign government. On December 15, 1978, President Jimmy Carter announced in a joint communique with Peking that the People's Republic of China and the United States would formally recognize each other. On January 1, 1980, diplomatic relations between the two nations resumed. If a president recognizes a foreign country, diplomatic relations with it are thereby established. Most policies, however, require an intricate set of positive actions on the part of many people to be implemented.

Policy implementation is the stage of policy making between the establishment of a policy (such as the passage of a legislative act, the issuing of an executive order, the handing down of a judicial decision, or the promulgation of a regulatory rule) and the consequences of the policy for the people whom it affects. If a policy is inappropriate, if it cannot alleviate the problem for which it was designed, it will probably be a failure no matter how well it is implemented. But even a brilliant policy poorly implemented may fail to achieve the goals of its designers. Since the people who originally enact public policies are usually not the same people who implement them, there is considerable room for misunderstanding and distortion of decision makers' intentions.

Implementing a public policy may include a wide variety of actions: issuing and enforcing directives; disbursing funds; making loans; awarding grants; signing contracts; collecting data; disseminating information; analyzing problems; assigning and hiring personnel; creating organizational units; proposing alternatives; planning for the future; and negotiating with private citizens, businesses, interest groups, legislative committees, bureaucratic units, and even other countries.

In this chapter we examine the president's efforts to implement policies. We shall find that, despite the unquestioned importance of implementation, it receives relatively low priority in the White House. We also find that the president faces an uphill fight in implementing the policies for which he is responsible. Thus, we focus on the obstacles to effective policy implementation, including communication, resources, implementors' dispositions, bureaucratic structure, and executive follow-up, to understand better the difficulties the president faces.

Before we move on, there is an important point that we should clarify. The president's role in implementation is not always as direct as in giving a speech, negotiating with Congress, or making decisions. Moreover, implementation typically occurs over an extended period of time and far from the confines of the White House. In addition, the implementation of federal policy usually requires the efforts of many people, often thousands, at the federal, state, and local levels and in the private sector. As a result, many observers of the presidency mistakenly restrict their discussions of the president as chief executive to actions he personally takes. To avoid this error we cast our view more broadly in order to understand the problems with which the president must contend as he seeks to carry out his responsibilities for implementing policies, including those he initiates, those established in previous administrations, and those passed over his objections.

IMPLEMENTATION PROBLEMS

Since policy implementation is so complex, we should not expect it to be accomplished in a routine fashion. Even presidents cannot assume that their decisions and orders will be carried out. Indeed, their experiences in recent years would turn even the most optimistic observers into cynics. Once again we see the validity of Richard Neustadt's warning that presidents are rarely in a position to simply issue commands and have them obeyed.

In 1962 President John Kennedy ordered U.S. Army troops located in Memphis to the campus of the University of Mississippi at Oxford to control rioting that resulted from the attempts of a black, James Meredith, to enroll. As the hours passed after giving the order, the commander-in-chief saw no progress toward Oxford. Frustrated, he demanded of Secretary of the Army Cyrus Vance, "Where are the troops?" No one seemed to know. When he talked on the phone to the general who supposedly was leading the troops, the general indicated he was awaiting orders from the Pentagon.[1] This was hardly Kennedy's only frustration in policy implementation. Kennedy once told an aide not to abandon the minor project of remodeling Lafayette Park across the street from the White House. "Hell," the president exclaimed, "this may be the only thing I'll ever get done."[2]

President Richard Nixon also had implementation troubles. An air force general carried out his own bombing campaign in Southeast Asia while the president was trying to avoid confrontation in order to facilitate peace negotiations, and Justice Department officials insisted upon antitrust prosecutions that Nixon opposed. Nixon's White House chief of staff, H. R. Haldeman, later wrote that by his third year in office the president "realized that he was virtually powerless to deal with the bureaucracy in every department of government. It was no contest."[3]

Given the frustration that presidents experience, we should not be surprised when President Carter complained, "Before I became president, I realized and I was warned that dealing with the federal bureaucracy would be one of the worst problems I would have to face. It has been even worse that I had anticipated."[4]

The experiences of recent presidents in implementation are summarized by Richard Cheney, President Gerald Ford's White House chief of staff:

> There is a tendency before you get to the White House or when you're just observing it from the outside to say "Gee, that's a powerful position that person has." The fact of the matter is that while you're here trying to do things, you are far more aware of the constraints than you are of the power. You spend most of your time trying to overcome obstacles getting what the President wants done."[5]

LACK OF ATTENTION TO IMPLEMENTATION

Policy implementation has had a low priority in most administrations. Presidents have many obligations, of which implementing policy is only one. Policies must be developed, decisions made, legislation passed, controversies defused or contained, and the public courted, to name only the most obvious. Moreover, presidents often lack experience in administration and find other tasks more compatible with their skills and interests.

Foreign affairs are always a top priority of presidents because of the inherent importance of these issues and the unique constitutional responsibilities of presidents for them. Besides, presidents often feel they can accomplish more in the international arena than at home wrestling over domestic issues with an unresponsive Congress or a recalcitrant executive branch. Many presidents bring to office a strong interest in international relations. Ceremonial functions performed in the role of chief of state are traditions maintained by the president to broaden his public support. All of these activities typically receive priority over implementation.

In addition, the incentives to invest time in implementation are few. The president has only a short time in office and, at least in his first term, must constantly think about reelection. This encourages a short-run view in the White House, and presidents are more likely to try to provide the public with immediate gratification through the passage of legislation or the giving of speeches than with efforts to manage the implementation of policies. As one Office of Management and Budget official put it:

> The people in the White House are there for such a short time. The pressure is on making some impact and getting some programs passed. There is not enough time or reward in thinking carefully about effectiveness and implementation. The emphasis is really on quantity, not quality. The President could never be reelected on the effectiveness theme. "We didn't do much, but it is all working very well." Do you think a President could win with that?[6]

Presidents know they will receive little credit if policies are managed well, because it is very difficult to attribute effective implementation to them personally. Moreover, to most people most of the time the functioning of government is not very visible. Both citizens and the press, when they pay attention to government at all, are most interested in controversial scandals, the passage of new policies, or ceremonial functions. Policies such as inflation or civil rights that have an immediate and direct effect on their lives attract their attention. Yet even here the press and public are mainly concerned with the impact of policies, not the process of their implementation. Although implementation directly influences the final results, this does not seem to be enough to entice the mass public and the press that caters to it to turn their attention to policy implementation.

As a result of these incentives, presidents direct a comparatively small amount of their time to policy implementation. Similarly, too little consideration is given to problems of implementation in the formulation of policies. Again, the proper incentives are missing. According to a Carter aide: "We all believe there should be more planning. The President has stressed the need for more caution. But when we fall behind, the President will impose a deadline. It is still a political system; and political systems are interested in results, not implementation."[7]

Thus, despite the president's clear responsibility for policy implementation, it typically receives relatively little attention from the White House. Although this may seem inevitable, given our discussion above, it is not without its costs. As President Reagan's assistant for communications, David Gergen, commented: "It's unfortunately true that the management of the bureaucracy becomes one of the lowest priorities of almost every administration that comes to this city. Every administration pays a heavy price for it before it's over."[8]

COMMUNICATION OF PRESIDENTIAL DECISIONS

The first requirement for effective implementation of presidential decisions or policies for which the president is responsible is that those who are to implement a decision must know what they are supposed to do. Policy decisions and implementation orders must be transmitted to the appropriate personnel before they can be followed. Naturally, these communications need to be accurate, and they must be accurately perceived by implementors. Implementation directives must also be clear. If they are not, implementors may be confused about what they should do, and they will have discretion to impose their own views on the implementation of policies, views that may be different from those of the president. Consistency in the communication directives is also crucial. Contradictory decisions confuse and frustrate administrative staff and constrain their ability to implement policies effectively.

Before subordinates can implement a presidential decision, they must be aware that the decision has been made and an order to implement it issued. This is not always as straightforward a process as it may seem. Ignorance or misunderstanding of decisions frequently occurs. Although the executive branch has highly developed lines of communication throughout the bureaucracy, this does not guarantee that communications will be transmitted successfully. The Bay of Pigs fiasco illustrates this point. On April 17, 1961, a force of 1,200 Cuban refugees, recruited, trained, and supplied by the U.S. Central Intelligence Agency (CIA), landed 90 miles south of Havana with the announced goal of overthrowing the Communist-oriented regime of Fidel Castro. Within three days the "invasion" had been crushed, inflicting a disastrous blow to American prestige, not to mention that of the new president, John F. Kennedy. The CIA never told the leader of the brigade sent to invade Cuba that the president had ordered the soldiers to go to the mountains and fight a guerilla war if the invasion failed. The CIA disregarded the president's order, which it thought might weaken the brigade's resolve to fight or encourage the brigade to go to the mountains too quickly.

Sometimes aides and other officials ignore presidential directives with which they disagree primarily to avoid embarrassment for their chief. Such orders are generally given in anger and without proper consultation. President Nixon especially liked to let off steam by issuing outrageous orders. At one time he instructed Secretary of State William Rogers to "fire everybody in Laos," and he often told aides to "go after" reporters and once ordered that all reporters be barred from Air Force

One. These and similar outbursts were ignored by H. R. Haldeman and the aides close to Nixon. They knew the president would view things differently when he calmed down.[9] In situations such as these, close associates of presidents have provided them safe outlets for their frustrations and protected them from their worst instincts.

In most instances, implementors have considerable discretion in interpreting their superiors' decisions and orders. Orders from the White House are rarely specific. Personnel at each rung in the bureaucratic ladder must use their judgment to expand and develop them. Obviously this process invites distortion of communications, and the further down in the bureaucracy presidential implementation directives go, the greater the potential for distortion. Moreover, as we shall see, subordinates do not always interpret the communications of superiors in a way that advances the goals of the president. Bureaucrats often use their discretion to further their personal interests and those of their agencies. Interest groups also take advantage of the discretion granted bureaucrats by pushing for their own demands at intermediate and low decision-making levels.

It is for these reasons that observers of the federal bureaucracy often recommend that presidents and other high officials make every attempt to commit their directives to writing (in detail where possible), use personalized communications where appropriate, and show persistence in attempting to convey accurately their orders to those who actually implement policies.

In general, the more decentralized the implementation of a public policy, the less likely that it will be transmitted to its ultimate implementors accurately. Decentralization usually means that a decision must be communicated through several levels of authority before it reaches those who will carry it out. The more steps a communication must traverse from its original source, the weaker the signal that is ultimately received will be. A president can tell a secretary of state to go to another country and deliver a policy pronouncement to its prime minister, with little concern that his message will not be accurately transmitted. But he cannot have the same confidence about messages aimed at caseworkers in a social security office or soldiers in the field. The distance between the White House and the implementors is too great.

Many laws which the president is responsible for implementing are actually carried out by persons in the private sector, and the president's transmission of policy directives to them is more problematical than to an organized bureaucracy. For example, thousands of loan officers in banks, stores, and automobile dealerships must be informed concerning consumer credit laws. The vastness of the credit bureaucracy causes problems in disseminating information to the public. Borrowers as well as lenders need to be aware of the law so that they will know if they have been denied credit illegally and what their legal remedies are. Since most Americans use credit, the number of people involved in the transmission of credit information numbers into the tens of millions. Because the number of people is so great and the information is relatively complex for the average person, the president and the bureaucracy he heads face great difficulties accurately transmitting policy decisions to the typical consumer.

At times, executives and their staffs prefer *not* to transmit policy directives personally; they would rather get others to communicate for them. President Johnson wanted Secretary of the Treasury Henry Fowler to apply "jawboning," or powerful persuasion, to try to lower interest rates. Because Fowler opposed such efforts, Johnson decided not to communicate his wishes to the secretary directly. Instead he called House Banking Committee Chairman Wright Patman, a supporter of "jawboning," and asked him to pressure Fowler. Any time a step is added to the chain of communication, the potential for distortion is increased. Those who speak for others will have their own styles, their own views, and their own motivations. Not even presidents can depend upon other people to transmit directives exactly as they would desire.

Some presidents do not have personalities that are well-suited to direct communication. This seems to have been particularly true of Richard Nixon. The president feared rejection and confrontation and adopted an indirect administrative style to avoid possible unpleasantness. He even handed the phone to his chief of staff, Alexander Haig, so the latter could tell Gerald Ford he had been selected to become vice president. He spoke elliptically to those who disagreed with him to avoid being rebuffed and typically failed to issue unambiguous orders directly to his subordinates. He did not like to say no personally or to impose discipline on recalcitrant officials. When he found opposition within his administration, either he tried to accomplish his objectives without his adversaries' being aware of it or he had intermediaries take them written or verbal orders. The president shunned personal efforts at persuading or inspiring subordinates.[10]

Nixon's unwillingness to communicate directly with his subordinates fostered an environment in which discipline and cohesion were often low. It also revealed disunity in his administration that outsiders could exploit, further eroding cohesion. Officials in positions of power, such as Secretary of State William Rogers, could increase their discretion by implementing orders with which they disagreed only if they were transmitted personally to them by the president, which they rarely were.[11]

In 1971 President Nixon employed another type of roundabout means of communication in an attempt to make the Federal Reserve Board more responsive to his wishes. He had an aide, Charles Colson, leak to the press a "shot across the bow" of Arthur Burns, the board's chairman. The story was that the president's advisers were urging him to increase the size of the board, a threat to Burns, and that Burns was hypocritically asking for a raise while opposing raises for other federal employees. The fact that neither of these points was true (the president later had to deny them) undoubtedly influenced Nixon's choice of transmission channels.

The press also may serve as a means of presidential communicating in more straightforward ways. Those in the White House often believe that since most high-level bureaucrats read the *New York Times* and the *Washington Post*, they can communicate with these officials about policy matters more rapidly through news stories than through normal channels. The White House also uses other media outlets such as television, newsmagazines, and specialized publications to send messages to government officials. Such messages may indicate a policy decision or position, or they may signal that an official White House statement was merely to appease special interests and should not be taken literally.

Others may use the press to elicit information from the White House. They may ask friends in the press to probe White House officials or the president at a press conference to learn whether the president is planning an action or to determine if a presidential aide's request for action really represents the president's views.

No matter who initiates the communication, the press is likely to transfer it more rapidly than will official channels. On the other hand, the information provided in a story or as a response to a reporter's question is unlikely to be sufficient for guiding the implementation of a complex policy. Indeed, it may be in error. Yet it is to the nuances contained in such communications that ears in Washington are often most attuned.

If policies are to be administered as the president desires, his implementation directives must not only be received, but they also must be clear. Often the instructions transmitted to implementors are vague and do not specify when or how a program is to be carried out, however. Lack of clarity provides implementors with leeway to give new meaning to policies, meaning that sometimes inhibits intended change or brings about unintended change.

The lack of clarity in many implementation orders can be attributed to several factors. Perhaps the most important is the sheer complexity of policy making. When they establish policy, neither the president nor Congress have the time or expertise to develop and apply all the requisite details for how it will be carried out. They have to leave most (and sometimes all) of the details to subordinates, usually in the executive branch. Thus, although it is the president's responsibility to implement policies of the national government, no matter who initiates them, he must delegate much of this responsibility to others.

The difficulty in reaching consensus on the goals of policies also inhibits clarity in implementation directives. In the United States we share wide agreement on the goals of avoidance of war, equal opportunity, and efficiency in government, but this consensus often dissolves when specific policy alternatives are under consideration. Lyndon Johnson once said, "If the full implications of any bill were known before its enactment, it would never get passed."[12] Clearly, imprecise decisions make it easier for presidents to develop and maintain winning decisional coalitions. Different people or groups can support the same policy for different reasons. Each may hold its own conception of the goal or goals the program is designed to achieve. Ambiguous goals also may make it less threatening for groups to be on the losing side of a policy conflict, and this may reduce the intensity of their opposition.

The problems of starting up a new program may also produce confusion in implementation instructions. Often the passage of a new policy is followed by a period of administrative uncertainty in which there is a considerable time lag before any information on the program is disseminated. This period is followed by a second one in which rules are made but are then changed quickly as high-level officials attempt to deal with the unforeseen problems of implementing the policy and of their own earlier directives.

A cynical yet realistic explanation for lack of clarity in federal statutes is that Congress does not want them to be detailed. Congress would rather let executive-branch agencies provide the specifics, not because of the latter's expertise, but in order to let the agencies take the blame for the rules that turn out to be unworkable or unpopular. Title IX of the Education Act Amendments of 1972 stated that "no person in the United States shall, on the basis of sex, be excluded from participation in, be denied the benefits of, or be subject to discrimination under an education program or activity receiving Federal financial assistance." Such broad language allowed Congress to sidestep many touchy questions and leave their resolution to the president and his appointees. Moreover, individual members of Congress can gain credit with their constituents by intervening on their behalf regarding the application of regulations. In addition, if goals are not precise, Congress cannot be held accountable for the failure of its policies to achieve them. All of this only adds to the president's burden in guiding the bureaucracy.

Sometimes efforts are made to restrict the discretion of implementors. The Voting Rights Act of 1965 reduced the discretion of local voting registrars by limiting the use of literacy tests or similar voter qualification devices. In some cases the administration of voting registration was physically taken over by federal officials so that local officials could not inhibit voter registration. Another example of limiting implementors' discretion occurred in early 1973 when the Nixon administration issued new rules that restricted the way funds could be expended to aid the poor through social services. Funds could be used only for persons with specifically defined conditions of need and then only under a system of detailed accounting of the services provided. This was an attempt by the Nixon administration to restrict the options available to social workers.

It is generally easier for the president to reduce the discretion of officials with orders to stop doing something than to start doing something. For example, an absolute ban on providing funds for abortions for poor women is more likely to be unambiguous and more likely to be noticed if it is violated than an order to begin implementing a new policy. The implementation of most policies, however, requires positive actions, not prohibitions. Moreover, usually a series of positive actions extending over a long period of time and involving the technical expertise of numerous persons throughout a bureaucratic hierarchy are necessary to implement a policy. The complexity of such policy making makes it very difficult for a president to communicate and enforce rules that effectively reduce the discretion available to most policy implementors.

Vague policy decisions often hinder effective implementation, but directives that are too specific may also adversely affect implementation. Implementors sometimes need the freedom to adapt policies to suit the situation at hand. A myriad of specific regulations can overwhelm and confuse personnel in the field and may make them reluctant to act for fear of breaking the rules. Strict guidelines may also induce a type of goal displacement in which lower-level officials become more concerned with meeting specific requirements than with achieving the basic goals of the program. By rigidly adhering to the letter of a regulation, they may become so bogged down in red tape that the purpose of the rule is forgotten or defeated. Conversely, implementors sometimes simply ignore rigid regulations.

Inconsistency as well as vagueness in guidance from the president may provide operating agencies with substantial discretion in the interpretation and implementation of policy, discretion that may not be exercised to carry out a policy's goals. Environmental policy during the Nixon administration is an example. The president made a rhetorical commitment to supporting the National Environmental Policy Act (NEPA), but in practice his policy priorities were not significantly tied to environmental matters. Similarly, the Office of Management and Budget, the president's principal tool for controlling the federal bureaucracy, did not treat environmental policy goals as a major consideration in the evaluation of the activities of all federal agencies as NEPA intended. Federal officials received inconsistent signals from the White House concerning the importance of environmental policy and were left to resolve the question largely on their own.

Many of the factors that produce unclear communications are also responsible for inconsistent directives. The complexity of public policies, the difficulties in starting up new programs, and the multiple objectives of many policies all contribute to inconsistency in policy communications. Another reason that decisions are often inconsistent is that the president and top officials are constantly attempting to satisfy a diverse set of interests that may represent views on both sides of an issue. Policies that are not of high priority to the president may simply be left to flounder in a sea of competing demands.

RESOURCES

Implementation orders may be accurately transmitted, clear, and consistent, but if the president lacks the resources necessary to carry out policies, established at his discretion or by Congress, implementation is likely to be ineffective. Important resources include money, staff of sufficient size and with the proper skills to carry out their assignments, and the information, authority, and facilities necessary to translate proposals on paper into functioning public services.

Money

Sometimes the problem the president faces in implementing policy and delivering services is simply a lack of money. Elliot Richardson, when he was secretary of the Department of Health, Education and Welfare, discovered that the funds Congress appropriated for programs permitted his department to reach only very small percentages of those eligible for the benefits. When his staff estimated the cost of having the department's service-delivery programs reach each eligible person, it turned out to exceed the entire federal budget for that year! Thus, frustration is likely to characterize many of the chief executive's efforts to provide services to large numbers of people.

In many policies, especially in the social welfare area, money is an end in itself. For the most part, for example, money is the essence of social security programs. Money also underlies limitations of other resources as well, however, especially staff and facilities.

Staff

Certainly an essential resource in implementing policy is staff. In an era in which "big government" is under attack from all directions, it may seem surprising to learn that a principal source of implementation failure is inadequate staff. Although about five million military and civilian personnel work for the federal executive branch, and therefore the president, there are still too few people with the requisite skills to do an effective job implementing many policies. We must evaluate the bureaucracy, not only in terms of absolute numbers, but also in terms of its capabilities to perform desired tasks.

The federal government provides a wide range of services through its own personnel, such as national defense, immigration control, and maintenance of recreational facilities. Each of these and others like them are labor-intensive policies, and thus the services they provide are directly related to the size and quality of the staff available to the relevant agencies over which the president presides. Yet there is substantial evidence that agencies and departments are woefully understaffed. For example, the navy is short thousands of chief petty officers, millions of illegal aliens reside in the United States, and the facilities in our national parks are deteriorating.

Other federal policies require monitoring of the behavior of others, including state and local officials administering federal grants or enforcing federal regulations and private citizens obeying federal laws. Effective monitoring of federal programs and requirements is an enormous task and the staff available to the chief executive to do the job is strikingly inadequate. Just think of how many people it would take to enforce complex guidelines for federal education grants in 20,000 school districts. Or consider the task of monitoring pollution from tens of thousands of primary sources of water pollution in the United States, plus countless thousands of other sources in the form of sewers, irrigation return flows, and agricultural runoffs; more than 150 million polluting motor vehicles on the highways; about 2,000 potentially dangerous chemical plants and dump sites; between 2,000 and 40,000 sources of industrial air pollution, excluding small furnaces, in each of the fifty states; and more than 50,000 pesticides in use around the country. When one adds responsibilities for enforcing health and safety laws in millions of workplaces, civil rights laws in millions of locations, and so on, one begins to understand the dimensions of the president's problem.

Although staff size can be critical for almost every policy, it is more so for some than others. Insufficient staff is especially critical to implementation when the policy involved is one that imposes unwelcome constraints on people, whether these be the requirements of grant policies, regulatory policies, or criminal law. Since such policies generally involve highly decentralized activities, a large staff is necessary if this behavior is to be monitored. It is much easier for the chief executive to implement a policy such as social security that distributes benefits recipients desire. More personnel are required to enforce limitations on people than to write checks to them.

The president's executive-branch agencies do not even come close to meeting these needs. The fear of creating a totalitarian bureaucratic monster and the pressures to allocate personnel to more direct services, such as the provision of agricultural expertise to farmers, keep staffs that monitor implementation small. In addition, the scarcity of payroll funds coupled with the irresistible urges of policymakers to provide public services (at least in form) ensure that staffs will generally be inadequate to implement programs.

Because of lack of staff and because of traditional federal government deference to the states, federal programs rely heavily upon state agencies for their implementation. This, however, does not solve the president's problem of lack of staff at the federal level; it merely transfers the problem to the states. Since this shortage of personnel exists at every level of government, delegating the implementation of a policy to a lower level of government rarely alleviates the problem.

Skill as well as numbers is an important characteristic of staff for implementation. All too often the public officials on which the president relies are lacking in the expertise, both substantive and managerial, needed to implement policies effectively. Delegating responsibility for the implementation of a policy to a lower-level government jurisdiction once again usually only exacerbates rather than alleviates the problem.

One problem the president faces is the shortage of people with management skills among career executives. Often those with professional backgrounds are promoted until they become administrators and thus no longer use their professional skills. Yet they often do not have the management expertise required for their new positions. There is little training in management for top career officials, whether they arrived at their positions from professional or administrative backgrounds. Their superiors, political appointees with short tenures in office, lack incentives to invest in the long-term development of skills, and the career executives themselves have not pressed for management training.

Personnel with substantive skills are also often in short supply in the executive branch. This is especially true when a government agency is carrying out or regulating highly technical activities. Sometimes the necessary personnel are very difficult to hire because of the higher incomes and greater flexibility they can enjoy by working in the private sector. The military's problems in attracting physicians is a prime example. At other times, the needed staff may simply not exist even in the private sector, and a government agency must invest in developing expertise. The federal government's efforts to regulate energy prices and allocations in the 1970s illustrate both problems. No one really knew how to accomplish these tasks, and few people outside the energy companies had the background to understand the industry. Thus, employees of the Federal Energy Office relied upon "on the job training."

Information

Information is another essential resource in presidential policy implementation. This information comes in two forms. The first is information regarding how to carry out a policy. Executive-branch officials need to know what to do when they are given directives to act. The second form of essential information is data on the compliance of others with governmental rules and regulations. Implementors must know whether other persons involved in implementing policies are complying with the law.

As we saw earlier, implementation directives are sometimes vague because high-level decision makers do not know what to require of implementors. This insufficient knowledge hinders implementation directly as well as indirectly through the nature of communications.

Program information is particularly critical for new policies or those involving technical questions, such as the abatement of air pollution or the development of a new weapons system, because implementors are asked to meet goals neither they nor anyone else knows how to accomplish, at least in the short run. Routine functions, such as dispersing funds, building roads, training troops, hiring typists, or purchasing goods, are relatively straightforward in their operation, and a wealth of information exists on how to carry them out. But the implementors of a new policy such as controlling hospital costs or developing a jet fighter do not share these advantages. They lack the necessary information to establish appropriate standards and guidelines. Thus, it is one thing for Congress or the White House to mandate a change in policy, but it is something quite different for the executive branch officials who work for the president to figure out how to do it.

The lack of knowledge of how to implement some policies has several direct consequences. Some responsibilities will simply not be met, or they will not be met on time. Inefficiency is also likely to characterize the implementation of such policies. Some efforts will prove to be mistakes, and implementors will have to try again. Moreover, regulations may be inappropriate, causing other government units or organizations in the private sector to purchase equipment, fill out forms, or stop certain activities unnecessarily. Ideally, for example, before an agency such as the Environmental Protection Agency acts to implement a law by ordering costly changes in an industry or its products (such as automobiles), the agency should be able to predict the effects of the change on the economic health of the industry in question. Such information, however, is frequently lacking, and the president may be severely criticized as a result.

Implementation of policies often requires information on the compliance of organizations or individuals with the law. Compliance data, however, is usually difficult to obtain, in part because of the lack of staff. Thus, the president and his subordinates often have to rely upon information about compliance from those who are doing the complying. This occurs in a wide range of policies, including school desegregation, hospital care, and environmental protection. Quite naturally, this system of information raises questions about effective implementation. It should come as no surprise to us, then, when faulty welds are discovered in the trans-Alaskan pipeline, federal grants to state and local governments are misspent, or hazardous wastes are found to be polluting water supplies.

Even more problematic is the implementation of federal policies by the private sector. In these policies the president must typically rely on private individuals to alert federal officials to violations of the law. Unfortunately, private citizens do not often initiate action or provide information on noncompliance. For example, those who are most likely to suffer discrimination in housing, employment, credit, and education are also poorly educated and thus least likely to know about antidiscrimination laws and the remedies available to them. They are also, because of their poverty, least likely to have the resources to pursue their claims and often do not receive the necessary outside help. Moreover, because they usually must continue to deal with their adversaries, such as employers, landlords, and banks, they may fear retaliation against their efforts to secure their rights.

Authority

Authority is often a critical resource in policy implementation. Authority varies from program to program and comes in many different forms: the right to issue subpoenas; take cases to court; issue orders to other officials; withdraw funds from a program; provide funds, staff, and technical assistance to lower-level government jurisdictions; issue checks to citizens; purchase goods and services; or levy taxes. Policies that require government oversight or regulation of others in the public or private sectors are those for which authority is most likely to be inadequate. Usually there is sufficient authority to *give* aid to individuals or lower-level governments. It is in *constraining* them that the executive branch is weakest.

The president actually has relatively little direct authority. Congress vests most authority in subordinate executive officials. Sometimes agency officials simply lack authority, even on paper, to implement a policy properly. For example, the policy being implemented may provide no sanctions against those violating the law, or the agency may lack authority to initiate administrative or judicial actions. When formal authority does exist, it is frequently mistaken by observers for effective authority. But authority on paper is one thing; authority effectively exercised is quite another.

One of the potentially most effective sanctions is the withdrawal of funds from a program. But there are many reasons why this authority is less than it seems. Cutting off funds is a drastic action. It may be embarrassing to all those involved and antagonize the implementors of a program whose active support is necessary for effective implementation. Cutting off federal funds from projects also alienates the members of Congress from the areas losing the money. Requiring states or cities to repay misspent funds can also have severe political consequences. In general the White House does not even try to exercise this authority.

Representatives of a state or local power structure may also intervene to counter the authority of higher jurisdictions. In our decentralized political system, state and local interests are often quite powerful. California was supposed to comply with a federal law regarding the provision of minimum welfare grants by July 1, 1969. But it did not comply, and at the beginning of 1971 the Department of Health, Education and Welfare ordered the termination of federal welfare funds to California. In response to this action Governor Ronald Reagan called Vice President Spiro Agnew and HEW Secretary Elliot Richardson to try to reverse the decision. The next day HEW withdrew its termination order. Finally, after two years of delay, California raised its welfare grants on July 1, 1971.

We should also note that the withdrawal of funds is relevant only for policies that award grants to lower-level governments or private organizations. The federal government usually does not withhold funds if one of its own components is not implementing a program effectively. It rarely withholds funds from itself.

Executive-branch officials may be reluctant to exercise authority for a number of other reasons. Terminating a project or withdrawing federal funds may hurt most those whom the policy is designed to aid. Schoolchildren, the elderly, or the poor are often the real victims of cutbacks. If a company loses federal contracts because of racial or sexual discrimination, it may be forced to lay off workers. Those with the least seniority may be the minorities the policy is trying to help. Similarly, cutting off federal funds for the educationally disadvantaged because of misallocation is most likely to hurt students from poor families.

The desire for self-preservation keeps many of the president's agencies from withdrawing funds. Agencies like the Federal Highway Administration and the Department of Education are primarily involved in channeling grants to other levels of government. To survive they must give away money. If they fail to do so, they may look bad to Congress and superior executive officials. This may hurt them in their future quests for budgets and authority, resources of great significance for most bureaucrats. Thus, they may sacrifice the social objectives of a program to the "maintenance" objectives of the bureaucratic unit.

Although executive officials often lack effective authority over other public officials, this lack of control is small compared with their lack of authority over private individuals, groups, and businesses, upon whom the successful implementation of policies often depends. Therefore, they must make their policies attractive to the private sector. As a result of these efforts, the enforcement of policies such as those dealing with safety in the workplace, including coal mines, rarely results in serious penalties for noncompliance.

Lacking effective authority, federal officials realize that they require cooperation from other implementors if they are to implement programs successfully. Therefore, they often take a service rather than a regulatory orientation toward officials of lower-level jurisdictions, who actually implement many programs. In other words, federal officials approach implementation from the standpoint of asking officials of lower-level jurisdictions for assistance rather than from the standpoint of imposing the will of a higher-level jurisdiction upon them. The hope is that through such an approach lower-level officials will give them at least some of what they want.

A study of public housing programs in Chicago found that the Department of Housing and Urban Development (HUD) was not enforcing the antidiscrimination provisions contained in statutes or in court orders. Instead, it set as its basic standard of compliance a resolution by the Chicago Housing Authority (CHA) stating it was obeying the law! Even more curious were HUD's activities regarding specific violations. It forced CHA to adopt a rule to assign public housing on a first-come, first-served basis, but it allowed CHA to operate contrary to the rule. Similarly, HUD made CHA remove a rule giving neighborhood residents priority in housing but allowed the authority to continue to operate as if the rule still existed. Thus, the federal agency exacted compliance with formal details of federal law, but allowed the local agency to have its way in major policy matters.[13]

Facilities

Physical facilities may also be critical resources in implementation. An implementor may have sufficient staff, may understand what he is supposed to do, and may have authority to accomplish his task, but without the necessary buildings, equipment, supplies, and even green space implementation won't succeed. National parks are overcrowded; military equipment, ranging from rifles to spare parts for airplanes, are often in short supply; those patrolling our borders lack the appropriate ships and planes to prevent the smuggling of illegal drugs; and we lack adequate storage facilities for our national oil reserves.

There is also often a shortage of sophisticated equipment. Computers are essential to the implementation of modern defense policy; they issue paychecks, assign personnel, navigate ships, and track missiles. Nevertheless, studies of the military's computers have found that the Defense Department is saddled with thousands of obsolete machines that leave the military services ill-prepared for a modern war. Similar problems beset other agencies, such as the Internal Revenue Service and the Social Security Administration.

Although the president can request funds for new or additional facilities, both the White House and Congress may hesitate to raise taxes to pay for them. Moreover, as was the case for staff, Congress often prefers to spread resources over many policies rather than to fund fewer programs adequately. Internal government procurement rules ("red tape") may add additional burdens to those trying to purchase expensive equipment such as computers.

DISPOSITIONS

If implementors are well disposed toward a particular policy, they are more likely to carry it out as the president intended. But when implementors' attitudes or perspectives differ from the president's, the process of implementing a policy becomes infinitely more complicated. Many policies fall within a "zone of indifference." These policies will probably be implemented faithfully because implementors do not have strong feelings about them. Other policies, however, will be in direct conflict with the policy views or personal or organizational interests of implementors. When people are asked to execute orders with which they do not agree, inevitable slippage occurs between policy decisions and performance. In such cases implementors will exercise their discretion, sometimes in subtle ways, to hinder implementation. As President Ford said:

> There are bureaucratic fiefdoms out in the states or in various regions, and the people who occupy those pockets of power want to do things in their own way. They are pros at it. They have been disregarding Presidents for years, both Democratic and Republican.[14]

Implementors may oppose a policy, and their opposition can prevent a policy option from even being tried. For some time there had been a policy debate over whether there should be a work requirement for those receiving welfare payments and able to work. During the Nixon administration, however, many top officials concluded that welfare administrators would not enforce a work requirement provision, even in the face of presidential exhortations and congressional demands. Thus, they had to turn to other alternatives, such as tax incentives, to encourage welfare recipients to work.

On another occasion, Nixon ordered Secretary of Defense Melvin Laird to bomb a hideaway of Palestine Liberation Organization guerrillas, a move that Laird opposed. According to the secretary, "We had bad weather for forty-eight hours. The Secretary of Defense can always find a reason not to do something."[15] Thus, the president's order was stalled for days and was eventually rescinded.

The opposition of presidential subordinates to a policy may also defeat some of its immediate goals after it becomes law. Federal efforts to evaluate education programs fail unless local education officials are inclined to collect the requisite data. Often they are not. One reason that many funds for Title I of the Elementary and Secondary Education Act of 1965 were not spent on disadvantaged children (as the law required) was that many of the administrators in the U.S. Office of Education were not interested in enforcing the law.

In 1977 President Carter ordered federal agencies to discourage the development of low-lying areas in danger of damage by flooding. Twenty-five months later only fifteen of the seventy-five agencies that had received the directive had issued final regulations specifying how they were going to comply with the president's wishes. Forty-six of the agencies had not even taken the first step toward adopting regulations. The primary reason for this lack of action was not bureaucratic indolence. Instead, it was the opposition of agencies to the substance of the president's order.

Competing policy interests of implementors may hinder implementation efforts. During the 1973 Arab-Israeli Yom Kippur War, President Nixon ordered that supplies be sent to the Israelis. The order took four days to execute because of foot-dragging by the Pentagon, which feared alienating Arab countries and the Soviet Union. The Pentagon wanted to use civilian planes instead of Israeli planes at U.S. military bases to transport the supplies, but civilian planes were not readily available. Disagreement over which military planes to use ensued. Finally, the president had to call the secretary of defense and demand immediate action.

Differences in organizational viewpoints may also impede the cooperation between agencies that is so often necessary in policy implementation. In the early 1970s the State Department and the Bureau of Narcotics and Dangerous Drugs (BNDD) did not work well together to control illicit drugs, a high priority for the president. The latter's emphasis on individual cases rather than on an overall strategy to help other countries control drugs upset State Department officials because they sometimes caused gunfights, embarrassment of corrupt foreign officials, and torture of American citizens peripherally involved in drug trafficking. Therefore, the department resisted the expansion of the BNDD's foreign programs and tried to keep its agents under tight control. This, naturally, further frustrated BNDD agents.

There may also be differences in viewpoints within an agency between presidential subordinates with different program responsibilities. There was intra-agency conflict over the implementation of the National Environmental Policy Act. Secretaries of transportation, for example, had a difficult time getting development-oriented agencies in the department, such as the Federal Highway Administration, to consider seriously the environmental consequences of their projects.

Bureaucratic units also resist vigorously the efforts of others to take away or share the resources deemed necessary to accomplish their missions. Feuding over responsibility for an activity has often hindered policy implementation. J. Edgar Hoover directed the Federal Bureau of Investigation with an iron fist from 1924 until 1972. According to Richard Nixon, Hoover "had always been rigidly territorial when it came to the functions and prerogatives of the FBI. He totally distrusted the other intelligence agencies . . . and, whenever possible, resisted attempts to work in concert with them."[16] In 1970 the director cut off all liaison activities with the other intelligence agencies, such as the Central Intelligence Agency, the Defense Intelligence Agency, and the National Security Agency. This hindered President Nixon's efforts to control dissension at home. Hoover didn't want to share his territory with anyone.

Staffing the Bureaucracy

Implementors' dispositions may pose serious obstacles to policy implementation. But if existing personnel do not implement policies the way top officials desire, why are they not replaced with people more responsive to leaders?

APPOINTMENTS   The president has authority to appoint directly about 650 leading members of the executive branch. This total includes the White House staff, between 15 and 20 individuals in each of the cabinet-level departments, about 10 persons in each of the major independent agencies (such as the Veterans Administration and the National Aeronautical and Space Administration), the heads of some lesser agencies, and commissioners of the independent regulatory agencies (as their terms expire). In the entire executive branch of the federal government, there are roughly 5 million employees. Far less than 1 percent are appointed by the president and his designees. This is an obvious constraint on the ability of any administration to alter personnel.

After being elected, a president has less than three months to search for a new team to take over the government. Moreover, this must be done by the president-elect and aides who are exhausted from the long, arduous election campaign and have many other demands on their time, such as preparing a budget and a legislative program. Members of the cabinet and other appointees usually have little advance notice of their selection and are busy wrapping up their other responsibilities and doing their homework on the issues relevant to their new positions prior to their confirmation hearings. Thus, they, too, often resort to haphazard recruiting techniques when they make their appointments.

Presidents are also constrained politically in their appointments. Usually they feel these appointments must show a balance of geography, ideology, ethnicity, sex, and other demographic characteristics salient at the time. Thousands of persons are urged upon an administration by themselves, members of Congress, or people in the president's party. Few of these persons are qualified for available jobs, but due to political necessity, more than a few are appointed. Political favors may please political supporters, but they do not necessarily provide the basis for sound administration. Moreover, such appointments may result in incompatibilities with the president that lead to politically costly dismissals.

The interest groups that appointments are designed to please keep a watchful eye throughout a president's tenure in office on who is appointed to what position. Not only is "balance" important at the beginning of a new administration, but it remains a constraint on recruiting personnel. Thus, in the middle of a term White House aides may be ordered to find a Mexican-American woman to serve as U.S. treasurer. A president also might desire to reward new groups. After the 1972 presidential election, Richard Nixon wanted his cabinet and subcabinet to represent more accurately his broadened electoral coalition. This led to a renewed emphasis on the demographic characteristics of appointees, delays in filling positions, and, most significantly, compromises in the quality of some appointees, such as many of those placed in top positions in the Labor Department to please the president's new "hard hat" constituency. It also led to a humorous incident in which Claude Brinegar was selected as secretary of transportation partly on the basis of his Irish Catholic background. The White House was in error, however. Brinegar was really a German Protestant.

A different type of "political" constraint may arise if a strong member of an administration opposes a person the president desires to appoint. Usually the president can overcome this opposition within the ranks, but sometimes the price may be too high. In his second term President Nixon wanted to appoint John Connally secretary of state but did not do so because of the opposition of his chief adviser on national security matters, Henry Kissinger. Instead, Kissinger was named to head the State Department.

A surprising but nonetheless real limitation on personnel selection is that presidents often do not know individuals who are qualified for the positions they have to fill. Following his election in 1960, John F. Kennedy told an aide: "For the last four years I spent so much time getting to know people who could help me get elected President that I didn't have time to get to know people who could help me, after I was elected, to be a good President."[17] Thus, presidents often appoint persons they do not know to the highest positions in the federal government.

Early in their terms recent presidents have typically not imposed their preferences for subcabinet level officials upon those whom they appoint to head departments and agencies. (The Reagan White House did exercise a veto over these appointments, however.) The reason has no doubt partially been the lack of organization in the personnel system. In addition, however, there has been a concern that since top officials will be held accountable for agencies' performances, they should be able to appoint subordinates whom they like and who will complement their own abilities and help them accomplish their jobs. Naturally, top officials generally request this freedom. High officials also fight to name their subordinates because if they lose to the White House on personnel matters, their standing within their departments will drop.

As presidential terms extend from weeks into months and years, the White House's perspective sometimes changes. Frustrating problems in policy implementation often lead the president and his staff to take a more direct interest in personnel matters below the levels of department and agency heads. For example, in mid-1978 the Carter administration began a review of subcabinet officials with the object of weeding out those who were incompetent or disloyal. Tim Kraft was promoted to the position of assistant for political affairs *and* personnel (indicating an appreciation for the linkage between the two). Kraft and his staff began taking more interest in appointees: "We have told the personnel people in the departments that we want to be consulted on all appointments, whether they are presidential appointments or appointments to high GS [civil service] positions."[18]

Despite its frequent use, political clearance is often a crude process. Many policy views fit under a party label. Democrats range from very liberal to very conservative, and the range for Republicans is nearly as great. Moreover, political appointees may be motivated by materialistic or selfish aims and not necessarily be responsive to the president. A person may want an ambassadorship, or a young lawyer may seek experience in the Justice Department or a regulatory agency in hopes of cashing in on it later for a high-paying job in the private sector. Political appointees may also remain loyal to their home-state political organizations, interest group associations, or sponsors in Congress—rather than to the White House.

Conversely, if political appointees are viewed as too close to the

White House, they may be "shut out" in their departments and from their departments' client groups and thus be of limited usefulness to the president. No matter how loyal to the president appointees are, they need to know what to do and how to do it once they obtain their positions. People with these capabilities, as we have seen, are not easy to find. Moreover, too many political lieutenants in a department may separate the top executive from the bureaucracy and its services. They may also decrease the executive's opportunities to build personal support within the bureaucracy through communication, consultation, and access.

CIVIL SERVICE   Below appointed officials in the federal hierarchy rank most executive-branch employees. Almost all civilian employees are covered by the protection of personnel systems designed to fill positions on the basis of merit and protect employees against removal for partisan political reasons. The military has a separate personnel system designed to accomplish the same goals.

Traditionally, there has been substantial distrust between "political" executives and the rest of the bureaucracy. Distrust of the implementation efforts of the federal bureaucracy has been especially prominent in the administration of Republican presidents. Nixon's White House chief of staff, H. R. Haldeman, complained that real policy decisions were made by civil servants who viewed a Republican administration as a "transient phenomenon."[19]

Research on high-level bureaucrats during the Nixon presidency supports this view of a hostile executive branch. There were few Republicans in the senior civil service, especially in social welfare agencies such as Health, Education and Welfare and Housing and Urban Development, and the Democrats tended to provide considerably more support for liberal domestic policies than Republicans (or Republican presidents). Thus, the quip that "even paranoids may have real enemies" is particularly applicable to the Nixon administration.[20]

While it is possible for an incompetent or recalcitrant civil service employee to be dismissed, this rarely happens. In a 1978 press conference President Carter announced that "last year . . . only 226 employees lost their jobs for inefficiency."[21] More dramatically, press secretary Jody Powell later exclaimed, "It is damn near impossible to fire someone from this government for failure to do their job."[22] It simply takes more time, expertise, and political capital to fire a civil servant than most officials have or are willing to invest in such an effort. Well aware of this situation, high federal officials must look to other means to remove unresponsive bureaucrats from positions in which they can obstruct implementation of the president's policies.

Both the frustration presidents often experience as a result of their dependence on the bureaucracy and the necessity of altering its makeup through indirect measures are captured in the following statement by President Nixon to his director of the Office of Management and Budget, George Schultz:

> You've got to get us some discipline, George. You've got to get it, and the only way you get it, is when a bureaucrat thumbs his nose, we're going to get him. . . . They've got to know, that if they do it, something's going to happen to them, where anything can happen. I know the Civil Service pressure. But you can do a lot there. There are many unpleasant places where Civil Service people can be sent. We just don't have any discipline in government. That's our trouble. . . . We got to get it in these departments. . . . So whatever you—well, maybe he is in the regional office. Fine. Demote him or send him to the Guam regional office. There's a way. Get him the hell out.[23]

Transferring unwanted personnel to less troublesome positions is one of the most common means of quieting obstructive bureaucrats. In President Carter's words, it is "easier to promote and transfer incompetent employees than to get rid of them."[24] Transferring unwanted personnel is much easier when the civil servants in question opt not to use the technicalities and protections of the civil service system or their allies in Congress and interest groups. Ironically, these are the type of persons most likely to be dedicated to the notion of a civil service and therefore the ones an executive would probably least desire to replace.

Transferring personnel is not a panacea for the problems of implementors' dispositions, because it doesn't solve problems, it just relocates them. And some bureaucrats successfully resist transfer. In 1966 differences between Assistant Secretary of State Abba Schwartz and Passport Office Director Frances Knight were publicized. Knight opposed her superior's more liberal interpretation of the State Department's passport and visa policy. Unable to dismiss Knight, Schwartz attempted to transfer her within the department. But Knight rallied support to her defense in Congress. The controversy was resolved by a departmental reorganization designed to eliminate the position held by Schwartz himself. Other techniques, such as early retirement, may also be used, but they are necessarily of limited utility.

In response to President Carter's request, Congress established in 1978 a voluntary Senior Executive Service for top civil service executives, which nearly all have joined. These officials will be easier to transfer and demote, but they will also be eligible for bonuses and substantial pay increases if their performance is outstanding. Although this policy directly affects only a small percentage of the civil service, those to whom it does apply are among the most powerful members of the career bureaucracy, and it may aid the president's efforts to improve the bureaucracy's implementation of federal policies.

"I'm leaving, sir, to become a disgruntled former Administration official."

Source: Drawing by Dana Fradon; © 1983 The New Yorker Magazine, Inc.

The Nixon administration abused the civil service system. Political referral units in the departments were established, procedures to "get" enemies were considered, a manual for training political executives in the manipulation of the merit system was put out by the White House, and appointments to key civil service positions received political clearance from the White House. Although these abuses were more widespread and systematic than in previous administrations, this was a culmination of a trend toward politicizing the bureaucracy; a trend emphasizing operational control of the executive bureaucracy, not traditional patronage.

These efforts were not uniformly successful. One reason was resistance from political executives. An additional problem was the long period of time (often many months) required to have an outsider cleared by the Civil Service Commission for a career position, and the higher the position the longer the clearance time involved. The Civil Service Reform Act of 1978 delegated to agency heads the authority to examine and hire potential civil service employees. Whether this will significantly speed up the process remains to be seen.

The Nixon and Ford administrations were able to place many persons who had favorable attitudes toward the Republican administrations' domestic policies in top career and politically appointed managerial positions. Yet, the number of vacancies the Nixon and Ford administrations were able to fill was limited. After eight years of Republicans in the White House, nearly 70 percent of the existing top career and political executives had assumed their positions before the Nixon administration. (The figure for career executives alone was 85 percent.) Thus, filling vacancies is unlikely to be a sufficient strategy to alter the attitudes in the bureaucracy. The president must also influence those already holding their jobs.[25]

Incentives

Changing the personnel in government bureaucracies is difficult, and it does not ensure that the implementation process will proceed smoothly. Another potential technique the president can use to deal with the problem of implementors' dispositions is to alter the dispositions of existing implementors through the manipulation of incentives. Since people generally act in their own interest, the manipulation of incentives by high-level policymakers may influence their actions. Increasing the benefits or costs of a particular behavior may make implementors more or less likely to choose it as a means of advancing their personal, organizational, or substantive policy interests.

As we have seen, the ability of top officials to exercise sanctions is severely limited. Rewards are the other side of the incentive coin, but they are even more difficult for executives to administer than penalties. Individual performance is difficult to reward with pay increases. In 1978 President Carter complained that "more than 99 percent of all federal employees got a so-called 'merit' rating."[26] Raises are almost always given "across-the-board," with everyone in the same category of employment receiving a similar percentage increase in salary regardless of differences in performance. The Civil Service Reform Act of 1978 provided for merit pay increases for many managers, supervisors, and top executives in the federal civil service, but the effect of this change remains to be seen. Usually personal performance can be rewarded only by promotions, and they are necessarily infrequent. In addition, presidential subordinates who oppose or who are indifferent to a policy are unlikely to employ incentives to further its implementation.

THE BUREAUCRATIC STRUCTURE

Policy implementors may know what to do and have sufficient desire and resources to do it, but they may still be hampered in implementation by the structures of the organizations in which they serve. Two prominent characteristics of bureaucracies are standard operating procedures and fragmentation. Both may hinder presidential policy implementation.

Standard Operating Procedures

Standard operating procedures are routines that enable public officials to make numerous everyday decisions. They have many benefits for the chief executive. They save time, and time is valuable. If a social security caseworker had to invent a new rule for every potential client and have it cleared at higher levels, few people would be helped. So detailed manuals are written to cover as many particular situations as officials can anticipate. SOPs also bring uniformity to complex organizations, and justice is better served if rules are applied uniformly. This is true for the implementation of welfare policies that distribute benefits to the needy, as well as for criminal law policies that distribute sanctions. Uniformity also makes personnel interchangeable. A soldier can be transferred to any spot in the world and still know how to carry out a function by referring to the proper manual, a substantial advantage for the commander-in-chief.

Although designed to make implementing policies easier, at least in theory, SOPs may be inappropriate in some cases and function as obstacles to action. Presidents have had many a plan thwarted by standard government practices. They certainly frustrated President Franklin D. Roosevelt:

> The Treasury is so large and far-flung and ingrained in its practices that I find it is almost impossible to get the action and results I want. . . . But the Treasury is not to be compared with the State Department. You should go through the experience of trying to get any changes in the thinking, policy, and action of the career diplomats and then you'd know what a real problem was. But the Treasury and the State Department put together are nothing as compared with the Na-a-vy. . . . To change anything in the N-a-a-vy is like punching a feather bed. You punch it with your right and you punch it with your left until you are finally exhausted, and then you find the damn bed just as it was before you started punching.[27]

Standard operating procedures may hinder policy implementation by inhibiting change. Designed for typical situations, SOPs can be ineffective in new circumstances. In 1962 the United States discovered the presence of Soviet missiles in Cuba and reacted by blockading the island. President John F. Kennedy was very concerned about the initial interception of Soviet ships, and he sent Secretary of Defense Robert McNamara to check with Chief of Naval Operations George Anderson on the procedures being followed. McNamara stressed to Anderson that the president did *not* want to follow the normal SOP whereby a ship risked being sunk if it refused to submit to being boarded and searched. Kennedy did not want to goad the USSR into retaliation. But Admiral Anderson was not cooperative. At one point in the discussion, he waved the *Manual of Naval Regulations* in the secretary's face and shouted, "It's all in here." To this McNamara replied, "I don't give a damn what John Paul Jones would have done. I want to know what you are going to do now."[28] The conversation ended when the admiral asked the secretary of defense to leave and let the navy run the blockade according to established procedures.

Sometimes SOPs cause organizations to take actions superior officials do not desire, as the Cuban missile crisis dramatically illustrates. Despite President Kennedy's explicit order that the initial encounter with a Soviet ship not involve a Soviet submarine, the U.S. Navy, according to established procedure, used its "Hunter-Killer" antisubmarine warfare program to locate and float above Soviet submarines within 600 miles of the continental United States. Also following standard "Hunter-Killer" procedures, the navy forced several Soviet submarines to surface. This drastic action was not ordered by the president or the secretary of defense. It "just happened" because it was the programmed response to such a situation. The highest U.S. officials, who ostensibly had authority over the navy, never imagined standard procedures would supplant their directives. SOPs become deeply embedded in an organization and are difficult to control, even in times of crisis.

New policies are the most likely to require a change in organizational behavior and are therefore the most likely to have their implementation hindered by SOPs. There is an old saying that the military is always prepared to fight the last war. The picture of American troops fighting in the early years in Vietnam as if they were on the plains of central Europe supports such a view.

Because of the difficulty SOPs sometimes place in the way of change, top policymakers may try to avoid giving an existing agency responsibility for a new program. As President Johnson once said, "The best way to kill a new idea is to put it in an old-line agency."[29] Thus, when the Office of Economic Opportunity was created in 1964, it was not placed in the Department of Health, Education and Welfare. Although creation of a new agency may facilitate policy implementation, such an approach is not always feasible because of the added costs of a new agency, political support for an old agency, or the need to coordinate related programs.

Fragmentation

A second aspect of bureaucratic structure that may impede implementation is fragmentation. Fragmentation is the dispersion of responsibility for a policy area among several organizational units.

The extent of government fragmentation is widespread. In the field of welfare, for example, more than one hundred federal human services programs are administered by ten different departments and agencies. The Department of Health and Human Services has responsibility for the Aid to Families with Dependent Children program; the Department of Housing and Urban Development provides housing assistance for the poor; the Department of Agriculture runs the food stamp program; and the Department of Labor administers manpower training programs and provides assistance in obtaining employment. In a May 1978 speech President Carter stated, "There are too many agencies doing too many things, overlapping too often, coordinating too rarely, wasting too much money—and doing too little to solve real problems."[30] The more actors and agencies involved with a particular policy and the more interdependent their decisions, the less the probability of successful implementation.

Over the years Congress has created many separate agencies and favored categorical grants that assign specific authority and funds to particular agencies in order to oversee more closely and intervene more easily in the administration of policies. Dispersing responsibility for a policy area also disperses "turf" to congressional committees. In water resource policy, three committees in the House and three committees in the Senate have authority over the Army Corps of Engineers, the Soil Conservation Service, and the Bureau of Reclamation, respectively. None of these committees wants to relinquish its hold over these agencies. Thus, the agencies and programs that deal with a common problem remain divided among three departments.

Like congressional committees, agencies are possessive about their jurisdictions. Usually department or agency heads vigorously oppose executive-branch reorganizations that encroach upon their sphere of influence. In his fiscal 1980 budget proposals, President Carter requested that funds for state drug abuse programs be divided into single, consolidated grants for mental health, drug, and alcohol abuse services. Congress refused to consent to this proposal, however. Professionals in the alcohol and drug abuse programs feared that their programs would be downgraded if they lost their separate legislative identities and were combined with mental health programs. They blocked the president's attempt to reduce program fragmentation.

Interest groups are a third force supporting fragmentation. When Lyndon Johnson tried to move the Maritime Administration from the Department of Commerce to the Department of Transportation, he was successfully opposed by the AFL-CIO. Although it made sense administratively to house the Maritime Administration with other transportation-related agencies, labor leaders feared a bureaucratic reorganization would jeopardize their close relationship with the Maritime Administration. Groups also develop close working relationships with congressional committees and do not want to lose their special access in a reorganization of committee jurisdictions that might follow an executive-branch reorganization.

Often a combination of interest groups and legislative committees oppose reorganization. The new Department of Education, proposed by President Carter, is composed almost exclusively of education programs from the old Department of Health, Education and Welfare. Head Start, Indian education, the school lunch program, GI bill benefits, manpower training, and some vocational and rehabilitation education programs remained where they were because of opposition to their being moved. For example, the Senate Agriculture Committee opposed change out of fear of losing oversight responsibility for child nutrition programs, and the American Food Service Association opposed change because it feared nutrition would not be a high priority with educators.

The nature of public policy also is a factor in producing fragmentation. Broad policies, such as those dealing with environmental protection, are multidimensional and overlap with dimensions of other policies, such as agriculture, transportation, recreation, and energy. Thus, presidents cannot easily organize government agencies around just one policy area.

Fragmentation implies diffusion of responsibility, and this makes coordination of policies difficult. The resources and authority necessary for the president to attack a problem comprehensively are often distributed among many bureaucratic units. After passage in 1966 of President Johnson's Demonstration Cities and Metropolitan Development Act, the Department of Housing and Urban Development requested the cooperation of other agencies. The act gave grants to selected cities to restructure the entire environment of neighborhoods chosen for demonstration projects. Funds could be used for education, antipoverty, and other social programs, as well as for housing and physical improvements. HUD especially wanted priority given to grant applications growing out of Model Cities programs, flexibility in the administration of grant regulations, a substantial percentage of urban program money earmarked for local Model Cities projects, and the employment of newly created community development agencies (CDAs) as a single channel for all federal aid affecting the model neighborhood. This was not to be.

Urban renewal officials within HUD itself were reluctant to cooperate with the CDAs by giving them a voice in planning renewal projects or reviewing authority over final plans. There were problems in coordinating other HUD programs as well. Worse than this, however, were the actions of other departments and agencies. There was a problem channeling HEW funds through the CDAs. Most HEW funds were categorical aid grants allocated according to statutory formulas and state plans. In addition, many HEW bureau chiefs and regional officials were unsympathetic to HUD's requests. The Department of Labor did not cooperate much on manpower training programs, and the Office of Economic Opportunity was opposed to coordination because of its commitment to its own community action agencies.

Duplication in the provision of public services is another result of bureaucratic fragmentation. For example, in 1978 President Carter complained, "There are . . . at least 75 agencies and 164,000 Federal employees in police or investigative work. Many of them duplicate or overlap state and local law enforcement efforts unnecessarily."[31]

Fragmentation may result in two or more agencies working at cross-purposes. According to Richard Nixon:

> One department's watershed project, for instance, threatens to slow the flow of water to another department's reclamation project downstream. One agency wants to develop an electric power project on a certain river while other agenices are working to keep the same area wild. Different departments follow different policies for timber production and conservation, for grazing, for fire prevention and for recreational activities on the federal lands they control, though the lands are often contiguous.[32]

Not only do such conflicts defeat the purposes of the programs involved, but they also force the president's highest level aides and departmental executives to spend great amounts of time and energy negotiating with one another. This is wasteful, and it may result in compromises representing the lowest common denominators of officials' original positions. Unfortunately, bold and original ideas may be sacrificed for intragovernmental harmony.

The fragmentation of program responsibilities is often so great that it confuses and even overwhelms those who are supposed to be served by the programs the president is administering. Speaking about federal aid for community economic development, President Carter pointed out the existence of:

- over eleven different business assistance programs in more than ten agencies;

- 46 sewage-related programs in five different departments, two independent agencies, and eight regional commissions;

- at least 77 different housing programs in 15 different agencies;

- 60 transportation grant programs in the Department of Transportation and 25 other agencies;

- and 24 programs administered by ten agencies for employment and training.[33]

With such an array of programs, no wonder many state and local officials find federal assistance too complicated to master! The possibilities for aid may be great in number, but the expertise to match the relevant program with the appropriate qualifications and needs of a jurisdiction is often not available, especially in small communities.

Sometimes responsibility for a policy area is so fragmented that certain functions fall between the cracks. Some tasks do not fit neatly within an agency's formal authority. A former intelligence official writes of serving in a Scandinavian embassy and hiring someone to read the local Communist literature. From this a useful chart showing the hierarchy of the Communist party was developed. The project was cut from the budget, however, because coverage of the Communist movement was considered to be a CIA function, yet the CIA could not carry out this function because it was "overt," and the CIA was a clandestine organization.[34] Thus, the project fell between the divisions of organizational responsibility, and useful information was not available to the White House or others in government.

FOLLOW-UP

Because of all the hindrances to effective policy implementation, it seems reasonable to suggest that implementation would be improved if presidents followed up on their decisions and orders to see that they have been properly implemented. The following example illustrates the importance of follow-up.

In 1970 President Nixon ordered the CIA to destroy its stockpile of biological weapons. CIA Director Richard Helms relayed the president's order to the deputy director for plans (the head of the covert action division), and he in turn relayed it to a subordinate. Five years later two lethal toxins were discovered in a secret cache. A middle-level official had disobeyed the president's order, later retired, and his successor had assumed that the storage of the toxins had official approval. When called before Congress, Helms testified that he had undertaken no follow-up check on his own order, and when asked who told him the toxins were destroyed, he replied, "I read it in the newspapers." Indeed, if the official who discovered the toxins had not received a directive from the new CIA director, William Colby, to be on the constant lookout for illegal action, he might not have checked on the legality of the toxins, and they would still be sitting there.[35]

The importance of follow-up was made apparent to Nixon at many other points in his administration. Once he ordered the demolition of two old Department of Defense buildings on the Mall near the White

House, but it took more than a year to get them down. White House aide William Safire explains:

> Because the President of the United States took a continuing interest, because at least two of his aides were made to feel that its success was a crucial test of their ability and because the President kept prodding, issuing orders, refusing to be "reasonable," a few miserable buildings were finally knocked down and their occupants reassigned.

After the demolition the president called together his aides. With "pride, relief, and wonderment," he told them, "We have finally gotten something done."[36]

Thus a president must constantly check up on his orders. Nevertheless, most recent presidents, including Nixon himself, have not followed this advice. Follow-up on the whole has been haphazard. They and their staffs have been too busy with crisis management, electoral politics, or getting legislation passed to delve into the details involved in monitoring policy implementation. Moreover, presidents lack systematic information about the performance of agencies.

Follow-up is more easily said than done. An aide to President Franklin D. Roosevelt wrote:

> Half of a President's suggestions, which theoretically carry the weight of orders, can be safely forgotten by a Cabinet member. And if the President asks about a suggestion a second time, he can be told that it is being investigated. If he asks a third time a wise Cabinet officer will give him at least part of what he suggests. But only occasionally, except about the most important matters, do Presidents ever get around to asking three times.[37]

One technique presidents could use to increase their capacity to follow up on their decisions is to enlarge the size of their personal staffs. This strategy can create additional burdens for the White House, however. Because chief executives can personally deal effectively with only a few people, they are forced to relay implementation orders and receive feedback through additional layers of their own staffs. This, in turn, increases both the possibility of communication distortion and the burden of administration, which the staff is supposed to lighten. The more authority is delegated to persons at the top of a hierarchy, the more possibilities there are for inadequate coordination, interoffice rivalries, communication gaps, and other typical administrative problems. Moreover, a large number of aides with limited access to a top official such as the president increases the chance of their carrying out orders given in anger. Those with limited access will be less likely to know the executive well enough or have enough confidence to hold back on implementing their supervisor's instructions.

A large staff for a president has another drawback. Only a few people can credibly speak for the president. If too many people begin giving orders in the president's name, for example, they will undermine the credibility of all those claiming to speak for him. This credibility is important for aides trying to help the president implement policies. As one Carter aide explained: "If you are perceived by people in a given agency as being close to the president because you have an office in the West Wing, your phone calls will be returned more rapidly and your requests for information or action will be taken more seriously."[38]

Presidential assistants carry the contingent authority of the president, authority that is essential to accomplish anything at all since under the law presidential assistants have no authority of their own. But presidential authority is undermined if numerous people attempt to exercise it.

Excessively vigorous staff involvement in implementation decisions may cause other problems. For example, some observers of recent presidential administrations have concluded that as larger numbers of bright, ambitious, energetic assistants probe into the activities of departments and agencies, they will bring more issues for decision to the president, issues that were formerly decided at lower levels in the bureaucracy. Bureaucrats will begin to pass the buck upward, and more and more decisions must then be made by the White House. This can easily make the Executive Office of the President top-heavy and slow. Involvement in the minutiae of government also may divert resources (including time) from the central objectives and major problems of a president's administration. In addition, if White House aides become intimately involved in the management of government programs, they may lose the objectivity necessary to evaluate new ideas regarding "their" programs.

Overcentralization of decision making at the highest levels may have other negative consequences. It may discourage capable people from serving in government posts where their authority is frequently undercut. It may lower morale and engender resentment and hostility in the bureaucracy. This may impede future cooperation; decrease respect for lower officials among their subordinates; reduce the time bureaucratic officials have for internal management because they must fight to maintain access to and support of the chief executive; and weaken the capability of agencies to streamline or revitalize their management. Similarly, too much monitoring of subordinates' behavior may elicit hostility or excessive caution and lack of imagination in administering policy.

At the beginning of his second term of office in 1973, President Nixon introduced throughout the executive branch a system of follow-up called management by objectives. It was a loose system designed to circulate information about the goals of bureaucratic units, define responsibility for achieving those goals, and assess progress toward meeting them. Conversely, it did not impose objectives on the bureaucracy, carry out performance audits, apply sanctions, offer rewards, make decisions, control actions, or provide plans for achieving results.

Although its aims were modest enough, management by objectives did little to improve implementation in the executive branch. It was often difficult to obtain meaningful objectives from agencies. "Ending crime," for example, was too utopian and too broad to be useful. Sometimes agencies were vague about their objectives to avoid alienating congressional committees and interest groups. Another problem was that many of the objectives were to develop a plan or pass legislation and therefore were not closely related to implementation. It was hard to quantify the objectives of policies such as research or diplomacy, and agencies chose "safe" objectives to state and monitor, not objectives they would have a difficult time achieving. In short, agencies seriously adopted management by objectives when it was in their interests to do so, not because the president desired it. Neither the White House nor the Office of Management and Budget, which had overall responsibility for the new system, was much interested in the information produced by management by objectives, and President Nixon did not devote much time to program management. Not surprisingly, a few years after it began, management by objectives was all but forgotten.

A different factor inhibiting follow-up is secrecy. Secretly executed policies, such as those implemented by the CIA, require few reports to Congress or to superiors in the executive branch. Consequently, officials' actions are not routinely monitored. Since members of Congress risk criticism for violating national security if they make public any secret information, they are reluctant to do so and have incentives to forgo their responsibility for oversight and follow-up of certain secret policies. When President Johnson's fear of leaks regarding decisions on the war in Vietnam led him to restrict his direct communications to a few top officials (the Tuesday lunch group), he did without a prearranged agenda or minutes of the meetings which would have recorded decisions and made possible follow-up on them.

An organization's personnel may be aware of implementation problems but fail to report them to the president or other administration officials. There are several reasons for this. An obvious one, which we noted earlier, is that subordinates may fear that reporting implementation failures will reflect poorly on their own performance and also possibly anger their superiors. Employees may also have a natural loyalty to their organization or to others in the organization who might be hurt by their negative reports. Finally, the informal norms against reporting negative information may be very strong. Thus, employees may withhold information from their superiors to escape social ostracism in their peer groups.

Some employees ignore problems they don't want to see. They don't like to think that a policy that they helped administer is not working. Or they may feel that their superiors will not pay attention to their reports anyway, so why bother? Indeed, superiors may reinforce such views by failing to act on evidence of implementation failure.

Organizations may fail to report problems in policy implementation for political reasons, such as the fear of losing public or legislative support for their programs. Also, within some organizations rivalries between headquarters and field personnel make the latter reluctant to expose themselves to negative reactions to their implementation efforts.

When information indicating poor implementation is made available to top executive-branch officials, in many instances they fail to use it. One reason for this is that information coming from the field is often circumstantial, inconsistent, ambiguous, unrepresentative—in sum, unreliable. In addition, information arrives in fragments at different places, without integrated patterns of timing, content, or form. High-level officials may not be in a position to see the whole as the sum of a program's numerous parts. Moreover, it is difficult for them to cull useful follow-up information from the tremendous volume of information they receive, particularly given the many pressing demands competing for their time and attention, such as those for substantive policy changes. Thus, it takes dedicated, sensitive leaders to both assemble and interpret correctly information on the actions of implementors.

While there are limitations on performing follow-up properly, this does not mean follow-up cannot work. And we have seen substantial evidence that it needs to be done. One study found that the Nixon administration's efforts to monitor and evaluate the actions of welfare caseworkers, especially to review them for errors that allowed ineligible persons to receive funds under the Aid to Families with Dependent Children program, had a significant influence on reducing the number of persons receiving welfare. (Unfortunately, it appears that this approach also resulted in many eligible persons not receiving welfare payments.)[39]

CONCLUSION

The president faces many obstacles in implementing public policies. Although he is the "chief executive," he typically is not in a position to command his own branch's bureaucracy, much less Congress and the private sector. Moreover, he operates in an environment of scarce resources and few incentives to devote time and energy to implementation.

Improving implementation will be very difficult. The roots of most implementation problems are embedded deeply in the fabric of American government and politics, as we have seen. Moreover, as long as presidents remain more concerned with shaping legislation to pass in the

Congress than with the implementation of the law after it is passed, as long as they persist in emphasizing public relations rather than policy, and as long as "crisis" situations continue to dominate their time, little progress is likely to be made in improving policy implementation. Moreover, until the public provides incentives for officials to devote more attention to policy implementation and to develop better administrative skills, these priorities probably will not change. Given both the low visibility of most policy implementation activities and the lack of interest of most Americans in government and politics, the prospects for a change in incentives are not very favorable.

NOTES

1. Lawrence F. O'Brien, *No Final Victories* (New York: Ballantine Books, 1974), p. 142.

2. John Herbers, "Nixon's Presidency: Centralized Control," *New York Times*, March 6, 1973, p. 20.

3. H. R. Haldeman, *The Ends of Power* (New York: Times Books, 1978), p. 149.

4. President Carter, quoted in G. Calvin Mackenzie, "Personnel Appointment Strategies in Post-War Presidential Administrations" (paper delivered at the Annual Meeting of the Midwest Political Science Association, Chicago, April 1980), introductory page.

5. Richard Cheney, quoted in Stephen J. Wayne, "Working in the White House: Psychological Dimensions of the Job" (paper delivered at the Annual Meeting of the Southern Political Science Association, New Orleans, November 1977), p. 10.

6. Quoted in Paul C. Light, *The President's Agenda: Domestic Policy Choice from Kennedy to Carter* (Baltimore: Johns Hopkins University Press, 1982), p. 145.

7. Quoted in ibid., p. 152.

8. "How Much Can Any Administration Do?" *Public Opinion*, December/January 1982, p. 56.

9. See, for example, William Safire, *Before the Fall: An Inside View of the Pre-Watergate White House* (New York: Doubleday, 1975), pp. 112–13, 285–87, 353, 566–67; Haldeman, *The Ends of Power*, pp. 58–59, 111–12, 185–87.

10. See, for example, Henry Kissinger, *White House Years* (Boston: Little, Brown, 1979), pp. 26, 28–29, 45–46, 48, 141–42, 158–59, 264, 482, 729, 806, 879, 887, 900, 909, 917, 994.

11. Ibid., pp. 28–29, 264, 900.

12. Lyndon Johnson, quoted in Doris Kearns, *Lyndon Johnson and the American Dream* (New York: Harper and Row, 1976), p. 137.

13. Frederick A. Lazin, "The Failure of Federal Enforcement of Civil Rights Regulations in Public Housing, 1963–1971: The Co-optation of a Federal Agency by its Local Constituency," *Policy Sciences* 4 (September 1973): 263–73.

14. Gerald R. Ford, "Imperiled, Not Imperial," *Time*, November 10, 1980, p. 30.

15. Melvin Laird, quoted in Seymour M. Hersh, *The Price of Power: Kissinger in the Nixon White House* (New York: Summit, 1983), pp. 235–36.

16. Richard M. Nixon, *RN: The Memoirs of Richard Nixon* (New York: Grosset and Dunlap, 1978), pp. 472–73, 513.

17. John F. Kennedy, quoted in Kenneth P. O'Donnell and David F. Powers, *Johnny, We Hardly Knew Ye: Memories of John Fitzgerald Kennedy* (New York: Pocket Books, 1972), p. 270.

18. Dom Bonafede, "Carter Sounds Retreat from 'Cabinet Government,' " *National Journal*, November 18, 1978, pp. 1852–57; "Rafshoon and Co.," *Newsweek*, January 29, 1979, p. 23.

19. Haldeman, *Ends of Power*, p. 149.

20. Joel D. Aberbach and Bert A. Rockman, "Clashing Beliefs within the Executive Branch: The Nixon Administration Bureaucracy," *American Political Science Review* 70 (June 1976): 456–68.

21. Brooks Jackson, "Carter Aide Blasts Civil Service System as Being Inefficient," *New Orleans Times-Picayune*, April 23, 1978, sec. 1, p. 26.

22. "Press Conference Text," *Congressional Quarterly Weekly Report*, March 11, 1978, p. 655.

23. Richard M. Nixon, quoted in Aberbach and Rockman, "Clashing Beliefs within the Executive Branch," p. 457.

24. "Civil Service Reform," *Congressional Quarterly Weekly Report*, March 11, 1978, p. 660.

25. Richard L. Cole and David A. Caputo, "Presidential Control of the Senior Civil Service: Assessing the Strategies of the Nixon Years," *American Political Science Review* 73 (June 1979): 399–413.

26. "Press Conference Text," p. 655.

27. Franklin D. Roosevelt, quoted in M. S. Eccles, *Beckoning Frontiers* (New York: Knopf, 1951), p. 336.

28. Quoted in Graham T. Allison, *Essence of Decision: Explaining the Cuban Missile Crisis* (Boston: Little, Brown, 1971), pp. 131–32.

29. Rowland Evans and Robert Novak, *Lyndon B. Johnson: The Exercise of Power* (New York: Signet, 1966), p. 430.

30. "Carter Criticizes Federal Bureaucracy," *Congressional Quarterly Weekly Report*, June 3, 1978, p. 1421.

31. Ibid.

32. Richard Nixon, "Government Reorganization—Message from the President," in Stanley Bach and George T. Sulzner, eds., *Perspectives on the Presidency: A Collection* (Lexington, Mass.: Heath, 1974), p. 257.

33. "Carter Criticizes Federal Bureaucracy," p. 1421.

34. William Colby, *Honorable Men: My Life in the CIA* (New York: Norton, 1975), pp. 101–02.

35. Ibid., pp. 440–41; "Intelligence Failures, CIA Misdeeds Studied," *Congressional Quarterly Weekly Report*, September 20, 1975, p. 2025.

36. Safire, *Before the Fall*, pp. 250–260.

37. Jonathan Daniels, *Frontiers on the Potomac* (New York: Macmillan, 1946), pp. 31–32.

38. Wayne, "Working in the White House," pp. 16–17.

39. Ronald Randall, "Presidential Power versus Bureaucratic Intransigence: The Influence of the Nixon Administration on Welfare Policy," *American Political Science Review* 73 (September 1979): 795–810.

SELECTED READINGS

Aberbach, Joel D., and Bert A. Rockman. "Clashing Beliefs within the Executive Branch: The Nixon Administration Bureaucracy." *American Political Science Review* 70 (June 1976): 456–68.

Allison, Graham. *Essence of Decision*. Boston: Little, Brown, 1971.

Bardach, Eugene. *The Implementation Game: What Happens after a Bill Becomes a Law*. Cambridge, Mass.: MIT Press, 1977.

Chambers, Raymond L. "The Executive Power: A Preliminary Study of the Concept and Efficacy of Presidential Directives." *Presidential Studies Quarterly* 7 (Winter 1977): 21–36.

Cole, Richard L., and David A. Caputo. "Presidential Control of the Senior Civil Service: Assessing the Strategies of the Nixon Years." *American Political Science Review* 73 (June 1979): 399–413.

Derthick, Martha. *Uncontrollable Spending for Social Services Grants.* Washington, D.C.: Brookings Institution, 1975.

Edwards, George C., III. *Implementing Public Policy.* Washington, D.C.: Congressional Quarterly, 1980.

Heclo, Hugh. *A Government of Strangers: Executive Politics in Washington.* Washington, D.C.: Brookings Institution, 1977.

Jones, Charles O. *Clean Air.* Pittsburgh: University of Pittsburgh Press, 1975.

Kaufman, Herbert. *Administrative Feedback.* Washington, D.C.: Brookings Institution, 1973.

Lazin, Frederick A. "The Failure of Federal Enforcement of Civil Rights Regulations in Public Housing, 1963–1971: The Co-optation of a Federal Agency by Its Local Constituency." *Policy Sciences* 4 (September 1973): 263–73.

Macy, John W.; Bruce Adams; and J. Jackson Walter. *America's Unelected Government: Appointing the President's Team.* Cambridge, Mass.: Ballinger, 1983.

Malek, Frederic V. *Washington's Hidden Tragedy: The Failure to Make Government Work.* New York: Free Press, 1978.

Mazmanian, Daniel, and Jeanne Nienaber. *Can Organizations Change? Environmental Protection, Citizen Participation, and the Corps of Engineers.* Washington, D.C.: Brookings Institution, 1979.

Moore, Mark H. "Reorganization Plan #2 Reviewed: Problems in Implementing a Strategy to Reduce the Supply of Drugs to Illicit Markets in the United States." *Public Policy* 26 (Spring 1978): 229–62.

Murphy, Jerome T. *State Agencies and Discretionary Funds.* Lexington, Mass.: Lexington Books, 1974.

Nathan, Richard P. *The Administrative Presidency.* New York: Wiley, 1983.

Pressman, Jeffrey L., and Aaron B. Wildavsky. *Implementation.* Berkeley: University of California Press, 1973.

Radin, Beryl A. *Implementation, Change, and the Federal Bureaucracy.* New York: Teachers College Press, 1977.

Rose, Richard. *Managing Presidential Objectives.* New York: Free Press, 1976.

Sapolsky, Harvey M. *The Polaris System Development: Bureaucratic and Programmatic Success in Government.* Cambridge, Mass.: Harvard University Press, 1972.

Williams, Walter, et al. *Studying Implementation: Methodological and Administrative Issues* (Chatham, N.J.: Chatham House, 1982).

13

The President and the Judiciary

The president's interactions with the Congress and the bureaucracy are constant and receive considerable attention. His relations with the third branch of government, the judiciary, are in many ways more intermittent and less visible. Nevertheless, the chief executive has important relationships with the courts. He has an opportunity to influence public policy for years to come through his nominations to the bench. The executive branch, operating through the solicitor general's office, is also a frequent litigant in the federal courts, especially at the Supreme Court level. Such litigation provides another opportunity for the president to influence judicial decisions. In addition, as chief executive the president may end up with responsibility for enforcing court decisions, even though he was not directly involved in them. Sometimes enforcing the law actually means complying with decisions directed at the White House. Although such instances are not common, they may provide moments of high political drama and have important consequences for our political system. Finally, the Constitution gives the president the right to exercise some judicial powers himself. He can grant pardons, amnesty, and clemency for those accused or convicted of federal crimes.

JUDICIAL SELECTION

One of the president's responsibilities with far-reaching consequences is his duty to nominate federal judges. This task involves him in intimate negotiations with senators and interest groups and may rise to prominence in presidential campaign platforms. In this section we examine the process of judicial selection for the federal courts and the types of persons who become federal judges.

Selection of Lower-Court Judges

We begin with the federal district courts and the courts of appeals, which include most federal judges and which handle most federal cases. The president nominates persons to fill these slots for lifetime service. The Senate must confirm each nomination by a majority vote. Because of the Senate's role, the president's discretion ends up being much less than it appears.

Senatorial courtesy is the customary manner in which the Senate disposes of state-level federal nominations for such positions as judgeships and U.S. attorneys. Under this unwritten tradition, nominations for these positions are not confirmed when opposed by a senator from the state in which the nominee is to serve (all states have at least one federal district court) or, in the case of courts of appeals judges, the state of the nominee's residence if the senator is of the same party as the president. To invoke the right of senatorial courtesy, the relevant senator usually simply states a general reason for his opposition. Other senators then honor their colleague's views and oppose the nomination, regardless of their personal views or the candidate's merits.

The first instance of senatorial courtesy occurred in 1789, when President George Washington failed to have Benjamin Fishbourn confirmed as naval officer of the port of Savannah because of the opposition of Georgia's two senators. Since that time senatorial courtesy has become more and more established. By 1840, senators were virtually naming federal district court judges. In addition, at times senatorial courtesy has been successfully invoked by a senator not of the president's party. Also, on a few occasions, the Senate has failed to observe senatorial courtesy, as it did for Senator Theodore G. Bilbo of Mississippi in 1936 and Senator W. Lee David of Texas in 1947.

A related practice began in the mid-1950s when the Senate Judiciary Committee initiated the practice of circulating a "blue slip" to the senators from the state in which a prospective judge was to serve, asking for permission to hold a hearing. Since these go to all senators, even those not from the president's party could object to a nominee by not returning the slip to the committee. Senators have not exercised this prerogative very often to defeat a nomination, however, and in 1979 the chairman of the Judiciary Committee, Edward Kennedy, announced that the committee would reserve the right independently to review and overrule a senator's failure to return a slip. After several years, the issue has not yet been pressed by a senator or the White House.

When a president fails to heed the tradition of senatorial courtesy, the results can be embarrassing. On April 1, 1976, President Ford nominated William B. Poff to a federal judgeship in Virginia. Virginia's Republican senator, William Scott, had previously given notice of his opposition to Poff and of his support for another candidate, Glenn Williams. It is important to note that Scott himself agreed that Poff was qualified for the position. He just felt Williams's philosophy was closer to his own. Thus, on April 15 Scott formally announced his opposition to Poff's nomination in a letter to the Senate Judiciary Committee, simply terming Poff "unacceptable." On May 5 the committee chairman, Senator James Eastland, moved to table the nomination, and it was tabled without objection.

The president is not without assets in such a situation, but he rarely will find it worthwhile to fight a senator over a district court judgeship. These judges seldom interfere with his policies. If he desires to do so, he can refuse to appoint anyone to the position in an attempt to pressure a senator into supporting his nominee to avoid a backlog of federal cases in his state. Or the president may make an appointment during a congressional recess at the end of a session. Although the nominee must still be confirmed in the next session of Congress, he may have had an opportunity to demonstrate his capabilities on the bench by then, and the Senate may be more deferential in its treatment of a sitting judge than of a more typical nominee.

Because of the strength of these informal practices, presidents usually check carefully with the relevant senator or senators ahead of time so they won't make a nomination that will fail to be confirmed. In many instances this is tantamount to giving the power of nomination to these senators. Typically, when there is a vacancy for a federal judgeship, the senator(s) of the president's party from the state where the judge will serve suggests one or more names to the attorney general and the president. If neither senator is of the president's party, the state's congressmen of the president's party or other state party leaders may make suggestions. Then the Department of Justice and the Federal Bureau of Investigation conduct competency and background checks on these persons, and the president usually selects a nominee from those who survive the screening process. It is very difficult for the president to reject in favor of someone else the recommendation of a senator of his party if the person recommended clears the hurdles of professional standing and integrity. Thus, the Constitution is turned on its head and the Senate ends up making nominations, which the president then approves.

The attorney general typically asks the Standing Committee on the Federal Judiciary of the American Bar Association (ABA) for its evaluation of potential nominees. Presidents have varied in the attention they pay to the committee's findings, with Eisenhower in his last two years in office giving it an effective veto over nominations. Most presidents, however, simply use the ABA evaluations as one of many inputs into their decision making, and the committee is largely powerless to stop a nomination once the president has made it. Moreover, the Carter administration broadened the participation of the legal community in the judicial selection process by asking the National Bar Association, a predominantly black lawyers' organization, and the Federation of Women Lawyers to evaluate potential nominees on their commitment to equal justice under law and their holding of racial, religious, or sexual biases. The Reagan White House returned to the earlier, more restricted system of formally consulting only the ABA.

Others have input in judicial selection as well. The ABA committee or the Department of Justice may ask sitting judges, usually federal judges, to evaluate prospective nominees. Sitting judges may also initiate recommendations to advance or retard someone's chances of being nominated. In addition, candidates for the nomination are often active on their own behalf. They have to alert the relevant parties that they desire the position and orchestrate a campaign of support on their behalf. As one appellate judge observed, "People don't get judgeships without seeking them. Anybody who thinks judicial office seeks the man is mistaken. There's not a man on the court who didn't do what he thought needed to be done."[1]

The president usually has more influence in the selection of judges to the federal courts of appeals than to federal district courts. Since the decisions of appellate courts are generally more significant than those of lower courts, the president naturally takes a greater interest in whom he appoints to these courts. At the same time, individual senators are in a weaker position to determine who the nominee will be because the jurisdiction of an appeals court encompasses several states. Although custom and pragmatic politics require that these judgeships be apportioned among the states, the president has discretion in how he does this and therefore has a greater role in recruiting appellate judges than district court judges. Even here, however, senators from the state in which the candidate resides may be able to veto a nomination.

Jimmy Carter attempted to alter the role of senators in the judicial selection process. Shortly after his election as president, Carter struck a deal with Senator James Eastland, chairman of the Senate Judiciary Committee, that the president would have a free hand in nominations to the federal courts of appeal but would continue to defer to senators in nominations to the federal district courts. The president then established the United States Circuit Judge Nominating Commission and appointed members to its thirteen panels. Each panel was composed of laypeople as well as lawyers and included women and minorities. When a vacancy occurred, the relevant panel interviewed potential nominees and recommended three to five persons to the president to fill the position, basing their evaluations on broad merit criteria. President Carter made his selection from this list of names.

In 1978 Congress added wording to an act creating new federal judgeships that asked the president to establish standards for selecting federal district court judges and emphasized the importance of merit selection and greater representation for women and minorities. President Carter subsequently requested senators to make special efforts to identify qualified women and minority candidates (he had no authority to force them to comply). In response senators from most states adopted the use of nominating commissions to recommend candidates for federal district courts. The selection of members and the composition and operation of the commissions varied widely, as did the use of the names they produced. Nevertheless, states with these commissions produced judges with higher ratings by the ABA and a greater percentage of women and blacks than states without commissions, although there were notable exceptions on both sides.

Things changed once again following Ronald Reagan's election as president. He abolished the Circuit Judge Nominating Commission and invited the Republican senator(s) from the relevant state (or Republican House members if there was no senator) to identify prospective candidates for federal judgeships. Senators were encouraged to apply screening devices to ensure that their recommendations were based on merit, but he specified no particular type of mechanism.

Backgrounds of Lower-Court Judges

What kind of people are selected as judges as a result of this process? The data in Tables 13-1 and 13-2 show that federal judges are not a representative sample of the American people. They are all lawyers (although this is not a constitutional requirement), and they are overwhelmingly white males. Jimmy Carter is the only president who has appointed a substantial number of women and minorities to the federal bench. Federal judges have also typically held office as a judge or prosecutor, and often they have been involved in partisan politics. This involvement is generally what brings them to the attention of senators and the Department of Justice when they seek nominees for judgeships. As former U.S. attorney general and circuit court judge Griffin Bell once remarked, "For me, becoming a federal judge wasn't very difficult. I managed John F. Kennedy's presidential campaign in Georgia. Two of my oldest and closest friends were two senators from Georgia. And I was campaign manager and special, unpaid counsel for the governor."[2]

Perhaps the most striking finding in Tables 13-1 and 13-2 is the fact that presidents rarely appoint someone to a judgeship who does not share their party affiliation. Merit considerations obviously occur after partisan screening. Judgeships are patronage plums that may serve as rewards for political service to either the president or senators of his party, as consolation prizes for unsuccessful candidates, or even to "kick upstairs" an official to remove him from an executive-branch post. When

Table 13–1. Backgrounds of Recent Federal District Court Appointees

	Reagan*	Carter	Ford	Nixon	Johnson
Total number of appointees	68	202	52	179	122
Occupation (%)					
Politics/gov't	7.4	4.0	21.2	10.6	21.3
Judiciary	36.8	44.6	34.6	28.5	31.1
Large law firm	11.8	14.0	9.7	11.3	2.4
Moderate size firm	27.9	19.8	25.0	27.9	18.9
Solo or small firm	11.8	13.9	9.6	20.0	23.0
Professor of law	4.4	3.0	—	2.8	3.3
Other	—	0.5	—	—	—
Experience (%)					
Judicial	44.1	54.5	42.3	35.1	34.3
Prosecutorial	42.7	38.6	50.0	41.9	45.8
Neither one	30.9	28.2	30.8	36.3	33.6
Party (%)					
Democrat	2.9	94.1	21.2	7.8	94.3
Republican	97.1	4.5	78.8	92.2	5.7
Independent	—	1.5	—	—	—
Past party activism (%)	64.7	60.4	50.0	48.6	49.2
Religious origin or affiliation (%)					
Protestant	63.2	60.4	73.1	73.2	58.2
Catholic	30.9	27.2	17.3	18.4	31.1
Jewish	5.9	12.4	9.6	8.4	10.7
Ethnicity or race (%)					
White	95.6	78.7	88.5	95.5	93.4
Black	—	13.9	5.8	3.4	4.1
Hispanic	2.9	6.9	1.9	1.1	2.5
Asian	1.5	0.5	3.9	—	—
Sex (%)					
Male	95.6	85.6	98.1	99.4	98.4
Female	4.4	14.4	1.9	0.6	1.6

Source: Sheldon Goldman, "Reagan's Judicial Appointments at Mid-Term: Shaping the Bench in His Own Image," *Judicature* 66 (March 1983): 338–39.
*1981–1982.

the president nominates someone of the other party for a judgeship, it is usually because of ideological congruity with the nominee or to obtain support in a state where his party is weak.

Partisanship also plays a role in the creation of judgeships. Because of their keen interest in them, members of Congress are reluctant to cre-

Table 13–2. Backgrounds of Recent Federal Courts of Appeals Appointees

	Reagan*	Carter	Ford	Nixon	Johnson
Total number of appointees	19	56	12	45	40
Occupation (%)					
Politics/gov't	—	5.4	8.3	4.4	10.0
Judiciary	68.4	46.6	75.0	53.3	57.5
Large law firm	10.6	10.8	8.3	4.4	5.0
Moderate size firm	5.3	16.1	8.3	22.2	17.5
Solo or small firm	—	5.4	—	6.7	10.0
Professor of law	15.8	14.3	—	2.2	2.5
Other	—	1.8	—	6.7	—
Experience (%)					
Judicial	73.7	53.6	75.0	57.8	65.0
Prosecutorial	21.1	32.1	25.0	46.7	47.5
Neither one	21.1	37.5	25.0	17.8	20.0
Party (%)					
Democrat	—	89.3	8.3	6.7	95.0
Republican	100.0	5.4	91.7	93.3	5.0
Independent	—	5.4	—	—	—
Past party activism (%)	57.9	73.2	58.3	60.0	57.5
Religious origin or affiliation (%)					
Protestant	57.9	60.7	58.3	75.6	60.0
Catholic	31.6	23.2	33.3	15.6	25.0
Jewish	10.5	16.1	8.3	8.9	15.0
Ethnicity or race (%)					
White	94.7	78.6	100.0	97.8	95.0
Black	5.3	16.1	—	—	5.0
Hispanic	—	3.6	—	—	—
Asian	—	1.8	—	2.2	—
Sex (%)					
Male	100.0	80.4	100.0	100.0	97.5
Female	—	19.6	—	—	2.5

Source: Goldman, "Reagan's Judicial Appointments at Mid-Term," pp. 344–45.
*1981–1982.

ate judicial positions to be filled by a president of the minority party in Congress. For example, Democrats in Congress rejected President Eisenhower's efforts to create new judgeships in every year of his second term, 1957–1960, even though he offered to name Democrats to half the new positions. In 1962, however, a similar bill easily passed Congress with

Democrat John Kennedy in the White House. This partisan behavior was nothing new. In 1801 the newly elected Jeffersonians repealed a law creating separate judges for the circuit courts of appeal that had been passed by the outgoing Federalists a few months earlier.

There is no doubt that various women's, racial, ethnic, and religious groups desire to have as many of their members as possible appointed to the federal bench. At the very least judgeships have symbolic importance for them. Thus, presidents face many of the same pressures for representativeness in selecting judges that they experience in naming their cabinet.

What is less clear is what policy differences result from presidents' appointing persons with different backgrounds to judgeships. The number of female and minority group judges has been too few and their service too recent to serve as a basis for generalizations about their decisions. There have been many members of each party appointed to the federal bench, however. It appears that, at least on economic issues, Republican judges are more conservative than Democratic judges. On other matters, however, party affiliation may bring no more uniformity to the courts than it does to Congress.

Selection of Supreme Court Justices

Like lower-court judges, justices of the Supreme Court must be approved by a majority of those voting in the Senate. There have been no recess appointments to the Court since the Senate voiced its disapproval of the practice in 1960. When the chief justice's position is vacant, the president may nominate either someone already on the Court or someone from outside it to fill the position. Usually presidents choose the latter course to widen their range of options, but if they decide to elevate a sitting associate justice, he or she must go through a new confirmation by the Senate.

The president operates under many constraints in selecting persons to serve on the lower federal courts, especially the district courts. Although many of the same actors are present in the case of Supreme Court nominations, their influence is typically quite different. The president is vitally interested in the Court because of the importance of its work and will generally be intimately involved in the recruitment process.

Unlike the case for federal judges, presidents have been personally acquainted with most of the people they have nominated to the Court, reflecting their involvement in the selection process, and it is not unusual for an administration official to receive a nomination. Presidents also often rely on the attorney general and the Justice Department to identify and screen candidates for the Court. Richard Nixon relied heavily upon recommendations from John Mitchell; Edward Levi was crucial in Presi-

"*Do you ever have one of those days when every-thing seems un-Constitutional?*"

Source: Drawing by Joe Mirachi; © 1974 The New Yorker Magazine, Inc.

dent Ford's selection of John Paul Stevens; and William French Smith led the effort to recruit Sandra Day O'Connor for Ronald Reagan.

There are few matters as important to justices on the Supreme Court as the ideology, competence, and compatibility of their colleagues, and thus it is not surprising that they, especially chief justices, often try to influence nominations to the Court. Former president and chief justice William Howard Taft was especially active during his tenure in the 1920s, and Warren Burger played a prominent role in the Nixon administration. Nevertheless, although presidents will listen to recommendations from justices, they feel no obligations to follow them.

Senators play a much less prominent role in the recruitment of Supreme Court justices than in the selection of lower-court judges, especially for the district courts. No senator can claim that the jurisdiction of the Supreme Court falls within the realm of his or her special expertise, interest, or sphere of influence. Thus, presidents typically consult with senators from the state of residence of a nominee after they have decided whom to select. At this point senators are unlikely to oppose a nomination because they like having their state receive the honor and are well aware that the president can simply select someone from another state if he chooses to do so.

Candidates for nomination are also much less likely to play a significant role in the recruitment process. Although there have been exceptions, most notably William Howard Taft, people do not usually campaign for a position on the Court. Little can be accomplished through such activity, and, because of the Court's standing, it might offend those who do play important roles in selecting nominees.

The American Bar Association's Standing Committee on the Federal Judiciary has played a varied but typically more modest role at the Supreme Court level than for nominations to lower courts. Between 1956 and 1970 the committee was asked to evaluate candidates for the Supreme Court only after the president had nominated them. The committee prefers to screen potential nominees before they are nominated, however, so it will not be in the position of opposing the president's choice. Indeed, it has never found a nominee unqualified to serve on the Court.

After Richard Nixon saw two of his nominees in succession fail to obtain Senate confirmation, he allowed the ABA committee to evaluate potential nominees before he announced nominations. But this arrangement proved unsatisfactory when in 1971 the committee failed to find Nixon's top choices for two vacancies on the Court to be qualified to fill the positions, and Attorney General John Mitchell withdrew the committee's prescreening privilege. Although it was restored for President Ford's single nominee, President Reagan does not appear to have consulted the committee in advance about his nomination of Sandra Day O'Connor.

Through 1983, 102 persons have served on the Supreme Court. Of the 139 nominees, 3 were nominated and confirmed twice, 8 were confirmed but never served, and 26 failed to secure Senate confirmation. The president, then, has failed 19 percent of the time to appoint the person of his choice to the Court, a percentage much higher than for any other federal position. Thus, although home-state senators do not play prominent roles in the selection process for the Court, the Senate as a whole does.

Four nominees have failed to receive Senate confirmation in this century: John J. Parker (1930), Abe Fortas (1968), Clement Haynesworth (1969), and G. Harrold Carswell (1970). Their difficulties are typical of those faced by unsuccessful candidates. Liberal and civil rights groups opposed Parker, Haynesworth, and Carswell, and organized labor was in active opposition against the first two as well. Fortas (who was already on the Court and who had been nominated as chief justice) was opposed by conservative interests and was charged with ethical violations, as was Haynesworth. Carswell was the only one of the four whose competence was seriously questioned. Haynesworth's and Carswell's troubles were compounded because they were Republican appointees facing a Democrat-controlled Senate, while Fortas was nominated at the end of President Johnson's term and Senate Republicans refused to confirm him in the hope that a Republican president would be elected and have the opportunity to nominate a new chief justice.

These examples indicate that nominations are most likely to run into trouble under certain conditions. A president whose party is in the minority in the Senate or who makes a nomination at the end of his term faces a greatly increased probability of substantial opposition and in some cases defeat. Equally important, opponents of a nomination usually must be able to question a nominee's competence or ethics in order to defeat a nomination. Ideological opposition is generally not enough, as the case of William Rehnquist, who was strongly opposed by liberals, illustrates. Questions of competence and ethics provide a rationale for opposition that can attract moderates and make ideological protests seem less partisan.

Characteristics of Justices

Competence and ethical behavior are important to presidents for reasons beyond merely obtaining Senate confirmation of their nominees to the Court. Skilled and honorable justices reflect well on the president and will likely do so for many years. Moreover, they are more effective advocates and thus can better serve the president's interests. In addition, presidents usually have enough respect for the Court and its work that they do not want to saddle it with a mediocre justice. Although the criteria of competence and character screen out some possible candidates, they still leave a wide field from which the president may choose. Other characteristics then play prominent roles.

Like their colleagues on the lower federal courts, Supreme Court justices share many characteristics that are quite unlike those of the typical American. All have been lawyers and all but two have been white males. Most have been in their fifties and sixties when they took office, from the upper-middle to upper class, and Protestants.

The only black (Thurgood Marshall) and woman (Sandra Day O'Connor) ever to sit on the court are currently serving (as of 1984). Race and sex have become more salient criteria in recent years. In the 1980 presidential campaign Ronald Reagan even promised to appoint a woman to the first vacancy on the Court if he were elected. Women and blacks may serve more frequently in the future because of increased opportunities for legal education and decreased prejudice against their judicial activity as well as because of their increasing political clout.

Geography once was a prominent criterion for selection to the Court, but it is no longer very important. Presidents do like to spread the slots around, however, as when Richard Nixon decided that he wanted to nominate a southerner. At various times there has been what some have termed a "Jewish seat" and a "Catholic seat" on the Court, but these are not binding on the president. For example, after a half century of having a Jewish justice, there has been none since 1969.

Partisanship remains an important influence on the selection of justices; only 13 of 102 members were nominated by presidents of a different party. Moreover, many of the 13 exceptions were actually close to the president in ideology as was the case in Richard Nixon's appointment of Lewis Powell. Herbert Hoover's nomination of Benjamin Cardozo seems to be one of the few cases where partisanship was completely dominated by merit as a criterion for selection.

The role of partisanship is not really surprising, even at the level of our highest court. Most of the president's acquaintances are in his party, and there is usually a certain congruity between party and political views. The president may also use Supreme Court nominations as a reward, as when President Eisenhower nominated Earl Warren as chief justice. As leader of the California delegation, Warren had played a crucial role in Eisenhower's obtaining the Republican nomination for president. Most justices have at one time been active partisans, which gave them visibility and helped them obtain the positions from which they moved to the Court.

Typically justices have held high administrative or judicial positions before moving to the Supreme Court. Most have had some experience as a judge, often at the appellate level, and many have worked for the Department of Justice. Some have held high elected office, and a few have had no government service but have been distinguished attorneys. The fact that not all justices, including many of the most distinguished ones, have had previous judicial experience may seem surprising, but the unique work and environment of the Court renders this background much less important than it might be for other appellate courts.

PRESIDENT–SUPREME COURT RELATIONS

At the top of two complex branches of government stand the president and the Supreme Court. Each has significant powers and in a system of shared powers such as ours, it is not surprising that the president is interested in influencing the Court. In this section we examine efforts of the White House to mold the Court through filling vacancies, setting its agenda, and influencing and enforcing its decisions. We also look at interbranch relations involving advising and other services.

Molding the Court

As we have noted, one of the most significant powers of the president is molding the Supreme Court through his nominations. Because justices serve for life, the impact of a president's selections will generally be felt long after he has left office. Because of this, the policy preferences of candidates for the Supreme Court are important to most presidents, and they typically make substantial efforts to ascertain them. When they succeed, they can slow or alter trends in the Court's decisions. Franklin Roosevelt's nominees substantially liberalized the Court, while Richard Nixon's turned it in a basically conservative direction.

Presidents and their aides survey candidates' decisions (if they served on a lower court), speeches, political stands, writings, and other expressions of opinion. They also turn for information to people who know the candidates well. The most direct means of learning candidates' policy views would be simply to ask them, but this must be done in a delicate manner. Most officials feel it is improper to question judicial candidates about upcoming judicial decisions, so conversations must be limited to broader discussions of issues. Ronald Reagan was reportedly favorably impressed with Sandra Day O'Connor's conservative views on social issues and politics in general in their prenomination talk.

As a result of all this effort, president are generally satisfied with the actions of their nominees, especially those who have prior judicial experience to examine. Nevertheless, it is not always easy to identify the policy inclinations of candidates, and presidents have been disappointed in their selections about a fourth of the time. President Eisenhower, for example, was displeased with the liberal decisions of both Earl Warren and William Brennan. Once when asked whether he had made any mistakes as president, he replied, "Yes, two, and they are both sitting on the Supreme Court."[3] Earlier, Woodrow Wilson was shocked by the very conservative positions of one of his nominees, James McReynolds. On a more limited scale, Richard Nixon was certainly disappointed when his nominee for chief justice, Warren Burger, authored the Court's decision calling for immediate desegregation of the nation's schools shortly after his confirmation. This did little for the president's "southern strategy."

Presidents make what in their views are errors in nominations to the Court for several possible reasons. They and their aides may have done a poor job of probing the views of candidates. Moreover, once on the Court, justices may change their attitudes and values over time because of new insights gained in their position, the normal process of aging, or the influence of other members of the Court (virtually all justices between 1801 and 1835 were strongly affected by Chief Justice John Marshall). Justices are also often constrained by their obligation to follow precedents (when they are clear).

Some presidents have been relatively unconcerned with ideology in their nominations. In a period of relative political and social calm or when there is a solid majority on the Court that shares his views and that is likely to persist for several years, a president might give less weight to policy preferences than to other criteria in choosing justices.

A president cannot have much impact on the Court unless he has vacancies to fill, of course. Although on the average there has been an opening on the Supreme Court every two years, there is a substantial variance around this mean. Franklin D. Roosevelt had to wait five years before he could nominate a justice. All the while he was faced with a Court that found much of his New Deal legislation unconstitutional. In more recent years Jimmy Carter was never able to nominate a justice. Indeed, between 1972 and 1984 there were only two vacancies on the Court. On the other hand, Richard Nixon was able to nominate four justices in his first three years in office.

Sometimes unusual steps are taken to enhance or limit a president's ability to fill vacancies. The size of the Supreme Court was altered many times between 1801 and 1869. In 1866 Congress reduced the size of the Court from ten to eight members so that Andrew Johnson could not nominate any new justices. When President Grant took office, Congress increased the number to nine, since it had confidence he would nominate members to its liking. This number has remained unchanged since then, and it now seems inviolate. Franklin D. Roosevelt attempted to "pack" the court in 1937 with his proposal to add a justice to the Court for every justice currently serving who was over seventy and had served ten years. This proposal was an obvious attempt to change the direction of Court decisions on his economic policies, and after a prolonged political battle Congress refused to approve it. The refusal, however, was given only after the Court made a strategic reversal and began approving liberal legislation. Thus, Roosevelt lost the battle but won the war.

The president's role in Supreme Court judicial selection is not limited to the nomination of justices. It extends to the creation of positions as well. Justices are typically not prone to retirement (in 1984 a majority of the justices were in their seventies), but presidents sometimes are frustrated enough at Court decisions to attempt to accelerate the creation of vacancies. Thomas Jefferson and his supporters tried to use impeachment to remove justices and thus gain control of the judiciary that was largely Federalist (and thus anti-Jefferson). This strategy was abandoned, however, when the Senate in 1805 failed to convict Justice Samuel Chase, who had made himself vulnerable with his partisan activities off the bench and injudicious remarks on it.

Thus, presidents have relied on indirect pressure. Theodore Roosevelt resorted to leaks in the press in an unsuccessful effort to induce two justices to resign. More recently, the Nixon administration orchestrated a campaign to force liberal justice Abe Fortas to resign after he was accused of financial improprieties.

Justices are not helpless pawns in the game of politics, of course, and may try to time their retirements so a president with compatible views will choose their successor. This is one reason that justices remain on the Court for so long, even when they are clearly infirm. William Howard

Taft, a rigid conservative, even feared a successor being named by Herbert Hoover!

Such tactics do not always succeed. In 1968 Chief Justice Earl Warren submitted his resignation to President Johnson, whom he felt would select an acceptable successor. When Johnson's choice of Abe Fortas failed to win confirmation, however, the opportunity to nominate the new chief justice passed to Warren's old California political rival, the newly elected president, Richard Nixon.

Arguments to the Courts

The president may influence what cases the courts hear as well as who hears them. The solicitor general is a presidential appointee who must be confirmed by the Senate and serves in the Department of Justice. It is he (not the attorney general) who supervises the litigation of the federal executive branch. In this position he plays a major role in determining the agenda of federal appellate courts. Although he exercises wide discretion, he is subject to the direction of the attorney general and the president, the latter of whom may play a role in major cases.

The solicitor general decides which of the cases lost by the federal government in the federal district courts or the courts of appeals will be appealed to the next higher court. The courts of appeals must hear properly appealed cases, but the Supreme Court, for all practical purposes, has complete control over its docket. Thus, it is significant that the court is far more likely to accept cases the solicitor general wants to be heard than those from any other party. Moreover, the amount of litigation involved is quite large. In recent years, the federal government has been a party to about half the cases heard in federal courts of appeals and the Supreme Court.

The executive branch also intervenes in cases to which it is not a party. The solicitor general files *amicus curiae* (friend of the court) briefs supporting or opposing the efforts of other parties to have the Court hear their cases. These cases range from school busing for racial integration to abortion rights to equal pay for women. Once again, the Court usually grants the government's request.

When a case reaches the Supreme Court the solicitor general supervises the preparation of the government's arguments in support of its position, whether it is a direct party or an amicus. These arguments are often reflected in Court decisions and thus become the law of the land. Since the government has participated in almost every major controversy decided by the courts in the past forty years, the potential influence of the executive branch on public policy through the courts is substantial. Moreover, both as a direct party or as an amicus, the federal government wins a clear majority of the time.

The government's success is due to several factors. The solicitor general builds credibility with the Court by not making frivolous appeals and in a few instances even by telling the Court the government should not have won cases in lower courts. Equally important, the solicitor general and his staff (again, not the attorney general) develop more expertise in dealing with the Court than anyone else, since they appear before it more frequently, and they provide the Court with high-quality briefs.

On a very rare occasion the president may directly attempt to influence a Court decision. Richard Nixon wanted the Court to slow down on busing children for school integration and felt a speech or position paper by him could influence it.[4] More directly, in a very unusual move in 1969 Department of Justice officials visited Justice Brennan and Chief Justice Warren to alert them that the administration was worried about the outcomes of some wiretapping cases that were on the Court's agenda. The administration was concerned that the Court's decisions would force the discontinuance of its surveillance of embassies or its prosecutions based on the information obtained from them. According to Warren, this visit had no influence on the Court's decision making.[5]

Enforcing Court Decisions

Another important relationship between the judicial and executive branches involves the enforcement of court decisions. Although the executive branch provides the federal courts with U.S. marshals, they are too few and lack sufficient authority to be of systematic aid, especially if a court order is directed against a coordinate branch of government. Thus, the courts often must rely on the president to enforce their decisions, especially their more controversial ones.

The Constitution is, not surprisingly, ambiguous as to the president's responsibility for aiding the judicial branch. Although it never explicitly discusses the point, the Constitution docs assign the president the responsibility to "take care that the laws be faithfully executed." Typically, presidents have responded to support the courts, or at least the rule of law. On several occasions, such as during the efforts of Presidents Eisenhower and Kennedy to integrate educational institutions, presidents have gone so far as to employ federal troops to ensure compliance with court orders.

Presidents may use the carrot as well as the stick to encourage others to comply with Court decisions. One of the most significant and controversial Supreme Court decisions of this century has been that of *Brown v. Board of Education*, 347 U.S. 483 (1954), calling for an end to segregation in the public schools. Compliance with this decision was a long and tortuous process, but it was aided by the passage of laws that provide federal aid only for school districts that do not segregate and that provide schools with extra funds to help ease the process of desegregation.

There have been exceptions to presidential cooperation, however. In

Worcester v. *Georgia*, 6 Peters 515 (1832), the Court found that Georgia had no authority over Cherokee Indian lands and that missionaries arrested there by the state were to be released. The Court also implied that it was the president's responsibility to enforce its decision. Georgia refused to comply with the decision, however, and President Andrew Jackson took no actions to enforce it. He is reputed to have stated, "Well, [Chief Justice] John Marshall has made his decision, now let him enforce it."

Other Relationships

In the earliest years of our nation the line of separation between the executive and judicial branches was vague and often crossed. President George Washington consulted with the chief justice on a range of matters and received written advisory opinions on matters of law. Washington even used the first two chief justices as diplomats to negotiate with other countries. The chief justice was also placed on a commission to manage the fund for paying off the national debt.

This interbranch cooperation did not last long, however. The diplomatic efforts of justices were criticized by many, the Court decided against providing further advisory opinions, and informal consultation between the White House and justices declined. The Court also refused to examine pension claims for the secretary of the treasury. The years of the Jefferson presidency were marked by the hostility of the president toward the judiciary, which was populated primarily by his Federalist political enemies.

The most notable formal exceptions in recent years to a strict separation between the two branches have been Justice Robert Jackson's service as chief American prosecutor at the Nuremberg trials of Nazi leaders following World War II and Chief Justice Earl Warren's chairing the commission investigating the assassination of President Kennedy. Abe Fortas received a great deal of criticism for his activities as an informal adviser to President Johnson. This type of relationship has occurred from time to time, however, principally between justices and the presidents who appointed them, continuing a pattern established before the justice reached the Court. Felix Frankfurter continued to advise Franklin D. Roosevelt after he took his seat on the court, as did Chief Justice Fred Vinson for Truman, Louis Brandeis for Woodrow Wilson, and a number of others throughout our history.

More striking perhaps is the fact that Chief Justice Warren Burger appears to have discussed issues pending before the Court with and reported internal activities of the Court to President Nixon and other top administration officials.[6] This would seem like a breach of the separation of powers, especially since the executive branch often appears before the Court. Burger also appears to have asked Nixon to use his influence with congressional Republicans to discourage them from proceeding with their attempt to impeach Justice William O. Douglas.

COMPLYING WITH THE COURT

It is one thing for the White House to enforce a court decision against someone else, and something quite different for it to comply with an order directed at the president when he has lost a case in the Supreme Court. At that point interesting constitutional questions arise that have the potential for substantial interbranch conflict. As we will see, however, presidents typically do comply with court orders, a task made easier by the general deference of the courts to the chief executive.

Presidential Compliance

The Constitution is ambiguous as to which branch shall have the final say in interpreting it. Jefferson, for example, argued that each branch has the authority to interpret the Constitution regarding its own actions. Thus, the president would be the final judge of his own conduct. Others disagreed and felt the Supreme Court should be the ultimate judge of the constitutionality of the executive's activities.

The Court made some progress in resolving this question in *Marbury* v. *Madison*, 1 Cranch 137 (1803). The case involved the requests of Marbury and others to have the Supreme Court order Secretary of State James Madison to deliver their commissions as justices of the peace in the District of Columbia. Congress had created these positions at the end of President John Adams's term, and he had appointed Federalists to serve in them but had not gotten their commissions to them by the time he left office. The new president, Thomas Jefferson, wanted to appoint fellow party members to the positions and therefore refused to deliver the commissions after he took office.

The Court held that although Marbury and his co-plaintiffs were entitled to receive their commissions, the law that gave the Supreme Court original jurisdiction over the case was unconstitutional. Thus, the Court could not order the president or his secretary of state to act. It thereby avoided a confrontation with Jefferson. At the same time, the Court proclaimed the administration's actions to be unlawful and, more significantly, asserted its right to make the final judgment on the constitutionality of actions of the other branches of government.

Marbury did not really settle the question of the president's obligation to accept and follow the Court's interpretation of the Constitution, because the president could argue that the law the Court voided pertained directly to the judicial branch. It was not until the *Dred Scott* v. *San-*

ford, 19 Howard 393 (1857), case that the Court again declared an act of Congress unconstitutional, and this time the law was not directly related to the judiciary. In the meantime the question of the final arbiter of the Constitution remained open.

Several presidents, including Jefferson, Lincoln, and Franklin D. Roosevelt, have threatened privately to disobey Court decisions that went against them, but in each case defiance was unnecessary because the Court supported them. The most blatant instance of a president's threatening to disobey a Court order occurred in a case in which the Court was asked to enjoin President Andrew Johnson from administering military governments in southern states following the Civil War. In oral argument before the Court, the president, speaking through his attorney general, let it be known that he would not comply with a decision enjoining him from implementing the laws. The Court, in turn, found in *Mississippi* v. *Johnson*, 4 Wallace 475 (1867), that it lacked jurisdiction to stop the president from performing his official duties that required executive discretion. We should also note that Johnson had vetoed these bills when Congress passed them, but he faced impeachment if he failed to execute them.

Nevertheless, presidents typically have obeyed Court decisions, even if it were costly to do so. There are two prominent examples of this in recent years that we will briefly examine. Near the end of President Truman's tenure and during the Korean War the United Steelworkers of America gave notice of an industry-wide strike. Concerned about steel production during wartime, the president ordered the secretary of commerce to seize and operate the steel mills. The steel companies then asked the courts to find the president's actions unconstitutional, and in *Youngstown Sheet and Tube Co.* v. *Sawyer*, 343 U.S. 579 (1952), the Supreme Court did so. It found that the president lacked the inherent power under the Constitution to seize the steel mills and that Congress had chosen not to give him statutory power to do so. Thus, in a rare occurrence, the president was ordered to reverse his actions, and Truman immediately complied.

The Watergate scandal produced another important case involving presidential prerogatives. Special Prosecutor Leon Jaworski subpoenaed tapes and documents relating to sixty-four conversations President Nixon had with his aides and advisers. Jaworski needed the material for prosecution of Nixon administration officials. The president claimed that executive privilege protected his private conversations with his assistants and refused to produce the subpoenaed material. Thus, the case worked its way quickly to the Supreme Court.

In *United States* v. *Nixon*, 418 U.S. 683 (1974), the Court unanimously ordered the president to turn the subpoenaed material over to the special prosecutor. Although Nixon had threatened not to comply with anything less than a "definitive" decision, he obeyed the Court and was forced to resign about two weeks later. The Court held that a claim of executive privilege unrelated to military, diplomatic, or national security matters cannot be absolute and in this case must give way to considerations of due process of law in criminal proceedings. Moreover, the justices reaffirmed that it was they and not the president who must be the final judge in such matters.

Presidents have not always been responsive to court orders, however. For example, in *United States* v. *Burr*, 25 Fed. Cas. 187 (No. 14,964) (1807), President Jefferson was subpoenaed to appear at the treason trial of Aaron Burr and to produce a letter. Jefferson refused to appear at the trial, but he did provide the document, stressing that he did so voluntarily and not because of judicial writ. Similarly, President James Monroe was subpoenaed as a witness in a trial, but he sent a written response instead.

The Civil War raised many difficult constitutional questions for the Court and the president. One set of cases found President Abraham Lincoln simply ignoring court orders. The president had suspended the writ of habeas corpus, and in the most famous of these cases, a citizen held prisoner by the military without the benefit of the normal constitutional rights sued for his freedom. Chief Justice Roger Taney ordered his release, but Lincoln refused to give him up to the U.S. marshal sent to bring him into court. The chief justice (on circuit duty) then held in *Ex parte Merryman*, 17 Fed. Cas. 144 (No. 9,487) (1861), that the president had exceeded his constitutional authority, but Lincoln simply ignored the decision and Merryman remained under arrest. Lincoln argued that he had not violated the Constitution but that it would be better for the president to violate a single provision to a limited extent than to have anarchy because of failure to suppress the rebellion in the South.

Another aspect of presidential compliance with Court decisions is the administration of laws that the Court has approved and that the president opposes. This issue has arisen most directly in the claims of some presidents to the right to decide not to execute laws they viewed as unconstitutional, even if they had received court approval. Jefferson's opposition to the Alien and Sedition Acts passed under his predecessor, John Adams, and upheld by the courts, led him to stop all prosecutions and pardon all those convicted under these laws when he took office. Andrew Jackson dismantled the Bank of the United States although the Court had approved it as constitutional.

This issue has never been really resolved, and presidents have often been lax in administering laws that they opposed. In modern times the Nixon administration was ordered by federal courts to enforce more strictly laws to eliminate segregation and sex discrimination in public educational institutions. Such court orders are rare, however.

If presidents are dissatisfied with Supreme Court decisions, their first thought is usually directed toward appointing new members with views similar to theirs. There are some other options, however. They might join in congressional efforts to remove certain types of cases from the Court's appellate jurisdiction. Congress has succeeded in such an action only once, however—on jurisdiction to hear appeals on certain writ of habeas corpus cases following the Civil War—and in this case the president supported the Court.

The president might support efforts to pass a constitutional amendment to overturn a Court interpretation of the Constitution. President Reagan supported amendments to allow prayer in public schools and to prohibit abortions. Such efforts rarely succeed, however. On the other hand, when the Court has made a statutory interpretation, it can be reversed by simply changing the law to clarify the intentions of those supporting the policy. In a notable example, in 1953 President Eisenhower supported legislation that deeded federal mineral rights on offshore lands to the states after the Court had held in 1951 that the federal government owned the rights.

Deference to the President

A principal reason that complying with judicial decisions has rarely posed a problem for the president is the small number of instances in which the courts have held presidential actions to be in violation of the Constitution. Rarely have even these decisions interfered significantly with the president's policies, the *Youngstown* case being a major exception. More typically these cases have dealt with matters such as presidential instructions to customs officials or the suspension of the writ of habeas corpus.

Most presidential actions are not based upon the president's prerogatives under the Constitution and therefore do not lend themselves to constitutional adjudication. Effective opposition to most presidential policies must focus on the broader political arena. Moreover, it is especially difficult to prevent the president from acting. Most challenges occur only after the fact. On some occasions it is possible to oppose the president through challenging the constitutionality of laws he supported and Congress passed. Such efforts are rarely successful, but they were important during the early years of the New Deal, as we have seen. In the end, however, President Roosevelt prevailed.

In the area of foreign and defense policy the Court has interpreted the Constitution and statutes to give the president broad discretion to act. In general the history of litigation regarding challenges to the president's actions in the field of national security policy has been one of avoidance, postponement of action, or deference to the chief executive. The judiciary has been content to find that discretionary actions of the executive branch were beyond its competence to adjudicate.

Since the Civil War, presidents have been allowed especially broad powers in wartime. In the war between the states the Supreme Court approved President Lincoln's deployment of troops during hostilities in the absence of a declaration of war and gave the chief executive discretion to determine the extent of force the crisis demanded and when an emergency existed. Similarly, it upheld the president's blockade of the South, expansion of the army and navy beyond statutory limits, calling out the militia, and most of his suspensions of habeas corpus.

In World War I, Congress delegated President Woodrow Wilson broad authority to regulate communications, transportation, and the economy; to draft soldiers; and even to censor criticism, all with the approval of the Court. Franklin D. Roosevelt exercised even broader economic powers during World War II: he relocated Japanese-Americans from the West Coast to relocation centers and confiscated their property, and he bypassed the courts to establish special military commissions to try Nazi saboteurs, again with the Court's okay.

During the period of U.S. military involvement in Vietnam, there was never a declaration or other formal congressional authorization for the war. Many people, including many legal authorities, felt that U.S. participation in the war without a formal declaration by Congress was unconstitutional, and several dozen cases were brought in federal court by opponents of the war to challenge various aspects of its legality. Yet the Supreme Court simply refused to hear all but one of these cases and never issued a written opinion regarding the war. A combination of deference to the president and pragmatic politics (what would happen if the war were declared unconstitutional while troops were engaged in combat?) rendered the Court irrelevant to the issue.

It is interesting that in times in which presidents are most likely to stretch their power, that is, in wartime, the courts are the least likely to intervene. When they do, the war may be over. For example, following both the Civil War and World War II, the Supreme Court held that civilians could not be tried by military tribunals when the civilian courts were open. In each case, however, the president at which the decision was directed was no longer living.

Outside of war, the courts have found that the president also has substantial discretion to act in the foreign affairs and defense areas. He has broad prerogatives to act in negotiating international agreements, withholding state secrets from the public, allocating international airline routes, terminating treaties, making executive agreements, recognizing foreign governments, protecting U.S. interests abroad with military activities, punishing foreign adversaries, executing international agreements, and acquiring and divesting foreign territory.

In the domestic sphere the president's prerogatives are closely linked to maintaining order. Thus, the president has discretion to declare and terminate national emergencies and even martial law. He may also call out the militia or the regular armed forces to control internal friction and keep the peace.

Of course, the president does not always receive supportive decisions from the courts. President Nixon, for example, was told he could not impound funds appropriated by Congress, engage in electronic surveillance without a search warrant, or prevent the publication of the Pentagon papers. He also was forced to turn over the Watergate tapes. Yet Nixon's presidency was atypical. Most presidents operate under few constraints from the courts.

It is not unusual for actions of executive-branch officials to be found to be in violation of statutes passed by Congress, usually for exceeding the discretionary limits in the law. In these situations the judiciary is finding that the law, not the Constitution, must be changed, or perhaps just clarified, before the president's agents can take certain actions. Depending on the prevailing view in Congress, this may pose little problem for the president. At any rate, rarely are the issues involved central to his program.

JUDICIAL POWERS

In addition to enforcing court orders, presidents have some judicial instruments of their own. They can issue pardons, grant clemency, and proclaim amnesty. These powers are exclusively theirs and theirs alone.

Over the years the exercise of this judicial authority by presidents has sparked controversy. Ford's unconditional pardon of his predecessor, Richard Nixon, in 1974 became a major political issue that adversely affected his electability two years later. Issued prior to a conviction or even an indictment of the former president, the pardon "for all offenses against the United States which Richard Nixon has committed or may have committed or taken part in during the period from January 20, 1969, through August 9, 1974," precluded any criminal prosecution. Although Ford was accused of subverting the legal process, his power to issue the pardon was not disputed.[7] Whether Nixon's acceptance of it amounted to an admission of guilt is also unclear.

In addition to the issuance of unconditional pardons, presidents can grant conditional ones. In 1974 the Supreme Court upheld President Eisenhower's commutation of a death sentence provided that the individual never be paroled. In 1972 President Nixon granted executive clemency to former labor leader James Hoffa on the condition that he refrain from further union activities.

Presidents may also issue general amnesty to those who have impeded war efforts. President Lincoln exercised this authority in 1863 in an effort to persuade southern deserters to return to the Union. His successor, Andrew Johnson, granted a universal amnesty in 1868 to all those who participated in the insurrection in order to heal the wounds of the Civil War. Twentieth-century presidents have used this power to pardon those convicted of crimes who subsequently served in the military and to prevent the imposition of wartime penalties (still on the books) on those who failed to register for the draft during peacetime.

The most sweeping and controversial amnesty proclamation in recent times occurred in 1977. Implementing one of his campaign promises, President Carter pardoned all Vietnam draft resisters and asked the Defense Department to consider the cases of military deserters during that war on an individual basis. Congress attempted to undercut Carter's general pardon by prohibiting the use of funds to execute his order. It was unsuccessful, however, because the president's directive to the Justice Department did not require a separate appropriation.

CONCLUSION

The president is involved in vital relationships with the judicial branch, especially the Supreme Court. He attempts to influence its decisions through the process of selecting judges and justices and the arguments of his subordinates before the courts. There are strong congressional constraints on him in the selection of judges, however, and presidents sometimes err in their choice of nominees. Although the executive branch has skilled litigators before the federal appellate courts and has a clear record of success, the chief executive is ultimately dependent upon the judgment of members of a branch of government much more independent of him than the legislature.

A judicial decision does not end the president's relationship with the courts on an issue. In the capacity as chief executive the president may be obliged to enforce decisions, a responsibility that sometimes conflicts with his policy goals. Moreover, although the judiciary is generally deferential to the president, he may be ordered to comply with a holding against an action of his. Such decisions do not touch most of what presidents do, but in some instances they do hamper their actions. Thus, the president's relations with the courts are characterized both by conflict and by harmony, and influencing judicial decisions remains an important, but at times frustrating, priority for the White House.

NOTES

1. Quoted in J. Woodford Howard, Jr., *Courts of Appeals in the Federal Judicial System: A Study of the Second, Fifth, and District of Columbia Circuits* (Princeton: Princeton University Press, 1981), p. 101.

2. Griffin Bell, quoted in Nina Totenberg, "Will Judges Be Chosen Rationally?" *Judicature* 60 (August–September 1976): 93.

3. Dwight Eisenhower, quoted in Henry J. Abraham, *Justices and Presidents: A Political History of Appointments to the Supreme Court* (New York: Oxford University Press, 1974), p. 246.

4. William Safire, *Before the Fall: An Inside View of the Pre-Watergate White House* (Garden City, N.Y.: Doubleday, 1975), pp. 237–38, 242.

5. Earl Warren, *The Memoirs of Chief Justice Earl Warren* (Garden City, N.Y.: Doubleday, 1971), pp. 337-42.

6. John Ehrlichman, *Witness to Power: The Nixon Years* (New York: Simon and Schuster, 1982), p. 133.

7. There were many allegations of a deal between the two men. Some observers accused Ford of having agreed to the pardon in exchange for his nomination as vice president by Nixon. Ford vehemently denied that such an agreement had been made in sworn testimony before the House Judiciary Committee in 1974.

SELECTED READINGS

Abraham, Henry J. *Justices and Presidents: A Political History of Appointments to the Supreme Court*. New York: Oxford University Press, 1974.

Bond, Jon R. "The Politics of Court Structure: The Addition of New Federal Judges, 1949–1978." *Law and Policy Quarterly* 2 (April 1980): 181–88.

Chase, Harold. *Federal Judges: The Appointing Process*. Minneapolis: University of Minnesota Press, 1972.

Danelski, David J. *A Supreme Court Justice Is Appointed*. New York: Random House, 1964.

Goldman, Sheldon. "Reagan's Judicial Appointments at Mid-Term: Shaping the Bench in His Own Image." *Judicature* 66 (March 1983): 334–47.

Grossman, Joel B. *Lawyers and Judges: The ABA and the Politics of Judicial Selection*. New York: Wiley, 1965.

Harris, Richard. *Decision*. New York: Dutton, 1971.

Schmidhauser, John R. *Judges and Justices: The Federal Appellate Judiciary*. Boston: Little, Brown, 1979.

Scigliano, Robert. *The Supreme Court and the Presidency*. New York: Free Press, 1971.

Slotnick, Elliot E. "The ABA Standing Committee on Federal Judiciary: A Contemporary Assessment, Part I." *Judicature* 66 (March 1983): 348–62.

Stidham, Ronald S., Robert A. Carp, and C. K. Rowland. "Patterns of Presidential Influence on the Federal District Courts: An Analysis of the Appointment Process." *Presidential Studies Quarterly* 14 (Fall 1984): 548–60.

14

Studying the Presidency

Although many people find the presidency the most fascinating subject in American politics, unfortunately it is not a topic that is easy to research. This chapter is an overview of studying the presidency. It is not a "how to" essay, nor is it a bibliographic review of the vast literature on the chief executive. Serious discussion of either topic could fill entire books.

Instead, this chapter is designed to alert students to the implications, both positive and negative, of adopting particular research approaches and methodologies. Armed with this awareness, researchers should be able better to understand the advantages and limitations of various research designs. Thus, they should be in a better position to choose one that comes closest to meeting their needs. The last portion of the chapter tries to ease the task of research by presenting some of the more accessible and useful sources of data on the presidency.

APPROACHES

There are many approaches to studying the presidency, ranging from those that are concerned with the constitutional authority of the office to those dealing with the personality dynamics of a particular president. By "approaches" we mean orientations that guide researchers to ask certain questions and employ certain concepts rather than others. In this section we focus on some of the principal approaches employed by political scientists who study the presidency. The categories we use are neither mutually exclusive nor completely comprehensive. The goal here is to increase our sensitivity to the implications of different approaches for what is studied, how a subject is investigated, and what types of conclusions may be reached rather than to create an ideal typology of scholarship on the presidency. Similarly, our focus is on approaches per se rather than on a critique of the work of individual authors or on a comprehensive review of the literature.[1]

Legal Perspective

The oldest approach to studying the presidency is what we shall term the "legal" perspective. Its principal focus is on the president's formal powers. Studying these involves scholars in analysis of the Constitution, laws, treaties, and legal precedents. Key questions concern the sources, scope, and use of the president's formal powers, including their legal limitations.[2] Since these have changed over time, there is typically a heavy historical orientation to the legal approach.

The legal perspective, with its emphasis on the historical development of the office and the checks and balances in the Constitution, also lends itself to discussion of the president's place in our system of government, both as it is and as scholars think it ought to be. Thus, there is often a clear prescriptive or normative element in these studies.

The range of issues involving presidential authority is great. Illustrations from the past decade include the right of the president to impound funds appropriated by Congress, the scope of the president's lawmaking power when he issues executive orders and proclamations, President Reagan's hiring freeze in 1981, the president's use of the pocket veto during brief congressional recesses, the constitutionality of the legislative veto, and claims of executive privilege. Foreign policy issues have also reached the courts. These include the conduct of the Vietnam War by Presidents Johnson and Nixon without explicit congressional authorization, President Carter's termination of the U.S. defense treaty with Taiwan and his settlement of the Iranian assets and hostage issues, and the president's use of executive agreements as substitutes for treaties.

Although the legal perspective is an important one and although it has a deservedly honored place both in political science and in a nation that prides itself on the rule of law, it also has limitations. A major one is that it neglects most of what the president does. Only a small portion of the president's behavior is prescribed by the wording of the Constitution, treaties, laws, or court decisions. Thus, most of the president's relationships with, for example, the public, the Congress, the White House staff, and the bureaucracy do not fall easily within the purview of the legal perspective. Instead, this behavior falls under the heading of informal or extraconstitutional powers. Similarly, since the focus of the legal perspective is on the presidency itself, topics such as the press's coverage of the presidency, the public's evaluation of the president, and other relationships that involve nongovernmental actors are largely ignored.

Equally significant, the legal perspective does not lend itself to explanation. Studies focusing on the boundaries of appropriate actions do not seek to explain why behavior occurs or what its consequences are. Moreover, the fact that scholars employing this approach often rely heavily upon case studies inevitably makes the basis of their generalizations somewhat tenuous.

Thus, although studies adopting the legal perspective make important contributions to our understanding of American politics, they do not and cannot answer most of the questions that entice researchers to study the presidency. For this we must turn to alternative approaches.

Institutional Perspective

A second basic approach to the study of the presidency focuses on it as an institution in which the president has certain roles and responsibilities and is involved in numerous structures and processes. Thus, the structure, functions, and operation of the presidency become the center of attention. These concerns are broad enough to include agencies such as the Office of Management and Budget and units in the White House such as the legislative liaison operation. Scholars following this approach can move beyond formal authority and investigate, for example, the formulation, coordination, promotion, and implementation of the president's legislative program or the president's relationship with the media.[3] As with the legal perspective, scholars employing the institutional approach often trace the persistence and adaptation of organizations and processes over time. This gives much of the literature a historical perspective and also lends itself to evaluations of the success of institutional arrangements.

The institutional approach plays a crucial role in helping us to understand the presidency. Although at one time much of the work that falls under this heading emphasized formal organizational structure and rules, such as organization charts of the White House or procedures in the budgetary process, in more recent years the focus has moved to the behavior of those involved in the operation of the presidency. This has increased the utility of institutional research. By focusing on processes and behavior, scholars collect empirical data on a variety of activities. Quite clearly, it is necessary to know what political actors are doing before we can discuss the significance of their behavior, much less examine analytical questions of relationships such as those pertaining to influence. By seeking to identify patterns of behavior and study interactions, such as those between the White House and the Congress, OMB, or media, institutional research not only tells us what happens but, more significantly, starts us on the road toward understanding *why* it happens. When scholars examine, say, presidential efforts to influence the media, they are focusing on typical and potentially significant behavior that may explain patterns of media coverage of the White House. The question of taking the final step and *testing* for such a relationship leads us to a discussion of limitations of this research.

There are two principal limitations to the institutional approach. First, there is typically a heavy emphasis on description at the expense of explanation. We know a great deal more about how presidents have organized their White House staffs, for example, than the differences it makes for the kinds of advice they receive. In other words, we know more about the process per se than about its consequences. This in turn provides a tenuous basis for the prescriptive aspect of some institutional research. We cannot have confidence in recommendations about presidential advisory systems, for example, until we understand the impact of different arrangements.

The second limitation is that in their emphasis on organizations and processes, some institutional studies downplay or even ignore the significance of other factors such as political skills, ideology, and personality. Indeed, the implicit assumption that emerges from the often extensive attention scholars devote to structures and processes is that they are very significant. This may not always be the case, however. Using the example above, it may be that the world view that a president brings to the White House is more important in influencing his decisions than the way he organizes his advisers. Similarly, ideology, party, and constituency views may be more important than the White House legislative liaison operation in influencing congressional votes on the president's program.

Power Perspective

In the political power approach to the study of the presidency, best represented by Richard Neustadt's *Presidential Power*,[4] researchers shift their focus from institutions to the people within them. The fundamental premise of this research is that it is the exploiting of political influence rather than the expanding of legal authority or the adjusting of institutional mechanisms that is the key to the president's success. It rejects the assumption that the president effectively wields power or that he possesses enough power to meet his responsibilities.

Since researchers employing this approach view power as a function of personal politics rather than formal authority or position, they turn their attention to the internal dynamics of the presidency. They find the president operating in a pluralistic environment in which there are numerous actors with independent power bases and perspectives different from his. Thus, the president must marshal his resources to persuade others to do as he wishes.

Power is a concept that involves relationships between people, so this approach forces researchers to try to explain behavior and to seek to develop generalizations about it. Moreover, the necessity for the president to attempt to exercise influence in several arenas leads those following the power perspective to adopt an expansive view of presidential politics that includes both governmental actors, such as the Congress, bureaucracy, and White House staff, and those outside of government, such as the public, the press, and interest groups. In studying presidential interactions the dependent variables, what authors are trying to explain, are many and may include congressional or public support for the president, presidential decisions, press coverage of the White House, bureaucratic policy implementation, or a set of policy options prepared by the bureaucracy for the president.[5] Because there are no assumptions of presidential success or the smooth functioning of the presidency, the effect of bureaucratic politics and other organizational factors in the executive branch are as important to investigate as behavior in more openly adversarial institutions such as Congress.

Although the power approach examines a number of questions left unexplored in other approaches, it also slights certain topics. With its focus on relationships, it does not naturally lend itself to investigation of questions of the president's accountability, the limitations of his legal powers, or the day-to-day operation of the institution of the presidency.

Some commentators are bothered by the top-down orientation of the power approach, that is, viewing the presidency from the perspective of the president.[6] They feel that it neglects the question of examining the presidency from the perspective of the American political system and that it carries an implicit assumption that the president should be the principal decision maker in American politics and that he should typically get what he wants. These critics argue that such premises are too Machiavellian and that an evaluation of the goals and means of presidents must be added to analyses of power.

Others feel that the depiction of the president's environment as basically confrontational, with conflicting interests of political actors creating centrifugal forces the president must try to overcome, is exaggerated. Moreover, the heavy emphasis placed on power or influence may lead analysts to underestimate the importance of ideology or other influences on behavior.[7]

Psychological Perspective

Perhaps the most fascinating and popular studies of the presidency are those that approach the topic from the perspective of psychological analysis. The most well known of these focus on psychopathology, essentially the negative manifestations of inner needs and ego defenses. They are based on the premises that personality is a constant and that personality needs may be displaced onto political objects and become unconscious motivations for presidential behavior. Some of these studies take the form of psychobiographies of presidents,[8] while others are attempts to categorize presidents on the basis of selected personality dimensions.[9]

Personality is an important factor in behavior and adds an important element to the study of the presidency. We need to take what goes on inside a president's head into account if we are to understand his behavior as president. Such a perspective forces us to ask why presidents behave as they do. It also forces us to look beyond external factors, such as advisers, Congress, the media, and interest groups, that may attempt to influence the chief executive for answers to this question. If they were not strongly affected by their personalities, presidents would neither be very important nor merit such attention.

Psychological analysis is also applied to the study of the presidency in broader ways. Presidents and their staffs have cognitive processes through which they view the world and that affect their perceptions of why people and nations behave as they do, how power is distributed, how the economy functions, and what the appropriate roles are of government, presidents, and advisers. Their cognitive processes also function to screen and organize an enormous volume of information about the complex and uncertain environment in which they function. Objective reality, intellectual abilities, and personal interests and experiences merge with personal needs, such as those to manage inconsistency and maintain self-esteem, to influence the decisions and policies that emerge from the White House. Cognitive processes simplify decision making and lessen stress, especially on complex and controversial policies such as the war in Vietnam. Group dynamics may also influence decision making, limiting the appraisal of alternatives by group members. Efforts to sort out the impact of these factors are only in their early stages, but there is little question that we cannot claim to understand presidential decision making until we do so.[10]

Although psychological studies can sensitize us to important personality factors that influence presidential behavior, they are probably the most widely criticized writings on the presidency. A fundamental problem is that they often display a strong tendency toward being reductionist. That is, they focus very heavily upon the variable of personality to the exclusion of most other factors in their attempts to explain behavior. As a result, they convey little information about the institution of the presidency or the relationships between psychological and institutional variables. Alternative explanations for behavior are rarely considered in psychological studies.

A related drawback is that psychological studies have a tendency to focus on the negative aspects of a presidency. Scholars, like others, are quite naturally drawn to investigate problems. Thus, the principal focus often becomes the relationship between the personality flaws of the president and what the author feels to be some of the chief executive's most unfortunate actions. This reinforces the reductionist tendency because it is usually not difficult to find plausible parallels between psychological and decisional deficiencies.

The availability of data is also a problem for psychological studies. It is difficult to discern unconscious motivations or cognitive processes and to differentiate their impact from that of external factors. Often authors must rely upon biographical information of questionable validity about the behavior and environment of presidents, stretching back to their childhoods.

Summary

Each of the four approaches to studying the presidency—the legal, institutional, power, and psychological perspectives—has advantages and disadvantages for the researcher. Each is more useful for answering some questions than for answering others, each informs us about a different aspect of the presidency, and each focuses on certain variables at the expense of others. Moreover, while the power and psychological perspectives are stronger on their concerns for explanation, the legal and institutional orientations are better at providing broad perspectives on the presidency.

Those thinking of doing research on the presidency should carefully determine what it is they want to investigate *before* selecting an approach, because not all approaches will be relevant to answering their questions. Selecting an approach is not the last decision one must make in deciding on a research project, however. Appropriate methods must be employed as well as the proper overall orientation.

METHODS

Although the American presidency has always been a prime topic of research interest for political scientists, our progress in understanding the institution has been very slow. One reason for this is that scholars have generally relied upon modes of analysis that do not easily lend themselves to examining questions on basic relationships of the presidency. In this section we explore some of the methods used by scholars to study the presidency, paying special attention to their advantages and limitations. This is not a "how to" discussion of methodology. Instead, our goal is to understand that some methods are more useful than others for investigating important questions regarding the presidency. Throughout, we should keep in mind that methods are not ends in themselves but rather techniques for examining research questions generated by the approaches discussed above.

Traditional Methods

The typical work on the presidency has focused on describing events, behavior, and personalities. Many studies, written by journalists or former executive-branch officials, rely heavily upon personal experiences for data. Unfortunately, such anecdotal material is generally subjective, fragmentary, and impressionistic. When explanations of the causes and consequences of presidential relationships do occur, the data base is typically composed of a single or a small number of examples. There is usually no possibility of controlling for alternative explanations. Thus, we must be very cautious about reaching generalizations based on this type of analysis, even when the anecdotes on which they are based come from eyewitnesses. In reading the memoirs of aides to Lyndon Johnson or Richard Nixon, one finds very different perceptions of the president and his presidency. As Henry Kissinger tells us about the Nixon White House staff, "It is a truism that none of us really knew the inner man. More significant, each member of his entourage was acquainted with a slightly different Nixon subtly adjusted to the President's judgment of the aide or to his assessment of his interlocutor's background."[11]

The commentary and reflections of insiders, whether participants or participant observers, are limited by their own perspectives, which may be rather narrow. Proximity to power can hinder rather than enhance one's perspective and breadth of view. The reflections of those who have served in government may be colored by the strong points of view they advocated or by a need to justify their decisions and behavior while in office. Faulty memories add a further element of uncertainty to such data. Moreover, proximity to power does not necessarily bring insiders insight or understanding of the process in which they have participated. Few insiders are trained to think in analytical terms of generalizations based on representative data and controls for alternative explanations.

Let us illustrate the problem with a few examples. One of the crucial decision points in America's involvement in fighting in Vietnam occurred during July 1965 when President Johnson committed the United States to large-scale combat operations. In his memoirs the president describes his process of making a decision on this issue, and he goes to considerable lengths in interpreting this complex event to show that he considered all the options available at this time very carefully.[12] One of his aides later provided a detailed account of the dialogue between Johnson and some of his advisers.[13] It shows the president probing deeply for answers, challenging the premises and factual bases of options, and playing the devil's advocate. Yet in a recent book a presidency scholar has argued persuasively that this "debate" was a charade, staged by the president to lend legitimacy to the decision he had already made.[14]

Another useful example, this one focusing on attributions of influence, is President Johnson's efforts at obtaining the support or at least the neutrality of Senate Finance Committee chairman Harry Byrd of Virginia on the 1964 tax cut. Hubert Humphrey reported in his memoirs that Johnson cajoled Byrd into letting the tax bill out of committee, relying on Lady Bird's charm, liquor, and his own famous "treatment."[15] Presidential aide Jack Valenti tells a different story, however. He writes that the president obtained the senator's cooperation by promising to hold the budget under $100 billion.[16] Thus, we have two eyewitnesses reporting on two different tactics employed by the president and each attributing Senator Byrd's response to the presidential behavior that he observed.

To confuse matters further, Henry Hall Wilson, one of the president's congressional liaison aides, indicates that both eyewitnesses were wrong. According to Wilson, when the president proudly told his chief congressional liaison aide, Lawrence O'Brien, about his obtaining Byrd's agreement to begin hearings on the tax cut on December 7, O'Brien replied, "You didn't get a thing. I already had a commitment for the 7th."[17] In other words, Johnson's efforts were irrelevant. Both eyewitnesses were wrong in attributing influence to him.

Even tapes of conversations in the Oval Office may be misleading. As Henry Kissinger explains regarding the Watergate tapes,

> Anyone familiar with Nixon's way of talking could have no doubt he was sitting on a time bomb. His random, elliptical, occasionally emotional manner of conversation was bound to shock, and mislead, the historian. Nixon's indirect style of operation simply could not be gauged by an outsider. There was no way of telling what Nixon had put forward to test his interlocutor and what he meant to be taken seriously; and no outsider could distinguish a command that was to be followed from an emotional outburst that one was at liberty to ignore—perhaps was even expected to ignore.[18]

We have seen, then, that there are a number of limitations to the use of insider accounts. It does not follow that these are not useful. On the contrary, they often contain numerous insights that may guide more rigorous research, and they provide invaluable records of perceptions of participants in the process and events of the presidency. As long as the researcher understands the limitations of these works and does not accept them at face value, they can be a considerable asset.

Not all studies of the presidency that employ traditional methods are written by insiders. Many, such as Richard Tanner Johnson's *Managing the White House*,[19] are written by scholars, based primarily on the observations of others. Many of these observations are repeated and become the conventional wisdom. As a consequence, new studies based on old sources may add little to our knowledge of what happened or our understanding of why.

Problems also arise when researchers make assertions about the behavior of the public. They often fail to look at available systematic data. For example, most discussions of the president's relationships with the public include a section on the influence of "rally events," dramatic international events involving the United States that provide the president with a sudden surge of popular support. The problem with such discussions is that they are not based on examinations of relevant data. When we do examine the data (see Chapter 4) we find that sudden surges of, say, 10 percent in presidential approval rarely occur, and the events that seem to generate them are highly idiosyncratic and do not seem to differ significantly from other events that were not followed by sizable surges in presidential approval. Moreover, most potential rally events fail to generate much additional approval for the president.[20]

Quantitative Analyses

Research on the presidency, then, has often failed to meet the standards of contemporary political science, including the careful definition and measurement of concepts, the rigorous specification and testing of propositions, the employment of appropriate quantitative methods, and the use of empirical theory to develop hypotheses and explain findings.

As we might expect, research on the presidency, taken as a whole, has not advanced our understanding of the institution very far. We lack a fundamental understanding of why things happen as they do. We have generally not focused on explanations, the relationships between two or more variables, but on descriptions. This situation presents a striking paradox: The single most important institution in American politics is the one that political scientists understand the least.

To increase our understanding of the presidency we need to move beyond the description of the institution and its occupants and attempt to explain the behavior we observe. In addition, we must seek to reach generalizations rather than being satisfied with discrete, often ad hoc analyses. To explain we must examine relationships, and to generalize we must look at these relationships under many circumstances. Quantitative analysis can be an extremely useful tool in these endeavors.[21]

There have been three principal constraints on using quantitative analysis to study the presidency. The first, the frequent failure to pose analytical questions, has already been discussed. The second constraint has been the small number of cases, or presidents. Viewing the presidency as a set of relationships, however, helps to overcome this problem. Although there may be few presidents, there are many persons involved in relationships with each president, including the entire public, the membership of Congress, the federal bureaucracy, and world leaders. It is these relationships on which we can profitably focus, and because there are so many people interacting with the president in one form or another, we are no longer inhibited by the small universe of presidents.

This leads us to the third perceived constraint on the quantitative study of the presidency: lack of data. Since scholars of the presidency have typically been more interested in description than analysis, they have often been primarily concerned with "inside" data on the president and the presidency. As we have seen, however, this usually is only one side of a relationship, and we need to be looking at both sides if we are to develop reliable explanations.

When we pose analytical questions, we are naturally led to search for data on the causes and consequences of presidential behavior. For example, we may ask what the president wants from other political actors, what he is trying to get people to do. Among other things, the president wants support from the public; positive coverage from the media; votes for his programs from Congress; options, information, and analyses from his advisers; and faithful policy implementation from the bureaucracy. Thus, we can look for data on these political actors, whose behavior is usually the dependent variable, that is, what we are trying to explain, in our hypotheses. Similarly, we can seek data on independent variables, that is, causes of behavior toward the president, such as the determinants of public opinion, congressional support, and bureaucratic faithfulness.

The advantage of quantitative analysis of the presidency can be seen in the quantitative studies that have been done already. For example, one of the most crucial relationships of the presidency is the president's standing in the public. Why are presidents as popular (or as unpopular) as they are? We are just beginning to make some headway in the investigation of this question.[22] Related to these studies are those of the attitudes and beliefs of children toward the presidency and the president.[23] This research has come out of the subfield of political socialization. Substantial progress in understanding public support for the president, a factor of great significance to the operation of the presidency, would simply be impossible without the use of quantitative analysis and the technique of survey research.

The other side of this relationship is the president's leadership of public opinion. We know presidents devote considerable efforts to this task, but without quantitative analyses our understanding of the impact of presidential efforts to lead or manipulate public opinion will remain almost completely conjectural. Fortunately, a few scholars have begun to explore this area with quantitative techniques, including experimentation. Some have focused on the public's response to presidential leadership,[24] while others are concerned with variance in the content of what the president presents to the public.[25] Other efforts have focused on the important questions of the nature of media coverage[26] and its effect on public approval and expectations of the president.[27]

The study of presidential-congressional relations has also been advanced through the use of quantitative analysis. We have been able empirically to test propositions about the extent of presidential coattails, the pull of the president's party affiliation, the influence of the level of the president's public approval and electoral support, and the significance of presidential legislative skills.[28] Many of our findings have been counterintuitive, and none of them would have been possible without the use of quantitative analysis. As in the case of the president's public support, we have only scratched the surface of the utility of quantitative techniques.

Even more exciting is the prospect of applying quantitative analysis to entirely new areas of presidency research. One such area in which quantitative analysis would be useful is that of presidential decision making, including presidential advisory systems. Nearly every student of the presidency has at one time or another discussed in lectures, writings, or both, how the organization of the White House staff influences presidential decisions, probably illustrating the point with examples like Richard Nixon's infamous "Berlin Wall." Yet it is difficult to show that the organization of the White House staff has any influence whatsoever on presidential decisions. This is not to say that it has no effect; it is to point out, however, that we cannot have confidence in conclusions based on our present understanding of presidential decision making. We need to measure information flow, including the options, information, and analyses placed before the president, in different organizational structures and with different personalities on the top. Only then will we be able to state with confidence how organizational structure affects the options and information received by the president.

We are also interested in other influences on presidential decision making. Who influences the president? An article by Cole and Wayne illustrates the utility of applying quantitative analysis to such questions.[29] How do external constraints and pressures, such as public opinion, the state of the economy, and international events, affect presidential decisions and decision making? Some progress is being made. Studies have examined the effect of a crisis situation on decision-making processes;[30] the influence of the public's approval of the president on the scheduling and conduct of press conferences;[31] and staff attitudes and communication and influence patterns in domestic policy making.[32]

Another area inviting quantitative analysis is that of policy implementation. Scholars have generally given the president's role as "executor" of the law limited attention, and most of what attention it has received has been of an anecdotal or case-study nature. First, we must identify the variables critical to successful implementation, such as communications, resources, implementors' dispositions, bureaucratic structure, and follow-up mechanisms. Then we need to develop measures of them as well as of implementation itself. Some very interesting survey work has been done on dispositions.[33] Finally, to make much headway toward understanding presidential policy implementation, we should employ quantitative methods to relate, systematically and empirically, possible causes with possible effects.

The proper use of quantitative analysis, like any other type of analysis, is predicated upon a close linkage between the methods selected and the theoretical arguments underlying the hypotheses being tested. A theoretical argument requires an emphasis on explanation, that is, *why* two variables are related. If closer attention is given to the use of theory in research on the presidency, our understanding of the institution will increase more rapidly than it has in the past.

Despite its utility for investigating a wide range of questions dealing with the presidency, quantitative analysis is not equally useful for studying all areas of the presidency. The research situations in which quantitative analysis is least likely to be useful are those in which there is a lack of variance in the variables under study. If the focus of research is just one president and the researcher is concerned not with the president's interactions with others but with how factors such as the president's personality, ideas, values, attitudes, and ideology influence his decisions, quantitative analysis will be of little help. The independent variables are unlikely to vary much during a term in office. Similarly, factors in the president's environment, such as the federal structure of U.S. government or the basic capitalist structure of our economy, vary little over considerable periods of time, and it is therefore difficult to employ quantitative analysis to gauge their impact on the presidency.

If we are able to move beyond case studies of a single president or a single country to make comparisons across different presidents and different nations, such studies would provide us a firmer basis for confidence in our conclusions. Whether all the necessary factors can be controlled to make such comparisons useful is an open question, however.

Quantitative analysis is also unlikely to be useful for the legal approach to studying the presidency. There are well-established techniques for interpreting the law, and scholars with this interest will continue to apply them.[34]

Normative questions and arguments have always occupied a substantial percentage of the presidency literature, and rightly so. Can quantitative analyses aid scholars in addressing these concerns? The answer is "partially." Let us illustrate this with the example of what has probably been the central normative concern regarding the presidency: its power.

To reach conclusions about whether the presidency is too powerful or not powerful enough requires a three-part analysis. The first is an estimation of just how powerful the presidency is. Quantitative analysis can be of great utility in measuring and explaining the power in the presidency in a large range of relationships. For example, it can aid us in understanding the president's ability to influence Congress or the public. The significance of quantitative studies for the first part of this normative analysis, then, is clear.

The second step in answering the question of whether the presidency is too powerful or not powerful enough requires an analysis of the consequences of the power of the presidency. In other words, given the power of the presidency, as determined in part one, what difference does it make? Are poor people likely to fare better under a weak or a powerful presidency, for example? Are civil rights and civil liberties more or less likely to be abused?

To answer these and similar questions rigorously requires that we correlate levels of power with policy consequences. This does not have to be done quantitatively, of course, but such analyses will be more convincing if we have empirical measurements of economic welfare, school integration, wiretapping, military interventions, and other possible consequences of presidential power as well as measures of mediating variables.

Quantitative analyses will be of much less utility in arriving at conclusions to the third part of the analysis concerning presidential power: Do we evaluate the consequences of power levels determined in part two of the analysis positively or negatively? Whether we like or dislike the consequences will determine our ultimate answer to the question of how powerful the presidency should be. Our evaluation of these consequences will, of course, be determined by our values. Nevertheless, it is important to remember that quantitative analysis can be very useful in helping us to arrive at the point where our values dominate our conclusions.

In short, quantitative analysis leads us to examine theoretical relationships, and it has considerable utility in testing and refining them. While it cannot replace the sparks of creativity that lie behind conceptualizations, it may produce findings upon which syntheses may be built. Conversely, quantitative analysis may also reveal findings contrary to the conventional wisdom and thus prod scholars into challenging dominant viewpoints. To this extent it may also be useful in theory building.

No one should be under the illusion that quantitative analysis is easy to do or that there is consensus either on appropriate methods or on indicators. Some authors will inevitably employ indicators that lack validity and reliability and tests that are inappropriate. Their conclusions are likely to be incorrect. In addition, findings can and should be refined as our indicators and tests are refined. In essence, quantitative analysis poses methodological problems precisely because it attempts to measure concepts and to test for relationships carefully. Studies that do not involve such concerns are able to avoid methodological questions, but often at the expense of analytical potential.

Case Studies

One of the most widely used methods for studying the presidency is the case study. There are innumerable studies of individual presidents, presidential decisions, and presidential involvement in specific areas of policy and policy making.

The case-study method offers the researchers several advantages. It is a manageable way to present a wide range of complex information about individual and collective behavior involving the presidency. Since scholars have typically found it difficult to generate quantitative data regarding the presidency, the narrative form often seems to be the only available option.

Conversely, case studies are widely criticized on several grounds. First, they have typically been used more for descriptive than for analytical purposes. As we shall note below, however, this failing is not inherent in the nature of case studies. A more intractable problem is the idiosyncratic nature of case studies and the failure of authors to employ common analytical frameworks. This makes the accumulation of knowledge difficult because scholars are often, in effect, talking past each other. In the words of a close student of case studies:

> The unique features of every case—personalities, external events and conditions, and organizational arrangements—virtually ensure that studies conducted without the use of an explicit analytical framework will not produce findings that can easily be related to existing knowledge or provide a basis for future studies.[35]

Naturally, reaching generalizations about the presidency on the basis of unrelated case studies is a hazardous task.

Despite these drawbacks, case studies can be very useful in increasing our understanding of the presidency. For example, analyzing several case studies can serve as the basis for identifying problems in decision making[36] or in policy implementation.[37] These in turn may serve as the basis for recommendations to improve policy making. Case studies may also be used to test hypotheses or disconfirm theories, such as propositions about group dynamics drawn from social psychology.[38] Some authors employ case studies to illustrate the importance of looking at aspects of the presidency that have received little scholarly attention, such as presidential influence over interest groups.[39]

On a broader scale, Richard Neustadt used several case studies to help generate his influential model of presidential power.[40] Graham Allison used a case study of the Cuban missile crisis to illustrate the utility of three models of policy making.[41]

Writing a case study that has strong analytical, as opposed to descriptive, content is difficult to do. It requires considerable skill, creativity, and rigor. It is very easy to slip into a descriptive gear. Those who embark on preparing case studies are wise to remind themselves of the pitfalls discussed earlier. It is especially important to have an analytical framework in mind before one begins to provide direction to data gathering and the line of argument.

DATA SOURCES

Doing research requires data, and the difficulty of obtaining data has been one of the greatest frustrations of presidency scholars. Although data on the presidency usually do not come as neatly packaged and are not as easily generated as, say, data on Congress, there are many readily accessible sources of data that a researcher may exploit. This section provides an overview of data sources on the presidency. It is not designed to be comprehensive but rather to point students to the data sources and finding aids that are likely to be the most helpful in their research, some of which are, unfortunately, rarely used.

Locating the Law

A student wishing to research legal questions regarding the president's authority or questions regarding the substance of presidential policy making may need to locate the text of a statute, treaty, regulation, or court decision. In addition, one may need to know whether these are still in force and how others have interpreted them. Fortunately, the task is not as difficult as it may first appear.[42]

The *U.S. Statutes at Large* contains public laws, private laws (legislation intended for the relief of private parties, especially claims against the national government and exceptions to immigration and naturalization requirements), reorganization plans, joint resolutions, concurrent resolutions, and proclamations issued by the president. Since volume 52 (1938), each volume contains the laws enacted during a calendar year. Citations are to volume and page, as in 94 Stat. 2957.

After volume 64 (1950), treaties and other international agreements were no longer printed in the *Statutes at Large*. Instead, they are printed in a series entitled *United States Treaties and Other International Agreements*. Citations are given to the volume and then page number, as in 31 UST 405. Each volume has a country and subject index. All the treaties and other international agreements prior to 1950 have been collected in a single work: *Treaties and Other International Agreements of America, 1776–1949*.

Laws enacted at one point are later modified or repealed by Congress. To find the permanent body of U.S. law, one turns to the *United States Code*. In the last fifty years new editions of the code have been published in 1934, 1940, 1946, 1952, 1958, 1964, 1970, and 1976. Supplements to the code are issued after each session of Congress. The code consists of fifty titles organized by subject matter such as the Congress, the President, and Armed Forces. Index references are to title, section, and year, as in 3 USC 246 (1976) and 3 USC 53 (Supp. II, 1978). West Publishing compiles U.S. law in *U.S. Code Annotated*, which is well indexed and includes many editorial aids for researchers.

The *Federal Register* includes all presidential proclamations and executive orders that have general applicability and legal effect as well as other presidential directives, including memoranda, presidential determinations, letters, directives, reorganization plans, designations, and lists of messages transmitting budget recissions and deferrals. The *Federal Register* is published each weekday, except for official holidays. A typical citation would be 48 Fed. Reg. 2311 (1983), designating the volume, page, and year, respectively. An index cumulated over the past year is published monthly. The earliest forms for executive orders were not numbered. Clifford Lord compiled these executive orders in the *List and Index of Executive Orders: Unnumbered Series*. The first volume is a chronological listing of titles (up to January 11, 1941), and the second volume is a subject index.

The subject matter of the *Federal Register* is codified into fifty titles that generally parallel those of the *United States Code*. Each of the fifty titles is published annually in pamphlet form. The pamphlets contain all rules, regulations, and orders in force at the time and collectively are entitled the *Code of Federal Regulations* (CFR). Citations are by title and section, as in 19 CFR 123 (1980). The CFR is indexed annually.

The full decisions of the Supreme Court are published in bound volumes of the *United States Reports*. Citations are in the form of *Baker* v. *Carr*, 369 U.S. 186 (1962), which indicates that the decision may be found in volume 369, beginning on page 186. The first ninety volumes of the *Reports* were named after court reporters, Dallas, Cranch, Wheaton, Peters, Howard, Black, and Wallace, instead of having consecutive volume numbers. Thus, references take the form of *McCulloch* v. *Maryland*, 4 Wheaton 316 (1819). An invaluable aid is the "citator" or citation book, which tells the student whether a decision is still valid and authoritative. A decision by a lower court may be affirmed, reversed, or modified. Many college libraries also contain privately published texts of Supreme Court decisions entitled *Supreme Court Reporter* (beginning with the 1882 term) and *United States Supreme Court Reports, Lawyers' Edition* (which also includes summaries of the justices' opinions).

The *Index to Legal Periodicals* and since 1980 the *Current Law Index* cite articles from several hundred legal journals and newspapers. The coverage of the *Current Law Index* is more comprehensive and its indexing is more refined and specific than that of the *Index to Legal Periodicals*.

General Sources

There are two general collections of presidential documents and several general indexes that students of the presidency may find helpful for a wide variety of research projects.[43] The *Weekly Compilation of Presidential Documents (Weekly Comp.)* is a selective compilation of press releases and generally contains presidential proclamations, executive orders, addresses, remarks, letters, messages, and telegrams, memoranda to federal agencies, communications to Congress, bill signing statements, presidential press conferences, communiques with foreign heads of state, appointments, and nominations. The *Weekly Comp.* began August 2, 1965, and is published each Monday for the week ending the previous Saturday. Each issue contains a cumulative index to issues in the current quarter, and separate indexes are published semiannually and annually.

Unfortunately, the *Weekly Comp.* does not use a standard, controlled vocabulary. Thus, it is necessary to examine all possible synonyms for the topic of research. Another difficulty is that all index terms are grouped under broad generic headings such as Addresses and Remarks, Communications to Congress, and Letters, Messages, Telegrams, and Statements by the President. Researchers who are unsure as to the index term under which their research topic falls must consult the listings under each type of heading.

The National Archives has published official compilations of the presidential papers of Presidents Hoover, Truman, Eisenhower, Kennedy, Johnson, Nixon, Ford, and Carter. Each annual volume contains an index but not a cumulative index. KTO Press, however, has published single-volume indexes for each administration from Truman through Nixon. Private presses have published papers of Washington, Adams, Jefferson, Madison, Wilson, and Eisenhower.

Another useful index to valuable primary documents is *The Federal Index*, which is published monthly. It indexes diverse publicly and privately published sources, including the *Congressional Record, Federal Register, Weekly Comp., Washington Post*, the *Code of Federal Regulations*, the *U.S. Code*, House and Senate bills, and other documents of the federal government.

The Monthly Catalog of United States Government Publications has been the basic bibliography of U.S. government publications. Each issue lists government publications for that month, organized by the agency or congressional committee that issued them. There is an index at the end of each issue, and indexes are cumulated semiannually, annually, and every five years. Before 1976 the *Monthly Catalog* was indexed only by subject; since then it has been indexed by author, title, subject, series, key words, and other criteria.

The American Statistics Index is a comprehensive source of information regarding all executive-branch publications. It employs a standard vocabulary and provides lengthy annotations of each monograph. This valuable source lessens considerably the burden of conducting a thorough review of a subject.

Congressional Quarterly publishes an annual review of important presidential activities (e.g., *President Reagan's First Year*). These include transcripts of press conferences and major speeches and coverage of policy developments, nominations, relations with Congress, and similar matters. The *National Journal* provides regular coverage of the White House and the executive branch and even publishes the White House phone list semiannually.

Congress

The Congressional Information Service's *Index to Congressional Publications and Public Laws* is the best source for locating congressional documents, which are often excellent sources of information on the presidency.[44] The *Index* has two parts. One is an annual volume that includes a subject and name index, a title index, and indexes by bill, document, and report numbers for all significant congressional documents published that year. Cumulative indexes are published every four or five years. The second annual volume contains detailed abstracts describing the contents of the publications of all congressional committees, including quotations from the testimony of witnesses at hearings, statements from committee reports, and lists of those testifying at hearings. The abstracts are an efficient means for obtaining a sense of the substance of congressional hearings and the principal arguments in committee reports. Also useful are the detailed legislative histories that list all of the documents relevant to each bill enacted into law during the year. These histories are found at the end of each abstract volume.

The Congressional Information Service's *U.S. Serial Set Index, 1789–1969* is the only complete index to the materials published in the Serial Set of congressional documents. It is composed of twelve chronological units of several volumes each. Each unit includes one volume with a finding list arranged by report and document numbers and several additional volumes arranged by subject.

The Congressional Quarterly *Weekly Report* is an indispensable aid to following the current activities of Congress, the president's interactions with it, and the substance of public policy. Both in the *Weekly Report* and its yearly *Almanac*, Congressional Quarterly provides an extraordinary amount of quantitative data on congressional roll-call voting, election results, and many other matters. The *Weekly Report* also carries the president's veto messages and transcripts of his press conferences. It has a cumulative, quarterly index.

The *Almanac* provides an extensive review of the past year organized by substantive policy area in addition to the data mentioned above. The volumes entitled *Congress and the Nation* are similar to the *Almanac*, but each volume covers a four-year period coterminous with a presidential term. The *Guide to Congress* provides useful background on the president and Congress, and the *Guide to U.S. Elections* and its biennial paperback supplements are the best single source of presidential election statistics available anywhere. They are even disaggregated by congressional districts.

Finally, the Inter-University Consortium for Political and Social Research (ICPSR), located at the University of Michigan, provides data in the form of machine-readable tapes to its member universities. On Congress these include roll-call voting records since 1789 and, for more recent years, indexes of voting records calculated by Congressional Quarterly and various interest groups.

Public Opinion

The president's relationship with the public is of great importance to any administration, but, with the exception of election studies, it has been common for students of the presidency to make assertions about what the public is thinking and why it is doing so without marshaling systematic evidence to support their assertions. Fortunately, there is an enormous amount of data on public evaluations of the president, voting behavior, and other relevant public attitudes waiting to be exploited.

The ICPSR makes its extensive biennial election studies, covering the years 1948–1982, available to members. These studies contain questions on a wide range of matters, including evaluations of the president, in addition to purely electoral concerns. The ICPSR also archives opinion surveys of elites, bureaucrats, children (useful for socialization studies), and the general public.

Since 1965, results of Gallup polls have been published in the monthly *The Gallup Report* (formerly the *Gallup Political Index* and the *Gallup Opinion Index*). Gallup polls since 1935 have been compiled in a set of volumes entitled *The Gallup Poll*. Gallup polls, as well as those from the Roper Poll and many other polling organizations, are available from the Roper Center, which is affiliated with the University of Connecticut, Williams College, and Yale University.

A number of surveys relevant to studying the presidency are archived at the Louis Harris Data Center at the University of North Carolina at Chapel Hill, and many libraries now receive press releases containing new Harris Poll results. Similarly, the National Opinion Research Center (NORC), affiliated with the University of Chicago, contains numerous relevant surveys of public opinion taken over the past four decades.

The Press

Mediating between the president and the public is the press. It plays a vital role in the operation of the presidency, but it also has often been overlooked by researchers. As we noted earlier, many of the materials that the White House formally prepares for the press are available in the *Weekly Comp.*, and transcripts of press conferences are available from several sources, including the *New York Times*.

Turning to the other side of the relationship, news coverage of the president is a much-discussed and, until recently, a rarely studied phenomenon, particularly in nonelection periods. The Television Archive at Vanderbilt University contains video tapes of television news programs, and researchers can use the elaborate indexes it publishes to order tapes of specified time periods or subject matters. The ICPSR's holdings include a data collection of media content. In addition, most libraries contain indexes of daily newspapers, including the *New York Times*, *Washington Post*, *Chicago Tribune*, *Los Angeles Times*, and *Wall Street Journal*, and the *Reader's Guide to Periodical Literature*, which indexes magazine coverage. These can be used to help the student focus on media coverage of the president as well as to trace the president's activities. Magazines such as the *Columbia Journalism Review* and the *Washington Journalism Review* regularly carry commentary on press coverage of Washington.

Presidential Libraries

A resource of enormous potential importance are the presidential libraries, although they have not been widely used by students of the presidency.[45] Presidential libraries contain millions of pages of memos, reports, letters, and so forth, from a president's White House years; a collection of relevant books, articles, and audiovisual materials; and oral histories. Libraries exist for all presidents since Herbert Hoover with the exceptions of Richard Nixon and Jimmy Carter. Unfortunately, they are widely dispersed, being located in West Branch, Iowa (Hoover), Hyde Park, New York (Roosevelt), Independence, Missouri (Truman), Abilene, Kansas (Eisenhower), Dorchester, Massachusetts (Kennedy), Austin, Texas (Johnson), and Ann Arbor, Michigan (Ford).

The holdings in these libraries can be very useful for someone researching the presidency. Reading background material can be useful before interviewing persons involved in the issues or processes one is studying. Most people will use the libraries as ends in themselves, however. The material in them can help set the general context of events one is studying, trace the development of a policy, or understand the operation of the White House. Each library provides extensive finding guides and well-trained archivists to aid researchers.

Unfortunately, there are a number of factors that limit the utility of presidential libraries for students of the presidency. One is that they are spread around the country. A second factor inhibiting research is the filing system. White House files are kept for ease in operating the presidency and not for the future convenience of political scientists. If one wants to research the question of the impact of cognitive processes on decision making in the war in Vietnam, for example, one cannot simply go to a set of files with such a heading. The task will be an extremely lengthy one, requiring the reading of material in thousands of files. In addition, not all top presidential aides leave extensive files, and there are not always records of oral advice or small meetings. Many records may be classified.

The researcher must also be sensitive to possible distortions in the records that do exist. Some advisers write self-serving memos that will make them look good in the light of history and exaggerate their own role in the policy-making process. Moreover, some memos from the president or documents prepared at his request served the purpose of his letting off steam and were never officially issued or were never meant to be taken seriously.

The oral histories in the libraries vary greatly in length and quality. Although some provide real insight into a president and his presidency, others are rambling accounts of an anecdotal nature. Nevertheless, they may prove very useful in a project, and since many important officials have died, there is no other way to "interview" them. Many oral histories, unlike other materials in the presidential libraries, are available on interlibrary loan.

Interviews

Much of what occurs in the operation of the presidency is not open to public observation. The executive branch, especially at its peak, is not as accessible as Congress. Moreover, many potentially important topics of research such as those involving interpersonal interactions may not be well represented by a trail of paper. Thus, researchers seeking to understand the presidency may find it necessary and beneficial to interview the participants themselves. The researcher should also keep in mind that it is not only the most prominent members of an administration who have worthwhile things to say. Lower-level officials have a great deal of knowledge and may have more time for interviews and fewer political axes to grind. Thus, they may be fertile sources of information.

Despite their obvious utility, interviews are not an unmixed blessing. Some participants may refuse to be interviewed, especially while they are in office, because they fear political repercussions or because they are simply too busy. Those who consent to interviews may forget or repress data, or they may be unable to communicate in terms of the concepts the investigator is employing. There are also the ever-present problems of lack of candor and embellishment on behalf of themselves or their administration.

To exploit successfully the value of interviews requires considerable skill and hard work. Although this is not the place for an extensive discussion of the do's and don'ts of interviewing,[46] both careful preparation and personal interaction skills are essential. Sophisticated understanding of the context of interviewees' positions and of the issues with which they deal are necessary to elicit useful comments. Also necessary is a sensitivity to the needs of interviewees, because their confidence must be won if they are to speak candidly.

CONCLUSION

There are few topics in American politics that are more interesting or more important to understand than the presidency. Researching the presidency is not a simple task, however. There are many reasons for this, including the relative sparsity of previous research that applied the approaches and methods of modern political science. There are fewer models to follow than we would like. The obstacles to studying the presidency may also be an opportunity, however. Few questions regarding the presidency are settled; there is plenty of room for committed and creative researchers to make important contributions to our understanding of this uniquely American institution. The prospects for significant research will be enhanced if investigators are aware of the implications of the approaches and methods they employ and choose those that are best suited to shedding light on the questions they wish to study.

NOTES

1. For a more extensive discussion of approaches to studying the presidency see Stephen J. Wayne, "Approaches," in George C. Edwards III and Stephen J. Wayne, eds., *Studying the Presidency* (Knoxville: University of Tennessee Press, 1983), pp. 17–49.

2. The classic work on the legal perspective is Edward S. Corwin's *The President: Office and Powers*, 4th rev. ed. (New York: New York University Press, 1957); an excellent recent example is Louis Fisher, *Presidential Spending Power* (Princeton: Princeton University Press, 1975).

3. See, for example, Stephen J. Wayne, *The Legislative Presidency* (New York: Harper and Row, 1978); and Michael Baruch Grossman and Martha Joynt Kumar, *Portraying the President: The White House and the News Media* (Baltimore: Johns Hopkins University Press, 1981).

4. Richard E. Neustadt, *Presidential Power: The Politics of Leadership from FDR to Carter* (New York: Wiley, 1980).

5. See, for example, George C. Edwards III, *Presidential Influence in Congress* (San Francisco: Freeman, 1980); *Implementing Public Policy* (Washington, D.C.: Congressional Quarterly, 1980); and *The Public Presidency* (New York: St. Martin's, 1983).

6. See Bruce Miroff, "Beyond Washington," *Society* 17 (July/August 1980): 66–72.

7. See Peter W. Sperlich, "Bargaining and Overload: An Essay on *Presidential Power*," in Aaron Wildavsky, ed., *The Presidency* (Boston: Little, Brown, 1969), pp. 168–92.

8. See, for example, Alexander L. George and Juliette L. George, *Woodrow Wilson and Colonel House: A Personality Study* (New York: Dover, 1964).

9. The most notable example is James David Barber's *The Presidential Character: Predicting Performance in the White House*, 2nd ed. (Englewood Cliffs, N.J.: Prentice-Hall, 1977).

10. Some relevant studies include Alexander L. George, *Presidential Decisionmaking in Foreign Policy: The Effective Use of Information and Advice* (Boulder, Colo.: Westview Press, 1980); Bruce Buchanan, *The Presidential Experience: What the Office Does to the Man* (Englewood Cliffs, N.J.: Prentice-Hall, 1978); John D. Steinbruner, *The Cybernetic Theory of Decision* (Princeton: Princeton University Press, 1974); Irving L. Janis, *Groupthink: Psychological Studies of Policy Decisions and Fiascoes*, 2nd ed. (Boston: Houghton Mifflin, 1982).

11. Henry Kissinger, *Years of Upheaval* (Boston: Little, Brown, 1982), p. 1182.

12. Lyndon B. Johnson, *The Vantage Point: Perspectives of the Presidency, 1963–1969* (New York: Popular Library, 1971), pp. 144–53.

13. Jack Valenti, *A Very Human President* (New York: Norton, 1975), pp. 317–19.

14. Larry Berman, *Planning a Tragedy: The Americanization of the War in Vietnam* (New York: Norton, 1982), pp. 105–21.

15. Hubert H. Humphrey, *The Education of a Public Man: My Life and Politics* (Garden City, N.Y.: Doubleday, 1976), pp. 290–93.

16. Valenti, *A Very Human President*, pp. 196–97. See also Russell D. Renka, "Bargaining with Legislative Whales in the Kennedy and Johnson Administration" (paper presented at the Annual Meeting of the American Political Science Association, Washington, D.C., August, 1980), p. 20.

17. Transcript, Henry Hall Wilson Oral History Interview, April 11, 1973, by Joe B. Frantz, p. 16, Lyndon B. Johnson Library.

18. Kissinger, *Years of Upheaval*, pp. 111–12.

19. Richard Tanner Johnson, *Managing the White House* (New York: Harper and Row, 1974).

20. Edwards, *The Public Presidency*, pp. 242–47.

21. For a more extensive discussion of quantitative analysis of the presidency see George C. Edwards III, "Quantitative Analysis," in Edwards and Wayne, eds., *Studying the Presidency*, pp. 99–124.

22. The literature on this question is vast. See, for example, Samuel Kernell, "Explaining Presidential Popularity," *American Political Science Review* 72 (June 1978): 506–22; Stephen J. Wayne, "Great Expectations: Contemporary Views of the President," in Thomas Cronin, ed., *Rethinking the Presidency* (Boston: Little, Brown, 1982); and Edwards, *The Public Presidency*, chap. 6 and sources cited therein.

23. The literature on children's attitudes and beliefs is also very extensive. See, for example, Fred I. Greenstein, "The Benevolent Leader Revisited: Children's Images of Political Leaders in Three Democracies," *American Political Science Review* 69 (Dec. 1975): 1371–98; Jack Dennis and Carol Webster, "Children's Images of the President and of Government in 1962 and 1974," *American Politics Quarterly* 3 (Oct. 1975): 386–405 and sources cited therein.

24. Lee Sigelman, "Gauging the Public Response to Presidential Leadership," *Presidential Studies Quarterly* 10 (Summer 1980): 427–33; Carey Rosen, "A Test of Presidential Leadership of Public Opinion: The Split-Ballot Technique," *Polity* 6 (Winter 1973): 282–90; Lee Sigelman and Carol K. Sigelman, "Presidential Leadership of Public Opinion: From 'Benevolent Leader' to Kiss of Death?" *Experimental Study of Politics* 7, no. 3 (1981): 1–22.

25. Lawrence C. Miller and Lee Sigelman, "Is the Audience the Message? A Note on LBJ's Vietnam Statements," *Public Opinion Quarterly* 42 (Spring 1978):71–80; John H. Kessel, "The Parameters of Presidential Politics," *Social Sciences Quarterly* 55 (June 1974):8–24, and "The Seasons of Presidential Politics," *Social Science Quarterly* 58 (December 1977): 418–35.

26. Grossman and Kumar, *Portraying the President*, chap. 10.

27. David L. Paletz and Richard I. Vinegar, "Presidents on Television: The Effects of Instant Analysis," *Public Opinion Quarterly* 41 (Winter 1977–1978):488–97; Dwight F. Davis, Lynda L. Kaid, and Donald L. Singleton, "Information Effects of Political Commentary," *Experimental Study of Politics* 6 (June 1978):45–68,and "Instant Analysis of Televised Political Addresses: The Speaker Versus the Commentator," in Brent D. Ruben, ed., *Communication Yearbook I*, (New Brunswick, N.J.: Transaction Books, 1977), pp. 453–64; Thomas A. Kazee, "Television Exposure and Attitude Change: The Impact of Political Interest," *Public Opinion Quarterly* 45 (Winter 1981):507–18.

28. Edwards, *Presidential Influence in Congress*, chaps. 3–7, and *The Public Presidency*, pp. 83–93 and sources cited therein.

29. Richard L. Cole and Stephen J. Wayne, "Predicting Presidential Decisions on Enrolled Bills: A Computer Simulation," *Simulation and Games* 11 (September 1980):313–25.

30. Lee Sigelman and Dixie Mercer McNeil, "White House Decision-Making under Stress: A Case Analysis," *American Journal of Political Science* 24 (November 1980):652–73.

31. Jarol B. Mannheim and William W. Lammers, "The News Conference and Presidential Leadership of Public Opinion: Does the Tail Wag the Dog?" *Presidential Studies Quarterly* 11 (Spring 1981):177–88.

32. John H. Kessel, *The Domestic Presidency: Decision-Making in the White House* (North Scituate, Mass.: Duxbury, 1975).

33. Joel D. Aberbach and Bert A. Rockman, "Clashing Beliefs within the Executive Branch: The Nixon Administration Bureaucracy," *American Political Science Review* 70 (June 1976):456–68; Richard L. Cole and David A. Caputo, "Presidential Control of the Senior Civil Service: Assessing the Strategies of the Nixon Years," *American Political Science Review* 73 (June 1979):399–413.

34. For more on legal analysis of the presidency, see Louis Fisher, "Making Use of Legal Sources," in Edwards and Wayne, eds., *Studying the Presidency*, pp. 182–98.

35. Norman C. Thomas, "Case Studies," in Edwards and Wayne, eds., *Studying the Presidency*, pp. 50–78.

36. See, for example, Alexander L. George, "The Case for Multiple Advocacy in Making Foreign Policy," *American Political Science Review* 66 (September 1972):765–81.

37. See, for example, Edwards, *Implementing Public Policy*.

38. See Janis, *Groupthink*.

39. See, for example, Bruce Miroff, "Presidential Leverage over Social Movements: The Johnson White House and Civil Rights," *Journal of Politics* 43 (February 1981):2–23.

40. Neustadt, *Presidential Power*.

41. Graham T. Allison, *Essence of Decision: Explaining the Cuban Missile Crisis* (Boston: Little, Brown, 1971).

42. For a more extended discussion on locating the law, students should see Fisher, "Making Use of Legal Sources," in Edwards and Wayne, eds., *Studying the Presidency*, pp. 188–98.

43. For a more extended discussion of general sources of data on the presidency, see Jennifer DeToro, "A Guide to Information Sources," in Edwards and Wayne, eds., *Studying the Presidency*, pp. 127–55.

44. For a more extended discussion of congressional sources of data, see G. Calvin Mackenzie, "Research in Executive-Legislative Relations," in Edwards and Wayne, eds., *Studying the Presidency*, pp. 156–81.

45. For detailed discussions of researching in presidential libraries, see Martha Joynt Kumar, "Presidential Libraries: Gold Mine, Booby Trap, or Both?" and Larry Berman, "Presidential Libraries: How *Not* to Be a Stranger in a Strange Land," in Edwards and Wayne, eds., *Studying the Presidency*, pp. 199–256.

46. For detailed discussions of the proper techniques for interviewing presidential aides, see Dom Bonafede, "Interviewing Presidential Aides: A Journalist's Perspective," and Joseph A. Pika, "Interviewing Presidential Aides: A Political Scientist's Perspective,"

in Edwards and Wayne, eds., *Studying the Presidency*, pp. 257–302. See also Lewis Anthony Dexter, *Elite and Specialized Interviewing* (Evanston, Ill.: Northwestern University Press, 1970).

SELECTED READINGS

Edwards, George C., III, and Stephen J. Wayne, eds., *Studying the Presidency*. Knoxville, Tenn.: University of Tennessee Press, 1983.

Appendix A

Nonelectoral Succession, Removal, and Tenure

The Constitution and statutes provide for contingencies that might require the selection, removal, or replacement of a president outside the normal electoral process. In addition to the provisions of Article 1 (Impeachment) and Article 2 (Impeachment and Succession), there have been three amendments (numbers 20, 22, and 25) and three laws concerning succession and term of office. This appendix will examine these contingency arrangements. It will also briefly describe the impeachment process and the two most serious attempts to remove a sitting president. The Constitution and statutes provide for methods of succession and removal.

SUCCESSION

The principal reason for creating the vice presidency was to have a position from which the presidency would automatically be filled should it become vacant. Death, resignation, and impeachment constitute clear-cut situations in which this succession mechanism would work. Eight presidents have died in office and one has resigned. In each of the nine instances, the vice president became president.

One contingency the founding fathers did not consider was temporary or permanent disability while in office. On a number of occasions, presidents have become disabled, unable to perform their duties and responsibilities. James Garfield, shot by a disappointed job seeker, lingered for almost three months before he died. More recently, Ronald Reagan was unconscious for two hours and hospitalized for twelve days following an attempt on his life. Other presidents have been incapacitated by natural causes. Wilson suffered a stroke that disabled him for much of the last year of his administration, while Eisenhower's heart attack, ileitis operation, and minor stroke severely limited his presidential activities in 1955, 1956, and 1957.

During none of these periods did vice presidents officially take over. In fact, Chester Arthur and Thomas Marshall, Garfield's and Wilson's vice presidents, respectively, avoided even the appearance of performing presidential duties for fear that their actions would be wrongfully construed. Vice President Richard Nixon did preside at Cabinet meetings in Eisenhower's absence but did not assume the president's other responsibilities. George Bush, away from the capital at the time Reagan was shot, flew back to Washington immediately to be available if needed. However, to avoid any appearance of impropriety, he had his helicopter land at the vice president's residence even though he was scheduled to meet at the White House with senior presidential aides.

It was not until 1967 that procedures were established for the vice president to become acting president in the event of the president's disability. The Twenty-fifth Amendment to the Constitution permits the vice president to exercise the duties and powers of the presidency if the president declares in writing that he is unable to do so or if the vice president and a majority of the principal executive department heads reach that judgment. The president may resume his office when he believes that he is able unless the vice president and a majority of the principal executive department heads object. In that case Congress must make the final determination. The procedures, however, are weighted in the president's favor. Unless Congress concurs in the judgment that the president is disabled, the president is entitled once again to exercise the duties and powers of his office.

Another important provision of this amendment provides for filling the vice presidency should it become vacant. Prior to 1967, it had been vacant sixteen times. The procedures permit the president to nominate a new vice president who takes office upon confirmation by a majority of both houses of Congress. Gerald Ford and Nelson Rockefeller were the only two vice presidents who assumed office in this manner. Ford was nominated by President Nixon in 1973 upon the resignation of Spiro T. Agnew. After succeeding to the presidency upon Nixon's resignation, Ford nominated Rockefeller.

While the presidency and vice presidency have never been vacant at the same time, Congress has provided for such a contingency should it arise by establishing a line of succession. The most recent succession law was enacted in 1947. It puts the Speaker of the House next in line to be followed by the president pro tempore of the Senate and the department heads in order of their seniority, beginning with the secretary of state. The provision for appointing a new vice president, however, makes it less likely that legislative and executive officials would ever succeed to the presidency, barring a catastrophe.

REMOVAL

In addition to providing for the president's replacement, the constitutional framers also thought it necessary to provide for his removal. They believed that it was too dangerous to wait for the electors' judgment in the case of a president who had abused his authority. Impeachment was considered an extraordinary remedy but one that could be used against executive officials, including the president and vice president, who violated their public trust.

Article 2, section 4, of the Constitution spells out the terms. The president, vice president, and other executive officials can be removed from office for treason, bribery, or other high crimes and misdemeanors. Precisely what actions would be considered impeachable offenses is left for Congress to determine.

The House of Representatives considers the charges against the president. If a majority of the House votes in favor of any of them, a trial is held in the Senate with the chief justice of the Supreme Court presiding. The House presents its case against the president. The latter, who may be represented by outside counsel, defends himself against the charges. A two-thirds vote of the Senate is required for conviction. If the president is convicted, he is removed from office. He may still be subject to civil or criminal prosecution.

Only one president, Andrew Johnson, has ever been impeached. The incident that sparked his impeachment was Johnson's removal of Secretary of War Edwin Stanton. Congress had passed a law over Johnson's veto that required appointees to remain in office until the Senate approved their successor. Known as the Tenure of Office Act (1867), it permitted the president some discretion during a congressional recess but required the Senate's advice and consent after Congress reconvened. In the absence of senatorial approval, the office reverted to its previous occupant.

During a congressional recess, Johnson removed Stanton. The Senate refused to concur in the removal upon its return. Under the law, Stanton was entitled to his old job. However, the president once again removed him. Upon his removal for a second time, the House of Representatives passed a bill of impeachment against the president. The Senate trial lasted six weeks. In its first vote the Senate fell one short of the required two-thirds. A ten-day recess was called by those favoring Johnson's removal. Extensive lobbying ensued, but when the Senate reconvened, no one changed their vote. Johnson was acquitted. The Tenure of Office Act was subsequently repealed during the Cleveland administration.

A second attempt to impeach a sitting president occurred in 1973. When Richard Nixon dismissed Archibald Cox, the special prosecutor who had been investigating charges of administration wrongdoing in the Watergate affair, members of Congress called for Nixon's removal. The Judiciary Committee of the House of Representatives began hearings on the president's impeachment. During the course of these hearings, the committee subpoenaed tapes of conversations which the president had held with aides in the White House, conversations that had been secretly recorded by the president. Claiming that these were privileged communications, Nixon refused to deliver the tapes, although he did send edited transcripts of them to the House committee. Not satisfied with this response, the House took its case to court and won. The Supreme Court ordered Nixon to release the tapes. When he did so, they revealed his early knowledge of the break-in and his participation in the cover-up. This information heightened calls for the president's ouster.

The House Judiciary Committee approved three articles of impeachment against Nixon. It looked as if the full House would vote to impeach him and that the Senate would vote to convict him. Faced with the prospect of a long trial and probable conviction, Nixon resigned on August 9, 1974.

TENURE

Electoral defeat and impeachment prematurely conclude a presidency—at least from the incumbent's perspective. Initially the Constitution imposed no limits on the number of times a president could be elected. Re-eligibility was seen as a motive to good behavior. Beginning with Washington, however, an unofficial two-term limit was established. Franklin Roosevelt ended this precedent in 1940 when he ran for a third term and won.

Partially in reaction to Roosevelt's twelve years and one month as president, a Republican-controlled Congress passed and the states ratified the Twenty-second Amendment to the Constitution. It prevents any person from being elected to the office more than twice. Moreover, it limits to one election a president who has succeeded to the office and has served more than two years of his predecessor's term.

Eisenhower was the first president to be subject to the provisions of the amendment. Since none of his successors has served two full terms, it is difficult to assess the amendment's impact on the operation of the presidency. It is feared, however, that making the president a lame duck in the second term of his administration may reduce his political power and his capacity to mobilize public backing for his programs and policies. On the other hand, his motives might not be impugned and his capacity to mobilize a bipartisan coalition improved. This might result in a weaker domestic presidency but in a stronger foreign policy one. It would certainly affect his incentives for policy making in each of these spheres.

Appendix B

The Constitution of the United States with Provisions on the Presidency Highlighted

We the People of the United States, in Order to form a more perfect Union, establish Justice, insure domestic Tranquility, provide for the common defence, promote the general Welfare, and secure the Blessings of Liberty to ourselves and our Posterity do ordain and establish this CONSTITUTION for the United States of America.

ARTICLE I

Section 1. All legislative Powers herein granted shall be vested in a Congress of the United States, which shall consist of a Senate and House of Representatives.

Section 2. (1) The House of Representatives shall be composed of Members chosen every second Year by the People of the several States, and the Electors in each State shall have the Qualifications requisite for Electors of the most numerous Branch of the State Legislature.

(2) No Person shall be a Representative who shall not have attained to the Age of twenty-five Years, and been seven Years a Citizen of the United States, and who shall not, when elected, be an Inhabitant of that State in which he shall be chosen.

(3) [Representatives and direct Taxes[1] shall be apportioned among the several States which may be included within this Union, according to their respective Numbers, which shall be determined by adding to the whole Number of free Persons, including those bound to Service for a Term of Years, and excluding Indians not taxed, three fifths of all other Persons.][2] The actual Enumeration shall be made within three Years after the first Meeting of the Congress of the

[1]The Sixteenth Amendment replaced this with respect to income taxes.
[2]Repealed by the Fourteenth Amendment.

United States, and within every subsequent Term of ten Years, in such Manner as they shall by Law direct. The Number of Representatives shall not exceed one for every thirty Thousand, but each State shall have at Least one Representative; and until such enumeration shall be made, the State of New Hampshire shall be entitled to choose three, Massachusetts eight, Rhode-Island and Providence Plantations one, Connecticut five, New York six, New Jersey four, Pennsylvania eight, Delaware one, Maryland six, Virginia ten, North Carolina five, South Carolina five, and Georgia three.

(4) When vacancies happen in the Representation from any State, the Executive Authority thereof shall issue Writs of Election to fill such Vacancies.

(5) The House of Representatives shall choose their Speaker and other Officers; and shall have the sole Power of Impeachment.

Section 3. (1) The Senate of the United States shall be composed of two Senators from each State, [chosen by the Legislature][3] thereof, for six Years; and each Senator shall have one Vote.

(2) Immediately after they shall be assembled in Consequence of the first Election, they shall be divided as equally as may be into three Classes. The Seats of the Senators of the first Class shall be vacated at the Expiration of the second Year, of the second Class at the Expiration of the fourth Year, and of the third Class at the Expiration of the sixth Year, so that one-third may be chosen every second year; [and if Vacancies happen by Resignation, or otherwise, during the Recess of the Legislature of any State, the Executive thereof may make temporary Appointments until the next Meeting of the Legislature, which shall then fill such Vacancies.][4]

(3) No person shall be a Senator who shall not have attained to the Age of thirty Years, and been nine Years a Citizen of the United States, and who shall not, when elected, be an Inhabitant of that State for which he shall be chosen.

(4) The Vice President of the United States shall be President of the Senate, but shall have no Vote, unless they be equally divided.

(5) The Senate shall choose their other Officers, and also a President pro tempore, in the Absence of the Vice President, or when he shall exercise the Office of President of the United States.

(6) The Senate shall have the sole Power to try all Impeachments. When sitting for that Purpose, they shall be on Oath or Affirmation. When the President of the United States is tried, the Chief Justice shall preside: And no Person shall be convicted without the Concurrence of two thirds of the Members present.

(7) Judgment in Cases of Impeachment shall not extend further than to removal from Office, and disqualification to hold and enjoy any Office of honor, Trust or Profit under the United States: but the Party convicted shall nevertheless be liable and subject to Indictment, Trial, Judgment and Punishment according to Law.

Section 4. (1) The Times, Places and Manner of holding Elections for Senators and Representatives, shall be prescribed in each State by the Legislature thereof; but the Congress may at any time by Law make or alter such Regulations, except as to the Places of choosing Senators.

(2) The Congress shall assemble at least once in every Year, and such Meeting shall [be on the first Monday in December,][5] unless they shall by Law appoint a different Day.

Section 5. (1) Each House shall be the Judge of the Elections, Returns and Quali-

---

[3]Repealed by the Seventeenth Amendment, section 1.
[4]Changed by the Seventeenth Amendment.
[5]Changed by the Twentieth Amendment, section 2.

fications of its own Members, and a Majority of each shall constitute a Quorum to do Business; but a smaller Number may adjourn from day to day, and may be authorized to compel the Attendance of absent Members, in such Manner, and under such Penalties as each House may provide.

(2) Each House may determine the Rules of its Proceedings, punish its Members for disorderly Behavior, and, with the Concurrence of two thirds, expel a Member.

(3) Each House shall keep a Journal of its Proceedings, and from time to time publish the same, excepting such Parts as may in their Judgment require Secrecy; and the Yeas and Nays of the Members of either House on any question shall, at the Desire of one fifth of those Present, be entered on the Journal.

(4) Neither House, during the Session of Congress, shall, without the Consent of the other, adjourn for more than three days, nor to any other Place than that in which the two Houses shall be sitting.

Section 6. (1) The Senators and Representatives shall receive a Compensation for their Services, to be ascertained by Law, and paid out of the Treasury of the United States. They shall in all Cases, except Treason, Felony and Breach of the Peace, be privileged from Arrest during their Attendance at the Session of their respective Houses, and in going to and returning from the same; and for any Speech or Debate in either House, they shall not be questioned in any other Place.

(2) No Senator or Representative shall, during the Time for which he was elected, be appointed to any civil Office under the Authority of the United States, which shall have been created, or the Emoluments whereof have been increased during such time; and no Person holding any Office under the United States, shall be a Member of either House during his Continuance in Office.

Section 7. (1) All Bills for raising Revenue shall originate in the House of Representatives; but the Senate may propose or concur with Amendments as on other Bills.

(2) Every Bill which shall have passed the House of Representatives and the Senate, shall, before it become a Law, be presented to the President of the United States; If he approve he shall sign it, but if not he shall return it, with his Objections to that House in which it shall have originated, who shall enter the Objections at large on their Journal, and proceed to reconsider it. If after such Reconsideration two thirds of that House shall agree to pass the Bill, it shall be sent, together with the Objections, to the other House, by which it shall likewise be reconsidered, and if approved by two thirds of that House, it shall become a Law. But in all such Cases the Votes of both Houses shall be determined by Yeas and Nays, and the Names of the Persons voting for and against the Bill shall be entered on the Journal of each House respectively. If any Bill shall not be returned by the President within ten Days (Sundays excepted) after it shall have been presented to him, the Same shall be a Law, in like Manner as if he had signed it, unless the Congress by their Adjournment prevent its Return, in which Case it shall not be a Law.

(3) Every Order, Resolution, or Vote to which the Concurrence of the Senate and House of Representatives may be necessary (except on a question of Adjournment) shall be presented to the President of the United States; and before the Same shall take Effect, shall be approved by him, or being disapproved by him, shall be repassed by two thirds of the Senate and House of Representatives, according to the Rules and Limitations prescribed in the Case of a Bill.

Section 8. (1) The Congress shall have the Power To lay and collect Taxes, Duties,

Imposts and Excises, to pay the Debts and provide for the common Defense and general Welfare of the United States; but all Duties, Imposts and Excises shall be uniform throughout the United States;

(2) To borrow money on the credit of the United States;

(3) To regulate Commerce with foreign Nations, and among the several States, and with the Indian Tribes;

(4) To establish an uniform Rule of Naturalization, and uniform Laws on the subject of Bankruptcies throughout the United States;

(5) To coin Money, regulate the Value thereof, and of foreign Coin, and fix the Standard of Weights and Measures;

(6) To provide for the Punishment of counterfeiting the Securities and current Coin of the United States;

(7) To establish Post Offices and post Roads;

(8) To promote the Progress of Science and useful Arts, by securing for limited Times to Authors and Inventors the exclusive Right to their respective Writings and Discoveries;

(9) To constitute Tribunals inferior to the supreme Court;

(10) To define and punish Piracies and Felonies committed on the high Seas, and Offenses against the Law of Nations;

(11) To declare War, grant Letters of Marque and Reprisal, and make Rules concerning Captures on Land and Water;

(12) To raise and support Armies, but no Appropriation of Money to that Use shall be for a longer Term than two Years;

(13) To provide and maintain a Navy;

(14) To make Rules for the Government and Regulation of the land and naval Forces;

(15) To provide for calling forth the Militia to execute the Laws of the Union, suppress Insurrections and repel Invasions;

(16) To provide for organizing, arming, and disciplining the Militia, and for governing such Part of them as may be employed in the Service of the United States, reserving to the States respectively, the Appointment of the Officers, and the Authority of training the Militia according to the discipline prescribed by Congress;

(17) To exercise exclusive Legislation in all Cases whatsoever, over such District (not exceeding ten Miles square) as may, by Cession of particular States, and the Acceptance of Congress, become the Seat of the Government of the United States, and to exercise like Authority over all Places purchased by the Consent of the Legislature of the State in which the Same shall be, for the Erection of Forts, Magazines, Arsenals, dock-Yards, and other needful Buildings;—And

(18) To make all Laws which shall be necessary and proper for carrying into Execution the foregoing Powers, and all other Powers vested by this Constitution in the Government of the United States, or in any Department or Officer thereof.

Section 9. (1) The Migration or Importation of such Persons as any of the States now existing shall think proper to admit, shall not be prohibited by the Congress prior to the Year one thousand eight hundred and ight, but a tax or duty may be imposed on such Importation, not exceeding ten dollars for each Person.

(2) The Privilege of the Writ of Habeas Corpus shall not be suspended, unless when in Cases of Rebellion or Invasion the public Safety may require it.

(3) No Bill of Attainder or ex post facto Law shall be passed.

(4) No Capitation, or other direct, Tax shall be laid, unless in Proportion to the Census or Enumeration herein before directed to be taken.[6]

(5) No Tax or Duty shall be laid on Articles exported from any State.

(6) No Preference shall be given by any Regulation of Commerce or Revenue to the Ports of one State over those of another: nor shall Vessels bound to, or from, one State, be obliged to enter, clear, or pay Duties in another.

(7) No Money shall be drawn from the Treasury, but in Consequence of Appropriations made by Law; and a regular Statement and Account of the Receipts and Expenditures of all public Money shall be published from time to time.

(8) No Title of Nobility shall be granted by the United States: And no Person holding any Office of Profit or Trust under them, shall, without the Consent of the Congress, accept of any present, Emolument, Office, or Title, of any kind whatever, from any King, Prince, or foreign State.

Section 10. (1) No State shall enter into any Treaty, Alliance, or Confederation; grant Letters of Marque and Reprisal; coin Money; emit Bills of Credit; make any Thing but gold and silver Coin a Tender in Payment of Debts; pass any Bill of Attainder, ex post facto Law, or Law impairing the Obligation of Contracts, or grant any Title of Nobility.

(2) No State shall, without the Consent of the Congress, lay any Imposts or Duties on Imports or Exports, except what may be absolutely necessary for executing its inspection Laws: and the net Produce of all Duties and Imposts, laid by any State on Imports or Exports, shall be for the Use of the Treasury of the United States; and all such laws shall be subject to the Revision and Control of the Congress.

(3) No State shall, without the Consent of Congress, lay any duty of Tonnage, keep Troops, or Ships of War in time of Peace, enter into any Agreement or Compact with another State, or with a foreign Power, or engage in War, unless actually invaded, or in such imminent Danger as will not admit of delay.

ARTICLE II

Section 1. **(1) The executive Power shall be vested in a President of the United States of America. He shall hold his Office during the Term of four Years, and, together with the Vice-President, chosen for the same Term, be elected, as follows:**

(2) Each State shall appoint, in such Manner as the Legislature thereof may direct, a Number of Electors, equal to the whole Number of Senators and Representatives to which the State may be entitled in the Congress, but no Senator or Representative, or Person holding an Office of Trust or Profit under the United States, shall be appointed an Elector.

[The Electors shall meet in their respective States, and vote by Ballot for two persons, of whom one at least shall not be an Inhabitant of the same State with themselves. And they shall make a List of all the Persons voted for, and of the Number of Votes for each; which List they shall sign and certify, and transmit sealed to the Seat of the Government of the United States, directed to the President of the Senate. The President of the Senate shall, in the Presence of the Senate and House of Representatives, open all the Certificates, and the Votes shall then be counted. The Person having the greatest Number of Votes shall be the President, if such Number be a Majority of the whole

[6]Changed by the Sixteenth Amendment.

Number of Electors appointed; and if there be more than one who have such Majority, and have an equal Number of Votes, then the House of Representatives shall immediately choose by Ballot one of them for President; and if no Person have a Majority, then from the five highest on the List the said House shall in like Manner choose the President. But in choosing the President, the Votes shall be taken by States, the Representation from each State having one Vote; A quorum for this purpose shall consist of a Member or Members from two-thirds of the States, and a Majority of all the States shall be necessary to a Choice. In every Case, after the Choice of the President, the Person having the greatest Number of Votes of the Electors shall be the Vice-President. But if there should remain two or more who have equal Votes, the Senate shall choose from them by Ballot the Vice-President.][7]

(3) The Congress may determine the Time of choosing the Electors, and the Day on which they shall give their Votes; which Day shall be the same throughout the United States.

(4) No person except a natural born Citizen, or a Citizen of the United States, at the time of the Adoption of this Constitution, shall be eligible to the Office of President; neither shall any Person be eligible to that Office who shall not have attained to the Age of thirty-five Years, and been fourteen Years a Resident within the United States.

(5) In case of the Removal of the President from Office, or of his Death, Resignation, or Inability to discharge the Powers and Duties of the said Office, the same shall devolve on the Vice-President, and the Congress may by Law provide for the Case of Removal, Death, Resignation or Inability; both of the President and Vice-President, declaring what Officer shall then act as President, and such Officer shall act accordingly, until the Disability be removed, or a President shall be elected.[8]

(6) The President shall, at stated Times, receive for his Services, a Compensation, which shall neither be increased nor diminished during the Period for which he shall have been elected, and he shall not receive within that Period any other Emolument from the United States, or any of them.

(7) Before he enter on the Execution of his Office, he shall take the following Oath or Affirmation:—"I do solemnly swear (or affirm) that I will faithfully execute the Office of President of the United States, and will to the best of my Ability, preserve, protect and defend the Constitution of the United States."

Section 2. (1) The President shall be Commander in Chief of the Army and Navy of the United States, and of the Militia of the several States, when called into the actual Service of the United States; he may require the Opinion in writing, of the principal Officer in each of the executive Departments, upon any subject relating to the Duties of their respective Offices, and he shall have Power to Grant Reprieves and Pardons for Offenses against the United States, except in Cases of Impeachment.

(2) He shall have Power, by and with the Advice and Consent of the Senate, to make Treaties, provided two-thirds of the Senators present concur; and he shall nominate, and by and with the Advice and Consent of the Senate, shall appoint Ambassadors, other public Ministers and Consuls, Judges of the supreme Court, and all other Officers of the United States, whose Appointments are not herein otherwise provided for, and which shall be established by Law: but the Congress may by Law vest the Appointment of such inferior

[7]This paragraph was superseded in 1804 by the Twelfth Amendment.
[8]Changed by the Twenty-fifth Amendment.

Officers, as they think proper, in the President alone, in the Court of Law, or in the Heads of Departments.

(3) The President shall have Power to fill up all Vacancies that may happen during the Recess of the Senate, by granting Commissions which shall expire at the End of their next Session.

Section 3. He shall from time to time give to the Congress Information of the State of the Union, and recommend to their Consideration such Measures as he shall judge necesssary and expedient; he may, on extraordinary Occasions, convene both Houses, or either of them, and in Case of Disagreement between them, with Respect to the Time of Adjournment, he may adjourn them to such Time as he shall think proper; he shall receive Ambassadors and other public Ministers; he shall take Care that the Laws be faithfully executed, and shall Commission all the Officers of the United States.

Section 4. The President, Vice President and all civil Officers of the United States, shall be removed from Office on Impeachment for, and Conviction of, Treason, Bribery, or other high Crimes and Misdemeanors.

ARTICLE III

Section 1. The judicial Power of the United States, shall be vested in one supreme Court, and in such inferior Courts as the Congress may from time to time ordain and establish. The Judges, both of the supreme and inferior Courts, shall hold their Offices during good Behavior, and shall, at stated Times, receive for their Services a Compensation which shall not be diminished during their Continuance in Office.

Section 2. (1) The judicial Power shall extend to all Cases, in Law and Equity, arising under this Constitution, the Laws of the United States, and Treaties made, or which shall be made, under their Authority;—to all Cases affecting Ambassadors, other public Ministers and Consuls;—to all Cases of admiralty and maritime Jurisdiction;—to Controversies to which the United States shall be a Party;—to Controversies between two or more states;—[between a State and Citizens of another State];⁹—between Citizens of different States;—between Citizens of the same State claiming Lands under Grants of different States, and [between a State, or the Citizens thereof, and foreign States, Citizens or Subjects.]¹⁰

(2) In all Cases affecting Ambassadors, other public Ministers and Consuls, and those in which a State shall be Party, the supreme Court shall have original Jurisdiction. In all the other Cases before mentioned, the supreme Court shall have appellate Jurisdiction, both as to Law and Fact, with such Exceptions, and under such Regulations as the Congress shall make.

(3) The trial of all Crimes, except in Cases of Impeachment, shall be by Jury; and such Trial shall be held in the State where the said Crimes shall have been committed: but when not committed within any State, the Trial shall be at such Place or Places as the Congress may by Law have directed.

Section 3. (1) Treason against the United States, shall consist only in levying War against them, or in adhering to their Enemies, giving them Aid and Comfort. No Person shall be convicted of Treason unless on the Testimony of two Witnesses to the same overt Act, or on Confession in open Court.

⁹Restricted by the Eleventh Amendment.
¹⁰Restricted by the Eleventh Amendment.

(2) The Congress shall have Power to declare the Punishment of Treason, but no Attainder of Treason shall work Corruption of Blood, or Forfeiture except during the Life of the Person attainted.

ARTICLE IV

Section 1. Full Faith and Credit shall be given in each State to the public Acts, Records, and judicial Proceedings of every other State. And the Congress may by general Laws prescribe the Manner in which such Acts, Records and Proceedings shall be proved, and the Effect thereof.

Section 2. (1) The Citizens of each State shall be entitled to all Privileges and Immunities of Citizens in the several States.

(2) A Person charged in any State with Treason, Felony, or other Crime, who shall flee from Justice, and be found in another State, shall on demand of the executive Authority of the State from which he fled, be delivered up, to be removed to the State having Jurisdiction of the Crime.

(3) [No Person held to Service or Labor in one State, under the Laws thereof, escaping into another, shall, in Consequence of any Law or Regulation therein, be discharged from such Service or Labor, but shall be delivered up on Claim of the Party to whom such Service or Labor may be due.]¹¹

Section 3. (1) New States may be admitted by the Congress into this Union; but no new State shall be formed or erected within the Jurisdiction of any other State; nor any State be formed by the Junction of two or more States, or Parts of States, without the Consent of the Legislatures of the States concerned as well as of the Congress.

(2) The Congress shall have Power to dispose of and make all needful Rules and Regulations respecting the Territory or other Property belonging to the United States; and nothing in this Constitution shall be so construed as to Prejudice any Claims of the United States, or of any particular State.

Section 4. **The United States shall guarantee to every State in this Union a Republican Form of Government, and shall protect each of them against Invasion; and on Application of the Legislature, or of the Executive (when the Legislature cannot be convened) against domestic Violence.**

ARTICLE V

The Congress, whenever two-thirds of both Houses shall deem it necessary, shall propose Amendments to this Constitution, or, on the Application of the Legislatures of two-thirds of the several States, shall call a Convention for proposing Amendments, which, in either Case, shall be valid to all Intents and Purposes, as part of this Constitution, when ratified by the Legislature of three-fourths of the several States, or by Conventions in three-fourths thereof, as the one or the other Mode of Ratification may be proposed by the Congress; Provided that no Amendment which may be made prior to the Year One thousand eight hundred and eight shall in any Manner affect the first and fourth Clauses in the Ninth Section of the first Article; and that no State, without its Consent, shall be deprived of its equal Suffrage in the Senate.

¹¹This paragraph has been superseded by the Thirteenth Amendment.

ARTICLE VI

(1) All Debts contracted and Engagements entered into, before the Adoption of this Constitution, shall be as valid against the United States under this Constitution, as under the Confederation.

(2) This Constitution, and the Laws of the United States which shall be made in Pursuance thereof; and all Treaties made, or which shall be made, under the Authority of the United States, shall be the supreme Law of the Land; and the Judges in every State shall be bound thereby, any Thing in the Constitution or Laws of any State to the Contrary notwithstanding.

(3) The Senators and Representatives before mentioned, and the Members of the several State Legislatures, and all executive and judicial Officers, both of the United States and of the several States, shall be bound by Oath or Affirmation, to support this Constitution; but no religious Test shall ever be required as a Qualification to any Office or public Trust under the United States.

ARTICLE VII

The Ratification of the Conventions of nine States, shall be sufficient for the Establishment of this Constitution between the States so ratifying the Same.

DONE in Convention by the Unanimous Consent of the States present the Seventeenth Day of September in the Year of our Lord one thousand seven hundred and Eighty seven and the Independence of the United States of America the Twelfth. In Witness whereof We have hereunto subscribed our Names.

Go. WASHINGTON
President and deputy from Virginia

ARTICLES IN ADDITION TO, AND AMENDMENT OF, THE CONSTITUTION OF THE UNITED STATES OF AMERICA, PROPOSED BY CONGRESS, AND RATIFIED BY THE LEGISLATURES OF THE Several STATES, PURSUANT TO THE FIFTH ARTICLE OF THE ORIGINAL CONSTITUTION.

AMENDMENT I[12]

Congress shall make no law respecting an establishment of religion, or prohibiting the free exercise thereof; or abridging the freedom of speech, or of the press; or the right of the people peaceably to assemble, and to petition the Government for a redress of grievances.

[12]The first ten amendments were adopted in 1791.

AMENDMENT II

A well regulated Militia, being necessary to the security of a free State, the right of the people to keep and bear Arms, shall not be infringed.

AMENDMENT III

No Soldier shall, in time of peace be quartered in any house, without the consent of the Owner, nor in time of war, but in a manner to be prescribed by law.

AMENDMENT IV

The right of the people to be secure in their persons, houses, papers, and effects, against unreasonable searches and seizures, shall not be violated, and no Warrants shall issue, but upon probable cause, supported by Oath or affirmation, and particularly describing the place to be searched, and the persons or things to be seized.

AMENDMENT V

No person shall be held to answer for a capital, or otherwise infamous crime, unless on a presentment or indictment of a Grand Jury, except in cases arising in the land or naval forces, or in the Militia, when in actual service in time of War or public danger; nor shall any person be subject for the same offense to be twice put in jeopardy of life or limb; nor shall be compelled in any criminal case to be witness against himself, nor be deprived of life, liberty, or property, without due process of law; nor shall private property be taken for public use without just compensation.

AMENDMENT VI

In all criminal prosecutions, the accused shall enjoy the right to a speedy and public trial, by an impartial jury of the State and district wherein the crime shall have been committed, which district shall have been previously ascertained by law, and to be informed of the nature and cause of the accusation; to be confronted with the witnesses against him; to have compulsory process for obtaining witnesses in his favor, and to have the Assistance of Counsel for his defense.

AMENDMENT VII

In Suits at common law, where the value in controversy shall exceed twenty dollars, the right of trial by jury shall be preserved, and no fact tried by a jury, shall be otherwise reexamined in any Court of the United States, than according to the rules of the common law.

AMENDMENT VIII

Excessive bail shall not be required, nor excessive fines imposed, nor cruel and unusual punishments inflicted.

AMENDMENT IX

The enumeration in the Constitution, of certain rights, shall not be construed to deny or disparage others retained by the people.

AMENDMENT X

The powers not delegated to the United States by the Constitution, nor prohibited by it to the States, are reserved to the States respectively, or to the people.

AMENDMENT XI[13]

The Judicial power of the United States shall not be construed to extend to any suit in law or equity, commenced or prosecuted against one of the United States by Citizens of another State, or by Citizens or Subjects of any Foreign State.

AMENDMENT XII[14]

The Electors shall meet in their respective states and vote by ballot for President and Vice-President, one of whom, at least, shall not be an inhabitant of the same state with themselves; they shall name in their ballots the person voted for as President, and in distinct ballots the person voted for as Vice-President, and they shall make distinct lists of all persons voted for as President, and of all persons voted for as Vice-President, and of the number of votes for each, which

[13]Adopted in 1798.
[14]Adopted in 1804.

lists they shall sign and certify, and transmit sealed to the seat of the government of the United States, directed to the President of the Senate;—The President of the Senate shall, in presence of the Senate and House of Representatives, open all the certificates and the votes shall then be counted;—The person having the greatest number of votes for President, shall be the President, if such number be a majority of the whole number of Electors appointed; and if no person have such majority, then from the persons having the highest numbers not exceeding three on the list of those voted for as President, the House of Representatives shall choose immediately, by ballot, the President. But in choosing the President, the votes shall be taken by states, the representation from each state having one vote; a quorum for this purpose shall consist of a member or members from two-thirds of the states, and a majority of all the states shall be necessary to a choice. [And if the House of Representatives shall not choose a President whenever the right of choice shall devolve upon them, before the fourth day of March next following, then the Vice-President shall act as President, as in the case of the death or other constitutional disability of the President.][15]—The person having the greatest number of votes as Vice-President, shall be the Vice-President, if such number be a majority of the whole number of Electors appointed, and if no person have a majority, then from the two highest numbers on the list, the Senate shall choose the Vice-President; a quorum for the purpose shall consist of two-thirds of the whole number of Senators, and a majority of the whole number shall be necessary to a choice. But no person constitutionally ineligible to the office of President shall be eligible to that of Vice-President of the United States.

AMENDMENT XIII[16]

Section 1. Neither slavery nor involuntary servitude, except as a punishment for crime whereof the party shall have been duly convicted, shall exist within the United States, or any place subject to their jurisdiction.

Section 2. Congress shall have power to enforce this article by appropriate legislation.

AMENDMENT XIV[17]

Section 1. All persons born or naturalized in the United States, and subject to the jurisdiction thereof, are citizens of the United States and of the State wherein they reside. No state shall make or enforce any law which shall abridge the privileges or immunities of citizens of the United States; nor shall any State deprive any person of life, liberty, or property, without due process of law; nor deny to any person within its jurisdiction the equal protection of the laws.

Section 2. Representatives shall be apportioned among the several States according to their respective numbers, counting the whole number of persons in each State, excluding Indians not taxed. But when the right to vote at any election for the choice of electors for President and Vice-President of the United States,

[15]Superseded by the Twentieth Amendment, section 3.
[16]Adopted in 1865.
[17]Adopted in 1868.

Representatives in Congress, the Executive and Judicial officers of a State, or the members of the Legislature thereof, is denied to any of the male inhabitants of such State, being twenty-one years of age, and citizens of the United States, or in any way abridged, except for participation in rebellion, or other crime, the basis of representation therein shall be reduced in the proportion which the number of such male citizens shall bear to the whole number of male citizens twenty-one years of age in such State.

Section 3. No person shall be a Senator or Representative in Congress, or elector of President and Vice-President, or hold any office, civil or military, under the United States, or under any State, who, having previously taken an oath, as a member of Congress, or as an officer of the United States, or as a member of any State legislature, or as an executive or judicial officer of any State, to support the Constitution of the United States, shall have engaged in insurrection or rebellion against the same, or given aid or comfort to the enemies thereof. But Congress may by a vote of two-thirds of each House, remove such disability.

Section 4. The validity of the public debt of the United States, authorized by law, including debts incurred for payment of pensions and bounties for services in suppressing insurrection or rebellion, shall not be questioned. But neither the United States nor any State shall assume or pay any debt or obligation incurred in aid of insurrection or rebellion against the United States, or any claim for the loss or emancipation of any slave; but all such debts, obligations and claims shall be held illegal and void.

Sectiion 5. The Congress shall have power to enforce, by appropriate legislation, the provisions of this article.

AMENDMENT XV[18]

Section 1. The right of citizens of the United States to vote shall not be denied or abridged by the United States or by any State on account of race, color, or previous condition of servitude.

Section 2. The Congress shall have power to enforce this article by appropriate legislation.

AMENDMENT XVI[19]

The Congress shall have power to lay and collect taxes on incomes, from whatever source derived, without apportionment among the several States, and without regard to any census or enumeration.

AMENDMENT XVII[20]

The Senate of the United States shall be composed of two Senators from each State, elected by the people thereof, for six years; and each Senator shall have one

[18]Adopted in 1870.
[19]Adopted in 1913.
[20]Adopted in 1913.

vote. The electors in each State shall have the qualifications requisite for electors of the most numerous branch of the State legislatures.

When vacancies happen in the representation of any State in the Senate, the executive authority of such State shall issue writs of election to fill such vacancies: *Provided*, That the legislature of any State may empower the executive thereof to make temporary appointments until the people fill the vacancies by election as the legislature may direct.

This amendment shall not be so construed as to affect the election or term of any Senator chosen before it becomes valid as part of the Constitution.

AMENDMENT XVIII[21]

Section 1. After one year from the ratification of this article the manufacture, sale, or transportation of intoxicating liquors within, the importation thereof into, or the exportation thereof from the United States and all territory subject to the jurisdiction thereof for beverage purposes is hereby prohibited.

Section 2. The Congress and the several States shall have concurrent power to enforce this article by appropriate legislation.

Section 3. This article shall be inoperative unless it shall have been ratified as an amendment to the Constitution by the legislatures of the several States, as provided in the Constitution, within seven years from the date of the submission hereof to the States by the Congress.

AMENDMENT XIX[22]

The right of citizens of the United States to vote shall not be denied or abridged by the United States or by any State on account of sex.

Congress shall have power to enforce this article by appropriate legislation.

AMENDMENT XX[23]

Section 1. The terms of the President and Vice-President shall end at noon on the 20th day of January, and the terms of Senators and Representatives at noon on the 3rd day of January, of the years in which such terms would have ended if this article had not been ratified; and the terms of their successors shall then begin.

Section 2. The Congress shall assemble at least once in every year, and such meeting shall begin at noon on the 3rd day of January, unless they shall by law appoint a different day.

Section 3. If, at the time fixed for the beginning of the term of the President, the President elect shall have died, the Vice-President elect shall become President. If a President shall not have been chosen before the time fixed for the beginning of his term, or if the President elect shall have failed to qualify,

[21]Adopted in 1919. Repealed in section 1 of the Twenty-first Amendment.
[22]Adopted in 1920.
[23]Adopted in 1933.

then the Vice-President elect shall act as a President until a President shall
have qualified; and the Congress may by law provide for the case wherein
neither a President elect nor a Vice-President elect shall have qualified, declaring who shall then act as President, or the manner in which one who is to
act shall be selected, and such person shall act accordingly until a President
or Vice-President shall have qualified.

Section 4. The Congress may by law provide for the case of the death of any of
the persons from whom the House of Representatives may choose a President
whenever the right of choice shall have devolved upon them, and for the case
of the death of any of the persons from whom the Senate may choose a Vice-
President whenever the right of choice shall have devolved upon them.

Section 5. Sections 1 and 2 shall take effect on the 15th day of October following
the ratification of this article.

Section 6. This article shall be inoperative unless it shall have been ratified as
an amendment to the Constitution by the legislatures of three-fourths of the
several States within seven years from the date of its submission.

AMENDMENT XXI[24]

Section 1. The eighteenth article of amendment to the Constitution of the United
States is hereby repealed.

Section 2. The transportation or importation into any State, Territory, or posses-
sion of the United States for delivery or use therein of intoxicating liquors, in
violation of the laws thereof, is hereby prohibited.

Section 3. This article shall be inoperative unless it shall have been ratified as an
amendment to the Constitution by conventions in the several States, as provided in the Constitution, within seven years from the date of the submission
hereof to the States by the Congress.

AMENDMENT XXII[25]

Section 1. No person shall be elected to the office of the President more than
twice, and no person who has held the office of President, or acted as President, for more than two years of a term to which some other person was
elected President shall be elected to the office of the President more than
once. But this Article shall not apply to any person holding the office of President when this Article was proposed by the Congress, and shall not prevent
any person who may be holding the office of President, or acting as President,
during the term within which this Article becomes operative from holding the
office of President or acting as President during the remainder of such term.

Section 2. This article shall be inoperative unless it shall have been ratified as
an amendment to the Constitution by the legislatures of three-fourths of the
several States within seven years from the date of its submission to the States
by the Congress.

[24]Adopted in 1933.
[25]Adopted in 1951.

AMENDMENT XXIII[26]

Section 1. The District constituting the seat of Government of the United States shall appoint in such manner as the Congress may direct:

A number of electors of President and Vice-President equal to the whole number of Senators and Representatives in Congress to which the District would be entitled if it were a State, but in no event more than the least populous State; they shall be in addition to those appointed by the States, but they shall be considered, for the purposes of the election of President and Vice-President, to be electors appointed by a State; and they shall meet in the District and perform such duties as provided by the twelfth article of amendment.

Section 2. The Congress shall have power to enforce this article by appropriate legislation.

AMENDMENT XXIV[27]

Section 1. The right of citizens of the United States to vote in any primary or other election for President or Vice-President, for electors for President or Vice-President, or for Senator or Representative in Congress, shall not be denied or abridged by the United States or any state by reasons of failure to pay any poll tax or other tax.

Section 2. The Congress shall have power to enforce this article by appropriate legislation.

AMENDMENT XXV[28]

Section 1. In case of the removal of the President from office or of his death or resignation, the Vice-President shall become President.

Section 2. Whenever there is a vacancy in the office of the Vice-President, the President shall nominate a Vice-President who shall take office upon confirmation by a majority vote of both Houses of Congress.

Section 3. Whenever the President transmits to the President pro tempore of the Senate and the Speaker of the House of Representatives his written declaration that he is unable to discharge the powers and duties of his office, and until he transmits to them a written declaration to the contrary, such powers and duties shall be discharged by the Vice-President as Acting President.

Section 4. Whenever the Vice-President and a majority of either the principal officers of the Executive departments or of such other body as Congress may by law provide, transmit to the President pro tempore of the Senate and the

[26]Adopted in 1961.
[27]Adopted in 1964.
[28]Adopted in 1967.

Speaker of the House of Representatives their written declaration that the President is unable to discharge the powers and duties of his office, the Vice-President shall immediately assume the powers and duties of the office as Acting President.

Thereafter, when the President transmits to the President pro tempore of the Senate and the Speaker of the House of Representatives his written declaration that no inability exists, he shall resume the powers and duties of his office unless the Vice-President and a majority of either the principal officers of the executive departments or of such other body as Congress may by law provide, transmit within four days to the President pro tempore of the Senate and the Speaker of the House of Representatives their written declaration that the President is unable to discharge the powers and duties of his office. Thereupon Congress shall decide the issue, assembling within forty-eight hours for that purpose if not in session. If the Congress, within twenty-one days after receipt of the latter written declaration, or, if Congress is not in session, within twenty-one days after Congress is required to assemble, determines by two-thirds vote of both houses that the President is unable to discharge the powers and duties of his office, the Vice-President shall continue to discharge the same as Acting President; otherwise, the President shall resume the powers and duties of his office.

AMENDMENT XXVI[29]

Section 1. The right of citizens of the United States, who are 18 years of age or older, to vote shall not be denied or abridged by the United States or any state on account of age.
Section 2. The Congress shall have power to enforce this article by appropriate legislation.

(D.C. VOTING RIGHTS)[30]

Section 1. For purposes of representation in the Congress, election of the President and Vice President, and article V of this Constitution, the District constituting the seat of government of the United States shall be treated as though it were a State.
Section 2. The exercise of the rights and powers conferred under this article shall be by the people of the District constituting the seat of government, and as shall be provided by the Congress.
Section 3. The twenty-third article of amendment to the Constitution of the United States is hereby repealed.
Section 4. This article will be inoperative, unless it shall have been ratified as an amendment to the Constitution by the legislatures of three-fourths of the several States within seven years from the date of its submission.

[29]Adopted in 1971.
[30]Proposed Amendment passed by Congress and sent to the states for ratification on August 28, 1978.

Appendix C

Presidential Elections, 1789–1984

Year	Candidates	Party	Popular Vote	Electoral Vote
1789	**George Washington**			69
	John Adams			34
	Others			35
1792	**George Washington**			132
	John Adams			77
	George Clinton			50
	Others			5
1796	**John Adams**	Federalist		71
	Thomas Jefferson	Democratic-Republican		68
	Thomas Pinckney	Federalist		59
	Aaron Burr	Democratic-Republican		30
	Others			48
1800	**Thomas Jefferson†**	Democratic-Republican		73
	Aaron Burr	Democratic-Republican		73
	John Adams	Federalist		65
	Charles C. Pinckney	Federalist		64
1804	**Thomas Jefferson**	Democratic-Republican		162
	Charles C. Pinckney	Federalist		14
1808	**James Madison**	Democratic-Republican		122
	Charles C. Pinckney	Federalist		47
	George Clinton	Independent-Republican		6
1812	**James Madison**	Democratic-Republican		128
	DeWitt Clinton	Federalist		89
1816	**James Monroe**	Democratic-Republican		183
	Rufus King	Federalist		34

Year	Candidate	Party	Popular Vote	Electoral Vote
1820	**James Monroe**	Democratic-Republican		231
	John Quincy Adams	Independent-Republican		1
1824	**John Quincy Adams†**	Democratic-Republican	108,740 (30.5%)	84
	Andrew Jackson	Democratic-Republican	153,544 (43.1%)	99
	Henry Clay	Democratic-Republican	47,136 (13.2%)	37
	William H. Crawford	Democratic-Republican	46,618 (13.1%)	41
1828	**Andrew Jackson**	Democratic	647,231 (56.0%)	178
	John Quincy Adams	National Republican	509,097 (44.0%)	83
1832	**Andrew Jackson**	Democratic	687,502 (55.0%)	219
	Henry Clay	National Republican	530,189 (42.4%)	49
	William Wirt	Anti-Masonic		7
	John Floyd	National Republican	33,108 (2.6%)	11
1836	**Martin Van Buren**	Democratic	761,549 (50.9%)	170
	William H. Harrison	Whig	549,567 (36.7%)	73
	Hugh L. White	Whig	145,396 (9.7%)	26
	Daniel Webster	Whig	41,287 (2.7%)	14
1840	**William H. Harrison***	Whig	1,275,017 (53.1%)	234
	(John Tyler, 1841)			
	Martin Van Buren	Democratic	1,128,702 (46.9%)	60
1844	**James K. Polk**	Democratic	1,337,243 (49.6%)	170
	Henry Clay	Whig	1,299,068 (48.1%)	105
	James G. Birney	Liberty	62,300 (2.3%)	

Year	Candidates	Party	Popular Vote	Electoral Vote
1848	Zachary Taylor* (Millard Fillmore, 1850)	Whig	1,360,101 (47.4%)	163
	Lewis Cass	Democratic	1,220,544 (42.5%)	127
	Martin Van Buren	Free Soil	291,263 (10.1%)	
1852	Franklin Pierce	Democratic	1,601,474 (50.9%)	254
	Winfield Scott	Whig	1,386,578 (44.1%)	42
1856	James Buchanan	Democratic	1,838,169 (45.4%)	174
	John C. Fremont	Republican	1,335,264 (33.0%)	114
	Millard Fillmore	American	874,534 (21.6%)	8
1860	Abraham Lincoln	Republican	1,865,593 (39.8%)	180
	Stephen A. Douglas	Democratic	1,382,713 (29.5%)	12
	John C. Breckinridge	Democratic	848,356 (18.1%)	72
	John Bell	Constitutional Union	592,906 (12.6%)	39
1864	Abraham Lincoln* (Andrew Johnson, 1865)	Republican	2,206,938 (55.0%)	212
	George B. McClellan	Democratic	1,803,787 (45.0%)	21
1868	Ulysses S. Grant	Republican	3,013,421 (52.7%)	214
	Horatio Seymour	Democratic	2,706,829 (47.3%)	80
1872	Ulysses S. Grant	Republican	3,596,745 (55.6%)	286
	Horace Greeley	Democratic	2,843,446 (43.9%)	66
1876	Rutherford B. Hayes	Republican	4,036,572 (48.0%)	185
	Samuel J. Tilden	Democratic	4,284,020 (51.0%)	184
1880	James A. Garfield* (Chester A. Arthur, 1881)	Republican	4,449,053 (48.3%)	214
	Winfield S. Hancock	Democratic	4,442,035 (48.2%)	155
	James B. Weaver	Greenback-Labor	308,578 (3.4%)	

Year	Candidate	Party	Popular Vote (%)	Electoral Vote
1884	**Grover Cleveland**	Democratic	4,874,986 (48.5%)	219
	James G. Blaine	Republican	4,851,981 (48.2%)	182
	Benjamin F. Butler	Greenback-Labor	175,370 (1.8%)	
1888	**Benjamin Harrison**	Republican	5,444,337 (47.8%)	233
	Grover Cleveland	Democratic	5,540,050 (48.6%)	168
1892	**Grover Cleveland**	Democratic	5,554,414 (46.0%)	277
	Benjamin Harrison	Republican	5,190,802 (43.0%)	145
	James B. Weaver	People's	1,027,329 (8.5%)	22
1896	**William McKinley**	Republican	7,035,638 (50.8%)	271
	William J. Bryan	Democratic; Populist	6,467,946 (46.7%)	176
1900	**William McKinley***	Republican	7,219,530 (51.7%)	292
	(Theodore Roosevelt, 1901)			
	William J. Bryan	Democratic; Populist	6,356,734 (45.5%)	155
1904	**Theodore Roosevelt**	Republican	7,628,834 (56.4%)	336
	Alton B. Parker	Democratic	5,084,401 (37.6%)	140
	Eugene V. Debs	Socialist	402,460 (3.0%)	
1908	**William H. Taft**	Republican	7,679,006 (51.6%)	321
	William J. Bryan	Democratic	6,409,106 (43.1%)	162
	Eugene V. Debs	Socialist	420,820 (2.8%)	
1912	**Woodrow Wilson**	Democratic	6,286,820 (41.8%)	435
	Theodore Roosevelt	Progressive	4,126,020 (27.4%)	88
	William H. Taft	Republican	3,483,922 (23.2%)	8
	Eugene V. Debs	Socialist	897,011 (6.0%)	

Year	Candidates	Party	Popular Vote	Electoral Vote
1916	Woodrow Wilson	Democratic	9,129,606 (49.3%)	277
	Charles E. Hughes	Republican	8,538,221 (46.1%)	254
1920	Warren G. Harding*	Republican	16,152,200 (61.0%)	404
	(Calvin Coolidge, 1923)			
	James M. Cox	Democratic	9,147,353 (34.6%)	127
	Eugene V. Debs	Socialist	919,799 (3.5%)	
1924	Calvin Coolidge	Republican	15,725,016 (54.1%)	382
	John W. Davis	Democratic	8,385,586 (28.8%)	136
	Robert M. La Follette	Progressive	4,822,856 (16.6%)	13
1928	Herbert C. Hoover	Republican	21,392,190 (58.2%)	444
	Alfred E. Smith	Democratic	15,016,443 (40.8%)	87
1932	Franklin D. Roosevelt	Democratic	22,809,638 (57.3%)	472
	Herbert C. Hoover	Republican	15,758,901 (39.6%)	59
	Norman Thomas	Socialist	881,951 (2.2%)	
1936	Franklin D. Roosevelt	Democratic	27,751,612 (60.7%)	523
	Alfred M. Landon	Republican	16,681,913 (36.4%)	8
	William Lemke	Union	891,858 (1.9%)	
1940	Franklin D. Roosevelt	Democratic	27,243,466 (54.7%)	449
	Wendell L. Wilkie	Republican	22,304,755 (44.8%)	82
1944	Franklin D. Roosevelt*	Democratic	25,602,505 (52.8%)	432
	(Harry S. Truman, 1945)			
	Thomas E. Dewey	Republican	22,006,278 (44.5%)	99
1948	Harry S. Truman	Democratic	24,105,587 (49.5%)	303
	Thomas E. Dewey	Republican	21,970,017 (45.1%)	189
	J. Strom Thurmond	States' Rights	1,169,063 (2.4%)	39
	Henry A. Wallace	Progressive	1,157,172 (2.4%)	

Year	Candidates	Party	Popular Vote	Electoral Vote
1952	**Dwight D. Eisenhower**	Republican	33,936,234 (55.2%)	442
	Adlai E. Stevenson	Democratic	27,314,992 (44.5%)	89
1956	**Dwight D. Eisenhower**	Republican	35,590,472 (57.4%)	457
	Adlai E. Stevenson	Democratic	26,022,752 (42.0%)	73
1960	**John F. Kennedy***	Democratic	34,227,096 (49.9%)	303
	(Lyndon B. Johnson, 1963)			
	Richard M. Nixon	Republican	34,108,546 (49.6%)	219
1964	**Lyndon B. Johnson**	Democratic	43,126,233 (61.1%)	486
	Barry M. Goldwater	Republican	27,174,989 (38.5%)	52
1968	**Richard M. Nixon**	Republican	31,785,148 (43.4%)	301
	Hubert H. Humphrey	Democratic	31,274,503 (42.7%)	191
	George C. Wallace	Amer. Independent	9,899,557 (13.5%)	46
1972	**Richard M. Nixon†**	Republican	45,767,218 (60.6%)	520
	(Gerald R. Ford, 1974)			
	George S. McGovern	Democratic	28,357,668 (37.5%)	17
1976	**Jimmy Carter**	Democratic	40,274,975 (50.6%)	297
	Gerald R. Ford	Republican	38,530,614 (48.4%)	240
1980	**Ronald Reagan**	Republican	43,899,248 (51.0%)	489
	Jimmy Carter	Democratic	36,481,435 (42.3%)	49
	John Anderson	Independent	5,719,437 (6.6%)	
1984	**Ronald Reagan**	Republican	52,606,797 (59.0%)	525
	Walter F. Mondale	Democratic	36,450,613 (41.0%)	13

*Died in office.
†Resigned.
‡Chosen by the House of Representatives.
Note: Because only the leading candidates are listed, popular vote percentages do not always total 100%.

Index

"... The scholarship is extraordinary."
—G. Calvin Mackenzie, Colby College

"... it is one of the most comprehensive treatments of the presidency available."
—Eric L. Davis, Middlebury College

This book is an examination of the difficult office of the presidency today and of the skills needed to overcome obstacles to achieve political and policy goals. Edwards and Wayne cover not only the political and political office, but the psychological, behavioral, and institutional dimensions of the well. The authors discuss the psychological, behavioral elements as tions, elections (including the 1984 results), decision making, policy implementation, and relations with Congress and the judiciary. Considerable attention is given to the public aspects of the presidency, especially to the mass media's impact on and use by the president.

In their view of the presidency as a multifaceted institution, best understood by adopting a variety of approaches and techniques, the authors draw on the best available contemporary research.